Computer Graphics Techniques

Lunch at First Sight (Brian Wyvill)

David F. Rogers   Rae A. Earnshaw
Editors

Computer Graphics Techniques

Theory and Practice

With 190 Figures in 212 Parts, 49 in Color

Springer-Verlag
New York Berlin Heidelberg
London Paris Tokyo Hong Kong

David F. Rogers
Aerospace Engineering Department
U.S. Naval Academy
Annapolis, Maryland 21402
USA

Rae A. Earnshaw
University of Leeds
Leeds LS2 9JT
United Kingdom

Cover illustration: The Hubble Space Telescope (Lee Butler and Mike Muuss)
The Hubble Space Telescope was modeled by Lee Butler, using BRL-CAD.
The image was rendered by Lee Butler and Mike Muuss using REMRT, a network
distributed ray-tracer running in parallel on all four processors of a Cray X-MP/48,
three different four-processor Silicon Graphics 4D/240 workstations, and two Silicon
Graphics 4D/25 workstations. The accurate star background was generated from the
Yale Bright Star Catalog.
This image is one frame from an animation sequence being jointly developed by The
Ballistic Research Laboratory and The Space Telescope Science Institute.

Library of Congress Cataloging in Publication Data
Computer graphics techniques : theory and practice / David F. Rogers
  Rae A. Earnshaw.
     p.   cm.
   Papers from an International Summer Institute on the State of the
Art in Computer Graphics held at the University of Exeter and
sponsored by the British Computer Society Graphics and
Displays Group and by the Computer Graphics Society.
   Includes bibliographical references.
   ISBN 0-387-97237-4 (alk. paper)
   1. Computer graphics—Congresses.   I. Rogers, David F., 1937–
II. Earnshaw, Rae A., 1944-   III. International Summer Institute
on the State of the Art in Computer Graphics (1988 : University of
Exeter).   IV. British Computer Society. Computer Graphics and
Displays Group.   V. Computer Graphics Society.
T385.C5915   1990
006.6—dc20   90-31346

Printed on acid-free paper

Typeset by Nancy A. Rogers using TEX. Photocomposition on a Chelgraph IBX-2000.
Printed and bound by South Seas (Hong Kong).

9 8 7 6 5 4 3 2 1

ISBN 0-387-97237-4 Springer-Verlag New York Berlin Heidelberg
ISBN 3-540-97237-4 Springer-Verlag Berlin Heidelberg New York

Contents

Introduction

Computer Graphics Techniques–
Theory and Practice

This is the second volume derived from a State-of-the-Art in Computer Graphics Summer Institute. The current volume represents a snapshot of a number of topics in computer graphics. These topics include: raster algorithms, color—both theory and practice, the generation of realistic images, animation, modeling in CADCAM, networking for graphics, and graphics standards.

Many of the papers first present a background introduction to the topic followed by a discussion of current work in the topic. The volume is thus equally suitable for nonspecialists in a particular area, and for the more experienced researcher in the field. It also enables general readers to obtain an acquaintance with a particular topic area sufficient to apply that knowledge in the context of solving current problems.

The volume is organized into seven chapters as follows: Algorithms for Graphics, Color In Computer Graphics, Realistic Image Generation, Animation, Modeling and CADCAM, Graphics and Networking, and Graphics Standards.

In the first chapter Jack Bresenham addresses some of the details of rasterization algorithms. He aptly illustrates, by example, that these details are of a nontrivial nature and that various implementations can yield both different and surprising results.

The second chapter discusses color in computer graphics. The first paper by Gary Meyer discusses color theory and human color vision. He treats the color vision system as a signal-processing device and shows that the fundamental spectral sensitivity functions have many of the characteristics of a simple sampling device. He uses these results to suggest the selection of interface colors for individuals with color defective vision.

The second paper by Maureen Stone addresses the very real and very difficult practical problem of reproducing in print the high quality monitor images generated in computer graphics. She discusses the theoretical and practical fundamentals of the process of reproducing a color image on paper, shows how this process can reduce the quality of the resulting image, and provides practical guidance on obtaining the best results. She illustrates that practical advice by supplying the color separations for both her paper and for Frank Crow's paper and for the frontispiece by Brian Wyvill.

The third chapter contains three papers on realistic image generation. The first by Frank Crow addresses the fundamental problems that occur when a continuous image is either digitally sampled or when an attempt is made to digitally generate a continuous image. The result is manifested in a phenomenon known in computer graphics as aliasing. Crow discusses and illustrates techniques for antialiasing the resulting image, i.e., techniques for making the human visual system perceive a digital image as continuous. As usual, he provides detailed examples for comparison.

One technique for cheaply adding interest to a computer graphics image is to add texture to it. In his second paper Crow discusses texturing techniques both from a fundamental and a practical point-of-view. He points out that aliasing is a severe problem in texturing and suggests various methods for dealing with it.

Realism in computer graphics is a never ending quest. The next paper, by Roy Hall, discusses algorithms for realistic image synthesis. He points out that there are really two fundamental reasons for continuing to seek realism in computer graphics images—simulation and emulation. Simulation tries to accurately model physical behavior, while emulation or illusion tries to provide the impression of realism by empirically approximating what we observe. Prior to radiosity techniques most computer graphics images were illusionary in nature. Hall throughly discusses the various image generation techniques and places them in scientific perspective.

In the fourth chapter Brian Wyvill explores the subject of animation. He discusses and compares both kinematic and dynamic motion control in animation and carries this forward by exploring the control of the deformation of soft objects. Animation is becoming increasingly important not only in its own right as an entertainment media but also as a valuable element in scientific visualization. Imparting motion to scientific results introduces a fourth dimension that frequently yields valuable and unique insights into the investigated phenomena.

In the fifth chapter on modeling and CADCAM Malcolm Sabin and Mike Pratt review past research and discuss current state-of-the-art research in sculptured surfaces and constructive solid geometry. In his first paper Sabin provides a concise and detailed historical review of the development of sculptured surface techniqes from conic lofting to the latest rational B-spline techniques. These techniques are currently used in all major industries for design and manufacturing of products as diverse as shower shampoo bottles, airplanes, yachts, ships, and automobiles.

Sabin's second paper addresses the very important question of interrogating these surfaces to obtain the requisite information to both judge a design and to manufacture it. For example, the surface normal is needed to position the tool for numerical control machining of the surface, an offset surface is required for developing the shape of supporting structure or for 'skinning' a surface, the intersection of surfaces is required in a number of applications including developing a fillet surface.

In the third paper in this chapter, Mike Pratt provides an historical introduction to solid modeling. He presents the development of the three most freqently used techniques: cellular subdivision, constructive solid modeling and boundary representation. Although each of these techniques developed more or less independently, today the designer's needs dictate that a successful system allows access to all of these methods. For example, sculptured surfaces are generally represented using a boundary representation. However, the design of a complex vehicle generally dictates that a sculptured surface representation is most efficient for the 'skin' while constructive solid geometry representation is most efficent for the internal mechanism. Pratt also discusses the emerging concept of design by 'feature line'. Finally, he addresses the very important problem of data exchange between solid modeling systems and the progress that is being made towards developing an international standard.

With the advent of reasonably low cost scientific workstations with reasonable to outstanding graphics capabilities, scientists and engineers are increasingly turning to computer analysis for answers to fundamental questions and to computer graphics for presentation of those answers. Although the current crop of workstations exhibit quite impressive computational capability, they are still not capable of solving many problems in a reasonable time frame, e.g., executing computational fluid dynamics and finite element codes or generating complex ray traced or radiosity based images.

In the sixth chapter Mike Muuss of the U.S. Army Ballistic Research Laboratory shows how both local area and campus wide networks can be used to make the requisite computational power immediately accessable. He specifically discusses accession and use of medium and large scale (CRAY) parallel and vector processors over networks for this task. He further illustrates the concept with a concert example of parallel processing for graphical display on a network of loosely coupled workstations (which may themselves be parallel processors). He develops the rationale and discusses a practical implementation of an algorithm for dividing the work among the processors including the details of the dispatching algorithm and the design of the distribution protocol. He shows, by example, that the efficiency for a system of this type is excellent.

Finally, in Chapter 7 Gunther Pfaff reviews current progress in graphics standards, including PHIGS, GKS, GKS-3D, the computer graphics metafile (CGM), and the computer graphics interface (CGI). A number of application areas in which on-going research and development is taking place as well as anticipated trends in standards are summarized.

Computer graphics pioneers looked to the time when computer graphics would come of age, when anticipated developments would become the reality of today. This has now happened. The contributors to this volume have made it very clear that computer graphics is not just a potential tool, it is a real tool for solving practical problems.

The continuing development and availability of powerful scientific and engineering workstations at affordable prices has advanced the state-of-the-art significantly. Images can be generated, rendered, and displayed in real time; interaction and modification of reasonably complex images is almost instantaneous. Using networks allows very powerful computational capabilities to be brought to bear, in new and novel ways, on previously unsolvable problems. In the coming decade, desk-top systems and networked supercomputers will make unprecedented power available to the scientist and engineer. Computer graphics and animation will help the scientist and engineer to better understand and appreciate the results of these numerical experiments.

Today, the print publishing industry is making significant strides in the development and presentation of even more efficient and higher quality images. Both increased understanding and increased computerization will continue to raise this standard.

Graphics standards are already producing greater uniformity of software interfaces—the key to greater transportability and to greater migration of programs and data across high-speed networks. Engineering design and manufacture has benefited substantially from the modeling systems currently in use. Integration of the various modeling techniques into a single scheme will increase both the ease and the efficiency of the designer's task. It enhances his problem-solving capability and capacity. We look to even greater developments in the future in the areas of image and print generation, the modeling of the design process, and the animation and rendering of images. The computer is an information processing machine, and in the context of computer graphics is processing pictorial information in one form or another. In order to fully exploit this capability, greater attention needs to be paid to the utilization of networks and parallel processors and the efficient display of the resulting image both on a monitor and in print.

Acknowledgements. The papers in this volume formed the basis of an International Summer Institute on The State of the Art in Computer Graphics held at the University of Exeter, Exeter, United Kingdom, in the summer of 1988. We are very grateful to our co-sponsors: the British Computer Society (BCS) Computer Graphics and Displays Group, and the Computer Graphics Society (CGS). We also thank the Association for Computing Machinery (ACM) for their co-operation and support. Our thanks and appreciation go to Mrs. Frances Johnson, Conference Officer at the University of Leeds, for all her help and support with the practical arrangements for the Institute. Our thanks and appreciation also to all those delegates who attended from many countries and contributed by their discussion, interaction and, inspiration. The following countries were represented: Australia, Austria, Belgium, Canada, Federal Republic of Germany, Finland, Netherlands, Norway, Portugal, Spain, Sweden, Switzerland, the UK, and the USA.

Especial thanks and appreciation go to Gerhard Rossbach of Springer-Verlag, Computer Science Editor, USA West Coast Office, Santa Barbara, California who organized the typesetting and production and to Nancy A. Rogers, who computer typeset the book using TeX.

A volume such as this is the result of many months of planning and preparation, and we thank all those who have assisted us. Colleagues, students, contributors, and publisher—we thank you all for your forbearance and patience, and for enduring our persistence in seeking to bring this project to a successful conclusion.

David F. Rogers
Annapolis, Maryland, USA

Rae A. Earnshaw
Leeds, United Kingdom

1 Algorithms for Graphics

Attribute Considerations in Raster Graphics

Jack E. Bresenham

Abstract

Graphic attributes such as Line_Width, Line_Style, Pixel_Color, Write_-Logic, and Transformation_Matrix should be completely specified and consistently implemented for application portability and device-independent processing to be realized. Picture equivalence can be enhanced by clear understanding and accurate, forthright documentation of underlying reference model attribute behavior for geometric and cosmetic effects. Considered here are aspects of visual consequences for several alternative interpretations of attribute association and transformation of geometric primitives. The argument is made that comprehensive specification of attributes and their consistent interaction with geometric object construction needs to receive increased attention.

Introduction

Intersystem and intrasystem consistency are desirable objectives for graphics implementations. Consistency is enhanced when construction, rendering, and approximating practices are openly discussed, clearly documented, and generally well understood. Different interpretations of a process or approximation model can lead to presentation of noticeably different visual pictures. Treated in this paper are alternatives for consideration when attributes are applied to geometric objects.

A graphics interface specification typically includes declarations by which various attributes can be associated with geometric constructs. For example, in Computer Graphics Interface (CGI) [CGI86; Bono88] attributes of width, color, style, logical writing mode, and a shape-and-positioning transformation matrix can be applied to a geometric object's presentation on a display viewsurface. Such attribute association is equally applicable to all geometric entities including specifically lines, circles, ellipses, and rectangles. Alternative graphics specifications such as the Computer

Graphics Metafile (CGM) standard, IBM's Graphical Data Display Manager (GDDM) program product, the Graphical Kernel System (GKS) standard, Xerox's Interpress [Inte84; Spro84] architecture, the Programmer's Hierarchical Interactive Graphics System (PHIGS) standard, and Adobe's PostScript [Post86a; Post86b] architecture each provide similar attribute and geometric primitive declarations.

As attributes are defined, it is helpful to pin down applicability, scope, and intended behavior while also taking careful note of potential side effects or special cases that can accrue. Should Line-Width, for example, be a geometric property subject to full transformation or should it be merely a cosmetic property of the final rendering not subject to transformation? If a wide line is taken to be an area bounded by the locus of points a distance w along the normal on each side of a geometric primitive curve, must an implementation actually render an accurate representation of the theoretical normal locus, or is a less accurate tracing of yet a different curve acceptable? How 'close' to the 'true' curve is the alternative curve that later is then itself approximated? Can the total posttransformation error be estimated easily? How should self-intersecting bounding curves for a 'wide line' area be processed; a scanline parity area fill could leave open gaps within the bounding envelope.

Before a graphics implementation is specified and work begun, computer architects and graphics developers need to consider a number of pertinent questions. If, for example, drawing a wide ellipse involves transforming the locus of curves factored from an eighth-degree equation [Salm96], should conformance testing consider the actual method an implementation employs and label as nonconforming those products that fail to approximate the theoretical curves obtained either from the eighth-order parallel curve itself or from actual calculation of multiple points along a closely spaced sequence of normals? Can an implementation arbitrarily select, for convenience, a simpler, but different, piecewise curve reference to transform and to which width and style will be added later? Or would an equally acceptable approach be to revise the definition of Line-Width to match anticipated practice?

Since multivendor considerations and standards activity also affect a product development effort, other relevant questions can transcend one's immediate implementation. Is a single or preferred practice desirable to assure portability, consistency, and robust visual and mathematical behavior under all possible attribute combinations and transformations? Should theory and implementation closely match, or can standardized concepts and principles be defined without regard to implementation practicality? Are quantitative error measures and controls necessary adjuncts to accompany forthright description of an implementation's approximation methodology? Or is it acceptable (perhaps at least safer) to leave users in the dark by omitting or minimizing descriptive documentation of one's approximation methodology and its integrity under, for example, anisotropic transformation extremes?

One even can wonder if there might be merit in pursuing some degree of standard practices model for a raster rendering level of layered graphics function. For several decades in computer development, floating point forms and precision were left to the imagination and perceived innovation of each vendor. Eventually, the need for a consistent, interchangeable standard practice led to today's IEEE floating point standard. Although computer interconnection has its seven-layer OSI model, computer graphics seems not yet to have evolved to such an ordered structuring of agreed functional layers.

In the absence of standard rendering conventions, a likely event could be that graphics conformance testing will ignore the actual picture displayed. Conformance testing well may have to ignore visual picture equivalence and accept multiple interpretations of attribute application so long as incoming language structure is correctly parsed. After all, many ordinary instances can be relatively insensitive to side effects or exceptional circumstances. Only those programmers who attempt to use the full capability implied in a definition may notice picture differences. What price and worth do robustness, fidelity, and completeness warrant? Is computer graphics concerned primarily with picture appearance and visual effect, or is computer graphics concerned primarily with structure of graphic data bases and attendant language syntax and semantics?

As a first illustration, alternative interpretations of segment transformation matrix application in CGI will be examined. Then Line_Width and Line_Style considerations will be discussed.

Transformation_Matrix

In CGI, that which is transformed has been decided several different ways during the course of debate over the past several years. Sometimes locus transformation was in favor; at other times, reference-point-only transformation was dominant.

Locus transformation assumes that a geometric shape such as an axially aligned rectangle or a three-point circular arc is defined in the pretransformation coordinate space and that the locus of all points comprising the original geometric shape is transformed. With locus transformation, 2D shapes change in accordance with the treatment of coordinate transformations found in standard mathematical texts. Anisotropic scaling, for example, would cause a circle to become an ellipse. Shearing could cause a rectangle to degenerate into a parallelogram.

Reference-point-only transformation assumes that geometric shape is defined in the posttransformation coordinate space and that only locating or reference definition points are transformed. After transformation of the defining reference points, the geometric shape is fitted to the new, posttransformation values. Simple rotation, for example, would never reorient sides of an axially aligned rectangle primitive to be other than parallel to the coordinate axes. Rotation could, though, cause an axially aligned rectangle to degenerate into a single line. Scalars are not transformable. Special exception conventions must be adopted to deal with specifications such as a center point and scalar radius declaration for a full circle primitive which later can be subject to anisotropic scaling.

In the CGI draft ISO DP/9636 document circulated for formal comment in the second quarter of 1987, only defining reference points were subject to transformation; geometric curve shapes were not transformed as a locus of points from the pretransformation coordinate space. Before that public draft and again later, after the close of public comment, transformation matrix applicability was discussed at length at Valbonne and San Diego during the third quarter of 1987. It now has once again been voted to be determined as applicable to the full locus of points in the original, pretransformation shape of a geometric primitive.

Locus transformation does seem to be the CGI choice now (August 1988). The next draft DP-level document should reflect the change repudiating treatment of geometric transformation described in ISO DP/9636. To be sure of the final decision, though, a graphics architect, programmer, or user would be well advised to read the next draft DP-level ISO document in late 1988 or early 1989 and then to read the final ISO standard when it is published after the final public review, response, and revision cycle is complete.[†]

What difference does locus or reference-point-only transformation make? If only isotropic scaling transformation is permitted, it makes no difference for line, circle, and ellipse shapes. CGM has used that constraint to avoid the problem up to now. If rotation and anisotropic scaling are precluded, even the geometric shape of an axially aligned rectangle specified by its diagonally opposite corners will be unaffected by the choice of locus or control-point-only transformation. If anisotropic transformation or rotation is allowed, there potentially can be a significant visual difference in some instances. For transformation examples with noticeable visual effects from unequal x and y scaling and rotation, a three-point circular arc will be examined in detail; then an axially aligned rectangle will briefly be considered.

In CGI, one means of specifying a circular arc is to give three defining control or reference points on the circle's circumference. CGI permits

---

[†]Public comment on proposed standards is always welcomed. Too often in the past, corporate and individual apathy has resulted in few comments from other than those already directly involved in promulgating standards at ISO and ANSII. The best way to assure a good graphics standard is to get a copy of the next public draft, read it thoroughly and carefully, and then submit your own corporate or personal comments. Get involved; don't sit back complacently. If you can't find a sponsor to participate directly on standards committees, please do share your own expertise by responding to calls for comment on draft standards.

any affine transformation of a line segment, circular arc, or elliptical arc. Specifically, anisotropic or unequal scaling in x and y and shearing are supported. If only translation, rotation, and equal x and y scaling are permitted then an implementation either can fit a circle to the three reference points and transform that locus shape or, alternatively, it can first transform the three defining points and, after transformation, can then fit a circle to the new posttransform three points. Identical results, at least within some numerical calculation error tolerance, can be achieved with the equal scaling only, no shearing constraint, so the question effectively is moot in the isotropic transformation instance.

With locus transformation and unequal scaling of x and y permitted, however, circles can cease to be circles. Anisotropic transformation will change the shape of a circle into an ellipse. Lines map to lines. Ellipses map to ellipses (including a circle as a degenerate ellipse; an ellipse drawing routine always would be capable of coping with a circle overspecified as an ellipse). Circles, though, map to ellipses, and rectangles can map to parallelograms.

To observe how CGI chose between a locus or a reference-point-only transformation model, let's look at a contrived, specific numerical example to highlight some pertinent facts. By considering the CGI declaration of

CIRCULAR ARC THREE POINT CLOSE–PIE

it can be seen that unequal scaling in x and y can produce very different pictures depending upon

(a) whether an original conceptual locus is transformed; or

(b) whether only reference points are transformed and the geometric primitive shape is then fitted to the new, posttransformation defining points.

This three-point circular arc construction should fit a circular arc through the three ordered points and then draw the two radial lines connecting each end point of the arc to the circle's center point. It produces a pie-shaped area object, a sector of a circle, which selectively can be filled with color. What happens when the 'pie slice' is subject to anisotropic transformation? In the presence of transformation, is a circle to be fitted to the three points before or after their transformation?

Original object specification in pretransformation Virtual Device Coordinate (VDC) space will be noted by coordinates (x, y), while posttransformation VDC coordinates will employ (u, v) for contrast. The CGI transformation matrix is applied to a point (x, y) as

$$\begin{bmatrix} u \\ v \end{bmatrix} = \begin{bmatrix} M_{11} & M_{12} & M_{13} \\ M_{21} & M_{22} & M_{23} \end{bmatrix} \begin{bmatrix} x \\ y \\ 1 \end{bmatrix}$$

or

$$u = M_{11}x + M_{12}y + M_{13}$$
$$v = M_{21}x + M_{22}y + M_{23}$$

so that, as well,

$$x = (M_{22}u - M_{12}v + (M_{12}M_{23} - M_{22}M_{13}))/(M_{11}M_{22} - M_{12}M_{21})$$
$$y = (-M_{21}u + M_{11}v + (M_{13}M_{21} - M_{11}M_{23}))/(M_{11}M_{22} - M_{12}M_{21})$$

For simplicity, let $M_{13} = M_{23} = 0$ to ignore the Euclidean operation translation. Let $M_{11} = 1$, $M_{12} = 0$, $M_{21} = 0$, and $M_{22} = 1/2$ such that any point (x, y) is transformed to (u, v) simply as

$$\begin{bmatrix} u \\ v \end{bmatrix} = \begin{bmatrix} 1 & 0 \\ 0 & 1/2 \end{bmatrix} \begin{bmatrix} x \\ y \end{bmatrix} \qquad \text{so} \qquad \begin{matrix} u = x & x = u \\ v = y/2 & y = 2v \end{matrix}$$

Two closed, pie-designated areas can be solved from their respective three-point specifications:

3-point definition			3-point definition		
Arc 1: (BLUE) pretransform			Arc 4: (GREEN) pretransform		
$x_1 = 13$	$x_2 = 0$	$x_3 = -13$	$x_1 = -13$	$x_2 = 0$	$x_3 = 13$
$y_1 = 0$	$y_2 = 13$	$y_3 = 0$	$y_1 = 0$	$y_2 = -13$	$y_3 = 0$

One method is to find the respective perpendicular bisectors of the lines between (x_1, y_1) and (x_2, y_2) and between (x_2, y_2) and (x_3, y_3). The point at which the two perpendicular bisectors meet is the circle's center point, and the following can then be calculated for locus transformation:

Derived circle and lines	Derived circle and lines
Arc 1: Fitted curve center $(0, 0)$	Arc 4: Fitted curve center $(0, 0)$
Circular arc: $x^2 + y^2 = (13)^2$	Circular arc: $x^2 + y^2 = (13)^2$
$-13 \le x \le 13 \quad 0 \le y \le 13$	$-13 \le x \le 13 \quad -13 \le y \le 0$
Line 2: From $(-13, 0)$ to $(0, 0)$	Line 5: From $(13, 0)$ to $(0, 0)$
Line 3: From $(0, 0)$ to $(13, 0)$	Line 6: From $(0, 0)$ to $(-13, 0)$

When reference-point-only transformation is used, the pie constructions will use transformed reference points:

Revised 3-points			Revised 3-point		
Arc A: (BLUE) posttransform			Arc D: (GREEN) posttransform		
$u_1 = 13$	$u_2 = 0$	$u_3 = -13$	$u_1 = -13$	$u_2 = 0$	$u_3 = 13$
$v_1 = 0$	$v_2 = 6.5$	$v_3 = 0$	$v_1 = 0$	$v_2 = -6.5$	$v_3 = 0$

for which can be found two circles in posttransform coordinates:

Revised circle and lines	Revised circle and lines
Arc A: Circle center $(0, -9.75)$	Arc D: Circle center $(0, 9.75)$
Arc: $u^2 + (v + 9.75)^2 = (16.25)^2$	Arc: $u^2 + (v - 9.75)^2 = (16.25)^2$
$-13 \le u \le 13 \quad 0 \le v \le 6.5$	$-13 \le u \le 13 \quad -6.5 \le v \le 0$
Line B: $v = (-9.75/13)u - 9.75$	Line E: $v = (-9.75/13)u + 9.75$
From $(-13, 0)$ to $(0, -9.75)$	From $(13, 0)$ to $(0, 9.75)$
Line C: $v = (9.75/13)u - 9.75$	Line F: $v = (9.75/13)u + 9.75$
From $(0, -9.75)$ to $(13, 0)$	From $(0, 9.75)$ to $(-13, 0)$

The simplified 2×2 (translation ignored: $M_{13} = M_{23} = 0$) matrix for transformation of loci can be used to demonstrate that a line transforms into a line and a circle, in general, can be transformed into an ellipse. Although a line maps into a line, slope and intercept do potentially change. Pretransformation parallel lines remain parallel posttransformation. Perpendicular and other intersecting lines still intersect but at a different angle posttransformation. The general transformation is neither angle-preserving for line, circle, or ellipse intersections nor eccentricity-preserving for circle and ellipse shapes.

In the absence of translation ($M_{13} = M_{23} = 0$) an origin-centered circle

$$x^2 + y^2 = r^2$$

transforms into the ellipse

$$((M_{21})^2 + (M_{22})^2)u^2 - 2(M_{11}M_{21} + M_{12}M_{22})uv \\ + ((M_{11})^2 + (M_{12})^2)v^2 = E^2$$

where $E = r(M_{11}M_{22} - M_{12}M_{21})$.

In like manner, the line

$$y = (P/Q)x + I_y$$

transforms into the line

$$(QM_{11} + PM_{12})v = (QM_{21} + PM_{22})u + I_y Q(M_{11}M_{22} - M_{12}M_{21})$$

Figure 1 shows the two different pictures obtained from contrasting assumptions of locus or reference-point transformation applied to our illustrative example. Locus transformation abuts two half ellipses, each with semiminor and semimajor axes of 6.5 and 13 units, respectively. Reference-point-only transformation, by contrast, produces two overlapping snowcone-shaped sectors of circles having a radius of 16.25 units; one circle is centered at $(0, -9.75)$ while the other has its center at $(0, 9.75)$.

LOCUS

Posttransformation curves

Original circles changed to ellipses

BLUE	GREEN
Arc 1: Elliptical arc	Arc 4: Elliptical arc
$(x/13)^2 + (y/6.5)^2 = 1$	$(x/13)^2 + (y/6.5)^2 = 1$
$-13 \leq x \leq 13 \quad 0 \leq y \leq 6.5$	$-13 \leq x \leq 13 \quad -6.5 \leq y \leq 0$
Radial lines	Radial lines
Line 2: From $(-13, 0)$ to $(0, 0)$	Line 5: From $(-13, 0)$ to $(0, 0)$
Line 3: From $(0, 0)$ to $(13, 0)$	Line 6: From $(0, 0)$ to $(-13, 0)$

REFERENCE-POINTS-ONLY

Posttransformation curves

New circles fitted to posttransform reference points

BLUE	GREEN
Arc 1: Circular arc	Arc 4: Circular arc
$x^2 + (y + 9.75)^2 = (16.25)^2$	$x^2 + (y - 9.75)^2 = (16.25)^2$
$-13 \leq x \leq 13 \quad 0 \leq y \leq 6.5$	$-13 \leq x \leq 13 \quad -6.5 \leq y \leq 0$
Radial lines	Radial lines
Line 2: From $(-13, 0)$ to $(0, -9.75)$	Line 5: From $(13, 0)$ to $(0, 9.75)$
Line 3: From $(0, -9.75)$ to $(13, 0)$	Line 6: From $(0, 9.75)$ to $(-13, 0)$

If the two graphic objects were drawn into a cleared frame buffer with a logical writing mode of EXCLUSIVE OR or OR, then the color of the overlapped portion of the reference-point approach is generally nonpredictable and nonportable. With locus transformation or with no transformation at all in the example, only the color of the line segment from $(-13, 0)$ to $(13, 0)$ is indeterminate. Logical operations aren't really well defined for multiple colors any more than they are for fruits and vegetables. Is the OR of an apple with a jalapeño pepper equal to a pinto bean or a banana? For colors in a raster display, the result of ORing blue with green depends upon how the manufacturer wired the color association with bit plane configuration.

In more flexible displays with a user-loadable color look-up table, the visible result is determined by table contents and bit plane logical pixel representation conventions. In any event, it is very unlikely that the outcome of EXORing magenta with lemon-lime will be a standard color across multiple vendors and multiple lines of equipment. From personal experience, I've observed that guaranteeing logical color mixing rules can be very difficult even when two projects with common announce/ship schedules are in the same building, separated only by two floors and minor philosophical differences in project team aspirations and expectations. For that matter, logical operation results in general will be unrelated to language binding representation of binary values as color specifiers. The actual, physical,

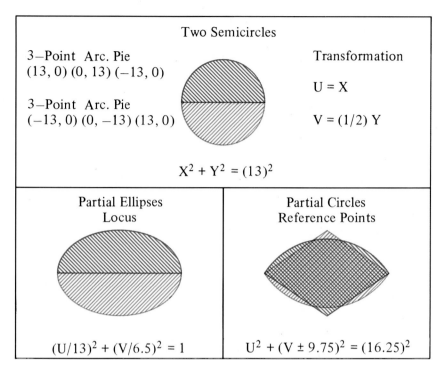

Figure 1. Locus contrasted to reference-point-only transformation.

device-dependent bit plane value usually is the key representation for pixel logical manipulation.

Incorporation of logical writing modes into a multicolor graphics architecture takes careful thought. Color is much more pervasive than a simple extension of monochrome. It affects basic line drawing conceptual framework and bit plane hardware organization. It calls into question just how abstract a data type a pixel should be. Rather than being satisfied with a pixel as merely a color designation abstraction, it may be that expert users will want access to ordered, positionally significant bit value format information for logical and arithmetical operations. Pixel arithmetic may even want a substructure of partitioned bit values in order to perform operations on RGB components as separate and independent values.

A motivation for considering CGI reference-point-only transformation seems, in part at least, to have been a desire to bend a generic, device independent graphics architecture to accommodate a unique perception of hardware rastering capability. Polygonal approximation with chords of an elliptical arc is usually a software task. Some vendors' display adapter VLSI chips, though, can draw an octant or more of a circle but are incapable of drawing incremental ellipses. Additionally, other vendors' graphics

software packages depend upon hardware circular arc capability. A desire
to reveal direct hardware circles at the user interface level could have contributed to pursuit of the reference-point-only transformation even though
it introduced logical inconsistencies in an overall graphics flow through the
geometric pipeline.

Direct circle drawing is not obviated by use of locus transformation.
Hardware circle capability still can be used efficiently with locus transformation. Typically, a 'set segment transform' operation is likely to be
invoked much less frequently than the draw command. It should not be
too difficult to test the transformation matrix to determine if circles still
will be circles posttransformation.

In the 2×3 CGI matrix used earlier, circle-to-circle transformation effect
is assured if

$$(M_{11})^2 + (M_{12})^2 = (M_{21})^2 + (M_{22})^2 \quad \text{and} \quad M_{11}M_{21} + M_{12}M_{22} = 0$$

At the time a new transformation matrix is invoked by replacement or
concatenation, it can be relatively efficient to test the new matrix and set
an appropriate flag to 'remember' whether circle direct rastering capability
can or cannot be used for subsequent drawing.

If the full test for circular shape invariant transformation is deemed too
time consuming with its six product terms, then an approximation will
catch many practical instances. If

$$M_{11} = M_{22} \quad \text{and} \quad M_{12} = -M_{21}$$

or if
$$M_{11} = -M_{22} \quad \text{and} \quad M_{12} = M_{21}$$

then hardware circle capability can safely be used. The computationally
less intensive approach of first transforming the three reference points, and
then using a polygon approximation in posttransform space can also safely
be used if an implementation has the space for exception processing. This
approach can then avoid transformation of each approximating chord's end
points when the test is successful and polygon approximation of circles is
done in unique software. The approximate test misses some opportunities, but it does catch simple scaling and ordinary rotation. Hardware
dependency seems a poor rationale for attempting to introduce reference-
point-only transformations as the one and only transformation method in
a comprehensive graphics architecture.

A parochial motivation for reference-point-only transformation also could
have been a vendor's investment in 'old' software which fit geometric shapes
after transformation was complete. Perhaps the assumption, possibly valid
at the time the programs originally were written, was that isotropic scaling would be adequate and sufficient. A reluctance either to rewrite or
to include explicit warning notice of an isotropic transformation-only constraint with an old set of products could have impeded progress toward a
consistent transformation pipeline.

Fortunately, most manufacturers cooperate in reaching consensus for standards and no such protectionist action is delaying CGI promulgation. Like the ongoing windows work in X3H3, there can be such opportunity from time to time to air questions as to whether standards should be innovative homologations of widespread practice and developing theory or whether standards should tend toward acceptance of one or a few vendors existing work on a more or less take-it-or-leave-it basis. Certainly the IEEE standard 802 for LANs demonstrates the practical possibility of creating rationale for a single multistrategy standard with coexisting, but mutually exclusive, diverse alternatives for perceived differences in common application intent.

CGI also has a specification

RECTANGLE

in which two VDC reference points define diagonally opposite corners of an axially aligned rectangle. It is a convenient shorthand by which a common, frequently used geometric primitive can be expressed more succinctly than could its polyline equivalent construct. Affine transformation can change corner angles from ninety degrees. The posttransformation figure shape can become a parallelogram having no side aligned with either of the coordinate axes rather than remaining a rectangle with all sides aligned parallel to coordinate axes. Just plain, ordinary, simple rotation with the reference-point-only approach can turn a RECTANGLE into a degenerate instance of a single line segment.

Interpress explicitly describes its MASKRECTANGLE command as being subject to a locus transformation and notes " ... for this reason, the mask on the page image may not be rectangular." Their approach assures consistent treatment as graphic objects flow through the processing pipeline while still providing the convenience of a compact designation for a frequently used construct.

Figure 2 illustrates the effect of locus or reference-point-only transformation for an axially aligned RECTANGLE as a geometric primitive. A graphics hardware chip may provide axially aligned rectangles as a basic hardware primitive (often as a BIT-BLIT). Biasing an entire graphics architecture strongly toward unique rastering hardware can be appealing but, given rapid advances in computer graphics technology, possibly short-sighted.

To me, consistency and robustness are more compelling considerations. A good implementation usually can deduce situations in which hardware can be directly applied to provide performance enhancements. Any graphics system architecture must be cognizant of efficiency and realizability; this, though, should not constitute a license to ignore extensibility and consistency.

Once a consistent transformation process is modeled, it is arguably advantageous to create separate extraordinary pseudogeometric primitives

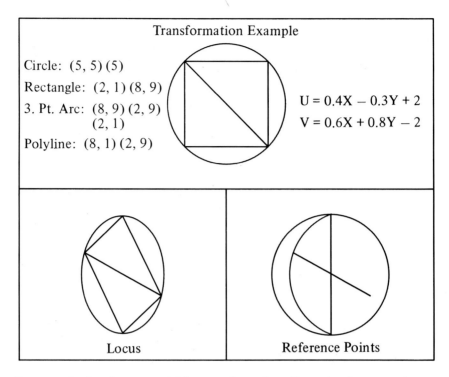

Figure 2. One's reference model for transformation affects visual presentation.

which by definition are transform-invariant. A new name probably would be a good idea. CHARACTER PRECISION TEXT or MARKER TYPE DOT are examples from CGI (ISO DP/9636).

Indiscriminate incorporation of many exceptional processing instances in an architecture might seem efficient in the short term. In the longer term, too many variants and exceptions make VLSI encapsulation of function much messier than would be the case with a 'clean' architecture having, perhaps, a few temporary deviations and vendor-unique registered extensions or grandfathered conformance. The key matter is simply to be careful to clearly identify those constructs in which locating or positioning values can be declared in a coordinate space that is different from the coordinate space in which implied geometric shape is to be formed. Such constructs need a unique processing pipeline distinct from the geometric pipeline.

A final point to consider when deciding how far rastering implications will be allowed to move toward the user interface is that of a proper subset. Will apparently equivalent constructions be treated consistently? A rectangle specified as

POLYLINE (0, 0) (10, 0) (10, 10) (0, 10) (0, 0)

will unequivocally be transformed as a locus. Does it make sense for its apparent equivalent shorthand subset of POLYLINE

RECTANGLE (0, 0) (10, 10)   or   RECTANGLE (0, 10) (10, 0)

to be transformed differently? Likewise, a circle and its polygonal approx-imation as chords of the circle should both behave comparably. A user resorting to his own approximation using polyline, perhaps for precise con-trol of dot/dash interval control, should not suddenly see a very different picture shape from that which he saw with a system-equivalent primitive and a solid style.

To me, locus transformation is clearly the consistent way and the pre-ferred convention for geometric primitives. Reference-point-only transfor-mation seems an inappropriate means of reflecting direct hardware at the user interface level. In 2D it is easy enough to detect conditions for which a transform will leave a circle a circle and when it will produce an ellipse from an original circle. With encouragement of a rational conformance philosophy, 'old' software can simply state it supports only isotropic trans-formations. A standard which looks toward the future without largely abandoning the past would seem more likely to gain widespread adoption.

Line_Width

In graphics system specification, it is not uncommon to find geometric con-structs originally defined at a simple level. These constructs then are ex-tended to more complex instances without consequences necessarily being either obvious or comprehensively described. Line_Width is an example. Is a wide line a line, an area, or a pair of parallel curves [Salm96] which may be filled or enveloped? Is Line_Width transformable or is Line_Width transform-invariant? What happens when the fuzzy concept of width is applied to circles and ellipses?

In traditional geometry, lines are 1D; they have length but no width. Traditionally, the geometric entity having both length and width has been called an area. Not so in computer graphics!

Lines in computer graphics now have optional width. These lines often offer end-treatment choices to close the otherwise unbounded, open-ended area implied by defining line width W only as being measured a distance $w = W/2$ along a normal on both sides of a traditionally zero width refer-ence line segment, circular arc, or elliptical arc.

However contradictory the combination of line and width may seem, the concept is taken in most computer graphics to be useful and practical. Many modern presentation devices have a pixel size so small that a one pixel 'wide' line is virtually invisible. Multiple pixel-wide lines are a necessary requirement with which any graphics architecture must deal. Rather than quibble about descriptive word choices, the significant matter is to provide a conceptual framework within which visible, multiple pixel line widths can be accommodated consistently.

Line_Width really needs to be defined in a manner that provides well-understood interaction with other attributes and geometric constructs. It would help if there were a clear understanding of the difference between wide line as a shorthand representation of a specific area and wide line as a new class of geometric primitive different from either areas or single pixel lines.

A clear, unequivocal, complete definition of how line width will be treated is essential. What geometric locus of points is implied? How will that locus be passed through the processing pipeline? What effect do other attributes such as Line_Style and logical writing mode contribute?

CGI specifies two very different line width modes. 'ABSOLUTE' width scaling is expressed in VDC units and is subject to all scaling and other transformation processing. 'SCALED' width scaling is expressed as a multiple of a device's minimum width line and is not subject to any scaling or other transformation processing. Neither mode implies a closed area definition; end caps and joins are purposefully being deferred to a future enhancement work item after ISO adoption of an initial CGI standard.

To me, the term 'geometric' width for loci which can be transformed as objects flow through the graphics-processing pipeline is more meaningful than the term 'absolute'. Here I shall use geometric width rather than absolute width. Likewise, I prefer the term 'cosmetic' width for that which is nontransformable as a multiple of a device's minimum line width and applicable only at displayed picture rendering time. I shall use the term cosmetic width rather than scaled width. Different size pen tips on a mechanical pen plotter represent cosmetic width for me, while an area on a 2D rubber sheet model illustrates geometric width.

Interpress 'strokewidth' provides geometric line width; its implied area is transformed with the applicable current transform just before rendering. PostScript also provides a geometric line width control 'setlinewidth' which is described as including " ... all points whose perpendicular distance from the current path, in user space, is less than or equal to one-half the absolute value of num."

Neither Interpress nor PostScript provides wide curves other than simple line segments. CGI implies provision of wide circular and elliptical arcs in addition to wide line segments. The Interpress and PostScript concept of reduction of any curve to a flattened path of concatenated simple line segments preceding transformation, stroking, and full attribute association is a very significant underlying principle.

CGI, by contrast, does not necessarily first reduce all curve primitives to their polyline approximations as zero-width reference sequences of line-segment chords. CGI has an implied intent that wide circular and elliptical arcs will be faithfully rendered and the proper parallel curves [Salm96] themselves will be approximated. Either approach can be useful; what's always needed is a clear description in an implementation's documentation. In many instances, the difference will be negligible. In other instances, especially those involving general transformation and shearing extremes, there is the possibility of noticeable visual differences for wide circles and ellipses. Introduction of bit plane writing logical modes, such as EXOR, also offers opportunity for visual differences.

Should one first approximate a reference curve, then transform that approximation, and finally apply width and style to the transformed approximation? Or should width and style first be applied to the true reference curve and then that result be transformed, and finally an approximation of the transformed true locus be displayed?

Many computer graphics uses will be relatively insensitive to whether approximation precedes or follows attribute association and transformation. If an implementation is to render faithfully the full definition of its implied attribute and geometric entity associations, it can make a difference whether attribute association follows or precedes approximation. A choice to transform an approximation or to approximate only after transformation also must be made. At a minimum, the length of line segments in an approximation will need to be carefully considered and error measures determined for deviation from the 'true, widened' curve or area. It is always helpful when documentation clearly and completely describes what is done.

The CGI definition of Line_Width is similar to that of PostScript and Interpress:

> The line width is measured perpendicular to the defining line (that is, it is independent of the orientation of the defining line). ... A wide line is aligned with its ideal zero-width defining line such that the distance between the defining line and either edge of the realized line is half the line width.

CGI's line width declaration applies to all geometric primitives including line segments, circular arcs, elliptical arcs, and axially aligned rectangles.

Examining a full circle can illustrate some consequences of the perhaps incomplete working definition of width as a distance $w = W/2$ measured along a normal on both sides of the circle's circumference.

Consider an axially aligned, standard ellipse

$$(x/a)^2 + (y/b)^2 = 1$$

The equation of the normal passing through any point (i, j) on the circumference is

$$b^2 i y - a^2 j x = ij(b^2 - a^2)$$

For any point (i, j) on the circumference of an origin-centered circle $x^2 + y^2 = r^2$, the line normal to the tangent at (i, j) reduces to simply

$$iy = jx$$

such that, when $y = j$, we find $x = i$ and, when $y = 0$, we find $x = 0$. Thus, the normal is seen to pass through the circle's center. We have a simple condition that radial rays constitute the normals along which width is measured a distance w on both sides of the circumferential point (i, j).

Obviously, then, as illustrated in Figure 3, a wide circle could be simply the area between

$$\text{an outer circle:} \quad x^2 + y^2 = (r + w)^2$$
$$\text{and an inner circle:} \quad x^2 + y^2 = (r - w)^2$$

Notice neither constraints nor limitations have been imposed on the magnitude of the width $W = 2w$. Neither has it been decided just how the area is determined and filled. Were it a partial arc, rather than a full circle, we've no knowledge of how to join the two disjoint partial arc boundary edges. We might perhaps, in time, want to modify the 'obvious' to provide more explicit guidance. For example, Figure 4 doesn't necessarily have an 'obvious' width.

With $r > w$, wide circle implementation could employ ordinary area fill using the two bounding concentric circles of radii $(r + w)$ and $(r - w)$. If circles are actually drawn as a polyline sequence of approximating chords forming a many-sided polygon, we'll need to establish a useful measure by which to determine closeness to the true curves being approximated. We definitely need to know what curves are actually approximated and what the effect of transformation is.

Figures 5, 6, and 7 illustrate some approximation alternatives. As can be seen in Figures 6 and 7, a mitered join of wide line segments needn't lie on the true curve width boundary. Transformation, especially shearing, can move the joining point even farther away from the true curve boundary. End point and joining conventions other than mitering also are popular. Using a butt join in Figure 7 would leave gaps in a 'wide' circle. Using circular end caps could, with anisotropic transformation, produce transformed line segments with elliptical ends.

For geometric width applied to its circle primitive, CGI requires the two concentric circular boundary-defining curves

$$x^2 + y^2 = (r + w)^2 \quad \text{and} \quad x^2 + y^2 = (r - w)^2$$

to be transformed conceptually. Only then, after transformation, would the potential pair of ellipses or possible pair of circles be approximated and the area between the two filled as the boundaries are traced out. (Geometric

Wide Circle

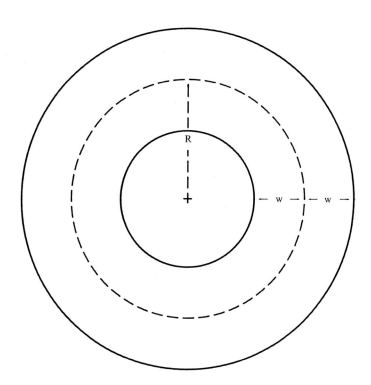

Figure 3. Line_Width applied to a circle.

line style also should be associated before transformation such that each dot, dash, or open gap subarea is transformed consistently.)

How good will the final visible wide circle be? What is a measure of closeness? Are there multiple sources of error? In the CGI intent, approximation is held until the last instance, and error measure can be taken to be a direct indication of how good a fit a circle or ellipse rendering procedure provides. An incremental circle algorithm can offer error measures of function residue magnitude, axial deviation, or radial deviation. With that must also be included any error estimate from center point and radius calculation imprecision or rounding. If chords are used, what measure determines approximation error from the true curve? Are chord end points

Width Exceeds Radius

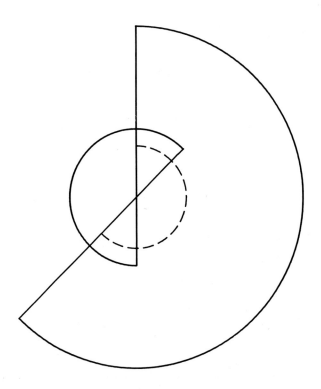

What is Width?

1) Drag Inked Rod
2) Pour Ink Along Reference
3) Favorite Area Fill, Say, Parity

Figure 4. Line_Width is not simply extended to circles.

Polygon Approximation

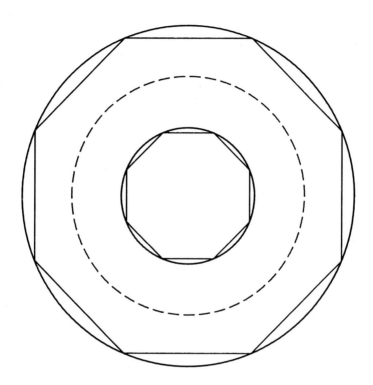

Figure 5. Approximation error measures need to be specified carefully.

rounded to integers before the line is quantized to add further sources of error?

Both Interpress and PostScript describe their use of trajectories and paths. Interpress [Inte84] provides line, not circle and not ellipse, as a basic primitive. A user provides his own approximation method for curves such as circles. Error measure and control thus are directly within the user's own purview. Only the accuracy of the underlying line rastering method is outside a user's control. A user may want to know whether end points are rounded or extrapolated to integers, what the normal or axial error measure of line approximation is, whether lines are retraceable from A to B and back from B to A, and other such approximation detail, but

Fat Lines $\neq$ Wide Circle

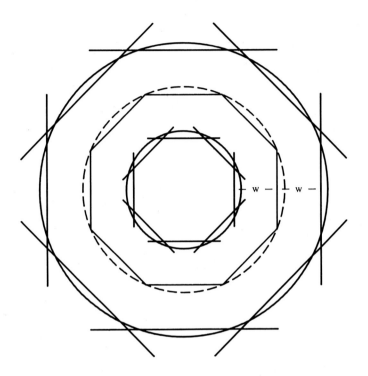

Figure 6. Width applied after polygonal approximation of a circle.

higher order curves do remain clearly a user prerogative. A user also must remember that his own approximation error will be subject to transformation as the concatenated trajectory is evaluated as a polyline reference string of concatenated line segments.

PostScript [Post86a] provides declarations for Bézier curves and circular arcs directly but, before drawing, reduces all curves to simple line segment sequences with PostScript's own internal approximation processing and a user's vague single control parameter 'flatness'. PostScript takes the approach that, first, the defining or reference circle

$$x^2 + y^2 = r^2$$

is approximated as a series of line segments. After this polyline path approximation of the reference curve, width will be applied to each pretrans-

Arc Needs Caps & Joins

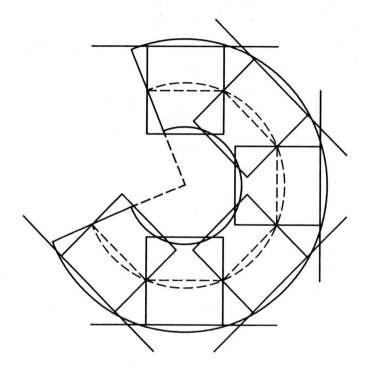

Watch "EXOR" Behavior

Figure 7. Line_Width can interact with 'exclusive or' pixel writing.

form line segment in the reference circle's implicit or explicit 'flattenpath' path reduction with stroking.

Rather than the original concentric pair of bounding circles being used, as shown in Figure 5, PostScript appears to use a concatenated sequence of line segments which are widened in a manner similar to that illustrated in Figures 6 and 7. It is an early approximation which subsequently will have all approximation errors transformed. It is, though, straightforward and unequivocal in the sense that actual rendering clearly is done with line segments approximating the zero-width circular, elliptical, or Bézier reference curve.

This early reduction of a reference circle to a polygon with width then determined for each approximating reference line segment, in contrast to reduction of the two bounding circles themselves, necessitates introduction of line joins for a full circle and line caps and joins for a wide partial arc. After these wide line segment approximations have been evaluated, together with whatever line end treatment has been deemed appropriate for joining, the resultant area will be transformed. If transformation scaling effect is greater than unity, the visible approximation will magnify the early pretransformation approximation to parallel pairs of line segments with their possibly mitered joins or butted end caps.

Polygonal chords are used to first approximate the reference circle, and then the width offsets from the chords are drawn as line segments. Included in a total error assessment should be measures such as a versine deviation of chords from the true reference arc periphery, line segment end point calculation accuracy (are end point values rounded before a line segment is drawn?), and line rendering error such as vertical displacement or normal deviation. The PostScript control 'flatness' appears to address only deviation from the posttransformation zero-width reference curve rather than from the true parallel curves [Salm96] traced by offset along the normals.

In our fat circle example, actual error measure properly would be deviation from the posttransformation form of the two pretransformation circles

$$x^2 + y^2 = (r + w)^2 \quad \text{and} \quad x^2 + y^2 = (r - w)^2$$

not from a posttransformation form of the single reference circle

$$x^2 + y^2 = r^2$$

For full evaluation of error, the actual pixel selection methodology could be included. Chords of a circle have, in infinite-precision arithmetic, a maximum deviation at their midpoint when deviation is measured along a radius. Actual rastering likely rounds finite-precision fractional end points to independent integers for x and y and then draws a slightly different line segment than that calculated for the chord with which error originally was assessed. This perturbed line segment then is quantized to add additional error to that which was calculated originally for the infinitely precise approximating chord's radial deviation.

Error claims without supporting detail of assumptions and analysis sometimes need to be taken with a grain of salt. I once worked on a product for which the architects had defined an interface in which a user could not always specify the partial arc he wanted. Our implementation then drew a partial arc slightly perturbed from that specified. How close the visible circular or elliptical partial arc was to that which a user actually wanted wasn't easily measured. Very small or very large arcs were rationalized to be unusual or degenerate situations which should not often occur. 'Not very often' can be a quickly encountered event.

A question, of course, soon arose during internal prerelease testing. Someone drew hundreds of small rivets on a railroad engine and was surprised by the variable radii circles produced. It turned out GDDM initial support revised circle commands into four or five partial arc commands, each of which could imply a different radius three-point arc owing to the GCP architectural dogma of only integer variables for three-point arc declarations. Lumpy, bumpy small circles were the subject of many meetings which affirmed our GX product met specification. Few meetings, though, really addressed how much sense the specification made or how the executive decision to provide less than full support exacerbated matters; no one wanted to face up to deleting three-point arc support until a comprehensive understanding of cumulative error propagation could be determined.

Today, I'm told, 'enhancements' to the original architecture permit fractional valued point specification, and GDDM passes on circle commands without revision. Users now can specify and get three-point circular and elliptical arcs close to what they expect. Comprehensive, cumulative error analysis usually is a good matter to pursue before specifications are frozen. Sometimes, though, it can be that only after the visual consequences are painfully obvious is there a common will to understand numerical analysis of error sources. Fractional valued points open up new exposures, but error analysis itself is not really the subject of this paper.

With anisotropic transformation, it will be necessary to know at what point error is measured, since the normal distance from equal angle chords to the edge of an ellipse is not a constant, as is the case for a circle. Usually one would expect analysis in the posttransformation coordinate space to be the basis for determination of the number of chords to be used in the pretransform space. Thus, the subsequent transformation needn't magnify too harshly the approximation errors, since the number of approximating line segments was determined with full knowledge of the subsequent transformation effect.

When anisotropic transformation is active, one needs to be a bit more careful about addressing measures for maximum error than when all transformation is isotropic. For circles which transform into ellipses, it is not unusual to use equal length chords around the circle that then transform into unequal length chords around the ellipse. The practice distributes more chords to high-curvature portions of an ellipse and fewer chords to those portions of the curve with low curvature. A good discussion of this circle-to-ellipse technique can be found in [Cohe71].

In the approach which first approximates the reference circle and then widens those approximating line segments, another error effect is introduced. Width is not rendered for the original curve. Width is associated only with the approximating line segments. One can ask how close does a mitered or beveled line edge come to the circle of radius $(r + w)$ or $(r - w)$ which would have been the theoretical boundary edge had widening taken place before approximation of a central reference circle by a polygon.

One also needs to decide whether a miter limit for beveling is applied pretransform or posttransform. If the visible picture is the objective of computer graphics and beveling is a cosmetic consideration, then posttransformation beveling determination would be in order.

It could be appropriate here to recall my old experience with an elementary lesson from Dr. Herriot's introductory course in numerical analysis at Stanford. One can produce an integer sum for a long series of numbers by adding all the fractional values and then rounding the fractional sum. Alternatively, one can first round each individual value and then add the integers. Many times the resultant sum will not differ much either way. In other instances, the final sum can differ dramatically depending upon which method was used. With unconstrained affine transformations possible, the final appearance of geometric entities can be sensitive to how and when approximations for width are made.

In graphics, it is always good to understand and clearly document how approximations are performed and at what point in the pipeline they're made in an implementation. Robustness is a useful concept to keep in mind. At a minimum, one should be careful to understand how a graphics system goes about its approximations and constructions.

Often, primitive behavior in the presence of anisotropic transformation and with an EXOR logical writing mode is a good test for robustness and consistency properties. For example, set the logical writing mode to EXOR and try drawing the line segments from $(160, 0)$ to $(0, 0)$ to $(160, 4)$ with and without a transformation by $M_{11} = 1$, $M_{12} = -40$, $M_{13} = 0$, $M_{21} = 0$, $M_{22} = 40$, and $M_{23} = 0$ and a geometric width of $W = 3$ with some limit, say 10 degrees, below which mitered joins should be beveled.

Just how can width conceptually be associated with a curve? The following three models are among the possibilities.

One way to think about curve width is to set the defining reference curve in pretransform coordinate space and visualize an infinitely thin, zero-width rod of length $W = 2w$ centered on the reference curve. The rod is covered with an inexhaustible supply of unique ink in the color of one's choice. The rod is aligned such that its orientation always is perpendicular to the curve's tangent at the point the curve intersects the rod's midpoint. Carefully keeping the rod aligned as a normal to the curve, drag the rod's midpoint along the curve leaving an inked area trailing behind as the full curve length is traversed.

The unique ink also will need additional special properties to accommodate logical writing mode equivalents. With only a REPLACE, OVERPAINT, or OR logical mode, no attention need be paid to inking the same spot two or more times. The ink is smudge free! With logical modes such as EXOR the ink exhibits new properties. Every other time the rod inks the same spot, it acts as a solvent to remove the prior ink residue and leaves a clean, ink-free point. In logical AND mode the inking process only deposits ink at spots which already had ink and ignores those spots which had no ink prior to the widening operation.

If the original curve were to degenerate to a single point, it would not be clear what we should do, as there is no normal for orientation. At the ends of each non-zero-length line segment some convention would be appropriate for a final flourish immediately before removing the rod. If we were just to stop, a butt end cap would result. Were we to cut away half the rod and then rotate the remaining half-rod 180 degrees about the ending and starting reference points, we could have rounded end caps.

A second conception of width can be to constrain our rod's ink to dispersal only from an infinitesimally small point at each end of the rod; it draws an offset pair of old-fashioned zero-width curves as it travels along the reference curve. Curve widening proceeds as a two-step process. First the midpoint of the rod is dragged along the curve keeping the rod oriented along the normal to the reference curve while the locus of normals is traced.

As can be seen in Figures 8 and 9, the peripheries of a 'wide' ellipse may not be immediately intuitively obvious. Parallel curves [Salm96] can be complex. When dealing with equations of eighth order, one can expect the possibility of self-intersections, cusps, and loops.

As the second step we use another special ink which has the property that it always flows in both directions away from the reference curve up to, but never past, the most distant of self-intersecting boundary edges drawn on its side of the reference curve. Pour the ink along the reference curve and watch it fill in the area between each of the outer envelopes of the widened curve to achieve the same effect as the first technique in REPLACE logic. Alternatively, the ink flow on a side could stop as soon as it first encountered a bounding curve trace for a flood fill effect. If the curve is self-intersecting with loops, the full envelope would not be filled. (In either event, the inked area will represent a conceptual pixel mask enabling the real display bit map to be subsequently filled as the final step in rendering wide solid lines.)

Without a closed boundary, ink will spill out at each end of a nonclosed curve such as a quarter circle partial arc. To avoid a potentially messy situation we'll need to establish conventions for closure at each end of a wide line segment. A radial line or a line parallel to one of the axes could be added to complete a repertoire of rounded, mitered, axially sheared, annular, beveled, and butted end cap possibilities.

A third conceptual inking scheme can be to draw the boundaries as in the second scheme. Rather than pour in an ink which seeks the nearest or most distant edge of a self-intersecting boundary, as in the second scheme, we could simply invoke our implementation's ordinary area fill. In a horizontal scanline parity fill, any boundary self-intersections can produce a pattern of inked and ink-free areas within the bounding envelope of the normals. Don't forget, partial circles and full or partial ellipses can have self-intersecting sections.

Imposing constraints, such as width cannot exceed the radius of a circle, could obviate some exceptional circle instances. With three-point circular arcs permitted, it would be a user's responsibility to calculate the radius of each three-point circle. Such calculation is probably what the user sought to avoid in the first place when a three-point arc was selected.

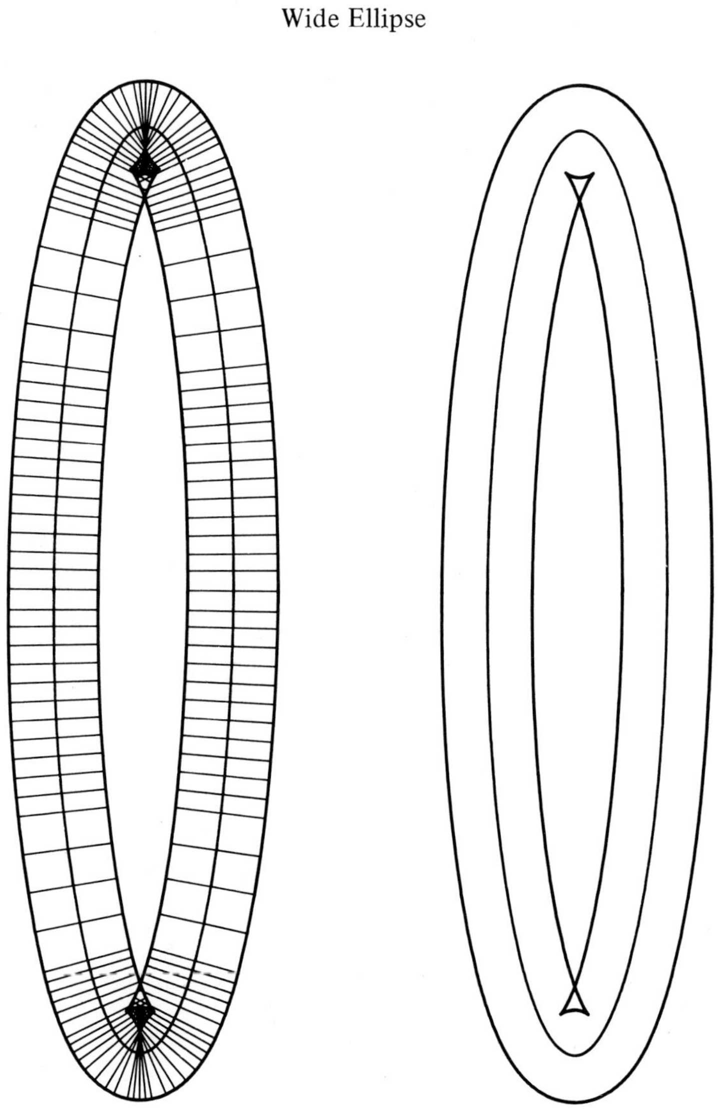

Wide Ellipse

Figure 8. Wide ellipses require eighth-order parallel curves.

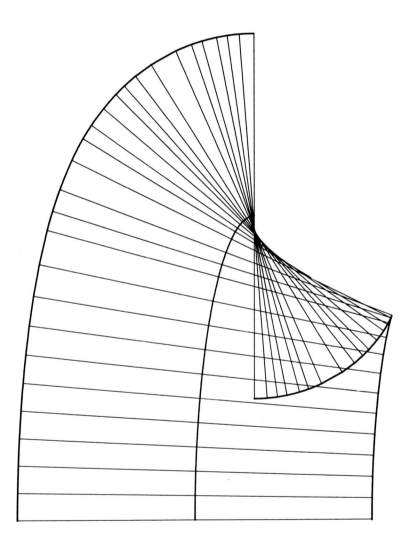

Figure 9. Line_Width can exceed the radius of curvature in an ellipse.

Consider now some consequences of the possible widening models described above. A couple of specific circles and widths can be illustrative:

(a) a circle of radius 10 with width of $W = 10$ such that $w = 5$;

(b) a circle of radius 10 with width of $W = 30$ such that $w = 15$.

Assume the logical writing mode is REPLACE. End shape is a missing piece of detail, so we'll assume radial line-segment closure of partial arcs to induce a proper sector of an annulus in most instances. In all variants of circle (a) the rendering of full, $1/4$, and $3/4$ circular arcs is then equivalent for all the width models.

When half the width $W = 2w$ exceeds the magnitude of the radius r, that is, $r < w$, the width models no longer give equivalent results. For the variants with circle (b) in which width exceeds the original radius, results differ. The first width method applied to case (b), full circle in REPLACE logic, is a solidly filled circle $x^2 + y^2 = (25)^2$. Were EXOR logic used for the full circle, the case (b) result could change to a filled ring between circles

$$x^2 + y^2 = (25)^2 \quad \text{and} \quad x^2 + y^2 = (5)^2$$

with the interior of the small central circle $x^2 + y^2 = (5)^2$ being clear. The $3/4$ circle as a scanline parity area fill will have empty gaps for the two quarter circles of

$$x^2 + y^2 = (5)^2$$

where $0 \le x \le 5$ and $0 \le y \le 5$ and where $-5 \le x \le 0$ and $-5 \le y \le 0$.

For theoretical width applied to lines and circles, the bounding width curves are, respectively, either a pair of parallel lines or a pair of concentric circles. If an implementation doesn't gracefully treat wide circles with $r < w = W/2$, a disclaimer would be appropriate. PostScript, for example, disclaims support of theoretical width for curves other than line segments by its reduction of all higher order curves to a flattened line segment path prior to application of its transformation matrix and stroking of width for polyline approximations of curves. Interpress also describes support only for lines as a basic primitive and overtly leaves higher curves to user subroutines. Whether one agrees or not, at least both implementations do document their behavior so a user can make informed judgments and can expect some degree of internal consistency.

CGI's width definition is likely to be challenging when fully implemented. As illustrated in Figures 8 and 9, the pretransformation parallel curve for a wide ellipse involves an eighth-degree equation [Salm96]. Contrary to popular lore, a wide ellipse cannot properly be formed by a pair of confocal ellipses. A few quick calculations for the ellipse

$$(x/25)^2 + (y/5)^2 = 1$$

to calculate the normal distance $5/2 = w = W/2$ units on either side of the ellipse at reference points of, say,

Reference ELLIPSE point		Wide 'INNER' point		Wide 'OUTER' point	
x	y	x	y	x	y
0	5	0	2.5	0	7.5
0	−5	0	−2.5	0	−7.5
15	4	14.629	1.528	15.371	6.472
−15	4	−14.629	1.528	−15.371	6.472
20	3	19.356	0.584	20.644	5.416
−20	3	−19.356	0.584	−20.644	5.416
25	0	22.5	0	27.5	0
−25	0	−22.5	0	−27.5	0

should be enough to establish that an ellipse will not fit either the inner or outer set of eight calculated points. One also could calculate points for reference ellipse abscissa values of

$$x = 22.51, \quad x = 24.6, \quad \text{and} \quad x = 24.996$$

to see a possible cusp indication in the first quadrant of the reference ellipse when widened.

The error analysis to quantify how close reference ellipse chords, subsequently widened as line segments, come to the true parallel curves should be interesting. For variety, try determining the 'inner' parallel curve for a width of 30 units ($w = 15$) with the above ellipse. In EXOR logic, I'm not sure just what to expect!

For the first quadrant of the standard ellipse

$$(x/a)^2 + (y/b)^2 = 1$$

the normal to the peripheral point (i, j) is

$$y = (a/b)^2(j/i)x + j(1 - (a/b)^2)$$

For any point (i, j) on the first quadrant boundary of the reference ellipse and a line width of W, then the two 'wide' points on the normal are

$$(i - w\cos(t), \ j - w\sin(t)) \quad \text{and} \quad (i + w\cos(t), \ j + w\sin(t))$$

where $w = W/2$ and $t = \arctan(a/b)^2(j/i)$ or, alternatively,

$$w\cos(t) = wb^2 i/(b^4 i^2 + a^4 j^2)^{1/2}$$
$$w\sin(t) = wa^2 j/(b^4 i^2 + a^4 j^2)^{1/2}$$

The preceding expressions for width were used to calculate points plotted in Figure 8 for the reference ellipse

$$(x/5)^2 + (y/25)^2 = 1 \quad \text{with} \quad W = 2w = 5$$

The width problem of a sometimes fuzzy reference model also applies to Line_Style. What shape are nonsolid lines originally; how faithfully are those shapes to be transformed for wide line arcs? How does EXOR affect overlapping wide line styles in a polyline sequence? Does Line_Style have originally rectangular areas for line segments yet use radial edges for closure as annular sectors for circles?

The line style shape question must be answered for both geometric and cosmetic line widths. Reducing all geometry to line segments before applying attributes certainly can reduce implementation complexity but only at the cost of some degree of loss in fidelity and accuracy. An error analysis should be documented to help users make informed decisions from quantitative measures and bounds.

We may want to think about why Line_Style exists, why it originally was included in an architecture. Is it meant only for cosmetic purposes to distinguish different lines within a common picture? If so, then forcing it to fully conform to transformation may be superfluous. Or is it to guarantee shape and structure definition as one would expect to see if examining a line style under a magnifying glass? If so, then it is not a cosmetic attribute but a geometric attribute and should flow through all transformation processes. In net, was the purpose of Line_Style meant to be a compact form of repetitive area specification within a line or edge or was Line_Style intended only to offer a means of visual emphasis, distinction, or highlighting?

As a concluding example of Line_Width, consider

$$\text{POLYLINE from } (40, 0) \text{ to } (0, 0) \text{ to } (40, 9)$$

with a width of 8 such that $w = 4$, and an anisotropic transformation matrix such that

$$u = x - (40/9)y \quad v = (40/9)y$$
$$x = u + v \qquad\quad y = (9/40)v$$

The wide-line locus envelope includes

'outer': $y = (9/40)x + 4.1$ and $y = -4$ intersecting at $(-36, -4)$

'inner': $y = (9/40)x - 4.1$ and $y = 4$ intersecting at $(36, 4)$

With axially aligned end caps, the unbeveled mitered boundary could be from $(-36, -4)$ to $(40, 13.1)$ to $(40, 4.9)$ to $(36, 4)$ to $(40, 4)$ to $(40, -4)$ to $(-36, -4)$.

The angle of the 'outer' bounding line pair from $(40, -4)$ to $(-36, -4)$ to $(40, 13.1)$ in x and y pretransform space is slightly less than 13 degrees. Should we therefore bevel the miter join? We certainly will get a different result than if we checked their posttransform intersection angle. After the two lines have had the above transformation applied, they intersect at a 90 degree angle.

The point to remember is that while geometric width boundaries and geometric line style areas should be determined prior to transformation, beveling is a posttransformation decision. The question to answer is: 'Are attributes such as mitered joins, beveled miters, circular end caps and the like meant to achieve geometric or cosmetic effects?' With isotropic transformation, of course, a decision usually can be made equally well in either pre- or posttransformation space. With anisotropic transformation, beveling, like a three-point circle's final shape, is a transformation-sensitive action. Notice also that had round end caps been specified, the posttransform end caps actually drawn in the example would need to be elliptical, not circular.

Conclusion

Seemingly obvious cases in graphics systems can actually carry a good bit of latitude in fuzzy definitions and permissive, nonportable implementations. As elementary concepts are extended, better, more definitive models may be worthwhile. Affine transformation, Line_Width, and Line_Style applied to lines, circles, and ellipses are representative examples. Comprehensive, complete, and consistent definitions for attribute processing and attribute interactions are usually well served by identifying one's motivation in providing an attribute. Is the effect intended to be geometric or cosmetic? Is the attribute applied pre- or posttransformation? Geometric line width, for example, should be applied pretransformation, while the refinement of beveling joined segments is a posttransformation action.

To the best of the author's knowledge, there is no standard agreement even on rendering concepts as basic as which pixels should appear for an EXOR rastered, wide polyline from device coordinates $(40, 0)$ to $(0, 0)$ to $(40, 1)$ and whether or not the polyline result should match identically, pixel for pixel, the rendering of the two lines separately drawn individually from $(40, 0)$ to $(0, 0)$ and from $(40, 1)$ to $(0, 0)$.

Attention to picture rendering should address a number of questions such as the following. Are the common pixels shared in the rastered form of the two component lines self-canceling when doubly selected or, like an area fill, are they visible, since area pixels are filled only once each between bounds? Are single pixel lines and wide lines compatible in their EXOR treatment of shared pixels? Should attributes be applied before or after approximation? Should approximation come before or after transformation? Should width be applied to an approximation of a reference curve or should the theoretical parallel curves themselves be approximated?

There could be merit in a separate, lower level of graphics specification layer which addresses alternatives for geometric raster renderings and approximations as its only topic of standardization. Perhaps higher level interface specifications need not fully and comprehensively resolve such detail as: 'Precisely how does a wide, dot/dash line style appear after anisotropic transformation as the edge of a wide ellipse drawn in an EXOR logical writing mode?' An architecturally layered conceptual model comparable to OSI's seven-layer approach could be interesting.

ADDENDUM

Version 3.0 of Xerox's Interpress introduced direct declaration of circular arcs and Bézier curves. Interpress, like Adobe's PostScript, now would appear to take full architectural responsibility for accuracy and robustness of approximation and attribute behavior should users apply affine transformation extremes to wide curves. References [Inte84] and [Spro84] describe Version 2.1, which included only line support.

Acknowledgments. Thanks are owed Rae Earnshaw and Dave Rogers for instigating preparation of this paper. As well, discussions at various times with Nancy Bull, Janet Lyn, L.J.B., David Floyd, Bob Sproull, Bryan Roberts, Brian Middleton, Alan Middleditch, Shawn Kerrigan, Adrian Gay, Mike Davis, and Richard Chandler were very helpful and thought-provoking. Illustrative figures were prepared by C. Brown McFadden and James Hammond. Faye Martin found a copy of reference [Salm96] for me. Texas Instruments' donation of a TI34010 development board with a full complement of accompanying software for graphics teaching and research at Winthrop College is very much appreciated. Special thanks also are expressed to IBM for their making possible Winthrop College participation in the X3H3.3 CGI graphics standardization committee.

REFERENCES

[Bono88]
Bono, P.R., and Arnold, D.B., *CGM and CGI: Metafile and Interface Standards for Computer Graphics*, New York: Springer-Verlag, 1988.

[CGI86]
Computer Graphics Interface. ISO/DP9636. Information Processing System—Computer Graphics—Interfacing techniques for dialogues with graphical devices. Functional Specification, 8 December 1986 (X3H3/86-188a).

[Cohe71]
Cohen, D., On Linear Difference Curves, in *Advanced Computer Graphics, Economics, Techniques and Applications*, Parslow, R.D., and Green, R.E., Eds., pp. 1143–1177, New York: Plenum Press, 1971.

[Inte84]
Interpress, *Electronic Printing Standard*, Xerox Corp., Stamford, CN, Ver. 2.1, April 1984.

[Post86a]
PostScript, Language Reference Manual, Adobe Systems, Reading, MA: Addison-Wesley, April 1986.

[Post86b]

PostScript, Language Tutorial and Cookbook, Adobe Systems, Reading, MA: Addison-Wesley, May 1986.

[Salm96]

Salmon, G., *A Treatise on Conic Sections*, 10th Ed., pp. 172–175 and pp. 334–339, London: Longmans, Green and Co., 1896.

[Spro84]

Sproull, R.F., and Reid, B.K., *Introduction to Interpress*, Xerox Corp., Stamford, CN, April 1984.

2 Color in Computer Graphics

Image Synthesis and Color Vision

Gary W. Meyer

Abstract

The first two stages of the human color vision system are introduced and are used to solve color selection problems in computer graphic image synthesis. In describing these initial portions of the visual pathway, the color vision system is treated as a signal-processing device that interprets the spectral energy distributions reaching it from the environment. The first stage of the color vision system, the fundamental spectral sensitivity functions, is shown to have many of the characteristics of a simple sampling device. These fundamental spectral sensitivity functions are suggested as being useful in selecting colors for individuals who have color-defective vision. The second stage of the color vision system, the opponent fundamentals, is shown to have a form that is optimal from a statistical communication theory viewpoint. These opponent fundamentals are demonstrated as providing a useful guide in the selection of wavelengths for synthetic image generation.

Introduction

The nature of the human color vision system plays an integral role in the creation of computer graphic images. The accurate synthesis of color for realistic images, the proper selection of color for informative displays, and the correct reproduction of color on an output device all depend on an understanding of how our color vision system works. This paper provides an introduction to the first two stages of the human color vision system and shows how the characteristics of these elements of our visual system can be used to solve computer graphic color selection problems.

The approach that is taken in this paper to introducing the color vision system is to draw on recent work that treats it as a signal-processing device. Given the information content of the spectral energy distributions that the visual system must be capable of interpreting, the type of receptor system that should be expected is derived. The transmission of the color signal beyond the receptors constitutes the second stage of the color vision system, and it is shown to have a form that is optimal from a statistical

communication theory viewpoint. Once the basic nature of each stage
has been motivated using this signal-processing approach, it is compared
with existing psychophysical data and is expressed in terms of the CIE
XYZ system.

After each of the first two stages of the color vision system has been
introduced, it is used to solve a specific computer graphics color selection
problem. The fundamental spectral sensitivity functions, which constitute
the first stage of the color vision system, are shown to be useful in selecting
colors for individuals who have color defective vision. A view of the world
as seen by a person who has color defective vision is synthesized, and guidelines are given for choosing colors that will not be confused by persons who
have the most common forms of color defective vision. The second stage of
the color vision system, the opponent fundamentals, are used to guide the
selection of wavelengths for synthetic image generation. It is shown that
wavelengths selected using the opponent fundamentals give better results
than wavelengths selected using either the fundamental spectral sensitivity
functions or the CIE XYZ matching functions.

The Fundamental Sensitivities

All color reproduction work in computer graphics is based on the fundamental spectral sensitivity functions that are active in the human visual
system. In this section, it is first suggested that the number and the shape
of these functions is related to the frequency content of the spectral energy distributions that the functions must interpret. Next, the fundamental spectral sensitivity functions are expressed in terms of the CIE XYZ
matching functions by drawing upon the fact that color blindness is caused
by the lack of one of the functions. Finally, a color-blind view of the world
is synthesized, and color scales that are unambiguous to both color-normal
and color-blind observers are derived. Since a significant portion of the
population is color blind, the design of displays for color-deficient users is
an important topic in computer graphics.

USE OF FOURIER ANALYSIS TO DERIVE THE NUMBER AND SHAPE OF THE HUMAN SPECTRAL SENSITIVITY FUNCTIONS

Fourier analysis can be used to suggest what both the number and the approximate shape of the human spectral sensitivity functions should be. The
spectral energy distributions that occur in nature are relatively smooth and
therefore require a low sampling rate. Evolution has produced a system
that not only takes advantage of this fact but is also capable of handling discontinuous spectral energy distributions such as those produced by modern
day lasers.

Number and Shape of Sensitivities Suggested by Fourier Analysis

The sampling theorem can be used to determine the rate at which samples must be taken in order to fully characterize a signal. Consider a function $f(\lambda)$ with Fourier transform $F(\omega)$. If the spacing between samples of $f(\lambda)$ is T, the Fourier transform of the resulting sampled function will consist of the original Fourier transform $F(\omega)$ replicated at intervals of $1/T$. If $F(\omega)$ is band limited so that ω is zero for $|\omega| > \omega_c$, then there will be no overlap between adjacent copies of $F(\omega)$ if $T \leq 1/(2\omega_c)$. This means that the original frequency representation $F(\omega)$ can be recovered from the sampled version of the function, and the original function $f(\lambda)$ can be reconstructed. If this Nyquist sampling criteria $T \leq 1/(2\omega_c)$ is not used, there will be overlap between adjacent copies of $F(\omega)$ making it impossible to recover the original function.

The sampling theorem can be extended to handle situations where the distance between samples is nonuniform [Yen56; Free65; Helm61]. Given the Nyquist sampling criteria T for a band limited function $f(\lambda)$, it can be shown [Yen56] that it suffices that there be N distinct samples for every interval of length NT. The position of each of the samples within the interval is unimportant. With this information, the original function $f(\lambda)$ can be uniquely reconstructed.

Determining the appropriate sampling rate for the human visual system requires Fourier analysis of the most probable set of spectral energy distributions encountered by the human organism during its evolution. The best available data for this task are the spectral reflectances of natural formations compiled by E. L. Krinov [Krin47]. As can be seen in Figure 1, the three classes of reflectance type identified by Krinov are all represented by very smooth curves. This implies that the frequency content of these curves is quite low and that the sampling rate necessary to fully characterize them is also very low. Let us defer the discussion of the work that has been done to precisely determine the frequency content of these curves and assume for the moment that a sampling rate of three samples over the visible spectrum is sufficient. Recalling that the spacing between samples need not be uniform, one plausible sampling array is shown in Figure 2.

As mentioned earlier, a function cannot be reconstructed from samples taken at less than the Nyquist rate. This means that if the sampling rate is fixed, functions that contain frequencies above the Nyquist limit cannot be reconstructed from their samples. The best that one can hope to do is to control the distortion by low-pass filtering the function before sampling it until no frequencies beyond the Nyquist limit are present. This can be accomplished in the frequency domain by multiplication with the desired filter, or it can be done in the spatial (or time, or wavelength) domain by convolution with the Fourier transform of the filter. In practice, the convolution need only be performed at those locations where samples will ultimately be taken. Although spectral energy distributions reflected from natural formations probably influenced the trichromatic nature of

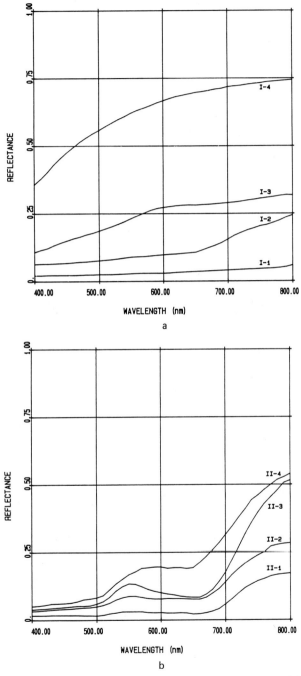

Figure 1. Spectrophotometric classification of natural formations (after Krinov [Krin47]). (a) Class I, bare areas, soils, buildings, and dry vegetation. (b) Class II, vegetative formations.

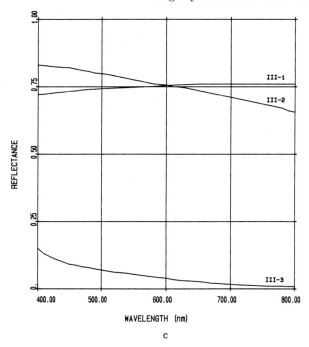

Figure 1. (cont.) (c) Class III, snow and water surfaces.

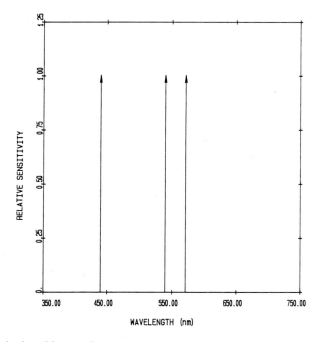

Figure 2. A plausible sampling array.

the human color vision system, there are numerous other spectral energy distributions in nature for which three samples would be inadequate. A prefilter like the one in Figure 3 is necessary in order to band limit the signal to less than one and a half cycles over the visual range. If this filter is transformed into the wavelength domain and the resulting convolution mask is positioned at the sample locations in Figure 2, the result is as shown in Figure 4. As we shall see later, these sensitivity functions bear a strong resemblance to the ones actually present in the human visual system.

Fourier Analysis of the Human Color Vision System

Determining the sampling rate that is necessary in order to fully characterize the spectral energy distributions that reach our eyes is a difficult task that involves a certain amount of subjective judgment. Fourier analysis assumes that the function being studied repeats itself indefinitely. In the case of spectral energy distributions that begin and end abruptly at approximately 400 and 800 nanometers (nm), a significant amount of high-frequency information is introduced that has nothing to do with the basic shape of the curves themselves. Low-frequency information such as the average value, linear trend, or quadratic trend can be removed from the function to minimize this effect. However, in this case, the impact on the

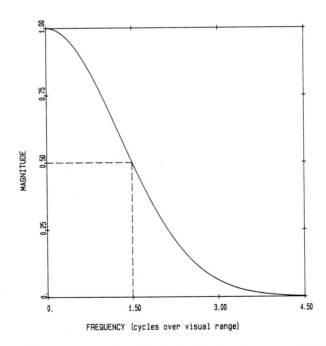

Figure 3. Prefilter necessary to band limit signal to less than one and a half cycles over the visual range.

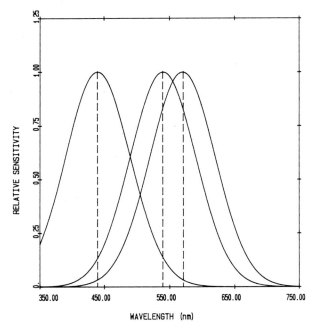

Figure 4. Prefilter convolution mask positioned at sample locations.

final result could be significant because this information is a major component of these spectral reflectance curves. The ends of the curves can also be tapered so as to provide a smooth transition when the curves are placed end to end. Figure 5 shows the result of applying these techniques to curve II-3 from Figure 1.

In spite of the difficulties that are involved, there have been several recent attempts to characterize the human color vision system as a device that low-pass filters and then samples the signals that it receives. In Buchsbaum and Gottschalk [Buch84] it was shown that frequency-limited functions having only three degrees of freedom produce a set of chromaticity coordinates that covers a significant region of the CIE chromaticity diagram. Cohen [Cohe64] applied characteristic vector analysis to 150 Munsell samples and found that three degrees of freedom were sufficient to represent the reflectances of these color chips. Maloney [Malo86] examined the power spectra of both the Munsell color samples and the Krinov [Krin47] reflectances of natural formations. His analysis showed that as much as 0.97 of the spectral energy was below the frequency limit (in cycles/nm) necessary to characterize the reflectances using only three samples. He concludes, however, that five to seven samples are necessary to perfectly represent all of the reflectances examined.

The low-pass filtering characteristics of the spectral sensitivity functions have been examined in Barlow [Barl82]. There it was shown that spectral energy distributions with frequency content as low as two cycles over

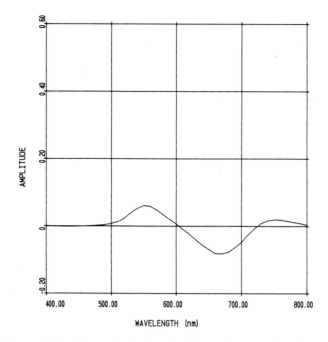

Figure 5. Curve II-3 with quadratic trend subtracted out and ends tapered.

the visible spectrum were significantly demodulated by the low-pass filter characteristics of the spectral sensitivity functions. The effect was quite strong for the long and medium wavelength fundamentals but was not as significant for the narrower short wavelength fundamental.

The extent to which the human color vision system can be thought of as a well-designed device for sampling spectral energy distributions is a question that is still open to debate. The answer to the question depends on what is selected as the collection of spectral energy distributions to be sampled, the importance that is placed on a perfect reconstruction of every curve in this collection, and the significance that is attached to aliasing artifacts produced by functions from outside the basic group of curves to be sampled. Nevertheless, the evidence to date does suggest that the color vision system has many of the characteristics of a simple sampling device.

GEOMETRIC PROPERTIES OF A COLOR SPACE BASED ON THE HUMAN SPECTRAL SENSITIVITY FUNCTIONS

Tristimulus values can be computed from the hypothetical spectral sensitivity functions derived by Fourier analysis in the preceding section and can be plotted in a 3D coordinate system. For 'color-blind' people, this color space collapses to a plane containing two of the original coordinate axes if it is accepted that 'color blindness' is caused by the lack of one of the spectral sensitivity functions. Certain geometric relationships hold between the coordinate systems of these 'dichromats' and the coordinate system of normal 'trichromats'. These geometric relationships remain invariant under a linear transform.

The SML Color Space

The short $(\bar{s}(\lambda))$, medium $(\bar{m}(\lambda))$, and long $(\bar{\ell}(\lambda))$ wavelength spectral sensitivity functions that were postulated by Fourier analysis resolve a spectral energy distribution $E(\lambda)$ into tristimulus values S, M, and L. This can be expressed mathematically as:

$$S = \int E(\lambda)\bar{s}(\lambda)d\lambda$$

$$M = \int E(\lambda)\bar{m}(\lambda)d\lambda$$

$$L = \int E(\lambda)\bar{\ell}(\lambda)d\lambda \qquad (1)$$

If two different spectral energy distributions yield the same tristimulus values, then they are indistinguishable to the visual system. It is this fact that makes color reproduction practical.

These tristimulus values can be plotted in an SML coordinate system. In this 3D space, the above integral expression is replaced by vector addition. Each wavelength λ_i of the spectral energy distribution $E(\lambda)$ produces a component vector $(E(\lambda_i)\bar{s}(\lambda_i),\ E(\lambda_i)\bar{m}(\lambda_i),\ E(\lambda_i)\bar{\ell}(\lambda_i))$. All such component vectors pass through the equal energy spectrum locus and lie on a cone-shaped surface called the cone of realizable color. Because the cone is convex, the sum of the component vectors that yield the tristimulus value must lie in the interior domain of the cone.

If a spectral energy distribution is scaled up or down (as it often is in a practical situation), the resulting tristimulus values produce a straight line that passes through the origin of SML space. The direction of this line can be described by erecting a unit plane and noting where the line intersects it. This point of intersection is identified by chromaticity coordinates s and m, which are computed from the expressions

$$s = \frac{S}{S + M + L} \qquad m = \frac{M}{S + M + L} \qquad (2)$$

Dichromatic Color Space

It is now generally accepted that 'color blindness' is caused by the lack of one of the fundamental spectral sensitivity functions. This is called 'dichromacy'; the three versions of it are known as protanopia (lack of the long wavelength function), deuteranopia (lack of the medium wavelength function), and tritanopia (lack of the short wavelength function). To quantify dichromatic color vision, distimulus values are computed instead of tristimulus values. These two coordinates are plotted on a 2D plane instead of in a 3D space, and chromaticity coordinates are found on a unit line instead of on a unit plane. Specifically, the SM, SL, and ML planes in SML space are the color planes for protanopia, deuteranopia, and tritanopia, respectively. Each edge of the unit plane in SML space becomes the unit line on which dichromatic chromaticity coordinates are plotted for each of the planes. Figure 6 shows how the color space for protanopia is derived from SML space.

A tristimulus coordinate is converted into a distimulus coordinate by orthographic projection onto the appropriate dichromatic plane. This means that there is a family of lines in SML space, each with constant trichromatic chromaticity, that all reduce to the same line with constant dichromatic chromaticity in the SM, ML, or SL planes. This family of lines all lie in the plane in SML space that contains both the line with constant dichromatic chromaticity and the axis of the missing fundamental. The intersection of this plane of constant dichromatic chromaticity with the unit plane in SML space produces what is called a line of dichromatic confusion. It is given this name because one of the three types of dichromats will not be able to distinguish between any of the trichromatic chromaticities that form this line. The intersection point of the lines of dichromatic confusion marks the spot where the axis of the missing fundamental pierces the unit plane. These are referred to as the dichromatic confusion points (see Figure 6).

Linear Color Space Transforms

Color-matching can be considered to be a linear process because it obeys the laws of proportionality and scaling. There are, therefore, an infinite number of equivalent color spaces that can be reached by a linear transform of SML space. These new color spaces contain unit planes that are intersected by the planes of constant dichromatic chromaticity once they are transformed from SML space. The three new sets of dichromatic confusion lines that are produced each intersect at the point where one of the transformed S, M, or L axes pierce the unit plane of the new space (see Figure 6). If the new space is called XYZ space (the significance of this choice of notation will become clear later) and the new dichromatic confusion points are called (x_p, y_p), (x_d, y_d), and (x_t, y_t), then the new matching functions $\bar{x}(\lambda)$, $\bar{y}(\lambda)$, and $\bar{z}(\lambda)$ can be expressed in terms of the fundamental spectral sensitivity functions $\bar{s}(\lambda)$, $\bar{m}(\lambda)$, and $\bar{\ell}(\lambda)$ by the relation

$$
\begin{bmatrix} \bar{x}(\lambda) \\ \bar{y}(\lambda) \\ \bar{z}(\lambda) \end{bmatrix} = \begin{bmatrix} x_t & x_d & x_p \\ y_t & y_d & y_p \\ 1 - x_t - y_t & 1 - x_d - y_d & 1 - x_p - y_p \end{bmatrix} \begin{bmatrix} k_t \bar{s}(\lambda) \\ k_d \bar{m}(\lambda) \\ k_p \bar{\ell}(\lambda) \end{bmatrix} \quad (3)
$$

where k_t, k_d, and k_p are normalization factors.

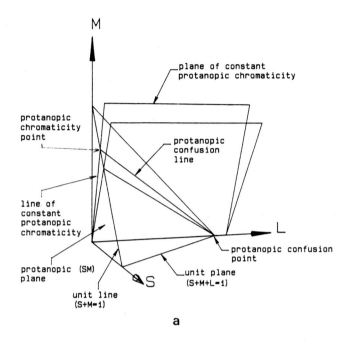

a

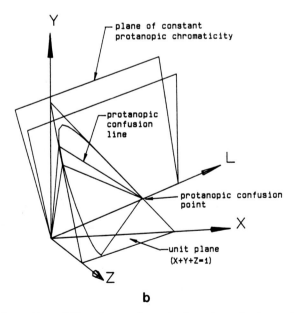

b

Figure 6. Intersection of the planes of constant protanopic chromaticity defines the position of the L-axis (a) in SML space; (b) in CIE XYZ space.

Derivation of the Human Spectral Sensitivity Functions From Available Psychophysical Data

To this point in the paper, the number and shape of the spectral sensitivity functions have been hypothesized, a color space based on these functions has been introduced, the possible geometric relationship between the color spaces of dichromats and trichromats has been suggested, and the effect of linear transformations of these color spaces has been demonstrated. This section seeks to solve Eq. (3) for the fundamental spectral sensitivities $\bar{s}(\lambda)$, $\bar{m}(\lambda)$, and $\bar{\ell}(\lambda)$. First, a set of color-matching functions $\bar{x}(\lambda)$, $\bar{y}(\lambda)$, and $\bar{z}(\lambda)$ are selected from the available psychophysical data. Next, the dichromatic confusion points (x_p, y_p), (x_d, y_d), and (x_t, y_t) are chosen. Finally, the relative sensitivities of the spectral sensitivity functions are derived. Once these pieces of information have been established, the matrix in Eq. (3) can be inverted and the fundamental spectral sensitivities can be solved for.

The Choice of Color-matching Functions

The correct way to determine color-matching functions is by measuring the radiant power of each of three primaries used to match a monochromatic stimulus. The only set of experiments in which these measurements were actually made is the Stiles two-degree pilot data [Stil55]. Although the discrepancies between this data and the 1931 CIE standard-observer matching functions described below are not great, the Stiles color-matching functions should be used for careful vision research [Este79]. Unfortunately, these data are not widely available.

The 1931 CIE XYZ standard-observer matching functions are based on color-matching experiments that were performed by Guild [Guil31] and Wright [Wrig28]. Because of technological limitations at that time, the amounts of the primaries were measured by a brightness-matching procedure instead of by making radiometric measurements. This imbedded two assumptions into the color-matching data that are being challenged today: (a) that brightness-matching is an additive process and (b) that the luminous efficiency function is a linear combination of the color-matching functions themselves. The CIE used the mean results of Guild [Guil31] and Wright [Wrig28] to define standard-observer matching functions $\bar{x}(\lambda)$, $\bar{y}(\lambda)$, and $\bar{z}(\lambda)$, where $\bar{y}(\lambda)$ is the luminous efficiency function.

Judd [Judd51] determined that the luminous efficiency function was in error at short wavelengths. A new luminous efficiency function was proposed and a new set of color-matching functions was derived from the Guild [Guil31] and Wright [Wrig28] data. Although these modified standard-observer matching functions have been widely used in vision research, they have not been applied to practical colorimetry.

In this paper, the 1931 CIE standard-observer matching functions $\bar{x}(\lambda)$, $\bar{y}(\lambda)$, and $\bar{z}(\lambda)$ will be used. This makes it possible to use phosphor chromaticity coordinates that are published in terms of the CIE standard observer. It also introduces only a small error and in return makes the results of the research accessible to a wider audience.

The Choice of Confusion Points

Table 1 summarizes the proposals that have been made for the protanopic, deuteranopic, and tritanopic confusion points. From this array of possible confusion points, the protanopic, deuteranopic, and tritanopic points proposed by Estevez [Este79] will be used here. This has been done for the following reasons: (a) the points are expressed in terms of the 1931 CIE system and not the 1951 Judd modification of this system; (b) there are unresolved discrepancies among the many other proposed sets of points; (c) the problems inherent in averaging confusion points to obtain new confusion points are avoided; and (d) all three points are evaluated simultaneously, not one point at a time.

To determine the protanopic and deuteranopic confusion points, Estevez [Este79] first uses previous estimates of these confusion points to find the two wavelengths that protanopes and deuteranopes consider to be neutral with respect to source B. The intersection of a line through each of these wavelengths and source B with the line $x + y = 1$ yields the protanopic and deuteranopic confusion points. Estevez [Este79] locates the tritanopic confusion point from the intersection of lines that connect wavelength pairs that, according to Wright [Wrig52], have the same dichromatic coordinates.

The Relative Sensitivity of the Fundamentals

Although there were many alternatives to be considered, the selection of the color-matching functions and the confusion points could be made with confidence because there was a substantial amount of evidence upon which to base a decision. This is not true of the relative sensitivity of the fundamentals because this question has not been given much study. The work of

Table 1. Proposed value for the protanopic, deuteranopic, and tritanopic confusion points.

Source	Protanopic		Deuteranopic		Tritanopic	
	x_p	y_p	x_d	y_d	x_t	y_t
Pitt35, Judd44	0.747	0.253	1.08	−0.08		
Pitt43, Judd49					0.18	0.0
Judd49, Judd50					0.165	0.0
Thom53, Wrig52[†]	0.7465	0.2535			0.1748	0.0044
Judd66, Nime70	0.75	0.25			0.17	0.0
Nime70			1.29	−0.29		
Nime70			1.53	−0.53		
Vos70[†]			1.4	−0.4		
Walr74[†]					0.1747	0.0060
Este79	0.73	0.27	1.14	−0.14	0.171	−0.003

[†]Used 1951 Judd matching functions.

Vos and Walraven [Vos70] and Walraven [Walr74] represents almost all the work that has been done in this area. Consequently, the approach taken in these two articles is adopted here.

To start, make the assumption that the output of the short, medium, and long wavelength receptors gets matrixed into red/green ($\bar{\ell}(\lambda)/\bar{m}(\lambda)$), yellow/blue (($\bar{\ell}(\lambda) + \bar{m}(\lambda))/\bar{s}(\lambda)$), and black/white ($\bar{s}(\lambda) + \bar{m}(\lambda) + \bar{\ell}(\lambda)$) signals. The fact that hue remains constant with a change in intensity for the wavelengths 475.5 nm and 570 nm leads to the relationship

$$\frac{\bar{\ell}(570)}{N_\ell} = \frac{\bar{m}(570)}{N_m} \tag{4}$$

$$\frac{\bar{\ell}(475.5) + \bar{m}(475.5)}{N_\ell + N_m} = \frac{\bar{s}(475.5)}{N_s} \tag{5}$$

where N_ℓ, N_m, and N_s are the number of each type of receptor in the retina. With the assumption that the black/white channel has spectral sensitivity that is equivalent to the luminous efficiency function and the realization that $\bar{m}(\lambda) = \bar{\ell}(\lambda) = 0$ at the S axis and that $\bar{s}(\lambda) = 0$ at the M and L axes, $\bar{s}(\lambda)$ can be solved for in terms of the $\bar{x}(\lambda)$, $\bar{y}(\lambda)$, and $\bar{z}(\lambda)$ matching functions when the dichromatic confusion points are known. Given $\bar{s}(\lambda)$, $\bar{m}(\lambda)+\bar{\ell}(\lambda)$ is known (because the three must sum to the luminous efficiency function), and it follows from Eq. (5) that

$$\frac{N_\ell + N_m}{N_s} = \frac{\bar{\ell}(475.5) + \bar{m}(475.5)}{\bar{s}(475.5)} = \frac{1}{16} \tag{6}$$

In order to determine the ratio between N_ℓ and N_m, the Stiles-Weber coefficients [Stil46] are used. This leads to

$$\frac{N_\ell}{N_m} = \frac{\bar{\ell}(570)}{\bar{m}(570)} = 2 \tag{7}$$

Given these two results, the ratios of each type of receptor become $N_\ell : N_m : N_s = 32 : 16 : 1$.

This approach to determining the relative sensitivity of the fundamentals has its strengths and weaknesses. As pointed out in Walraven [Walr74], the above ratio of receptor populations makes it possible for each type of receptor to be laid out in a manner that is consistent with the overall hexagonal pattern of the receptors on the retina. The 2:1 ratio of long wavelength to medium wavelength receptors is close to the 1.6:1 ratio suggested by Ingling [Ingl83]. On the other hand, Burns et al. [Burn84] have argued strongly against the use of unique hues as balance points for either of the two opponent mechanisms.

The Resulting Fundamental Sensitivities

Given the dichromatic confusion points that were selected previously in the section on linear color space transformation and the ratios between the fundamentals that were given in Eqs. (6) and (7), the fundamental spectral sensitivity functions can be expressed as

$$
\begin{bmatrix} \bar{s}(\lambda) \\ \bar{m}(\lambda) \\ \bar{\ell}(\lambda) \end{bmatrix} = \begin{bmatrix} 0.0000 & 0.0000 & 0.0127 \\ -0.2606 & 0.7227 & 0.0562 \\ 0.1150 & 0.9364 & -0.0203 \end{bmatrix} \begin{bmatrix} \bar{x}(\lambda) \\ \bar{y}(\lambda) \\ \bar{z}(\lambda) \end{bmatrix} \tag{8}
$$

where $\bar{x}(\lambda)$, $\bar{y}(\lambda)$, and $\bar{z}(\lambda)$ are the 1931 CIE XYZ matching functions selected previously in the section on the choice of color-matching functions. Figure 7 shows the resulting curves.

Given the fundamental spectral sensitivity functions, we can now take a closer look at the SML coordinate system that was first introduced in the section discussing the SML color space. When the tristimulus values $\bar{s}(\lambda_i)$, $\bar{m}(\lambda_i)$, and $\bar{\ell}(\lambda_i)$ are plotted for each wavelength λ_i in the visible spectrum, the equal energy spectrum locus in Figure 8 results. The cone of realizable color is created by extending vectors out from the origin of SML space and through the equal energy spectrum locus. All possible SML tristimulus values must lie within the shell that results (see Figure 8).

DICHROMATIC VISION AND COMPUTER GRAPHICS

The human spectral sensitivity functions, which were derived from psychophysical experiments performed on dichromats, can be used in conjunction with computer graphics hardware to gain additional insights into the nature of dichromatic vision. A color image can be transformed so that a trichromat can see how this picture appears to a dichromat, and guidelines for designing computer graphic displays for use by dichromats can be derived.

A Dichromat's View of the World

Synthesizing a view of the world as seen by a dichromat depends on data obtained from people who are protanopes or deuteranopes in one eye and trichromats in the other eye. The weight of evidence from research on these people is that the hue circuit for normal trichromats becomes a hue line for protanopes and deuteranopes with blue and yellow as the end points for the line and a neutral gray at the midpoint. In the primary experiment used to obtain these results, wavelengths of light from across the spectrum were presented to the dichromatic eye, and the subject was allowed to vary the wavelength of a spectral light focused on the trichromatic eye until a match with the dichromatic eye was obtained. In all cases only one of two wavelengths was used to match all of the spectral lights. One of these occurred in the blue portion of spectrum at approximately 575 nm, and the other occurred in the yellow portion of the spectrum at approximately 470 nm. At about 500 nm the subjects reported that the test light appeared neutral and could not be matched by either of the above two spectral lights.

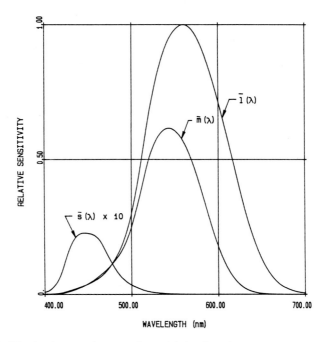

Figure 7. The fundamental spectral sensitivity functions.

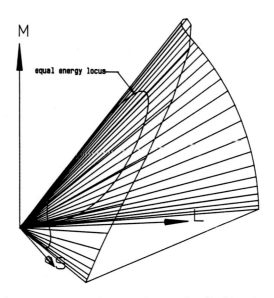

Figure 8. Equal energy spectrum locus and cone of realizable color in SML space. (Fundamental spectral sensitivities were all normalized to 1.0 to plot the equal energy spectrum locus.)

With this experiment as a starting point, a view of the world as seen by a dichromat has been synthesized [Meye88b]. The *RGB* values for each pixel were first transformed into CIE *XYZ* space and the chromaticity and luminance were determined. Next, the confusion line that passes through the chromaticity point of each pixel was found. The point of intersection between this confusion line and the major axis for each type of dichromat represents the color as it would appear to that type of dichromat (see Figure 9). The major axes were defined as the lines through 473 nm and 574 nm for protanopes, the line through 477 nm and 578 nm for deuteranopes, and the line through 490 nm and 610 nm for tritanopes. The position of these axes was based on the above color-matching experiment and on the uniform chromaticity diagram proposed by Farnsworth [Farn43]. This new chromaticity and the original luminance were then transformed back into *RGB* space. If the new color fell outside the monitor gamut, it was adjusted by either holding its dominant wavelength constant and reducing its purity, or by holding its chromaticity constant and adjusting its luminance. In some cases both types of adjustment were required. The resulting pictures for each type of dichromat are shown in Figure 10.

Figure 9. Axes of colors actually seen by protanopes and adjustments made to a single chromaticity point in order to create a protanopic version of an image.

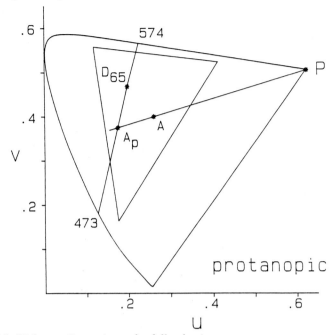

Figure 10. Dichromatic versions of a full color image.

Color Selection for Dichromats

Colors to be avoided when designing displays for dichromats are obviously those colors that they cannot separately distinguish. Just as a trichromat cannot tell the difference between colors that have the same SML tristimulus value, a dichromat cannot distinguish between colors that have the same SM, ML, or SL distimulus value. Expressed in another way, if the dichromatic chromaticity and luminance are the same for two colors, a dichromat will not be able to tell them apart. If, in addition, the trichromatic chromaticity and luminance for the colors are the same, a trichromat will not be able to distinguish between them. The confusion lines on a trichromat's chromaticity diagram indicate those colors that have constant dichromatic chromaticity. If it is assumed that to a first order the luminance for trichromats and dichromats is the same (the differences are discussed in Wyszecki and Stiles [Wysz82]), then two colors that lie on the same confusion line and have the same luminance will be indistinguishable to the appropriate dichromat.

Colors that appear different to a dichromat and are thus to be preferred in display design for dichromats are those which at least differ in luminance and preferably do not lie on the same confusion line in the chromaticity diagram. The best such color scales would be those that are more or less orthogonal to the confusion lines. The colors used to produce the dichromatic version of the full color picture in Figure 10 have such a property (see

Figure 9). They also correspond to the colors actually seen by a dichromat. Since tritanopia is so rare and the confusion lines for protanopia and deuteranopia are almost parallel, it is possible to select a single color scale that will accommodate virtually all color-defective users [Meye88b].

The Opponent Fundamentals And Their Use In Synthetic Image Generation

In realistic image synthesis, color is determined by finding the wavelength composition of the light that reaches the image plane. Doing this efficiently depends on modeling the correct number and spacing of wavelengths across the visible spectrum. It has recently been shown that the opponent representation of the fundamental spectral sensitivity functions that has long been postulated as the second stage of human color vision is optimal from the point of view of statistical communication theory. This result is used in this section to guide the selection of wavelengths for synthetic image generation. Gaussian quadrature with the opponent fundamentals as weighting functions is used to choose the wavelengths. This approach is compared with using Gaussian quadrature with the fundamental spectral sensitivity functions or the CIE XYZ matching functions.

AN OPTIMAL COLOR SPACE FOR COLOR SYNTHESIS

The determination of color in a computer-generated scene involves both a modeling and a synthesis step. As the environment is modeled, reflectances are assigned to materials and emittances are associated with light sources. Synthesis involves the application of a sophisticated lighting model to compute spectral energy distributions on a wavelength-by-wavelength basis [Cook82; Hall83]. Eventually, the spectral energy distributions are resolved to tristimulus values and are displayed on a color reproduction device.

The obvious system in which to represent the tristimulus values that result from the image synthesis process would appear to be the SML coordinate system that is based on the fundamental spectral sensitivity functions of the human visual system. Equation 8 relates the fundamental spectral sensitivities $\bar{s}(\lambda)$, $\bar{m}(\lambda)$, and $\bar{\ell}(\lambda)$ to the 1931 CIE standard-observer color-matching functions $\bar{x}(\lambda)$, $\bar{y}(\lambda)$, and $\bar{z}(\lambda)$. The spectral sensitivities and the SML color space that result from this transformation are shown in Figures 7 and 8, respectively.

While the SML coordinate system is the straightforward choice for the space in which to represent tristimulus values, a color space should be chosen that minimizes any errors that might be inherent in the color calculations. The color space used should ensure that the minimum number of wavelengths are used in the synthesis process, since the expensive lighting model calculations may have to be repeated at each wavelength. These wavelengths should be positioned in the visible spectrum so that they are located at the positions most important for accurate color rendition.

A transform of the SML coordinate system is sought that directs the axes through the most dense regions of tristimulus values and that assigns a priority to each axis depending on the proportion of the coordinates which lie along its direction. Some clues as to the nature of this transformation can be obtained by examining SML space. The overlap between the $\bar{m}(\lambda)$ and $\bar{\ell}(\lambda)$ spectral sensitivity functions in Figure 7 leads to high correlation between the M and L portions of an SML tristimulus value. This can be seen in Figure 8 where the locus for the equal energy spectral energy distribution makes a loop in the LM plane at a 45 degree angle to the L and M axes. On the other hand, the lack of overlap between the $\bar{s}(\lambda)$ spectral sensitivity functions and either the $\bar{m}(\lambda)$ or the $\bar{\ell}(\lambda)$ spectral sensitivity functions leads to a low correlation between the S and either the L or M portions of an SML tristimulus value.

The discrete Karhunen-Loeve expansion can be used to find such a transform. Buchsbaum and Gottschalk [Buch83; Gott83] were the first to apply this technique to the study of human color vision. A transform of the form

$$\begin{bmatrix} A \\ C_1 \\ C_2 \end{bmatrix} = [T] \begin{bmatrix} S \\ M \\ L \end{bmatrix} \tag{9}$$

is sought where the new coordinates A, C_1, and C_2 are prioritized in such a way that the mean squared error is minimally affected as the coordinates are distorted or even selectively eliminated. It can be shown [Fuku72] that this will happen when the rows of the transformation matrix $[T]$ are the eigenvectors of a covariance matrix

$$\begin{bmatrix} C_{SS} & C_{SM} & C_{SL} \\ C_{SM} & C_{MM} & C_{ML} \\ C_{SL} & C_{ML} & C_{SS} \end{bmatrix} \tag{10}$$

With the assumption that there is minimal correlation between the wavelengths that compose the spectral energy distribution impinging on the eye [Meye88a], the terms of the matrix become

$$C_{SS} = \int \bar{s}(\lambda)\bar{s}(\lambda)d\lambda \qquad C_{SM} = \int \bar{s}(\lambda)\bar{m}(\lambda)d\lambda$$

$$C_{MM} = \int \bar{m}(\lambda)\bar{m}(\lambda)d\lambda \qquad C_{SL} = \int \bar{s}(\lambda)\bar{\ell}(\lambda)d\lambda$$

$$C_{LL} = \int \bar{\ell}(\lambda)\bar{\ell}(\lambda)d\lambda \qquad C_{ML} = \int \bar{m}(\lambda)\bar{\ell}(\lambda)d\lambda \tag{11}$$

where $\bar{s}(\lambda)$, $\bar{m}(\lambda)$, and $\bar{\ell}(\lambda)$ are the fundamental spectral sensitivity functions defined in Eq. (8).

Substituting the fundamental spectral sensitivities as defined in Eq. (8) into Eq. (11), then forming the transformation matrix in Eq. (9) from the eigenvectors of the covariance matrix in Eq. (10), and concatenating the matrices in Eqs. (8) and (9) leads to the following transformation from 1931 CIE XYZ space to the original AC_1C_2 space

$$\begin{bmatrix} A \\ C_1 \\ C_2 \end{bmatrix} = \begin{bmatrix} -0.0177 & 1.0090 & 0.0073 \\ -1.5370 & 1.0821 & 0.3209 \\ 0.1946 & -0.2045 & 0.5264 \end{bmatrix} \begin{bmatrix} X \\ Y \\ Z \end{bmatrix} \tag{12}$$

The eigenvalue ratio is

$$102.4 : 2.29 : 0.0221 \tag{13}$$

between A, C_1, and C_2, respectively. This determines the amount by which the mean squared error increases when the corresponding coordinate is deleted.

The new AC_1C_2 space is depicted in Figure 11. The A axis, as predicted by the eigenvalue ratio in Eq. 13, passes through the loop of the equal energy locus in Figure 8 that lies at 45 degrees with respect to the L and M axes and hence passes through the most dense region of tristimulus values. The C_1 axis is positioned in such a way as to pick up the difference

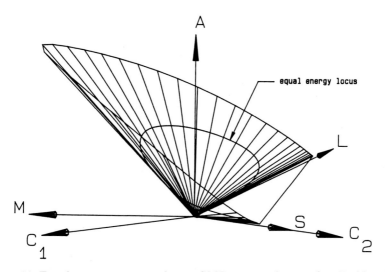

Figure 11. Equal energy spectrum locus, SML-axes, and cone of realizable color in AC_1C_2 space.

between the L and M coordinates. The least important coordinate, the C_2 coordinate according to the eigenvalue ratio, is positioned along the relatively insensitive S axis.

Spectral sensitivity functions that result from the transformation given in Eq. (12) are similar in shape to the opponent fundamentals that have been suggested for the human visual system. These $\bar{a}(\lambda)$, $\bar{c}_1(\lambda)$, and $\bar{c}_2(\lambda)$ sensitivities are shown in Figure 12. The achromatic channel, designated as A, corresponds closely to the photopic luminous efficiency function $\bar{y}(\lambda)$. The chromatic channels, designated as C_1 and C_2, correspond to the red/green and yellow/blue functions of the classical opponent fundamentals.

USING GAUSSIAN QUADRATURE TO COMPUTE TRISTIMULUS VALUES

Given the spectral sensitivities $\bar{a}(\lambda)$, $\bar{c}_1(\lambda)$, and $\bar{c}_2(\lambda)$, the tristimulus values A, C_1, and C_2 are computed by evaluating the integrals

$$A = \int E(\lambda)\bar{a}(\lambda)d\lambda$$

$$C_1 = \int E(\lambda)\bar{c}_1(\lambda)d\lambda$$

$$C_2 = \int E(\lambda)\bar{c}_2(\lambda)d\lambda \qquad (14)$$

To minimize the expense of computing these integrals, an integration technique is needed that will yield the highest accuracy while using the fewest wavelengths to perform the calculation. Gaussian quadrature can be used to achieve this result [Meye88a]. In this approach, numerical techniques are employed that use the $\bar{a}(\lambda)$, $\bar{c}_1(\lambda)$, and $\bar{c}_2(\lambda)$ spectral sensitivity functions as the Gaussian quadrature weighting functions. In Wallis [Wall75] and MacAdam [Maca81] the computation of 1931 CIE XYZ tristimulus values is accomplished using this approach.

Given a function $f(x)$, a weighting function $w(x)$, and an interval (a, b), the Gaussian rules for integration are [Cont72]

$$\int_a^b f(x)w(x)dx \simeq \sum_{i=0}^n H_i f(x_i) \qquad (15)$$

where the coefficients H_i are determined by

$$H_i = \int_a^b \ell_i(x)w(x)dx \quad (i = 0, \cdots, n)$$

$$\ell_i(x) = \prod_{\substack{j=0 \\ j \neq 1}}^n \frac{(x - x_j)}{(x_i - x_j)} \quad (i = 0, \cdots, n) \qquad (16)$$

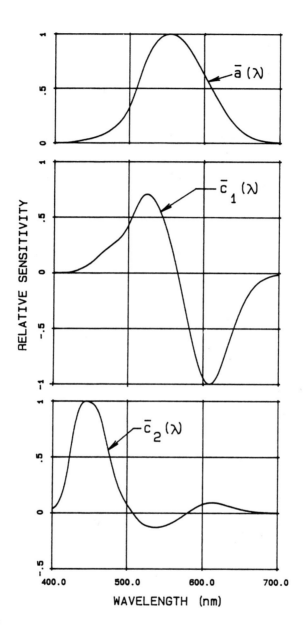

Figure 12. Spectral sensitivities for AC_1C_2 space.

The abscissas $x_0, x_1, \cdots, x_n$ are the zeroes of a family of polynomials $P_n(x)$ orthogonal to $w(x)$ over the interval (a, b).

To apply Gaussian quadrature to evaluation of the integrals in Eq. (14), (a) substitute $E(\lambda)$ for $f(x)$ and $\bar{a}(\lambda)$, $\bar{c}_1(\lambda)$, or $\bar{c}_2(\lambda)$ for $w(x)$ in Eq. (15); (b) compute the coefficients H_i by using Eq. (16); and (c) find the wavelengths $\lambda_0, \lambda_1, \cdots, \lambda_n$ as the zeroes of the $n+1$ order polynomials orthogonal to $\bar{a}(\lambda)$, $\bar{c}_1(\lambda)$, and $\bar{c}_2(\lambda)$. The results for orders 1 through 10 are given in Table 2. The interval of integration was taken to be 380 to 770 nm.

Examination of Table 2 reveals one of the limitations of applying Gaussian quadrature to this problem. Certain orders of integration are undefined for the functions $\bar{c}_1(\lambda)$ and $\bar{c}_2(\lambda)$ because they take on negative values [Stro66]. The other limitation of this approach is that the spectral energy distribution $E(\lambda)$ must be continuous. Most, but not all, spectral energy distributions are continuous. This fact is confirmed by the Fourier analysis in the section on fundamental sensitivities, which revealed a low-frequency content for the spectral reflectances of natural formations, and by Moon [Moon45], where it was shown that low-order polynomials could be used to represent the spectral reflectances of many common materials.

A test was performed to compare the computation of tristimulus values using the new AC_1C_2 fundamentals with the computation of tristimulus values using either the SML spectral sensitivity curves defined by Eq. (8) or the CIE XYZ matching functions. The spectral reflectances of the Macbeth Color Checker chart [Mcca76] were multiplied by CIE standard illuminant C to produce spectral energy distributions for the test. Tristimulus values were computed using Gaussian quadrature with the AC_1C_2, SML, and CIE XYZ functions as weighting functions. The difference between these computed tristimulus values and the actual tristimulus values was measured as a distance in CIE L*a*b* space [CIE78]. It was found that, in all cases, the AC_1C_2 fundamentals produced a more accurate result for the number of wavelengths used to perform the integration than either the SML or CIE XYZ fundamentals (Figure 13).

A particularly efficient set of wavelengths is obtained by using the major peaks of the AC_1C_2 fundamentals to guide the selection of the wavelengths. The first row of Table 3 shows the result of using first-order quadrature for the C_2 fundamental, second-order quadrature for the C_1 fundamental, and third-order quadrature for the A fundamental. This allocates (a) one wavelength to the C_2 fundamental that has only one peak and is the least important (according to the eigenvalue ratio in Eq. 13); (b) two wavelengths to the C_1 fundamental that has two peaks and is the second most important; and (c) three wavelengths to the A fundamental that has only one peak but is the most important of the three fundamentals. By using two of the wavelengths from the C_1 fundamental to also calculate the A fundamental, a particularly efficient four-wavelength set is obtained. New coefficients for the A component can be determined by the use of Eq. (16).

Table 2. Wavelengths and weights necessary to compute AC_1C_2 tristimulus values using Gaussian quadrature.

Order	A		C_1		C_2	
	λ_i	H_i	λ_i	H_i	λ_i	H_i
1	559.2	1.05638	undefined		456.4	0.54640
2	516.9	0.52827	490.9	0.31824	444.0	0.51004
	601.5	0.52811	631.4	−0.46008	631.6	0.03636
3	483.0	0.15908			386.9	0.01859
	557.7	0.71695	undefined		447.7	0.49780
	632.3	0.18035			644.9	0.03001
4	457.6	0.04639	450.8	0.04863		
	529.3	0.50400	509.9	0.33007		
	592.5	0.46254	618.4	−0.47764	undefined	
	660.5	0.04346	679.3	−0.04290		
5	441.3	0.01727				
	506.7	0.25935				
	562.3	0.56306	undefined		undefined	
	621.0	0.20904				
	688.4	0.00766				
6	429.4	0.00697	428.3	0.00607		
	484.6	0.10576	468.2	0.08951		
	537.8	0.47284	518.5	0.30806	undefined	
	590.4	0.39430	610.9	−0.43681		
	644.8	0.07519	658.3	−0.10674		
	713.4	0.00131	723.6	−0.00193		
7	419.1	0.00261			401.2	0.01622
	465.0	0.04337			433.3	0.25009
	517.7	0.30092			466.4	0.27643
	564.7	0.47041	undefined		546.5	−0.04131
	614.0	0.21567			618.3	0.03706
	665.6	0.02311			664.7	0.00779
	732.0	0.00030			729.5	0.00013
8	409.6	0.00089	407.3	0.00031		
	450.0	0.02039	443.1	0.02106		
	499.3	0.15315	481.0	0.11686		
	543.0	0.42595	524.3	0.28008		
	588.1	0.34893	605.5	−0.38470	undefined	
	634.2	0.10036	645.7	−0.16389		
	684.4	0.00662	693.1	−0.01134		
	744.4	0.00010	748.3	−0.00022		
9	401.6	0.00031			390.6	0.00309
	439.0	0.01036			419.2	0.08580
	482.0	0.07168			444.1	0.27309
	525.0	0.31122			473.2	0.18523
	566.1	0.40479	undefined		543.1	−0.04554
	608.6	0.21487			616.0	0.03344
	651.8	0.04113			654.9	0.01064
	700.9	0.00199			701.9	0.00063
	752.5	0.00004			752.5	0.00001

Table 2. *Continued.*

Order	A		C_1		C_2	
	λ_i	H_i	λ_i	H_i	λ_i	H_i
	395.6	0.00013	389.9	0.00001	389.1	0.00234
	430.7	0.00542	426.3	0.00367	416.8	0.06757
	467.5	0.03658	455.9	0.04038	441.5	0.26510
	509.3	0.18889	491.7	0.13564	470.8	0.20992
10	547.0	0.38063	528.8	0.24852	548.1	−0.05047
	586.4	0.31151	601.2	−0.33288	580.7	0.01304
	626.4	0.11678	636.4	−0.20508	623.2	0.03172
	667.6	0.01572	674.8	−0.03047	663.3	0.00685
	714.4	0.00070	719.2	−0.00156	710.4	0.00033
	757.7	0.00002	759.2	−0.00006	756.2	0.00001

When this is done and the set of four wavelengths is used to compute tristimulus values for the Macbeth Color Checker chart, the accuracy that is achieved is quite good, as can be seen in Table 3.

APPLICATION OF WAVELENGTH SELECTION TO IMAGE SYNTHESIS

In realistic image synthesis, the behavior of light in an environment is modeled on a wavelength-by-wavelength basis. The wavelength selection technique that was developed in the preceding sections can be used to select the number and spectral spacing of the wavelengths to be simulated. By employing a global illumination model, the behavior of light in the environment at each of these wavelengths can be modeled, and the color of the light reaching each point of the plane on which the image is to be formed can be determined. In this section, the wavelength selection technique is used to synthesize a picture of a simple scene.

Table 3. Results from using Gaussian quadrature to compute tristimulus values of Macbeth Color Checker chart.[†]

A		C_1		C_2		$L^*a^*b^*$
λ_i	H_i	λ_i	H_i	λ_i	H_i	error
483.0	0.15908	490.9	0.31824	456.4	0.54640	5.432
557.7	0.71695	631.4	−0.46008			
632.3	0.18035					
490.9	0.18892	490.9	0.31824	456.4	0.54640	5.429
557.7	0.67493	631.4	−0.46008			
631.4	0.19253					

[†] In the second row, wavelengths from the C_1 component have also been used for the A component.

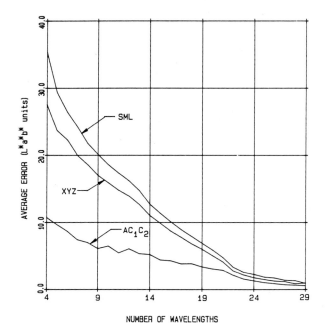

Figure 13. Average error produced when using Gaussian quadrature in three different color spaces to compute tristimulus values for Macbeth Color Checker chart.

The radiosity method was used to simulate the propagation of electromagnetic energy in the environment. This technique, first applied to computer graphics by Goral et al. [Gora84], is based on the assumption that the environment can be discretized and that each of the resulting surfaces either emits or reflects in a pure diffuse (Lambertian) manner. The energy flux (energy per unit area per unit time) leaving the surface is the radiosity of the surface, and it is directly proportional to the intensity of the radiation leaving the surface. The relation between the radiosities of all the surfaces in the environment is given by the algebraic expression

$$B_{i\lambda} = E_{i\lambda} + \rho_{i\lambda} \sum_j F_{ij} B_{j\lambda} \tag{17}$$

where

$B_{i\lambda}$ = radiosity at wavelength λ of surface i,

$E_{i\lambda}$ = energy emitted at wavelength λ from surface i per unit area per unit time,

$\rho_{i\lambda}$ = reflectance at wavelength λ of surface i,

F_{ij} = form factor representing the fraction of energy leaving surface i that reaches surface j,

$B_{j\lambda}$ = radiosity at wavelength λ of surface j.

The expression for computing the form factors is:

$$F_{ij} = \frac{1}{A_i} \int_{A_i} \int_{A_j} \frac{\cos\phi_i \cos\phi_j}{\pi r^2} \, dA_i \, dA_j \qquad (18)$$

where

A_i = area of surface i,

A_j = area of surface j,

r = distance between dA_i and dA_j,

ϕ_i = angle between surface normal of i and the line that connects dA_i and dA_j,

ϕ_j = angle between surface normal of j and the line that connects dA_j and dA_i.

From the above, a system of simultaneous linear equations can be formulated and solved for the radiosities. The method has been extended to handle hidden surfaces by Cohen and Greenberg [Cohe85], and it was this version of the technique that was used to perform the calculations.

A picture of a single scene consisting of a desk, a lamp, a chair, and the Macbeth Color Checker chart was created using the radiosity method and the wavelength selection technique. Spectral energy distributions were assigned to the light sources in the scene, spectral reflectances were selected for the surfaces in the environment, and Eq. (17) was used to compute the radiosity of each surface at a particular wavelength. The wavelengths that were selected to perform the calculation are the four wavelengths given in Table 3. The image that resulted is shown in Figure 14.

Conclusions

The fundamental spectral sensitivity functions have important implications for computer graphics research. Fourier analysis of the reflectances of natural formations shows that the number and the shape of the fundamental spectral sensitivity functions may have been determined by the low-frequency content of the spectral energy distributions that these functions were intended to interpret. Fundamental spectral sensitivity functions can be expressed in terms of CIE XYZ matching functions if the dichromatic confusion points are known. Research available on people who have one color-normal eye and one color-blind eye makes it possible to synthesize

Figure 14. Image modeled using only the four wavelengths given in the second row of Table 3.

a view of the world as seen by color-blind persons. This leads to the recommendation that color scales with chromaticity loci orthogonal to the protanopic and deuteranopic confusion lines are optimal for the major types of color blindness.

An opponent color space, such as AC_1C_2 space, has important properties for realistic image synthesis. Better color accuracy is achieved with fewer wavelengths when the wavelengths are selected based on AC_1C_2 space than when they are chosen using either CIE XYZ space or SML space. Within AC_1C_2 space itself, the A coordinate is most important, the C_1 coordinate is second most important, and the C_2 coordinate is least important. This information can be used to select wavelengths for synthetic image generation and leads to a particularly efficient four-wavelength set that roughly corresponds to the four peaks of the opponent fundamentals themselves.

Acknowledgments. Radiosity software was modified from a version first written by Michael Cohen, Phil Brock, and Dave Immel. Color blindness research was done in conjunction with Prof. Donald P. Greenberg. This work was performed at the Cornell University Program of Computer Graphics and was partially funded by the National Science Foundation under Grant DCR-8203979.

74   Gary W. Meyer

REFERENCES

[Barl82]
Barlow, H.B., What causes trichromacy? A theoretical analysis using comb-filtered spectra, *Vision Res.*, Vol. 22, pp. 635–643, 1982.

[Buch83]
Buchsbaum, G., and Gottschalk, A., Trichromacy, opponent colours coding and optimum colour information transmission in the retina, *Proc. Roy. Soc. London Ser. B*, Vol. 220, pp. 89–113, 1983.

[Buch84]
Buchsbaum, G., and Gottschalk, A., Chromaticity coordinates of frequency-limited functions, *J. Opt. Soc. Amer. Ser. A*, Vol. 1., pp. 885–887, 1984.

[Burn84]
Burns, S.A., Elsner, A.E., Pokorny, J., and Smith, V.C., The Abney effect: Chromaticity coordinates of unique and other constant hues, *Vision Res.*, Vol. 24, pp. 479–489, 1984.

[CIE78]
CIE Recommendations on Uniform Colour Spaces, Colour-difference Equations, and Psychometric Colour Terms, Supplement No. 2 to Publication CIE No. 15, *Colorimetry* (E-1.3.1) 1971, Bureau Central de la CIE, Paris, 1978.

[Cohe64]
Cohen, J., Dependency of the spectral reflectance curves of the Munsell color chips, *Psychon. Sci.*, Vol. 1, pp. 369-370, 1964.

[Cohe85]
Cohen, M., and Greenberg, D.P., The hemi-cube: A radiosity solution for complex environments, *Comput. Graph.*, Vol. 19, pp. 31–40, 1985 (SIGGRAPH 85).

[Cont72]
Conte, S.D., and deBoor, C., *Elementary Numerical Analysis: An Algorithmic Approach*, 2nd Ed., New York: McGraw-Hill, 1972.

[Cook82]
Cook, R.L., and Torrance, K.E., A reflectance model for computer graphics, *ACM Trans. Graph.*, Vol. 1, pp. 7–24, 1982.

[Este79]
Estevez, O., On the fundamental data-base of normal and dichromatic color vision, Ph.D. Thesis, University of Amsterdam, Krips Repro Meppel, Amsterdam, 1979.

[Farn43]
Farnsworth, D., The Farnsworth-Munsell 100-hue and dichotomous tests for color vision, *J. Opt. Soc. Amer.*, Vol. 33, pp. 568–578, 1943.

[Free65]
Freeman, H., *Discrete-Time Systems: An Introduction to the Theory*, New York: John Wiley and Sons, 1965.

[Fuku72]
Fukunaga, K., *Introduction to Statistical Pattern Recognition*, New York: Academic Press, 1972.

[Gora84]
Goral, C., Torrance, K.E., Greenberg, D.P., and Battaile, B., Modeling the interaction of light between diffuse surfaces, *Comput. Graph.*, Vol. 18, pp. 213–222, 1984 (SIGGRAPH 84).

[Gott83]
Gottschalk, A., and Buchsbaum, G., Information theoretic aspects of color signal processing in the visual system, *IEEE Trans. Systems, Man Cybernet.*, Vol. SMC-13, pp. 864–873, 1983.

[Guil31]
Guild, J., The colorimetric properties of the spectrum, *Philos. Trans. Roy. Soc. London Ser. A*, Vol. 230, p. 149, 1931.

[Hall83]
Hall, R.A., A Methodology for Realistic Image Synthesis, Master's Thesis, Cornell University, Ithaca, August 1983.

[Helm61]
Helms, H.D., Generalizations of the Sampling Theorem and Error Calculations, Ph.D. Dissertation, Princeton University, Princeton, January 1961.

[Ingl83]
Ingling, C.R., Simple-opponent receptive fields are asymmetrical: G-cone centers predominate, *J. Opt. Soc. Amer.*, Vol. 73, pp. 1527–1532, 1983.

[Judd44]
Judd, D.B., Standard response functions for protanopic and deuteranopic vision, *J. Res. Nat. Bur. Standards*, Vol. 33, pp. 407–437, 1944.

[Judd49]
Judd, D.B., Response functions for types of vision according to the Muller theory, *J. Res. Nat. Bur. Standards*, Vol. 42, pp. 356–371, 1949.

[Judd50]
Judd, D.B., Tritanopia with abnormally heavy ocular pigmentation, *J. Opt. Soc. Amer.*, Vol. 40, pp. 833–841, 1950.

[Judd51]
Judd, D.B., Report of U.S. Secretariat Committee on Colorimetry and Artificial Daylight, in *CIE Proceedings*, Vol. 1, Part 7, p. 11, 1951.

[Judd66]
Judd, D.B., Fundamental studies of color vision from 1860 to 1960, *Proc. Nat. Acad. Sciences*, Vol. 55, pp. 1313–1330, 1966.

[Krin47]
Krinov, E.L., *Spectrol, naye, otrazhatel'naya sposobnost' prirodnykh obrazovanii*, Izadeltel'stvo Akad. Nauk, USSR, 1947 (translation by G. Belkov, National Research Council of Canada, Technical Translation TT-439, 1953).

[Maca81]
MacAdam, D.L., *Color Measurement: Theme and Variations*, Berlin: Springer-Verlag, 1981.

[Malo86]
Maloney, L.T., Evaluation of linear models of surface spectral reflectance

with small numbers of parameters, *J. Opt. Soc. Amer. Ser. A*, Vol. 3, pp. 1673–1683, 1986.

[Mcca76]
McCamy, C.S., Marcus, H., and Davidson, J.G., A color-rendition chart, *J. Appl. Photographic Engrg.*, Vol. 2, pp. 95–99, 1976.

[Meye88a]
Meyer, G. W., Wavelength selection for synthetic image generation, *Comput. Vision, Graph., Image Process.*, Vol. 41, pp. 57–79, 1988.

[Meye88b]
Meyer, G. W., Color defective vision and computer graphic displays, *IEEE Comput. Graph. Appl.*, Vol. 8, pp. 28–40, September 1988.

[Moon45]
Moon, P., Polynomial representation of reflectance curves, *J. Opt. Soc. Amer.*, Vol. 35, pp. 597–600, 1945.

[Nime70]
Nimeroff, I., Deuteranopic convergence point, *J. Opt. Soc. Amer.*, Vol. 60, pp. 966–969, 1970.

[Pitt35]
Pitt, F.H.G., Characteristics of dichromatic vision, Med. Res. Council, *Rep. Committee Physiol. Vision XIV*, Spec. Rep. Ser. No. 200, London, 1935.

[Pitt43]
Pitt, F.H.G., The nature of normal trichromatic and dichromatic vision, *Proc. Roy. Soc. London*, 132B, pp. 101–117, 1944.

[Stil46]
Stiles, W.S., A modified Helmholtz line element in brightness-colour space, *Proc. Phys. Soc. (London)*, Vol. 58, p. 41, 1946.

[Stil55]
Stiles, W.S., and Burch, J.M., Interim report to the Commission Internationale de l'Eclairage, Zurich, 1955, on the National Physical Laboratory's investigation of colour-matching, *Optica Acta*, Vol. 2, p. 168, 1955.

[Stro66]
Stroud, A.H., and Secrest, D., *Gaussian Quadrature Formulas*, Englewood Cliffs: Prentice-Hall, 1966.

[Thom53]
Thomson, L.C., and Wright, W.D., The Convergence of the tritanopic confusion loci and the derivation of the fundamental response functions, *J. Opt. Soc. Amer.*, Vol. 43, pp. 890–894, 1953.

[Vos70]
Vos, J.J., and Walraven, P.L., On the derivation of the foveal receptor primaries, *Vision Res.*, Vol. 11, pp. 799–818, 1970.

[Wall75]
Wallis, R., Fast computation of tristimulus values by use of Gaussian quadrature, *J. Opt. Soc. Amer.*, Vol. 65, pp. 542–545, 1975.

[Walr74]
Walraven, P.L., A closer look at the tritanopic convergence point, *Vision Res.*, Vol. 14, pp. 1339–1343, 1974.

[Wrig28]
Wright, W.D., A re-determination of the trichromatic coefficients of the spectral colors, *Trans. Opt. Soc. London*, Vol. 30, p. 141, 1928.

[Wrig52]
Wright, W.D., The characteristics of tritanopia, *J. Opt. Soc. Amer.*, Vol. 42, pp. 509–521, 1952.

[Wysz82]
Wyszecki, G., and Stiles, W.S., *Color Science: Concepts and Methods, Quantitative Data and Formulae*, 2nd Ed., New York: John Wiley and Sons, 1982.

[Yen56]
Yen, J.L., On Nonuniform Sampling of Bandwidth-Limited Signals, *IRE Trans. Circuit Theor.*, Vol. CT-3, pp. 251–257, 1956.

Color Printing for Computer Graphics

OR: HOW TO GET IT OFF YOUR SCREEN AND ONTO PAPER, IN COLOR

Maureen C. Stone

Abstract

Members of the computer graphics community are expert at producing high-quality images on monitors. Rarely, however, are they satisfied with the results of reproducing these images on paper. Part of this dissatisfaction is inevitable as some aspects of images rendered on monitors can never be reproduced on paper. However, part of the problem is simply ignorance, and knowledge of the strengths and weaknesses of printing systems can be used to produce better results. This paper explains why transferring a monitor image to a printed page is difficult and presents some techniques that can be used to improve the results.

Introduction

Much work in the computer graphics research community is focused on the production of high-quality images on monitors. Often, these images are carefully constructed to provide scientifically accurate renderings of a simulated scene [Meye86]. Even if the rendering is not physically based, great care is taken to produce the desired appearance on the display. For many projects, a single *tour de force* image is the ultimate proof of the research. However, if these images are to be distributed or published, they must be transferred to slides or paper. Reproducing the picture so that it maintains the same appearance as the monitor image is an interesting and challenging problem.

A related problem is printing in color the output of current desktop publishing systems. A significant difference, however, is that the ultimate output of these systems is intended to be printed pages. This means that it is possible to design interfaces that take advantage of the existing modes of operation in the graphic arts community. The display is only intended to be an approximate representation of some standard, printed color guide such as the one provided by the Pantone ® color system. However, the use of color monitors in these systems and the desire or expectation of users for the print to 'look the same' as the monitor means that the issues presented here are also relevant to these systems.

Traditional graphic arts practice is an obvious source of information about high-quality printing and color image reproduction. The use of computer monitors for previewing and page makeup, plus the evolution of desktop publishing systems toward treating the offset printing industry as a high-quality form of digital printer, does mean that customers now expect to see on the print what they see on the monitor. However, while the carefully controlled monitors in graphic arts environments provide a more accurate preview of the printed page than the typical computer monitor, significant skill is still needed to predict the actual appearance of the printed page from the monitor image.

What does it mean to accurately reproduce a monitor image on paper? There is no single answer. Industries that specialize in color reproduction such as printing, photography, movies, and television all define a good reproduction in terms of what the individual customer wants and is willing to pay for. High-quality reproduction inevitably involves specialists who can accurately predict and control the myriad complexities of the different color processes. Therefore, it seems unlikely that a single, correct definition of monitor-to-print reproduction can be found that is independent of the cost or the application.

This paper will focus on the problem of preparing computer-generated images for offset printing, the technology used by most scientific journals, newspapers, and popular magazines. The first part of this paper will survey traditional publishing and printing practice. The second will focus on the color reproduction problem in a scientific manner, presenting some current results in this area.

Introduction to Commercial Printing and Publishing

Back in the days before computer professionals were expected to do their own typesetting, the traditional way to get a manuscript published was to hand a draft of the manuscript to a publisher. Production of the camera-ready version of the text was divided between the copy editor, responsible for the text, and the graphic designer, responsible for the illustrations as well as the overall design of the publication. A third person, the production editor, was responsible for keeping track of all the pieces. The output of this process was printed pages, either in a book or a journal. This process is summarized in Figure 1. The important point of this diagram is that each of the boxes represents a staff of specialists whose procedures were designed both to maximize the quality of their individual contribution and to optimize the coordination between the different steps in the process. Modern computer technology has made it possible for the author to be responsible for all of these steps; such is progress.

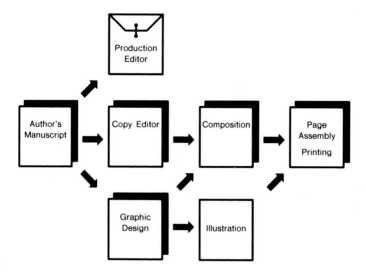

Figure 1. Traditional graphic arts processes involve considerable parallelism in the procedures for publishing a manuscript. The author's manuscript is copied and sent to the production editor, the copy editor, and the design/illustration department. Edited pages are typeset by the composition staff who are guided by the design of the document. The typeset manuscript and the illustrations are then assembled into pages in preparation for printing.

In the figure, Page Assembly and Printing share the same box. There is a good reason for this. Different types of illustrations require different types of preparation for printing. Some of these preparation steps can be performed by the original illustrator. Others are performed by the printer or yet another set of experts who specialize in making the color separations for photographic imagery. For color printing, the entire page may be collected together only on the printing plate. Many of these special procedures are driven by the nature of offset printing and are not required for digital printers. Obviously, however, anyone wanting to use computer tools to generate artwork for offset printing must be aware of the requirements of the technology. This section provides a primer for such hardy souls. A trip to the graphic arts or business sections of a good book store can produce a number of different texts that discuss making camera-ready artwork [Beac86]. While none are currently oriented directly toward the computer market, they can provide additional detail about the conventional state-of-the art.

OFFSET PRINTING

Offset printing is a lithographic process, which means that the printing plate is flat rather than etched or engraved. Different parts of the surface are treated to repel or attract water; those that attract water repel ink and vice versa. To make a better contact with the paper surface, the image is *offset* onto a rubber sheet (called a blanket), and the print is made by pressing the blanket onto the surface of the paper. This works better than pressing the plate and the paper together because the rubber is a softer surface than the plate (usually a sheet of aluminum), and therefore can conform to the paper surface more effectively.

Offset printing is a bilevel process; at each point on the page either there is ink or there is not. Different gray levels are produced using a technique called *halftoning*, which reproduces the different tones using patterns of dots of different sizes. Halftone patterns will be described in more detail below. To produce different colors, the page is printed with different inks, one color per offset impression. Therefore, the artwork to be printed must be separated into its component colors, one per *color separation*. For each color there is one plate and one pass through the printer (or stage of the printer). It is impossible to align the multiple passes precisely, so the color separations must be designed to tolerate some misalignment.

Offset printing plates are generated photographically. A light-sensitive emulsion on the plate surface is exposed through a film containing the image to be printed. The plate is then developed to harden the surface. The plates for the different color separations are prepared separately, by hand, providing another opportunity for misalignment. The fact that the plates are prepared photographically means that the film images must have high contrast and the transition from opaque to clear on the film must be sharp. Otherwise, the image of the film on the plate will be overly sensitive to the exposure time. While the platemaker can compensate for failures in the film processing, it is a time-consuming and unreliable process. Most authors are not going to be working directly with the printer, so it is extremely important that the films for platemaking be correctly produced.

Process Color vs. Custom Color

Process color for offset printing reproduces color by combining three primary inks: cyan, magenta, and yellow. A fourth ink, black, is often added to improve contrast. Different colors can be produced by halftoning the four color separations. Halftoning, however, can produce visible texture patterns, especially along edges and in thin lines and text. Furthermore, the range of colors that can be produced by the standard primaries, while large, is ultimately limited. To produce a specific color with no halftoning, or to produce colors outside of the standard gamut, the printer can mix an ink of precisely the correct color, a *custom color*, and print with it. The Pantone ® system is an example of a standard set of custom colors that is commonly used in the graphic arts community.

Adding custom colors to a job already requiring the four process colors is an additional expense. However, many illustrations can be reproduced better with a small number of custom colors than by halftoning the process colors, reducing the overall cost of the job. Custom colors may also be halftoned and combined, producing shades and tints of the different colors.

Producing the color separations for an existing continuous-tone image, such as a color photograph or painting, was originally done by photographing the image through a set of color filters corresponding to the standard process colors. Now, it is common to use a digital scanner and film plotter. Companies exist that only produce color separations and proofs, although some large printing companies have the equipment in-house. The standard output of this operation is a set of three or four halftoned films, one for each color separation, plus a proof made from those films. The films and proof form the standard interface between the color separator and the printer. Significant effort has been spent to make the commercial proofing processes reliable and stable. How well the proof matches the final print, however, depends on how well the colors of the printing inks are controlled (which varies widely with cost) and how well the printer sets up and controls the press.

Producing the color separations for custom colors is not done photographically. The original illustrator or another specialist called a *paste-up artist* or *production artist* separates the image into a set of *mechanicals* that the printer can photograph to make the films for platemaking. A mechanical is a black/white image on paper, often attached to a mounting board for stability. Mechanicals do not usually contain the halftone patterns used on the press. Areas to be halftoned are left uncolored and are marked with the color and type of screen (halftone pattern) required. When the printer makes the films, such areas are photographed through a screen of the requested type. If the page includes photographs or other artwork that must be separated photographically, a rectangular area is left on the page for the printer to add the halftoned films.

The choice between custom and process color is dictated by the contents of the manuscript and by the budget. Illustrations that contain color photographs or other continuously shaded images must be produced using process color. Adding custom color above that increases the cost. However, limiting production to one or two custom colors will be less expensive than using process color.

PRODUCING ART FOR PRINTING

The full page mechanical is the standard form of communication between the designer of the page and the printer. When an author offers to produce camera-ready art, it means this artwork will become part of the mechanical submitted to the printer. If the author cannot supply artwork that meets the accepted standards, it will have to be redone.

One of the most important technical issues having to do with making mechanicals, and ultimately for designing the page content, is to compensate for the alignment and resolution limitations of offset printing. Typical halftone screen resolution is 150 lines/inch, that is, a pattern of dots spaced at 0.0067-inch (0.17-mm) intervals. Typical misalignment between colors is about the same size. These numbers suggest a minimum feature size of around 0.2 mm (1/2 point) and a minimum overlap of the same size between adjacent colored areas. These numbers are suggested as comfortable limits for conventional printing. If you have a special arrangement with a printer for your work of art, smaller tolerances can be achieved. Note also that the limits for film or even the photographic paper used in phototypesetters are much smaller. However, it's not enough to get it on film; it has to be printable.

A complete treatment of how to produce mechanicals or color separations is beyond the scope of this paper. Furthermore, many of the conventions for labeling, crop marks, alignment marks, and other instructions to the printer are highly individual and must be determined through discussions with the printer or publisher. However, even if the author is not going to produce mechanicals, he or she can apply some techniques for designing illustrations that will make them more effective when printed.

The following rules of thumb address some of the more common problems found when trying to reproduce illustrations designed on a digital system:

All small features should appear in only one color separation and should not be halftoned.

Text should be produced as a single color separation whenever possible. The colored 'halos' produced by misalignments decrease readability.

Consider the final size when designing illustrations. What looks good filling half a page is not the same as what looks good two inches tall. Try to design the illustration at a size no larger than twice the final size, and scale it to the final size for fine-tuning design decisions.

Final copy for text, lines, and solid areas should be produced at an effective resolution of approximately 1000 spots/inch. Note that the printer can easily scale such illustrations, so if you only have a low-resolution printer, you can print the image larger than final size to increase the effective resolution.

For continuous-tone colored images, transparencies produced on a film recorder provide the highest quality original for the color separation process. Photographing the monitor can introduce barrel distortion, and the image may contain visible scan lines.

All multicolored printed originals will be conventionally separated and halftoned by the printer. If the image already contains a halftone pattern, moiré patterns may be introduced. This applies to the output of digital color printers as well as images from magazines or posters.

Lines and flat-filled areas will look better if they are separated as mechanicals even if the colors used are the standard process colors. An illustration involving a continuous-tone image combined with text and lines will look better if the two components are separated and produced independently.

When separated as mechanicals, adjacent areas of different colors must overlap rather than abut. Visible white lines will appear between the colored areas otherwise.

Each layer of the mechanical or color separation must be clearly labeled and contain four alignment marks, one in each corner. If you intend to produce mechanicals or color separated films, check with your publisher/printer for the local conventions.

Very few digital systems sold for desktop publishing have the resolution or film-processing capabilities needed to make commercial-quality halftones. If you intend to generate halftones, provide your printer with an example early on to be sure they are acceptable.

The next section discusses the principles of color separation for continuous-tone images (process color) in some detail. This provides both a practical example of some of the problems encountered when reproducing color images and, as digital color printers are becoming more prevalent, some potentially useful information about producing color on printers.

Principles of Color Separation

This section provides an introduction to the process and terminology used for making digital color separations for offset printing. The definitive work in the field is by John Yule [Yule67] while Miles Southworth [Sout79] provides a more trade-oriented description of color separation techniques. These days, most commercial color separation production houses use specialized digital scanners and printers for producing halftone films. The companies that provide this hardware rarely publish their algorithms, but when they do, it is often in the proceedings of the annual Technical Association of the Graphic Arts conference [TAGA].

There have been some efforts to provide guidelines for making film separations directed toward making it easier for the printer to match the proof [Brun86]. One is a set of recommendations for standard printing inks, proofing colors, and proofing densities, "Recommended Specifications Web Offset Publications, SWOP" [SWOP]. While not strictly controlled, these recommendations provide some mechanisms for insuring that a duplication of the proof is practical. The printer's skill and judgment, however, are still the most significant factors in the success of the reproduction.

Halftone Patterns

Halftone patterns are defined by the spacing of the dots measured in lines per inch (lines/inch), called *screen frequency*, and the percentage area covered by ink in the resulting patterns, called *dot area*. The dot spacing defines the sharpness of the resulting image, with 133–150 lines/inch screens being typical for magazine-quality offset printing. The percentage area defines the lightness or darkness of the resulting image. Figure 2 shows halftone patterns for different dot areas.

Figure 2a shows the round dots that would be produced using a traditional mechanical halftone screen, but other shapes can be used either to produce textures for artistic reasons or to accommodate a scanning output device such as a film plotter. When a halftone pattern is generated on a raster printer, a pattern like that shown in Figure 2b is often used [Holl80].

In color printing, the four separations are printed one over the other. To minimize interference between the different colors, the halftone patterns on each separation are oriented along lines at different angles. Mechanically, this difference is produced by rotating the halftone screen when photographing the image. Digitally, the effect of this rotation must be simulated. Typical screen angles are: 105, 75, 90, and 45 for cyan, magenta, yellow, and black, respectively, although some recommendations exchange the values for magenta and black. Figure 3 shows a close-up of a halftoned area illustrating the halftone pattern and screen angles for different colors.

When printed on film, a halftone pattern should contain only opaque and clear areas. Gray areas in the pattern will make the pattern overly sensitive to exposure time when making the printing plate. The dot area of a properly screened film can be accurately measured using a densitometer, which is a crucial tool for maintaining quality control of the film printing process. Film fog (which affects the transparency of the background film),

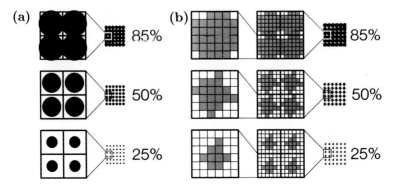

Figure 2. (a) Idealized halftone patterns for 25%, 50%, and 85% dot area. (b) Digitally produced halftone patterns for 25%, 50%, and 85% dot area using Holladay's algorithm. Original image by Chuck Haines, Xerox Corp.

Figure 3. Close-up of a halftoned image showing the halftone dots, four process colors, and rotated screen angles.

inadequately opaque dark areas, and insufficiently sharp edges will all invalidate this measurement and jeopardize the reproduction process. It is essential to use high-contrast film and to carefully control the development process to achieve reliable results.

TONE REPRODUCTION

The basic measure of a reproduction technology is its *tone reproduction curve*, abbreviated TRC. This function defines the mapping from the input gray or *tone values* to the output values. In traditional printing, these tone values are measured as *density*, a logarithmic function of reflectance. The tone reproduction curve relates density values in the original image to those in the reproduction, and ideal reproduction maps the original values to the identical values on the print. Where the original image is in digital form, however, the concept of a TRC must be redefined, since there is no set of density measurements available for the original image. The optimal mapping from monitor intensity to print density has not yet been defined, although a metric based on the colorimetric quantity L^* has been considered [Rhod88]. In practice, visually compensating the monitor and the printer so that a set of gray patches of different values (a gray step wedge) appears evenly spaced in lightness on both devices is adequate to ensure reasonable tone reproduction.

Another use of the term TRC describes the mapping between the requested tone values and those actually produced by the mechanics of the printing process. The spots produced by any mechanical device are not the idealized squares or disks shown in the illustrations above, so the bit patterns sent to the printer must be modified to accommodate the tone reproduction characteristics of the device. This compensation can be provided by a table that is the inverse of the tone reproduction curve for the device. When setting up a digital printer, it is very important to control the printing process so that the dot area or density requested is actually the same as what is produced on the film. This does not happen 'automatically' for most real devices.

GRAY BALANCE AND THE BLACK SEPARATION

One of the most important criteria for a good color reproduction process is that it be able to accurately reproduce the neutral colors in a picture. The three guns on a color monitor are usually balanced so that equal amounts of the primary colors produce a neutral gray color. In printing, it is not usually possible to use equal amounts of the primary colors to produce a gray. Figure 4 shows a 'gray wedge' made of equal parts of cyan, magenta, and yellow compared with one printed with black ink and one printed with balanced amounts of cyan, magenta, yellow, and black.

The process of adjusting the mix of the three primaries to produce a neutral color is called *gray-balancing*. It is a straightforward task to find an approximately neutral progression of grays from a set of color patches containing nearly equal amounts of the primary colors. This data is used to produce a table of values that compensates each of the primaries to produce a neutral gray scale. For example, a color whose ideal value is a 50% gray might actually be produced as [C: 50%, M: 47%, Y: 47%].

The three primary colors of the offset printing process are cyan, magenta, and yellow. In four-color printing, black is used as well. The black separation is used to accomplish two things in offset printing: to increase the contrast by increasing the density in the dark areas of the picture, and to replace some percentage of the three primaries for economic or mechanical reasons. For example, to keep the paper from getting too wet with ink on high-speed presses, the SWOP recommendations restrict the maximum dot area in any one region to 280% (four solid colors = 400%). To achieve this, it is necessary to substitute black ink for mixtures of cyan, magenta, and yellow, a process called *undercolor removal*, or more recently, *gray component replacement* (GCR). Printing is distinctly nonlinear, so it is difficult to predict how much black ink is required to match the density

Figure 4. Three renderings of a gray step wedge.

of the colored ink removed. If the replacement is not done correctly, dark areas of the print, which are subject to GCR, will actually appear lighter than supposedly lighter tones not subject to GCR.

Given that it is necessary to adjust the mix of cyan, magenta, yellow, and black to produce gray colors, what about colors that are nearly gray? If these are not compensated also, there will be a discontinuity in the color space. Most colors contain some amount of gray, called the gray component, which is simply $min[C, M, Y]$. For example, the color defined as [C: 100%, M: 75%, Y: 80%] has a gray component of 75%. The obvious solution is to balance the gray component exactly as we would a gray color, and this is sometimes done. For one printer, however, we found that we got better results by gray-balancing less than the full gray component for colors off the gray axis using a function inversely proportional to the color's distance from the gray axis. For this calculation, distance from the gray axis was defined as $max[C, M, Y] - min[C, M, Y]$. Both of these methods introduce black into the colored parts of the picture, which can cause hue shifts because the black ink has a color different from the color of the mixture of the primaries.

The only way to determine the correct mix of colors to produce a neutral is to print a number of patches with different mixtures of cyan, magenta, and yellow and compare them with a neutral gray standard. Once the gray balance is determined, experiments can be performed to generate the correct amount of black overprinting. The most conservative approach adds black only to make the dark colors darker (called a *skeleton black*). If GCR is required, the problem is much harder. For commercially available inks, the gray balance and black separation information is usually encoded in the scanning hardware. The author's experience with deriving the necessary GCR and black printer data for the SWOP recommendations (which require GCR) has been limited to reverse-engineering the results from a commercial system.

Why not replace all of the black in the print with black ink? This procedure is only possible with digital scanning systems, and some of the negative reactions to it by the graphic arts community may be traditional. However, there are some real problems with such an approach for offset printing. Such separations are very sensitive to alignment problems when printing. Offset alignment is not perfect, and such imperfections will produce hue shifts and white or colored gaps between parts of the image. Reproducing gray areas with only black ink limits the contrast available in the image; black alone is not as dark as black in combination with other colors, as can be seen by comparing Figure 4b with Figure 4c.

The correct way to handle the gray component and the black separation is a topic of much interest in the color printing field today. The use of computer-controlled scanners and printers has made a wide range of effects possible in a domain once limited to effects obtained by photographic masking [John85]. Many companies keep their precise algorithms proprietary.

QUANTIZATION EFFECTS

On raster devices, the set of brightness values available is quantized. Computer-driven displays typically restrict monitor output to 256 different levels per primary. For film output, the number of halftone patterns available is quantized by the resolution of the printer. Each halftone dot is built on an array of printer pixels, as shown in Figure 2. The maximum number of gray levels attainable for a particular array size is $N^2 + 1$, where N is the number of pixels along the edge of the array. The number of gray levels can be increased by making the array larger, with a corresponding decrease in image sharpness. Further quantization effects occur when approximating the different screen frequencies and angles.

In practice, the total number of levels obtainable may be significantly smaller than the ideal due to limitations in the printing process. A single pixel in isolation may not reproduce, so patterns with single dark pixels are effectively unpatterned. Similarly, single white pixels in a dark area may tend to fill in, so the darkest patterns will also be limited. For example, when we used a 10×10 array on a 1200 spots/inch (spi) printer to approximate a 120 lines/inch printing screen, after compensation there were only 80 intensity levels rather than the ideal 101.

Restricting the number of gray levels can produce visible contour lines on smoothly shaded portions of an image. This problem can be masked by adding small quantities of random noise to the picture, as shown in Figure 5. White noise works adequately, although some authors recommend 'blue' noise to minimize graininess [Ulic87, Chap. 8]. Commercial-quality digital systems generate around 200 different gray levels. For completely noiseless gray wedges, however, contour lines are still visible at screen values of around 30–40% (light gray). In fact, banding is visible in the same region on a carefully tuned monitor using 256 levels. These extreme cases are only a problem with synthetically generated images, because scanning an image adds noise to it as a side effect of the scanning system.

Figure 5. Step wedge quantized to 5 bits/pixel by zeroing the bottom three bits of an 8-bit byte. Random noise is gradually introduced, as indicated by the direction of the arrow, to a maximum of ±9 out of 255 possible values.

DIGITAL DATA EXCHANGE STANDARD (DDES)

The graphics arts industry has recognized the advantages of being able to interchange digital images and, to that end, is defining a format for exchanging images on magnetic tape. This format, DDES [DDES86], defines an image as an array of $CMYK$ pixels. The pixel values represent percentage dot area for the corresponding color. A vendor who supports DDES can convert an image stored on tape to halftoned films. This provides a digital link to the filmmaking equipment; however, the specification is in terms of $CMYK$ which is not standardized, so the actual color of the image will depend on the colors of the inks. In our limited experience, most United States vendors claim that they can use SWOP inks. However, we have been warned that the SWOP recommendations are not tightly controlled so that depending on them for color fidelity would be unsatisfactory.

In Europe, a method for specifying ink color has been standardized by the *Deutsche Industrie-Norm* (DIN), which is the German equivalent to the ANSI standardizing body. This provides better control over ink color than the United States SWOP recommendations. Overall, the European printing industry is reputed to have better specification and control systems that provide more uniform quality than their United States counterparts. The Japanese also are gaining a reputation for high-quality, low-cost printing. The author has no experience, however, with other than United States printers.

DIGITAL PRINTERS

While the previous discussion has been focused on offset printing, much of it can be applied to the different digital color raster printers available as computer peripherals. Most such printers are bilevel devices and must use halftoning to produce gray levels. The Holladay algorithms for generating digital halftones will produce satisfactory results on many digital printers, although the low spatial resolution of such printers (150–400 spi) limits the effective screen resolution significantly. The principles of tone reproduction, gray-balancing, and quantization can be applied to all printers. If the printer includes a black ink or toner, it can be used like the black separation in offset printing. However, because the technology is different, the way these principles are applied will be somewhat different. A summary of the important differences will be given here. For further information, see the recent work by Rhodes and Lamming [Rhod88].

The resolution of digital color printers is low compared with that of the film printing systems used to make the separations for offset printing, but the alignment between separations is usually much better than on an offset press. Because the four color passes can be more precisely aligned, alternatives to conventional halftoning patterns such as dithering, error diffusion, or dot-on-dot halftoning (halftoning without rotating the screens) may produce better results. However, the conventional halftoning pattern has evolved to provide a minimum of visual artifacts (distracting patterns, contour lines) and high stability under different printing conditions. A recent textbook [Ulic87] discusses black/white digital halftoning algorithms in detail, and a recent article [Knut87] presents a formal, mathematical description of these algorithms to the computer graphics community. The definitive work for digital color halftoning has yet to be written, however.

Defining the tone reproduction function that controls the mapping between the requested tone values and those actually produced by the mechanics of the printing process is very important in digital systems because the low resolution limits the number of available gray levels. The only way to determine the correct TRC is to print all of the available patterns generated by the halftoning algorithm and to measure them. The details of the halftoning algorithm will define the TRC, and it is difficult, if not impossible, to predict the TRC for one halftoning algorithm as opposed to another. For example, most printers have dot shapes that are direction-dependent, that is, a pattern of single dot lines, off and on, oriented one way may look very different when rotated 90 degrees. In some cases, this difference can be extreme. The author has seen an example where the first case produced a picket-fence pattern and the second case produced a solid area due to the ink spread.

Gray-balancing a digital printer is the same as finding the gray balance for offset printing; grayish patches must be compared with a gray standard. One additional difficulty with digital systems is that the halftone patterns may be so coarse as to make comparing the patch and the standard difficult. One looks gray, the other looks textured. Any technique that minimizes or defocuses the patterns will help: standing back a distance, removing corrective eyeglasses, etc. If the printer has a black ink or toner, good results may be obtained by using a black separation for printing. However, it is not safe to assume that adding black will always improve printer performance. The author has seen an example involving a a thermal transfer printer (wax melted on the paper) where adding black made the resulting color lighter because the black pass lifted off more color than it applied. Wet printing processes may smear or even wash off previously applied color. Again, nothing substitutes for testing the algorithms on the actual hardware involved.

Quantization is a significant problem for digital color printers. Those at 300 spi have the minimum resolution needed to print text and lines without visible jaggies, and this assumes special algorithms to tune the text rendering to the printer raster. Any halftoning algorithm at this resolution will produce a visible texture. For example, halftoning on a 300 spi printer with a 6×6 array of pixels produces an effective screen resolution of 50 lines/inch with a maximum of 37 gray levels. This is roughly equivalent to newspaper quality in effective screen resolution (graininess), and more limited in terms of the number of gray levels. These textures can destroy the legibility of text and of lines and will then look grainy under the best of circumstances. Furthermore, many commercially available color printers have a lower resolution than 300 spi. While rumors hint at 600 spi color printers, even this resolution will result in visible texturing of halftoned areas as it is still about a factor of four smaller than the resolutions used for offset.

An alternative to increasing the spatial resolution is to add a small number of levels to each color, changing the printer from a strictly bilevel device to one with multiple levels per color. These levels are obtained either by actually changing the darkness (density) of the ink or by changing the size of the spot. At typical printer resolutions (150–300 spi) a large increase in quality can be obtained by adding a very small number of gray levels to each color (as few as four). Because many of these devices are being driven by a market need to capture video images on paper, 64 levels will probably become a common offering. This, rather than increasing the spatial resolution of digital printers, will probably produce the most significant increase in printing quality for digital systems, especially for printing continuous-tone images.

Principles of Color Reproduction

The first part of this paper has focused on traditional graphic arts practice for color offset printing. Little was said about how this practice facilitated good color reproduction, or even what good reproduction is. The most general definition of color reproduction includes any task that involves duplicating a color or colors. More formally, however, the problem of duplicating single colors (for example, making several batches of identical paints) is called *color matching*. The term 'color reproduction' is reserved for reproducing collections of colors that form a picture, especially pictures of real scenes. The important distinction is that the collected colors in a scene are related, and these relationships are often much more important than any individual color.

The remainder of this paper will discuss the principles and problems associated with color reproduction. First is a survey of principles of color reproduction that apply to all color devices. The next section describes standard color measurement techniques and how they can be applied to color reproduction. The final section summarizes some experiments in digital color reproduction based on colorimetric principles.

HISTORY OF COLOR REPRODUCTION

The traditional industries involved in color reproduction are photography, graphic arts, television, and motion pictures. A classic work in this area is *The Reproduction of Colour* by R.W.G. Hunt [Hunt87]. For these industries, color reproduction means reproducing a real world scene onto film, paper, television monitor, or movie screen. None of these industries has produced a device-independent model for color reproduction. Color production is sufficiently complex that the usual emphasis is to master the process and then develop expertise in making the images 'look right.' Once the specific task is mastered, interest in solving the general problem is diminished.

In spite of all of the significant device-specific subtleties, which are unarguably very important for the best color reproduction, there do seem to be some principles that are common across technologies. Foremost is that there is no single definition of a good color reproduction. The average person is not very fussy about color images, as is demonstrated by the quality of the images displayed in color snapshots and on home television sets. However, the professional photographer, artist, or designer is very interested in accurate and effective color reproduction. Furthermore, specialists in the field of color reproduction are often concerned with differences that have only a subliminal effect on the average observer. It is essential, therefore, to clearly define the accuracy and quality required for the particular application when studying the problem of color reproduction.

The complexity of color-producing devices makes it very easy to generate unmistakably bad color reproductions. Some basic principles can describe why these are bad and suggest ways to improve them. Many of these same principles zcan be used to provide higher levels of quality. The rest of this section defines these basic color reproduction principles, emphasizing those that apply when transferring images from monitor to print.

Color Names

Imagine a picture with a purple sky or blue snow. Except in very unusual circumstances, everyone would agree that something was wrong with the reproduction. If, however, the sky were any shade of blue, or the snow any color recognized as white, far fewer people would complain about the reproduction. This example illustrates the role of color names in color reproduction: an image typically contains some reference objects whose colors correspond to a name in the viewer's mind. A reproduction that violates these names is wrong.

How colors map to names is difficult to predict quantitatively. A perceptually uniform color space like the Munsell color system [Muns41] can be divided into regions corresponding to different color names [Kell76]. However, the boundary between named regions is fairly sharp compared with the size of the regions. This means that given some color and its reproduction, measuring the distance between the value of the original and its reproduction is not sufficient to determine whether the color has changed its name.

The color of white is even more difficult to quantify because 'white' is defined as the brightest achromatic color in the environment. This definition covers a set of colors ranging from the reddish-orange light of the evening sky or a tungsten lamp to the blue-white of a fluorescent tube or a computer monitor. When the snow in a photograph looks blue, it looks blue in comparison to some other reference white, such as the paper white; the original snow may well have been blue on an absolute scale.

Maintaining the color of reference names is the primary rule of color reproduction. Fortunately, precise color matches are rarely important, since the space of color names is fairly coarsely quantized. However, small differences in critical regions of the color space can be very important. For example, commercial practice emphasizes sky, vegetation, and Caucasian skin as reference objects for natural scenes. Adding any hint of green or purple to skin tones is considered highly objectionable. Adding more red or brown, however, may go unnoticed. Color naming, and the set of common color names, seems basic to human perception [Uchi87]. Studying how this phenomenon can be quantified to help control reproduction is an interesting research problem.

GRAY SCALE AND TONE REPRODUCTION

As was emphasized in the section on printing, an important measure of the reproductive qualities of a color device is its gray scale. A color device is not truly under control until it is possible to produce a smooth, neutral range of tones from dark to light. Color monitors are well-behaved devices in this regard; they can be easily balanced so that equal amounts of the primary colors produce a neutral gray. Color printers and color photographic processes are more difficult to control.

Once the gray scale is neutral, the crucial question becomes how the gray values are distributed along it. In a reproduction system, the brightest achromatic color is defined as 'white' and the darkest is defined as 'black.' The ratio of the lightness of these colors defines the maximum *contrast* available on the device, that is, the maximum difference between light and dark. The term *dynamic range* is sometimes applied to scenes and reproduction processes with the same meaning as contrast. Quantization often limits the tone scale of digital systems independent of the contrast.

Issues of quantization and efficiency aside, less important than how a particular device's gray scale is arranged is how the gray tones in the original image map to the gray tones in the reproduction and hence the emphasis on tone *reproduction*. A common problem in reproduction is that the original image has a greater dynamic range than the output device. Therefore, compromises must be made to compress the information in the image onto the available values. Photographers are familiar with this process when printing film negatives onto paper: the paper has a smaller dynamic range than the film, which in turn (for pictures of the real world) has a smaller dynamic range than the original scene. The best reproductions compress the image nonlinearly as a function of the image content. That is, if the image has more information in the dark tones, these tones are spread over proportionally more of the available gray levels and vice versa.

Many experts in the field of color reproduction claim that tone reproduction is the single most important factor in effectively reproducing an image. As long as the reference color names are not compromised, the transformations applied to the colors are much less important than those applied to the neutral axis.

SATURATION

Most perceptually ordered color systems such as the Munsell system separate color into its hue, lightness, and some measure of the distance of the color from the neutral axis, called *chroma* or *saturation*. An image can be characterized by the overall level of saturation in the scene colors. Maintaining this characteristic saturation level is important in color reproduction.

There is strong evidence that the North American and Japanese publics prefer highly saturated images. Therefore, in commercial color reproduction systems it is common to boost the saturation of the reproduction beyond that of the original, often to the detriment of deliberately pastel images. This may be an attempt to compensate for the decrease in achromatic contrast in the reproduction; it may be just a matter of taste.

UNREPRODUCIBLE COLORS

Each different color reproduction technology can produce only a subset of all the colors found in nature. Unless an image is designed specifically for a particular medium, it will most likely contain colors that are not reproducible. How these colors are best approximated will ultimately be a function of the scene content. For example, imagine a scene with a colored ball sitting on a brightly lit table. The image of the ball contains a range of colors, dark to light, that are defined by the color of the ball and the color of the light source. If some of these colors are unreproducible, they must be changed in either hue or lightness. If only part of the ball changes hue, it will look like it has a colored blotch on it. If only part of the ball changes in lightness, it will no longer look like a shaded 3D object. Clearly all the colors in the ball should be changed to maintain the appearance of a shaded, 3D object of uniform color.

The most straightforward way to handle unreproducible colors is to smoothly transform the entire image to bring all the colors inside the set of producible colors. As in mapping the tone values to accommodate the limitations of the output device, these transformations are nonlinear and image-dependent. Ultimately, they require parsing the image content into objects and light sources, a problem for computer vision research. When considering computer-generated scenes, however, it is feasible to change the object color at the modeling level to minimize these problems.

Controlling Color Reproduction

The industries that specialize in color reproduction combine the use of measurement with skilled experts to control color reproduction. Traditionally, the skill of the specialist has been more important than color measurement; color reproduction is a craft rather than a science. This is slowly changing with the advent of computers in all forms of industry. The graphic arts industry now uses computer-controlled scanners, film plotters, and page makeup systems. Modern printing presses include equipment that can scan, evaluate, and adjust the press to maintain consistent quality. The skilled craftsman is still important, but the tools of the trade are irrevocably changing.

Color measurement as described in the next section is a reasonably mature science; most of the important standards have remained essentially unchanged since 1931. Applying this science to color reproduction, however, has been limited by the cost (in both time and money) of using it. Modern computer technology makes it possible to challenge the traditional assumptions about the cost and effectiveness of using color measurement to control color reproduction. The next sections discuss how color measurement can be applied to reproduction in a digital environment and provide an example of applying these principles to digital images.

Applying Color Measurement to Color Reproduction

Color measurement can be applied to color reproduction both to characterize color devices and to describe the transformations that must be applied to image colors to accommodate the characteristics of the output device. To understand how to use color measurement, it is important to understand what it tells us and, perhaps more importantly, does not tell us about the appearance of a color. The next section is a survey of classic *colorimetry*, the science of color measurement. The following section on *color appearance* surveys those aspects of color that are not adequately described by colorimetry. Finally, these concepts are combined with the principles of color reproduction to define *colorimetric color reproduction*.

Color Measurement

How do we measure color? Human beings see color when light is reflected off a colored object, transmitted through a colored filter, or emitted directly as from the phosphors of a color monitor. Light is a physical quantity, but color depends on the interaction of light with the human visual system and is thus a psychophysical phenomenon. Research in vision has determined physical properties of light that are well correlated with psychophysical properties of color. Colorimetry is the science of measuring color based on these physical properties, many of which have been standardized by the

Commission Internationale de l'Eclairage (CIE). There are several extensive reference works on color science and colorimetry [Wysz82; Maca81], and this section will provide only an overview of the important concepts and terminology.

Color can be defined as the response of an observer to a visual stimulus. This stimulus can be quantified as the spectrum of the light reaching the eye, that is, the energy of the light as a function of its wavelength. The *spectral reflectance* of an object is the percentage of the light energy reflected at each wavelength, and the 'color' of an object is most precisely defined as its spectral reflectance. The *stimulus* that reaches the eye, however, is the product of the spectral reflectance and the spectrum of the light falling on the object, so the perceived color of an object can never be separated from its illumination. These principles are summarized in the equations below.

Light + Object = Stimulus

Stimulus + Observer = Color

The most basic aspect of a stimulus that we can quantify is brightness. Human beings see light when stimulated by electromagnetic radiation of wavelengths roughly between 350 nm and 700 nm, but they do not see all these wavelengths equally well. The *luminance response curve* defines how efficiently the eye responds to light at each wavelength. Multiplying a stimulus by the luminance response curve and integrating produces a measure of how bright a color will appear, called *luminance*.

The stimulus is a spectrum, but radically different spectra can appear to be the same color, an effect that is formally called *metamerism*. This principle makes it possible to use three phosphors on a color monitor or three inks in offset printing to produce a wide range of colors. The number three in these systems is not coincidental; it is directly related to the physiology of human vision.

Imagine a color-matching experiment where an observer has three primary lights that can be adjusted to match a given color. Each color produced by the system can be defined entirely by the power of the primaries. These powers are called the *tristimulus values* for that set of primaries. It has been empirically proven that different observers will produce the same tristimulus values for a given color, or, conversely, any stimulus that reduces to the same tristimulus values will look the same to any standard observer. By standardizing the primaries, therefore, we can define any colored light with just three numbers rather than an entire spectrum.

The concept of tristimulus values can be applied to colored objects as well as colored lights by standardizing the illumination as well as the system primaries. The resulting color stimulus can then be reduced to three tristimulus values. Changing the illumination, however, will produce different tristimulus values from the same colored object. Furthermore, two objects that match under one set of lights will not necessarily match under any other set of lights unless the objects have the same spectral reflectance. A *metameric match* is one where the objects have different spectral reflectances but happen to match under a specific illuminant.

CIE Standards

The CIE is an international organization that has standardized a method for computing tristimulus values, notated X, Y, and Z, as a standard representation for colors. In 1931 the CIE standardized three primaries and a standard observer that are widely used by a variety of industries to define colors. There have been some revisions and extensions since then but the basic definition has not changed, and the 1931 standard is still the one most commonly used. The CIE has also standardized a number of illuminants; most relevant to this discussion are D5000, adopted by the graphic arts community for observing printed materials, and D6500, adopted by the television community for the white point of monitors.

The units for X, Y, and Z are power (watts). Within a reasonable range, multiplying the spectral power distribution by the same value at every wavelength does not change the perceived color, since the tristimulus values are multiplied uniformly by the same factor (effectively, the ambient light is made more intense). This fact can be used to produce a 2D representation that eliminates the intensity information by projecting the tristimulus values on the plane: $X + Y + Z = 1$. The resulting 2D representation is known as the *chromaticity coordinates* of the color. The commonly used chromaticity coordinates are x and y, where $x = X/(X + Y + Z)$ and $y = Y/(X + Y + Z)$.

The familiar CIE *chromaticity diagram* shown in Figure 6 is a plot of x vs. y. Included on this plot is a horseshoe-shaped curve called the *spectrum locus* that is defined by the chromaticity coordinates of the spectral (single-frequency) colors. The *purple line* is the line connecting the blue with the red end of the spectrum locus. The black-body radiation curve describes the chromaticity coordinates for black-body radiators of different color temperatures. All visible colors lie inside the region bounded by the spectrum locus and the purple line. All colors described as 'white' lie near the black-body curve.

Alternative coordinates for chromaticity are *dominant wavelength* and *purity*. The dominant wavelength of a color is the wavelength of the spectrum color whose chromaticity is on the straight line connecting the sample and the illuminant. Purity is the ratio of the distance from the illuminant to the sample to the distance from the illuminant to the spectrum locus. If the sample lies between the illuminant and the purple line, the *complementary dominant wavelength* is the intersection with the purple line of the extension of the line connecting the sample and the illuminant. Dominant wavelength and purity correspond roughly to the perceptual concepts of hue and saturation.

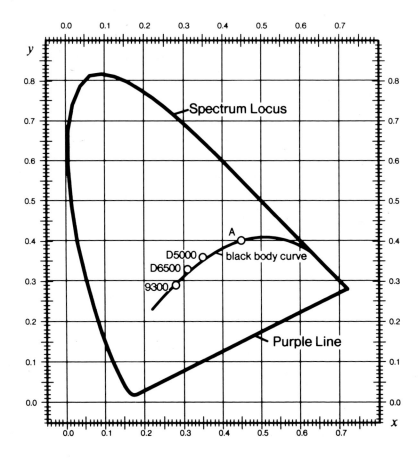

Figure 6. The CIE chromaticity diagram showing the spectrum locus, purple line, black-body curve, and the location of three standard illuminants: D5000, D6500, and A. Illuminant A corresponds to incandescent light. A typical computer graphics monitor white point (color temperature 9300°K) is also shown.

The CIE values of reflecting objects are generally computed in terms of reflectance rather than power. *Reflectance* is the ratio of the power of the reflected light to the power of the incident light. Given the reflectance of the object and the power spectrum of the illuminant, it is easy to compute the power spectrum, i.e., color stimulus, for the color. The tristimulus values are normalized so that $Y = 100$ for 100% reflectance.

Luminance, reflectance, and the CIE tristimulus values can be measured with a *spectroradiometer* or *spectrophotometer* that samples the stimulus at a number of different wavelengths, multiplies it by the color-matching functions, then sums the results to perform the integration and produce X, Y, Z. Such a device generates complete spectral information for objects and light sources. A *colorimeter* contains three filters whose transmittances are close to the color-matching functions. Measuring the total light energy through each filter defines the tristimulus values. A colorimeter is not as accurate an instrument as a spectroradiometer and cannot be used to measure complete spectral information.

CIELAB, CIELUV

The Euclidean distance between two colors defined as tristimulus values is not a good measure of how similar the colors appear. That is, the minimum perceptible difference between colors corresponds to a different distance in different parts of the color space. Several attempts have been made to derive perceptually uniform color spaces from the tristimulus values. Two that have been standardized by the CIE are CIELAB and CIELUV.

These two systems are derived from ones that already existed in different industries at the time the CIE addressed the problem of standardizing a uniform color space. The CIE recommendations recognize both spaces as being better than tristimulus values for comparing colors, although neither was found to be truly uniform nor significantly better than the other. To maximize acceptance, the decision was made to standardize them both. The intent of the standard is to formally define the *just noticeable difference* (JND) between two colored samples. The samples must be viewed under identical conditions and, since the standard was written for reflective colors, the definition of a match must include a specification of the light source.

Both of the systems use a metric for lightness called L^* (L-star), which is proportional to the cube-root of the luminance. L^* is defined with respect to a reference white so it always falls in the range of 0 (black) to 100 (white). The other two axes, a^* and b^* for CIELAB or u^* and v^* for CIELUV, define the colorfulness of a color. One convenient way of visualizing these systems is in polar coordinates around the L^* axis. *Hue angle* is the angle with respect to the positive a^* or u^*, and *chroma* is the distance radially from the origin.

A single JND is a Euclidean distance of one in either system. Maintaining any color reproduction process to a JND of 10 or less is quite difficult. Single JND values are more commonly applied to paints, inks, and other colorants.

COLOR APPEARANCE

The color definition introduced above emphasized the difference between *stimulus* and *color*. Tristimulus values (a measure of the stimulus) determine whether two colors seen in identical visual environments are identical in appearance. They do not, however, completely determine the *color*, which can be strongly influenced by other factors such as surface gloss and texture, the ambient light level in the room, other objects in the observer's field of view, what the viewer was looking at previously, and so on. These additional factors are often combined together under the designation *color appearance* and include many aspects of color vision and perception.

The goal of color reproduction is to duplicate the appearance of the original. It can easily be shown that this does not mean duplicating the tristimulus values, point for point, in the image. Consider the following example. A typical white point for a monitor is (x: 0.313, y: 0.329), Y: 25.0. A typical measured white point of a printed page (blank paper viewed in an ANSI standard viewing booth [ANSI72]) is (x: 0.345, y: 0.367), Y: 526. On the printed page, a color with the same tristimulus values as the white point of the monitor appears not white but a dark blue near gray. Duplicating the tristimulus values is wrong in two ways: it isn't light enough, and it isn't the color that is perceptually 'white' on the new device. Normalizing the luminance can fix the first problem but not the second.

The goal of this section is to present a brief overview of the factors affecting color appearance, particularly those that apply to color reproduction. Readers interested in more information on this topic should consider reading *The Perception of Color* by Ralph Evans [Evan74]. Hunt's book has a small section on color appearance also [Hunt87, pp. 123–133]. Modern texts on color vision [Boyn79, Hurv81] contain relevant information as well.

Adaptation and Color Constancy

The perception of color remains remarkably constant under variation in the ambient light. This consistency is demonstrated in two ways. One is the wide range of different 'normal' lighting conditions found in nature. Sunlight varies in color and intensity throughout the day; buildings are lit by lights ranging in color from incandescent to fluorescent. However, only when making direct comparisons do people become aware of the change in color of objects as a result of these lighting changes. Not so the spectroradiometer, which will produce radically different tristimulus values for the same object under different light sources.

The second demonstration is the typical nonuniformity of light in the environment. Shadows and reflections change the intensity and color of the light throughout most rooms, yet this effect is easily ignored by observers asked to name the colors of objects in the room. An example relevant to this discussion is the significant variation in intensity (as much as 30%) across the surface of a typical computer monitor. Most users, except those that have tried to make any measurements from the monitor, have never noticed this variation.

Adaptation accounts for the wide range of colors people are willing to consider white. When the illumination is colored, the eye compensates until the 'white' objects look neutral. For example, if you view a monitor (either computer graphic or television) in a dimly lit room, the screen will look white. However, if you look into the room through a window the monitor often looks very blue because your visual system is adapted to a different white point.

Adaptation affects color reproduction because it tells us that the human eye is optimized to derive the color of objects independent from the absolute light levels in the environment. Therefore, object color, relative brightness, and contrast are much more important than absolute brightness or color. The most important application of this fact is in rendering the achromatic colors. It seems clear that these colors should be defined relative to the rendering medium. That is, the white point of the monitor should map to the point called white on the paper, and similarly for black. The neutral colors should then interpolate smoothly between these two colors.

The Effect of Surrounding Colors

Most readers will be familiar with optical illusions where two patches of the identical color are displayed surrounded by differently colored backgrounds. The two colors appear radically different. A simple example of this phenomenon is shown in Figure 7. The two gray squares are identical, but the one on the dark background appears to be lighter than the one on the light background.

Monitor images are often shown on black backgrounds that intensify the color. Images printed on pages, however, are usually surrounded by white. A black background tends to diminish the perceived contrast and increase the perceived saturation [DeMa71]; a white background seems to increase contrast and diminish saturation. The contrast effect helps the printed image, since printers generally have less contrast than monitors (especially monitors viewed in a darkened room). The saturation effect, on the other hand, puts the printer at a double disadvantage, since monitors can physically produce a much more saturated range of colors.

Sharpness

The human visual system is optimized to find edges in scenes. Any abrupt change in lightness or in the rate of change of lightness is a candidate for an edge. *Mach bands*, which are edges seen in nonuniformly changing

Figure 7. The effect of background color on the perception of color. The two gray squares are identical.

gradients, are an example of the second phenomenon [Evan74, p. 211]. The mind finds edges where an instrument would find none. This tendency of the eye to enhance edges can be a problem, since it aggravates quantization effects. However, it can also be used to advantage to increase the sharpness of the reproduction as in the practice of unsharp masking in the graphic arts [Hunt87, p. 274; Yule67, pp. 325–326].

A good reproduction duplicates or even enhances the spatial characteristics of the original as well as the colors. Monitor images have limited resolution and can appear blurry or 'soft' when printed over a large area. Traditional antialiasing techniques exaggerate this effect. Though the sharpness of offset printing is itself limited by the halftone screen frequency, techniques to enhance sharpness can be included in halftone patterns [Hou83, p. 85; Ulic87, pp. 334–337]. The best solution is to reproduce high-resolution originals whenever possible. With the edge-enhancing mechanisms built into modern scanners, providing twice the resolution of the screen frequency, i.e., 300 spi for a 150 line screen measured along the printed image dimensions (not the original film dimensions) will produce good results.

Monitors vs. Printers

The contrast and brightness of a color monitor are very much dependent on how it is viewed. In absolute terms, monitors are very dim, so the addition of even low levels of ambient light decreases the contrast significantly. The contrast and brightness of a printed page, however, are enhanced by increasing the amount of light reflected from the image. This means that people tend to prefer to look at monitors in the dark and prints under bright light. To properly adjust (formally, *adapt*) to two such disparate lighting environments will typically take several minutes, so there can never be any true side-by-side comparison of monitor and print images; reproducing the appearance of the monitor means reproducing what the designer of the image remembers of its appearance on the monitor. This quickly becomes a process of enhancing the most important image features to accommodate the output medium. Deriving algorithms that make it easy to make, or even anticipate, these adjustments is the goal of digital color reproduction.

COLORIMETRIC COLOR REPRODUCTION

Colorimetry based on the existing CIE standards is useful in color reproduction as a way to quantitatively describe device behavior. To characterize a device, measurements are taken that define a correspondence between the values of the device primaries and the tristimulus values of the generated color. Once a device characterization is established, it is possible to define the device gamut, the set of all possible colors produced by the device. Specifying device gamuts in a standard form provides a quantitative way to compare them.

Accurate monitor characterization has been well studied but is not yet used in common practice [Cowa86, Mott88]. What is common is to derive an 'ideal' characterization based on the tristimulus values of the primary colors, to assume black is at (X: 0, Y: 0, Z: 0), and to ignore the effects of ambient illumination and nonlinearities in the individual monitor. This provides a simple linear transformation (3×3 matrix) between RGB values and tristimulus values that is assumed to be a reasonable approximation for a properly gamma-corrected monitor viewed in a dark room.

To characterize an offset printer it is necessary either to model the ink, paper, and halftone productions [Pobb72] or to sample the entire gamut at regular intervals and interpolate [Saun86; Schr86; Ston88]. The second approach is more attractive because it is simpler to implement and more general. The same technique can be applied to digital printers that do not use conventional halftoning techniques or to any color-producing device, including monitors. To apply this technique to four-color offset printing, it is convenient to first define black as a function of cyan, magenta, and yellow. Once the function for the black separation is fixed, the gamut of the printer can be derived from a set of color charts generated by varying cyan, magenta, and yellow in uniform steps. These charts are measured to produce a piecewise linear function that maps between tristimulus values and cyan, magenta, and yellow.

The gamut for a device can be visualized as a solid shape in the 3D space of tristimulus values. An image, therefore, is a set of points (tristimulus values) that must lie inside the gamut of the target device to be reproducible. Different reproduction principles are modeled as different geometric relationships between image point sets and device gamut solids.

This way of stating the problem leads to a model of color reproduction as a transformation of the original image colors, defined in terms of tristimulus values, to values that provide the same appearance in the reproduction. The research question is: what are these transformations, and how are they generated? Furthermore, it is clear that the information provided by the tristimulus values alone is inadequate to generate the transformation, so another aspect of the research is determining what other information needs to be included with the image to make it possible to construct the correct transformation.

No one yet knows exactly what these transformations are or how to derive them from an image. However, the model is gaining some acceptance in the research communities studying color reproduction. The next section describes a project in the computer graphics community to apply this model to reproducing computer graphics images.

An Experiment in Colorimetric Color Reproduction

CIE tristimulus values were first used as the basis for publishing computer graphics images in a project to produce the color figures for the proceedings of the AIC (*Association Internationale de la Coleur*) conference on *Color in Computer Generated Displays* [Ston86]. Conference participants supplied digital images and characterizations of their monitors, the digital pipeline from pixel values to color separations was measured and characterized, and a transformation, called a *gamut mapping*, was generated for each image to map it from monitor to print. This work has been reported in detail elsewhere [Ston88; Ston86].

The project suggested a methodology for publishing computer-generated images but left many points for further exploration. To investigate more extensively how to improve the quality and accuracy of published computer graphics imagery, ACM SIGGRAPH has funded a project to develop state-of-the-art techniques for publishing color images in *Computer Graphics* and *ACM Transactions on Graphics*. This section provides a status report on that project. It describes the current production pipeline, formally defines gamut mapping, and then presents some examples to illustrate the issues that need to be addressed in reproducing computer graphics imagery.

REPRODUCTION PIPELINE

In this project, we are interested in transforming images generated in typical computer graphics environments to color separations that can be printed by typical printers. This is in contrast to an experiment where both the design and printing environments are tightly controlled. We are therefore forced to concentrate on problems that have a large effect on the quality of the reproduction and to ignore the inevitable small variations. The intention is to accept images specified as calibrated *RGB* pixel values and to produce SWOP standard color separations and proofs. Currently the project has no special arrangement with any printer, so the term 'print' actually means 'proof.' This implies trusting the printer's skill to get the proofs reproduced.

Typical computer graphics imagery is developed on a monitor that accepts an 8-bit voltage value (a maximum of 256 levels) for each color. There is usually a look-up table associated with each color that maps the 8 bits for each color in the frame buffer to the output voltage. This look-up table is typically used for gamma correction and is intended to make the monitor's output intensity a linear function of voltage. Once the monitor is prop erly gamma-corrected, a linear transformation can be generated to convert between monitor voltages and tristimulus values. This transformation is formed from the tristimulus values for the device primaries (red, green, and blue) and is only correct if no ambient light is falling on the monitor.

An *image* is defined as a set of pixel values in the frame buffer, that is, the color values before gamma correction. As defined above, a characterization for this image provides a mapping between these values and tristimulus values. If the definition of the appearance of the image is how it looked on a particular monitor, the image characterization will be derived from the monitor characterization.

To produce the proofs, the DDES standard [DDES86] provides a digital link to the equipment used to make offset films. DDES is a magnetic tape format for specifying color images in terms of cyan, magenta, yellow, and black pixel values. The pixel values define the percentage dot area desired at each point for the corresponding ink. The DDES values can be characterized by generating and measuring a printed color chart. We have chosen to make black a function of cyan, magenta, and yellow to simplify the resulting sampled function. The result of the characterization is a piecewise linear function for converting between tristimulus values and the three printing primaries.

Figure 8 illustrates this pipeline. Gamut mapping is the step that converts monitor tristimulus values to printer tristimulus values. The next section describes this process in more detail.

GAMUT MAPPING

Reproducing a monitor image on a printer requires us to consider three gamuts: the monitor, the printer, and the image. A reproduction algorithm can either define a single mapping that takes the monitor gamut to the printer gamut or it can produce a custom map for each different image. Graphic arts practice tells us that the highest quality will be achieved with a custom map for each different image, i.e., a mapping that takes the image gamut to the printer gamut. However, there are several reasons for considering the relationship between the monitor gamut and the printer gamut.

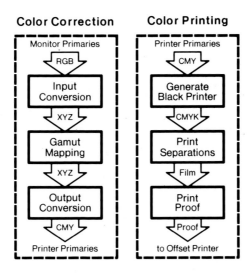

Figure 8. A block diagram showing the process used to convert images designed on a monitor to digitally produce color separations for offset printing.

First, constructing custom maps is time-consuming, and many applications are better served by trading quality for efficiency. Therefore, a single transformation that maps the entire monitor gamut aesthetically onto the printer gamut is extremely useful. Such a transformation can be used alone or as a starting point for more sophisticated, image-specific mappings.

Second, information about the appearance of the original image can be derived from the relationship between the image gamut and the monitor gamut. The most obvious example is the definition of black and white. A story illustrating this problem goes as follows. At one time, a hot research topic in computer graphics was the modeling of fog. Much effort, therefore, went into the production of foggy scenes, that is, blurry, low-contrast pictures. Inevitably, when it came time to publish a paper on these algorithms, the first attempt to reproduce these pictures was ruined by someone in the reproduction pipeline 'improving' the contrast and destroying the fog. Without a reference to the designer's definition of black and white, there was no way to tell that the picture was supposed to be gray.

Finally, the colors in an image are related to one another in a way that often can be derived more easily from the original monitor-relative representation than by considering the tristimulus values. For example, a common problem in reproducing monitor imagery is handling the vivid blue colors obtained by specifying the blue monitor primary alone. Most of these colors are not reproducible on the printer gamut. Algorithms that consider each color individually often project out-of-gamut colors to the surface of the printing gamut, which means that a shaded blue area may end up all the same color. By considering these colors relative to the monitor gamut, we can redefine blue in a way that smoothly transforms all the related colors together.

Gamut Visualization

The gamut of a calibrated device can be visualized as a solid in the Cartesian space of tristimulus values. All realizable colors lie inside this solid. Similarly, the pixels that make up an image displayed on a calibrated device define points in the same 3D space. Once the devices and the images are calibrated, we can discuss the different color transformations in terms of transforming points (pixel values) to fit inside characteristic solids (device gamuts).

However, viewing raw tristimulus values does not provide much intuition about an image. It is much more informative to separate the lightness from the colorfulness of an image as is done in the traditional CIE chromaticity diagram. This diagram has the additional feature that for the simplified monitor characterization described above, colors specified as RGB combine along straight lines in the xy plane. An alternative to the chromaticity diagram is to convert the tristimulus values to CIELUV or CIELAB and make a projection on the u^*v^* or a^*b^* planes. While the use of these systems for viewing the effect of color reproduction algorithms is not proven, it can be argued that they are more accessible than the chromaticity diagram.

Figure 9 shows a typical monitor and printer gamut displayed in each of these three forms. In each of these figures the color of the outline is intended as a label, that is, the reddest point of the device gamut is colored pure red. In all three representations the monitor gamut is larger than the printer gamut. Figure 9a shows the triangular monitor gamut nearly enclosing the roughly six-sided printing gamut. The white points of the two gamuts are marked with white dots. The white point of the printer gamut is to the right of and above the monitor white point.

Figures 9b and 9c show this same data projected on the a^*b^* and u^*v^* planes, respectively. Here, the white points are not specifically marked because, in the CIELAB and CIELUV representations, white is always $L = 100$ and (a^*, b^*) or $(u^*, v^*) = (0, 0)$. This occurs because these systems are defined with respect to a reference white. Precisely what this reference white should be in monitor-to-print transformations has not been

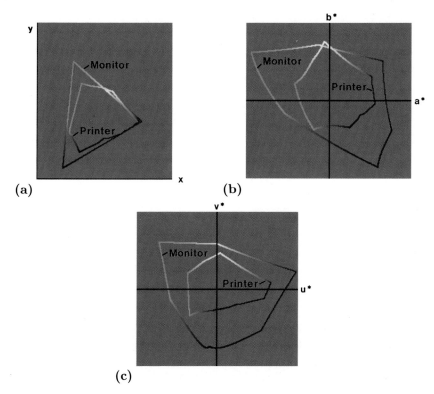

(a)

(b)

(c)

Figure 9. A typical monitor and printer gamut. (a) Gamuts overlaid on the CIE chromaticity diagram. Note that the white points do not align. The upper white point is the printer white. (b) Gamuts overlaid on the CIELAB a^*b^* plane. (c) Gamuts overlaid on the CIELUV u^*v^* plane.

determined. In these diagrams, the monitor reference white is the point where $R=G=B=$maximum voltage. For the printer, the reference white was chosen to be the color of the paper viewed under a D5000 light source. Using two different values for the reference white has the effect of mapping the white point on each device to the same CIELAB or CIELUV value. While this method of aligning the white points of the two gamuts has not been proven optimal, it is adequate for many applications.

The figures in Figure 9 are projections of a 3D solid. Figure 10 shows the monitor and printer gamuts overlaid on plots of L^* vs. a^* and L^* vs. b^*. Note that while the ideal monitor gamut goes through $(0, 0, 0)$, the black point for the measured printing gamut is much higher. Also, the neutral gray values of the ideal monitor gamut are vertically aligned at $a^* = b^* = 0$ whereas the neutral axis of the printer is tilted. A similar diagram could be constructed for L^* vs. u^* and L^* vs. v^*. It is less clear what an equivalent profile would be for chromaticity values due to a lack of a well-defined black point in that system.

Another interesting lightness profile plots the maximum brightness for each of the saturated colors (see Figure 11). This figure was generated by interpolating between each of the primary and secondary colors for each gamut, plotting L^* vs. hue angle. Note that the L^* value is higher for the monitor than for the print except for yellow. Also, the printer magenta more nearly aligns with the monitor red than with the monitor magenta. The hue values for cyan are very different between the two devices as well. A similar profile could be constructed for the CIELUV system, or by plotting dominant wavelength vs. reflectance (or vs. L^*).

Each of these color spaces provides a slightly different way of viewing the device gamuts. Which one is preferred is still highly a matter of individual taste. In this paper, the CIELAB color space is used because it has a perceptually uniform lightness axis, it has a distinct black as well as a distinct white point, hue can be represented as a single number (hue angle), and the author prefers its shape over that of the CIELUV gamut.

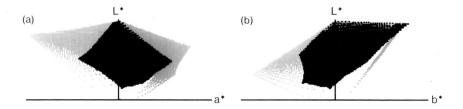

Figure 10. A typical monitor (gray) and printer (black) gamut overlaid (a) on the CIELAB a^*L^* plane (b) on the CIELAB b^*L^* plane. Note that the black points of the two gamuts are different.

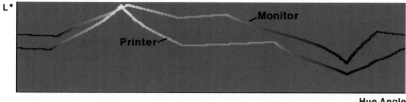

Figure 11. A plot to show the difference in maximum brightness for the primary colors of a typical monitor and printer. The color at each point indicates the color with respect to the device primaries. Note that hue angle 0 is red for the monitor and magenta for the printer.

Image Visualization

The most obvious way to view an RGB image is to render it on a monitor. Even if the local monitor is quite different from the originating monitor, it is usually possible to get some idea of the appearance of the image by simply putting the RGB values into the frame buffer of the local monitor and looking at it. If the image and the local monitor are calibrated, it is possible to do a better job of matching the original colors, except for those that are outside of the local device's gamut, of course.

This method of viewing an image exposes an important problem with the simplified characterization for monitors presented above. People are notoriously free about fiddling with the contrast and brightness knobs of their monitors. The assumption, therefore, that the gamma correction makes the monitor linear in intensity is usually wrong, and thus the assumption that the pixel values can be linearly transformed to luminance is also wrong. Furthermore, the ambient viewing conditions strongly affect the perceived brightness and contrast of the image. The best solution to this problem is currently unknown. Assuming that the monitor characterization was carefully done so that the luminance value is correct, there is still no way to include the effect of the ambient light in the linear model. If the monitor is viewed in a room with no ambient light, the viewer's adaptation when viewing the monitor will be extremely different than when viewing the print, and maintaining the correct appearance of an image across such radically different viewing conditions is not yet understood. Finding the best way to calibrate the lightness scale for the monitor/image characterization is the next critical step in this project.

The distribution of these lightness values can be informative. It is straightforward to make a histogram for an image that maps lightness to frequency of use. This gives a profile for the image that defines whether it is high or low contrast and where in the lightness range the information lies. Assuming the characterization is correct, it is possible to construct a diagram such as the ones shown in Figure 12. The independent variable is the L^* value computed from the monitor characterization quantized to 256 levels. The dependent variable is the number of pixels in the image at that value. In Figure 12a, the image has the bulk of its information in the darker colors with a small sprinkling of colors at the higher values. Figure 12b shows a scene that has values more evenly distributed across the lightness scale.

The colors in an image can be plotted on the a^*b^* plane, as shown in Figure 13. Each color in the image has been converted to CIELAB and plotted. The color of the dots is a label just like the color of the gamut outlines. The lightness of the dot is proportional to its lightness value. The color of the dot corresponds to its position on the a^*b^* plane. Viewing images on these diagrams helps to identify problem colors that are far outside the printing gamut. Note that there may be other problem colors, because the picture may contain a color that is available on the printing gamut but only at a much lower brightness level. The figure plotted in Figure 13a has a limited range of colors, principally dark blues and grays, with a noticeable line of bright colors streaking toward blue. Such a line usually indicates a shaded object or tone wedge. In contrast, the image plotted in Figure 13b has colors spread much more uniformly around the gamut with three distinct streaks: one toward magenta, one toward red-orange, and one toward blue. In these figures, the printer and monitor gamuts are outlined as in Figure 9.

Constructing Gamut Transformations

A gamut mapping is a function that maps image tristimulus values to the printer tristimulus values. The best transformation is image dependent and currently requires an expert to construct it. However, it is possible to describe some of the principles involved in defining the transformations.

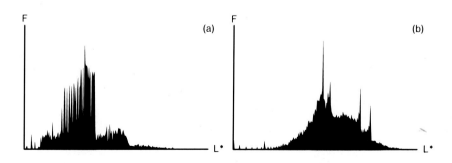

Figure 12. The horizontal axis is L^*, the vertical axis is frequency of occurrence. (a) The image shown is dark. (b) The image shown is brighter and has a wider range of lightness values.

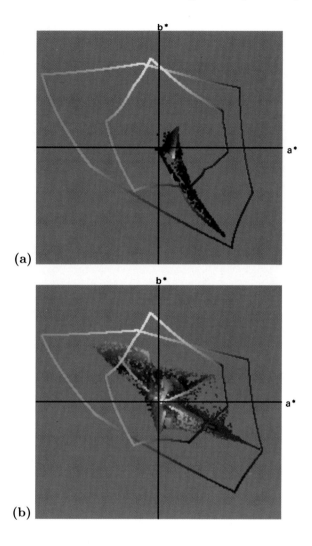

Figure 13. Image colors plotted on the CIELAB a^*b^* plane. The lightness of the point indicates the lightness of the pixel value. (a) An image with a limited range of colors. (b) An image with a wide range of colors.

Furthermore, for many images an acceptable reproduction can be achieved by algorithmically applying some of these principles.

Mapping the Lightness Scale

The gamut transformation should maintain relative rather than absolute lightness values. If the dynamic range of the printer and the monitor are different, the image must be scaled to fit. The most elegant transformation would be nonlinear and would accommodate the image content, as is common in photography. The easiest transformation, however, is a linear scale.

White and black should be transformed so that 'white' maps to the paper and 'black' to the darkest printed black. There is a question as to whether the monitor or the image should define white and black, especially if the image contains a picture of a light source. Is white the color of the light in the picture, or the color of the white point for the monitor? Also, it is possible to imagine special illustrations, such as one trying to show how blue the monitor is compared with white paper, where mapping white and black would be the wrong thing to do. However, these are unusual cases; mapping white and black is generally the right thing to do.

Graphic arts practice tells us that the way the lightness profile of an image is reproduced is very important to the quality of the reproduction. The tone reproduction affects the contrast and the overall brightness of the image. Maintaining contrast is considered a very important factor in the reproduction process. High overall contrast is often considered a mark of quality although maximizing contrast is not always appropriate, as the example of the foggy pictures demonstrates. The fact that contrast is a ratio emphasizes again that the relative relationships between the color values in the picture are more important than the absolute relationships.

The concept of tone reproduction is key to transferring images between any two devices, but the definitive way to map or even define the lightness values of a monitor in such a way that the TRC for monitor-to-print reproduction can be computed has yet to be found. Recent work [Rhod88] suggests that using L^* to make this mapping is effective. However, using L^* based on the simple, linear monitor characterization is inadequate unless the monitor is very carefully set up.

Mapping the Chromatic Values

The principles for mapping the chromatic values are similar to those for mapping the lightness scale except that they are applied in two dimensions. Few images sample the color space uniformly, so mappings can be made that distribute the important parts of the image over the color space. However, it is important to maintain the correct relationship between colors in an image.

In each of the color gamuts, the colors interpolate smoothly from the most saturated colors on the gamut surface toward the neutral axis. Also, the colors are distributed smoothly from light to dark. Any transformation that maintains this relationship will maintain a reasonable appearance for shaded objects. That is, scaling the gamut (linearly or nonlinearly) with respect to the neutral axis is acceptable, but adding discontinuities to it is not. Considering the CIELAB space as hue, lightness, and chroma provides an effective way to discuss such a transformation. A gamut map that changed only the chroma for all the colors would desaturate the picture without changing the relative lightness of the colors. If the mapping was a uniform scaling, the relative saturation relationship between the colors would be maintained. However, uniformly scaling the monitor gamut shown in Figure 9b until it fit inside of the printer gamut would leave large sections of the printer gamut unused due to the difference in shapes. As people quickly develop a sense of where the limits of each device lie (for example, what is the reddest red) such a mapping would be highly unsatisfactory. A nonlinear transformation that smoothly collapsed the monitor gamut onto the printer gamut while maintaining the hue and lightness is preferable.

There exists a simple-to-compute transformation that maps the entire monitor gamut surface onto the printer gamut surface; the transformation $CMY = [1,1,1] - [R,G,B]$. To understand what is meant by this transformation, it is necessary to discuss the printing part of the production pipeline a little further. The black separation is a function of CMY, so it does not enter into this discussion at this point. If the CMY values are derived from the trivial equation above, tone wedges from cyan [R: 0, G: 1, B: 1], magenta [R: 1, G: 0, B: 1], and yellow [R: 1, G: 1, B: 0] to white will map to tone wedges on the print that are linear in dot area for each of the printing primaries. As the DDES standard is written in terms of dot area, this makes the optimal use of the resolution available for specifying the image color. Similarly, red, green, and blue will shade smoothly to white as overlaid values of two of the printing primaries.

Away from the surface of the gamut, the cyan, magenta, and yellow values must be gray-balanced and, for the darker colors, the black separation must be added. For the SWOP standard, it is necessary to do gray component replacement as well. These transformations are invisible in the model presented here. They should be performed so that the neutral axis defined by $C=M=Y$ (or $R=G=B$) is gray and varies smoothly from light to dark. Exactly how the gray scale varies in lightness can be controlled somewhat independently of the chromatic parts of the gamut. The tone wedges running from the primaries to black should do so smoothly without abruptly changing hue. Developing and implementing this model has been the first significant milestone of the project.

This transformation is far from ideal because it changes both the hue (notice the difference between the printer cyan and the monitor cyan) and the relative lightness of the colors, as can be seen by comparing the gamuts in Figures 9 and 11. However, it does smoothly map the monitor gamut to completely fill the printer gamut, avoiding the problem of handling out-of-gamut colors.

Out-of-gamut Colors

The gamut diagrams shown above clearly indicate that the colors on the surface of the monitor gamut are much more saturated and brighter than those on the surface of the printer gamut. This difference in chromatic contrast is probably the most significant source of disappointment when transferring monitor images to print. Some of this dissatisfaction can only be avoided by educating users about the limits of printing technology; the vivid blue produced by the monitor's blue phosphor alone cannot be matched on any print media, nor can the electric yellow-greens and bright magentas found on the monitor be reproduced using standard offset printing inks and papers. Users who intend to print their images should simply avoid these colors.

Colors that lie outside of the gamut must be mapped to some color on the gamut, usually by making the color less saturated, darker, or both. In some circumstances, however, it may be desirable to change the hue also. For example, the brightest, most saturated blue on the printing gamut is closer to cyan (blue-green) than to the blue-purple of the monitor phosphor. If bright blue is what is important, changing the hue will give better results.

The current methodology is to apply global gamut mappings that bring the bulk of the image gamut inside the printing gamut. Then, any remaining out-of-gamut colors are projected a short distance onto the surface of the gamut.

RESULTS

The AIC conference proceedings [Ston86] contains several examples of images that were generated by the techniques discussed in this paper. In this original effort, we mapped the tristimulus values for each image by visualizing the device gamuts as solids in the coordinate system defined by the CIE tristimulus values XYZ. This work highlighted the need for aligning the neutral axis, especially the black point, and emphasized the importance of considering the tristimulus values relative to the device gamut. The switch to using CIELAB for visualization and gamut mapping was motivated much more by the convenience of manipulating the gamut in terms of its normalized neutral axis, chroma, and hue than by any belief in the uniformity of the color space for measuring the effect of a color reproduction system.

Within the context of this current project, the bulk of the effort to date has gone into correctly setting up the printing pipeline and writing the tools to generate the different views of the device and image gamuts shown in the figures in this paper. The current gamut mapping tools are quite simple and include only a remapping to normalize the gray scale plus a way to globally increase the saturation of the printed picture. The values of cyan, magenta, and yellow are derived by inverting red, green, and blue.

Two examples of applying the current system to computer-generated images are shown in Figures 14 and 15. Figure 14 shows an image generated at the University of Waterloo Graphics Lab by Mike Sweeney. This print is not a good reproduction because the balls appear bright blue on the monitor image, whereas the printed colors are purple and much darker than in the original. Furthermore, the shading on the balls is much less visible on the print than on the monitor image. The reproduction of the image

in Figure 15, generated at Xerox PARC by Mik Lamming, was more successful. While there are noticeable hue shifts compared with the original,
none of the important scene colors crossed a color name boundary. The
most obvious differences are in the color of the wine glass (the original is
less red) and the color of the sky (the original is less purple).

Figures 16–19 show how the gamut mapping transformed the image colors for each of these examples. Each figure shows the image colors, the
monitor gamut, and the printer gamut plotted on the a^*b^*, a^*L^*, and b^*L^*
planes. In the a^*b^* plot, the lightness of the image colors indicates the
lightness of the color in the image. The monitor and printer gamuts are
indicated as colored outlines, as in Figure 13. On the a^*L^* and b^*L^* plots,
the monitor gamut is displayed in white and the printer gamut in black.
The image colors have all been modified to show bright, saturated values
that contrast well with the black and white device gamuts.

Figure 16 shows the original image colors for Figure 14. The blue balls
show as a blue streak on the a^*b^* plot. The ball color is shown to be the
color of the blue monitor primary because the streak in the a^*b^* plot runs
out toward the bluest point of the monitor gamut. On the other two views,

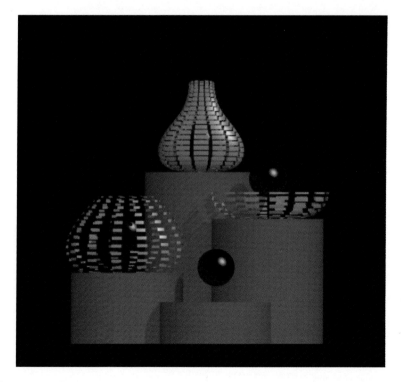

Figure 14. 'Dali Vases' by Michael J. Sweeney, University of Waterloo Computer
Graphics Lab, reproduced using the simple gamut mapping described in the text.
The balls should be a lighter and brighter blue.

Figure 15. 'Mik's Test Image' by Mik Lamming, Xerox PARC/EDL, reproduced using the simple gamut mapping described in the text. This is an acceptable reproduction of the original image.

the blue colors lie along a path from dark blue near black (L^* near zero) to a bright, saturated blue (near the edge of the gamut) to a light blue near white (L^* near maximum). This corresponds to the dark shading, the bright blue of the fully lit ball, and the white highlight. Most of the colors associated with the balls lie outside the printer gamut.

Figure 17 shows the printed image colors for Figure 14. On these diagrams all of the image colors lie inside the printing gamut. On the a^*b^* plot the blue balls are represented as a streak that points at the 'bluest' point of the printing gamut (full cyan plus full magenta). While mathematically this is 'blue' ($[C:1, M:1, Y:0] = [1, 1, 1] - [R:0, G:0, B:1]$), visually it is purple, which causes the color name change. The other two plots show that the path indicating the gradation of the ball colors from dark to light has been significantly compressed. The b^*L^* plot shows best how the blue colors have been forced into the 'bluest' point of the printing gamut. The L^* value for this point is much lower than that of the monitor, making the printed balls significantly darker than the original.

Figures 18 and 19 show the colors in Figure 15. These plots emphasize that this image is much more colorful than the previous example, as is obvious from looking at the picture. Individual objects are much less easy

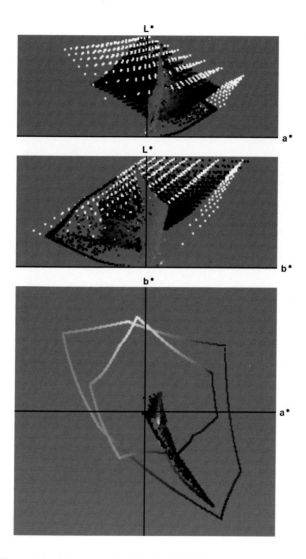

Figure 16. The original image colors for the Dali Vases overlaid on the monitor and printer gamuts. Notice that many of the blue colors lie outside of the printer gamut.

to recognize, although the streak toward magenta ([R: 1, G: 0, B: 1]) in the a^*b^* plot of the original image is clearly the pink wine glass. As in the case of the balls, many of this object's colors are outside of the printing gamut. The plots of the printed image colors, Figure 19, show the wine glass colors mapped to printing magenta. This color is significantly more red than the corresponding value on the monitor. How this set of colors is

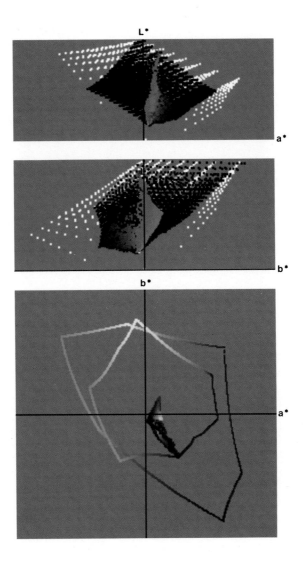

Figure 17. The printed image colors for the Dali Vases overlaid on the monitor and printer gamuts. All colors now lie inside the printer gamuts.

transformed is quite clear on the a^*b^* plot and the a^*L^* plot. Comparing the b^*L^* plots, however, is a little more difficult. The printed values for the magenta colors appear to be significantly desaturated. In reality, this is a problem with using a projection for viewing 3D data. From the a^*b^* plot, it is clear that the magenta colors have been transformed to lie nearly orthogonal to the b^*-axis.

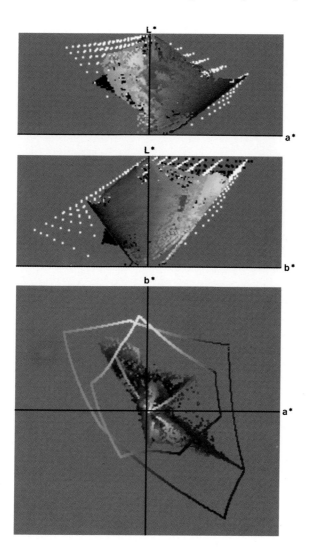

Figure 18. The original image colors for Mik's Test Image overlaid on the monitor and printer gamuts. This image is much more colorful than the previous example.

CONCLUSIONS AND FUTURE WORK

Using a digital reproduction pipeline, controlling the way the gray scale is mapped, and applying simple gamut transformations to accommodate the print medium can provide a significant improvement over traditional methods of printing computer graphics images. These methods have been demonstrated in the examples shown here and in the 1988 SIGGRAPH

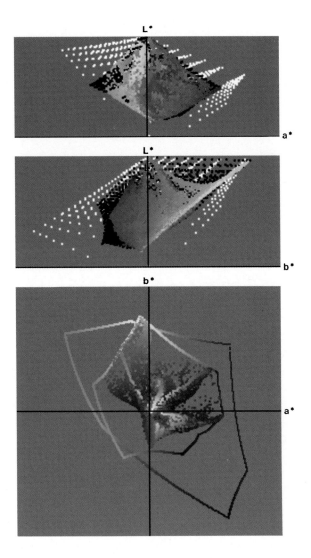

Figure 19. The printed image colors for Mik's Test Image overlaid on the monitor and printer gamuts.

proceedings [SIGG88]. The front cover, title page, one image from the back cover, and one image on the interior of the proceedings were produced using our system. These simple methods will fail if the original image colors lie significantly outside of the printing gamut. In our experience, pure blue ([R: 0, G: 0, B: 1]) has produced the most problems. Comparing the monitor gamut with the printing gamut suggests that most of the pure monitor primary and secondary colors will produce problems. Images that carefully model realistic scenes tend to contain few of these problem colors.

Designers of illustrative or surrealistic images, however, often choose pure monitor colors and so create pictures that are difficult to print.

Further developing the gamut transformations should produce interesting results. Visualizing the image and device gamuts in the CIELAB color space suggests developing gamut mappings based on the CIELAB representation, especially expressed as lightness, chroma, and hue. However, while manipulating CIELAB values makes it easier to address the two basic principles of normalizing the white point and aligning the neutral axis, duplicating monitor CIELAB values on a printer will not usually produce an acceptable reproduction. A minimum transformation must align both the white and black points of the monitor or image gamut with the printer gamut. Further work is necessary to determine the optimal way to perform even this basic transformation.

The monitor and printer characterizations, while adequate for initial testing and demonstration, need additional work. For some images we have found it necessary to deviate from the theoretically correct lightness mapping to produce a reasonable reproduction. We need to find a more accurate way to capture the lightness information in a monitor image, including all the relevant factors such as the effect of the ambient illumination and the actual linearity of the monitor. This characterization needs to be simple enough to produce that it can be accurately supplied with each image.

The initial characterization of the printer gamut shows irregularities in the dark colors that may be measurement error or may be problems with the black separation and gray component replacement. Whether or not such irregularities are visually significant, they can produce numerical difficulties when transforming between CMY and XYZ and projecting out-of-gamut colors. Further work in this area is also needed to improve the maximum obtainable contrast. That is, we would like to make our black darker, especially because so many computer graphics images include a black background.

Conclusions

To date, the vast majority of the research in computer graphics has been directed toward producing monitor images. The most common applications of these images have been video, and, to a lesser extent, film. The link between these media and computer graphics monitors is the fact that they are viewed in dim or dark environments and that the color produced is emissive. Even with these media, however, the problem of reproducing the monitor appearance is nontrivial. An attempt to apply the principles of color measurement and gamut transformations to this problem is currently being considered by a group interested in High Definition TV [DeMa88].

When moving from monitors to print, the reproduction problems become even more complex. Printed pages are not typically viewed in dark rooms, and the colors produced are limited by the physics of reflective surfaces, inks, and colorants. While desktop publishing, the use of computers in the graphic arts industry, and the introduction of digital color printers to the computer graphics community all demand solutions to this problem, it is unrealistic to expect to find a single, ideal solution. The history of color reproduction industries suggests that a range of solutions, each varying in cost and quality, will emerge instead.

The computer graphics research community should demand the best quality reproduction of their computer-generated images. To achieve this, however, improvements need to be made in the way that practitioners use and control their monitors. *RGB* is not a precise or even a very accurate description of typical monitor primaries. A single value of gamma, arbitrarily defined, does not guarantee monitor linearity in intensity or luminance. And the practice of designing ultra-saturated images in lightless environments produces unprintable pictures.

The solution to these problems is not to dictate a precise standard for monitor usage or to limit the production of images to brightly lit rooms. After all, that beautiful, glowing image may still be reproducible on a slide. The more useful approach is to develop ways to characterize the monitor, image, and environment that capture the information important for generating the best monitor-to-print transformations. Along with these techniques must come guidelines to help the author design the image so it will continue to illustrate the desired effect even after it is printed. After all, many of the colors selected in computer graphics are arbitrary. Why not pick ones that will reproduce well?

Acknowledgments. The work on colorimetric color reproduction is a continuation of work begun with John C. Beatty and William B. Cowan, University of Waterloo Computer Graphics Lab. Many of the concepts are the result of this collaboration. Thanks go to Xerox Corporation and ACM SIGGRAPH for funding this effort. Special thanks go to Richard J. Beach for sponsoring this work both in his management role at Xerox and as Editor-in-Chief of SIGGRAPH. The color separations generated in this work are produced at Kedie-Orent, Sunnyvale, CA.

REFERENCES

[ANSI72]
Viewing Conditions for the Appraisal of Color Quality and Color Uniformity in the Graphic Arts, ANSI PH2.32-1972, American National Standards Institute, Inc., New York, 1972.

[Beac86]
Beach, M., Shepro, S., and Russon, K., *Getting It Printed*, Portland, OR: Coast to Coast Books, 1986.

[Boyn79]
Boynton, R.M., *Human Colour Vision*, New York: Holt, Rinehart and Winston, 1979.

[Brun86]
Bruno, M.H., *Principles of Color Proofing*, Salem, NH: Gama Communications, 1986.

[Cowa86]
Cowan, W. B., and Rowell, N.L., Phosphor constancy and gun independence in color video monitors, *Color Res. Appl.*, Vol. 11, Suppl. (June 1986), pp. S34–S38, 1986.

[DDES86]
Digital Data Exchange Specification (DDES)^{TM}, Dunn Report^{TM}, Vol. IV, No. 6, June 1986.

[DeMa71]
DeMarsh, L.E., Optimum reproduction of color, in *Proc. of the 1971 Inter-Society Color Council*, pp. 95–97, 1971.

[DeMa88]
DeMarsh, L.E., HDTV Production Colorimetry, presented at InterSociety Color Council Meeting, May 8–10, 1988.

[Evan74]
Evans, R.M., *The Perception of Color*, New York: John Wiley and Sons, 1974.

[Holl80]
Holladay, T.M., An optimum algorithm for halftone generation for displays and hard copies, in *Proc. of Society for Information Display*, Vol. 21, pp. 185–192, Playa del Rey, CA: Society for Information Display, 1980.

[Hou83]
Hou, H.S., *Digital Document Processing*, New York: John Wiley and Sons, 1983.

[Hunt87]
Hunt, R.W.G., *The Reproduction of Color*, 4th Ed., New York: John Wiley and Sons, 1987.

[Hurv81]
Hurvich, L.M., *Color Vision*, Sunderland, MA: Sinauer, 1981.

[John85]
Johnson, T., Polychromatic colour removal — Revolution or evolution? in *Proc. of the Technical Association of the Graphic Arts (TAGA)*, pp. 1–15, Rochester, NY: Technical Association for the Graphic Arts, 1985.

[Kell76]
Kelly, K., and Judd, D., COLOR, Universal Language and Dictionary of Names, National Bureau of Standards Special Publication 440, 1976. (available from U. S. Government Printing Office, Washington, DC 20402, Stock No. 003-003-01705-1.)

[Knut87]
Knuth, D., Digital halftones by dot diffusion, *ACM Trans. Graph.*, Vol. 6, pp. 245–273, 1987.

[Maca81]
MacAdam, D., *Color Measurement, Theme and Variations*, 2nd Revised Ed., Berlin: Springer-Verlag, 1981.

[Meye86]
Meyer, G.W., and Greenberg, D.P., Color education and color synthesis in computer graphics, *Color Res. Appl.*, Vol. 11, Suppl. (June 1986), pp. S39–S44, 1986.

[Mott88]
Motta, R.J., The colorimeteric calibration of a CRT imaging system for color appearances research, *Proc. of Society for Information Display*, Vol. 30, July 1989.

[Muns41]
Munsell, A.H., *A Color Notation*, 9th Ed., Baltimore, MD: Munsell Color Company, 1941. The latest *Book of Color* is available from Munsell Color Company, 2441 North Calvert Street, Baltimore, MD 21218.

[Pobb72]
Pobboravsky, I., and Pearson, M., Computation of Dot Areas Required to Match a Colorimetrically Specified Color Using the Modified Neugebauer Equations, Report No. 150, Information Service Graphics Arts Research Center, Rochester Institute of Technology, Rochester, NY: 1972.

[Rhod88]
Rhodes, W.L., and Lamming, M.G., Towards WYSIWYG Color, Xerox Palo Alto Research Center Technical Report EDL-88-2, April 1988.

[Saun86]
Saunders, B., Visual matching of soft copy and hard copy, *J. Imaging Technol.*, Vol. 12, pp. 35–38, 1986.

[Schr86]
Schreiber, W.F., A color prepress system using appearance variables, *J. Imaging Technol.*, Vol. 17, pp. 200–210, 1986.

[SIGG88]
Comput. Graph., Vol. 22, August 1988 (SIGGRAPH 88).

[Sout79]
Southworth, M., *Color Separation Techniques*, 2nd Ed., Graphics Arts: Livonia, 1979.

[Ston86]
Stone, M., Cowan, W.B., and Beatty, J.C., A description of the reproduction methods used for the color pictures in this issue of *Color Research and Application*, *Color Res. Appl.*, Vol. 11, Suppl. (June 1986), pp. S83–S88, 1986.

[Ston88]
Stone, M., Cowan, W.B., and Beatty, J.C., Gamut mapping and the printing of digital color images, *ACM Trans. Graph.*, Vol. 7, pp. 249–292, 1988.

[SWOP]
Recommended Specifications Web Offset Publications, S.W.O.P. (available from Graphic Arts Technical Foundation, 4615 Forbes Ave, Pittsburgh, PA 15213).

[TAGA]

Technical Association of the Graphic Arts, RIT T&E Center, One Lomb Memorial Drive, P.O. Box 9887, Rochester, NY 14623.

[Uchi87]

Uchikawa, K., and Boynton, R.M., Categorical color perception of Japanese observers: comparison with that of Americans, *Vision Res.*, Vol. 27, pp. 1825–1833, 1987.

[Ulic87]

Ulichney, R., *Digital Halftoning*, Cambridge, MA: The MIT Press, 1987.

[Wysz82]

Wyszecki, G., and Stiles, W.S., *Color Science*, 2nd Ed., New York: John Wiley and Sons, 1982.

[Yule67]

Yule, J.A.C., *Principles of Color Reproduction*, New York: John Wiley and Sons, 1967.

3 Realistic Image Generation

Antialiasing

Franklin C. Crow

Abstract

Aliasing causes familiar defects in raster computer graphics due to the sampling and reconstruction of an 'ideal' image defined by the input data. Although there are simple ways to reduce the effects of aliasing, they are either expensive or compromise image quality. More effective ways of reducing aliasing require some understanding of the problem. Such understanding leads to various ways of applying approximations of a low-pass filter to the ideal image. A test pattern is used to show the effectiveness of various filters for this purpose. Filtering at all pixels is expensive. Therefore, cost reduction techniques are presented that attempt to limit filtering to those places where shading changes abruptly. Temporal aliasing is also a problem to be dealt with, and recent attention to this problem is surveyed. However, the most significant recent efforts have used stochastic sampling techniques, that provide a unified solution to both spatial and temporal aliasing.

Effects and Their Causes

Those who work with digital imagery are familiar with the symptoms of aliasing. In still images, jagged edges caused by the regular structure of dots making up the image are often evident (Figure 1a). In animated sequences the jagged edges come alive, with rows of little stairsteps running back and forth along the edges of objects. Small or narrow objects can suffer random changes in shape and can even disappear in places (Figure 1b). Regular arrays of shapes, such as the windows on the side of a tall building, may appear to 'swim', or undulate, in an animated sequence.

The term 'aliasing' refers to the effect caused by 'sampling' (taking discrete measurements of) a signal at an inadequate number of regular intervals. A 12-cycle signal sampled at ten regularly spaced positions appears identical to a 2-cycle signal over the same interval sampled at the same positions. Thus, the 2-cycle signal is an 'alias' of the 12-cycle signal (Figure 2).

Use of an inadequate sampling interval when synthesizing digital images causes small errors in representing the positions of the edges that characterize the image. These errors, in turn, cause all of the problems mentioned above. Unfortunately, technological limits and standardized equipment

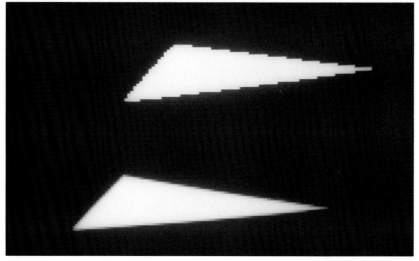

a

b

Figure 1. Aliasing effects. (a) Jagged edges; (b) disappearing detail.

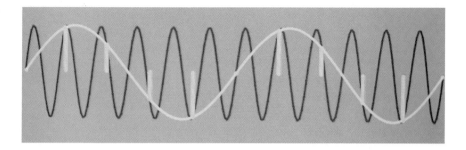

Figure 2. A 2-cycle 'alias' of a 12-cycle signal.

prevent most of us from choosing our sampling interval. Therefore, we are left trying to make the best of what we have.

To put it another way, the effects of aliasing are caused by attempts to force the positions of details in an image to coincide exactly with the positions of the individual spots ('pixels') of the physical image structure. In virtually all computer-driven displays capable of showing shaded images, the physical image structure consists of a regular array of pixels upon which individually calculated intensities are displayed. An image is most simply calculated by representing the color of a single surface at each of these pixels.

However, if a pixel can represent only one surface, then the boundaries between objects in the image must fall between pixel positions. This forces such boundaries to be jagged in shape except where they are perfectly aligned with the pixel array (e.g., horizontally or vertically). Such boundaries can be made to appear smooth by blending the colors of two or more surfaces at the pixels involved. Methods for calculating that blend and deciding when it is necessary to do so provide the basis for the methods suggested below.

If a display is viewed from an adequate distance, details the size of a pixel cannot be resolved. Therefore, variation in intensity over a few pixels can be used to 'suggest' the position of an edge. By such means it is technically feasible to make an image that is indistinguishable from one of much greater resolution. In order to do this we must achieve the same level of intensity at each pixel as would be seen over the equivalent small area in an image of much higher resolution. This can be done by properly considering all the details that contribute to the area represented by each pixel.

In theoretical terms, aliasing cannot be entirely eliminated. In practical terms, however, it can be diminished to the point where it is undetectable. All successful techniques for diminishing aliasing involve increasing the amount of information upon which the image is based. The array of pixels making up an image represent samples from a conceptual scene defined by the input data. The information content of the image can be improved by increasing the number of samples or by taking more information into account when taking each sample.

Treatments of the theoretical underpinnings of the aliasing problem can be found in [Crow77; Kaji81; Mitc88; Oppe75]. Algorithms for solutions to various aspects of the problem have appeared in [Catm78; Catm80; Crow77; Crow78; Crow81; Cook86; Fuch79; Feib80; Gupt81; Mitc87; Warn80].

Easy Solutions

The most straightforward way to reduce the effects of aliasing is to increase the resolution at which the image is calculated. For example, four pixels may be calculated for every pixel on the display. The displayed intensity may then be made the average of the four calculated intensities. Attempts have been made to measure the costs and benefits of this approach [Crow81].

Increasing the resolution, while generally easy to implement, can be very expensive. In general terms, the cost of generating an image varies directly with the number of scanlines for calculations involving the surface definition (vertices, edges, etc.), and with the square of the number of scanlines for calculations involving the shade of an individual pixel [Whit82]. Therefore, higher resolution can be very expensive where highlights, texture, or other expensive shade calculation techniques are applied. Furthermore, even for the least expensive shading techniques, the cost of generating the image rises directly with the resolution.

Many of the effects of aliasing may be lessened by processing the image after it has been computed (postprocessing). For example, where the effects are subtle, as along edges across which there is only small contrast, adding noise or blurring the image may be sufficient. For high-contrast edges, a combination of edge detection and smoothing algorithms can have quite satisfactory results [Bloo83]. Standard thresholding techniques may be used to determine where high-contrast details are to be found. Local edge slopes may then be determined by following the edges, and pixels may be blended by utilizing the local slope.

The performance of methods that process the completed image is fairly straightforward. Blurring techniques are usually applied globally. Therefore, performance is a function of the extent of the blur (how many pixels are involved in the calculation of a single blurred pixel) and the square of the image resolution. Noise addition may in some cases be provided gratis by the equipment (e.g., very grainy photographic film) or display algorithms (e.g., dithering techniques). In other cases it should cost no more than one or two simple operations per pixel.

Edge-smoothing techniques, on the other hand, require two stages. First, edges must be found. This requires a pass over the entire image, making nearest-neighbor comparisons. Cost is a function of the square of the resolution. Then, edges must be processed by blending colors in pixels along edges. The cost of this stage is dependent on the amount of high-contrast detail in the image. When the image is synthesized from geometric data (as opposed to painted, etc.), the first stage may be simplified by recording edge information as the image is generated and then checking for contrast only where edges are known to lie.

While blurring and edge-smoothing techniques may be used to enhance the appearance of images, such methods can NOT recover detail that has been lost in the process of making the image. Small or thin objects may still disappear or be distorted. While a still image may be processed to remove clear evidence of aliasing, animated sequences can still reveal problems. Most problems may be avoided by insuring that the data describing the image contains no details below a certain size. However, this will usually require human intervention or much more carefully prepared data than is desirable.

Understanding the Nature of the Problem

The methods of the previous section have disadvantages because of ineffectiveness in the case of postprocessing techniques and expense in the case of higher-resolution techniques. To do better, it is necessary to have a better understanding of the problem.

The process of making a synthetic image involves taking samples of a 2D function defined by the surface elements forming the input data (transformed polygons, patches, etc.). The simplest algorithm for determining the color of a pixel is to find all surface elements intersecting a ray emanating from the eye. The intersecting surface closest to the eye determines the color of the pixel.

Using this method, anything not touched by a ray will be lost. Since the rays are infinitesimally thick, an infinitesimal portion of the ideal image is actually represented. In particular, details small enough to lie between rays can be missed entirely.

As was stated above, more information must be brought to bear on the problem of computing the shade of a pixel. Instead of using a ray emanating from the eye we should be using a solid angle, thus forming a cone. The area of each visible surface falling within the cone must be computed. To a first approximation, the color of a pixel is simply the average of the colors of all surfaces represented weighted by their respective areas covered within the solid angle.

Calculating such areas is equivalent to a signal-processing operation know as 'convolution'. We 'convolve' a 'filter' with an image by superposing the filter function over the image function at each pixel position and integrating over the product of the two. The effect of a convolution, for the cases in which we are interested, is to smooth over abrupt changes in color, thus diminishing the strength of higher spatial frequencies in the image.

Fourier theory says that the highest frequency that can be represented in a digital image is one that has a cycle of two pixel widths. Taking a sine wave of that frequency and using the Fourier transform to find the corresponding spectrum, we get an impulse function at the highest representable frequency (Figure 3a).

Constructing a frequency function that is constant up to the highest representable frequency and then drops to zero, we then take the inverse Fourier transform to find that the corresponding spatial representation is the sinc ($\sin x/x$) function with a central lobe having a width of two times the interpixel distance (Figure 3b).

Now, it turns out that convolving with a filter function has the same effect as multiplying by the corresponding spectrum. Thus, convolving with the sinc function is the same as eliminating frequencies above a sharp cutoff, exactly what we want to do.

Unfortunately, the sinc function is infinite in extent and therefore impossible to apply as a practical filter. However, we can use the general shape of the sinc function to lead us to a practical filter shape. The most important feature to note is that most of the area lying under the sinc function is in the two-pixel-wide central lobe.

A test pattern was generated to try different filter shapes, with the results shown in Figure 4. Each image shows a synthesized test pattern made using the filter function shown at the bottom. The hatch marks represent pixel spacing. The commonly used filter shapes are (a) an impulse function, or no filter; (b) 16 samples/pixel; (c) 64 samples/pixel weighted over a four-pixel area; (d) 64 samples per single-pixel area; (e) 256 samples/pixel weighted over a four-pixel area; (f) a box function over a single-pixel area, or Fourier window; (g) the triangle function; (h) the central lobe of the sinc function.

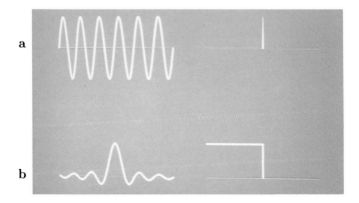

Figure 3. Spatial and frequency domain images of (a) $\sin x$ and (b) $(\sin x)/x$.

Filters wider than two pixels such as (i), a weighted version of the three inner lobes of the sinc function, are sometimes used.

It should be clear from Figure 4 which filters work best on an extreme case. However, it is important to test various filters on images typical of those to be used in a given environment (see Figures 5 and 6). The more effective filters are also more expensive. In cases where there are no small, highly contrasting details, the less expensive filters will often be adequate. However, line drawings and text are two examples of very common imagery that includes lots of small, highly contrasting details.

Restricting the Domain of Application

Different features in an image require differing amounts of care to hide aliasing. Broad areas in which the shade changes slowly can be reproduced with very little information. On the other hand, areas with sharp detail carry a much greater density of information and must be treated more carefully. Areas with extremely fine detail, of course, may not be representable given the display resolution. In such cases, the proper representation is a smudge of the correct intensity.

Expensive antialiasing measures can be practical if it can be determined where they are really necessary in advance of their application. As was seen in the previous section, it is possible to isolate those pixels which contribute to the problem by looking for contrast thresholds. Knowledge of the surface

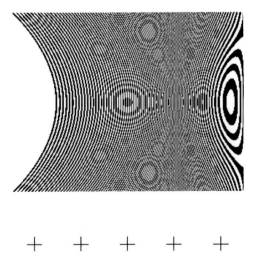

Figure 4. Effects of various filter functions. (a) Impulse (equivalent to a single sample/pixel).

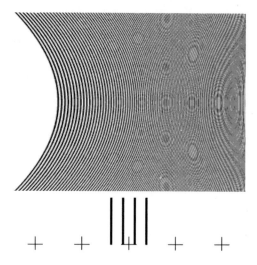

Figure 4. (*Continued*) (b) Four impulses across one interpixel distance (16 samples/pixel).

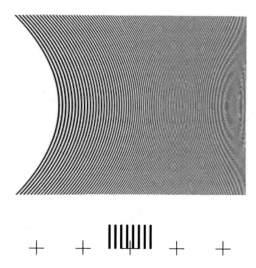

Figure 4. (*Continued*) (c) Eight weighted impulses in two interpixel distances (64 samples/pixel).

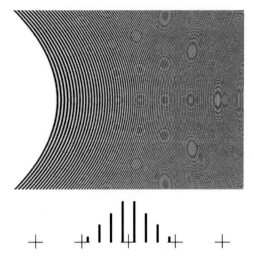

Figure 4. (*Continued*) (d) Eight impulses across one interpixel distance (64 samples/pixel).

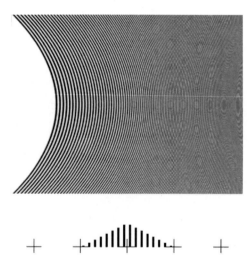

Figure 4. (*Continued*) (e) Sixteen weighted impulses in two interpixel distances (256 samples/pixel).

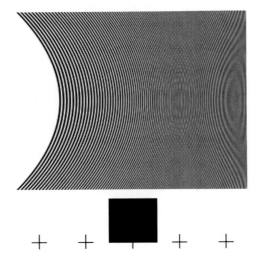

Figure 4. (*Continued*) (f) Box function across one interpixel distance.

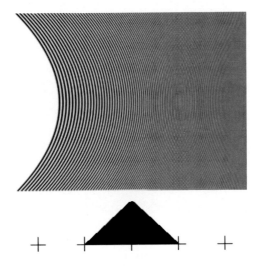

Figure 4. (*Continued*) (g) Triangle across two interpixel distances.

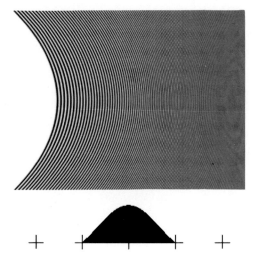

Figure 4. (*Continued*) (h) Central lobe of sinc function across two interpixel distances.

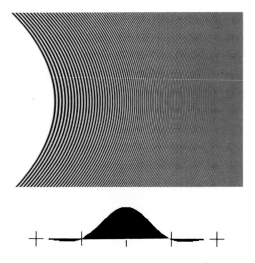

Figure 4. (*Continued*) (i) Weighted sinc function across four interpixel distances.

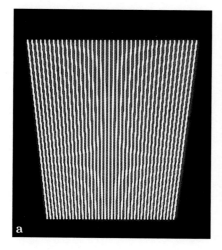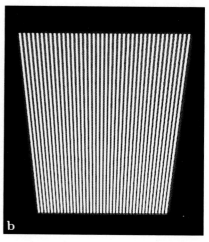

Figure 5. Lines scan-converted using (a) a one-pixel box filter (left) and (b) a two-pixel triangular filter (right).

definitions from which the image is to be made allows the display algorithm to know where those high-contrast details are likely to occur. Using such knowledge, the domain of application of antialiasing techniques may be restricted to just those areas where they are needed. Furthermore, such information can be used during the generation of the image, avoiding loss of detail which is not recoverable after the image is generated.

Currently, most practical images have large regions of sparse detail. It is therefore inefficient to use brute force techniques such as computing the entire image at a much higher resolution and then averaging many samples into one displayed pixel. This may not be true for future images of much greater complexity. For the moment, however, algorithms that treat detailed areas with special care remain important enough for study.

Generally, the pixels that need special care are those which contain part of one of the edges defining a surface. If the pixel is considered to represent a very small image from the scene being generated, then the color of each surface visible within that image must contribute to the color of the pixel. The pixel color is determined by summing all the contributing surface colors, each weighted by the area it subtends within the pixel and the height of the filter function over that area. Therefore, where an edge passes through a pixel, the surface colors on either side of the edge are blended by a weighted average.

During the generation of an image involving objects with smooth, non-glossy, untextured surfaces, all aliasing problems must occur where the defining edges of surfaces pass through pixels. Therefore, the domain of application of antialiasing measures may be restricted to those pixels. In

Figure 6. Images calculated at 4096 lines and then (a) averaged eight lines into one interpixel distance (equivalent to 64 samples/pixel) to make the top 512-line image and (b) averaged with weighting 16 lines into two interpixel distances (256 samples/pixel) to make the bottom 512-line image.

an image of a simple environment, this greatly reduces the amount of computation required. On the other hand, as image complexity grows, the number of pixels that must be processed for antialiasing becomes more significant. However, it remains quite expensive to make pictures of a complexity great enough to suggest that global methods such as those of the previous section would be more efficient.

Frequently, curved surfaces are represented by polygonal approximations. This poses a problem in that it is necessary to use a large number of polygons to approximate a curved surface closely enough to avoid a polygonal silhouette. This means that the large majority of edges defining the surface are not evident in the image and thus require no antialiasing measures.

Therefore, one way to cut down the number of pixels subject to additional computation would be to use nonlinear surfaces such as piecewise continuous patches. Algorithms for direct rendering of nonlinear surfaces are more difficult to implement, generally less efficient, and sometimes more restrictive than those for polygonal surfaces [Blin80]. On the other hand, subdivision schemes that produce a collection of small polygons from nonlinear surfaces are widely used today. Such methods make it easy to concentrate efforts on patch boundaries.

The high-contrast edges in an image of a smoothly curved surface fall along the silhouette of the surface. If the silhouette can be characterized in the data, then only those pixels involved in the silhouette of the object need be treated for aliasing. There is a relatively easy way to determine silhouette edges. In a polygonally approximated surface, silhouette edges are those edges shared by a polygon on the visible side of the surface (a 'frontfacing' polygon) and one on the far side of the surface (a 'backfacing' polygon). Hidden-surface algorithms generally cull the backfacing polygons before rendering a surface [Suth77]. If a data structure that provides pointers to the neighbors of a given polygon is used (Figure 7), silhouette edges may be determined straightforwardly.

Therefore, for curved surfaces, edges that require special attention are those that are shared by a frontfacing and a backfacing polygon or those that belong to only one polygon. The latter case consists of those polygons that lie along the edge of an open surface (one that does not close on itself). When subdividing patches, it is sometimes possible to keep track of which subpatches lie on the silhouette, thereby isolating the resulting polygons for more careful treatment.

Calculating Subpixel Areas

In order to calculate the intensity of a pixel which represents parts of more than one surface, the area covered by each surface within the pixel must be estimated. Area-estimation algorithms can take a number of different forms [Crow77; Feib80; Abra85]. However, the algorithm must be relatively quick if it is to be used with complicated scenes.

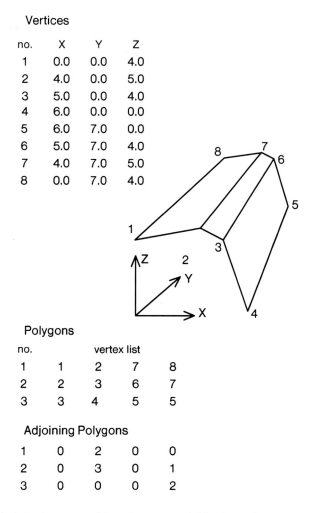

Vertices

no.	X	Y	Z
1	0.0	0.0	4.0
2	4.0	0.0	5.0
3	5.0	0.0	4.0
4	6.0	0.0	0.0
5	6.0	7.0	0.0
6	5.0	7.0	4.0
7	4.0	7.0	5.0
8	0.0	7.0	4.0

Polygons

no.		vertex list		
1	1	2	7	8
2	2	3	6	7
3	3	4	5	5

Adjoining Polygons

1	0	2	0	0
2	0	3	0	1
3	0	0	0	2

Figure 7. A data structure with pointers to neighboring polygons.

There are two widely used models for the area subtended by a pixel: (a) The image may be considered a grid wherein each square hole represents a pixel area. In this model, pixels abut and completely fill the image area (Figure 8). (b) The image may be modeled more closely to its physical realization on a CRT. Here, the pixels are larger and overlap one another by half (Figure 9). In addition, the importance of a subarea varies over the pixel; details toward the middle of the pixel area are weighted more heavily in computing the pixel intensity. Various weighting functions have been used [Crow77; Kaji81], all of which are similar in general shape to the Gaussian distribution of intensity produced by a focused electron beam (i.e., symmetric, with most of the weight in the middle).

Figure 8. Pixels modeled as abutting squares.

Obviously, area-estimation algorithms based upon the first model can be somewhat simpler [Catm78; Crow78]. The differences between these models, however, can be quite important when treating areas of fine, highly contrasting detail [Crow81] and when rendering lines and characters [Crow78; Kaji81; Naim87]. For the most part, images have been made with the simpler model [Catm78, Fuch79, Pitt80] with varying degrees of success.

Area-estimation is most correctly done by calculating a simplified hidden-surface algorithm at each affected pixel [Catm78; Fuch79]. However, quite adequate images can be made by simpler approximations.

In order to compute a mini-hidden-surface algorithm at a pixel, either a 'scan-order' algorithm [Catm78] or a 'cookie-cutter' (polygon subdivision) algorithm [Weil77] must be used. The scan-order algorithms tend to be complicated and thus hard to implement. The cookie-cutter algorithms have yet to be fully exploited. They also have turned out to be complicated and hard to implement. In addition, the primary example [Weil77] is not well suited to complicated images, since its computational cost increases with the square of the number of polygons involved.

Many hidden-surface algorithms have been inspired by the universal dominance of random-access frame buffers. Relatively simple algorithms can be constructed by sorting the surfaces involved to a 'priority' order (closest surfaces have highest priority) and then writing the surfaces to the frame buffer in order. However, when the surfaces are individually scan-converted, there is no way to distinguish whether two surfaces that partially cover the same pixel area both cover the same part of the pixel (overlap), cover different parts of the pixel (abut), or do some of both (Figure 10).

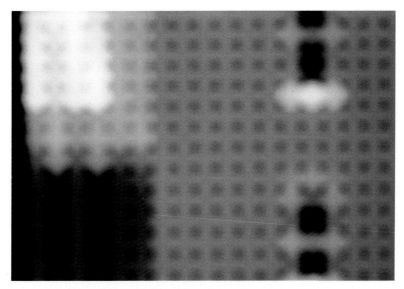

Figure 9. Pixels modeled as overlapping Gaussian bumps.

In the simplest case, the 'painter's algorithm', surfaces are scan-converted in reverse-priority order. Thus, the most distant surface is written to the frame buffer first. Subsequent surfaces are then written over earlier surfaces to hide them. If only part of a pixel is covered by a surface, then the proper color for the pixel is a weighted average of the color already stored for the pixel and the color of the surface being scan-converted. The weight for each color must be only the percentage of the pixel area covered by the surface. The painter's algorithm models the situation where all surfaces partially overlap.

Unfortunately, a smooth surface modeled by polygons will reveal its seams when rendered with the painter's algorithm (Figure 11). As neighboring polygons are rendered, the first polygon to be rendered will fill pixels along the polygon edge with a color representing a blend of the background color and the polygon color. When the neighboring polygon is rendered, the previously painted pixels along the common edge will be given a color blended from the first blend and the color of the new polygon. Therefore, some of the background color will show through along polygon edges.

A reversed painter's algorithm in which polygons are painted front-to-back is slightly more successful. Here an additional few bits per pixel can be used to store the 'coverage' (the fraction of the pixel's area that is covered by a surface) for each pixel [Carp84]. Now when neighboring polygons are rendered, the first one will give its color to the pixel and store the fraction of the pixel covered. The neighboring polygon now can blend its color for the pixel with the previous color, knowing what fraction of the polygon is covered by each. The coverages are then summed. Note that this assumes that surfaces abut. Pixels that are not completely covered are filled in by a

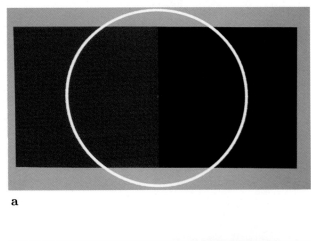

a

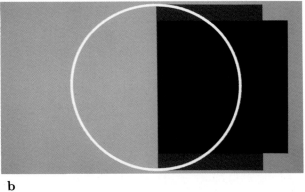

b

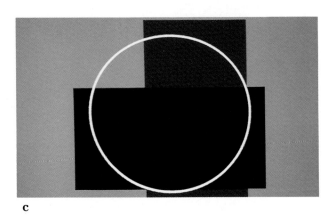

c

Figure 10. Effects of surface-to-pixel geometry (a) Abutting surfaces; (b) over-lapping surfaces; (c) partially overlapping surfaces.

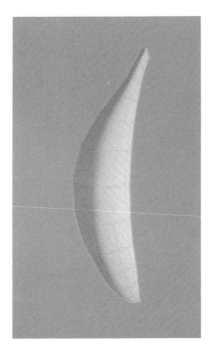

Figure 11. Seams show through when using the painter's algorithm.

background process which blends background color with previously written colors using the coverage information.

This method has problems where backfacing polygons are retained. Since multiple polygons contributing to a pixel are assumed to be abutting, the coverage is overestimated when they overlap instead. This causes edges to be incorrectly represented at contour edges where a backfacing and a frontfacing polygon affect the same pixel (Figure 12). Since backfacing polygons need only be retained where the inside of a surface can be seen, this problem can be avoided much of the time by modeling the inside of an open surface as an additional surface spaced a small distance inside the outer surface. As long as the wall thickness thus defined leaves sufficient distance between the inner and outer surfaces to sort them, there will be no problems.

If backfacing polygons are avoided, most images can be made without worrying much about the distinction between overlapping and abutting surfaces. Other cases when completely overlapping surfaces occur within a pixel are infrequent, involving separate shapes that line up perfectly behind one another. Small errors will also occur where partially overlapping surfaces are treated as overlapping. Where the silhouettes of two shapes intersect, for example, a small error will be made at the pixel where the intersection occurs. This has not proven to be noticeable in practice.

In general, it should be somewhat less expensive to use either of the

Figure 12. Jagged edges due to improper calculation of overlapping surfaces.

above approaches than to calculate a mini-hidden-surface algorithm at every point. The area within the pixel covered by each surface must be calculated no matter what algorithm is used. Additional computation to find what part of which surface covers what other can only add to the cost. However, it should be noted that the cookie-cutter algorithms work in such a way as to allow calculation of only the visible portion of areas partially covering the pixel. So, at least for this purpose, they can be regarded as superior.

Shading and Texture

So far we have concentrated on handling aliasing problems caused along the edges or silhouettes of objects. Modern shading techniques have opened a wealth of new opportunities for aliasing defects by allowing small details to be created independently of surface edges. For example, when highlights are to be calculated on a cylindrical surface, it is possible to produce long, thin, bright features in the image which, if improperly treated, appear jagged [Crow81].

We have made successful images by using higher resolution in highlights where needed. Since highlights can be calculated independently of the remaining shading components, it is possible to calculate the highlights at a higher resolution when necessary to get a better representation. The problem lies in deciding when such efforts are justified. Without a heuristic rule for selecting difficult cases, highlights are very expensive.

We have used a heuristic approach that estimates local surface curvature based on the surface normal vectors used to calculate the highlights. By using a threshold curvature, highlight resolution can be selectively increased (Figure 13). Unfortunately, we do not have an algorithm for selecting the threshold, which is thus determined manually by feedback, a process open to unforeseen errors.

An alternative technique softens highlights by changing the surface glossiness where small highlights are expected. A less glossy surface produces a more diffuse highlight spread over a wider area. This has an effect similar to applying a low-pass filter such as those described in an earlier section.

The addition of texture to surfaces has allowed some spectacular images to be produced. Very roughly, texture is provided by taking intensities from an image of the texture desired and mapping them onto the surface being scan-converted. Variations on this scheme allow environmental reflections, color patterns, or surface relief to be represented [Blin76; Blin78; Feib80]. However, texture can look absolutely horrible if aliasing ruins it (Figure 14).

Unfortunately, properly calculating the shade of an individual pixel in a textured region involves integrating over a region of the texture image. This is especially expensive when there is a significant mismatch between the density of the texture-image pixels and the scan-converted pixels. In these cases, large numbers of texture-image pixels may have to be integrated when computing the intensity of a scan-converted pixel. Integrating over large numbers of texture pixels to get a color for display can be avoided by

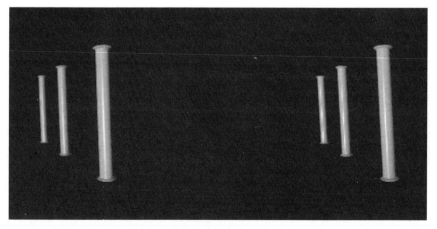

Figure 13. Jagged and antialiased highlights.

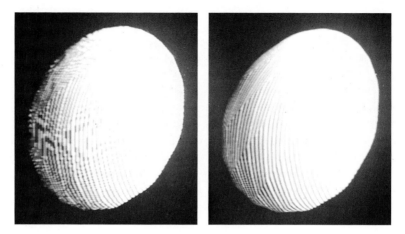

Figure 14. Jagged and antialiased texture.

selectively band limiting the texture function at such places.

Catmull and Smith [Catm80] have published another approach to texture mapping that decomposes the 2D mapping process into two passes of a 1D process. This considerably simplifies the process, so much so that it can be implemented in hardware [Ampex]. Unfortunately, as of this writing the two-pass method has yet to be demonstrated in an all-purpose image-generation system. The current use is primarily for manipulating video images in their entirety.

Antialiasing of texture is more thoroughly covered in the following chapter of this volume, which is devoted solely to texture.

Temporal Aliasing

In addition to the problems discussed up to this point, there is another form of aliasing that can cause problems in animated imagery. Each frame of an animated sequence is a sample in time of a continuous function. Sampling in time poses the same problems with aliasing as does sampling in space. A frame from a computer-generated sequence has typically represented a single, infinitesimally short sample in time. The effects of the resulting aliasing are perhaps most familiar to us from experiences with conventional motion picture images. The most common effect results in spoked wheels that appear to run backward (most often seen in 'Westerns').

In computer-generated animation, the effects of aliasing in time are most noticeable when either some object in the image or else the simulated camera is moving rapidly. In such cases the image appears to hop across the screen in a series of jumps, sometimes creating the illusion of multiple images, rather than moving smoothly. If we apply the lessons learned from spatial antialiasing, we can propose to either (a) increase the sample rate or (b) somehow integrate over time to get a blurred representation of fast-moving objects.

As with spatial antialiasing, increasing the sample rate is not the best solution or even possible in all cases. The rate at which images are presented cannot be changed under normal circumstances. Standard film presentation provides the viewer with 24 frames per second, each frame flashed twice to limit flicker. Increasing the sampling rate would suggest calculating several frames and averaging them to get each presented frame. Unfortunately, for small numbers of frames this simply leaves the impression of multiple copies of fast-moving objects. Calculating a sufficient number of frames to make this method effective appears to be unnecessarily expensive.

When preparing images for video presentation, the situation is slightly better. Current broadcast standards call for interlaced displays. Generally, one produces a single image for all scanlines at once. However, the sampling rate in time can be effectively doubled by taking advantage of the fact that the odd-numbered lines are presented in between presentations of the even-numbered lines. By calculating half-frames (only the even-numbered or odd-numbered lines) at twice the time rate, temporal aliasing can be greatly diminished.

As for our second approach, for several years researchers in computer animation have been looking for a practical method of presenting objects properly blurred by motion. Early thoughts on the subject were severely hampered by the desire to make images inexpensively enough to be able to afford animation. In recent years, there has been a greater willingness to spend previously incomprehensible amounts of computer time on computer imagery with the result that algorithms for motion-blurred imagery are appearing in increasing numbers.

Reeves [Reev83] modeled a class of objects by sets of particles and then blurred fast-moving particles by representing them with a line connecting the extreme positions occupied by the particle during the sample period. Korein and Badler [Kore83] implemented a system using blurred discs to represent figures and proposed a more general algorithm.

Potmesil and Chakravarty [Potm83] used a postprocessing blurring function. Their approach was to take pixels from a rendered portion of an image and blur them after scan conversion. They used a convolution algorithm for doing the blurring that operates by multiplying the frequency-domain versions of the image and the convolution filter. This technique, when combined with matting techniques for combining images [Carp84], could be quite effective.

All of these algorithms for blurring depend either on modifying the data before scan conversion [Reev83; Kore83] or postprocessing the pixels after scan conversion [Potm83]. A more integrated approach was first reported by Cook et al. [Cook84]. In this approach, multiple samples are generated at each pixel. Instead of varying just the spatial position of each sample, as is customary for this approach to antialiasing, the temporal position of each sample is varied as well.

Stochastic Sampling

Antialiasing by calculating at higher resolutions has been and continues to be widely used. Until recently the resolution was increased merely by increasing the density of the raster, or sampling grid. Contrasting the way an image is formed on a raster with the way an image is formed on film indicates an alternative and more effective procedure. Film grains are randomly scattered over the image area with the result that an inadequate density of grains make the image noisy. Noisiness is accepted as less deleterious to the image than aliasing. Therefore, it takes a smaller number of extra samples to generate an acceptable image if they are randomly distributed than if they are regular.

Irregular sampling does not remove the principal objection to supersampling as a remedy for antialiasing. Important features may still be missed. However, it eliminates regular, repetitive artifacts. It is largely this regularity that makes the artifacts annoying and obvious.

This idea has occurred to a number of researchers, and their techniques have been well explored recently [Dipp85; Gran85; Lee85; Max85; Cook86; Mitc87; Mitc88]. There has been considerable discussion of the proper way to locate the randomly distributed samples. Some have used a standard raster grid and then randomly perturbed the pixel positions by less than one interpixel distance [Cook86; Dipp85]. Others have precalculated tables of positions using various algorithms for approximating Poisson distribution of pixels [Dipp85; Mitc87]. The argument has been made that Poisson distribution may be optimal since it is found in nature, in particular in the primate retina.

Once the sample values are computed the pixel values must be constructed. This is not an obvious process. Ideally, the samples should be fit to a smooth surface with no frequencies above the half-cycle-per-pixel limit. Then this surface should be sampled at the regular pixel sites. Various approximations to this are possible by summing the sample values, weighted by a suitable filter, which lie within a given neighborhood of each pixel. Mitchell and Netrevali have treated this problem recently [Mitc87; Mitc88].

As mentioned earlier, uniform use of extra samples is expensive. Therefore, good methods are needed for supersampling adaptively, that is, only where extra detail will be found. This is impossible to do perfectly for ray-tracing algorithms, which sample the scene rather than generating the image driven by the input. However, using hints, such as sharp variations in intensity across small distances in the image, adaptive supersampling has been made to work quite well [Whit80; Dipp85; Lee85]. Furthermore, when the image is built by directly scan-converting surface elements, choosing sites for supersampling is trivial [Cook86].

There remains much to learn about doing only that work which will improve the image. Kajiya has made a stab at characterizing this using 'importance sampling' [Kaji86]. Clearly, images can be made more efficiently by more complicated software that avoids unnecessary samples. On the other hand, simpler algorithms are more amenable to more cost-effective hardware implementation. As computer hardware becomes easier to synthesize, issues of how to implement rendering algorithms will only get more complicated. The remedies for aliasing should continue to develop for a long time.

REFERENCES

[Abra85]
Abram, G., Westover, L., and Whitted, T., Efficient alias-free rendering using bit-masks and look-up tables, *Comput. Graph.*, Vol. 19, pp. 53–59, 1985 (SIGGRAPH 85).

[Ampex]
ADO: Ampex Digital Optics (special effects system for TV studios), Ampex Corporation, Redwood City, CA.

[Blin76]
Blinn, J.F., and Newell, M.E., Texture and reflection in computer generated images, *CACM*, Vol. 19, pp. 542–547, 1976.

[Blin78]
Blinn, J.F., Computer Display of Curved Surfaces. PhD Thesis, University of Utah, Salt Lake City, Utah, December 1978.

[Blin80]
Blinn, J.F., Carpenter, L.C., and Lane, J.M., Scan line methods for displaying parametrically defined surfaces, *CACM*, Vol. 23, pp. 23–34, 1980.

[Bloo83]
Bloomenthal, J., Edge inference with applications to anti-aliasing, *Comput. Graph.*, Vol. 17, pp. 157–162, 1983 (SIGGRAPH 83).

[Carp84]
Carpenter, L., The A-buffer, an anti-aliased hidden surface method, *Comput. Graph.*, Vol. 18, pp. 103–108, 1984 (SIGGRAPH 84).

[Catm78]
Catmull, E., A hidden-surface algorithm with anti-aliasing, *Comput. Graph.*, Vol. 12, pp. 6–11, 1978 (SIGGRAPH 78).

[Catm80]
Catmull, E., and Smith, A.R., 3-D transformations of images in scanline order, *Comput. Graph.*, Vol. 14, pp. 270–285, 1980 (SIGGRAPH 80).

[Cook84]
Cook, R.L., Porter, T., and Carpenter, L., Distributed ray tracing, *Comput. Graph.*, Vol. 18, pp. 137–145, 1984 (SIGGRAPH 84).

156   Franklin C. Crow

[Cook86]
Cook, R.L., Stochastic sampling in computer graphics, *ACM Trans. Graph.*, Vol. 5, pp. 51–72, 1986.

[Crow77]
Crow, F.C., The aliasing problem in computer-generated shaded images, *CACM*, Vol. 20, pp. 799–805, 1977.

[Crow78]
Crow, F.C., The use of grayscale for improved raster display of vectors and characters, *Comput. Graph.*, Vol. 12, pp. 1–5, 1978 (SIGGRAPH 78).

[Crow81]
Crow, F.C., A comparison of anti-aliasing techniques, *IEEE Comput. Graph. and Appl.*, Vol. 1, pp. 40–48, 1981.

[Dipp85]
Dippe, M.A.Z., and Wold, E.H., Anti-aliasing through stochastic sampling, *Comput. Graph.*, Vol. 19, pp. 69–78, 1985, (SIGGRAPH 85).

[Feib80]
Feibush, E.A., Cook, R.L., and Levoy, M., Synthetic texturing using digital filters, *Comput. Graph.*, Vol. 14, pp. 294–301, 1980 (SIGGRAPH 80).

[Fuch79]
Fuchs, H., and Barros, J., Efficient generation of smooth line drawings on video displays, *Comput. Graph.*, Vol. 13, pp. 260–269, 1979 (SIGGRAPH 79).

[Gran85]
Grant, C.W., Integrated analytic spatial and temporal anti-aliasing for polyhedra in 4-space, *Comput. Graph.*, Vol. 19, pp. 79–84, 1985 (SIGGRAPH 85).

[Gupt81]
Gupta, S., and Sproull, R., Filtering edges for grey-scale displays, *Comput. Graph.*, Vol. 15, pp. 1–5, 1981 (SIGGRAPH 81).

[Kaji81]
Kajiya, J.T., and Ullner, M., Filtering high quality text for display on raster scan devices, *Comput. Graph.*, Vol. 15, pp. 7–15, 1981 (SIGGRAPH 81).

[Kaji86]
Kajiya, J.T., The rendering equation, *Comput. Graph.*, Vol. 20, pp. 143–150, 1986 (SIGGRAPH 86).

[Kore83]
Korein, J., and Badler, N., Temporal anti-aliasing in computer generated animation, *Comput. Graph.*, Vol. 17, pp. 377–388, 1983 (SIGGRAPH 83).

[Lee85]
Lee, M.E., Redner, R.E., and Uselton, S.P., Statistically optimized sampling for distributed ray tracing, *Comput. Graph.*, Vol. 19, pp. 61–67, 1985 (SIGGRAPH 85).

[Max85]
Max, N., and Lerner, D.M., A two-and-a-half-D motion blur algorithm,

Comput. Graph., Vol. 19, pp. 85–93, 1985 (SIGGRAPH 85).

[Mitc87]
Mitchell, D.P., Generating antialiased images at low sampling densities, *Comput. Graph.*, Vol. 21, pp. 65–72, 1987 (SIGGRAPH 87).

[Mitc88]
Mitchell, D.P., and Netravali, A.N., The sampling and reconstruction problem in computer graphics, *Comput. Graph.*, Vol. 22, pp. 221–228, 1988 (SIGGRAPH 88).

[Naim87]
Naiman, A., and Fournier, A., Rectangular convolution for fast filtering of characters, *Comput. Graph.*, Vol. 21, pp. 233–242, 1987 (SIGGRAPH 87).

[Oppe75]
Oppenheim, A.V., and Schafer, R.W., *Digital Signal Processing*, Englewood Cliffs: Prentice-Hall, 1975.

[Pitt80]
Pitteway, M.L.V., and Watkinson, D.J., Bresenham's algorithm with grey scale, CACM, Vol. 23, pp. 625–626, 1980.

[Potm83]
Potmesil, M., and Chakravarty, I., Modeling motion blur in computer-generated images, *Comput. Graph.*, Vol. 17, pp. 389–399, 1983 (SIGGRAPH 83).

[Reev83]
Reeves, W.T., Particle systems — A technique for modeling a class of fuzzy objects, *ACM Trans. Graph.*, Vol. 2, pp. 91-108, 1983.

[Turk82]
Turkowski, K., Anti-aliasing through the use of coordinate transformations, *ACM Trans. Graph.*, Vol. 1, pp. 215–234, 1982.

[Suth77]
Sutherland, I.E., Sproull, R.F., and Schumaker, R.A., A characterization of ten hidden-surface algorithms, *Comput. Surveys*, Vol. 6, pp. 1–55, 1977.

[Warn80]
Warnock, J.E., The display of characters using grey-level sample arrays, *Comput. Graph.*, Vol. 14, pp. 302–307, 1980 (SIGGRAPH 80).

[Weil77]
Weiler, K.J., and Atherton, P.A., Hidden-surface removal using polygon area sorting, *Comput. Graph.*, Vol. 11, pp. 214–222, 1977 (SIGGRAPH 77).

[Whit80]
Whitted, J.T., An improved illumination model for shaded display, *CACM*, Vol. 23, pp. 343–349, 1980.

[Whit82]
Whitted J.T., Processing requirements for hidden-surface elimination and realistic shading, in *Proc. IEEE Spring Comput. Conf.* (February 1982), New York: IEEE Press, 1982.

Texture

Franklin C. Crow

Abstract

Texture applied to a surface adds interest and realism without complicating the underlying surface description. Texture values can be produced by space-filling functions—$f(x, y, z)$—or 2D functions—$f(x, y)$. A computed texture value can be used to modify color, reflectance properties, transparency, or other properties of a surface that determine its shading. It may further be used to perturb the shading parameters to produce the appearance of a bumpy surface, or to actually displace the surface, producing 'real' bumps.

Photographic images provide a convenient source of 2D functions for enhancing realism through texture. This has motivated much study of methods for mapping 2D textures onto surfaces. Similar applications of texture mapping allow reflections of the surrounding environment and representation of complex or multitudinous light sources. Sampling texture functions leads to aliasing problems that may be dealt with in various ways. Finally, different texturing techniques are appropriate for different levels of detail. Making smooth transitions between different forms of texture poses interesting problems.

Introduction

The progress of realism in computer-synthesized images was greatly aided by the introduction of surface texture in the mid-1970s [Catm74; Blin76; Blin78]. Surface-texturing techniques allowed much more interesting images to be made without having to produce more complicated underlying surface descriptions. Since then many texturing techniques have been explored, and texture has come to be an expected feature in up-to-date image-synthesis systems.

APPLICATION OF TEXTURE VALUES

Texture is generally applied by evaluating a texture function at each displayed pixel where a textured surface is represented. The texture value can then be used to modify the surface shading in a number of different ways. The most straightforward use of the texture value is to use it as a surface intensity ranging from zero to one. Where the texture value is one, the surface maintains its color. Where it is zero, the color goes to zero. In between, the surface color is darkened appropriately. Figure 1 shows an egg with a striped texture applied using this rule.

If three texture values are supplied by the texture function (e.g., a red, green, and blue texture triple), then the texture itself may provide the surface color. This is particularly appropriate when a photograph is used to provide a 'natural' texture, as in Figure 2. Since a large percentage of man-made objects have painted or printed surfaces, such objects are often represented quite well by varying just the color across an otherwise smooth surface. Items made of metal, plastic, or cardboard generally have smooth painted or printed surfaces.

On the other hand, objects made from natural materials, such as wood, exhibit variations in reflectivity across the surface as well as variations in color. Similarly, painted or printed patterns may use materials (paints, inks) with differing reflective properties. Generally, variation in reflectivity coincides with accompanying variations in color. In shading functions capable of rendering highlights, the contribution of the highlight may be modified by a texture value before being combined with the remainder of the shading function to implement variations in reflectivity, as seen in Figure 3.

Transparent glass and plastic objects often exhibit variations in transparency. These variations can be produced by painting or printing patterns on the surface or by incorporating materials with different properties in the mix from which the object is molded, blown, or extruded. A texture value

Figure 1. Texture as intensity (egg) and transparency (glass).

Figure 2. Natural images, vertex colors, and space functions as texture.

Figure 3. Variations in reflectivity. The brown texture is matte.

may be used to vary the transmittance of a surface to achieve such effects. An example may be seen in the glass shown in Figure 1.

Many man-made objects exhibit low-relief texture. A surface may be made more interesting or less slippery, for example, by adding some bumpiness or roughness. In other cases, low-relief texture can be an artifact of the process, as in a plastered wall, a woven carpet, or paint applied with a roller. This sort of surface is simulated well by techniques developed initially by Blinn [Blin78]. His method uses texture values to perturb the local orientation of the surface before calculating the shading. The surface is thus made to appear bumpy without actually displacing the surface. An example is shown in Figure 4.

Where higher relief is to be represented, actual displacement of the surface is necessary. This has been accomplished in at least four ways: (a) The data describing the shape can be algorithmically expanded [Csur79]; (b) the surface can be subdivided using stochastic techniques to displace new vertices [Four82; Haru84]; (c) the surface can be displaced using texture values during a subdivision algorithm [Hill87]; (d) The surface can be diced into subpixel-sized micropolygons, which are then displaced by texture values [Cook84; Cook87].

A texture function can be used to modulate any parameter that can be varied over a surface, even to the presence or absence of the surface. Trees, for example, can be represented by a few very simple polygons with bivalued texture maps determining presence or absence of a leaf. This technique is used by Evans and Sutherland in their CT-6 visual system for training systems.

The examples above span the obvious applications of texture. However, as new shading techniques arise, texturing techniques can be applied anew.

Figure 4. A texture used both for intensity mapping and bump mapping.

We can certainly envision texture values modulating characteristics such as hairiness or index of refraction. Only our imaginations limit us.

CHOOSING TEXTURE VALUES

A texture function must return a value or set of values within a given range in response to input values from a domain in two and sometimes three dimensions. For a simple example, take the function $\sin(cy)$. This could be applied as a *solid* texture function providing objects with regular stripes. On the other hand, it could be applied as a *surface* texture, putting stripes on each polygon or patch independently.

To apply a function as a solid texture, the surface represented in an image must be intersected with the function and evaluated at each point represented by a pixel in the image. This requires carrying the untransformed surface coordinates along through the entire transformation, clipping, and scan conversion pipeline. Alternatively, an inverse transformation can be applied to recover the original coordinates.

To apply a function as a surface texture, some mapping must be available that takes the surface of an object or each of its *surface elements* (polygons, patches, etc.) into the domain of the texture function. Normally, we refer to this style of texture use as *texture mapping*. There are numerous different ways of achieving a mapping between the texture function domain and a surface, a number of which are described below.

Both of these general methods, solid texture and surface texture mapping, require evaluating (sampling) the texture function at discrete points. This gives rise to *aliasing* problems [Crow77; Crow86] whenever the points lie too far apart in the domain of the texture function. Solutions to this problem range from predistorting the texture function to better fit the distribution of evaluation points to elaborate and expensive schemes for approximating a discrete integral over the area represented by a pixel. This problem is visited many times below.

TEXTURE FUNCTIONS

The texture function is a fascinating study by itself. Simple analytic functions have some use [Peac85]. However, algorithmic functions [Perl85] and especially image-based functions [Catm74; Blin78] have proven to be more effective. Often, texture is used for realism. In such cases, photographic images of the type of texture desired are much easier to come by than believable analytic or algorithmic approximations.

On the other hand, where solid texture is required or desired, photographic imagery is less satisfactory. An image may be extruded through space to be used as a solid texture [Peac85], but this hasn't been terribly useful. Recent progress in volumetric imagery used in CAT scan reconstructions suggests the possibility of 3D natural imagery as texture. However, limited access to CAT equipment and the huge storage required for volume data of useful resolution has apparently discouraged efforts of this sort.

Algorithmic simulations or approximations of natural processes [Yaeg86] have been effective under some circumstances. Given a large enough library of such functions, one might be able to do as well as with natural imagery. Some examples in later sections should help to illustrate this. However, it is vastly easier to develop a collection of texture functions with a camera than with the intensive creative work required for algorithmic textures. At the moment practicality makes algorithms the dominant source for solid texture and images the dominant source of surface texture.

THE ROLE OF TEXTURE

Texture techniques are useful when the general shape of an object would provide insufficient detail but the exact details of the surface are of no importance. If an egg is to be viewed from any distance, a matte off-white surface will approximate it sufficiently. If it is to be viewed more closely, the bumpy nature of the surface will require the use of one of the above texture techniques for an adequate rendition. However, if it is to be viewed from microscopic distance, the structure of the shell material becomes important, and texture techniques will not be applicable.

Happily, the character of most scenes is such that texture techniques are almost always useful. Although texture is widely used, the realm of texture techniques has by no means been exhaustively explored. We have seen very little activity in time-varying texture, only slightly more in multiple textures, and a great deal of pioneering work remains to be done on integrated use of different textures at different distances from a surface. Texture should remain an area to which research contributions can be made for a long time.

What follows is for the most part an expansion of the above. The simulation of texture effects without using texture is discussed in the next section. Thereafter, solid and surface texture are treated in more detail. The problem of mapping a texture function to a surface is given an entire section to itself. Finally, shorter sections on surface displacement and levels of detail lead to a brief roundup of areas where much research remains to be done.

Surface Shading Without Texture

Surface characteristics may be expressed without the use of a texture function as such. For example, the shininess of a surface can be characterized by specular reflectance added to the surface color [Warn69] and by simulated highlight reflections from the light sources [Phon75]. Different materials reflect light in different ways. Blinn [Blin77] and then Cook and Torrance [Cook82] described better reflectance models for varying materials.

Effects such as sparkling highlights and glowing filaments have been produced by adding randomly drawn, bright colored lines radiating from those pixels that represent bright areas. The appearance of neon tubes can be given by shading functions based on the eyepoint position rather than the light-source position.

Simply by assigning colors on a vertex-by-vertex basis, effects similar to texture may be obtained. Figure 5 shows apparent texturing produced by algorithmic assignment of appropriate color and transparency values to selected vertices.

The egg and glass in Figure 5 are both surfaces of revolution constructed from rectangular polygon meshes. This makes it relatively easy to assign a darker color to regularly spaced vertices of the egg. The spiral pattern on the glass is similarly constructed by skewing a pattern of stripes on the polygon mesh, the vertices falling within the stripes having opaque values.

The banana in Figure 2 gets its green extremities and brown ends from vertex colors laboriously assigned by hand using a text editor. However, it is easy to conceive of an interactive vertex coloring system that would make this sort of thing much easier.

When the above sort of color variation is sufficient to achieve the desired effect, then the greater expense of texturing within polygons or patches can be avoided. Furthermore, there is another advantage to vertex coloring in that it adds no additional aliasing problems to those inherent in the rendering system.

Solid Texture

Solid texturing requires the intersection of a space-filling function with selected visible surfaces in an image. This poses two problems: (a) three-space coordinates must be recovered at each pixel for the surface represented there; (b) the space-filling functions themselves must be defined. Interesting functions don't come all that easily.

The original three-space coordinates of the surface may be recovered by applying the inverse of the transform, taking the surface from the space in which it is defined to the image space. Texture space coordinates can then come from applying any transformations into texture space. However, it is frequently more efficient to carry the texture space coordinates of the surface along, interpolating them just as you would other surface characteristics.

In particular, when the surface is approximated by polygons, color and other surface characteristics are traditionally determined by bilinear interpolation between polygon vertices, as in Gouraud shading [Gour71]. Therefore, the incremental cost of obtaining the shading values and thus the texture space coordinates is very small for each pixel. However, it should be noted that linearly interpolated texture tends to reveal the underlying polygonal structure that Gouraud shading obscures.

166   Franklin C. Crow

Figure 5. Apparent surface texture from vertex colors.

Where the surface is defined by patches or other primitives, the texture space coordinates may be treated similarly. When the image pixels are determined by patch subdivision, then the texture space patch is subdivided in lock-step with the corresponding patch defined in the space in which the image is built.

TEXTURE SPACE MAPPING

Normally, the texture would be expected to stick with an object as it moves around. To get the texture to stick with the surface, the texture space must be carried untransformed through to the stage where shading functions are evaluated. However, other effects are possible by changing the space from which the texture coordinates are taken.

If the texture space coordinates are carried through the transform taking definition space coordinates to world space coordinates (the space in which the entire scene is assembled), then the object will appear to move through the texture as the object moves around the scene. This could be useful for creating images of a shape moving through a complicated pattern of light and shadow or in a medium with changing light patterns, such as might be found in an underwater scene.

The chiaroscuro caused by the complex shadows of the leaves of a tree could be easily produced by extruding the image of the tree as seen from the light source through the world space to define a three-space texture function. Objects intersected with this function would then have their shading modified to produce the effect of light and shadow. Of course, care would have to be taken to avoid producing the texture on self-shadowed parts of the object.

One can imagine that many other useful mappings exist. Time-varying transforms could be used for many effects. For example, an old-style rotating barber pole could be simulated using one of the example functions below. The effect of motion could be achieved by either using a rotation matrix varying in time or by translating along the axis of the pole through the texture space over time. See [Wyvi87] for some other examples.

EXAMPLES OF TEXTURE SPACE FUNCTIONS

Simple space functions are easy to come up with. The example given in the introductory section, $f(x, y, z) = \sin(cy)$, gives the world striations. However, interesting space functions take some imagination. Hopefully, the following simple examples will stimulate some ideas. Note in the following that terrestrial coordinates are used. Looking from the South, x is East (to the right), y is North (ahead), and z is height (up).

The red and green checkered pattern shown on the egg in Figure 2 is produced by a real program similar to the following pseudocode. The code implements a space-filling function that is the 3D analog of a checkerboard. Hint: when implementing this, make sure you understand the behavior of your 'MOD' function about zero.

```
red: RGBCOLOR := [0.9, 0.2, 0.2];
green: RGBCOLOR := [0.4, 0.9, 0.2];
xTrue, yTrue, zTrue, isRed: BOOLEAN;
xTrue := (x MOD 2) = 1;  yTrue := (y MOD 2) = 1;  zTrue := (z MOD 2) = 1;
isRed := xTrue XOR yTrue XOR zTrue;
IF isRed THEN RETURN[red] ELSE RETURN[green];
```

The garish colored egg in Figure 6 uses the following function providing a simple superposition of three sine waves modulating red along the x-axis, green along the y-axis, and blue along the z-axis. Note from Figure 6 that while the result is understandable on a CRT, even a well-corrected conversion to color printing can make the correspondence between the image and the texture function hard to see.

```
r,g,b: REAL;
r:= (Sin[10.0*x] + 1.0)/2.0;
g:= (Sin[10.0*y] + 1.0)/2.0;
b:= (Sin[10.0*z] + 1.0)/2.0;
RETURN[ [r,g,b] ];
```

The 'barber-pole' function is produced by applying a rotation transformation to a sine wave along the x-axis. The angle of rotation is linear in z. This function is used to modulate the transparency of the glass in Figure 1.

```
r,g,b,angle,intensity: REAL;
angle := 3.1416*z;
intensity:= Sin[40.0*(x*cos[angle] + y*sin[angle])];
intensity:= (intensity + 1.0)/2.0;
r:= 1.0;
g:= intensity;
b:= intensity;
RETURN[ [r,g,b] ];
```

More interesting, organic, texture space functions can be built upon randomized space-filling 'noise' functions [Perl85]. Given such a function, elaborate textures such as that on the teapot in Figure 7 can be produced with slightly more imaginative functions similar to the latter two above.

The teapot texture is based on a function implemented by Perlin in the following way. A table of pseudorandom numbers is imposed on a 3D integer grid. A texture value is determined by interpolating between the eight bounding grid points of a *voxel* (the cube defined by a set of eight grid points) in texture space. A cubic function is used to smooth the interpolation with the intention of avoiding high spatial frequencies in

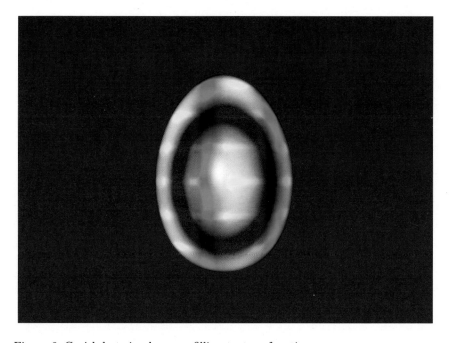

Figure 6. Garish but simple space-filling texture function.

Figure 7. Teapot with pseudonatural solid texture.

the resulting texture function. The result is a space-filling noise function concentrated about a controlled band of frequencies.

The noise function is further modified by repeated application in a $1/f$ style characteristic of fractal functions [Mand77]. At each step of an iteration the texture space coordinates are doubled, effectively scaling the spatial frequencies of the noise function by two. Applying the noise function to the scaled space coordinates, the resulting value is scaled by half the value used in the previous iteration and added to a running sum. The result is a function with decreasing power at increasing frequencies similar in characteristics to many natural phenomena.

To produce the teapot texture, Perlin's function is evaluated at the texture space coordinates resulting from each pixel representing the teapot surface. The output of the natural phenomena function is included in a weighted sum with the x and y coordinates from texture space. Taking the sine function of the result yields a space filled with distorted waves radiating from the z-axis. Where the function is negative, it is perturbed by a secondary function providing higher frequency distorted waves varying along the z-axis. Where the function is positive, it is perturbed by another secondary function providing somewhat less higher frequency distorted waves varying along the x-axis. Taking this fundamental method, adjusting parameters, and randomly trying this and that yielded the teapot texture in a couple of hours of pure enjoyment.

Interesting as it is, the teapot texture has severe drawbacks. Unlike a natural texture, it does not continue to be interesting as you get closer to it. The detail in the texture is limited by the length of the $1/f$ iteration in the natural phenomena function. Because the noise function is relatively expensive to evaluate, there is a practical limit on the length of the iteration, since it must be done anew for each pixel.

To make a truly interesting texture, the natural phenomena function should be modified to accept an input specifying the texture range spanned by the pixel being colored. Given the range, suitable limits on the iteration can be set to give an appropriate level of detail. Note that the lower limit of the iteration must remain constant to ensure inclusion of the larger terms of the iteration. However, given the usual pattern of calculating adjacent pixels consecutively, the earlier terms of the iteration will change very slowly.

A scheme for caching the earlier terms and reevaluating them only when sufficiently distant from the point where the cached evaluation was computed would bound the iteration from below. Given such a scheme, the computational expense of the natural phenomena function should remain relatively constant over a wide range of viewing distances. It remains, however, for the texture function to do something interesting with the smaller variations in magnitude from the natural phenomena function at higher frequencies.

SAMPLING AND ANTIALIASING

When evaluating a texture function at discrete intervals and then displaying the result on discrete pixels, we are sampling and reconstructing the function. This exposes us to all the problems of aliasing. Solid texture is still relatively new and not much has yet been done about the problem.

For limited ranges of viewing distance, choosing a function with appropriate frequency characteristics avoids aliasing. A texture without sharp edges and small features won't cause problems. Also, for many images a texture function without strong features, one consisting largely of random noise, will tend to mask aliasing artifacts.

However, the aliasing problem must be addressed at some point. The most effective technique put forth so far is the 'natural phenomena' function described above. If the $1/f$ iteration is chosen properly, based on the pixel extent in texture space, aliasing should not be visible.

No antialiasing methods have yet appeared in the literature that will handle sharp-edged functions such as the cube tessellation function shown on the egg in Figure 2 and described algorithmically above. There are certainly brute force techniques that could be applied. The function could be sampled several times in the vicinity of a center point provided by the texture coordinates. The resulting samples could then be averaged, possibly weighted by proximity to the center point. The average could then be applied as the texture value.

It may be that no more samples would be required for this than are used in the recently developed techniques for jittered sampling applied to scan conversion [Cook86; Mitc87]. This area is still open for research.

EXTENSIONS AND PROBLEMS

Recent development on surface reconstruction from computer-aided tomography and other sources of volume imaging data [Herm79; Levo88; Reyn88; Dreb88] begs the question of whether we should be using 'real' solid textures scanned from real objects. Researchers at the University of North Carolina at Chapel Hill have considered scanning a log in a CAT machine, for example, to get a solid texture for wooden objects.

This idea poses all sorts of interesting problems. Is it possible to use replications of a natural solid texture to fill a large region? Methods discussed below for using replicated 2D texture images on surfaces can probably be extended.

How much resolution will be necessary to make effective use of such texture? A cube with 128 pixels on a side includes $2^7 \times 2^7 \times 2^7$ pixels, 2 megapixels. With 512 pixels on a side, 128 megapixels are involved.

How can you antialias natural solid texture? Multiple samples can be used as above. However, there are a number of more efficient methods discussed in the next section on surface texture. Unfortunately, to varying degrees, they require even more storage.

Perlin suggested the use of time-varying functions for portraying fire and other dynamic phenomena. This poses exciting possibilities that remain largely unexplored.

Surface Texture

In contrast to solid texture, where direct evaluation of a texture function has been the usual approach, surface texturing has been dominated by techniques based on storage of the texture in a table. The reasons for this are made clear by noting the difficulty of the methods discussed in the section on solid texture. It is no easier to come up with interesting 2D texture functions than it is to come up with 3D ones. However, it is ever so much easier to produce 2D images by many different means than it is to get true volume imagery. This helps explain the dominance of 2D texturing techniques in current practice.

The fact that surface texturing techniques were developed some ten years before solid texture is almost certainly due to the advent of the frame buffer and the subsequent explosion of applications of stored 2D imagery. Catmull [Catm74] saw the natural correspondence between the addressing of a scanned image and the parametric space used to develop the bicubic patches he was working with. Blinn [Blin78] noted a few years later how easy it was to produce patterns for textures using the tools he and others had developed for painting and image manipulation on frame buffers.

Meanwhile, Williams [Will78] and others at the New York Institute of Technology were discovering increasingly interesting and varied ways of using stored images. The few years between the development of the frame buffer and the wide availability of virtual memory and large resident storage on smaller computers allowed image-based surface texturing to get well established before competing methods were developed.

A great deal of attention has been paid to the problem of how to map 2D image data onto surfaces. In contrast to solid data where the mapping is normally trivial, surface texture cannot be evenly distributed over the surface of an object in any generally applicable way. The problem is a reversal of the problem that has intrigued cartographers over centuries: that posed by putting the surface of the earth on a rectangular piece of paper.

The remainder of this section is devoted to the calculation, preparation, and storage of 2D texture functions. The following section is devoted to the problem of mapping from the texture function to the surface.

Texture Sources

Many methods have been used to develop texture. All of the techniques described in the previous section on solid texture could easily be adapted to two dimensions. However, there has been little activity of this sort. It takes considerably less mathematical insight to use image data.

Scanners have long been available for converting photographic imagery into stored sample arrays suitable for use as textures, and such imagery has been widely used. However, photographic imagery has its limits. The ideal function for bump mapping, for example, would be a function of height rather than intensity or color.

To get a texture map for tree bark, Bloomenthal [Bloo85] obtained an x-ray image of a plaster cast of an actual piece of bark. The result, a thickness function of the bark, was precisely what is needed for bump mapping.

Blinn [Blin78] often used images produced by hand on an early digital paint system for his texture work. He also used inverse Fourier transforms of digital paintings as texture, a technique he called 'Fourier synthesis'. The digital paintings were taken as frequency spectra and then transformed to spatial images for use as texture. This gave texture images with the desired formlessness and uniform character. Lewis [Lewi84] later described more fully realized but similar techniques.

Video frame-grabbers are now so widely available and inexpensive that more examples of animated texture are bound to appear. The Ampex ADO and Quantel Mirage provide a form of texture mapping using video imagery mapped onto simple surfaces as special effects for television. More recently, a system mapping video over much more complex surfaces was described by Oka et al. working at a Sony research center [Oka87].

One problem with sampled images as texture is that, once sampled, images are only useful over a small range of resolutions. When expanded, it becomes obvious that there is limited detail—the images become annoyingly fuzzy. When shrunk, there is unusable detail, which makes aliasing a potential problem.

As shown in the previous section, 2D algorithmic or analytic functions can be designed to avoid aliasing artifacts by limiting spatial frequencies to prescribed ranges. Norton, Rockwood, and Skomolski [Nort82] showed some examples of functions composed of sine waves and described a 'clamping' method for limiting the spread of frequencies to those appropriate for the area covered by a pixel.

Gagalowicz and Ma [Gaga85] describe a texture-synthesis method based on analysis of natural textures. They synthesize a texture function based on statistical analysis of an image. This function captures the characteristics of the texture without retaining any of the prominent features of the image. The resulting function can then be applied without as much concern for position or texture image boundaries. Since the frequency characteristics are known, aliasing can be kept under control.

Burt and Adelson [Burt83] describe an application using multiple-filtered versions of an image, each representing a limited range of spatial frequencies. Their application was the joining of dissimilar images. However, their basic method has been applied to texture mapping as well.

Edge Matching

Texture functions with finite extent (e.g., images) are usually applied repeatedly over a surface. It becomes critically important to arrange the function so that it can be seamlessly abutted with copies of itself. The pixels along the right-hand edge must closely match those on the left edge; top and bottom edges must match as well.

A photograph that appears to be evenly lit will often exhibit gross disparities when opposite edges are compared. Various image-processing techniques may be applied to remove subtle gradations in shading. Other techniques, such as that of Burt and Adelson mentioned above, can be used to force smooth joins between arbitrarily dissimilar edges. However, if the edges are grossly mismatched, the results can be arbitrarily unsatisfactory as repeated texture patterns.

Image edges can be matched straightforwardly using *vignetting*. All edges of the image are *faded* (interpolated) to a common shade. If the image is forced to black all around, then the edges have to match. However, unless this is done with great subtlety on an image of suitable character, the pattern of repeated texture images will be obvious.

Blinn's digitally painted textures mentioned previously ensured well-matched edges by using a solid-color background. A successful technique used at the New York Institute of Technology employs a paint program with several helpful tools such as a 'brush' that can blend adjacent regions. Using scrolling and panning in the frame buffer, the texture image can be manipulated to put the join between opposite edges in the middle of the screen. The image is then touched up by hand to match the edges.

Images with large discrete features will generally make the repetition of texture obvious. It is better to use an image with fairly uniform character across the image. Bloomenthal's tree bark mentioned previously is a good example. The overall character of the tree bark image is uniform. Burt and Adelson's algorithm serves to join the quite dissimilar edges.

SAMPLING AND ANTIALIASING

The dominance of image-based methods for texture has lead to extensive efforts at avoiding aliasing problems. The problem, as was seen in earlier sections, is to limit the spatial frequencies to those matching the area represented at a pixel.

Early antialiasing methods described by Blinn and Newell [Blin76] and then Feibush, Levoy, and Cook [Feib80] calculated a weighted sum of all texture pixels that mapped into the area covered by a pixel. This general method is prohibitively expensive where many texture pixels map into one image pixel. Each of many texture pixels must be retrieved and then added to a weighted sum, which involves a lot of work for each image pixel.

Multiresolution Texture Images

Williams [Will83] noted that by precalculating smaller texture images, wherein each pixel is a weighted sum of a set of pixels from the original image, much of the pixel-summing computation could be reused across many pixels. Williams' solution requires that the texture area mapped to each pixel be square, a rather loose approximation that produces fuzzier imagery than more exacting methods

While scan-converting a surface, the texture coordinate offset from one pixel to the next is noted and used to select a texture image that has pixels which roughly match the size of the offset. If neighboring pixels map to places in the texture that are eight texture pixels apart, then a one-eighth-size texture image is appropriate.

At that time (early 1979), all work at Williams' site was being done on 512 × 512 pixel frame buffers. Williams noted that an RGB texture image fit neatly into such a frame buffer in the following way: Three 256 × 256 pixel images are stored in the lower and left quadrants of the frame buffer, leaving the upper right quadrant unfilled. Half-resolution images are then computed and three 128 × 128 pixel images stored similarly in the upper right quadrant. This leaves the upper right quadrant of the upper right quadrant empty. Recursive application of the process fills the frame buffer (save the upper rightmost pixel) with successively half-sized, averaged texture maps.

Texture images are then stored at factors of two in resolution, each pixel in a smaller image being the average of four pixels from the next larger image. At each pixel, the scan conversion process provides a texture coordinate pair and offsets to the next texture coordinate pair. The integer part of the offset, if greater than one, determines which two sizes of texture map to use.

The texture coordinates are scaled appropriately, and four texture pixels are retrieved from each map. The texture coordinates are then used to interpolate between the four pixels to best approximate the value that should lie exactly at the coordinates. Having recovered two pixel values (or colors), the fractional part of the texture offset is then used to interpolate between them.

The first set of interpolations serves to smooth out changes between adjacent texture pixels and to handle the case where many image pixels map into one texture pixel. The final interpolation serves to smooth transitions between texture maps at different scales.

The general idea of a nested hierarchy of texture images has appeared in a number of places. The concept was used in early versions of the General Electric visual flight simulator hardware around 1962 [Roug69]. Dungan et al. [Dung78] discuss a hierarchy where each nested image is half the size of the next larger one. In these cases the texture was applied only to flat surfaces representing ground planes, etc. Multiresolution images are also used in various applications within the field of image processing.

The importance of this approach is that texture values are computed in constant time. A constant-time algorithm can generally be implemented in hardware to run in real time. Furthermore, for nearly all situations, the constant-time algorithms run much faster than those that must sum over all texture pixels which map into an image pixel.

Integrated Texture Images

Crow [Crow84] and Perlin independently discovered a method generalizing the set of possible prepared texture areas to rectangular areas aligned with the texture image axes. This works particularly well on texture images with primarily rectilinear patterns such as checkerboards (Figure 8).

An image can be integrated by summing its pixels. Texture values that represent the average pixel value over a subimage from the texture can be had by dividing the integral over that area by the area. A table can be built as follows from which values representing the integral of axis-aligned rectangles can be easily calculated.

Consider a table where each entry represents the sum of all pixel values lying to the left of and below a given position. Such a table, often called a *summed-area table*, is easily computed iteratively from a texture image. Indexing the table in the same way as the texture image, table entry (x_1, y_1) would represent the sum of all pixels with x coordinates less than or equal to x_1 and y coordinates less than or equal to y_1.

The sum over a rectangular area bounded on the bottom left by (x_l, y_b) and on the top right by (x_r, y_t) is then recovered by four accesses to the summed-area table T (see Figure 9)

$$S = T(x_r, y_t) - T(x_l, y_t) - T(x_r, y_b) + T(x_l, y_b)$$

S is then divided by $(x_r - x_l)(y_t - y_b)$ to get the average pixel value.

Figure 8. Checkerboard texture. From top, aliased, multiresolution, summed area.

As in the multiresolution texture images above, interpolation between table values is used to more accurately place the corners of a texture rectangle and to allow smooth variation between texture values when texture pixels spread over multiple image pixels. Note that this is unnecessary where a large area of texture is involved as the resultant sum will be changed insignificantly.

Glassner [Glas86] extended the application of summed-area tables by using repeated applications of the texture retrieval algorithm. An image pixel, if considered a square area, forms an arbitrary quadrilateral image in the texture. The difference between this quadrilateral and the axis-aligned rectangle provided by the summed-area table can be reduced by removing smaller and smaller rectangular regions from the initial one. Therefore, repeated retrievals from the summed-area table can improve the fit to the pixel image.

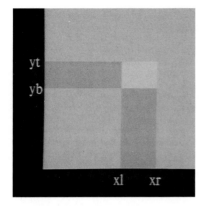

Figure 9. Recovery of texture values from a summed-area table.

Glassner implemented his scheme along with an additional table that helps to measure the variance in a texture region. Using the variance to determine how close an approximation is needed, he claims an increase in texture accesses of only 50 percent or so. This is largely due to the fact that only a small minority of pixels in a given image map into large regions of texture. Nonetheless, his adaptive technique allows the work to be concentrated where it is needed.

Perlin suggested extending integrated texture to repeated integrations to get weighted sums of texture pixels instead of a simple average. Heckbert [Heck86] implemented the idea and was able to show improvements. A second integration allows recovery of a rectangle weighted by a pyramid shape using nine texture accesses instead of four.

The disadvantage of repeated integrations is that they require high-precision arithmetic (greater than 32 bits) for the stored tables. However, for good texture functions (small features, evenly distributed) it may be possible to fit smooth, easily evaluated functions to the stored tables. Given the fitted functions, only the differences from the functions would need to be stored. The differences have a chance of staying within 32 bits in length. Of course, this incurs the additional overhead of evaluating the fitted functions for each texture retrieval.

Summed-area tables were independently discovered and were used in the image-processing community. Furthermore, the concept shows up in probability as well. Linear use of summed functions to integrate appears widely. See Crow [Crow78] for one example.

In an excellent recent survey, Heckbert [Heck86] compares integrated textures, multiresolution textures, and a hybrid method that combines multiresolution texture with multiple texture retrievals in a weighted sum. A weighted average of multiple texture pixels was shown to yield the best absolute result. However, it appears that methods using a small (or, hopefully, constant) number of retrievals from a prepared texture function will provide the best quality consistent with reasonable cost. This area continues to inspire good, original research.

Mapping Texture to Surfaces

Before texture can be applied to a surface, how the texture fits over the surface must be determined. Catmull's [Catm74] technique used shapes consisting of bicubic patches. The parameters of the bicubic patch formulation provided an obvious index into the texture image. Therefore, each patch contained a replica of the texture image. This approach has been used often, most visibly on the Utah teapot [Blin76; Crow87].

A generalization of this idea allows an array of polygons or patches to be superposed on a replicated array of texture images. Where a shape is a simple surface of revolution, for example, it is generally composed of a rectangular array of surfaces. The surface may be conceptually split open at a seam and flattened to a rectangular array. A single texture image or multiple copies of one may be mapped to this array. The mapping results in texture coordinates associated with each vertex in the shape.

An advantage of a more global mapping is that the mapping may be scaled, translated, rotated, or skewed for additional effect as shown on the striped egg in Figure 1. The texture may even be animated. Figure 10 shows a simulated paper web. In an animated sequence the texture slides along the web giving the appearance of a moving web, when actually only the texture-mapping transform is being translated, a substantially easier modeling task.

Given texture coordinates at the vertices, the coordinates at pixels can be found by interpolation, linear interpolation in the case of polygons and up to bicubic for appropriate patches. The interpolation process can easily provide texture coordinate offsets between adjacent pixels for use by the antialiasing algorithms described in the last section.

Caution must be exercised when using linear interpolation of texture values. Perspective distortion must be taken into account if interpolating over more than a small number of pixels. Perspective effects will cause the texture to appear to sag and to move strangely during animation.

These effects can be avoided by using adaptive subdivision techniques which guarantee that distortion due to linear interpolations will stay below a given threshold. However, large areas can be interpolated using a more complex formula including a perspective divide at each pixel. See Heckbert [Heck86] for a thorough treatment of this problem.

Where the polygon or patch mesh is irregular or the shape consists of an assembly of simpler pieces, different mapping techniques must be employed. A popular technique uses the normal vector to the surface to determine which texture value to retrieve. This technique was pioneered by Blinn and Newell [Blin76] for *environment mapping*.

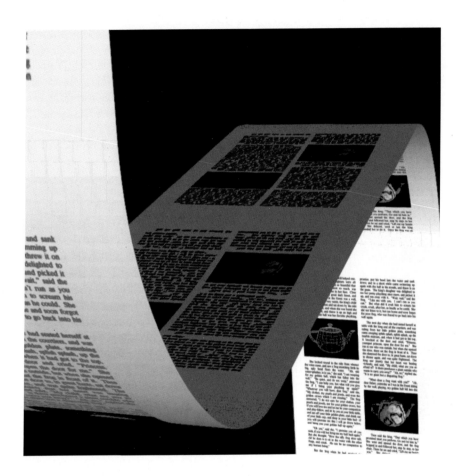

Figure 10. A simulation of a printer web.

Environment mapping simulates an enveloping environment for the shape by using a texture image representing an unwrapped spherical surface similar to some map projections used to represent the surface of the Earth. A reflected vector calculated from the eyepoint direction and normal vector is converted to spherical coordinates. The resulting azimuth and elevation are used to address the texture image.

Environment maps have advantages for representing light sources or lighting in general. The lighting environment can be made into an image and used as an environment map. The advantage lies in being able to have an arbitrarily complex lighting scheme at constant cost. Furthermore, using the antialiasing schemes described above, light source reflections (highlights) are automatically antialiased, a difficult task for direct highlight calculation methods.

The same general mapping technique can be used to apply texture to a surface. Instead of using a reflected vector, the normal vector is used directly to pick off a texture value. Bier [Bier86] has done a thorough investigation of this approach. He points out that undulations in the surface cause wide excursions in the direction of the surface normal which can, in turn, cause the texture to vary excessively (even invert) over the surface.

Bier suggests using a ray from the centroid of the object through its surface to pick off a texture value. This improves the situation but fails for those objects that have projections or concavities which cause a ray from the centroid to pierce the surface more than once.

Barr [Barr84] proposes a decal-like paradigm in which an area of texture is placed in proximity to the surface and then mapped to it using nearness and the direction of the surface normal to pick off texture values. This opens a promising area of research which hasn't been followed up well as yet. However, the problem of stitching together decals to completely cover a surface looks no easier than that of mapping replicated texture images.

Ma and Gagalowicz [Ma85] show a mapping based on a starting point and propagation of a local coordinate system along geodesic curves on the surface. This shows some promise as long as the surface can be broken into locally simple pieces. They slice their objects by sets of parallel planes to accomplish this. However, it appears that complex areas such as branch points in a surface still cannot be handled automatically.

Complex shapes composed of multiple pieces having concavities and/or projections, or just tortuously convoluted, don't lend themselves to any of the mapping schemes described thus far. Solid texturing avoids the mapping problem but poses difficulties in describing natural surface textures. Finding ways of stitching together patches of texture to cover arbitrary surfaces remains a fertile area for further research.

Surface Displacement and Modification

The solid and surface texturing schemes described in the previous sections are fine for variations in surface color and transparency characteristics and even low relief. However, surface texture in reality is a richer domain involving a continuum of relief ranging from bumpy surfaces like stucco to extremely complex phenomena such as hair and clothing.

A class of higher relief textures can be developed based on local displacement of the surface according to a texture function. This technique extends what can be accomplished with texture function methods. For example, it is possible with this technique to view lumpy surfaces closely enough to see the self-occlusions caused by one lump hiding another. Surfaces with large displacements such that the shape of the profile is clearly modified are also possible.

Displacement mapping, as it has come to be called, extends the technique of *bump mapping* to actual surface displacements. This, of course, must be accomplished through a subdivision process that dices the polygon or patch into small enough pieces to express the surface undulations. As the surface is subdivided, the texture function is used to displace the resulting vertices.

Pixar [Cook87] dices patches into subpixel-sized *micropolygons* that are then displaced by the texture function. This process can run very efficiently where a texture image is mapped directly to the patch being diced. In this case the appropriate texture value can be read directly from the coordinates used for dicing the patch. Simple scaling giving multiple texture images per patch or multiple patches per texture image maintains this simplicity.

The Pixar algorithm is predicated on the idea that patches will be diced into micropolygons. If large surface displacements occur over small areas, the micropolygons could be stretched to significantly larger sizes, possibly causing problems with their display algorithm. At the time of their paper, they claimed not to have tried this.

Hiller [Hill87] built a similar displacement mapping system on top of the author's rendering system at Xerox PARC. In this implementation, polygons are adaptively subdivided until it can be determined that further subdivisions would not displace the edges of the subpolygons enough to make a difference in the resulting image. The adaptive termination of the algorithm allows for arbitrary excursions in the resulting surface. It remains to be seen how useful that will be.

There are limits to what can be expressed with displacement mapping. For example, a displacement map offers only a height field. Therefore, a surface can't fold back on itself or produce cave-like hollows. Other techniques must be used to model hairy or spiny surfaces or add high relief with loops and hollows in the surface.

To get surfaces that have more relief than provided by displacement maps, additional structures must be layered over the polygons or patches. An early example of this was described by Csuri et al. [Csur79]. Here, a surface of revolution served as a base for a large number of long, thin polygons that radiated from the surface. While very limited in scope, the method made some interesting images of wire-brush-like objects.

More recently, Miller [Mill88] has produced very convincing images of hairy surfaces by drawing carefully colored line segments from specified points on the polygons of an underlying surface. He has also produced scaly surfaces by attaching polygons rather than lines to the underlying surface.

The attachment points of the hairs/scales are determined either by a regular grid for man-made effects such as a brush, or by a dithered grid for more natural surfaces. Given the underlying surface and the attachment points, all of the techniques developed for particle systems [Reev83] can be applied to produce textured surfaces.

Of course, using an array of attachment points on a surface allows the attachment of anything that can be rendered. One can envision a texture of attached doorknobs or decorations using full-dimensional figures as on a Grecian frieze. One advantage of treating such things as texture is that the hidden-surface problem is eased, since rendering order can be controlled by the order of surface elements on the underlying surface as long as the attached shapes don't interlock.

Unifying Texture Over Levels of Detail

A long-standing problem in computer graphics lies in controlling the level of detail in an image or animated sequence when objects may be seen from vastly different distances. Flight simulator databases often contain multiple descriptions of objects, sparse descriptions for distant views and detailed ones for closeups. Texture techniques offer a range of detail that could be used similarly.

Texturing by color variation, by bump mapping, and by surface displacement spans a hierarchy of levels of detail that can be useful in representing the same surface at different sizes in an image. However, to gracefully segue from one description to the next will require that all these techniques be controlled by the same texture function or derivatives of the same function.

A continuous effective zoom into a surface starting with a single color at a very great distance and then working through color mapping, bump mapping, and displacement mapping as the surface is approached has yet to be demonstrated.

Hiller [Hill87] described using the same texture for bump mapping and displacement mapping. This works reasonably well since both techniques require a height field. However, as seen in Figure 4, using the same function for intensity mapping and bump mapping is less successful. The height map of the bump texture determines shading that changes with the relative position of the light source. This sort of variation isn't possible with conventional intensity mapping. It remains to be seen whether some sort of derived intensity map can be used effectively in a texture hierarchy for levels of detail.

There are other models for surface development that take care of multiple levels of detail quite naturally; for example, fractal and other stochastic models develop detail adaptively. Note, however, that even these surfaces pose some problems. As a surface is subdivided, there is no guarantee that the shade over a small section of surface after subdivision will be the same as that before subdivision. Visible artifacts are most certainly possible. Nonetheless, as long as reasonably unobtrusive changes take place, adaptively subdivided surfaces can be zoomed quite successfully.

A technique frequently seen in movies about Dr. Jekyll and Mr. Hyde can be used to segue between very different representations. Here, both representations are used over a fairly wide range with a mix of the two appearing in the image. This is similar to the linear interpolation between texture maps at different scales used in the multiresolution texture maps discussed above. Unfortunately, the effectiveness of this technique is directly related to the similarity of the interpolated images.

There are some important unsolved problems remaining in this area. It is not at all clear how one could gracefully segue from any kind of ordinary texture map into a hairy surface based on attachment points, for example. Kajiya [Kaji85] and Miller [Mill88] both discuss anisotropic reflection models that could serve to represent certain kinds of hairiness from a distance. But how do you get from there to a particular representation of individual hairs?

Areas Needing Further Work

It is pretty clear from the above that a number of issues concerning texture remain unresolved at this time. The following list will serve as a summary.

Rich texture definitions. Solid texture functions give us the possibility for truly interesting surfaces that continue to show detail at many magnifications, as do the recently popular Mandelbrot and Julia sets. As yet, this hasn't been demonstrated except for stochastic terrain models.

Natural solid texture sources. Methods for reconstructing surfaces from volume data make it clear that natural objects could be scanned and stored as solid textures. Ever expanding memory capacity should make such textures possible if not practical. This just awaits somebody doing it.

Better antialiasing. Techniques for preparing texture maps for use at different resolutions and methods of refining the areas mapped to a pixel can be improved as can frequency bounds on the detail returned by algorithmic texture functions.

Mapping to arbitrary surfaces. Mapping texture to surfaces with hollows, projections, and branches remains difficult.

Time-varying texture. Some very rudimentary probes at time-varying texture were described above. However, some truly interesting dynamic images should be possible through texture techniques. There should be some interesting effects possible by running simultaneous animations, the output of one serving as a texture map to the other.

Fuzziness. It ought to be possible to represent fuzzy surfaces in a way that captures what one sees from a distance at which the individual hairs can't be distinguished.

Texture offers much added richness to our imagery at a bounded cost. It has proven very useful over the past decade. It now remains to integrate it better with more and less detailed descriptions, to generalize it to a broader range of effects, and to find ways to speed up its execution without incurring deleterious defects in the resulting images.

REFERENCES

[Barr84]
Barr, A.H., Decal Projections, SIGGRAPH 84, Course No. 15, Mathematics of Computer Graphics, July 1984.

[Bier86]
Bier, E.A., and Sloan, K.R., Jr., Two-part texture mappings, *IEEE Comput. Graph Appl.*, Vol. 6, pp. 40–53, 1986.

[Blin76]
Blinn, J.F., and Newell, M.E., Texture and reflection in computer generated images, CACM, Vol. 19, pp. 542–547, 1976.

[Blin77]
Blinn, J.F., Models of light reflection for computer synthesized pictures, *Comput. Graph.*, Vol. 11, pp. 192–198, 1977 (SIGGRAPH 77).

[Blin78]
Blinn, J.F., Simulation of wrinkled surfaces, *Comput. Graph.*, Vol. 12, pp. 286–292, 1978 (SIGGRAPH 78).

[Bloo85]
Bloomenthal, J., Modeling the mighty maple, *Comput. Graph.*, Vol. 19, pp. 305–311, 1985 (SIGGRAPH 85).

[Burt83]
Burt, P.J., and Adelson, E.H., A multiresolution spline with application to image mosaics, *ACM Trans. Graph.*, Vol. 2, pp. 217–236, 1983.

[Catm74]
Catmull, E.E., A Subdivision Algorithm for Computer Display of Curved Surfaces, UTEC-CSc-74-133, Department of Computer Science, University of Utah, Salt Lake City, UT, December 1974.

[Cook82]
Cook, R.L., and Torrance, K.E., A reflectance model for computer graphics, *ACM Trans. Graph.*, Vol. 1, pp. 7–24, 1982.

[Cook84]
Cook, R.L., Shade trees, *Comput. Graph.*, Vol. 18, pp. 223–231, 1984 (SIGGRAPH 84).

[Cook86]
Cook, R.L., Stochastic sampling in computer graphics, *ACM Trans. Graph.*, Vol. 5, pp. 51–72, 1986.

[Cook87]
Cook, R.L., Carpenter, L., and Catmull, E., The Reyes image rendering architecture, *Comput. Graph.*, Vol. 21, pp. 95–102, 1987 (SIGGRAPH 87).

[Crow77]
Crow, F.C., The aliasing problem in computer-generated shaded images, *CACM*, Vol. 20, pp. 799–805, 1977.

[Crow78]
Crow, F.C., The use of grayscale for improved raster display of vectors and characters, *Comput. Graph.*, Vol. 12, pp. 1–5, 1978 (SIGGRAPH 78).

[Crow84]
Crow, F.C., Summed area tables for texture mapping, *Comput Graph.*, Vol. 18, pp. 207–212, 1984 (SIGGRAPH 84).

[Crow86]
Crow, F.C., Advanced image synthesis—Anti-aliasing, in *Advances in Computer Graphics I*, pp. 419–440, Enderle, G., Grave, M., and Lillehagen, F., Eds., New York: Springer-Verlag, 1986.

[Crow87]
Crow, F.C., The origins of the teapot, *IEEE Comput. Graph. Appl.*, Vol. 7, pp. 8–19, 1987.

[Csur79]
Csuri, C., et al., Towards an interactive high visual complexity animation system, *Comput. Graph.*, Vol. 13, pp. 289–299, 1979 (SIGGRAPH 79).

[Dreb88]
Drebin, R.A., Carpenter, L. and Hanrahan, P., Volume rendering, *Comput. Graph.*, Vol. 22, pp. 65–74, 1988 (SIGGRAPH 88).

[Dung78]
Dungan, W., Jr., Stenger, A., and Sutty, G., Texture tile considerations for raster graphics, *Comput. Graph.*, Vol. 12, pp. 130–134, 1978 (SIGGRAPH 78).

[Feib80]
Feibush, E.A., Levoy, M., and Cook, R.L., Synthetic texturing using digital filters, *Comput. Graph.*, Vol. 14, pp. 294–301, 1980 (SIGGRAPH 80).

[Four82]
Fournier, A., Fussell, D., and Carpenter, L., Computer rendering of stochastic models, *CACM*, Vol. 25, pp. 371–384, 1982.

[Gaga85]
Gagalowicz, A., and Ma, S.D., Model driven synthesis of natural textures for 3-D scenes, in *Proc. Eurographics 85*, pp. 91–108, September 1985.

[Glas86]
Glassner, A., Adaptive precision in texture mapping, *Comput. Graph.*, Vol. 20, pp. 297–306, 1986 (SIGGRAPH 86).

[Gour71]
Gouraud, H., Computer display of curved surfaces, *IEEE Trans. Comput.*, Vol. 20, pp. 623–629, 1971.

[Haru84]
Haruyama, S., and Barsky, B.A., Using stochastic modeling for texture generation, *IEEE Comput. Graph. Appl.*, Vol. 4, pp. 7–19, 1984.

[Heck86]
Heckbert, P.S., Survey of texture mapping, *IEEE Comput. Graph. Appl.*, Vol. 6, pp. 56–67, 1986.

[Herm79]
Herman, G.T., and Liu, H.K., Three-dimensional display of human organs from computer tomograms, *Comput. Graph. Image Process.*, Vol. 9, pp. 1–21, 1979.

[Hill87]
Hiller, M., Three Dimensional Texture Trees, Master's Thesis, Mass. Institute of Technology, Cambridge, MA, June 1987.

[Levo88]
Levoy, M., Display of surfaces from volume data, *IEEE Comput. Graph. Appl.*, Vol. 8, pp. 29–37, 1988.

[Lewi84]
Lewis, J.P., Texture synthesis for digital painting, *Comput. Graph.*, Vol. 18, pp. 245–292, 1984 (SIGGRAPH 84).

[Ma85]
Ma, S.D., and Gagalowicz, A., Determination of local coordinate systems for texture synthesis on 3-D surfaces, in *Proc. Eurographics 85*, pp. 109–118, September 1985.

[Mand77]
Mandelbrot, B.B., Fractals—Form, Chance, and Dimension, San Francisco: W.H. Freeman, 1977.

[Mitc87]
Mitchell, D.P., Generating antialiased images at low sampling densities, *Comput. Graph.*, Vol. 21, pp. 65–72, 1987 (SIGGRAPH 87).

[Nort82]
Norton, A., Rockwood, A.P., and Skomolski, P.T., Clamping: A method of antialiasing textured surfaces by bandwidth limiting in object space, *Comput. Graph.*, Vol. 16, pp. 1–8, 1982 (SIGGRAPH 82).

[Oka87]
Oka, M., et al., Real-time manipulation of texture-mapped surfaces, *Comput. Graph.*, Vol. 21, pp. 181–188, 1987 (SIGGRAPH 87).

[Peac85]
Peachey, D.R., Solid texturing of complex surfaces, *Comput. Graph.*, Vol. 19, pp. 279–286, 1985 (SIGGRAPH 85).

[Perl85]
Perlin, K., An image synthesizer, *Comput. Graph.*, Vol. 19, pp. 287–296, 1985 (SIGGRAPH 85).

[Phon75]
Phong, B.T., Illumination for computer generated images, *CACM*, Vol. 18, pp. 311–317, 1975.

[Reyn88]
Reynolds, R.A. et al., Realistic presentation of three-dimensional medical datasets, in *Proc. Graph. Interface 88*, pp. 71–77, June 1988.

[Reev83]
Reeves, W.T., Particle systems—A technique for modeling a class of fuzzy objects, *ACM Trans. Graph.*, Vol. 2, pp. 91–108, 1983.

[Roug69]
Rougelot, R.S., The General Electric computer color TV display, in *Pertinent Concepts in Computer Graphics*, pp. 261–281, Faiman, M., and Nievergelt, J., Eds., Urbana: University of Illinois Press, 1969.

[Warn69]
Warnock, J.E., A Hidden Surface Algorithm for Computer Generated Half-Tone Pictures, Department of Computer Science, University of Utah (TR 4-15), Salt Lake City, UT, June 1969 (available through NTIS No. AD-753-671).

[Will78]
Williams, L., Casting curved shadows on curved surfaces, *Comput. Graph.*, Vol. 12, pp. 270–274, 1978 (SIGGRAPH 78).

[Will83]
Williams, L., Pyramidal parametrics, *Comput. Graph.*, Vol. 17, pp. 1–12, 1983 (SIGGRAPH 83).

[Wyvi87]
Wyvill, G., Wyvill, B., and McPheeters, C., Solid texturing of soft objects, *IEEE Comput. Graph. Appl.*, Vol. 7, pp. 20–26, 1987.

[Yaeg86]
Yaeger, L., Upson, C., and Myers, R., Combining physical and visual simulation—Creation of the planet Jupiter for the film '2010', *Comput. Graph.*, Vol. 20, pp. 85–93, 1986 (SIGGRAPH 86).

Algorithms for Realistic Image Synthesis

Roy Hall

Abstract

The quest for realism in computer graphics takes several forms. The prevalent approaches are either to simulate the real process to produce a result analogous to reality, or to examine reality and then to empirically generate techniques which create an appearance that mimics reality. These two approaches to generating realistic imagery and the resulting algorithms are reviewed.

Introduction

All it takes is for the rendered image to look right.—Blinn (1985)

Realism is a key concern in the field of computer graphics. A study of the literature reveals great emphasis on realism in rendering, modeling, and animation. While realism is an area of concentration, we seldom pause to define the term. It may be that realism is an elusive goal because it does not mean the same thing to each of us.

Realism is one of the primary demands of computer graphics users. Users cry out for increasingly complex rendered environments, reflection, texture, refraction, subtle shading, fog, shadows, models and motion for natural phenomena, etc. The list is endless. Yet it is inevitable that the same user who cries out for these facilities also wants sufficient control to turn these facilities on and off, and to be able to effect the operation so the behavior is not 'realistic'. This presents a dilemma for the software professional when creating image-generation tools.

The concept of realism does not present a static target. The history of art provides vivid illustration of this. Through the centuries, art provides a window into the ideas and attitudes of its time. Art reflects the perception of the world, the 'reality' of its time. A review of art through the ages certainly shows an evolution in the interpretation of realism.

There was a time when paintings that do not even have correct perspective were considered to be 'realistic'. The first black and white pictures were called 'realistic', as were the first moving pictures. The experience of realism has gone through such upheaval during the last century that there are people who do not accept the landing on the moon as a real event regardless of the quality of the associated imagery or other supporting evidence.

The perception of realism results from an interplay between real stimulation of the senses with the perceptual and intellectual interpretation of the stimuli. Basically, this means that realism is subjective. What we accept as realistic is based on our expectations and/or experience. As we become more sophisticated viewers, our expectations become more sophisticated. The imagery we accepted as realistic yesterday pales in comparison to what we expect a realistic image to look like today.

This paper discusses realism in computer graphics. Specifically, the evolution of expectations for realism and the algorithms to meet these expectations are reviewed. Many of the observations expressed here are personal opinion. Fortunately, the algorithms are not affected by whether or not you agree with the observations. Due to the scope of the material, this is primarily a survey of algorithms with some hints for the implementation of those that the author has used.

Why Do We Create Imagery?

The primary purpose of generating imagery is to communicate information. In the words of Samuel Taylor Coleridge, *"A picture is an intermediate something between a thought and a thing."* Imagery can let us:

'see' things that don't currently exist because they are only in design or visualization stages;

'see' things that cannot otherwise be observed because they are outside the realm of our visual perception;

'see' things that could not exist—that is, we can create data and display concepts that are inconsistent with a 3D reality;

'see' abstract concepts or concepts for which the true visual reality is confusing.

Bob Abel, a pioneer in advertising communication, has said of commercials that, *"The most successful commercial is one that you remember because it reminds you of something you've never seen before."* The essence of that statement is that for effective communication you need sufficient realism to make something familiar and sufficient fantasy or novelty to make it memorable.

Obviously, the nature and requirements of the communication depend upon the application. However, no matter what the nature, realism plays the part of making imagery understandable within the framework of our experience.

WHAT IS REALISTIC?

Attempting to quantify realism can lead to nothing but controversy. It is often said that *beauty is in the eye of the beholder*. This is also true of realism. Because the demands of each application are different, realism can only be evaluated in the context of the application. Some definitions of realistic include:

creating an experience that is indistinguishable from the real experience;

generating the same stimulus as the real environment;

generating the same perceptual response as a real scene;

creating the impression of a real scene.

Flight simulators are an example of an application judged by the first definition. The success of the flight simulation depends on the fidelity of the simulated experience to the experience of flight. The computer-generated visuals are but a small component of the overall experience. Other elements include the recreation of the cockpit interior and the motion experience. Realism is not evaluated by comparison of generated imagery with photographs but instead is evaluated by the quality of the experimental clues communicated to the pilot. For example, the scale of surface textures and runway details such as tire skid marks are important visual clues for speed and altitude during an approach.

Generating the same stimulus as a real scene is the motivation for attempting to exactly model all of the interactions between light and an environment. This is a very literal interpretation of realism. This approach suffers from the inability of display equipment to reproduce the dynamic intensity range and the color range found in nature. Additionally, there is great complexity in this type of modeling because of the complexity of the environments that surround us.

Producing the same perceptual response is an alternative to producing the same stimulus as the real environment. An example of this type of processing would be to add diffraction rings or stars around very bright highlights that cannot be reproduced on the display. Essentially, this requires that the correct stimulus information is passed through a perceptual model to determine what should be displayed to create the correct perception.

Creating the impression of realism takes advantage of the human ability to fill in missing details given sufficient information. This is an extremely subjective approach and is difficult, if not impossible, to quantify.

The process of creating and understanding imagery is schematically described in Figure 1. Each of the definitions of reality plug into the process

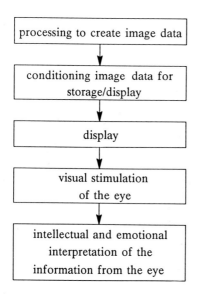

Figure 1. Steps in image creation and interpretation.

at different points. If the display hardware could faithfully reproduce the calculated results, the second definition would be the easiest to match. This requires the modeling of well-understood physical phenomena and the application of this model to environments of nearly unlimited complexity. At any other stage, a perceptual model or, what is even more difficult to quantify, an intellectual interpretation model, is required in order to generate the required imagery.

SIMULATION OR EMULATION?

I use the term simulation to refer to the process of trying to accurately model physical behavior as explained by current theory (Figure 2). I use the term illusion or emulation to refer to the process of trying to create the impression of realism by empirically approximating what we observe (Figure 3). Most computer-generated imagery prior to radiosity techniques was created primarily through emulation. Radiosity and subsequent approaches attempt simulation.

The reason that simulation was only toyed with prior to radiosity was the lack of sufficient computing power. Early researchers in image synthesis identified the theoretical information important for simulation of realism but did not have sufficient resources to apply this information. As noted by Appel [Appe68], *"many problems need to be solved such as the effect of illumination by direct and diffuse lighting, atmospheric diffusion, back reflection, the effect of surface texture, tonal specification, and the transparency of surfaces."*

In examining the question of whether it is most desirable to include

Figure 2. Radiosity solution simulating the physical behavior of light. (Courtesy of The Program of Computer Graphics, Cornell University.)

these effects by rigorous simulation or by emulation, Michael Mills [Mill85] asked *"Is there a better—or at least more sophisticated—way of conceiving the task of depiction in computer graphics than as a contest with reality, a quest to 'fool' the perceptual system via imitation of the real world?"* While this question cannot be answered here, the relationship between theory and practice is discussed. The discussion of techniques is primarily a discussion

Figure 3. Empirical approximation using reflection, bump, and texture mapping; negative intensity light sources; and multiple object representations. (Courtesy of Wavefront Technologies, Inc.)

of current practice, most of which is emulation or gross approximation. The presentation of these techniques highlights the differences between actual phenomena and methods being used to represent that phenomena.

In summary, simulation attempts to apply the principles of physics and optics to model the real interactions between light and materials as accurately as possible. Illusion attempts to present the appearance of reality without going through the pains of simulating reality. The algorithms used to create realistic appearance, whether by rigid simulation of real processes or by empirical approximations that create realistic appearance, all have trade-offs between quality and speed.

ELEMENTS OF REALISM

The advances in computer graphics that have done the most to improve the realism of imagery revolve around increased complexity and attention to subtle detail. The world around us is rich in detail and subtlety. Early in my experimentation with imagery I was impressed by how much I expected—but how little I knew about—how an image really should look. To explain that, let me recount an early experience in ray tracing. When I created my first ray-traced crystal ball, I was ecstatic—it was so realistic. I spent the next couple of weeks looking for and studying crystal balls to see what they really looked like. Later, I learned there was a bug in the refraction algorithm that made images incorrect. It was discovered only by chance about six months into the use of the code for image generation. Nobody had noted the problem in that six-month period. Although the images were incorrect, there was great complexity, and the behavior was somewhat reasonable. This was sufficient to preserve the impression of realism.

To summarize, the conclusions derived from my observations about the perception of realism in computer imagery are:

the impression of realism does not necessarily require correct imagery in terms of geometric detail as long as the general behavior is reasonable;

that high image complexity is primary in creating the perception of realism;

that subtle shading and surface detail are key in creating the perception of realism (they are actually a component of high complexity);

everything real is 3D—the perception of 3D from 2D imagery is greatly enhanced by motion.

These observations are not meant to imply that approximations should be substituted for realistic simulation but to provide a clue about why many of the techniques used in image generation are successful. Examples of approximation techniques that are very successful are the cloud and terrain generation of Gardner [Gard84; Gard85], the fractal terrain generation of Carpenter [Carp80] and Voss [Voss85], and the stochastic fire and plant generation by Reeves [Reev83; Reev85] and Smith [Smit84].

The advances that added detail and subtlety are milestones in the evolution of image-generation techniques. In summary, a brief list of these milestones includes:

geometric smoothing [Gour71; Phon75];

antialiasing [Crow77; Crow81];

mapping material and geometric parameters onto surfaces [Catm75; Blin76; Blin78; Crow84; Will83];

reflection mapping [Blin76];

improved illumination models [Phon75; Blin77; Whit80; Cook82; Hall83];

fractals, particle systems, and other data generators [Carp80; Max81; Blin82; Reev83; Reev85; Smit84; Voss85];

recursive ray tracing [Whit80];

distributed ray tracing [Cook84a];

radiosity techniques [Gora84];

hybrid radiosity/ray-tracing techniques [Wall87].

The following sections in this presentation address each of these advances in terms of the algorithms applied to image generation. Since antialiasing and texture mapping are being addressed in detail by Dr. Frank Crow elsewhere in this volume, the treatment of these areas will be brief.

Many techniques are available for generating spectacular imagery. Often these techniques require special programs and tremendous operator inter-action in order to generate the desired results. Typically, this creates a condition in which the computer is part of the problem rather than be-ing part of the solution when creating imagery. A challenge for research is to continually develop new techniques. A challenge for industry is to turn these techniques into tools that help solve the problem rather than becoming part of it.

EVALUATING IMAGE REALISM

While we often discuss the notion of realism in computer graphics, we seldom test the results, unlike other disciplines that design experiments to test and verify hypotheses. Typically, we drag people in front of monitors to look at isolated images and ask, 'what do you think?' At the early levels of development, this may have been sufficient. At current levels of image sophistication, subjective observation of isolated images cannot provide any conclusive evaluation of improvements in realism.

The only effort I am aware of to objectively evaluate imagery was pre-sented by Meyer et al. [Meye86]. In their experiments, the real environ-ment and the image were displayed side-by-side through cameras in a very controlled fashion. It was reported that when observers were asked to indicate which display was the computer-generated image, they "*did no better than they would have simply by guessing*". Their experiments also included radiometric measurements and comparison of measurements with the generated image data.

While this testing effort is a monumental step forward in creating an awareness of the problem of evaluating realism, there is still a long way to go in defining a methodology that can be uniformly applied. As we attempt to push the limits of realistic simulation, better techniques for image evaluation will be vital. These techniques will require test images, test environments, real environments, and some method for comparing and evaluating the closeness of the generated imagery to the real environment.

With this in mind, let us consider some of the algorithms for realistic image synthesis.

Geometric Smoothing

Many image-generation techniques rely on polygonal approximations for geometry. Rendering this description results in a faceted appearance if no smoothing algorithms are applied. The polygonal approximation provides a common representation for most geometric representations. Additionally, this representation is simple to render.

One method of smoothing polygonal geometry is to subdivide surfaces to subpixel size during tessellation (subdivision into polygons). While the results are effective, there are also problems with the approach:

subpixel subdivision can create more polygons than the renderer can handle;

subpixel subdivision can create enough polygons to seriously degrade rendering performance;

the correct subdivision depends on the position in the image and changes during animation sequences.

All other methods of simulating a smooth surface interpolate vertex information across the face of the polygon. The first interpolation approach was presented by Gouraud [Gour71]. He suggested that instead of computing a single color for a polygon, the colors should be computed at polygon vertices and interpolated over the face of the polygon. Original implementations were in scanline algorithms using incremental update techniques for each pixel. This allowed for linear interpolation of the color using only three add operations per pixel.[†] Several problems with this approach have been identified:

Pronounced Mach banding occurs at polygon boundaries due to discontinuities in the first derivative of intensity [Phon75]. The rate of change is constant across a polygon but usually does not match the rate of change in adjacent polygons.[‡]

Shading is not invariant with scanline orientation (Figure 4) [Duff79]. This causes 'shimmering' or 'crawling' of highlights when objects are in motion.

[†] There is a start-up cost for each polygon on a scanline; however, this was minimal because the environments used at that time had very few polygons.

[‡] Mach banding is a perceptual phenomena noted by E. Mach in the 1860s. Mach bands are caused when the first derivative (rate of change) of intensity across a scene is discontinuous. The perceptual mechanism of the eye enhances the discontinuity by making it appear lighter or darker than the surroundings.

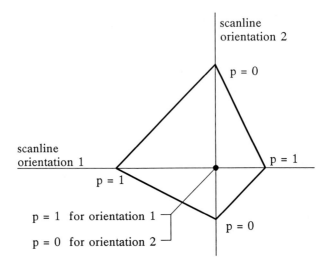

Figure 4. Variation as a function of scanline orientation [Hall88].

If illumination models generate highlights, the highlights are easily mis-placed or completely omitted (Figure 5) [Phon75]. This effect is exaggerated with animation, again causing 'shimmering' and 'crawling'.

These problems stem either from performing the interpolation after the color computation or from performing the interpolation in screen coordi-nates. Geometric information critical to the shading is lost once the color is computed. Interpolating the color does not reflect the variation in ge-ometry and presents false shading information.

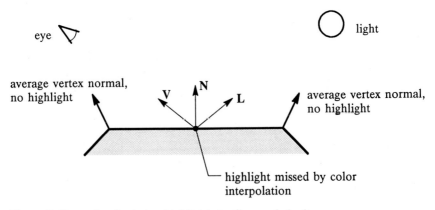

Figure 5. Example of missing highlights in Gouraud shading.

Phong [Phon75] presented a smoothing technique that interpolates the surface normal. This provides geometric information required for color computation and produces much better results. However, there is a great increase in cost because the illumination model must be evaluated at every pixel.

The perspective transformation is nonlinear. As a result, the interpolation in screen space introduces undesirable image anomalies that are sensitive to screen orientation. Interpolation in object space eliminates these anomalies but requires the object space location of the visible surface. Ray-tracing techniques perform all computations in object space and provide this information. Appendix A, Interpolating Polygon Vertex Information, details the implementation of object space interpolation for polygonal data.

The implementation of this technique interpolates the three components of the normals at the polygon vertices and then normalizes the result. The illumination model is then used to compute the color for the pixel.

The results of this approximation are very successful for creating the illusion of a smoothly curved surface. However, the surface is still polygonal, and any silhouette edges will be polygonal. Von Herzen and Barr [VonH87] present an adaptive subdivision technique that provides finer subdivision at silhouette edges to provide a smooth appearance.

Antialiasing

Aliasing results from the discrete sampling of a continuous signal (the image) at a rate too low to capture the frequency of the signal. In imagery, this means misrepresentation of high spatial frequency elements such as edges and texture details. Antialiasing techniques (see Crow, this volume) are closely related to rendering techniques.

Mapping Parameters Onto the Surface

Parameter mapping is one of the most effective methods of adding surface detail in the form of color patterns and roughness textures. The methodology is very similar to geometric smoothing. The interpolated parameter is a mapping index, and a look-up procedure is performed using this mapping index to find the mapped parameter value to be incorporated into the visible point data before color computation. A schematic of the methodology is given in Figure 6. The details of implementation vary greatly (see Crow, this volume). The remainder of this discussion of texture addresses some global implementation issues.

In the general case, the mapping is a look-up of a parameter from either a 1, 2, or 3D array of data. Examples are using a simple 1D gradation, a 2D image, or a 3D block of data. Any material or geometric parameter that describes the visible point for which color is being computed can

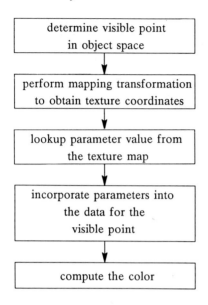

Figure 6. Schematic of the texture mapping process.

be mapped.[†] Approaches to mapping include separate mapping of all parameters with direct substitution into the material, separate mapping of all parameters and factoring the mapped parameters with the assigned parameter, using the mapping as an index into a complete material description, or a combination of these methods.

DIRECT SUBSTITUTION OF VALUES

Direct substitution typically uses a separate map for each color component that is mapped, i.e., ambient, diffuse, and specular, and a separate map for each scalar parameter such as the specular exponent, transparency, etc. Any combination of specified parameters and mapped parameters is used. The advantage is the speed of direct substitution and the selective mapping of parameters. The disadvantage is the number of mapping interpolations required if many parameters are mapped and the need to build new textures for minor alterations.

USING MAPPED VALUES AS MULTIPLIERS

Using mapped values as multipliers follows the same methodology as substitution except that the mapped parameter is multiplied by the specified material parameter. If the identity material parameter is specified the

---

[†]In practice, any of the material parameters can be mapped, and the surface normal can be mapped. Mapping the location of the point or a displacement for the point affects visibility and is not done in general practice. Cook [Cook84b] alludes to the mapping of displacement, but no details of the technique are presented.

result is the same as direct substitution. If minor color shifts or contrast adjustments are required, the specified material properties can be used to alter the map values. The advantage is the greater flexibility over direct substitution. The disadvantage is the increased computation for factoring instead of substituting values.

MAPPING COMPLETE MATERIALS

This approach is useful for modeling surfaces that are inlays of a variety of different homogeneous materials. A single interpolation is required, followed by a single map look-up to determine which material should be used. The advantage is the large volume of information that can be embodied in a single map look-up. The disadvantage is the lack of flexibility.

COMBINED TECHNIQUES

Combined techniques combine the material index map with material property maps. For example, consider a surface that is an inlay of wood, mother of pearl, and silver. In addition to the map to determine which material should be used, a parameter mapping is required to get the wood grain pattern or texture of the pearl. Figure 7 describes the combined mapping techniques used to generate a surface that is an inlay of copper, silver, and wood grain.

BUMP MAPPING

Another important mapping is bump mapping, or roughness mapping. Bump mapping emulates a geometric disturbance of the surface by adding a perturbation to the surface normal. Bump mapping is not as simple to implement as material parameter mapping.

The idea behind bump mapping is that the surface normal is perturbed to match the normal of the roughness texture. The shading then matches the shading that would be created by the actual texture, except that shadows and silhouette details are missing because the modeled surface position is not moved. A topological description of the roughness texture is processed to create slope maps in the directions of the principle axes of the texture. The texture look-up determines the slope of the surface relative to the surface normal in the principle axes of the texture. A new normal is computed by adding perturbation vectors factored by the slope to the normal vector and then normalizing the result (Figure 8).

A difficult aspect of bump mapping is determining the perturbation vectors to be multiplied by the slope values. If the mapping of a geometry naturally follows the description of the geometry, as in the case of parametric surfaces when the application of the texture follows the parametric axes, the perturbation vectors are well defined. However, in the general case of

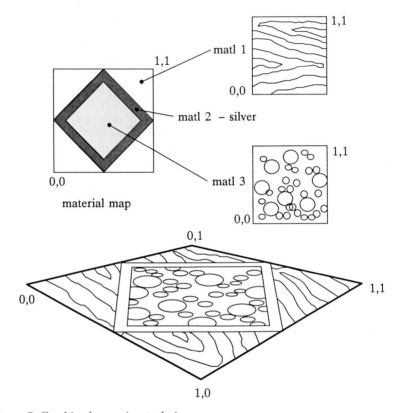

Figure 7. Combined mapping techniques.

a polygonal geometry that has been mapped by some arbitrary mapping function, the perturbation vectors must be derived from the mapping description. Appendix B, Perturbation Vectors for Bump-mapped Polygons, describes a general method for determining the perturbation vectors.

Reflection Mapping

Reflection mapping is a 'poor man's ray tracing'. It is very effective for capturing the 'feel' of reflective surfaces at a fraction of the computational expense of ray tracing. It is particularly effective when the surfaces are in motion and the reflections cannot be scrutinized. The technique, introduced by Blinn and Newell [Blin76], extends the local reflection model by including information from the reflection direction and using a simple look-up table to determine the color from any reflection direction.

The reflection map is an image that is projected onto the inside of a global environment sphere that surrounds the objects being rendered (Figure 9).

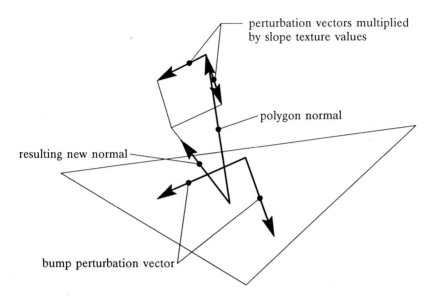

Figure 8. Bump mapping procedure.

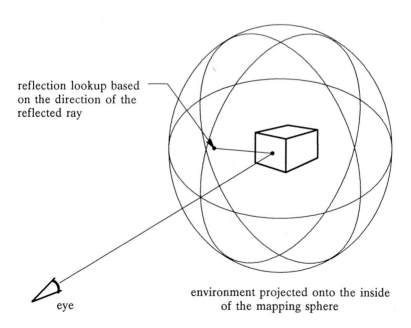

Figure 9. Concept of reflection mapping [Hall88].

The mapping is conceptual in the sense that there is no global sphere and the look-up procedure implicitly performs this projection. The concerns in implementing reflection mapping are to minimize the impact of the 'seam' where the reflection texture wraps back on itself and to minimize computational expense. The seam is generally positioned in front of the viewer (what is directly in front of the viewer is seldom reflected), and a look-up scheme, as detailed in Figure 10, is used. The expense of the arctangent computation can be minimized by using a look-up table.

The reflection map is often a simple gradation representing ground and sky. For more demanding applications, a map of a specific environment is constructed. A point centered in the reflective objects is used as a view point and six views are constructed using frustums formed by the diagonals of a cube surrounding the view point (Figure 11). These six views are then combined to create a reflection map. This map resembles photographs taken using a wide-angle lens (Figure 12) and is essentially a very wide-angle image of the environment. Figure 13 provides a comparison of objects rendered with and without reflection mapping. Note that the reflection map can be blurred for rough surfaces to achieve a more realistic appearance. Details of this procedure are found in Hall [Hall86].

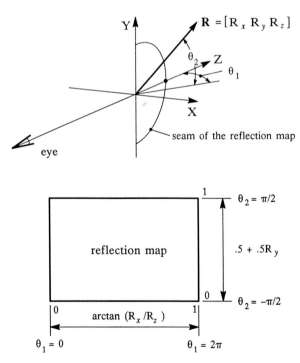

Figure 10. Reflection mapping look-up scheme.

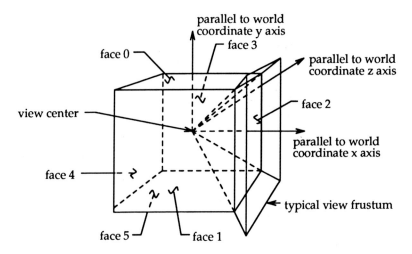

Figure 11. View cube for reflection map generation [Hall86].

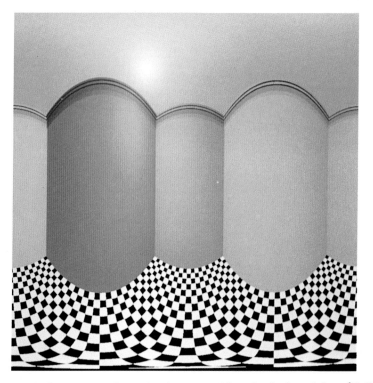

Figure 12. Reflection map for a simple room with a checkerboard floor [Hall88].

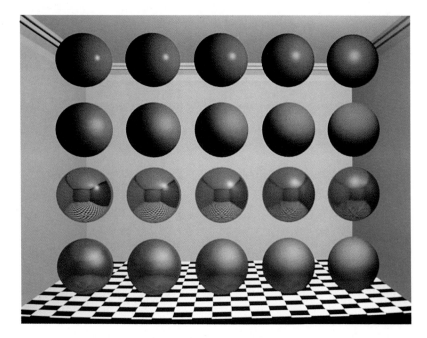

Figure 13. Comparison of metallic objects rendered with (bottom) and without (top) reflection mapping [Hall88].

Improved Illumination Models

The application of research in physics and optics to computer graphics constitutes an evolution governed by the current visible-surface algorithms, by what is considered computationally reasonable, and by the level of realism that is acceptable. The illumination models used fall into three general classifications: empirical, transitional, and analytical. The shading techniques that evolved with these models fall into three corresponding classifications: incremental, ray-tracing, and radiosity methods (Table 1). In addition, a hybrid classification has recently emerged that combines the radiosity and ray-tracing approaches.

Early illumination models were empirical in nature. They were evaluated after the geometry was transformed into the perspective space (screen space) used for visible surface computation. The same incremental techniques used to exploit scanline coherence in visible surface determination were also applied to the illumination computations. These models and application techniques were an adjunct development to scanline visible surface algorithms.

Transitional models use prior work in physics and optics to improve the earlier empirical models. These models demonstrate an increasing concern for color, shading, and visual detail in imagery supported by the increasing computational power of the hardware. These illumination models require the use of Euclidean geometry (object space geometry) prior to perspective transformation so that reflections, refractions, and shadows are geometrically correct. Initially, ray tracing was restricted to very smooth reflective surfaces. Cone tracing and distributed ray tracing attempt to extend the ray-tracing methodology to include diffuse environments.

Analytical approaches make the illumination model the driving force for the application of energy equilibrium techniques to computer imagery. In addition to maintaining true geometry, the movement of light energy

Table 1. Classification of shading technique and illumination models [Hall88].

Rendering Technique	Reference	Shading and Illumination Additions
Perspective (screen space) geometry:	[Bouk70]	Constant color across polygons
scanline techniques, incremental	[Warn69; Romn69]	Distance attenuation, primitive highlights
updating, empirical	[Gour71]	Color interpolation across polygons
illumination	[Newe72]	Pseudo transparency
	[Phon75; Duff79; Bish86]	Normal interpolation across polygons, refined highlights
Euclidean (object space) geometry:	[Catm75; Blin76]	Texture mapping, reflection mapping
ray tracing, empirical	[Blin77]	Incoherent reflection
and theoretical illumination	[Kay79]	Distance attenuation and refraction in transparent materials
models	[Whit80]	Recursive coherent reflection, refraction
	[Hall83]	Incoherent transmission
	[Cook84a; Aman84]	Distributed sampling and area sampling
	[Kaji85]	Anisotropic illumination
	[Kaji86]	Energy equilibrium in distributed ray tracing

Table 1. *Continued*

Rendering Technique	Reference	Shading and Illumination Additions
Energy equilibrium: radiosity, energy equilibrium models	[Cook82]	Spectral character of highlights, energy formulation
	[Gora84]	Diffuse energy equilibrium
	[Cohe85; Nish85; Cohe86]	Complex diffuse environments including shadows
	[Imme86]	Specular highlights in radiosity solutions
	[Max86; Rush87; Nish87]	Atmospheric effects
Hybrid techniques	[Wall87]	Radiosity diffuse, ray traced specular

through the environment must be modeled to provide the information required to evaluate the illumination model. Initially, radiosity techniques were restricted to ideally diffuse reflective surfaces. The introduction of specular effects soon followed.

The hybrid rendering technique integrates radiosity and ray-tracing techniques to handle diffuse and specular effects, respectively. Each technique is used to model the illumination components for which it is best suited. Translucency and refraction are also included in the hybrid model.

These four classifications describe a shift in research from solving the hidden-surface problem, to creating realistic appearance, to simulating the behavior that creates the appearance.

Illumination models have received sufficient attention in graphics texts and articles that any additional discussion here is not warranted. In addition to the original articles, other references are Newman and Sproull [Newm79], Foley and Van Dam [Fole84], Rogers [Roge85], and Hall [Hall88].

Fractals, Particle Systems, and Other Data Generators

Increasing the complexity of the rendered environment requires increasing the complexity of the database. Texture mapping produces an apparent increase in complexity, but there are limits to the effects it can produce. Renderings of natural environments such as mountains, forests, fields, and water require great geometric complexity if they are to create an impression of realism.

The problem in portraying natural phenomena is twofold. The first part of the problem is creating the data that is required to model the environment. The second part of the problem is selecting rendering techniques that can accommodate the volume of data that describes the environment.

Fractal, graftal, particle systems, and other data generators procedurally create complex data representations from a minimum amount of input data. This has tremendous implications for rendering. Most commercial rendering systems use algorithms that will accept a very limited number of polygons (several hundred thousand) because the rendering algorithm must sort all data before starting (scanline or incremental algorithms) or because the entire database must be accessible (ray-tracing algorithms). When dealing with large natural databases, other rendering techniques must be explored.

Sutherland et al. [Suth74] characterized the visible surface algorithms that were in use at that time. They identify sorting as the major task of visible surface determination and consideration of coherence as the means for accelerating the sorting.[†] Perspective transformation, clipping, and visibility sorting were performed on the entire database at the same time. This study was made in an era of very simple geometric environments and slow serial processors.

The Z-buffer approach presented by Catmull [Catm74] was a departure from previous algorithms because it treats polygons independently and writes them into a buffer of the entire frame that includes a depth value at every pixel. If the current polygon is in front of the polygon currently stored in a pixel, that pixel is overwritten; otherwise, the polygon is ignored for the pixel. This approach requires a buffer large enough for the entire image, which was problematic at the time but is well within current technology limits. The A-buffer presented by Carpenter [Carp84] solves the aliasing problems inherent in the Z-buffer algorithm and maintains the independent processing of each polygon. This is a promising technique for use with procedural data generators although, to the author's knowledge, it is not available in any commercial rendering systems.[‡]

Some of the procedural data-generation techniques use special-purpose rendering programs ([Max81; Blin82; Reev83]). While this allows optimizing of the rendering technique for a specific class of data, it presents problems in a generalized rendering environment where several different classes of objects are available to users. Options for solving this dilemma in-

---

[†]Coherence is the probability that what is visible in one pixel is visible in the neighboring pixel; that what is visible on one scanline is likely to be visible on the adjacent scanline; and that, between two successive frames of an animation, what is visible in a pixel in one frame is likely to be visible in the same pixel in the next frame.

[‡]This technique is part of the Reyes (Renders everything you've ever seen) image-generation system at PIXAR. This system was used to generate the animation *The Adventures of André and Wally B.* This animation featured forest backgrounds composed of millions of polygons.

clude: developing a rendering technique that handles every class of data; developing a rendering technique that incorporates class-specific renderers and merges the results into a single image; and developing a technique that allows a collection of independent renderers to render separate images and then merges the resulting images into a single image.

Compositing is a technique common in animation in which many layers of artwork are overlayed and photographed; it is also common in optical effects where many 'elements' are photographically combined by exposing the film of each element and projecting it through a matte that allows exposure of only the portion of the film where the effect of the element is to be seen. This technique is common in computer-generated imagery so that elements—in this case, separate images—can be overlayed. The technique was presented by Wallace [Wall81] for use in computer-assisted cartoon animation. Extensions were presented by Porter and Duff [Port84] that more closely mimicked the optical effects operations used in filmmaking.

Duff [Duff85] extended the technique still further by incorporating depth information into the compositing step. Prior to this, the image layers used in compositing needed to be completely independent; that is, the objects in the back layer needed to be completely behind all of the objects in the front layer. The intersection of objects in the different layers was precluded. The extension by Duff allows objects in different layers to intersect and makes the resulting image independent of the compositing order. This is critical in making the technique general so that the user does not need to agonize about compositing strategies to combine images created by several different renderers.

Within the context of these procedural data generators, let us turn our attention to realism. Are these algorithms generating realistic imagery? Judging from the crowd reaction at SIGGRAPH presentations and at SIGGRAPH film shows, these algorithms are creating data that has a lot of appeal. However, most of the techniques have been generated through empirical efforts to create the desired effect. There is very little 'scientific' evidence that suggests an attempt to simulate the real process and very few comparisons to the 'real' phenomena being emulated; there is also no methodology for evaluating the results with reference to past techniques or to the new techniques continually under development.[†]

Recursive Ray Tracing

This rendering technique traditionally takes the approach of beginning the illumination computation at the eye. This technique naturally emerges from visible surface computation because the surfaces that must be shaded

---

[†]Some exceptions to this are the simulations of water waves in which there is a substantial body of hydrodynamic and wave theory [Max81; Peac86; Four86].

are those that are visible. This approach is exemplified in early illumination models.

The illumination expression is applied to the visible surface for each pixel. Consider the simple environment of Figure 14. If a point on patch three is visible, the illumination model is applied to the visible point. The question asked by the model is: *what information is required to evaluate the illumination model at this point?*

The earliest models obtained illumination information from light sources only. Global illumination, that illumination reflected from other surfaces in the environment, is accounted for by a global ambient illumination term. This assumes the environment is uniformly filled with light of some intensity coming from all directions (Figure 15).

The next step in technique began to consider illumination provided by other surfaces in the environment. To provide the required illumination information for evaluating the color of the visible surface, all other surfaces are queried to find out how they illuminate the visible surface. To determine the color of all the other surfaces, the illumination model is applied that, in turn, requires a query of all other surfaces (Figure 16).

It is readily apparent that if the environment is complex, the calculations for a single pixel become overwhelming. However, consider evaluating the color of a perfect mirror: The only color is that reflected back to the viewer from the direction of the reflected view ray. Reflection mapping, as previously described in the section on this subject, provides a simple, inexpensive method for computing this color.

Recursive ray tracing explicitly calculates the color by spawning rays through the environment in the reflected and refracted directions. The ray-tracing technique was first introduced by Appel [Appe67] as a method for visible surface determination.

This method was extended by Kay [Kay79] and made recursive by Whitted [Whit80] in his classic paper. Hall [Hall83] extended the illumination model to include work that was previously disjoint into a single model.

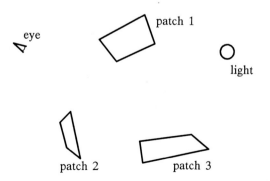

Figure 14. Simple environment for describing illumination [Hall88].

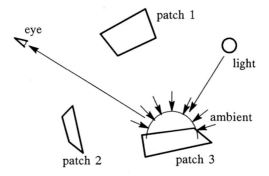

Figure 15. Early illumination models.

The beauty of the ray-tracing methodology is that it is conceptually and algorithmically very simple and elegant. It is very easy to implement, and it is an 'exact' solution for optically smooth surfaces. The problem is that most surfaces in the environment are not optically smooth. Additionally, the problem of determining what surface is visible to a ray can be computationally prohibitive for complex environments.

Minimizing the computational expense of ray tracing is accomplished by minimizing the number of rays and minimizing the expense of processing each ray. Hall [Hall83] presented a method for adaptively adjusting the recursive depth for each ray to reduce the number of rays. Adaptive control of the pixel sampling rate was explored by Whitted [Whit80] and Mitchell [Mitc87].

As Sutherland et al. [Suth74] noted, the visibility problem is primarily one of sorting. This is true for ray tracing as well as for any of the scanline algorithms they reviewed.

A large body of work exists that explores methods to minimize the expense of each ray by innovative sorting techniques. Among these efforts

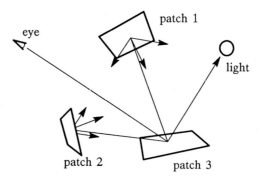

Figure 16. Recursive evaluation of the illumination model starting from the eye [Hall88].

are the work of Rubin and Whitted [Rubi80], Glassner [Glas84], Weghorst et al. [Wegh84], Kaplan [Kapl85], Kay and Kajiya [Kay86], Arvo and Kirk [Arvo87], and Snyder and Barr [Snyd87].

Distributed Ray Tracing

Initial ray-tracing solutions provided realistic solutions to environments of optically smooth surfaces—realistic in the sense that the images were very convincing and the theoretical foundation for the technique is sound. However, there are very few surfaces in our environment that even approach being optically smooth. Distributed ray tracing is an approach to rendering surfaces that are more typical of the environment.

The distributed ray-tracing approach is born from the notion that more than one sample is required to characterize an area event (such as the illumination from the global environment). One solution is to spawn a bundle of rays from every visible surface. Another solution is to spawn sampling volumes [Aman84] (Figure 17).

A problem with ray tracing bundles of rays is that there are increasing numbers of rays sampling information that has a decreasing influence on the final image. This devotes the greatest computation effort to the least meaningful information. Volume sampling is difficult to implement. Distributed ray tracing, as presented by Cook et al. [Cook84a], uses the standard ray-tracing approach of spawning a single reflection ray, a single refraction ray, and a single ray to sample each light source, and observes that since oversampling is required to prevent aliasing in a pixel, there are many rays available per pixel for sampling nonpoint information. Distributing these rays to adequately sample these events without adding extra rays is the key to the technique.

In this method, Cook et al. used 16 rays per pixel. If a single polygon is visible in the pixel, the 16 reflected rays would be nearly identical in standard ray tracing. By perturbing the direction of reflection, they essentially obtained a bundle of rays to sample the reflected direction. If, instead of considering a ray to the center of the light source, the 16 rays were distributed over the face of the light source, soft shadows could be

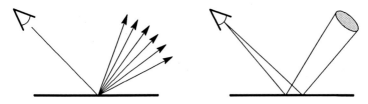

Figure 17. Ray tracing with ray bundles and volumes.

obtained. Note that no additional rays were required over traditional ray-tracing methods. Cook et al. note this method can also be used (a) to simulate depth-of-field by perturbing the view ray start position over the lens area of the eye, (b) to simulate motion blur by distributing the rays over the time of a single frame, and (c) to improve antialiasing by perturbing the view ray off of the sampling grid.

The key to the success of this technique is determining the distribution. Cook [Cook86] presented a method that divided the distribution range or area into uniform discrete ranges or areas and then randomly placed or 'jittered' the sample within that area. Figure 18 shows an example of a regular and a jittered sampling grid for a pixel. Consider a horizontal edge between a black and white field passing over the pixel at a constant rate. The pixel would take on discrete values of 0, $1/4$, $1/2$, $3/4$, and 1. The jitter-sampled pixel would take on 16 values as the edge passed over the pixel. Note, however, that the time-spacing of the 16 values would not be uniform. Cook notes that this method essentially eliminates banding but adds noise instead. Other discussions of the sampling technique are found in Lee et al. [Lee85], Dippé and Wold [Dipp85], and Kajiya [Kaji86].

Once again we return to the question of realism. The point sampling techniques provide us with a limited view of the interactions that occur in the environment. These are approximations that provide an acceptable approximation of the real phenomena, but the cost may be high. The results demonstrated in Kajiya's work were very impressive, but 40 rays per pixel were required. As noted by Whitted [Whit82], "*Unfortunately, the price of increased realism is a huge increase in computation costs.*"

Radiosity Techniques

Radiosity techniques take a different approach to computing illumination for a scene. Instead of starting from the eye and treating only the visible polygons, radiosity solutions start at the light source and trace light energy through the environment generating a complete illumination solution before viewing is even considered.

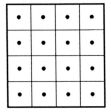
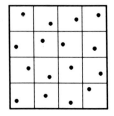

Figure 18. Uniform and jittered sampling grid for a pixel.

Consider once again the simple environment of Figure 14. Suppose that for each patch in the environment we could generate a coefficient that relates the intensity reflected or transmitted to a target patch to the intensity received from a source patch, $\xi_{target,source,active}$. We will use the notation $I_{source,destination}$ to denote the intensity from a source to a destination.

An ideal diffuse environment greatly simplifies the computations. The intensity leaving any surface is independent of direction for ideal diffuse surfaces. Thus, the ξ term becomes $\xi_{source,active}$ relating the intensity radiated in any direction from the active patch to the intensity received from the source. This requires n^2 coefficients, where n is the number of patches in the environment.

The diffuse environment is solved by recursively asking what the intensity is of the patches in the environment. The simple environment of Figure 19 is characterized by these relationships:

$$I_1 = \xi_{lgt,1}I_{lgt} + \xi_{2,1}I_2 + \xi_{3,1}I_3 \qquad (1a)$$

$$I_2 = \xi_{lgt,2}I_{lgt} + \xi_{1,2}I_1 + \xi_{3,2}I_3 \qquad (1b)$$

$$I_3 = \xi_{lgt,3}I_{lgt} + \xi_{1,3}I_1 + \xi_{2,3}I_2 \qquad (1c)$$

The first iteration provides illumination from the light source only (Figure 20). The intensities of the patches are zero at the beginning of the first iteration. The second iteration includes the first bounce of light from the surfaces (Figure 21). The total energy leaving a surface is always less than the energy incident on the surface. Rapid convergence is guaranteed due to this physical restriction on the validity of the ξ coefficients. It can readily be seen that for simple diffuse environments with few patches the technique of starting from the eye is not computationally prohibitive.

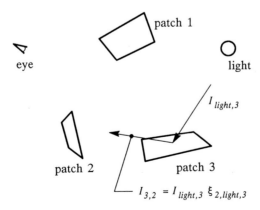

Figure 19. Notation for radiosity [Hall88].

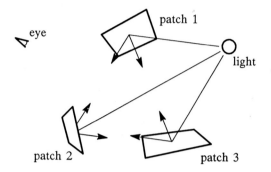

Figure 20. First approximation starting from the light [Hall88].

Goral et al. [Gora84] formalized this using a diffuse illumination model
of the form

$$I(\lambda) = \varepsilon(\lambda) + R_d(\lambda) \int^{2\pi} I_L(\lambda)(\mathbf{N} \cdot \mathbf{L}) d\omega \qquad (2)$$

where R_d is the diffuse reflectance, ε is the emissivity, and I_L is the intensity
from the $\mathbf{L}$ direction. Evaluation of the illumination model for a specific
patch, n, in the environment is approximated by summing contributions
from all patches in the environment

$$I_n(\lambda) = \varepsilon_n(\lambda) + R_{dn}(\lambda) \sum_{m=1}^{p} I_m(\lambda) F_{m,n} \qquad (3)$$

The form factor, $F_{m,n}$, is introduced as a notational convenience. It is a
factor that relates the energy density reaching patch n from patch m to
the intensity of patch m. The form factor is given by

$$F_{m,n} = \frac{1}{A_n} \int^{A_n} \int^{A_m} \frac{\cos \theta_n \cos \theta_m dA_m dA_n}{r_{m,n}^2} \qquad (4)$$

Figure 22 describes the form factor. The computation of form factors
is described in detail by Goral [Gora84][†] and is not repeated here. The
equation set that results from considering a complete n patch environment
is given in matrix form by

[†]The original presentation of radiosity was expressed in terms of energy flux
per unit area. Energy formulation results in an additional factor of π in the
denominator of the form factor. This discussion is presented in terms of intensity,
and the $1/\pi$ factor is included in the reflectance. Typically, $R_d(\lambda) = M(\lambda)/\pi$
where $M(\lambda)$ is the measured material curve.

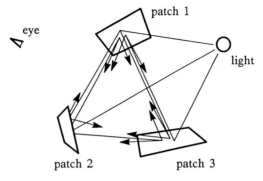

Figure 21. Second approximation starting from the light [Hall88].

$$
\begin{bmatrix}
1 - R_{d1}F_{1,1} & -R_{d1}F_{2,1} & \cdots & -R_{d1}F_{n,1} \\
-R_{d2}F_{1,2} & 1 - R_{d2}F_{2,2} & \cdots & -R_{d2}F_{n,2} \\
\cdot & \cdot & & \cdot \\
\cdot & \cdot & & \cdot \\
-R_{dn}F_{1,n} & -R_{dn}F_{2,n} & \cdots & 1 - R_{dn}F_{n,n}
\end{bmatrix}
\begin{bmatrix}
I_1 \\ I_2 \\ \cdot \\ \cdot \\ I_n
\end{bmatrix}
=
\begin{bmatrix}
\varepsilon_1 \\ \varepsilon_2 \\ \cdot \\ \cdot \\ \varepsilon_n
\end{bmatrix}
\quad (5)
$$

The form factor for a patch reflecting energy to itself is 0, so the diagonal terms reduce to 1. Cohen et al. [Cohe85; Cohe86] developed an extension to the radiosity method that provides a general methodology for approximating form factors and accounting for shadowing within the environment. This extension allows the rendering of more complex environments using radiosity techniques.

Cohen et al. observed that any two patches that have the same projection on the illuminating hemisphere had the same form factor. They proposed

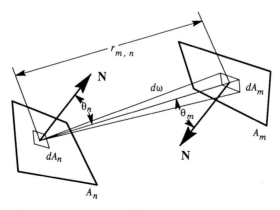

Figure 22. The form factor for radiosity (adapted from Goral et al. [Gora84]).

projecting the environment onto the illuminating hemisphere over a given patch by performing visible surface calculations from that patch. Each sample point in the visible surface projection represented some solid angle and a corresponding form factor, ΔF_q. The form factor for a particular patch was approximated by summing the form factors of the sample points, s, covered by the patch

$$F_{m,n} = \sum_{q=1}^{s} \Delta F_q \qquad (6)$$

Visible surface projection onto a hemisphere is difficult, and Cohen et al. suggest the use of a *hemicube*, or half of a cube, for the projection of visible surfaces (Figure 23).

The radiosity technique computes the intensity (color) of each patch independent of processing for display. A Gouraud shading algorithm was then used to render images with the vertex colors determined by averaging the colors of adjacent patches on a surface.

Additional description of radiosity techniques is found in Greenberg et al. [Gree86], which provides a good overview of the technique, Cohen et al. [Cohe86], which discusses techniques for subdividing the surfaces in the environment for efficient processing, Baum et al. [Baum86], which discusses extensions for efficient processing of dynamic environments for multiple frame animation, and Immel [Imme86], which presents an extension to the radiosity technique that demonstrates that it is possible to include specular or directional effects.

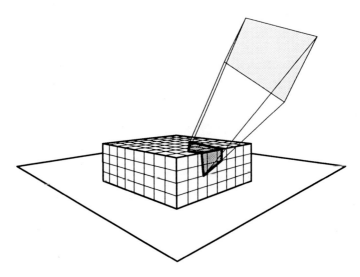

Figure 23. A hemicube for form-factor evaluation (adapted from [Cohe85]).

The radiosity technique demonstrates a rigorous simulation of the phenomenon of illumination in the world around us. The technique generates striking images. However, it is difficult to imagine that such an approach could be implemented or is appropriate for a highly complex natural environment such as a forest.

Hybrid Techniques

Wallace et al. [Wall87] presented a hybrid technique that combined radiosity and ray-tracing methods. Their approach was to break the illumination process into four components that they identified as the 'mechanisms' of illumination.

They noted that the incident illumination is the combination of a diffuse and a specular component. Each of these results in both a diffuse and a specular reflection. Thus, the reflected color is a summation of a diffuse incident to diffuse reflected component, a diffuse incident to specular reflected component, a specular incident to diffuse reflected component, and a specular incident to specular reflected component (Figure 24).

The hybrid method uses two passes for illumination calculation. The first pass is a view-independent pass similar to the diffuse radiosity computation, which computes the diffuse illumination of the scene. In addition to the

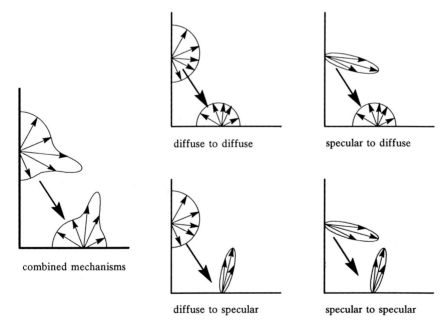

diffuse to diffuse   specular to diffuse

combined mechanisms

diffuse to specular   specular to specular

Figure 24. The four 'mechanisms' of illumination (adapted from [Wall87]).

diffuse-to-diffuse mechanism, this extends the form factor to account for specular-to-diffuse and specular-to-specular mechanisms. The second pass is a view-dependent pass similar to distributed ray tracing, which uses the results of the first pass to provide global illumination information and then selective sampling to provide the view-dependent, specular-to-specular, and diffuse-to-specular components.

Conclusions

> "[Many approaches to creating images] *at first seem like very special tricks, but, as we all know, a 'technique' is a 'trick' used more than once.*"—Blinn (1985)

There are a wide variety of techniques and algorithms available for generating imagery. All of these make trade-offs in speed, complexity, and realism. There is no universal solution to the problem of creating a renderer that is all things to all people. The selection of the correct algorithms requires an understanding of the application and its needs.

Realism is an elusive goal. The elusiveness is both a function of the complexity of the real world and of our inability to define and measure reality in imagery. If we are to continue to push at the bounds of reality, then it is necessary for us to clearly articulate the meaning and goals so that we can design methods to evaluate the progress made by new algorithms. The techniques and algorithms have outpaced our awareness to the extent that it is no longer sufficient to look at images and ask *'which is more realistic?'*

Appendix A

INTERPOLATING POLYGON VERTEX INFORMATION

Many of the techniques for increasing image complexity require the interpolation of properties defined at polygon vertices over the surface of the polygon. The success of these techniques, particularly for animation, is dependent upon the care with which interpolation is performed.

Scanline algorithms are very popular for visible surface determination. The scanline process is an incremental process that is very well suited to interpolation in screen coordinates. Figure A1 describes the incremental interpolation process. Interpolated parameters can be updated incrementally by a single add operation at each pixel during the processing of each scanline.

While the method can be efficiently implemented, it is not invariant if the orientation of the display grid changes (Figure 4); it is also not invariant because the nonlinear perspective transformation distorts distance

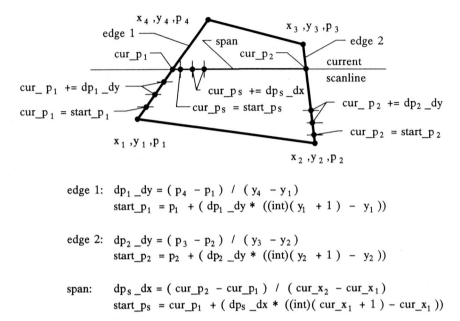

edge 1: $dp_1\_dy = (p_4 - p_1) / (y_4 - y_1)$
          $start\_p_1 = p_1 + (dp_1\_dy * ((int)(y_1 + 1) - y_1))$

edge 2: $dp_2\_dy = (p_3 - p_2) / (y_3 - y_2)$
          $start\_p_2 = p_2 + (dp_2\_dy * ((int)(y_2 + 1) - y_2))$

span: $dp_s\_dx = (cur\_p_2 - cur\_p_1) / (cur\_x_2 - cur\_x_1)$
          $start\_p_s = cur\_p_1 + (dp_s\_dx * ((int)(cur\_x_1 + 1) - cur\_x_1))$

Figure A1. Incremental parameter updating [Hall88].

relationships along the polygon edges (Figure A2).[†]

The solution to this problem is to perform interpolation in object space. The major implication is that the object space view ray and visible polygon intersection must be determined. Additionally, the interpolation becomes a mapping transformation rather than a simple incremental update. The mapping transformation can be simple or complex depending on the polygon configuration. Different interpolation strategies result in different generated images. The major concerns in selecting a strategy are orientation independence and behavior of the method at polygon boundaries. Orientation independence means that the results will be the same regardless of object orientation and/or display grid orientation. Perspective or screen space interpolation is not invariant as the orientation of the display grid changes.

The most simple and widely used interpolation method is a linear interpolation implemented using a linear transformation. This method allows a linear or first-order variation of a parameter over the surface of a polygon. The interpolated parameter will match in value at the adjoining polygon boundaries. However, it may be discontinuous in all derivatives. In the general case, the polygon must be triangular (Figure A3).

[†]The midpoint of an edge in screen space does not correspond to the actual midpoint of an edge unless the edge is parallel to the image plane (Figure A2).

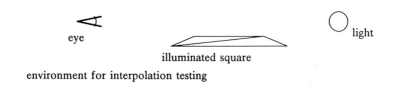

eye

illuminated square

light

environment for interpolation testing

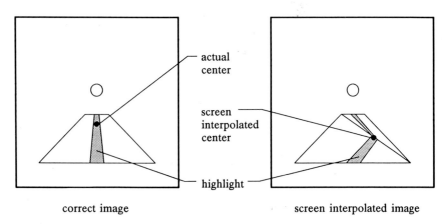

actual
center

screen
interpolated
center

highlight

correct image   screen interpolated image

Figure A2. Distortion resulting from nonlinearity of the perspective transform [Hall88].

The method transforms a point on the polygon into the mapped parameter space. The transformation is expressed by

$$[n \text{ parameters}] = \begin{bmatrix} n \times 3 \\ \text{mapping} \\ \text{transform} \end{bmatrix} \begin{bmatrix} pv_{i0} \\ pv_{i1} \\ 1 \end{bmatrix} \tag{A1}$$

The location of the visible point, pv, on the polygon is given by $pv = (pv_x, pv_y, pv_z)$. The transformation matrix has a row for each parameter to be interpolated over the polygon. Only two components of the intersection point are required for the mapping. The two components, pv_{i0} and pv_{i1}, are selected at the time the mapping transformation is generated. The selection is based upon minimum numerical error considerations. Given the location of a point on the polygon, the interpolated parameter values are given by the simple transformation.

To describe the generation of the mapping transformation matrix, consider a triangular polygon defined by three points, $p0$, $p1$, and $p2$, as shown in Figure A4. The polygon is defined by the corner vertices which, in turn, define the plane equation for the polygon.[†] The normalized plane equation

---

[†] The plane equation is determined by substituting the vertex locations into the plane equation and solving the resulting simultaneous equations. An alternate method using vector cross products is given in Sutherland et al. [Suth74].

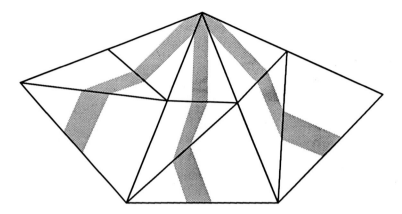

Figure A3. Distortion of linear interpolation on a nonrectangular polygon grid with a striped texture.

is given by

$$Ax + By + Cz = D; \qquad \sqrt{A^2 + B^2 + C^2} = 1 \qquad (A2)$$

Note that any point on the polygon is fully defined by only two of the three components. The third is determined using the plane equation. However, there is a boundary condition when one or two of the plane equation coefficients is 0. In this case, those components must be specified to uniquely locate the point. Minimum numerical error is assured by selecting the two components whose plane equation coefficients have the minimum absolute values. These components are referred to as the $i0$ and $i1$ components. Thus, pv_{i0} and pv_{i1} are either the (x, y), (y, z), or (x, z) coordinates of the visible point.

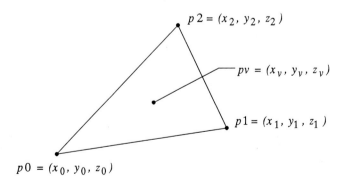

Figure A4. Notation for mapping transformation derivation.

Given vertex parameters $q0$, $q1$, and $q2$, the parameter value, qv, at the visible point is given by:

$$qv = \begin{bmatrix} q_a & q_b & q_c \end{bmatrix} \begin{bmatrix} pv_{i0} \\ pv_{i1} \\ 1 \end{bmatrix} \qquad (A3)$$

The matrix coefficients q_a, q_b, and q_c are determined by substituting the vertex locations and parameters into Eq. (A3) for each of the three vertices and solving the resulting simultaneous equations. This procedure is repeated for each of the parameters that will be interpolated resulting in an $n \times 3$ mapping transformation for the polygon.

Appendix B

PERTURBATION VECTORS FOR BUMP-MAPPED POLYGONS

Determining the perturbation vectors for bump-mapped polygons is necessary for a generalized rendering system. If polygons are generated from the tessellation of a parametric surface and a bump map is applied along the parametric axes of the surface, then the derivatives of the surface along the parametric axes will give perturbation vectors. However, for the case of generalized polygonal construction and/or arbitrary projections of the texture, the perturbation vectors must be computed based upon the mapping.

Consider an arbitrary triangular polygon as described in Figure B1. The polygon is defined in space by the vertex coordinates $p0$, $p1$, and $p2$. The projection of the bump map is defined by the texture vertices (u_0, v_0), (u_1, v_1), and (u_2, v_2). The unknown perturbation vectors are **U** and **V**.

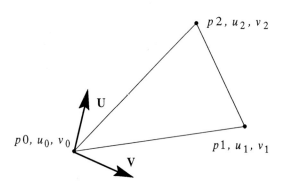

Figure B1. Notation for perturbation vector computation.

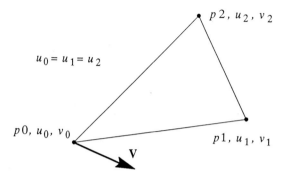

Figure B2. Notation for special case perturbation vector.

The relationships between vertices $p0$, $p1$, and $p2$ are expressed in terms of $\mathbf{U}$ and $\mathbf{V}$ by

$$p1 = p0 + (u_1 - u_0)\mathbf{U} + (v_1 - v_0)\mathbf{V} \qquad (B1a)$$

$$p2 = p0 + (u_2 - u_0)\mathbf{U} + (v_2 - v_0)\mathbf{V} \qquad (B1b)$$

These are expanded into the x, y, z components to create six equations with six unknowns. These equations are solved for $\mathbf{U}$ and $\mathbf{V}$ using standard linear equation solution techniques.

A special case arises when $u_0 = u_1 = u_2$ or $v_0 = v_1 = v_2$. In this case, either the $\mathbf{U}$ or $\mathbf{V}$ vector is undefined. The equation set is overdetermined and there is generally no solution for the remaining vector.

A solution used with success is to set the undefined vector to be a zero length vector[†] and define the other vector to be in the plane of the polygon starting at $p0$ and oriented such that the distance to points $p0$ and $p1$ is proportional to the u or v delta between the points. Figure B2 describes the notation for this system when $u_0 = u_1 = u_2$. The resulting relationships are given by

$$\begin{bmatrix} x_1 - x_0 & y_1 - y_0 & z_1 - z_0 \\ x_2 - x_0 & y_2 - y_0 & z_2 - z_0 \\ A & B & C \end{bmatrix} \begin{bmatrix} V_x \\ V_y \\ V_z \end{bmatrix} = \begin{bmatrix} v_1 - v_0 \\ v_2 - v_1 \\ 0 \end{bmatrix} \qquad (B2)$$

A, B, and C are the plane equation coefficients. The last equation assures the $\mathbf{V}$ vector is in the plane of the polygon by keeping the dot product with the normal equal to zero.

As a standard practice, the computed perturbation vectors are normalized. Normalization of these vectors assures that the features in the texture maintain the same apparent slope regardless of the scale of the texture.

[†]Since the entire polygon corresponds to a single u or v location on the texture map, the derivative in that direction must be zero.

REFERENCES

[Aman84]
Amanatides, J., Ray tracing with cones, *Comput. Graph.*, Vol. 18, pp. 129–135, 1984 (SIGGRAPH 84).

[Appe67]
Appel, A., The notion of quantitative invisibility and the machine rendering of solids, in *Proc. ACM Natl. Conf.*, pp. 387–393, New York: ACM Press, 1967.

[Appe68]
Appel A., Some techniques for shading machine renderings of solids, in *Proc. AFIPS 1968 Spring Joint Comput. Conf.*, Vol. 32, pp. 37–49, 1968.

[Arvo87]
Arvo, J., and Kirk, D., Fast ray tracing by ray classification, *Comput. Graph.*, Vol. 21, pp. 55–64, 1987 (SIGGRAPH 87).

[Baum86]
Baum, D.R., Wallace, J.R., Cohen, M.F., and Greenberg, D.P., The back-buffer: An extension of the radiosity method to dynamic environments, *The Visual Comput.*, Vol. 2, pp. 298–306, 1986.

[Bish86]
Bishop, G., and Weimer, D., Fast Phong shading, *Comput. Graph.*, Vol. 20, pp. 103–106, 1986 (SIGGRAPH 86).

[Blin76]
Blinn, J. F., and Newell, M.E., Texture and reflection in computer generated images, *CACM*, Vol. 19, pp. 542–547, 1976.

[Blin77]
Blinn, J.F., Models of light reflection for computer synthesized pictures, *Comput. Graph.*, Vol. 11, pp. 192–198, 1977 (SIGGRAPH 77).

[Blin78]
Blinn, J.F. (1978), Simulation of wrinkled surfaces, *Comput. Graph.*, Vol. 12, pp. 286–292, 1978 (SIGGRAPH 78).

[Blin82]
Blinn, J.F., A generalization of algebraic surface drawing, *ACM Trans. Graph.*, Vol. 1, pp. 235–256, 1982.

[Blin85]
Blinn, J.F., The ancient Chinese art of Chi-Ting, SIGGRAPH 85 Image Rendering Tricks Tutorial Course Notes.

[Bouk70]
Bouknight, W.J., A procedure for generation of three-dimensional half-toned computer graphics presentations, *CACM*, Vol. 13, pp. 527–536, 1970.

[Carp80]
Carpenter, L., Computer rendering of fractal curves and surfaces, *Comput. Graph.*, Vol. 14, p. 109, 1980 (SIGGRAPH 80).

[Carp84]
Carpenter, L., The A-buffer, an antialiased hidden surface method, *Comput. Graph.*, Vol. 18, pp. 103–108, 1984 (SIGGRAPH 84).

[Catm74]
Catmull, E.E., A Subdivision Algorithm for Computer Display of Curved Surfaces, Ph.D. Dissertation, University of Utah, Salt Lake City, Utah, 1974.

[Catm75]
Catmull, E.E., Computer display of curved surfaces, in *Proc. IEEE Conf. Comput. Graph., Pattern Recognition and Data Struct.* (May 1975), pp. 11–17, New York: IEEE Press, 1975.

[Cohe85]
Cohen, M.F., and Greenberg, D.P., The hemi-cube, a radiosity solution for complex environments, *Comput. Graph.*, Vol. 19, pp. 31–40, 1985 (SIGGRAPH 85).

[Cohe86]
Cohen, M.F., Greenberg, D.P., Immel, D. S., and Brock, P.J., An efficient radiosity approach for realistic image synthesis, *IEEE Comput. Graph. Appl.*, Vol. 6, pp. 26–35, 1986.

[Cook82]
Cook, R.L., and Torrance, K.E., A reflection model for computer graphics, *ACM Trans. Graph.*, Vol. 1, pp. 7–24, 1982.

[Cook84a]
Cook, R.L., Porter, T., and Carpenter, L., Distributed ray tracing, *Comput. Graph.*, Vol. 18, pp. 137–145, 1984 (SIGGRAPH 84).

[Cook84b]
Cook, R.L., Shade trees, *Comput. Graph.*, Vol. 18, pp. 223–231, 1984 (SIGGRAPH 84).

[Cook86]
Cook, R.L., Stochastic sampling in computer graphics, *ACM Trans. Graph.*, Vol. 5, pp. 51–72, 1986.

[Crow77]
Crow, F.C., The aliasing problem in computer-generated shaded images, *CACM*, Vol. 20, pp. 799–805, 1977.

[Crow81]
Crow, F.C., A comparison of antialiasing techniques, *IEEE Comput. Graph. Appl.*, Vol. 1, pp. 40–48, 1981.

[Crow84]
Crow, F.C., Summed-area tables for texture mapping, *Comput. Graph.*, Vol. 18, pp. 207–212, 1984 (SIGGRAPH 84.

[Dipp85]
Dippé, M.A.Z., and Wold, E., Antialiasing through stochastic sampling, *Comput. Graph.*, Vol. 19, pp. 69–78, 1985 (SIGGRAPH 85).

[Duff79]
Duff, T., Smoothly shaded renderings of polygonal objects on raster displays, *Comput. Graph.*, Vol. 13, pp. 270–275, 1979 (SIGGRAPH 79).

[Duff85]
Duff, T., Compositing 3-D rendered images, *Comput. Graph.*, Vol. 19, pp. 41–44, 1985 (SIGGRAPH 85).

[Fole84]
Foley, J., and Van Dam, A., *Fundamentals of Interactive Computer Graphics*, Reading, MA: Addison-Wesley Publishing Company, 1984.

[Four86]
Fournier, A., and Reeves, W.T., A simple model of ocean waves, *Comput. Graph.*, Vol. 20, pp. 75–84, 1986 (SIGGRAPH 86).

[Gard84]
Gardner, G.Y., Simulation of natural scenes using textured quadric surfaces, *Comput. Graph.*, Vol. 18, pp. 11–20, 1984 (SIGGRAPH 84).

[Gard85]
Gardner, G.Y., Visual simulation of clouds, *Comput. Graph.*, Vol. 19, pp. 297–303, 1985 (SIGGRAPH 85).

[Glas84]
Glassner, A.S., Space subdivision for fast ray tracing, *IEEE Comput. Graph. Appl.*, Vol. 4, pp. 15–22, 1984.

[Gora84]
Goral, C.M., Torrance, K.E., Greenberg, D.P., and Battaile, B., Modeling the interaction of light between diffuse surfaces, *Comput. Graph.*, Vol. 18, pp. 213–222, 1984 (SIGGRAPH 84).

[Gour71]
Gouraud, H., Continuous shading of curved surfaces, *IEEE Trans. Comput.*, Vol. C-20, pp. 623–629, 1971.

[Gree86]
Greenberg, D.P., Cohen, M.F., and Torrance, K.E., Radiosity: A method for computing global illumination, *The Visual Comput.*, Vol. 2, pp. 291–297, 1986.

[Hall83]
Hall, R.A., and Greenberg, D.P., A testbed for realistic image synthesis, *IEEE Comput. Graph. Appl.*, Vol. 3, pp. 10–20, 1983.

[Hall86]
Hall, R.A., Hybrid Algorithms for Rapid Image Synthesis, SIGGRAPH 86 Rendering Tricks Tutorial Course Notes.

[Hall88]
Hall, R.A., *Illumination and Color in Computer Generated Imagery*, New York: Springer-Verlag, 1988.

[Imme86]
Immel, D.S., Cohen, M.F., and Greenberg, D.P., A radiosity method for non-diffuse environments, *Comput. Graph.*, Vol. 20, pp. 133–142, 1986 (SIGGRAPH 86).

[Kaji85]
Kajiya, J.T., Anisotropic reflection models, *Comput. Graph.*, Vol. 19, pp. 15–21, 1985 (SIGGRAPH 85).

[Kaji86]
Kajiya, J.T., The rendering equation, *Comput. Graph.*, Vol. 20, pp. 143–150, 1986 (SIGGRAPH 86.

[Kapl85]
Kaplan, M.R., The uses of spatial coherence in ray-tracing, SIGGRAPH 85 State of the Art in Image Synthesis Course Notes, 1985.

[Kay79]
Kay, D.S., and Greenberg, D.P., Transparency for computer synthesized images, *Comput. Graph.*, Vol. 13, pp. 158–164, 1979 (SIGGRAPH 79).

[Kay86]
Kay, T.L., and Kajiya, J.T., Ray tracing complex scenes, *Comput. Graph.*, Vol. 20, pp. 269–278, 1986 (SIGGRAPH 86).

[Lee85]
Lee, M.E., Redner, R.A., and Uselton, S.P., Statistically optimized sampling for distributed ray tracing, *Comput. Graph.*, Vol. 19, pp. 61–67, 1985 (SIGGRAPH 85).

[Max81]
Max, N.L., Vectorized procedural models for natural terrain: Waves and islands in the sunset, *Comput. Graph.*, Vol. 15, pp. 317–324, 1981 (SIGGRAPH 81).

[Max86]
Max, N.L., Atmosphere illumination and shadows, *Comput. Graph.*, Vol. 20, pp. 117–124, 1986 (SIGGRAPH 86).

[Meye86]
Meyer, G.W., Rushmeier, H.E., Cohen, M.F., and Greenberg, D.P., An experimental evaluation of computer graphics imagery, *ACM Trans. Graph.*, Vol. 5, pp. 30–50, 1986.

[Mill85]
Mills, M.I., Image synthesis, optical identity or pictorial communication, in *Computer Generated Images, The State of the Art*, Magnenat-Thalmann, N., and Thalmann, D., Eds., pp. 3–10, New York: Springer-Verlag, 1985.

[Mitc87]
Mitchell, D.P., Generating antialiased images at low sampling densities, *Comput. Graph.*, Vol. 21, pp. 65–72, 1987 (SIGGRAPH 87).

[Newe72]
Newell, M., Newell, R., and Sancha, T., A solution to the hidden surface problem, in *Proc. ACM Natl. Conf.*, pp. 443–450, New York: ACM Press, 1972.

[Newm79]
Newman, W., and Sproull, R., *Principles of Interactive Computer Graphics*, 2nd Ed., New York: McGraw-Hill, 1979.

[Nish85]
Nishita, T., and Nakamae, E., Continuous tone representations of three dimensional objects taking account of shadows and interreflection, *Comput. Graph.*, Vol. 19, pp. 23–30, 1985 (SIGGRAPH 85).

[Nish87]
Nishita, T., and Nakamae, E., A shading model for atmospheric scattering considering the luminous intensity distribution of light sources, *Comput. Graph.*, Vol. 21, pp. 303–308, 1987 (SIGGRAPH 87).

[Peac86]

Peachy, D.R., Modeling waves and surf, *Comput. Graph.*, Vol. 20, pp. 65–74, 1986 (SIGGRAPH 86).

[Phon75]

Phong, B.T., Illumination for computer generated pictures, *CACM*, Vol. 18, pp. 311–317, 1975.

[Port84]

Porter, T., and Duff, T., Compositing digital images, *Comput. Graph.*, Vol. 18, pp. 223–231, 1984 (SIGGRAPH 84).

[Reev83]

Reeves, W.T., Particle systems—A technique for modeling a class of fuzzy objects, *Comput. Graph.*, Vol. 17, pp. 359–376, 1983 (SIGGRAPH 83).

[Reev85]

Reeves, W.T., and Blau, R., Approximate and probabilistic algorithms for shading and rendering structured particle systems, *Comput. Graph.*, Vol. 19, pp. 313–322, 1985 (SIGGRAPH 85).

[Roge85]

Rogers, D.F., *Procedural Elements for Computer Graphics*, New York: McGraw-Hill, 1985.

[Romn69]

Romney, G.W., Computer Assisted Assembly and Rendering of Solids, Ph.D. Dissertation, Department of Electrical Engineering, University of Utah, Salt Lake City, Utah, 1969.

[Rubi80]

Rubin, S. and Whitted, T., A three-dimensional representation for fast rendering of complex scenes, *Comput. Graph.*, Vol. 14, pp. 110–116, 1980 (SIGGRAPH 80).

[Rush87]

Rushmeier, H.E., and Torrance, K.E., The zonal method for calculating light intensities in the presence of a participating medium, *Comput. Graph.*, Vol. 21, pp. 293–302, 1987 (SIGGRAPH 87).

[Smit84]

Smith, A.R., Plants, fractals, and formal languages, *Comput. Graph.*, Vol. 18, pp. 1–10, 1984 (SIGGRAPH 84).

[Snyd87]

Snyder, J.M., and Barr, A.H., Ray tracing complex models containing surface tessellations, *Comput. Graph.*, Vol. 21, pp. 119–128, 1987 (SIGGRAPH 87).

[Suth74]

Sutherland, I. E., Sproull, R.F., and Schumacker, R.A., A characterization of ten hidden-surface algorithms, *Comput. Surveys*, Vol. 6, pp. 1–55, 1974.

[VonH87]

Von Herzen, B., and Barr, A.H., Accurate triangulation of deformed intersecting surfaces, *Comput. Graph.*, Vol. 21, pp. 103–110, 1987 (SIGGRAPH 87).

[Voss85]
Voss, R.F., Random fractal forgeries, in *Fundamental Algorithms for Computer Graphics*, Earnshaw, R.A., Ed., pp. 805–835, New York: Springer-Verlag, 1985.

[Wall81]
Wallace, B.A., Merging and transformation of raster images for cartoon animation, *Comput. Graph.*, Vol. 15, pp. 253–262, 1981 (SIGGRAPH 81).

[Wall87]
Wallace, J.R., Cohen, M.F., and Greenberg, D.P., A two-pass solution to the rendering equation: A synthesis of ray tracing and radiosity techniques, *Comput. Graph.*, Vol. 21, pp. 311–328, 1987 (SIGGRAPH 87.

[Warn69]
Warnock, J.E., A Hidden Surface Algorithm for Halftone Picture Representation, Ph.D. Dissertation, Department of Computer Science, University of Utah, Salt Lake City, 1969.

[Wegh84]
Weghorst, H., Hooper, G., and Greenberg, D.P., Improved computational methods for ray tracing, *ACM Trans. Graph.*, Vol. 3, pp. 52–69, 1984.

[Whit80]
Whitted, T., An improved illumination model for shaded display, *CACM*, Vol. 23, pp. 343–349, 1980.

[Whit82]
Whitted, T., Processing requirements for hidden surface elimination and realistic shading, *Proc. COMPCON 82*, February 1982.

[Will83]
Williams, L., Pyramidal Parametrics, *Comput. Graph.*, Vol. 17, pp. 1–11, 1983 (SIGGRAPH 83).

4 Animation

A Computer Animation Tutorial

Brian Wyvill

Abstract

This tutorial presents an overview of 3D computer animation. Techniques for modelling and rendering are briefly described and taxonomies of the available techniques are given. Methods for motion control are dealt with in greater detail and, again, a taxonomy of the different approaches to this topic is presented. The second part of the paper describes how implicit surfaces (known as SOFT objects) may be used for modelling and animation. Using this technique, models that change shape as they move can be easily set in motion.

Part I—Computer Animation

Introduction

In the last ten years, computers have become sufficiently fast and inexpensive to allow a computer animation industry to grow from almost zero to 150 million dollars by 1987. During this time the technology has advanced sufficiently to permit the making of landmark animated shorts, from Peter Foldes' *La Faim* (1974), with software by Nestor Burtnyk and Marcelli Wein [Burt76], to John Lasseter's *Luxo Junior* (1986) [Lass87], with software by Bill Reeves et al. from Pixar. The skeleton techniques used in *La Faim* were essentially 2D. The method employed extended the traditional animation concept of 'key framing'. When using this technique, an animator draws a character posed in two or more 'key' positions and uses the computer to generate interpolated drawings in the frames spanning between them. By contrast, *Luxo Junior* used 3D computer animation in which digital models of the characters and backgrounds are described in 3D space and are moved using a variety of techniques, such as by simulating the dynamics of each motion. The common thread binding these two animated pieces is not that a computer was used to produce the pictures, but that they both succeed as animated shorts because the artists who made them share the same skills that have always distinguished good animators.

The computer has allowed them to produce their art in an exciting new form and has opened the door to many other enthusiasts who may have the ideas and the ability to breathe life into a character but who lack traditional draughting skills. Although there are several commercially available animation systems, the best computer-animated films are generated by a team consisting of at least one animator and one computer scientist. Regardless of how sophisticated and general purpose the tools are that an animation package provides, animators often want to go beyond the capabilities offered, and require a programming solution. The technology is advancing extremely quickly: hardware becomes faster and cheaper, and the volume of literature describing new software techniques grows alarmingly each year. An animator buying a system today could be put out of business by his competitor who has tomorrow's system.

There are many applications of computer animation in industries other than entertainment and advertising. Flight and other simulators have attained a fair degree of sophistication, responding with real-time graphics to a user's inputs. Scientific visualisation uses the techniques of computer animation to present complex data in a more pleasing and intelligible form. Such applications are intimately linked with simulation, and techniques from that discipline are generally useful in others.

In this tutorial, the fundamentals of 3D animation are presented with particular emphasis on motion control, or on how to make models move. Of course, the work of an animator will always be judged by the final result, but a working knowledge of existing tools is a means to help him to convey the vision in his mind to the big (or little) screen with less tedious effort.

The Elements of 3D Computer Animation

In traditional animation, the end product is a series of cells that are overlaid and photographed for each film frame, often with additional optical effects such as pans and zooms added at the camera stage. Reaching this final production requires many steps, including designing characters and backgrounds and prototyping movements with flip books or by filming rough sketches (known as 'pencil tests'). Key frame drawings are made and the inbetween segments are drawn and tested; this leaves a series of pencil drawings that must be inked and painted, each character possibly being done in isolation on sheets of clear acetate. Backgrounds are painted, and the results are composited and photographed.

Model animation involves the building of a miniature world. High-tech cameras with periscope lenses are used to photograph the models, giving them a sense of scale. Every movement of each character must be carefully calculated and the model changed with skill and care. Like model animation, 3D animation also requires that the artist create a 3D world. Each character and background object must be crafted using one of a variety of digital techniques.

As with model animation, specifying the motions of these computer models is the most complex operation to be carried out and the one for which the least amount of packaged software is available. The computer animator has the advantage that the digital equivalent of a camera is weightless, sizeless, and can be moved along any desired path. Each frame of the 3D scene must be rendered: a view is chosen and the 3D model is projected as a 2D shaded image. This operation has been the subject of much research, and there are many techniques available for it. Usually, rendering algorithms present a trade-off between picture quality and computation time. There are steps beyond rendering: transferring the finished images to film or video, and subsequent editing. Since complex animation frames at high resolution cannot, in general, be manufactured in real time, this last step requires some special hardware and a talented film or video editor.

To manufacture the finished animation frames requires the following major steps:

modelling;

motion control;

rendering.

Figures 1, 2, and 3 summarise these three areas, showing a taxonomy of each. The following sections present brief descriptions of trends in modelling and rendering and a somewhat more detailed review of motion control. In the second part of this paper, a modelling method which uses implicit surfaces is described, and the way in which this technique is particularly appropriate for certain kinds of animation is shown.

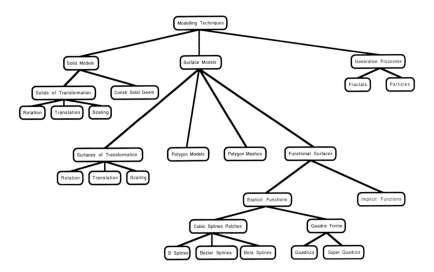

Figure 1. A taxonomy of modelling techniques.

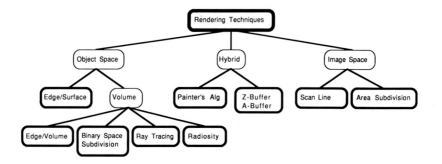

LIGHTING MODELS

Constant Shading   [Bouknight,80]
Colour Value Interpolation [Gouraud,71]
Surface Normal Interpolation [Phong,75]
Ray Tracing [Witted,80][Cook,82][Cook,84]
Radiosity [Cohen,85][Cohen,86][Greenberg,86]

TEXTURE MAPPING

2D Textures [Catmull,74][Blinn,76][Blinn,78][Feibush,80]
3D Textures [Perlin,85][Peachey,85][Wyvill,87]

Figure 2. A taxonomy of rendering techniques.

Modelling

Building models for computers to display is a natural application and was
accomplished in the 1950s on vector displays and graph plotters. Any
mathematical function which produces points on a surface in 3D space
could potentially form the basis of a modelling method. However, with
many such techniques it is difficult to achieve the desired shape and also
difficult to render the resultant surfaces. Since this tutorial is mainly concerned with motion control, only a brief explanation has been given for
the major areas of modelling. Figure 1 shows various classes of modelling
techniques. There are three main categories:

 surface modelling;

 solid modelling;

 generative processes.

SURFACE MODELLING

As the name implies, in surface modelling information is stored about the
surface of the model. A point in space is either on the surface or it is
not. A polygon mesh is an example of such a model. Some objects which
have many curved surfaces are best modelled using curved spline patches.
Patches are based on parametric cubic curves. Some of the latest work
done in this area permits the user to have fine control over the shape of the
patch; smooth curves and sharp changes in slope can be described using
beta splines [Bart87]. This technique allows the user to make a curved

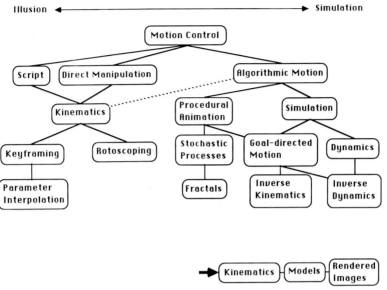

Figure 3. A taxonomy of motion control techniques.

surface patch and then smoothly join it to others, forming a solid object. Implicit surfaces, or SOFT objects, are different from parametric surfaces because they have a different mathematical definition, which is discussed in Part 2 of this paper. Like patches, they are defined by a set of keys but, unlike patches, they have the property that they can be blended merely by placing their 'keys' near each other. Part 2 presents methods for modelling and animating these surfaces.

SOLID MODELLING

In solid modelling, models are described by the volume of space that they occupy. A solid model has an inside and an outside. Constructive Solid Geometry (CSG) is a solid modelling technique where objects are built from primitives that are usually defined as quadrics (sphere, cylinder, plane, etc.). The primitives can be combined; for example, to make a hole through a sphere, a cylinder is subtracted from the sphere. CSG systems are often implemented using an octree data structure.

GENERATIVE PROCESSES

These can apply to either of the above categories: models can be generated by some algorithmic process, as with fractals [Mand77] or particle systems [Reev83]. A recent example of a generative process that has been used to produce 3D models is an extension of Conway's life game to 3D [Thal86].

COMPOSING MODELS

It may be appropriate to build one model from a variety of primitives. This is usually accomplished by structuring the model as a hierarchy, as the Graphicsland system does [Wyvi86a]. Figure 4 shows a tree built, using a recursive hierarchy, from polygons, with particle systems as leaves. Fractal mountains appear in the background.

Rendering

During the 1970s and 1980s, much research was put into the development of rendering algorithms. The main obstacle is that if a scene consists of n objects, then a naive algorithm will compare each object with every other object to check if it is occluded from a particular viewpoint ($O(n^2)$). If n is large, this is a time-consuming task. The class of rendering algorithms whose time complexity depends purely on n is known as *object space* algorithms. Another class of rendering algorithms work in *image space*, where the screen resolution or number of pixels becomes the dominant factor [Suth74].

One early algorithm simulates the paths of light rays: the *ray-tracing* algorithm sends out rays from the eye point through the scene and finds the intersections between the ray and any object on its path. Ray tracing has the benefit that rays can be traced recursively as they are transmitted through transparent objects and reflected from shiny ones. Rays can also

Figure 4. Graphicsland made from polygons, particles, and fractal mountains.

be traced from an object intersection point towards the light source(s); if an object is on the ray path then the intersection point is in shadow. (Figure 5 shows a ray-traced rabbit with shadows.) Early versions checked all m rays against all n objects in the scene. Since m can be tens of thousands, or millions, for antialiased scenes, the algorithm is slow. One way of speeding up ray tracing is to reduce the number of intersection calculations on a ray's path, either by surrounding each object, or hierarchy of objects, with a bounding volume, or by subdividing the scene space. In the latter case, the volume of the scene is split into cubic cells (*voxels*), and the objects are sorted into the voxels which contain them. (Some objects will appear in more than one voxel.) Each ray is intersected with each voxel that it must pass through and, if any objects are present in the voxel, only then is it necessary to check for intersections of the ray with those objects. Since many objects may be clustered in a few voxels, further subdivision may take place; in this case the voxel is often stored as an octree data structure [Glas84; Kay86; Clea88].

To manufacture highly realistic scenes great attention must be paid to the lighting model employed. An object may be partly illuminated by light reflected from other objects as well as by primary light sources. Most lighting models account for reflected light by adding a constant ambient light value into the illumination of every point. Recent work employs a technique known as *radiosity* [Imme86], in which each surface is broken into patches, and the illumination effect on each patch by every *other* patch in the scene is calculated. This technique produces excellent results but requires large amounts of computer time. An excellent book on illumination models including radiosity is [Hall89].

Surface detail is often added during the rendering stage rather than by trying to model small details. Early work on *texture mapping* was done by Catmull [Catm80] and Feibush [Feib80] in which 2D images were mapped onto 3D objects. Later work [Perl85; Peac85; Wyvi87] used 3D functions to specify the colour or direction of the reflection vector (surface normal) at any point in space. Figure 6 shows conventional textures on the walls

Figure 5. Ray-traced rabbit.

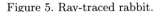

and 3D 'wood' texture on the four posts of the bed. A combination of sine waves with amplitude, frequency, and phase modulation in x, y, and z was used to create the 3D texture space in which the wood exists. For a full treatment of rendering algorithms, see the references at the end of this paper.

Animation—Controlling the Motion

To animate, we wish to simulate the appearance of motion of real objects. This motion control falls roughly into two classes:

   simulation;
   illusion.

To look natural, animation has to represent possible motion in the physical world. In this sense, the best animation is based on detailed simulation that accounts for the dynamics of the action. In such a simulation, a mathematical model representing the physical laws that govern the motion would, as a consequence, produce the desired effect. In many applications it is not necessary for an animation sequence to be an accurate dynamic model; unless the animation is intended to visualise the results of a simulation, it is only required to make the motion *appear* realistic to a human viewer. The technique of *faring* in hand animation can be regarded as a crude attempt to use a few simple rules to do this. Faring creates the *illusion* of

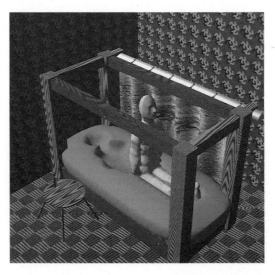

Figure 6. Creating the right impression.

acceleration that would be present in an accurate dynamic *simulation* of the same motion. The taxonomy of motion control (Figure 3) portrays this distinction.

At the lowest level, 3D computer animation is based on specifying the position and orientation of an object at some time. This *kinematic* description of animation can be manufactured by a whole variety of techniques. At the highest level an animator may wish to give a command such as 'walk to the door'; it would then be up to the system to calculate how that walk is to be achieved and finally to produce the kinematic description for the low-level part of the system (inverse kinematics). Such *goal-directed* animation is the subject of much current research with applications in robotics as well as the entertainment/advertising animation industry. At an intermediate level, for example, an animator may wish to show a falling human. Given the constraints and initial condition, the system can then formulate a set of differential equations that describe the fall. This *dynamics* approach should produce an accurate simulation of the motion provided the dynamic model is sufficiently detailed. To illustrate the difference between a dynamic simulation and the kinematic approach (aided by a script file or interactive system), consider a bouncing ball. The animator can define a ball and move the position of the ball along a damped sine curve as illustrated in Figure 7. The dynamic solution would calculate the position of the ball from the Newtonian equations

$$v^2 = u^2 + 2gs \qquad (1)$$

$$s = ut + gt^2/2 \qquad (2)$$

Provided the initial conditions were known, this very simple dynamic model could look quite reasonable except that the motion would not cease very accurately. In fact, the physical model used is incomplete. No term has been added for air resistance or to account for the material that the ball is made from. These factors would cause the motion to damp out. An example of using a dynamic solution applied to human animation is given in the later section on Chmilar/Herr experiment.

KEY FRAME INTERPOLATION

In hand animation, an animator will draw a character in some position, make a second drawing of the character in a new position, and then manufacture the inbetween frames. The digital equivalent to this is to interpolate between key positions of models. A simple approach would be to use linear interpolation between key frames but, in real life, objects don't start and stop suddenly—depending on the situation there is usually some kind of smooth acceleration. Neither should interpolation necessarily take place along a straight line in space. Particularly with camera moves, a series of straight line segments would make the motion appear discontinuous as

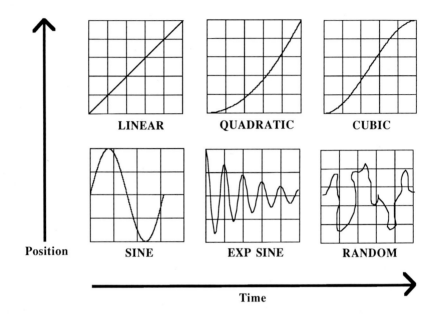

Figure 7. Sample motion curves.

the camera suddenly changed direction. A smooth curve would be far more natural.

Figure 8 shows another problem introduced by linear interpolation in space. To move the rod from $P1Q1$ to $P2Q2$ implies a rotation. Linear interpolation would make the rod change length as it rotated. Smooth motion curves can be applied to any part of the animation in both space and time: in space, as shown in Figure 8, and also in time to make the rod ease in and ease out of the motion (cubic curve) as it moves. Models, lights, cameras, fades, colours, and so forth can all follow some interpolated path according to a curve. The simplest method is to use a function such as a cubic polynomial, from which the position is sampled at any instant in time. Since the function is continuous, time between key frames can be scaled arbitrarily by the animator before the final sampling is taken. Some examples are given in Figure 7.

PARAMETRIC INTERPOLATION

Parametric systems use key frame interpolation at a slightly higher level than simple key frame systems. Each object is defined by a set of parameters, and the values of these parameters are interpolated between the keys.

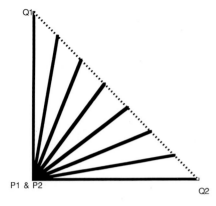

Figure 8. Using linear interpolation
for rotation doesn't work.

If a model is defined by surface patches, for example, the control points
can be interpolated and the patches reshaped from the new data. Examples of this type of system are BBOP or EM, both developed at the NYIT
Graphics Lab and described by Sturman [Stur84] and Hanrahan [Hanr85].
More elaborate control of the motion is discussed by Steketee [Stek85] in
a system that guarantees continuous acceleration while still having local
control of key points and the ability to join motions. Kochanek points
out that splines can avoid the discontinuities in the direction and speed of
motion that are produced by linear interpolation. She introduces the use
of three control parameters, bias, tension, and continuity, to provide the
animator with more control over the motion [Koch84].

As well as smooth motion through time, it is important that camera
moves follow smooth motion paths through space. Using Kochanek's spline
technique, the animator can place a camera at a number of key frames,
then interpolate smoothly between them through space and time. Similar
control can be applied to any other object. Sometimes a discontinuity in
time is required, for example when objects collide or interact. One way
of representing this motion is to apply a suitable motion curve: at any
time the position of the object can be found from a curve such as those
shown in Figure 7. Sometimes the animator will want more control than
that provided by say a damped sine wave. Kochanek's curves allow the
animator to smoothly change the 'continuity' parameter to produce the
desired results.

Sometimes the animator will want to change one model into another as
opposed to the normal inbetween problem of interpolating between different
positions of the same model. The main problem with such a *metamorphosis*
is that the source and destination models may not precisely match. If the
objects are polygonal, they may contain different numbers of polygons or
the polygons may not have the same numbers of vertices. These problems
are not found when using the same model in different positions. A more
detailed examination of metamorphosis is given in Part 2.

SCRIPTING SYSTEMS

Key frame animation has the advantage that an animator can interact with the motion and specify movements by direct manipulation. However, much animation is algorithmic in nature and difficult to specify interactively. For this reason, many systems allow the user to specify the animation in a script. There are many examples [Chua83; Thal85; Reyn82; Zelt82]. The Ani system [McPh84] is typical. Ani, part of the Graphicsland system, reads a script and produces a description of every frame in PG, a modelling language. It is a multiple track system. Instead of describing each key frame, each object pursues its own course of action; the animator creates tracks of animation and places objects on their own track. The object is moved by interpolation as in a parametric system; however, the difference is that the tracks are independent and a total description of each frame does not exist explicitly. A track is effectively a list of known events in time. A good example of such a system is Twixt [Gome85]. Scripts in this system are kept as a log of the animators input, which is purely interactive. An example of an animation script is given in the section on the Chmilar/Herr experiment.

A somewhat more powerful but less high-level approach than a scripting system is to extend an existing general-purpose programming language to provide an environment where it is easy to specify algorithmic animation while also offering the full power of a programming language. The MIRA animation system [Thal85] is a good example of the language Pascal extended to cope with animation.

Most animation systems store the models in some sort of hierarchy. A model is manufactured from different parts, each containing subparts, and so on. Each node in the hierarchy contains a geometric transformation matrix which defines how the part is translated, rotated, and scaled relative to its parent. For example, a train puffs smoke that moves along with the train; after 1/2 second the train continues leaving the smoke behind to disperse in the wind. The whole animation is then repeated every two seconds. A script system allows such algorithmic animation to be defined without the animator having to learn a full programming language. The problem is algorithmic: in each cycle, the smoke, which has its own local motion associated with it, must be attached to the engine. The easiest way is to move the smoke relative to the chimney until the smoke must be left behind. While the smoke is 'owned' by the chimney (which in turn is 'owned' by the train), everything that happens to the train (i.e., geometric transformations) also happens to the chimney and, in turn, to the puff of smoke. As soon as the chimney ceases to own the puff, the puff no longer moves with the train. However, the global position of the smoke in the world is required to remain the same. To achieve this, the puff must be attached to some object, in this case, the land after 1/2 second. Figure 9 shows the structure. One of the problems with altering the topology of an object in motion is what happens to the orphaned part, in this case, the puff of smoke. It has velocity and possibly some acceleration since it is travelling with the train. In the example, the puff will come to an abrupt halt unless the data structure carries sufficient information to allow the object to be eased out of its motion. Many animation systems have separate data structures for the model and for the animation. By using the modelling hierarchy to also store the motion control information, velocity and acceleration become information that is readily accessible when the topology of the system is altered dynamically.

ROTOSCOPING

When human animation was first attempted, movement data was often retrieved via *motion recording*. Rotoscoping was one such method, where joint coordinates were hand-digitized by viewing at least two orthogonal views of a previously recorded scene (on film or video) [Rids86]. Though such a technique was tedious, it began the trend toward analysing human motion for computer animation. Later techniques included the use of goniometers and (expensive) video scanning equipment to record 3D motion. The results allowed some of the first reasonable animation sequences of human figures, but the techniques used were ultimately too specific to adequately address the human animation problem.

INVERSE KINEMATICS

Direct kinematics seems to be used mostly in low-level animation systems where movements must be described by the animator. To simplify the methods for specifying motion, higher levels of description are needed. One

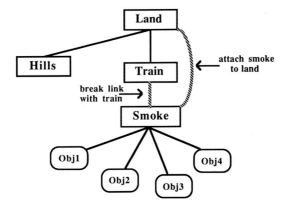

Figure 9. Animation Hierarchy (see example under script systems).

such method is inverse kinematics. Rather than calculate the position of a distal segment based on given joint rotations (as in direct kinematics), in inverse kinematics the joint rotations are calculated based on the position of the distal segment [Wilh87]. This allows for more natural movement specifications such as 'move hand to cup'.

Wilhelms [Wilh87] notes that inverse kinematics provides a method of constraining bodies within their world. A walking figure, for example, must have its feet constrained to the ground (the tendency is for a swing motion in which the foot drops below the ground level). Reach goals, often used in robotics, are also solved with inverse kinematics by specifying the location a robotic arm should reach for and letting the joint calculations be automatically generated. This leads us to a problem found in human animation but not in robotics: how is a movement made to appear human?

The manner in which a robot arm reaches its goal is not important (ignoring collisions for now); however, when animating human forms the motions must appear realistic. In what order and with what speed and extent do joints rotate to allow the distal segment to reach its goal? What constitutes a natural human motion is not clear. The redundancy of the human figure contributes to this problem. Even if one movement were determined, this solution would not generalise to other movements and certainly not to other limbs. To date, no adequate solution for this problem has been offered.

MOTION DYNAMICS FOR ANIMATION

Dynamics analysis considers mass, force, and the effects of both combined. It is a simulation of the world and therefore offers a more automatic approach than kinematics. Dynamics analysis also offers a more 'complete' analysis of a scene as it considers effects of bodies on each other. It is, however, computationally expensive and has therefore not been implemented in many systems until recent years.

Newton's second law [Wilh87] is the basis for the simulation used in dynamics:

$$F = ma$$

Dynamics equations are developed for each degree of freedom in a scene. A rigid, articulated figure with 18 degrees of freedom that is free to move or rotate in its environment has a total of 24 dynamics equations associated with it. Various types of equations can be used depending on the application. Lagrangian, Gibbs-Appell, and recursive dynamics equations are quite common.

To define the forces and torques acting on a body, several methods can be employed. One method is to provide automatic calculation of forces and torques that have known equations associated with them (such as gravity). Another method is to model springs and dampers for certain joints and segments. The final method relies on user input. Clearly, this input cannot be too complex if the system is to be useful.

Wilhelms [Wilh87] notes three problems associated with dynamics analysis:

the cost of the analysis is high;

a numerical instability exists when bodies are complex;

motion control is restricted to high levels only.

Wilhelms has implemented a system called Deva that uses dynamics analysis to animate rigid, articulated bodies [Wilh85]. Armstrong and Green have also been using dynamics analysis for motion control and have published several interesting results [Arms85].

The Chmilar/Herr experiment

To illustrate the difference between dynamics and kinematics, a somewhat ad hoc experiment where two animator/programmers were asked to make a short piece of animation showing a human figure falling from a diving board was conducted. The figure must make 3/4 of a somersault before reaching a mattress on the ground. The figure should then bounce from the mattress. Both animators assumed the figure to be limp.

THE KINEMATIC SOLUTION

To produce a kinematic solution requires that the animator has a keen eye for detail and is able to capture the essential parts of the motion to convey what is happening. Using the Graphicsland system the motion is prototyped, alterations are made, and a new cycle is begun; everything is done by trial and error. By observing a physical model it was seen that the man would do half a twist and obviously accelerate under gravity. As the figure began to fall he would rotate about the heel position until he left the platform. The man would then spin about his centre of mass. The major motions were blocked out and observed with a rigid stick figure. By trial and error, various motions of limbs were added. What followed was a critical adjustment of the various parameters (joint angles, etc.) that defined the motion. It became apparent that the hips should 'lead' the motion with other body parts following. It was also noticed that a pair of good flailing arms conveyed the idea that the figure was falling more convincingly than getting the acceleration of the figure precise. The final animation script in Ani is as follows.

```
# detailed body limb motions

spin upper_body x -15 1..6 smooth
```

```
spin upper_body x 30 9..15 smooth
spin upper_body x -15 20..21 steady
#
spin upper_body x -10 21..24 smooth
spin upper_body x 30 24..29 smooth
spin upper_body x -20 32..33 steady
#
spin upper_body x -5 33..35 smooth
spin upper_body x 17 35..38 smooth
spin upper_body x -12 38..39 steady

spin head x -14 1..9 smooth
spin head x 18 11..17 smooth
spin head x -4 20..21 steady

spin r_arm x 25 1..8 smooth
spin r_arm x -40 11..20 smooth
spin r_arm z -70 9..18 smooth
spin r_arm x 15 20..21 steady
#
spin r_arm z 40 21..24 smooth 22
spin r_arm x 40 21..23 smooth
spin r_arm x -80 23..32 smooth
spin r_arm x 40 32..33 steady
#
spin r_arm z 10 33..36 smooth 34
spin r_arm x 20 33..34 smooth
spin r_arm x -40 34..38 smooth
spin r_arm x 20 38..39 steady

spin l_arm x 22 1..7 smooth
spin l_arm x -34 11..20 smooth
spin l_arm z 50 14..20 smooth
spin l_arm x 12 20..21 steady
#
spin l_arm z -30 21..24 smooth 22
spin l_arm x 38 21..23 smooth
spin l_arm x -76 23..32 smooth
spin l_arm x 38 32..33 steady
#
spin l_arm z -10 33..36 smooth 34
spin l_arm x 18 33..34 smooth
spin l_arm x -36 34..38 smooth
spin l_arm x 18 38..39 steady

spin r_lower_arm x 30 10..18 smooth
spin r_lower_arm x -30 20..21 steady
```

```
spin l_lower_arm x 30 9..18 smooth
spin l_lower_arm x -30 20..21 steady

spin r_leg x 3 1..5 smooth
spin r_leg x 7 11..16 smooth
spin r_leg x -10 20..21 steady
spin r_leg z -20 12..16 smooth
spin r_leg z 23 16..20 smooth

spin l_leg x 3 1..5 smooth
spin l_leg x -10 11..15 smooth
spin l_leg x 7 19..20 steady
spin l_leg z -25 12..15 smooth
spin l_leg z 20 16..20 smooth
#
spin l_leg x -15 20..29 smooth 23
spin l_leg x 15 29..33 smooth 32
#
spin l_leg x -6 32..37 smooth 34
spin l_leg x 6 37..39 smooth

spin l_lower_leg x 3 1..6 smooth
spin l_lower_leg x -3 20..21 steady
#
spin l_lower_leg x 7 21..26 smooth
spin l_lower_leg x -7 32..33 smooth

spin r_lower_leg x 2 1..5 smooth
spin r_lower_leg x -2 20..21 steady
#
spin r_lower_leg x 6 21..25 smooth
spin r_lower_leg x -6 32..33 steady

spin lower_body x -20 14..20 smooth
spin lower_body x 20 20..21 steady
#
spin lower_body x 10 21..24 smooth
spin lower_body x -30 24..29 smooth
spin lower_body x 20 32..33 steady
#
spin lower_body x 8 33..35 smooth
spin lower_body x -22 35..38 smooth
spin lower_body x 14 38..39 steady

# major body motions

# spin on heels
spin body y -180 1
spin body y -180 8..20 slowin 16
```

```
move body 0 3.3 0 1    #translate body up to rotate around heels
move body 0 0 0 10     #translate to rotate around hips
rotate body x 270 1..20 slowin 14
move body 0 24 -6 1

# fall after 90 degrees reached
move body 0 20.7 -2.7 10
move body 0 0 -2.7 10..20 steady #NOTE: not slowin!

# bounce one
move body 0 4 -2.7 20..26 slowout
move body 0 0 -2.7 27..32 slowin

# bounce two
move body 0 2 -2.7 33..35 slowout
move body 0 0 -2.7 36..38 slowin
```

THE DYNAMIC SOLUTION

To solve the problem of the falling man by the dynamics approach requires a different set of skills compared with the kinematic. The essence of dynamics is that motions are described by differential equations. Two methods were considered:

consider forces and torques involved and use $F = ma$ and $\tau = I\alpha$;

consider energy and use Lagrange's equation.

It turned out that the first approach required a great deal of algebra to arrive at the required set of differential equations compared with using Lagrange's equation. Some of the reasons why Lagrange's equations are useful are:

physical intuition helps if you want to get the forces right;

dealing with energy (scalar) is somewhat easier than using vector quantities;

Lagrange's equation allows the easy use of constraint equations;

Lagrange's equation allows us to introduce new coordinates that can make the problem easier.

The major steps in deriving differential equations with Lagrange's equation are:

(a) pick suitable coordinates;

(b) write constraint relations between coordinates;

(c) write the kinetic and potential energy expressions;

(d) use Lagrange's equation to get the differential equations;

(e) differentiate the constraint relations to get enough equations so that all the accelerations can be solved for (accelerations are the crucial quantities to solve for in these problems);

(f) write expressions for the generalised forces; the limits on how far each limb can rotate, damping, the mattress force.

The first major difference between the dynamic and kinematic approaches is that the problem is too hard to solve dynamically without making some simplifying assumptions (at least in the one week that was allotted for this experiment):

the man lies in a vertical plane (Note: a full 3D version is being prepared);

the body has only three segments—body, arms, and legs;

the man is initially leaning over the edge of the diving board.

Two systems of differential equations are used:

System 1—Constraints are included to bind the feet to the diving board.

System 2—No constraints are included to bind the feet to the diving board.

Initially System 1 is used; when the body is below the board, System 2 is used. The final conditions for System 1 are the initial conditions for System 2.

Figure 10 shows the body model used for the animation. Since the left and right sides of the body do not work independently, only five coordinates are needed to describe the position of the body:

x, y = position of centre of mass of the body (mass = m)

θ = angle body makes with horizontal

θ_1 = angle legs make with horizontal

θ_2 = angle arms make with horizontal

Other coordinates are introduced for convenience:

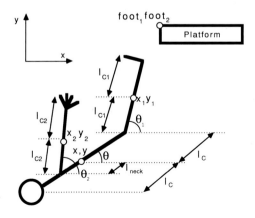

Figure 10. Body model for dynamic animation.

x_1, y_1 = position of centre of mass of the legs (mass = m_1)

x_2, y_2 = position of centre of mass of the arms (mass = m_2)

Moments of inertia for arms, legs, and body can be expressed as

$$I = \frac{1}{12}ml_c^2 \qquad I_1 = \frac{1}{12}m_1 l_{c_1}^2 \qquad I_2 = \frac{1}{12}m_2 l_{c_2}^2$$

Constraint Equations

$$x_1 = x + l_c \cos\theta + l_{c_1} \cos\theta_1$$

or

$$f_{1x} = x_1 - x - l_c \cos\theta - l_{c_1} \cos\theta_1$$

$$f_{1y} = y_1 - y - l_c \sin\theta - l_{c_1} \sin\theta_1$$

$$f_{2x} = x_2 - x + l_{\text{neck}} \cos\theta - l_{c_2} \cos\theta_2$$

$$f_{2y} = y_2 - y + l_{\text{neck}} \sin\theta - l_{c_2} \sin\theta_2$$

While the foot is constrained to the platform:

$$f_{\text{foot}_x} = \text{foot}_x - x_1 - l_{c_1} \cos\theta_1$$

$$f_{\text{foot}_y} = \text{foot}_y - y_1 - l_{c_1} \sin\theta_1$$

Kinetic Energy

$$T = \frac{1}{2}mv^2 + \frac{1}{2}I\omega^2$$

v = speed of centre of mass

ω = angular velocity of body about centre of mass

$v = \sqrt{x^2 + y^2}$ (x, y are components of the velocity vector)

$\omega = \dot{\theta}$

For our man:

$$T = \frac{1}{2}\left(m(\dot{x}^2 + \dot{y}^2) + m_1(\dot{x}_1^2 + \dot{y}_1^2) + m_2(\dot{x}_2^2 + \dot{y}_2^2)\right) + \frac{1}{2}(I\dot{\theta} + I_1\dot{\theta}_1 + I_2\dot{\theta}_2)$$

Potential Energy

$$U = mgy$$

where y is the height of centre of mass above some reference level.

For our man:

$$U = g(my + m_1 y_1 + m_2 y_2)$$

Lagrangian

$$\mathbf{L} = T - U$$

Generating the Differential Equations

$$\frac{\partial \mathbf{L}}{\partial q_i} - \frac{d}{dt}\frac{\partial \mathbf{L}}{\partial \dot{q}_i} + \sum_k \lambda_k \frac{\partial f_k}{\partial q_i} = -Q_i$$

where

$\mathbf{L}$ ≡ Lagrangian

q_i ≡ *i*th coordinate where $q_i = x, y, \theta, x_1, y_1, \theta_1, x_2, y_2, \theta_2$

f_k ≡ *k*th constraint equation where $f_k = f_{1x}, f_{1y}, f_{2x}, f_{2y}, f_{\text{foot}_x}, f_{\text{foot}_y}$

λ_k ≡ *k*th undetermined multiplier

Q_i ≡ force or torque applied to the *i*th coordinate

Solving for λ_k produces the value of the force that maintains the *k*th constraint. The Q_i values allow us to account for damping, the bounce on the mattress, and joint-limiting torques. Using Lagrange's equation will produce a set of differential equations that have to be solved for the various accelerations. Accelerations required are:

$$\ddot{x}, \ddot{y}, \ddot{\theta}, \ddot{x}_1, \ddot{y}_1, \ddot{\theta}_1, \ddot{x}_2, \ddot{y}_2, \ddot{\theta}_2$$

Using the above results in a linear system of nine equations for the 15 unknowns, which are the accelerations and:

$$\lambda_{1x}, \lambda_{1y}, \lambda_{2x}, \lambda_{2y}, \lambda_{\text{foot}_x}, \lambda_{\text{foot}_y}$$

The additional six equations are defined by the constraint equations. The accelerations are found by taking the second time derivative, giving:

$$\dot{f}_{1x}, \dot{f}_{1y}, \dot{f}_{2x}, \dot{f}_{2y}, \dot{f}_{\text{foot}_x}, \dot{f}_{\text{foot}_y}$$

We now have a system of differential equations that basically describe a triple pendulum (three sticks joined together).

Restoring Torque

Each joint has an equilibrium position and negative and positive limits, as indicated in Figure 11, which shows how the torque τ_{restore} increases away from the equilibrium position.

Damping

There are two types of damping forces:

linear damping force—$F_{\text{damping}} = -b\dot{x}$, where b is the damping constant ($b > 0$);

rotational damping torque—$\tau_{\text{damping}} = -b\dot{\theta}$, the force opposing the motion.

Mattress Force

Spring force acting on the centre of mass in a vertical direction only:

$$F_{\text{mattress}} = \begin{cases} 0 & \text{if } y > y_{\text{mattress}} \\ -k(y - y_{\text{mattress}}) & \text{if } y \leq y_{\text{mattress}} \end{cases}$$

Q_i's For Our Man

The following expressions summarise the generalised forces for each degree of freedom:

$$Q_x = -b_x\dot{x}$$

$$Q_y = -b_y\dot{y} + \begin{cases} 0 & \text{if } y > y_{\text{mattress}} \\ -k_y(y - y_{\text{mattress}}) & \text{otherwise} \end{cases}$$

$$Q_\theta = -b_\theta\dot{\theta}$$

$$Q_{x_1} = -b_{x_1}\dot{x}_1$$

$$Q_{y_1} = -b_{y_1}\dot{y}_1 + \begin{cases} 0 & \text{if } y_1 > y_{\text{mattress}} \\ -k_{y_1}(y_1 - y_{\text{mattress}}) & \text{otherwise} \end{cases}$$

$$Q_{\theta_1} = -b_{theta_1}\dot{\theta}_1 + \tau_{\text{restore}\theta_1}(\theta_1 - \theta)$$

$$Q_{x_2} = -b_{x_2}\dot{x}_2$$

$$Q_{y_2} = -b_{y_2}\dot{y}_2 + \begin{cases} 0 & \text{if } y_2 > y_{\text{mattress}} \\ -k_{y_2}(y_2 - y_{\text{mattress}}) & \text{otherwise} \end{cases}$$

$$Q_{\theta_2} = -b_{theta_2}\dot{\theta}_2 + \tau_{\text{restore}\theta_2}(\theta_2 - \theta)$$

MAKING THE ANIMATION

The symbolic arithmetic to produce the differential equations fortunately is handled by a commercial package (Macsyma). Macsyma code has been written that generates a program to do the simulation including calls to a commercial differential-equation-solving package. The values of the positions and angles are output at each display step. This constitutes a kinematic description for the animation program that handles the graphics of the man.

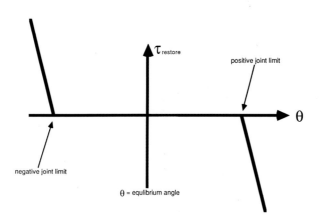

Figure 11. Joint limits.

CONCLUSIONS TO BE DRAWN FROM THE CHMILAR-HERR EXPERIMENT

The animation frames are shown in Figure 12. To view the two animations, the reader should flip the pages of this volume. The top right-hand corner contains the Chmilar-kinematic animation and the bottom right the Herr-dynamic animation. Except in simple cases, dynamic solutions take considerable effort. Even when the programming is minimised with better general-purpose software to solve dynamics problems, complex systems require large numbers of equations to be solved and correspondingly large amounts of computing time. Our man had only five degrees of freedom and produced nine differential equations. A more complete body model in 3D should have between 30 and 40 degrees of freedom; if further detail is required, such as finger joints, the number would be more than 200. In our experiment, the dynamic solution modelled the acceleration and subsequent bounce of the man more convincingly than did the kinematic. However, the kinematic solution was able to account for more detailed motion, and in 3D, such as the half twist on the body as it fell.

One problem with the dynamic approach is that it is difficult to achieve some particular motion. If the objective instead is to find out what happens when certain forces are applied, such as where a body might be flung in a car accident, then dynamic animation is effective.

Both the kinematic and dynamic solutions to such problems are very complex. What is required is a hybrid of the two approaches, with the dynamics sufficiently well integrated into the animation system to be a first cut at the final animation. In the final analysis the animator will use whatever tools best suit his purpose. It is the quality of the software tools that will distinguish the system he chooses.

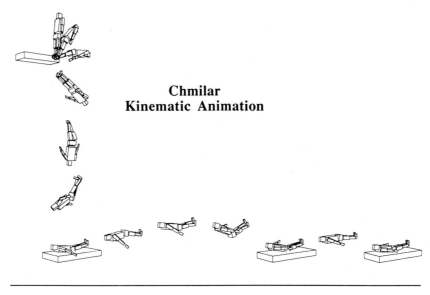

Chmilar
Kinematic Animation

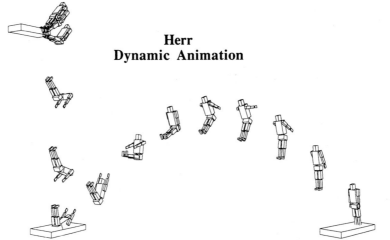

Herr
Dynamic Animation

Figure 12. Frames from the Chmilar-Herr experiment.

Part I—SOFT Objects

Introduction

The term SOFT objects refers to a particular method of representing 3D models that change shape as they move, thus enabling animators to go beyond rigid polygonal models, such as rotating logos, characteristic of computer-generated animation. A technique suited to representing such flexible surfaces was developed by Blinn to model constant energy surfaces in molecules (blobby molecules, see [Blin82]). Blinn used an isosurface in a scalar field defined by a number of key points. Perhaps the best way to visualise this idea is by analogy. Each key can be considered to be a hot star in space radiating heat. The isosurface, or contour, connects all the points which have the same temperature value. Each key can be associated with a *shape function*; the simplest is a sphere so that the key radiates heat equally in all directions. The temperature drops as the distance from the key increases. At some chosen temperature (the isovalue, corresponding to some particular distance away from the key) the spherical surface is found. As two keys approach each other (Figure 13), the space between the keys heats up, changing the shape of the isosurfaces.

It can be seen from the figure that the surfaces will bulge, then join. Eventually the keys will be coincident and form a new sphere. This method of defining surfaces is extremely useful in computer animation, since the keys can be moved independently to produce objects which change shape over time. To model a more complex surface than a sphere, many keys are used. It is relatively simple to check if a particular point in space is inside or outside the surface (hot or cold) by summing the contributions from each key and comparing the field value to the isovalue. The problem is to find out exactly where the surface should be.

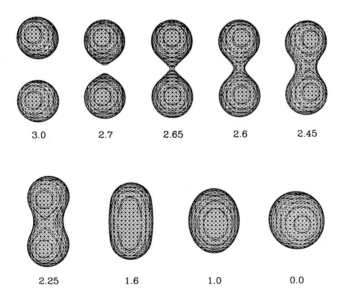

3.0   2.7   2.65   2.6   2.45

2.25   1.6   1.0   0.0

Figure 13. Two SOFT keys approach to form a single sphere.

Building a Model

As far as the modeller is concerned, the keys form a skeleton of the object. The railway engine in Figure 14 is a good example. The left-hand figure shows the keys that form the skeleton; in this case, each key is in the shape of an ellipsoid defined by a skeleton of three axes. The right-hand figure shows the effect of polygonising the surface. The keys are effectively covered in a polygon mesh that approximates the surface. Figure 15 is a rendered version of the railway engine, a frame from the film *The Great Train Rubbery*. The engine is moving through a region of *abstract texture space*. As it enters the space any point in space is given a colour defined by the 3D texture function. In this case, the well-known Mandril texture is

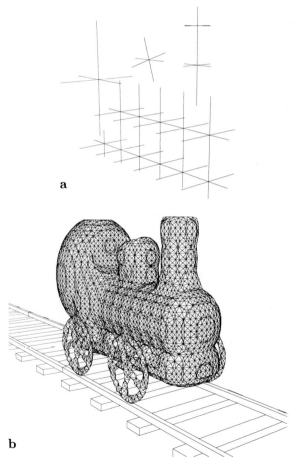

a

b

Figure 14. Train. (a) Skeleton. (b) Polygonal representation.

extruded along the direction of motion of the train producing an interesting visual effect. For further details, see Wyvill [Wyvi87].

FINDING AND RENDERING THE SURFACE

Various researchers have produced algorithms for rendering these surfaces. At about the same time, new algorithms for finding implicit surfaces along with field functions based upon a cubic function were developed in Japan (meta-balls, [Nish85]) and in Canada (SOFT objects, [Wyvi86d]). In the latter work the surface is sampled by uniformly subdividing space into cubic regions. Each cube can then be replaced by polygons that approximate the surface. This process has been referred to as clothing, but the more accurate term is *polygonisation*[Bloo88b]. In contrast, Blinn renders the surface directly from the function. Although it is possible to directly render implicit surfaces with techniques such as ray tracing, prototype surfaces built from polygons are extremely useful. Many workstations such as the Silicon Graphics Iris are capable of producing perspective images of large numbers of polygons per second. Keys can be moved interactively and, if the surface can be recalculated quickly enough, interactive editing can take place. Also, polygon renderers are common, so there is a large incentive to search for fast polygonisation algorithms. The efficiency of the earlier algorithm has been improved [Bloo88b; VonH87; Jeva88b]. Despite the abundance of names for these implicit surfaces, in our research we refer to them as SOFT objects. Over the last few years, a system for modelling and

Figure 15. Rendered version of the train in a scene from *The Great Train Rubbery*.

animating these SOFT objects has been built at the University of Calgary. The system is called Graphicsland, from which many of the examples in this paper are taken.

POSITIVE AND NEGATIVE KEYS

Each key contributes to the field. The contribution can be positive, as in Figure 13, or negative, as illustrated in Figure 16. Figure 6 also illustrates the use of negative keys. The crude human figure is made from positive keys. In fact, in Graphicsland this becomes a hierarchy of transformations of a single SOFT key, a primitive sphere which can be stretched to form an ellipsoid. It is relatively simple to replace the positive primitive by its negative counterpart; the man now becomes invisible and subtracts from a positive surface, thus leaving a man-shaped depression in the mattress.

IMPLICIT SURFACES

Two methods of producing 3D curved surfaces are commonly used in computer graphics:

parametric;
implicit.

Parametric surfaces define a set of points P such that

$$P = (x(u, v), y(u, v), z(u, v))$$

whereas implicit surfaces are simply formulated as

$$f(P) = 0$$

Isosurfaces or SOFT objects fall under the more general term of implicit surfaces. In computer graphics much attention has been paid to methods for modelling parametric surfaces (such as spline patches) but, until recently, implicit surfaces have been largely disregarded. The exception is some work done by Ricci [Ricc73], on a constructive geometry that he used to build and modify shapes. Ricci defined the shapes as the boundary between the half spaces $f(P) < 1$ and $f(P) > 1$, in other words, those

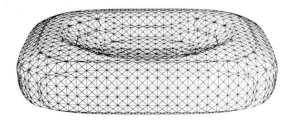

Figure 16. Negative key subtracts the dent from the positive superellipsoid.

points satisfying $f(P) = 1$. The Constructive Solid Geometry (CSG) that evolved has emphasized the operations performed on primitives, generally limiting these to quadrics. Ricci points out that implicit surfaces offer more succinct definitions than parametric surfaces. An example from a paper by Bloomenthal [Bloo88a] shows the following two definitions of a sphere

$$\text{(parametric)} \quad P = C + (r\sin(\theta)\cos(\phi), r\sin(\theta)\sin(\phi), r\cos(\theta)),$$
$$\theta \in (0, \pi), \quad \phi \in (0, 2\pi)$$

$$\text{(implicit)} \quad f(P) = |P - C| - r$$

The implicit formulation offers the designer freedom to arbitrarily constrain a surface; however, producing pictures of these generalised surfaces is far from straightforward.

FIELD FUNCTIONS

The shape of the primitives depends on the function used to define the field and is not restricted by the renderer. To polygonise the surface all that is required is to know if a point is inside or outside (hot or cold). To render the surface more precisely, for example, with ray tracing, the only additional information required is that the surface normal must be found at the point of intersection with a ray (e.g., [Jeva88a]). Thus, many mathematical functions lead to some interesting SOFT objects. In the original work done by Blinn, an exponential function was used. In our previous work in this area we used a cubic [Wyvi86d] where the distance r increases, the field value falls from a maximum of 1 $(r = 0)$ to 0 $(r = R)$. The value of R is a characteristic of a particular SOFT primitive, the distance beyond which it has no effect on its neighbours. Using the heat analogy, beyond R there is no radiated heat from the key. We chose the cubic coefficients so that the field and its derivative (with respect to r) dropped to zero. This enables fields to be combined efficiently and without approximation using large numbers of keys. The field at any point depends only on keys in that locality. The above formulation only allows keys with a spherical field to be defined. Blinn also mentions other shapes besides spheres such as general quadrics. Bloomenthal has produced some magnificent branching structures (ramiforms) based on a spline primitive (Figure 17) [Bloo88b].

Creating Ellipsoid Primitives

In order to find the position of the isosurface formed by a generalised version of the cubic field function, a few concepts have to be defined. The primitive shape is defined by the shape function (also referred to as the field function) around a key. The key is given by three vectors normal to each other, which intersect at the origin of the key. These can be thought of as the axes of

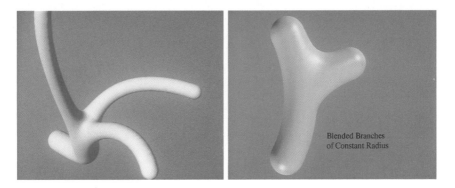

Blended Branches
of Constant Radius

Figure 17. Bloomenthal's ramiforms.

the primitive. The shape function defines the surface due to the key. At the origin of the key the field has a fixed value, due to that key, known as the force. In most of our examples, this value is fixed at plus or minus one. The contribution to the field due to the key decreases with distance from the origin until the radius of influence is reached when the contribution is deemed to be zero.

Figure 18 shows a 2D representation of the isosurface (in bold) due to a single key and the surface at which the force falls to zero (outer ellipse). Given a point P at distance r from the origin O of the key, the contribution of that key at some distance r is determined as follows:

(a) Calculate the distance R where the field value turns to zero along the line OP due to the key by solving the field function.

(b) If $r \leq R$, then the contribution is zero (Figure 18). Otherwise, the field is found from r and R (decay function).

The shape function must provide a continuous closed surface. A useful family of such functions called *superellipsoids* was made popular by the Danish scientist and poet, Piet Hein [Gard65] or more generally the family of superquadrics [Barr81]. The superellipsoids are found from the equation of the ellipsoid

$$\frac{x^2}{a^2} + \frac{y^2}{b^2} + \frac{z^2}{c^2} = 1 \tag{3}$$

where a, b, and c are the axes of the ellipsoid. Piet Hein observed that some pleasing shapes can be made by changing the power from 2 to some real power, n. The mattress in Figure 6 is a superellipse with $n = 4$. To make this useful for building SOFT objects the shape function must provide a means of calculating R (see Step (a) above).

The following function is formed by replacing x, y, z in Eq. (3) with $R\cos(\alpha)$, $R\cos(\beta)$, and $R\cos(\gamma)$ where α, β, and γ are the angles made by the axes of the key and the vector OP (Figure 18).

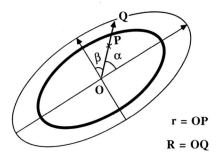

r = OP

R = OQ   Figure 18. 2D isosurface.

$$\frac{R^n \cos^n(\alpha)}{a^n} + \frac{R^n \cos^n(\beta)}{b^n} + \frac{R^n \cos^n(\gamma)}{c^n} = 1 \qquad (4)$$

where n is a real value. Figure 19 shows four primitives with values of n at 2 (an ellipsoid), 2.5, 3, and 4. As n is increased, the shape becomes more like a cube with rounded corners. This form of the superellipsoid provides a primitive defined by a key oriented at an arbitrary angle. The axes a, b, c can be used to alter the aspect ratio of the primitive. Since the axes are orthogonal, γ can be found in terms of α and β. Also, since OP and the key axes' vectors are known, the cosine can be evaluated with a few multiplications. The value of the field can now be found from the values of r and R. It has been found empirically that substituting r and R into the cubic function given in [Wyvi86d] provides good results. Reasonable results can also be obtained with fewer floating-point calculations using

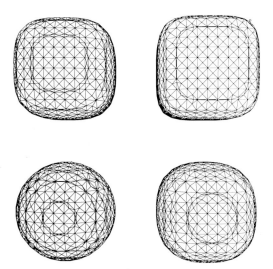

Figure 19. Super ellipsoids.

$$F = 1 - \frac{r^2}{R^2} \tag{5}$$

although, compared with the cubic, the surface blending is more rapid as keys approach each other. The contribution to the field F of some key can be scaled by the *force* characteristic of that key. The force can be positive or negative providing the user with further control on the shape of the objects being modelled.

Computing the Surface

The problem is to find the surface of an object given a set of *keys* and their field functions. In [Wyvi86d] an algorithm is described that finds the field value at successive points along one axis (starting at a control key); each point is the corner of a cube. In fact, it is part of a grid of cubes subdividing the object space. Near the key the value will be greater than the isovalue (hot). When the field falls below the isovalue, the surface has been crossed (the value becomes cold). It can then be determined which cube edges are cut by the surface by comparing the field value of each vertex to the isovalue. If the surface cuts a particular edge, the adjacent cube in the grid is manufactured and the process is repeated recursively until the entire surface has been covered by containing cubes. The surface can then be approximated by manufacturing a polygon (or set of polygons) in each cube. Details of this algorithm are given in [Wyvi86d].

IMPROVING THE SEARCH

Finding the surface that *clothes* the keys requires the evaluation of the field function at many different points in space. The field value at any point is the sum of the field values due to each key. However, the field function used falls to zero at some distance from the centre of the key. To reduce the number of field evaluations for each point we use space subdivision or cellular *clothing* in which the object space is divided into a 3D grid of cubic volumes or cells. The method employed is similar to that of ray tracers and other graphics rendering processes [Clea83]. Essentially, space is broken down into units that are more manageable. Each cell (unit) contains only those objects that affect it, in this case, a subset of the keys. When finding the isosurface, only those keys whose influence extends into the current cell need to be examined for their field contributions. In this way, checking every key point in the 3D space is avoided [Wyvi86d]. Bloomenthal [Bloo88b] found that octree subdivision could be faster than the original uniform subdivision. Jevans et al. have also experimented with this technique [Jeva88b].

The octree subdivision has a minimum and a maximum limit of recursion. This effectively controls the resolution of the polygonal surface and how accurately it reflects the functionally defined isosurface. The minimum limit ensures that the octree subdivision will proceed a minimum number of times regardless of the state of each node's vertices. This ensures that surfaces that are smaller than a cell will be found. The maximum limit stops the octree subdivision and effectively controls the resolution of the surface.

If all of the cells are subdivided equally, then as many polygons are produced over relatively flat areas as are used to represent extreme curvature. Since the polygons are subsequently passed to a renderer when shading is required, it is desirable to reduce the number of polygons. This can be done by having more octree subdivisions in areas of greater surface curvature. Von Herzen developed such a technique using *restricted quadtrees* [Herz87]. Bloomenthal and Jevans et al. have developed independently a method similar to this for use with SOFT objects [Bloo88b; Jeva88b]. One problem is that when two adjacent octree nodes have different levels of subdivision it is difficult to join the polygons in neighbouring nodes (Figure 20). Bloomenthal now has an elegant algorithm that solves this problem. Although there are considerable savings to be had in the rendering process through the use of irregularly subdivided surfaces, introducing this technique considerably reduces the performance of polygonising.

One other advantage to the cellular subdivision is that frame coherence can be exploited. The idea is that a cell will be flagged if any change has occurred in that cell since the last frame. Since each cell is independent of the other cells, i.e., all the information necessary to describe that region of space is contained in the cell, then only the field values at the vertices of the flagged cells need be re-evaluated.

Polygonising

Choosing a polygon mesh that approximates the surface within a cell is responsible for 75 percent of the time taken in clothing the surface. During the development of the new clothing algorithm, several new methods for

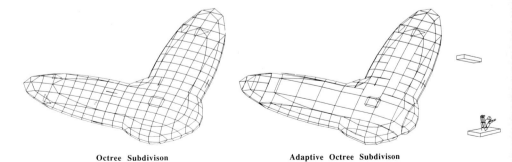

Octree Subdivison   Adaptive Octree Subdivison

Figure 20. Results of octree and adaptive octree subdivision.

building polygonal meshes from surface bounding boxes were explored. One very simple approach is to simply use the cubes representing each node as the polygons of the surface. This method is extremely fast but results in very crude approximations to the surfaces. The effect is like constructing the polygon mesh of many small boxes on its surface. This method can produce reasonable surfaces but only if the subdivision's upper limit is set unreasonably high.

To provide more accurate surfaces at lower subdivision levels an adaptation of the algorithm given in [Wyvi86d] has been found to give a fast and reasonably accurate response. Each cube (octree leaf node) has vertices that are either hot (field value > isovalue) or cold (field value < isovalue). Vertices on the surface are taken as hot. There are eight vertices at each node and thus 256 combinations of hot and cold. A table is constructed (once at initialisation time) which indicates the appropriate polygons to construct for each case. The cube vertices are numbered systematically so that the bits set in a single 8-bit byte represent the hot vertices. The byte is stored for each cube and is used to manufacture a pointer into the correct part of the table. The polygons themselves are algorithmically constructed as in [Wyvi86d] and are then stored in a look-up table. Our empirical results so far indicate that the use of the table increases the speed of this operation by more than one order of magnitude over the previous algorithm.

Animating SOFT Objects

Traditional animators often criticise 3D computer-generated animation for the stilted way in which objects move. Computer-generated objects or *characters* tend to lack the subtleties in motion seen in traditional animation. Characters do not have to be humanoid; objects can be given character such as the brooms in the sorcerer's apprentice sequence from Disney's *Fantasia*: in other words, they can be made to be anthropomorphic. The motion of such objects is controlled to a fine degree to characterise their movement. Characters tend to bend as they move and, at times, they must conform to their surroundings. A figure sitting in a chair is an example, as is flowing water. In computer animation, popular modelling techniques such as polygon meshes or spline patches do not lend themselves to the manufacture of objects that can be given this type of motion. SOFT objects lend themselves to representing models that undergo some kind of shape change. The intention is to let the animator design the skeleton of the character or object and then automatically *clothe* this skeleton with a surface. If the skeleton moves, then the surface changes its shape smoothly to conform. If the skeleton undergoes metamorphosis to a totally different skeleton or inbetweens to a skeleton in a new position, then a new surface is calculated at every frame. The surface is represented in such a way that it maintains nearly constant volume as the skeleton moves, thus providing convincing *character coherence*. This property of coherence is very important. Intuitively it means that, throughout metamorphosis, the model remains recognisable as the same character. A model built from keys can be moved without shape change by maintaining the relative spatial relationship between the keys in the absence of any influencing field. Achieving shape change without distorting the model beyond recognition requires that certain constraints be placed on the animation system. The following techniques can be used to animate a model built from a skeleton of SOFT keys to achieve shape change:

geometric transformation—Motion of keys relative to each other;

altering the field—Influence of global or local field;

changing key characteristic—Altering parameter describing a key.

The following sections describe how these methods can be used by high-level motion specifications to create the appropriate blended surfaces. Controlling the shape of the surface is still an open research issue. However, implicit surface methods provide a very fast way of producing blended surfaces that can approximate, say, a humanoid character. The methods described here are low level; they affect individual keys or groups of keys. It is intended that they can be assimilated into a higher level animation system as described in Part 1.

GEOMETRIC MOTION

By simply altering the relative spatial relationship between keys, a surface can be made to alter its shape. Figure 21 shows the skeleton of an arm with the position of the keys marked. By moving the keys with the skeleton, the surface blends smoothly and the arm appears to bend. There are two ways the skeleton can be replaced by the keys: by the animator, specifying for each skeleton part a key configuration, or procedurally by the system. The latter method can be applied once to the model or at every frame. If each limb is defined as a line, then soft keys can be evenly spaced along the length of the limb by simple linear interpolation. However, if the length of the limbs remains constant (as is normally the case), then it is quite adequate and usually more effective for the animator to interactively specify the keys at the start of the animation. The relationship between keys and skeleton remains constant throughout.

PATH DEFORMATION

Motion paths are extremely useful when applied to the keys of a SOFT object. A cartoon-like character can be made to conform to its surroundings by using the shape of an object to define the path that a group of keys must follow. This effect was demonstrated in the movie *SOFT* [Wyvi86b]. The

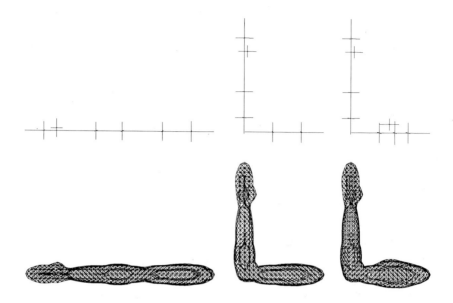

Figure 21. Bending an arm.

character in this case was a group of letters spelling the word 'SOFT'. Each letter was made from about 20 keys; the path was drawn up a flight of stairs by marking various positions and passing a spline through these points using a spline technique similar to that described in [Koch84]. In this technique each key in the character was moved to the interpolated path position at each frame. Each point along the path represented a position at a particular instance in time. Rather than define a separate path for each key, the keys were grouped so that each group was moved together to the next point in the path. Normally a group was chosen according to some spatial relationship, for example, all keys within a specific range of z values. To maintain 'character coherence' the relative positions of the keys within a group were constrained. In this case the amount each group was allowed to vary its position was constrained by the change along the path. Each key maintained its position relative to the group. It is the origin of the group that followed the path. The positions of the groups changed relative to the other groups by an amount specified in the path. Thus, the model was deformed whilst maintaining the overall shape and the character coherence property that distinguishes shape distortion from metamorphosis. When the letters were moved up the stairs in the movie $SOFT$, the direction of motion was along the negative z axis, so the groups were chosen as keys with the same z value. As each group advanced along the path, the y value of the group was altered according to the path specification (see [Wyvi86c] for frames from the film).

ALTERING THE FIELD

SOFT objects may also be animated by altering the field in which the objects exist. Local deformation can be achieved by moving other SOFT keys relative to these objects or by placing some global influence into the field. A good example of local deformation is shown in Figure 6. As the negative human figure lies on the mattress, his impression is left there. The mattress is deformed by the motion of some external influence. Global deformation is more difficult to specify in a completely general way. The field itself could have some external influence such as a plane of constant value. Objects approaching that plane will deform according to the value chosen. In Figure 22 a ball is shown approaching a plane held at the isovalue. The plane is of course invisible but is shown here as a grid of polygons in fact placed slightly higher than the plane itself. The ball deforms as it approaches the plane and returns to its original shape as it moves away.

CHANGING KEY CHARACTERISTIC

Each key is defined by three axes and a 'force'. The size and orientation of the axes may be changed and also the force, which is a scale factor applied to the key's contribution to the field. The effect of negative force has already been shown. By increasing the force, the effect on the neighbouring keys will be altered; the effect is very similar to changing the size of the axes of the key. Making the force negative produces animation effects that cannot be achieved by other means. Since SOFT objects remain blended if they are in close proximity, scaling an individual key can appear somewhat like a muscle bulging as an arm is bent. Figure 21 shows the same arm bending, only this time, the keys representing the muscle area are made larger. To achieve high-level control, the system would have to know that each time the arm is bent a proportional scaling must be applied to certain keys. This can be achieved in a script system by defining a method that is invoked each time the high-level command is issued to bend the arm. This kind of procedural animation is difficult to achieve in purely interactive systems.

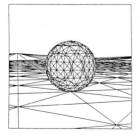 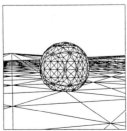 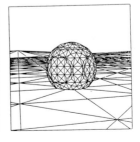

Figure 22. Global field deformation.

Inbetweening and Metamorphosis

SOFT objects are particularly useful for metamorphosis, or inbetweening. A method suitable for 2D (cartoon) models would have the character drawn on a vector-oriented display in two positions and the inbetween frames interpolated by the system. The simplest way to do this is to interpolate each point of the first (*source*) object to a corresponding point on the second (*destination*) object. Difficulties arise if the number of points is different on source and destination objects. New points have to be created or several points have to collapse onto a single point. Even if the number of points is the same on the two objects, if they are distributed in a different way the image will be scrambled as each point is interpolated. SOFT objects always guarantee a closed surface, so this problem does not arise. However, it is still easy to lose character coherence in the inbetween versions. Figures 23 and 24 illustrate these points.

Inbetweening is not only used to show motion of a character from one position to another, it can also be used to show metamorphosis from one character to another. If the characters are very different in shape and number of keys, then the scrambling problem is difficult to avoid. Peter Foldes used software by Burtnyk and Wein [Burt76] in the film *La Faim* and exploited this technique to good advantage. However, to avoid *scrambling* is a difficult and tedious task that requires very careful design of the keypoints for inbetweening.

Burtnyk and Wein developed a computer version of this technique using skeletons. These skeletons defined a conformal mapping from one key frame to the next. The space itself was distorted; thus, any line within the space was similarly distorted according to the mapping function. In contrast, 3D computer-generated characters are often moved by applying geometric transforms to the different parts, which changes their relative positions but does not necessarily give the characters as smooth a change of shape as can be achieved using the 2D techniques. However, the advantages of using 3D characters are considerable, as the computer can be used to render frames from any chosen camera position with the appropriate lighting all calculated automatically. An effective way of producing shape change in 3D animation is to use the inbetween technique. However, extending the 2D technique to 3D introduces new problems. Reeves points out [Reev81] that it is difficult to identify corresponding points (and polygons) on different characters. Even with functional representations, the parameters from which a surface is manufactured must be chosen so that the source model *matches* the destination model. Each of the parameters defining the *source* model must be changed to one of the parameters defining the *destination* model. The matching process chooses the appropriate *destination parameters* corresponding to the *source parameters*. At each intermediate stage during the inbetween, a model will be manufactured from an interpolated set of parameters.

In the following paragraphs several different heuristics for matching the

Polygons

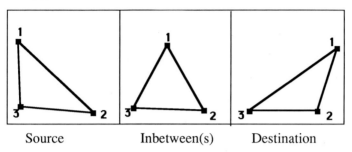

Source   Inbetween(s)   Destination

Order of points is critical

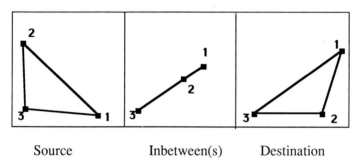

Source   Inbetween(s)   Destination

Figure 23. Inbetweening polygons.

models are presented. The shape of the intermediate models vary according to the chosen method, based on one or more of the heuristics.

HEURISTICS FOR POINT-MATCHING IN METAMORPHOSIS

In this section four approaches that we have found useful for defining the matching process are described. Although the SOFT object modelling system has been used to illustrate how these heuristics may be applied, the methods are general and can be extended to other modelling techniques. In practice, an animator will want to experiment with different combinations of these techniques to arrive at the desired effect.

We start with two models, the source model and the destination model. The source model must be made to change into the destination model. The

Soft Objects Avoid This problem

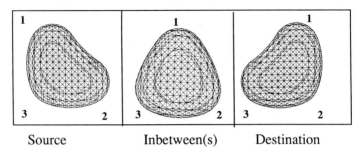

Source   Inbetween(s)   Destination

Order of points is critical but closed surface guaranteed

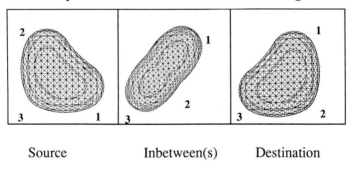

Source   Inbetween(s)   Destination

Figure 24. Inbetweening SOFT keys.

models are defined as a set of SOFT object keys as described above. Each key has the following properties:

axes vectors	**v1,v2,v3**
position	x, y, z
force	F

Each of these methods assumes that objects have been preprocessed so that there are the same number of keys defining each object. This may involve creating zero-weighted keys. A key can be weighted using the force, F, which scales the contribution to the field, or by scaling the axes. A zero-weighted key has its axis vectors set to zero, or $F = 0$. When a source key is inbetweened to a destination key, at each frame a new key is chosen which has an interpolated value for position, axes vectors, and force. The start or finish position of the new keys is chosen by the appropriate method.

Hand-matched

The simplest method of establishing which keys are to be interpolated is to to order the source and destination keys by hand and to process each pair in turn. Since the number of keys is small compared with the number of polygons in an equivalent model, this method is feasible for some objects. However, computer animation is generally moving toward higher levels of control, so this method is considered a last resort.

Hierarchical Matching

In this heuristic method it is assumed that each model is represented by a hierarchy of keys. Each node in the hierarchy has an arbitrary number of sibling nodes and one or zero child nodes. Nodes are matched at the same level in the hierarchy. An example is shown in Figure 25. The character with two bodies is matched to the character with three legs. It is assumed that the hierarchies are designed so that each level of the source object has an equivalent level in the destination object. If a rabbit is to change into a man, the heads will be matched, the front legs of the rabbit will be matched to the arms of the man, and so on (Figure 26). The main problem with this approach is that the hierarchies have to be constructed carefully. Not only do the levels have to match but, within a level, the nodes must either be ordered or labelled to match. Despite these drawbacks, this method is still preferable to ordering all the keys by hand and, for small sets of keys, with suitable interactive tools it is quite acceptable.

Cellular Inbetweening

In this technique the models are matched according to the space they occupy. The world is first divided into a 3D grid of cells. This is done by

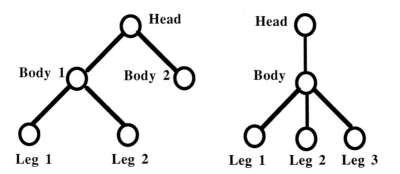

Figure 25. Hierarchical matching.

Surface Inbetweening

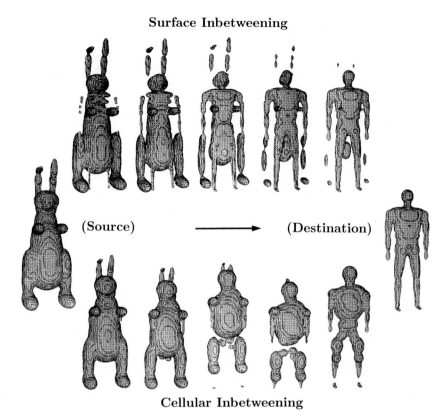

(Source) ⟶ (Destination)

Cellular Inbetweening

Figure 26. Rabbit to man inbetweening.

finding the extents of each model and manufacturing the corresponding rectangular box. Each box is then divided along the x, y, z axes by some user-defined amount. The two boxes may be different shapes, but they are divided into an equal number of cells. The keys are then sorted into the cellular grid, and the keys in each source grid cell are then interpolated to the keys in the corresponding grid cell of the destination model. The objects can have different sizes, but the method tries to maintain some sort of position coherence between source and destination objects. Figure 27 shows a 2D version of how the keys are matched. Circles with similar shading patterns are matched between source and destination. In the top diagram the points match exactly; for every key in every cell in the destination object there is a corresponding key in the corresponding cell in the source object. In the lower diagram there are some cells containing keys in the destination object for which there are no keys in the corresponding cell in the source object. In this case, a zero-weighted key (indicated as a small circle) will be manufactured in the source object. Similarly, keys that exist

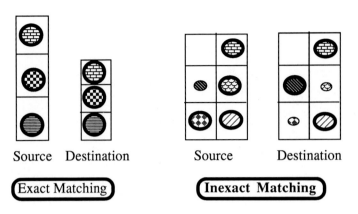

Source   Destination   Source   Destination

(Exact Matching)   **(Inexact Matching)**

Figure 27. Cellular matching.

in the source object are grown in the destination. An example of the use of cellular inbetweening is shown in Figure 26.

Surface Inbetweening

In this method no matching is necessary. All the keys from both source and destination objects define each intermediate model. However, the force property of each source key is weighted. The weighting is gradually changed from one to zero as the inbetween progresses. Also dependent on time is a second weighting applied to the force property of the destination keys. This value changes from zero to one. The shape of the weight value versus time curve controls the shape of the intermediate model. This is shown in Figure 28. A simple linear interpolation means that both source and destination objects are reduced to half the weight halfway through the simulation. In practice, this gives poor results, as the SOFT surfaces around each key no longer merge. If the source is weighted by a cosine function and the destination weighted by a sine function, each object is never weighted by less than $1/\sqrt{2}$. The objects can still be matched by one of the sorting techniques (hand, hierarchy, cellular), but the inbetweening process is different using surface inbetweening. An example is shown below.

Metamorphosis of Rabbit to Man

Figure 26 shows some frames from a metamorphosis in which a rabbit is changed to a man. The frames in the top row were produced using the surface inbetweening method, with a sin/cos decay weighting function. The cellular method in combination with the hierarchical technique was used to produce the frames on the bottom row. The man and rabbit were first broken into two equivalent hierarchies and the cellular method used within each pair of parts. Table 1 indicates how well the keys were matched. It can be seen from Figure 26 that the hierarchical/cellular approach succeeds

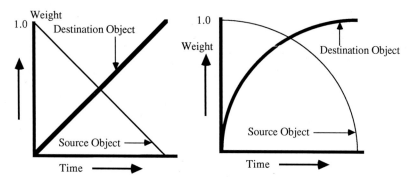

Figure 28. Surface inbetweening.

somewhat better than the surface method. Clearly other heuristics are necessary to stop the model from breaking apart. The actual inbetween is done along linear paths in space (although not in time), and it is the relationship between the paths that govern the intermediate shapes that are generated. The good point about this is that little effort is needed to get some sort of metamorphosis and, although the figure may break into separate parts, these parts will individually maintain a closed surface.

Lessons Learned from the Heuristics

The main lesson to be learned is that good results cannot be obtained from the few heuristics described here. Other constraints have to be placed on the keys before they can be made to form reasonable models in the inbetween stages. Further constraint-based heuristics may well prove a fruitful area of research.

Conclusion

Presented here is an attempt to impose some order on the many techniques in 3D computer animation. Particular attention has been paid to

Table 1. Matching the rabbit (R) and the man (M).

Part	M-Keys	R-Keys	Matched Keys	Number of Cells	Cells Used
Head	2	13	5	2^3	7
Torso	16	7	2	3^3	6
Left leg	13	3	6	2^3	6
Right leg	13	3	5	2^3	6
Left arm	1	9	3	2^3	4
Right arm	1	9	3	2^3	4

a relatively new area, the use of implicit surfaces for animation. Although there are still many outstanding problems to solve, such surfaces have an important role to play in the computer animator's store of techniques.

Acknowledgments. I would like to acknowledge the help of my fellow worker in implicit surfaces, Jules Bloomenthal of Xerox Parc, for the use of some of his material. I also thank my graduate students for their help in the preparation of this paper. I would particularly like to thank Jeff Allan, Mike Chmilar, Angus Davis, Anja Haman, Charles Herr, Dave Jevans, and Trevor Paquette. Mike Chmilar composed the kinematic animation and Chuck Herr slaved over a computer full of hot differential equations to produce the dynamics of the falling man. This research is partially supported by grants from the Natural Sciences and Engineering Research Council of Canada.

REFERENCES

[Arms85]
  Armstrong, W., and Green, M., The dynamics of articulated rigid bodies for purposes of animation, *Visual Comput.*, Vol. 1, pp. 231–240, 1985.

[Barr81]
  Barr, A., Superquadrics and angle-preserving transformations, *IEEE Comput. Graph. Appl.*, Vol. 1, No. 1, pp. 11–23, 1981.

[Bart87]
  Bartels, R.H., Beatty, J.C., and Barsky, B.A., *An Introduction to Splines For Use in Computer Graphics & Geometric Modeling*, Los Altos, CA: Morgan Kaufmann, 1987.

[Blin82]
  Blinn, J., A generalization of algebraic surface drawing, *ACM Trans. Graph.*, Vol. 1, p. 235, 1982.

[Bloo88a]
  Bloomenthal, J., Techniques for implicit modeling, Xerox PARC technical report P89-00106 (November 1988).

[Bloo88b]
  Bloomenthal, J., Polygonisation of implicit surfaces, *Comput. Aided Geom. Design*, Vol. 4, pp. 341–355, 1988.

[Burt76]
  Burtnyk, N., and Wein, M., Interactive skeleton techniques for enhancing motion dynamics in key frame animation, *CACM*, Vol. 19, p. 564, 1976.

[Catm80]
  Catmull, E., and Smith, A.R., 3D transformations of images in scanline order, *Comput. Graph. (Proc. SIGGRAPH 80)*, Vol. 14, pp. 279–285, 1980.

[Chua83]
  Chuang, R., and Entis, G., 3-D shaded computer animation—Step by step, *IEEE Comput. Graph. Appl.*, Vol. 3, No. 9, pp. 18–25, 1983.

[Clea83]
Cleary,J., Wyvill, B., Birtwistle, G., and Vatti, R., A parallel ray tracing computer, in *Proc. XI Association of Simula Users Conference (Paris)*, pp. 77–80, 1983.

[Clea88]
Cleary,J., and Wyvill, G., Analysis of an algorithm for fast ray tracing using uniform space subdivision, *Visual Comput.*, Vol. 4, pp. 65–83, 1988.

[Feib80]
Feibush, E.H., Levoy, M., and Cook, L., Synthetic texturing using digital filters, *Comput. Graph. (Proc. SIGGRAPH 80)*, Vol. 14, pp. 294–301, 1980.

[Gard65]
Gardner, M., Mathematical games, *Sci. Amer.*, Vol. 213, pp. 222–236, September 1965.

[Glas84]
Glassner, A.S., Space subdivision for fast ray tracing, *IEEE Comput. Graph. Appl.*, Vol. 4, No. 10, pp. 15–22, 1984.

[Gome85]
Gomez, J.E., Twixt: A 3D animation system, *Comput. Graph.*, Vol. 9, pp. 291–298, 1985.

[Hall89]
Hall, R., *Illumination and Color in Computer Generated Imagery*, New York: Springer-Verlag, 1989.

[Hanr85]
Hanrahan, P., and Sturman, D., Interactive animation of parametric models, *Visual Comput.*, Vol. 1, pp. 260–266, 1985.

[Imme86]
Immel, D.S., Cohen, M.F., and Greenberg, D.P., A radiosity method for non-diffuse environments, *Comput. Graph. (Proc. SIGGRAPH 86)*, Vol. 20, pp. 133–142, 1986.

[Jeva88a]
Jevans, D., and Wyvill, B., Ray Tracing Implicit Surfaces, Technical Report 88/292/04, University of Calgary, Dept. of Computer Science, Calgary, Alberta, Canada, 1988.

[Jeva88b]
Jevans, D., Wyvill, B., and Wyvill, G., Speeding up 3D animation for simulation, in *Proc. SCS Conference* (Proc. MAPCON IV (Multi and Array Processors)), pp. 94–100, 1988.

[Kay86]
Kay, T.L., and Kajiya, J.T., Ray tracing complex scenes, *Comput. Graph. (Proc. SIGGRAPH 86)*, Vol. 20, pp. 269–278, 1986.

[Koch84]
Kochanek, D., Interpolating splines with local tension, continuity and bias control, *Comput. Graph. (Proc. SIGGRAPH 84)*, Vol. 18, pp. 33–41, 1984.

[Lass87]
Lasseter, J., Principles of traditional animation applied to 3D computer

animation, *Comput. Graph.* (*Proc. SIGGRAPH 87*), Vol. 21, pp. 35–44, 1987.

[Mand77]
Mandelbrot, B.B., *The Fractal Geometry of Nature*, New York: W.H. Freeman, 1977.

[McPh84]
McPheeters, C., and Wyvill, B., A Tutorial Guide to the ANI Animation System, Technical Report 84/187/45, University of Calgary, Dept. of Computer Science, Calgary, Alberta, Canada, 1984.

[Nish85]
Nishimura, H., Hirai, A., Kawai, T., Kawata, T., Shirakawa, I., and Omura, K., Object modelling by distribution function and a method of image generation, *Journal of Papers Given at the Electronics Communication Conference 85*, J68-D(4), 1985 (in Japanese).

[Peac85]
Peachey, D., Solid texturing of complex surfaces, *Comput. Graph.* (*Proc. SIGGRAPH 85*), Vol. 19, pp. 279–286, 1985.

[Perl85]
Perlin, K., An image synthesizer, *Comput. Graph.* (*Proc. SIGGRAPH 85*), Vol. 19, pp. 287–296, 1985.

[Reev81]
Reeves, W., Inbetweening for computer animation utilizing moving point constraints, *Comput. Graph.* (*Proc. SIGGRAPH 81*), Vol. 15, pp. 263–269, 1981.

[Reev83]
Reeves, W., Particle systems—A technique for modeling a class of fuzzy objects, *ACM Trans. Graph.*, Vol. 2, pp. 91–108, 1983.

[Reyn82]
Reynolds, C.W., Computer animation with scripts and actors, *Comput. Graph.* (*Proc. SIGGRAPH 82*), Vol. 16, pp. 289–296, 1982.

[Ricc73]
Ricci, A., Constructive geometry for computer graphics, *Comput. J. (GB)*, Vol. 16, pp. 157–160, 1973.

[Rids86]
Ridsdale, G., Hewitt, S., and Calvert, T. W., The interactive specification of human animation, *Proc. Graph. Interface*, pp. 121–130, 1986.

[Stek85]
Steketee, S.N., and Badler, N.I., Parametric keyframe interpolation incorporating kinetic adjustment and phrasing control, *Comput. Graph.* (*Proc. SIGGRAPH 85*), Vol. 19, pp. 255–262, 1985.

[Stur84]
Sturman, D., Interactive keyframe animation of 3-D articulated models, *Proc. Graph. Interface*, pp. 35–40, 1984.

[Suth74]
Sutherland, I., Sproull, R., and Schumacker, R., A characteristic of ten hidden-surface algorithms, *Comput. Surveys*, Vol. 6, pp. 1–55, 1974.

[Thal85]
Thalmann, N., Thalmann, D., and Fortin, M., Miranim: An extensible director oriented system for the animation of realistic images, *IEEE Comput. Graph. Appl.*, Vol. 5, pp. 61-73, 1985.

[Thal86]
Thalmann, D., A lifegame approach to surface modeling and rendering, *Visual Comput.*, Vol. 2, pp. 384–388, 1986.

[VonH87]
Von Herzen, B., and Barr, A.H., Accurate triangulations of deformed intersecting surfaces, *Comput. Graph. (Proc. SIGGRAPH 87)*, Vol. 21, pp. 103–110, 1987.

[Wilh85]
Wilhelms, J., Using dynamic analysis to animate articulated bodies such as humans and robots, *Proc. Graph. Interface*, pp. 97–104, 1985.

[Wilh87]
Wilhelms, J., Towards automatic motion control, *IEEE Comput. Graph. Appl.*, Vol. 7, No. 4, pp. 11–22, 1987.

[Wyvi86a]
Wyvill, B., McPheeters, C., and Garbutt, R., The University of Calgary 3D computer animation system, *J. Soc. Motion Picture and Television Engr.*, Vol. 95, pp. 629–635, 1986.

[Wyvi86b]
Wyvill, B., SOFT, *SIGGRAPH 86 Electronic Theatre and Video Review*, Issue 24, 1986.

[Wyvi86c]
Wyvill, B., McPheeters, C., and Wyvill, G., Animating soft objects, *Visual Comput.*, Vol. 2, pp. 235–242, 1986.

[Wyvi86d]
Wyvill, G., McPheeters, C., and Wyvill, B., Data structure for soft objects, *Visual Comput.*, Vol. 2, pp. 227–234, 1986.

[Wyvi87]
Wyvill, G., Wyvill, B., and McPheeters, C., Solid texturing of soft objects, *IEEE Comput. Graph. Appl.*, Vol. 7, pp. 20–26, 1987 (originally presented at CG International 87, Tokyo, Japan).

[Zelt82]
Zeltzer, D., Motor control techniques for figure animation, *IEEE Comput. Graph. Appl.*, Vol. 2, No. 9, pp. 53–60, 1982.

5 Modeling and CADCAM

Sculptured Surface Definitions– A Historical Survey

Malcolm Sabin

Abstract

*Equations suitable for the representation of smooth surfaces have been pro-
gressively improved over the last three decades. This paper identifies the
mainstream landmarks, from conic lofting to NURBS, with a few side excursions on the way. Each method is explained with its advantages and
disadvantages.*

Introduction

This paper contains three main sections. In the first a chronological account
is given of the development of the main techniques used for representation
of smooth surfaces. It is a personal view, but I hope one that is not too
biassed or misleading.

The second section surveys the four main paradigms for sculptured surface description:

the directrix-generator form;

the multiple patches form;

the transfinite interpolation or blending form;

the carpet form.

Each is described in some detail.

The third section is a critical analysis of various aspects of the requirements for a sculptured surface system.

Although each of the main paradigms has its own flavour, the distinctions
are not absolute, and a given surface equation can often be described by
more than one of them. These ambiguities are elaborated. Because of these
ambiguities there is a useful distinction to be drawn between the external
description of a surface and its internal representation; thus, the ways in
which a surface designer could actually manipulate a computer model to
achieve his ends are discussed in their own right.

Certain surfaces are required that are defined, not independently, but in terms of other surfaces. A requirement becoming particularly pressing with the integration of surfaces into more general geometric modelling systems is the representation of a piece of surface whose boundary need not be part of the original surface definition. Finally, some methods that are not yet widely used are outlined, and both their promises and their problems are discussed.

Useful sources for surface descriptions are given in:

Hawthorne and Edwards [Hawt71];

Barnhill and Riesenfeld [Barn74a];

Barnhill and Boehm [Barn83];

Gregory [Greg86a]; and

Martin [Mart87].

Historical Introduction

PRE-COMPUTING METHODS

The first sculptured surfaces needing design were boats. The techniques for describing their shape emerged from manufacturing methods. Frames had to be shaped to give the lateral shape to the hull, but the requirement for smooth lines meant that the frames had to be coherent with each other. The planking between the frames automatically gave a smooth shape if the frames were consistent, and there was no need for information between the frames. This led to a technique of fairing, in which a 'nest' of frames was drawn, full-size, and graphical techniques were used to determine horizontal (waterline) and vertical (buttline) sections through them (graphical in the sense of done with a pencil on a drawing board, not computer graphical!). Full-size draughting of a reasonable size ship needed a very large drawing board and, in fact, the floor of the loft above the shed where the ship was being built was put to this use—hence the term 'mould-loft'.

Ships outgrew indoor construction, and lofting to a smaller scale became the standard practice in large shipyards. One-tenth scale became a standard for optical line-following flame cutters, which competed for a while with numerically controlled machines for cutting out frames of steel ships.

Full-scale lofting remained standard practice in the aircraft industry at least until the VC10 and still remains so today in the automotive industry.

In all these industries, if the horizontal and vertical sections did not look smooth, fairer versions of them would be drawn, and the same techniques were used to redetermine the frames again. If these were now wiggly they would be faired in turn, and the whole process would go around and around until a set of three views that were mutually consistent and were all looking fair were derived. The master would then actually be the frame sections, because these, together with certain waterlines that corresponded to floors in the structure, gave the shape of structural members from which shape the skinning was unable to depart. The key properties of graphical definitions were:

only a collection of curves across the surface was defined, not the surface as a whole;

the distinction between definition and interrogation was only partial, in that the definition itself contained the most important outputs;

determining the shapes of the few skew structural members was a major exercise, a challenge for a skilled loftsman.

By about 1965, most aircraft companies had adopted a direct numerical analogue of the traditional graphical techniques, and there was a lot of interest in lines fairing for the shipbuilding industry using numerical analysis. In both cases, the analogue was quite close, equations being used to define the 2D curves that the draughtsman would have drawn, rather than the surfaces that he was using the curves to define.

CONIC LOFTING

The analogue favoured in the aircraft industry was called 'conic lofting' because it used conic section curves (defined by second-degree equations) to model the long, sweeping curves found on aircraft fuselages.

The first description of conic lofting that I know of was the book by Roy Liming in 1944 [Limi44], and the earliest paper I have seen described the use of these techniques to define the fuselage of the Gloster Whittle, the first jet aircraft [Shel47] (document dated 1947), but reinventions of minor variations on this technique have appeared regularly ever since.

NUMERICAL LINES FAIRING

Uses in naval architecture had to deal with shapes not representable by conics, often having inflections (changes in sense of curvature), and the idea developed in this context was the least squares fitting of polynomials [Clen65]. The idea of least squares fitting was recognisably the automation of the process of fairing, i.e., the replacement of an unfair curve through a set of incompatible frames by a fairer version, which was then used to give a set of intercept points for the frames, to be faired in turn. Both numerical techniques retained the graphical properties that I identified previously:

the coefficients of the equations were for discrete 2D curves;

most of the required data lay in the curves directly represented;

calculating the occasional skew section was a challenge for a skilled mathematician.

Splines

When, in 1965, I started work on representation of sculptured shape, there were some newer ideas afoot. One was the mathematical idea of the spline curve, a curve that would interpolate as many given points as you wished without the gross misbehaviour of high-order polynomial interpolation, and without the discontinuities of slope (or even position) that traditional numerical interpolation techniques suffered. These spline curves 'cheated' by explicitly using multiple pieces, each with its own equation.

Autokon

An important application of these ideas was the Norwegian Autokon package [Mehl71], which used a proprietary variant of the spline idea to implement the numerical lines fairing ideas. This package was used during the 1960s and into the 1970s by the majority of European shipyards for definition of hull forms.

Parametric Surfaces

Other ideas just surfacing in the mid-1960s were based on the idea of representing a surface as such, not just a finite collection of curves across it. Particularly important were papers by Coons [Coon67] (not published until 1967 but much circulated before then in the 1964 version), Ferguson [Ferg64], and Freyman. These papers carried the concept of the 'patch', a vector-valued biparametric function that mapped a unit square in parameter space into a four-sided piece of surface only topologically square.

Ferguson and Freyman independently described the bicubic patch and its control by corner points and tangent vectors; Ferguson's methods became the basis of the FMILL surface milling facility in the APT language for the programming of numerically controlled machine tools.

Coons' paper also identified the extreme adaptability of the transfinite interpolation idea, matching the edges of this patch to almost any curves whatever. In fact, he found that it was easier to implement a restricted set of boundary curves, and thereby limited himself to the same surfaces that Ferguson had described. I have always been rather sad that bicubics have been called 'Coons patches' ever since, since this labelling does neither Steve Coons nor Jim Ferguson full justice.

I had the job of designing and building a system for day-to-day use in design of aircraft and, after a brief flirtation with a variant of conic lofting, I used a combination of the patch ideas with spline interpolation to get the patch boundaries for an array of patches forming a topologically rectangular network. In fact, the nearest system available in the literature before I started was a scalar-valued interpolation by Birkhoff and Garabedian [Birk60], which used a piecewise rational patch to fill in between spline boundaries. I disliked this method so much that it stimulated me to sort out the bicubic properly.

SPLINE CARPET

I spotted that the spline interpolator could be regarded as a differentiation operator and created a spline carpet. A few years later Robin Forrest found a description of a very similar but scalar-valued system by Inaba that predated mine, and in the summer of 1987 I discovered an identical system to mine described in a 1962 paper by Carl de Boor [deBo62].

This method passed spline curves through data points arranged in a topologically rectangular array by computing the values of tangent vectors that would give continuity of curvature at the knots of a curve through each row. This process determined the tangent vectors in both directions of the bicubic patches that filled the gaps between the curves. It also used the same spline operator to determine the twist vectors to give a surface with continuity of second as well as first derivative everywhere. This surface could be regarded as sliding a spline in one direction across a set of spline curves in the other, either way around. However, we also allowed explicit setting of individual tangent and twist vectors if the surface designer so wished.

These new techniques made the task of defining a surface a relatively unskilled job. It was necessary only to feed in the coordinates of a set of points on a topologically rectangular grid, and the spline interpolation did the rest. The definition itself, however, was of almost no direct use at all, and so the whole problem of how to get out the actually required data came to the fore.

In the operational context, the only possible way of displaying a surface for the judgement of those responsible for authorising a shape was as a nest of parallel plane sections, and the plane section problem was the main challenge in making the new methods acceptable (see Sabin, "Interrogation Techniques for Parametric Surfaces", in this volume).

The methods we found worked well, and our software, the Numerical Master Geometry (NMG), entered routine productive use in early 1967. Many of its routines are still in use today.

BÉZIER PATCHES

In 1971 Charles Lang's CAD group at Cambridge introduced the United Kingdom community to the ideas of Pierre Bézier. Bézier had built and put into use at Renault [Bezi71] a software system that used Bernstein polynomials as basis functions instead of the Hermite polynomials used by Ferguson and the splines in NMG.

What was special about these ideas was that they gave a much better set of 'handles' with which to control the shape of a single polynomial biparametric patch than was previously available. The 'twist vectors' were the particular part of the black magic of bicubics that NMG's splining had hidden but not really tamed. The Bézier representation used a set of control points, the positioning of which influenced the surface in a very natural and understandable way. Precise control of the boundary curves of a patch and of the cross-boundary slopes was combined with qualitative control of curvatures.

B-SPLINES

The next few years found a few problems with the Bézier methods: individual definition of many low-order patches was a tedious task, and high-order patches had very soft control in the interior. These residual difficulties were removed by the proposal of Gordon and Riesenfeld in 1974 [Gord74] that the B-spline functions described earlier by Schoenberg [Scho67] should be used as basis functions for a carpet of patches.

A simple summary is that the B-spline bears the same relationship to the interpolating spline as the Bézier method does to Lagrange interpolation or, alternatively, the same relationship to the Bézier method as the interpolating spline does to Lagrange interpolation. B-splines had the additional advantage that the Bézier methods could be regarded as the special case of a B-spline with only one span, and so all surfaces described Bézier-fashion could be handled by a B-spline system.

Since their original proposal, variants of B-splines have been proposed, but such versions as beta and nu splines do not appear to have any operational advantage in practice. Two variations, both visible in the original idea, are:

> to use the possibility of unequal intervals in the division of the parametric line into pieces; and

> to represent the surface in 4D space rather than 3D space, using homogeneous coordinates to project the result into real 3D space.

The combination of these, the Non-Uniform Rational B-Spline (NURBS), includes all widely used previous parametric surface representations and can exactly describe shapes with circular (conic) edges.

It is the current favourite for standardisation of surface representation.

Survey of Representations

DIRECTRIX-GENERATOR METHODS

Description

This class of methods is based on the simple idea of sliding a generator curve across a set of guidelines, thus sweeping out a surface. In any such method there are three essential constituents:

> a set of longitudinal curves or *directrices*;

> a *correspondence rule*, so that, to each point on any one of the curves, a

corresponding point on each of the others may be identified;

a *generator rule*, whereby a generator curve may be constructed through each such set of corresponding points.

A slight generalisation permits some of the directrices to be scalar-valued rather than point-valued: the concept remains that to any point on any directrix the corresponding value on all the others can be identified. It is also possible for the generator rule to treat some of the directrices as guide points rather than as points to be interpolated.

Note that for continuity of the resulting surface it is generally necessary that *all three* constituents have the required continuity. Correspondence discontinuity is easily overlooked. Examples of these methods are:

Shelley's Lofting of the E1/44 Fuselage [Shel47]

Directrices. Maximum section (circular), the aircraft nose (a degenerate conic with only one point), and an intermediate frame section defined as upper and lower conics (see Figure 1).

Correspondence rule. Intercepts of constant angle as seen from forward.

Generators. Longitudinal conics perpendicular to the x-axis at the front and parallel to the x-axis at the maximum section.

Traditional Conic Lofting of an Aircraft Fuselage

Directrices. Curves conic in side and plan view for the upper and lower profile curves, and for the curve of maximum width. Also for shoulder curves above and below the maximum width line (see Figure 2).

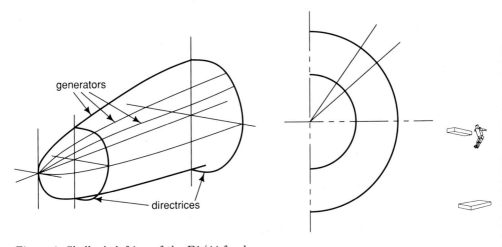

Figure 1. Shelley's lofting of the E1/44 fuselage.

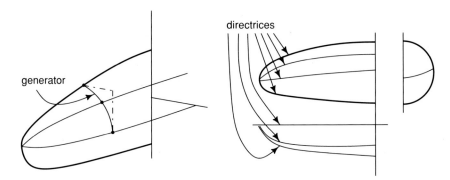

Figure 2. Traditional conic lofting of an aircraft fuselage.

Correspondence rule.   Equal x-value.

Generators.   One conic above the maximum width line, horizontal at the top and vertical at the side, interpolating the shoulder point, together with a similar conic beneath the maximum width line.

Advanced Conic Lofting

Directrices.   Curves as above for the profile and maximum width lines, but a scalar function replacing each shoulder curve, that scalar function being the fullness factor of the generator conic (see Figure 3).

Correspondence rule and generators.   As in traditional conic lofting.

Lockheed Master Dimensions

Generators.   Superellipses instead of conics. The superellipse is a curve of equation

$$(x/a)^n + (y/b)^n = 1$$

It fits into a right-angled quadrant and has one degree of freedom to control the fullness. The disadvantages are that its tangent triangle has to be right-angled (whereas for a conic it may be any triangle), and that the curvature at the end points is unbounded for $n < 2$ and zero for $n > 2$ (see Figure 4). I am not aware of any advantages.

Numerical Master Geometry (NMG)

Directrices.   Parametric splines through data points.

Correspondence rule.   Equal parameter.

Generators.   Parametric splines.

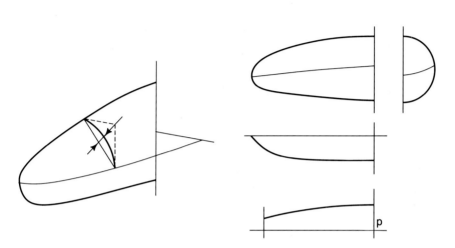

Figure 3. Advanced conic lofting.

DUCT

Directrices.   Spine curve, together with section properties (see Figure 5).

Correspondence rule.   Association of section properties with arc length along the spine.

Generators.   Originally superellipses, but cubics in later versions.

The various versions of DUCT have had many different choices of directrix and generator forms. It is an interesting comment that the changes of the spine curve equation from conic to lince (a curve in which the curvature varies linearly with arc length) to cubic, and of the generators from superellipse to cubics, never influenced the basic character of the package. In fact, the current version as described by Sturge [Stur86] is a multiple patch system, since the defining generators have a simpler form than the general generator.

The subtlety of continuity requirements is exemplified by the fact that to achieve a C^1 continuous surface, it is necessary for the spine curve to be C^2 continuous. A good example of this is the trombone, an archetypal duct of long tapering cross-section based on an obvious centre line. The obvious choice of spine curve, a sequence of straight lines and circular arcs, combined with a smoothly tapering bore, does in fact define a surface with slight creases where the straight parts meet the curves (Figure 6).

Surfaces of Revolution

An extreme example of the directrix-generator approach is the surface of revolution that has a single directrix, the shape of the profile curve with

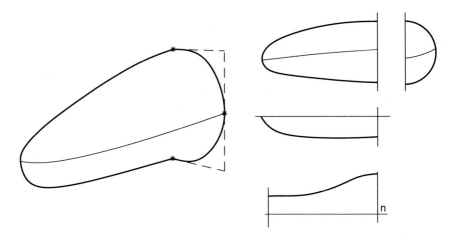

Figure 4. Lockheed Master Dimensions.

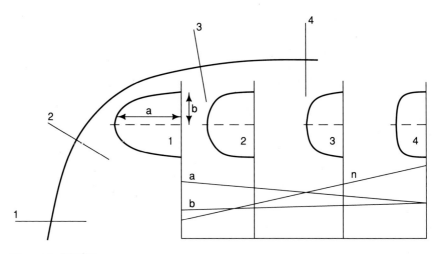

Figure 5. DUCT.

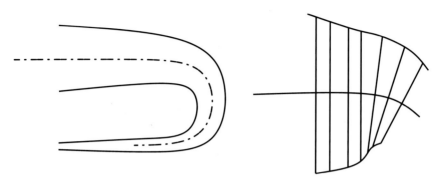

Figure 6. The trombone problem.

respect to the axis, the natural correspondence between anything and itself, and circular generators.

Ruled Surfaces

Another extreme example is the ruled surface. The directrices are the edges to be joined, and the generators straight lines. The correspondence chosen influences the shape of the surface. If the surface required is a wrapped or developable single-curvature surface, this defines a specific correspondence which, unfortunately, is often difficult to match exactly, even with a rational-based rather than a polynomial-based system.

Method-specific Problems

The main problem of explicit directrix-generator methods is that of handling regions without a single natural flow direction to them but in which the continuity properties of a unified definition are needed. The archetypal example is that of a slope-continuous wing–fuselage intersection blend, where the natural fore and aft flow of the fuselage and the spanwise flow of the wing cannot be combined into a single structure of directrices and generators (Figure 7). Shelley's solution [Shel47] for this specific problem was to construct directrices for a fillet surface by intersecting the basic surfaces with views of the required curves of tangency.

In general, obtaining tangency between surfaces other than for the trivial cases of symmetry or when the tangency curve is also a silhouette requires a significant amount of mathematical reasoning. Modification of a surface within a bounded region is far from easy.

The conic-lofting systems, into which the 'equal x' correspondence rule was built, suffered from needing three distinct cross-section algorithms. Sections perpendicular to the x-axis were generators and could be constructed as such. Sections far from perpendicular could be approximated

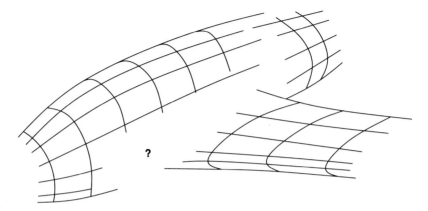

Figure 7. The topology problem.

by intersecting the plane with numerous generators. Those near to perpendicular, however, needed a dense set of longitudinal curves (waterlines or buttlines) to be constructed, and the section would be computed by cutting these with the section plane.

MULTIPLE PATCHES

Description

The unit (that piece with a single equation) of a conic-lofting surface is fairly large; the surface normal typically covers one-eighth of the unit sphere. The blending ideas discussed below brought the thought that, if a blended surface of that size were not quite the right shape, an extra curve could be inserted across the surface to provide the extra control. They also brought special cases by defining the bounding curves to have specific equations. Coons himself [Coon67] used parametric cubic bounding curves in his own implementations, which, when used with cubic blending functions to give slope continuity between adjacent patches, gave bicubic surfaces.

Bicubic patches had also been described by Ferguson [Ferg64] and by Freyman. For one reason or another, not obvious at the time nor easily distinguished now, the idea got around that one should use relatively large numbers of relatively small patches if they were bicubic. Perhaps the spline curve, able to interpolate large numbers of data points without gross misbehaviour, made it too easy to fit long runs of cubics together.

The new concept brought by these patches was the idea of a surface description that was:

Fully defined—the whole surface had an equation, not just curves across it. Although directrix-generator schemes are now understood as being just as full, they were perceived at the time to define only specific frame sections.

Axis-independent—the definition of a specific surface was in terms of points and vectors. Applying a solid body transform to these defining items had the effect of moving the defined surface by the same transform without any change of shape. The constant x correspondence conic-lofting methods were not invariant in the same way.

A bicubic patch can be described in terms of a bivariate polynomial

$$P(u, v) = \sum_{i=0}^{3} \sum_{j=0}^{3} A_{ij} u^i v^j$$

but this is not convenient for surface design because only one of the patch corners is directly controlled, and the differences between the effects of the high-order coefficients are not intuitively understood.

Far better is to use a set of Hermite basis functions

$$P(u, v) = \sum_{i=0}^{3} \sum_{j=0}^{3} A_{ij} f_i(u) f_j(v)$$

where

$$f_0(t) = 1 - 3t^2 + 2t^3$$

$$f_1(t) = 3t^2 - 2t^3$$

$$f_2(t) = t - 2t^2 + t^3$$

$$f_3(t) = t^3 - t^2$$

because the coefficients A_{ij} then become the corner points and the corner derivatives of the patch. This was not only more convenient for the design of individual patches, it also gave a fairly straightforward numerical method of enforcing tangency between adjacent patches.

The problem was the choice of values for the 'twist vectors', the mixed derivative coefficients, corresponding to the required values of $d^2P/dudv$ which did not have a readily describable geometric meaning, and it was thus rather difficult to choose values for them. NMG bypassed this problem by offering numerical differentiation to calculate a good value.

The Bézier description gave an even more satisfactory solution by using a slightly different basis in which the corresponding coefficients had a much more intuitive meaning.

$$P(u, v) = \sum_{i=0}^{3} \sum_{j=0}^{3} A_{ij} f_i(u) f_j(v)$$

where

$$f_0(t) = (1 - t)^3$$
$$f_1(t) = 3t(1 - t)^2$$
$$f_2(t) = 3t^2(1 - t)$$
$$f_3(t) = t^3$$

The coefficients are now all positions of points, which form a fairly regular array across the surface. Only the corner points actually lie on the surface, but the others control it in a highly ergonomic way. Moving one control point displaces every point of the surface, with most effect near the moved point.

For curves, there are certain theorems about the absence of inflections in the sequence of control points guaranteeing the absence of inflexions in the curve and, although the surface situation is rather more complicated, the same ideas are a trustworthy guide.

This approach also made it possible to describe surfaces of a higher order than bicubic with a good chance of getting more or less what you wanted first time. There are fairly straightforward conversions between the control point coordinates, the Hermite end points and tangent vectors, and the polynomial coefficients. These will be elaborated below, where they are also compared with B-splines.

All the forms above are called 'tensor product' or 'Cartesian product', because the set of basis functions in each case is generated as the product of a set of univariate functions of one parameter with a set of univariate functions of the other. This is not the most general parametric surface form, which is

$$P = \sum A_i f_i(u, v)$$

but is much more amenable for visualisation and control.

The less general tensor-product form has the elegant property that, provided each univariate function can be split into two, summing to the original, local increase in density of control can be achieved by splitting a patch into two, which will together have the same shape as the original. Small changes to control values then make small changes to the surface. Examples are:

APTLFT/FMILL

APTLFT/FMILL used bicubic patches with tangent vectors derived by a variant of splining, and zero twist vectors.

NMG

NMG used bicubics with uniform splining to give all the derivatives.

MULTIPATCH

MULTIPATCH used bicubics without aid in setting slope or twist vectors [Armi70].

UNISURF

Bézier's system, UNISURF, used Bézier surfaces of order up to 21 in each direction [Bezi71].

DUCT

Later versions of DUCT may be regarded as fitting rather complicated patches into the network of curves defined by the cross sections at the control points on the spine [Stur86].

Variants

Order

Bipolynomials can vary in order from the simple bilinear that interpolates any quadrilateral upwards. The order of most use historically is the bicubic, probably because it can give slope continuity easily and conveniently via the Hermite mechanism. Higher orders can be defined either by Hermite schemes, in which higher derivatives at the end points are specified, or by Bézier schemes. In both cases a higher order patch gives more degrees of freedom than a lower one, and this can be used to give increased density of control. However, in both cases each control 'handle' influences the whole of the patch.

In the Hermite case it rapidly becomes unrealistic to expect an operator to specify derivatives higher than at most the second. A part-Hermite, part-Lagrange form can push up to order six or seven, but I am not at all sure that it is worth even investigating.

In the Bézier case higher orders are more easily controlled because of the way the curve mimics the shape of the control polygon. However, with high orders the effect of a movement of the innermost control points becomes very low-geared, so that large movements of the control points are needed to achieve a required movement of the curve.

Many Bézier-based systems allow high-order surfaces because there are internal transformations that can push up the order of a surface originally defined as a low-order cubic or quadratic. For example, suppose that a curve $v_1 = f(u)$ (f polynomial) is defined across a patch, and we wish to represent the surface on one side of this curve as a patch with that curve as a boundary. Substituting $v' = v/v_1$ (or $v = v_1 v'$) into the surface equation produces a new representation of exactly the same surface, but with $v' = 1$ lying along the required curve. This new representation is of a higher order in u (Figure 8). It is also possible to apply some transformation to u in this example so that places where dv_1/du is infinite are dealt with accurately.

However, u' must be monotonic in u, and so this method of trimming is not fully general.

Non-four-sided patches

If patches are treated as independent entities, it is possible within the scheme of things for some of them to have other than four sides. The requirement is typically for a few n-sided patches to be included among a collection of mainly four-sided ones. In a C^2 continuous surface, the expectation that isoparametric lines should be feature lines running more or less along lines of curvature, implies that an n-sided patch is required for each umbilic point.

In the literature there are a number of three-sided patches [Barn74b; Greg86b; Char80; Fari79] and a few five-sided patches [Sabi83; Greg86b]. All are parametric, but the parametric domain has various possibilities.

For triangles, Barnhill [Barn74a] uses the unit triangle (0,0; 1,0; 0,1), but other authors use barycentric coordinates to give symmetry between the three sides. Symmetry of this kind is a useful aid in ensuring that the triangle can in fact be embedded among other patches with specified continuity: you only have to prove that it works across one edge, and the others follow by symmetry. Mapping a unit square into a triangular patch by shrinking one side to a point works only at a point such as the pole of a sphere, where all the patches at that point are similarly degenerate. The Barnhill, Gregory, and Charrot [Barn74b; Greg86b; Char80] triangles are defined as blends between their edges, Coons style, and specific patches can be constructed by choosing the edges to be, for example, parametric cubics with parametric cubic cross-slope variation. In such a case, each edge curve

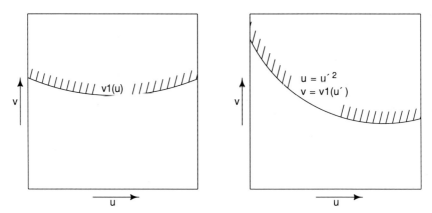

Figure 8. Bézier trimming.

is defined in the same way as the edges of the four-sided patches, and so continuity is assured. Both Sabin triangles are defined as specific patches, the 1968 one [Sabi68] as matching adjacent bicubics, the 1983 one [Sabi83] as matching adjacent Bézier quadratics.

Gregory and Charrot treat the pentagon as a mapping from a regular pentagon in the parameter plane and achieve continuity by using blending between predefined edge curves; Sabin [Sabi83] considers it as a mapping from a manifold in 5D space, one parameter zero on each side, the five parametric variables being related by a set of symmetric equations.

All of these methods give patches that behave plausibly as individual pieces of surface. None of them, however, give ease of modification to a region within the patch, since none of them permit easy subdivision without altering the shape of the patch.

Geometric Continuity

An alternative to the use of a single n-sided patch is to fit together n four-sided-patches around a singular vertex (Figure 9). Bézier's thesis [Bezi77] includes the necessary conditions for joining these patches together in such a way that, although continuity of first derivative with respect to parameter is lost between adjacent patches, continuity of tangent plane can still be maintained.

These methods, however, do not make it easy to smoothly join such

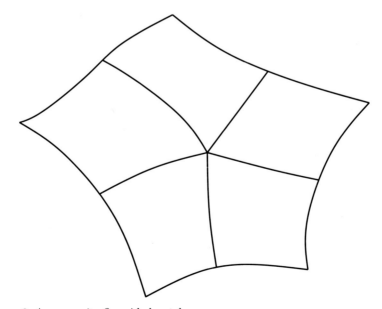

Figure 9. A composite five-sided patch.

assemblies with the regions around them unless the order of the inserted patches is increased drastically. Bézier's own system allowed for patches of up to order 21 primarily to permit this kind of manipulation. There are special cases when these methods do work, which are the cases where there is exploitable symmetry. If the cross tangent direction is constant across each of the three external boundaries of a triple (as at a suitcase corner), the variation of tangent vector magnitude can easily be shown not to introduce creases; in general, however, life is not so accommodating.

Interrogation of n-sided Patches

The fact that n-sided patches are not images of the unit parametric square complicates their interrogation (see the discussion in Sabin, "Interrogation Techniques for Parametric Surfaces," in this volume.)

Method-specific Problems

The setting of the twist vectors, necessary if a Hermite form is used, is not a convenient handle to use in surface description.

Multiple small patches give a data-management complication for the software and, unless the patches are arranged as a carpet, even more of one for the operator, who has to make sure that patches remain continuous while he modifies them.

Nonrectangular patches are available but do not fit very conveniently into a multiple patch management scheme.

TRANSFINITE PATCH METHODS

Description

Like the directrix-generator methods, the transfinite interpolation or 'blending' idea is another way of progressing from a network of curves to a fully defined surface. Here the concept is that each piece of surface is defined to match its boundary, where a boundary may be either a curve, in which case the pieces will match with continuity of position only, or a curve with an associated tangent plane at every point, in which case the pieces must meet with continuity of tangent plane. The best known of such methods is the Coons patch [Coon67], which fits a four-sided boundary. Specifically, the four sides have to satisfy certain conditions:

for a position-continuous surface, edges have to be position-continuous curves;

adjacent sides must match at the corners;

opposite sides must have a correspondence, so that any position on one side has a corresponding point on the other, and also must have a correspondence with a scalar going from 0 to 1 . In other words, the sides must be parametric.

Note that it is not necessary that a side be analytic. It can be piece-wise defined, using as many pieces as you like, and so a curve calculated across some other surface could be a perfectly good boundary for a Coons patch provided that it satisfied the three conditions above. The surface constructed is a parametric surface, the image of the unit square. The construction is most easily described by taking the scalar-valued version.

A surface $zz(u, v)$ (Figure 10) is to be constructed matching

$$
\begin{array}{lll}
z_1(v) & \text{along} & u = 0 \\
z_2(u) & \text{along} & v = 0 \\
z_3(v) & \text{along} & u = 1 \\
z_4(u) & \text{along} & v = 1
\end{array}
$$

The first step satisfies two of these conditions

$$zz_1(u, v) = z_1(v)(1 - u) + z_3(v)u$$

Clearly this function matches the requirements at $u = 0$ and at $u = 1$ (Figure 11a). However, it falls short of the required values along $v = 0$ by an amount $z_2(u) - zz_1(u, 0)$ and along $v = 1$ by an amount $z_4(u) - zz_1(u, 1)$ (see Figure 11b). This shortfall could be made up by adding to zz_1 the correction function

$$zz_2(u, v) = (z_2(u) - zz_1(u, 0))(1 - v) + (z_4(u) - zz_1(u, 1))v$$

which is zero on $u = 0$ and $u = 1$, and has the correct value on $v = 0$ and $v = 1$ (Figure 12). The total of these two functions thus has all the required interpolation properties. When expanded it becomes

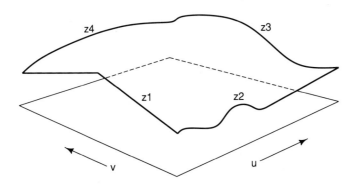

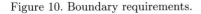

Figure 10. Boundary requirements.

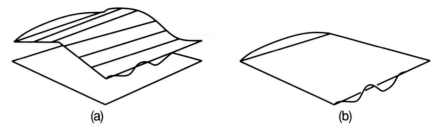

Figure 11. (a) First blending. (b) Residual boundary error.

$$zz(u,v) = zz_1(u,v) + zz_2(u,v)$$
$$= z_1(v)(1-u) + z_3(v)u$$
$$+ (z_2(u) - z_1(0)(1-u) - z_3(0)u)(1-v)$$
$$+ (z_4(u) - z_1(1)(1-u) - z_3(1)u)v$$
$$= z_1(v)(1-u) + z_2(u)(1-v) + z_3(v)u + z_4(u)v$$
$$- z_1(0)(1-u)(1-v) - z_3(0)u(1-v)$$
$$- z_1(1)(1-u)v - z_3(1)uv$$

As well as its generality of boundary, this method also has the nice property that, if an isoparametric line is computed across the patch and new patches are computed using this line as a defining boundary, the result is exactly the same as the original. This means that extra data can be inserted into a surface that almost meets the requirements and then moved slightly. The insertion does not completely upset the rest of the surface.

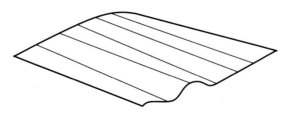

Figure 12. Boundary error correction surface.

Examples

Coons himself generalised this method to handle known boundary cross-slopes by means of further correction surfaces, and Barnhill, Gregory, and others have produced triangular and pentagonal patches that match boundary values and cross-slopes [Coon67; Barn74b; Greg86b; Char80].

When boundary cross-slopes are to be used it is necessary that they be consistent at the corners with the slopes along the adjacent sides. Ideally, the twists should also match, but Gregory has defined a method for handling any mismatch [Greg86b].

Gordon [Gord68] produced another generalisation by using splines instead of the linear interpolation used above, and by fitting those splines through sets of curves parallel in the parameter domain, not just opposite edges. With this view of the world, Coons' slope matching form is just the limit of the Gordon surface when there are two control curves around the boundary, and these approach the limit. The actual boundary curve and the cross derivative are the limit of the mean and the scaled difference of the two curves near a given point of the boundary.

Just as spline interpolation produces better continuity from a given order of piece than Hermite interpolation (Hermite interpolation needs cubics to give slope continuity; spline interpolation gives slope continuity from quadratics and curvature continuity from cubics), spline blending should give better continuity at a given level of performance than lots of individually fitted Coons' patches.

The Gordon method works over a topologically rectangular grid, but this can be of unequal intervals in either or both directions. In Gordon's system at General Motors, a second level of spline mapping is used to map any grid onto a tartan grid. Provided that this parameter map is also continuous in curvature and strictly monotonic, the surface remains curvature-continuous with respect to parameter.

Note that in the transfinite method the individual curves that are interpolated can have a piecewise structure unrelated to the spacing of the cross curves. If the implementor decides to permit only one type of bounding curve (the parametric cubic was chosen by Coons), this technique reduces to a way of making a finite-dimensional patch where the only freedom the operator has is in the choosing of a certain number of numerical coefficients. Such surfaces are not necessarily impossibly restrictive, but they are properly described in other parts of this paper.

Method-specific Problems

The version that uses individual patches is forced to use higher order surfaces to achieve continuity of a given derivative than the spline-blending variant. It is not particularly easy to define a cross-slope variation that suits the patches on both sides of a line of tangency. The full power of the method, with its ability to interpolate curves of any parametric equation whatever, is not easily delivered to the surface designer unless he is prepared to write pieces of program to evaluate points on his curves and to link these in with the bulk of the software. Since the method may be viewed as the blending between orthogonal directrix-generator surfaces, the difficulties of the directrix-generator methods apply here also, except that there do exist non-four-sided patch formulations.

CARPET METHODS

Description

The multiple patch methods made it necessary to be able to refer to a whole collection of individual patches as a unit; otherwise, invoking any interrogation would have been ridiculously long-winded. It is obviously desirable to record the adjacencies and sharing of handles between the patches, so that continuity can be maintained between them as automatically as possible. This can be done for general assemblies, but the simplest arrangement of patches, the regular array, gives the most benefit for minimal complication. It is possible to regard such an array as a single surface with piecewise defining basis functions.

NMG can be regarded in this light. Provided that no slopes are controlled except across a complete row of data points, its set of basis functions is the tensor product of the interpolating spline functions. The B-spline theory made this idea really respectable. It bears the same relationship to the NMG methods as does the Bézier technique to interpolating (Lagrange) polynomials, and gives the same advantage of complete control of the qualitative properties of the curve while sacrificing the precision of interpolation (see Table 1).

A B-spline is a piecewise basis function that is zero outside of a minimum-width region and positive within it. This minimum width depends on the order of the pieces and on the continuity required between them. The cubic B-spline has cubic pieces with second derivative continuity and has a width of four pieces. Such functions are used in sets with as many functions as are necessary to give a curve of the required length. Apart from at the ends, the members of such a set are all the same shape, only differing from one another in that they apply to successive ranges.

Associating a point coefficient with each term in the tensor product of two sets of B-spline functions gives a surface definition in which each coefficient influences the surface in a limited region nearby, but in which all the

Table 1. Relationships between curve systems.

	Polynomial	Spline
Interpolating	Lagrange	NMG
Variation diminishing	Bézier	B-spline

required continuity properties are automatically maintained. Examples are NMG (used in a restricted way) and many more recent proprietary systems.

Variants

Important variants are the following:

Uniform versus Nonuniform

The uniform B-spline is defined over a set of pieces all of the same parametric length; the nonuniform B-spline allows the pieces to vary in length. By having some pieces tend to the limit of zero length, we are able to include within a B-spline structure additional control when curvature continuity needs to be sacrificed for slope control or when even slope continuity is not required. For initial design there is little operational difference (except the ability to include slope discontinuities) but, when small changes are to be made in detailed areas, the ability to insert subdivisions (and thus short-wavelength features), which the nonuniform version gives, is very valuable. The details of nonuniform B-spline capability are covered below in the section on relationships between various bipolynomial methods.

Rational versus Polynomial

It is not possible to represent a circle as a polynomial

$$P = \sum_{i=0}^{n} A_i u^i$$

if P and A are interpreted as vectors in 3D space. However, an arc of a circle can be so represented if they are interpreted as vectors in 4D space of homogeneous coordinates. This brings the ability to join sculptured surfaces smoothly to parts whose shape is defined more conventionally, such as cylinders and cones, with no approximation error at all.

The Effects of the Weights as Design Handles

It is rather difficult to interpret the effects of the fourth coordinate on the Hermite control of a curve. They become much easier to understand in a Bézier framework, where each control point has associated with it a *weight*. The 4D coordinates are, first, the three 3D coordinates each multiplied by the weight, and the weight itself. Within a single piece of curve of any order, the weights can be redistributed to some extent between the Bézier points without changing the shape, because multiplying the weights by a geometric sequence merely corresponds to a reparametrisation.

We may therefore assume that both ends of the span have the same unit weight. (This assumption does not strictly carry over to the bivariate case, because it is not possible to get all four corners to unit weight simultaneously from some arbitrary initial set of weights. However, the restriction to unit corner weights does not appear to be cumbersome.)

The effect of increasing the weight of the tangent control point of a quadratic is to pull the curve towards the vertex of the tangent triangle (Figure 13.) In the symmetric case the value $w = 1$ gives the parabola; the value $w = \cos$ of half the angle turned through gives the circular arc. Values of w slightly less than one are typical of nice rounded curves. The values of w should always be positive if the tangent at the end of the curve is to point from the end point towards the next control point. This is also a sufficient condition for avoiding asymptotes in the curve, which will arise if the fourth coordinate becomes zero at any parameter value in the range used for the curve.

In the case of the cubic, the influences of the weights of the two tangent control points are similar. Increasing either weight pulls the curve towards that point. Increasing both of them pulls the curve towards the polygon.

For the surface case, increasing the weight of any control point pulls the surface towards that control point. It is not in my view proven that this additional handle provides any operational advantage over the movement of control points.

The rational facilities can be made available and not hinder the operator (except by a slight reduction in interrogation speed) because he can always leave the weights at the default of unity. However, I would not regard it as wise to sell the use of these facilities until a really difficult surface definition problem loomed that turned out to be unmanageable using the simpler homogeneous control interface of moving control points of the polynomial B-spline. The rational B-spline does not give such neat control as the rational Bézier, although the same principle of 'increase the weight: pull the curve' still applies.

For simple application of the B-spline ideas there has to be continuity of first derivative in all four dimensions, which means that the tangent control weights cannot all be less than one if the end point weights are held at unity.

To describe a circular arc as a rational B-spline requires the weights to increase towards the ends (Figure 14). Further, a longer series of spans which

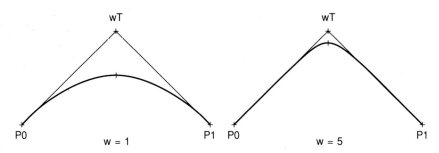

Figure 13. Effect of varying weight.

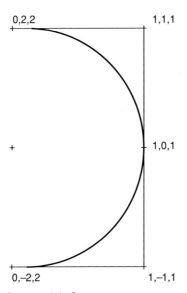

Figure 14. Rational B-spline semicircle.

all look alike turn out to be represented by an unequal interval B-spline, the intervals increasing towards the ends. Essentially, trying to represent a complete circle as a rational B-spline amounts to splitting the parameter interval between minus and plus infinity into pieces. The complete circle cannot be represented as a single rational B-spline without dynamic modification of the representation between pieces.

Order

There are two aspects of the B-spline that may be regarded as 'order'. One is the number of spans, which influences the density of control. The number of spans needs no comment. The other is the order of the individual pieces of which the spline is built, which does not influence the density of control except in the degenerate cases.

   With the development of B-spline theory it became possible to achieve slope continuity with quadratics, but parabolae give a much poorer approximation to circular arcs than do cubics, and the smoothness of quadratic splines is therefore suspect.

   High-order B-splines exist, giving progressively higher continuity between adjacent spans. Splines made up of nth-order polynomial pieces give continuity of $(n - 1)$th derivative. Because of the variation diminishing properties of all B-splines, there is no danger of ripples being introduced by the use of a high order, but the range of influence of each control point becomes wider as the order goes up, and the gearing on its own part of the curve becomes lower. Unless there is a definite requirement for higher order continuity, I see no reason for the use of high-order B-splines. Further discussion of B-splines can be found in [Roge90; Pieg87].

Method-specific Problems

The use of points lying off the surface in its definition gives some problems when attempting to capture an existing surface accurately. It is very likely that the first attempt will not be highly accurate, and modification will then need to be carried out.

The regularity of the array of patches prevents the inclusion of other than four-sided patches.

A combination of B-spline and interpolating spline methods that uses the interpolating spline to give a first approximation, which can be viewed either as a control point network or by conventional sections, and which can then be improved by B-spline techniques, should give the best of both worlds. At British Aircraft Corporation (BAC) we found the B-spline ideas a valuable way of deciding what modifications to make to the slopes and twist vectors.

Critical Analysis

DIFFERENT WAYS OF LOOKING AT THE SAME SURFACE

Overlap Between Paradigms

NMG may be viewed as a directrix-generator form (if you regard the data points as lying on a set of directrix curves), as a multiple patch form (if you expect to control a lot of the slopes and twists), or as a carpet form (if you expect to control none). Equally, a conic-lofting surface can be regarded as a patch. The individual pieces of a carpet are multiple patches and, if there is some coupling by common values between patches, they become to some extent a carpet. What is probably most important is not philosophical discussion but giving the surface designer the most convenient set of facilities for controlling the shape of the surface.

Relationships Between Various Bipolynomial Methods

Several of the methods described previously result in parametric bipolynomial surfaces. The Hermite cubic, the Bézier cubic, and the cubic B-spline are all ways of describing the same universe, and so it is possible to convert between these descriptions. These conversions are fairly straightforward, and an understanding of them means that ideas from all three sources can be used whenever the package itself demands it. In this section these relationships are spelled out for the univariate case. The tensor product idea generalises these results to the bivariate case.

All three variants are of the form

$$P = \sum_i A_i f_i(u)$$

using different cubic polynomials as their basis f and, therefore, coefficients A with different geometric interpretations. For a single cubic span, the Hermite and Bézier variants have the following basis functions

(Hermite)
$$f_0 = 1 - 3u^2 + 2u^3$$
$$f_1 = 3u^2 - 2u^3$$
$$f_2 = u(1-u)^2$$
$$f_3 = -u^2(1-u)$$

(Bézier)
$$f_0 = (1-u)^3$$
$$f_1 = 3u(1-u)^2$$
$$f_2 = 3u^2(1-u)$$
$$f_3 = u^3$$

which can be represented by the product of a 4×4 matrix with the vector of powers of u. Let U be the transpose of

$$\begin{bmatrix} u^3 & u^2 & u & 1 \end{bmatrix}$$

and F be the column of basis functions in each case. Then

(Hermite)
$$[F] = \begin{bmatrix} 2 & -3 & 0 & 1 \\ -2 & 3 & 0 & 0 \\ 1 & -2 & 1 & 0 \\ 1 & -1 & 0 & 0 \end{bmatrix} [U] = [H][U]$$

(Bézier)
$$[F] = \begin{bmatrix} -1 & 3 & -3 & 1 \\ 3 & -6 & 3 & 0 \\ -3 & 3 & 0 & 0 \\ 1 & 0 & 0 & 0 \end{bmatrix} [U] = [B][U]$$

$$[P] = [P_h][H][U] = [P_b][B][U]$$

where $[P_h] = [P_0, P_1, V_0, V_1]$ and $[P_b] = [P_0, T_0, T_1, P_1]$, and so

$$[P_h][H] = [P_b][B]$$

Thus
$$[P_h] = [P_b][B][H]^{-1}$$

and
$$[P_b] = [P_h][H][B]^{-1}$$

Let P_0 and P_1 be the start and finish points of the span, V_0 and V_1 the slope vectors at those points, and T_0 and T_1 the inner Bézier points. Then

$$V_0 = 3[T_0 - P_0] \qquad V_1 = 3[P_1 - T_1]$$
$$T_0 = P_0 + V_0/3 \qquad T_1 = P_1 - V_1/3$$

are the results of the matrix manipulation above (Figure 15). This enables easy and rapid conversion between the two forms.

Because of the triangular form of the Bézier matrix $[B]$, it is particularly easy to determine the derivatives at the ends of the span from the Bézier form

$$
\begin{aligned}
P(0) &= P_0 & P(1) &= P_1 \\
P_u(0) &= 3(T_0 - P_0) & P_u(1) &= 3(P_1 - T_1) \\
P_{uu}(0) &= 6(T_1 - 2T_0 + P_0) & P_{uu}(1) &= 6(T_0 - 2T_1 + P_1)
\end{aligned}
$$

Requiring position continuity between two Bézier segments (P_0, T_0, T_1, P_1) and (Q_0, U_0, U_1, Q_1) is sufficient to make them share the same control point position so that $Q_0 = P_1$.

If we require continuity of first derivative, we must satisfy the further condition $P_1 - T_1 = U_0 - Q_0$, which combined with the first gives

$$Q_0 = P_1 = [T_1 + U_0]/2$$

Because P_1 and Q_0 are constrained in this way we have lost them from the list of control points for the entire curve, and so the control point list is now

$$P_0 \, T_0 \, T_1 \, U_0 \, U_1 \, Q_1$$

and if a longer collection of slope-continuous pieces were being designed we would have as our control points just the inner Bézier points, the original span end points being retained only at the ends of the complete curve.

This is a useful concept for curve design. To modify a curve so that a bulge is added mainly in one span, the influence being restricted to at most two spans, one chooses a displacement for one of the inner Bézier control points (say, U_0) and changes the common point and the tangent vector there to suit (Figure 16).

For equal parametric intervals, the maximum displacement of this perturbation is 0.64 (say, two-thirds) of the movement of U_0 and occurs at a parameter value one-fifth of the way from Q_0 to Q_1. If the maximum movement is to be D, then the change in U_0 is $25D/16$, the movement of $P_1 (= Q_0)$ is $25D/32$ and the change in slope $75D/32$.

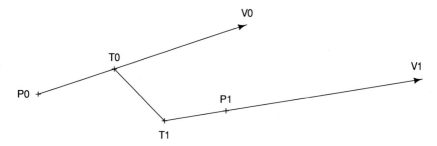

Figure 15. Conversion between Hermite and Bézier coefficients.

If we require continuity of second derivative between adjacent spans, the additional condition, derived from the end conditions given above, applies:

$$[U_1 - 2U_0 + Q_0] = [T_0 - 2T_1 + P_1]$$

or
$$U_1 - T_0 = 2[U_0 - T_1]$$

or
$$2T_1 - T_0 = 2U_0 - U_1$$

Each side of the last form can be interpreted as a point as far beyond T_1 as T_1 is from T_0, and as far beyond U_0 as U_0 is from U_1. Since the equation of second derivative continuity equates these two expressions, give the point a name, say, B_1.

Then
$$T_1 = [T_0 + B_1]/2$$
$$U_0 = [B_1 + U_1]/2$$

By replacing T_1 and U_0 in our list of effective control points by the new point B_1 and always computing T_1 and U_0 from it, we can ensure that the curve always retains second derivative continuity.

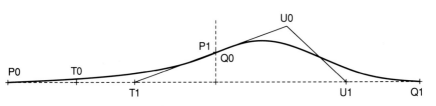

Figure 16. A local modification.

If this principle is applied all of the way along a curve with more pieces, we find that the new B points replace all the inner Bézier points except at the ends. At an intermediate span, we have

$$U_0 = [B_1 + U_1]/2$$

$$U_1 = [U_0 + B_2]/2$$

which may be solved to give (Figure 17)

$$U_0 = [2B_1 + B_2]/3$$

$$U_1 = [B_1 + 2B_2]/3$$

These points B are the B-spline control points, and so a quick conversion from a B-spline polygon to a Bézier polygon gets the inner points by dividing the chords of the polygon into thirds, and then the span end points by taking the midpoints of the pairs of slope control points. The above description has assumed a regular interval (uniform) B-spline for simplicity. In the unequal interval (nonuniform) case the equations are significantly more complex, but the logic of the argument still applies.

Calculating the B-spline polygon from a set of points and slopes that has been generated by splining is most easily done by constructing the inner Bézier points and then cantilevering outwards to give the B-spline points. Each control point can be worked out from either side; the two calculations should give the same answer if the splining has worked correctly.

Where a slope has been constrained, the two cantileverings will give different answers, and the vector difference between the two gives a measure of the discontinuity of second derivative. If this is parallel to the slope at the common point of the two spans, the discontinuity of curvature will be zero.

One of the useful operations with B-splines, if unequal intervals are permitted, is the splitting of a span into two. (This can be done because we can arbitrarily think of a single piece of cubic as two pieces by reparametrising.) This alters the control polygon, because a new control point becomes available and, in fact, the adjacent ones move to even out the control effect.

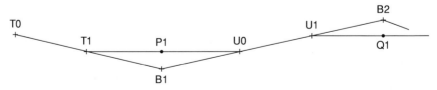

Figure 17. Conversion from B-spline to Bézier coefficients.

If a new knot is inserted at exactly the same place as an existing one, the mathematics treats this as the limiting case of a new knot very close to an original one. The effect of this is to move the original control point over in one direction and to create the new one displaced the other way. If this is done at every point of a long curve, the new control points turn out to be the inner Bézier points $(T_0\ T_1\ U_0\ U_1 \cdots)$ so the control by means of these points can be given the name 'Degenerate B-spline' to sound more impressive.

If a third knot is inserted at the same place, the extra control point turns out to be the common end point, $P_1 = Q_0$, enabling us to define a curve without slope continuity. This is obviously the best way of defining a sharp knuckle. An alternative is to superimpose the positions of a number of control points without multiple knots. This is fairly controllable using the B-spline approach, whereas passing an interpolating spline through the same point several times would cause horrible loops.

In the case of a cubic B-spline, if three consecutive control points are placed on a straight line, the curve will be tangent to that line, with zero curvature. If three are given the same position, the curve has zero first and second derivatives as it passes through that point. Because the third derivative is constant over a cubic span, the curve will come away from the repeated point along a straight line towards the next control point on each side. Again, this allows the definition of a knuckle, but the straight line portion may not be wanted.

THE SURFACE DESIGNER'S INTERFACE

There are two aspects to be considered, initial setting up of a surface and subsequent modification, which in turn may either be the global modification of the entire surface or the detailed modification of a small locality.

Initial Design

During the initial setting up phase, the various paradigms give the following kinds of handles.

Directrix-generator Methods:

   choice of generator form;
   choice of directrices;
   choice of correspondence rule.

It is relatively easy to use the full power of these methods if the surface designer is a programmer and is prepared to write a short routine for every surface so defined. If not, these choices are restricted to choosing one of a small number of predefined forms and values for its coefficients.

Transfinite Interpolation:

   choice of curves in network;

choice of blending method;

choice of correspondences.

Again, these can only be fully exploited if the surface designer can program. If not, they reduce to multiple patch or carpet methods.

Multiple Patch Methods:

The most sensible multipatch option today is the Bézier form, which gives the surface designer the following:

choice of surface order (number of control points in each direction);

choice of positions of control points.

This looks restricted, but a homogeneous control medium is one which is easily learned. A preprocessor to generate the Bézier form from the Hermite or from an interpolating spline or B-spline is a highly practical possibility.

Carpet Methods:

The most general form is the nonuniform rational B-spline, which offers

choice of surface order (number of control points in each direction);

choice of order of internal continuity;

choice of knot vector;

choice of positions of control points;

choice of control point weights.

This relative richness requires a lot of defaults to make it useful. It is likely that defaults of

second derivative continuity;

uniform knot vector; and

unit weights

would seldom need to be changed at the initial design stage.

Global Modification

The various paradigms give the following facilities for global adjustment of the surface such as might be required to give the specified displacement or metacentric height. Facilities amounting to a complete redesign of the surface are noted in parentheses.

Directrix-generator Methods:

modify the directrices;

(modify the correspondence rule);

(modify the generator rule).

Transfinite Interpolation:

Modify the curves.

Multiple patch (Bézier) Methods:

move control points, possibly several at once;
change order.

Provided that the change is an increase in order, there is an algorithm that computes the positions for the control points of the new surface such that it is the same shape as the original.

Carpet Methods:

move collections of control points;
change weights;
change knot vector;
change order or continuity.

Again, as long as the changing of knot vector, order, or continuity is in the direction of increasing the availability of control, i.e.,

insertion of knots;
increase of order; or
decrease of continuity

the change can be implemented by algorithm without changing the shape of the surface, following which, movement of the new control points can achieve delicate adjustment. In fact, reasonable ways of moving almost all of the control points at once can be defined as the sum of two B-splines, one with a relatively dense network, the other with a relatively coarse one. The latter is used for global modifications. The theory for this is that of discrete B-splines. Subdivision theory shows that a B-spline over a coarse knot vector can be expressed as the sum of the B-splines over a subdivision of that knot vector. A long wavelength modification can therefore be applied as the sum of a lot of minimum-width B-splines over the actual knot vector (Figure 18).

Local Modifications

Later in the design process there may be a need for local modification of relatively small parts of the shape to allow, for example, appropriate fairing between a prop-shaft and a ship hull. The various approaches offer the following capabilities.

Directrix-generator Methods:

These methods enable one to define a region of the original surface to be modified, and completely redesign a new surface for that part. This may be difficult if the modification region is not bounded by generators only.

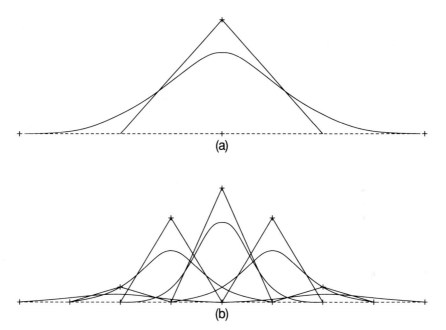

Figure 18. (a) Original knot vector and B-spline. (b) Equivalent component B-splines.

Transfinite Interpolation:

This method offers the ability to define a region of the original surface that is to be modified, and completely redesign a new surface for that part. The ability to split a surface is important here for the setting of the boundary of the region to be modified as close as possible around the area of interest.

Multiple Patch Methods:

With these methods one can identify whether the boundary can lie along existing patch boundaries and, if so, modify the patches affected. If not, one can partition the surface using Bézier trimming if necessary (see above) so that the boundary lies along an existing patch boundary.

Carpet Methods:

With these methods, if a nonuniform basis is used, one can insert additional knot lines if necessary and move control points. Clearly, facilities for insertion of a new knot line must be provided if the full power of the method is to be made available.

I believe that it should be possible with reasonable performance to allow the surface designer to indicate a region of one view of the lines plan that he wishes to alter, and for any necessary subdivision to be carried out. Pulling the middle of this region with cursor or dial would then carry all the lines on that view, whether they be waterlines, butts, or frame sections. When what is seen is regarded as reasonably satisfactory (or when the program detects that the operator has stopped changing the amount of bulge) the other two views of the new version would be calculated.

If the region to be modified has 20 lines each of 25 points, only 500 points need be recomputed and, provided that the modification lies within the view plane, this can be a simple re-evaluation from stored parameter values. Again, assuming that the computer used is large enough to hold the surface coefficients and the lists of parameter values in real memory, and assuming for the moment that the surface has bicubic pieces and the sending to the display is pipelined by Direct Memory Access somehow, the cycle time would be

$$500 \text{ points} \times 60 \text{ flops/point} \times 5 \text{ microseconds/flop}$$
$$= 150 \text{ milliseconds, giving six cycles per second}$$

This could be speeded up by computing once and for all the influence coefficients of the modification on each of the points, thus reducing the recomputation time to 4 flops/point and thus 10 milliseconds per cycle, but other overheads might dominate this.

Flops (floating point operations) are used as a measure here of computational cost because they are both more meaningful than 'instructions' (instruction sets differ so much from machine to machine that one may require five short instructions to achieve what another can do in one long one) and much easier to count. The fact that much of the computing time is taken in nonfloating-point tasks such as array subscripting, is taken care of by including an overhead within the microseconds-per-flop figure.

Why 60 flops per point?

$$x = (((((. * u + .) * u + .) * u + .) * v +$$
$$((. * u + .) * u + .) * u + .) * v +$$
$$((. * u + .) * u + .) * u + .) * v +$$
$$((. * u + .) * u + .) * u + .$$

$$y = (((((. * u + .) * u + .) * u + .) * v +$$
$$((. * u + .) * u + .) * u + .) * v +$$
$$((. * u + .) * u + .) * u + .) * v +$$
$$((. * u + .) * u + .) * u + .$$

Thirty each of $*$ and $+$.

Why 4 flops per point?

$$x = x_0 + a\frac{dx}{da}$$

$$y = y_0 + a\frac{dy}{da}$$

DERIVED SURFACES

Two important classes of surface are not defined independently but in terms of other surfaces. These are the offset surfaces, used for skin thicknesses and cutter centre surfaces, and fillet surfaces, where a concave corner is smoothed out. Developed surfaces are used as an aid in developing plates into the flat.

Offset Surfaces

Offsets are required for a number of purposes, notably for interrogating inside skins when the outside has been defined, for interrogating a cutter centre surface when model making by numerically controlled machine tools, and for determining the centre line of a fillet surface. Such offsets can be handled in either of two ways.

Approximate Method

Here the coefficients of another surface are computed so that the result lies as close to parallel to a first as is required. It is possible to achieve any required accuracy by subdivision of the offset surface, which is particularly easy if the original surface was defined with a carpet method. This is likely to be adequate for skin thicknesses.

However, the more complicated offsets for machining make it difficult to be certain that the required accuracy has been reached everywhere, and so very deep subdivision is likely to occur. If male and female dies are being machined for pressing of sheet material, it is highly important for the satisfactory working of the process that the offsets are compatible. Unfortunately, the obvious way of setting new patch control points gives a second-order error that goes opposite ways for the two surfaces, thus giving large thickness errors very easily. Further, modification of the original surface makes it necessary to recalculate the offset one.

Dynamic Method

This is the method used in NMG, which uses the result that any offset defined in terms of a parametric surface is itself a parametric surface. It is more expensive in evaluation time, because an extra layer of derivatives is required, together with the actual offsetting code, in the middle of every inner loop. However, its coding simplicity makes it my preference still. All the surfaces defined above have been parametric surfaces and so all may be offset dynamically.

Fillet Surfaces

Fillet surfaces are the surfaces inserted to smooth out the join between two previously defined surfaces that would otherwise meet at a concave intersection. Examples might be between a bulbous bow and the main hull, between the propshaft tunnel and the hull near the stern, or between the conning tower and the body of a submarine. They are distinguished from fairings that fill the gap between previously defined surfaces that are almost tangential anyway.

Fillets are usually thought of by the analogy of putting modelling clay into the concave corner and having the pattern maker run his thumb along, squeezing out unwanted clay and forming the remainder into a smooth surface tangential with those it joins. Numerical procedures can emulate this, perhaps using a ball bearing of exact radius rather than a thumb, but essentially sweeping out the fillet by line contact of a generating shape.

For the simplest case of a constant radius fillet, the procedure is simple to describe. Intersect the two surfaces, each offset by the fillet radius, to give the trajectory of the centre of the ball. Drop perpendiculars from each point of this curve on to each of the original surfaces (probably by reevaluating the original surfaces at the known parameter values) and construct a circular arc in the plane of these three points. Each such circular arc is a generator of the required fillet surface.

More complex fillet definitions can be elaborated into surface definitions in a similar way. In particular, the radius of the rolling ball can depend on the position of its contact point with the base surface. This will not give exactly circular generators but, if the radius is varying along the fillet, it hardly matters if it varies across it too.

The above description defines a discrete representation, which may be turned into a fully defined surface either by interpolation between the generators or by treating the above as a dynamic definition. Interpolation will not be strictly accurate even if Hermite interpolation is used to ensure that the fillet surface is truly tangential to the originals at every explicit point. Particular difficulty may be encountered if either of the original surfaces has a discontinuity of curvature. Dynamic definition will be very expensive.

Developed Surfaces

A convenient way of carrying out the calculation of the shape of plates in the flat before rolling is to have an auxiliary surface which is itself flat, corresponding point by point to the original. (For more detail, see Sabin, 'Interrogation Techniques for Parametric Surfaces,' this volume.)

Trimming and Bounding of Surfaces

Once a fillet surface itself is constructed, there is still the problem remaining that the original surfaces have to be trimmed. A variation available in principle for all of the surface definitions mentioned above is whether the boundary of the definition should be identical with the boundary of the surface.

It is generally accepted in geometric or volume modelling that the final boundary of the surface should not be forced to be the boundary of the definition. If it happens to be convenient for the two to coincide, then well and good, but if not, then coincidence should not be forced.

The alternative is for additional representation on top of the geometric form of the shape itself to represent what part of that form actually constitutes the hull or deck or whatever. This allows the hull–deck intersection to appear rather than having to be initially specified. The additional representation necessary is to associate with each surface a curve held both in parametric form and as a list of points. Each piece of this curve also indicates how it was originally derived, whether by intersection with another surface, a plane, or as a parameter line. As interrogations reach this curve they test whether they cross it, and when they do, they terminate the interrogation in an appropriate way, possibly continuing across on to the neighbour surface.

Having an explicit boundary becomes particularly valuable when prop-shaft tunnels, for example, penetrate the hull surface and cross-sections are required that follow the tunnel surface around the hole in the hull. It is indispensable when the most convenient way of describing a shape is as two surfaces with a fillet between them. Thomas [Thom84] and Palmer [Palm82] have addressed these questions in their Ph.D. theses.

Future Methods

Certain new techniques have been proposed but are not yet regarded as proven enough for commercial use. Five worthy of mention here are recursive division, other irregular B-spline-like surfaces, cyclides, multivariate B-splines, and implicit surfaces.

Recursive Division

One of the essential properties of a surface description method has to be the ability to change the density of description of the shape without altering the shape. This is because afterthoughts often require the addition of relatively short-wavelength features to a basically smooth shape. Also, no method will guarantee to provide exactly the ideal shape from very sparse data. Having got a good smooth shape that is not quite what is wanted, finer detail needs to be added or corrected.

In order to be able to make these finer changes, extra 'handles' need to be made available. This can be done with directrix-generator methods (unless they are very inflexibly implemented) by dividing the surface along a generator and altering the definition of one or more directrices on one side of the division. It may also be possible to define a new generator rule with more directrices together with a new set of directrices which, together with the new rule, give exactly the same shape as the old rule with the old directrices.

The B-spline method has a fairly simple procedure for such increase of density. This involves adding imaginary knot lines across the surface (imaginary because the amount of discontinuity of nth derivative across the new lines is zero), and computing what the set of control points is that gives the same surface. This computation of the new control points turns out to be evaluating fairly simple linear combinations of the original control points. For example, a quadratic B-spline surface can be doubled in control density in one direction by applying Chaikin's algorithm [Chai74] to each of the rows of control points extending in that direction. Suppose that $P_i\ (i = 1, n)$ are the control points in such a row. Then the construction

$$Q_{2i-1} = (3P_i + P_{i+1})/4$$
$$Q_{2i} = (P_i + 3P_{i+1})/4$$

gives a new row of points Q. Now modification of these points gives control of surface perturbations with only half the wavelength. Doubling in the other direction can be achieved by applying the same construction to the rows in the other direction. When this procedure is carried out a number of times it becomes very clear that the net of control points converges towards the surface itself.

This repeated division could be regarded as a way of constructing points close to the surface for interrogation, or even as the definition of the surface. Now, although the tensor product B-spline ideas can only be applied to give a strictly rectangular surface topology, simple linear combinations can be calculated quite plausibly for very general linkings of control points into control nets.

The Doo-Sabin [Doo78] construction is carried out as follows. Take any control network in which control vertices are joined by edges in loops in a polyhedron-like graph. (Such a graph will be referred to as a polyhedron, but this is loose terminology because the 'faces' need not be plane.) Within each face, construct a new face by creating a new control point corresponding to each old one around that face. The construction is a linear combination with weights w_i given by

$$Q_j = \sum_{i=0}^{n-1} w_i P_{i+j}$$

where n is the number of sides of the face,

$$w_0 = \frac{5+n}{4n}$$

and

$$w_i = \frac{3 + 2\cos\left(2\pi \frac{i}{n}\right)}{4n}$$

The points Q are the control vertices of a denser description of the same surface.

Each original edge separated two faces, each of which has a new one constructed in it, with a new edge corresponding to the given original one. These two new edges may be joined together to form a new (four-sided) face corresponding to the old edge. Each old vertex had a ring of faces around it, each of which has a new vertex corresponding to the original one. These new vertices may be joined together in cyclic order corresponding to the sequence of faces around the original vertex. The complete set of face-faces, edge-faces, and vertex-faces span a surface in the same way as the original polyhedron.

Experimentally, this procedure gives a smooth surface. It is also possible to argue the analytic structure of the limit surface as follows. The effect on the limit surface of moving just one original control point is bounded, because only certain control points are modified at each level of division, and the range of such a modification halves at each step. The series $1 + 1/2 + 1/4 \cdots$ has a finite limit. The number of control points influencing any particular piece of limit surface is therefore limited. If all of the points that influence a small region actually form a regularly rectangular topology, the limit surface in that region cannot tell that they are not embedded in a complete regular lattice and must therefore be the limit surface of that piece of a regular lattice.

The Doo-Sabin construction reduces to Chaikin's construction for a regular lattice, which has a piecewise biquadratic limit surface. Every new vertex has four neighbouring faces. Every new face-face has the same number of sides as its parent. Every new edge-face has four sides. Every new vertex-face has the same number of sides as its parent vertex had incident edges. The total number of non-four-sided faces therefore does not increase after the first iteration. This number is equal to the number of original non-four-sided faces plus the number of original non-four-valent vertices. Each non-four-sided face has the same centroid as its parent.

After many iterations, therefore, the control net takes the form of large areas of regular lattice, joining at a fixed number of isolated non-four-sided faces. The limit surface therefore consists of areas of biquadratic patches, meeting at 'rings' around these singular faces. As division proceeds these rings shrink.

The control points around such a ring form a configuration whose topology remains invariant through the division, although the scale shrinks. The members of the configuration after each step are all linear combinations of the members before the step, and so we can regard the division as a linear operator applied to the vertices of the configuration. The limit surface at the centroid of a non-four-sided face can be analysed in terms of the eigenproperties of the linear operator.

This analysis indicates that whatever the number of edges of the face, there is a well-defined limiting tangent plane at the centroid, and that estimators of curvature in any particular direction converge to a constant value, not in general zero.

Cubic Surfaces

Constructions that reduce to bicubic B-splines on a regular control network were suggested by Catmull and Clark [Catm78]. Unfortunately, these do not have well-behaved limit surfaces at the singular points. Although there is a well-defined tangent plane everywhere, there is either a local zero of curvature or else a local unboundedness of curvature estimator. Ball and Storry [Ball84] have identified how these ill-effects may be minimised.

In principle, higher order surfaces could be constructed, but I am not aware of any work to characterise them. There are also constructions that reduce to box-splines over a regular triangular control net, but all of these appear to have misbehaviour at the singular points [Loop87].

Operational Properties

The main difference between the recursive division definition and their special case, the tensor product B-spline surfaces, is that the control network need not be regular. The only conditions are that at least three edges must meet at each vertex and that each face must have at least three sides. It is thus very easy to arrange a net so that rows of control vertices flow along all the natural features of the shape.

An undesirable feature of the quadratic variant, shared with the regular biquadratic B-spline, is that the surface bulges rather too much towards each control point. Ideally, a set of control points located at the vertices of a cube would define a spherical limit surface. In fact, there is a bulge of over ten percent of radius. There is no obvious way of carrying out local increase in density of control in the way that unequal interval tensor product B-splines do. The method does extend naturally to the homogeneous coordinate rational form.

Irregular B-spline-like Surfaces

The recursive division surfaces have the advantage over regular B-splines of permitting the topology of the control network to vary to suit the natural flow of the lines of the shape being defined. Their disadvantage is that they consist of an infinite number of pieces, and so there is not much alternative to using division methods for interrogation. This stimulates the question as to whether there might not be some way of having an irregular topology, but filled in with finite patches instead of the rings of recursive division. With some limitations this is indeed possible. Two methods are available. The first is the approximation of recursive division by pieces that lose continuity of slope over small regions around the singular points (Figure 19).

Suppose that we approximate a ring of n vertices by a collection of n patches, one fitting into each corner, and all n meeting at the (known) centroid. Assume biquadratic patches. The central twist control point of each patch can be taken as the vertex of a given level of recursive division. The edge tangent intersections are all taken as midpoints between twist control points, and all patch corners except the central common point are taken as centroids of four surrounding twist control points. The central point is taken as the centroid of the n surrounding twist control points. Consider any pair of adjacent patches in this innermost ring. They have continuity of position along their common edge but, in general, do not have continuity of tangent plane. The amount of discontinuity may be regarded as a function of position along that edge, and it is zero at the outside of the ring. Further, its derivative is also zero at the outside.

In the case of a triangular ring the discontinuity is also zero at the centre. The worst angle of mismatch appears about one-third of the way from the centre to the outside and shrinks by a factor of two at every step. For the configuration of three patches forming an octant of a sphere, the mismatch is about four degrees.

In the case of four patches coming together at a vertex there is, of course, no error. In the case of larger numbers, there is a mismatch at the centre due to the twist control points being nonplanar, although if singular points are kept near spherical points of the surface, as they should be, this effect will be very small.

Alternatively, patch equations can be devised that are controlled in Bézier fashion such that if these patches are inserted in place of the rings

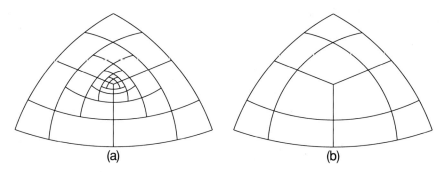

Figure 19. (a) Recursive division. (b) Truncated recursive division.

of recursive division, the fitting of the Bézier control points in the obvious way into a B-spline network gives continuity of tangent plane. There are published quadratic patches of three and five sides with fairly simple equations [Sabi83]. Higher numbers of sides can be derived from n-sided transfinite descriptions by using specific expressions for the boundary and the cross-boundary derivative, but these are likely to be expensive to evaluate.

Cyclides

During the early 1980s a group of students working under Tony Nutbourne [Nutb88] at the Cambridge Engineering Department sought surface analogues for simple cases of the implicit curve equation

$$c = f(s)$$

where c is the local curvature and s the arc length.

The major find resulting from this search was the cyclide surface, which was first explored by the Victorian geometers (Figure 20). (It is often called the Dupin cyclide after a French mathematician who published some of its properties.) The cyclide is a fourth-order algebraic surface $(f(P) = 0)$ with two sets of generators, the properties of which are:

(a) all generators are circles;
(b) all generators are lines of curvature;
(c) crossing generators cut orthogonally.

The cyclide contains as special cases the plane, sphere, cone, cylinder, and torus and may be given the mental image of a torus whose radius varies as you go around. The radius may change sign, in which case the surface passes through two singular points, analogous to the vertex of a

Figure 20. Cyclides.

cone. In fact, geometric inversion of such a cyclide with respect to one of its vertices gives a cone. Cyclides form a class of surfaces closed under inversion and under solid body transformations but not under affine or perspective transformations.

The algebraic geometry properties of the cyclide derive from the fact that it is a fourth-order surface that contains the absolute conic as a curve of self-intersection (a bispherical quartic). Because of this the plane section is simpler than that of most fourth-order surfaces, being only as complex as the intersection of two quadrics and therefore having a parametric form which needs one square root per point evaluated.

The intersection of two cyclides is an eighth-order curve (compared with the order 324 curve in which two bicubic patches can intersect) with a parametric form that requires the solution of a fourth-order equation in the evaluation of each point.

The cyclide has a biparametric form that is rational biquadratic and therefore a subset of rational bicubics or higher orders. Individual cyclide patches (pieces of cyclide bounded by generators) have even fewer freedoms than most biparametric patches. For example, the four corners always lie in a plane and, further, form a cyclic quadrilateral in that plane. They are unlikely, therefore, to be convenient tools for the description of sculptured surfaces. However, there are some results which indicate that arrays of such patches may become a useful tool when additional work has been done.

(a) Considering small perturbations from an initial configuration, an array of cyclide patches behaves in the limit (infinitesimal perturbation) like a biquadratic B-spline.

(b) If a cyclide patch is divided into nine subpieces (a 3 × 3 array) along lines of curvature, a finite perturbation exists that keeps all the pieces cyclide and retains slope continuity both internally and with the unaltered surface outside the array.

(c) Subarrays of 6 × 6 and larger have finite perturbations from arbitrary initial configurations, but those elaborated so far are not very well conditioned.

These results do not yet form an adequate basis for use of cyclide patches as sculptured surface building blocks, but new results in this theory may well make them a most exciting prospect [Mart82; dePo84].

Multivariate B-splines

In the approximation theory community a new way of looking at B-splines has gained favour over the last five years or so. One of the ways of deriving the univariate B-spline basis functions is as the projection of a simplex in n dimensions onto a straight line. For example, the first-order B-spline (the piecewise linear function) is given by the projection of a triangle onto a straight line; the quadratic B-spline is given by the projection of a tetrahedron. In each case the value of the function at a point is given by the residual cross-sectional 'volume' of the points projecting into that point (Figure 21).

This construction is not restricted to generating all the minimum-width univariate B-splines; by using polyhedra instead of simplices it generates all linear combinations of B-splines; by partitioning a large simplex into smaller ones it gives all the discrete B-spline and subdivision theory; by projecting onto a plane instead of a line it gives basis functions which are much more general than the tensor products of univariate functions. For example, the projection of a tetrahedron onto a plane gives a function with three or four linear pieces on triangles, forming a pyramid (Figure 22).

The parametric analogue of this method gives pieces of surface that are parametric polynomials over some tessellation of the parameter plane. The projection of a 4D simplex onto the plane gives a surface consisting of quadratic pieces (with plane sections that are conic sections in the parameter plane and therefore parametric curves) meeting with slope continuity.

Because any simplex can be subdivided before projection, there are subdivision algorithms that give completely local increase of density of control.

This theory may well give a powerful tool for terrain and function contouring when it has been explored further. The kind of problem still to be sorted out is that, given a set of points to interpolate, we do not know the best set of simplices to base our functions on.

There is even more to do before this method will be really useful for the representation of sculptured shapes. Because it still deals with a single parameter plane, it cannot make any contribution to the topology problem.

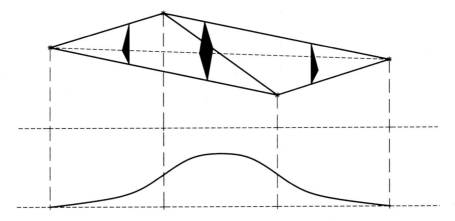

Figure 21. B-splines by projection.

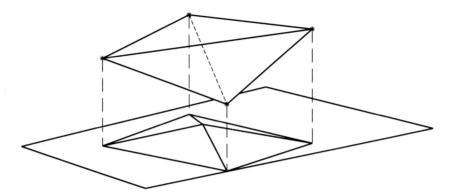

Figure 22. Bivariate B-spline.

Because it loses the preferred directions in the parameter plane, it also loses the confidence-building directrix-generator arguments about the good behaviour of the surface. The time to look at these methods again, therefore, is when they have been exploited in the contouring context [Dahm83].

Implicit Surfaces

In geometric modelling many of the surfaces dealt with are simpler in the implicit form

$$f(P) = 0$$

than in the parametric form, and so much of such software deals with the implicit surface equation. The desire to incorporate free-form surfaces into such geometric modellers has led to some work on free-form surfaces with implicit equation. Sederberg [Sede84; Sede85] has examined the Steiner surface, which is a quadratic triangle in parametric form, but which has a fairly simple implicit form. The cyclides have already been mentioned above.

One of the more interesting possibilities that may reach practical implementation sooner is the use of an implicit form fillet between implicit surfaces. Middleditch, Woodwark, Hoffman and Hopcroft [Midd85; Wood87; Hoff86], and Rockwood and Owen [Rock85] have all been investigating this area.

Acknowledgments. Most of the material presented in this paper was derived under contract to the Ministry of Defence, United Kingdom, and thanks are due for their permission to use this material. I would also like to thank Drs. John Duncan and Nicholas Prudden of the Ministry of Defence, Prof. Robin Forrest, and Dr. Alan Ball for their contributions.

Appendix: Variant Tree for Surface Definition

What Conceptual Basis?

Directrix-generator

  What generators?

    Splines

      What order?
        Quadratic
        Cubic
          What continuity?
            Slope
            Curvature

      Interpolating or B-spline?
        Interpolating
        B-spline with interpolated ends
        Interpolating with slope control points at ends.
        Interpolating with fixed end slopes

    Conics

      What control of end slopes? (end points are assumed)
        Fixed end slopes
        Tangent intersection point
        End angles

      What control of fullness?
        Fullness factor
        Shoulder point

    Superellipses
      What control of fullness?
        Shoulder point
        Exponent

    Polynomials
      What order?
        Quadratic
        Cubic
        Higher
        Variable

      Interpolating or Bézier?
        Lagrange
        Lagrange but with slope control points at ends
        Bézier

  What directrices?

    Space conics
      How specified?

As above

Conic projections
  How specified?
    As above

Splines
  How specified?
    As above

Polynomials
  How specified?
    As above

What Correspondence rule?

Equal parameter

Cut by fan of planes
  What fan?
    Parallel planes
    Linear system of planes
    Planes perpendicular to spine curve
      What spine?
        See directrices.

Cut by some other family of surfaces

Equal parameter with reparameterisation

Transfinite Patch Methods

What patch boundary curves?
  See directrices above

Independent patches or carpet?
  Separate patches
  Spline blended carpet

Patch grid?
  Rectangular grid only
    Grid?
      Equal intervals
      Unequal intervals (tartan grid)
  Triangular grid only
  Rectangles and triangles and pentagons mixed

Rational definition?
  Definition in 4D space projected to 3
  Definition in 3D space

Single Patches

What form?
  Bipolynomial

    How described?
      Hermite
      Bézier

What order?
    Quadratic
    Cubic
    Higher order
Other directrix-generator surfaces

Spline Carpet Methods

What order?
    Quadratic
    Cubic
    Higher

How specified?
    Interpolation
    B-splines
    Interpolation plus tangents/twists override
        Generality of override?
            Anywhere
            Across complete curves only
            Across complete edges only

Grid?
    Equal intervals
    Unequal intervals (tartan grid)

Rational definition?
    Definition in 4D space projected to 3
    Definition in 3D space

Recursive Subdivision

What order?
    Quadratic
    Cubic

What completion of singular region?
    Limit of division
    Fitted nonrectangular patches

Rational definition?
    Definition in 4D space projected to 3
    Definition in 3D space

Bounded?
    Natural boundary only
    Distinct boundary

References

[Armi70]
Armit, A.P.A., Computer Systems for Interactive Design of Three-dimensional Shapes, Doctoral Thesis, University of Cambridge, Cambridge, U.K., 1970.

[Ball84]
Ball, A.A., and Storry, D.J.T., Recursively generated B-spline surfaces, Proc. CAD84, Brighton, UK: Butterworth, 1984.

[Barn74a]
Barnhill, R.E., and Riesenfeld, R.F., Eds., *Computer Aided Geometric Design*, New York: Academic Press, 1974.

[Barn74b]
Barnhill, R.E., Smooth interpolation over triangles, pp. 45–70 in [Barn74a].

[Barn83]
Barnhill, R.E., and Boehm, W., Eds., *Surfaces in Computer Aided Geometric Design*, Amsterdam: North-Holland, 1983.

[Bezi71]
Bézier, P.E., Example of an existing system in the motor industry, *Proc. Roy. Soc. London Ser. A*, Vol. 321, pp. 207–218, 1971.

[Bezi77]
Bézier, P.E., Essai de Definition Numerique des Courbes et des Surfaces Experimentales, These de Doctorat d'Etat, l'Université de Pierre et Marie Curie, France, 1977 (2 vols.).

[Birk60]
Birkhoff, G., and Garabedian, H.L., Smooth surface interpolation, *J. Math. Phys.*, Vol. 39, pp. 258–268, 1960.

[Catm78]
Catmull, E., and Clark, J., Recursively generated B-spline surfaces on arbitrary topological meshes, *Comput. Aided Design*, Vol. 10, pp. 350–355, 1978.

[Chai74]
Chaikin, G.M., An algorithm for high-speed curve generation, *Comput. Graph. Image Process.*, Vol. 3, pp. 346–349, 1974.

[Char80]
Charrot, P., The Use of Triangular and Pentagonal Patches in the Numerical Representation of Surfaces, Doctoral Thesis, Brunel University, Uxbridge, U.K., 1980.

[Clen65]
Clenshaw, C., and Hayes, J.G., Curve and surface fitting, *Journal Institute Mathematics and Appl.*, Vol. 1, pp. 164–183, 1965.

[Coon67]
Coons, S.A., Surfaces for Computer Aided Design of Space Forms, Project MAC, Technical Report 41, Massachusetts Institute of Technology, Cambridge, MA, 1967.

[Dahm83]
Dahmen, W., and Micchelli, C.A., Recent Progress om Multivariate Splines, Research Report RC 9969 (No. 44209), IBM T.J.Watson Research Center, Yorktown Heights, NY, 1983.

[deBo62]
deBoor, C., Bicubic spline interpolation, *J. Math. Phys.*, Vol. 41, pp. 212–218, 1962.

[dePo84]
dePont, J., Essays on the Cyclide Patch, Doctoral Thesis, University of Cambridge, Cambridge, U.K., 1984.

[Doo78]
Doo, D., and Sabin, M.A., Behaviour of recursive division surfaces near extraordinary points, *Comput. Aided Design*, Vol. 10, pp. 356–362, 1978.

[Fari79]
Farin, G., Subsplines über Dreiecken, Doctoral Thesis, University of Braunschweig, Braunschweig, West Germany, 1979.

[Ferg64]
Ferguson, J.C., Multivariable curve interpolation, *J. ACM*, Vol. 11, pp. 221–228, 1964.

[Gord68]
Gordon, W.J., Spline Blended Bivariate Interpolation Through Curve Networks, GMR-799, General Motors Corporation, Warren, MI, 1968.

[Gord74]
Gordon, W.J., and Riesenfeld, R.F., Bernstein-Bézier methods for the computer aided design of free-form curves and surfaces, *CACM*, Vol. 21, pp. 293–310, 1974.

[Greg74]
Gregory, J., Smooth interpolation without twist constraints, in *Computer Aided Geometric Design*, pp. 71–88, Barnhill, R.E., and Riesenfeld, R.F., Eds., New York: Academic Press, 1974.

[Greg86a]
Gregory, J.A., Ed., *The Mathematics of Surfaces*, Oxford, U.K.: Clarendon Press, 1986.

[Greg86b]
Gregory, J.A., *N*-sided surface patches, pp. 217–232 in [Greg86a].

[Hawt71]
Hawthorne, W., and Edwards, G.R., Eds., A discussion on computer aids in mechanical engineering design and manufacture, *Proc. Roy. Soc. London Ser. A*, Vol. 321, pp. 143–248, 1971.

[Hoff86]
Hoffman, C., and Hopcroft, J., Quadratic blending surfaces, *Comput. Aided Design*, Vol. 18, pp. 301–306, 1986.

[Limi44]
Liming, R.A., *Practical Analytical Geometry wuth Applications to Aircraft*, New York: Macmillan, 1944.

[Loop87]
Loop, C.T., Smooth Subdivision Surfaces Based on Triangles, Master's Thesis, University of Utah, Salt Lake City, UT, 1987.

[Mart82]
Martin, R.R., Principal Patches for Computational Geometry, Doctoral Thesis, University of Cambridge, Cambridge, U.K., 1982.

[Mart87]
Martin, R.R., Ed., *The Mathematics of Surfaces II*, Oxford, U.K.: Clarendon Press, 1987.

[Mehl71]
Mehlum, E., and Sorensen, P.F., Example of an existing system in the shipbuilding industry: the Autokon system, pp. 219–234 in [Hawt71].

[Midd85]
Middleditch, A.E.,and Sears, K.H., Blend surfaces for set theoretic volume modelling systems, *Comput. Graph.*, Vol. 19, pp. 161–170, 1985 (SIGGRAPH 85).

[Nutb88]
Nutbourne, A.W., and Martin, R.R., *Differential Geometry Applied to the Design of Curves and Surfaces*, Chicester, UK: Ellis Horwood, 1988.

[Palm82]
Palmer, T.R., Sculptured Surfaces in Solid Object Modelling Systems, Doctoral Thesis, University of East Anglia, Norwich, U.K., 1982.

[Pieg87]
Piegl, L., and Tiller, W., Curve and surface constructions using rational B-splines, *CADJ*, Vol. 19, pp. 485–498, 1987.

[Rock85]
Rockwood, A.P., and Owen, J.C., Blending surfaces in solid modelling, in Proc. SIAM Conference on Geometric Modelling and Robotics, Farin, G., Ed., Albany, NY, 1985.

[Roge90]
Rogers, D.F., and Adams, J.A., *Mathematical Elements for Computer Graphics*, 2nd Ed., New York: McGraw-Hill, 1990.

[Sabi68]
Sabin, M.A., Parametric Surface Equations for Non-rectangular Regions, VTO/MS/147 British Aircraft Corporation, Weybridge, UK, 1968.

[Sabi83]
Sabin, M.A., Non-rectangular surface patches suitable for inclusion in a B-spline surface, in *Proc. Eurographics '83*, pp. 57–70, Hagen, T., Ed., Amsterdam: North Holland, 1983.

[Sede84]
Sederberg, T.W., Anderson, D.C., and Goldman, R.N., Implicit representation of parametric curves and surfaces, *Comput. Vision, Graph. Image Process.*, Vol. 28, pp. 72–84, 1984.

[Sede85]
Sederberg, T.W., Piecewise algebraic surface patches, *Comput. Aided Geom. Design*, Vol. 2, pp. 53–59, 1985.

[Shel47]
Shelley, J.H., The Development of Curved Surfaces for Aero-design, Gloster Aircraft Company, Hucclecote, Gloucester, UK, 1947.

[Stur86]

Sturge, D., Improvements to parametric bicubic surface patches, in *The Mathematics of Surfaces*, pp.47–58, Gregory, J.A., Ed., Oxford, U.K.: Clarendon Press, 1986.

[Thom84]

Modelling Volumes Bounded By B-spline Surfaces, Ph.D. Thesis, University of Utah, Salt Lake City, UT, 1984.

[Wood87]

Woodwark, J.R., Blends in solid modelling, in *The Mathematics of Surfaces II*, pp. 255–294, Martin, R.R., Ed., Oxford, U.K.: Clarendon Press, 1987.

Interrogation Techniques for Parametric Surfaces

Malcolm Sabin

Abstract

Almost all of the techniques currently in use for the description of smooth but complex surfaces can be regarded as mappings from a parameter space to physical space. Use of these definitions requires that it be possible to answer questions about these shapes such as 'what does the shape look like?' or 'what shape must templates be for manufacture or for mating structural members?' Techniques for interrogating numerical definitions to answer these questions are identified and their robustness and accuracy considered.

Summary

Almost all of the questions we can ask of a surface involve the calculation of curves of some kind across that surface. Such curves are sets of points satisfying either some algebraic or differential equation. Each type of interrogation has its own equation to satisfy. This paper, therefore, begins by giving the main examples of calculations that produce curves as their results. A major section on methods for computing such curves follows. In the next short section, the relative speed of these methods for the dominant calculation, that of plane sections for display, is discussed. Finally, interrogations that are not just the calculation of single curves are described and discussed. Essential further reading is the doctoral thesis of Geisow [Geis83], which analyses many aspects in much more depth than is possible here. Pratt and Geisow [Prat86] is also useful and is more accessible.

Notation

In the examples that follow

u, v denote the values of the parameters;

$\vec{P}$ denotes the vector of coordinates of the point at u, v;

$\vec{N}$ denotes the surface normal at $\vec{P}$;

$\vec{Q}$, $\vec{R}$ are fixed points;

$\vec{A}$, $\vec{B}$, $\vec{C}$ are fixed vectors;

S represents a complete surface;

P_u, P_v denote derivatives of P with respect to u and v;

$[\,]$ a vector expression;

$(\,)$ a scalar expression or arguments of a procedure

$\langle\,\rangle$ indicate normalisation of the enclosed vector;

$|\,|$ indicates the magnitude of the enclosed vector so that $|\langle\,\rangle| = 1$ identically

$\cdot$ denotes the dot product of two vectors;

$*$ denotes scalar multiplication or multiplication of a vector by a scalar;

$\otimes$ denotes the cross product of two vectors;

Examples of Interrogations

Isoparametric lines

$$u = \text{const} \qquad v_{\min} < v < v_{\max} \quad \text{or}$$
$$v = \text{const} \qquad u_{\min} < u < u_{\max}$$

Straight lines in the parameter plane

$$(u, v) = (u_{\min}, v_{\min}) + t(u_{\max} - u_{\min}, v_{\max} - v_{\min})$$

These are both examples of a parametric curve in the parameter plane, which is evaluated straightforwardly by taking successive values of the curve parameter at an appropriate spacing.

Plane sections

$$[\vec{P} - \vec{Q}] \cdot \vec{A} = 0$$

Intersections with an implicit surface

$$f(\vec{P}(u_1, v_1)) = 0$$

Silhouette lines

$$[\vec{P} - \vec{Q}] \cdot \vec{N} = 0$$

These problems reduce to the solution of some algebraic equation over the parameter plane. They can be typified by the calculation of plane sections.

Projection of a curve onto a surface

$$\left[\vec{P} - \vec{A}\right] \otimes \vec{N} = 0$$

Reflection of a curve in a surface

$$\left[\langle\vec{P} - \vec{A}\rangle + \langle\vec{P} - \vec{B}\rangle\right] \otimes \vec{N} = 0$$

These involve the calculation of a new point on the given surface for each point of a given data curve.

Intersections of two surfaces

$$\left[\vec{P}(u_1, v_1) - \vec{Q}(u_2, v_2)\right] = 0$$

This is a set of three algebraic equations over the 4D product of the two parameter planes.

Methods for Curve Interrogations

The issues that arise when designing software facilities are firstly those of representation—how should the curves be represented numerically—and secondly those of precision versus cost of storage. Whatever the method, at some stage it is necessary to calculate a sequence of points, which will approximate the complete curve by some interpolation rule.

Such sequences of points may be found by any of a number of methods, the main contenders being:

marching methods;

lattice methods;

subdivision.

We also consider various hybrids and the possibility that the result of an interrogation may be a parametric curve that can be evaluated at successive values of the parameter by a direct, noniterative calculation.

Marching

This is the method used in the Numerical Master Geometry (NMG) software and is probably the fastest of the three. It works by first seeking a starting point, probably at the edge of the surface being interrogated. Once such a point is found, the ratio of du to dv corresponding to a movement along the intersection curve is determined, and then the magnitudes of these steps in the parameter are determined. This step is made in the parameter plane, and the corresponding point position is evaluated. Because the second derivatives are not zero, this will typically not satisfy the interrogation condition, but it will provide a good starting point for Newton-Raphson iteration to a surface point that does satisfy the interrogation condition and that also satisfies some step-length condition.

Algorithm

Consider the example of the plane section algorithm, which produces the intersection of the surface $\vec{P}(u, v)$ with the plane

$$f(\vec{P}) = [\,\vec{P} - \vec{Q}\,] \cdot \vec{A} = 0$$

where $\vec{A}$ is assumed to be a unit normal vector.

For simplicity we require the curve to be generated in the form of a sequence of points lying on the curve and within a tolerance, *tol*, of the surface. The points should be generated approximately a distance s apart.

```
begin          find a startpoint u,v on the edge of the surface
      until {   evaluate P⃗,P⃗ᵤ,P⃗ᵥ from u,v
                P⃗_L := P⃗
                d_u := P⃗ᵥ·A⃗
                d_v := -P⃗ᵤ·A⃗
                T⃗  := P⃗ᵤ * d_u + P⃗ᵥ * d_v
                d  := sqrt(s * s/T⃗·T⃗)
                until {   u := u + d * d_u
                          v := v + d * d_v
                          evaluate P⃗,P⃗ᵤ,P⃗ᵥ from u,v
                          f := (P⃗ - Q⃗)·A⃗
                          r := (P⃗ - P⃗_L)·(P⃗ - P⃗_L) - s * s
                          f * f < tol
          and             r * r < 0.04 * s * s * s * s  }
          do              f_u := P⃗ᵤ·A⃗
                          f_v := P⃗ᵥ·A⃗
                          r_u := 2(P⃗ - P⃗_L)·P⃗ᵤ
                          r_v := 2(P⃗ - P⃗_L)·P⃗ᵥ
                          d := 1/(f_v * r_u - f_u * r_v)
                          d_u := (f_u * r - f * r_u)
                          d_v := (f * r_v - f_v * r)
                od
            u,v is outside the surface }
            do    append point P⃗ to output curve
            od
            determine point P⃗ where P⃗_L to P⃗ cuts the boundary
            append point P⃗ to output curve
end
```

A production algorithm would contain rather more tests to avoid the possibility of divide-by-zero, for example, and to ensure convergence within the iterative loop.

In this version all steps are roughly the same size. Substitution of more complex expressions in the calculation of r, r_u, and r_v, taking into account the angle turned through, can very easily make this method adaptive so that it bunches output points in sharply curved regions of the curve.

Basically, the same algorithm can be modified to intersect the parametric surface $\vec{P}(u, v)$ with any implicit surface $f(\vec{P}) = 0$ by inserting, after each evaluation of $\vec{P}$, calculation of $\vec{Q}$ and $\vec{A}$ to be local estimates at $\vec{P}$ of the tangent plane to the surface $f(\vec{P}) = 0$.

$$f := f(\vec{P})$$
$$\vec{A} := df/d\vec{P}(\vec{P})$$
$$Q := \vec{P} - f * \vec{A}/\vec{A} \cdot \vec{A}$$
$$\vec{A} := \langle \vec{A} \rangle$$

There are three problems with this method. First, the method is not guaranteed to find all intersections, although this is a problem of the starting method rather than of the marching. If a number of parallel sections were required, it might be very cost-effective to seek first all the points of minimum, maximum, or stationary extent in the direction perpendicular to the sections and join these with a spanning tree. Scanning all edges of this tree would find all the pieces of section at any station.

Second, the method is not guaranteed to be robust. Particularly at patch boundaries where there is a discontinuity of some kind, the Newton-Raphson procedure may not converge. The technique used to deal with this problem in NMG is pitch-halving, whereby if convergence is not achieved within a fixed number of iterations, another attempt is made to step from the previous good point, but only going half as far. In one case this is exactly the wrong thing to do. In the situation where the surface is offset from a basic surface with a slight discontinuity of the first derivative, there is a small discontinuity of position—a gap—in the theoretical result curve. Pitch-halving below the width of this gap ensures that no further progress can be made. An alternative, rejected for aesthetic reasons at the time, could be to interrogate each patch individually and to link the pieces of the resulting curve afterwards.

A more acceptable version of this would look at the detail of the patch structure only when a failure to converge had occurred. If, when a failure was detected, the major step had been across a patch boundary, the curve could be completed to the patch boundary and restarted from the far side.

This situation poses a real problem: should the result be a single curve or a number of pieces? The difference may not be visible on a display screen but could cause significant changes in the behaviour of a machine tool cutting along that path.

A related problem occurs when there is a saddle in the surface where the intersection plane is tangent and, therefore, the intersection curve has a theoretical crossing point. At such a point the local first derivatives do not give a well-defined path direction, and simple stepping fails. It is particularly difficult when this happens at the starting point so that the curve can never get going. The geometric modelling community has the technique of a 'help point' well away from the singularity from which the curve is traced out in both directions and subsequently reassembled. This seems an inappropriate complication for the surface modelling context.

Third, since the result curve should be terminated when it 'falls off the edge' of the defined surface, calculation of intersections that lie very close to the edge (within the prescribed tolerance) may be terminated prematurely in this method. This could be addressed by preliminary examination of the edge to determine whether any edge in its entirety was a solution. Alternatively, some measure of extrapolation could be permitted during the interrogation, termination of the result (to the accurate edge) being made only if the curve reached some further boundary outside the strict edge by more than the usual tolerance. This would require that some rule for extrapolation be defined.

Algebraic extension of the patches just inside the boundary would normally be expected to be satisfactory provided the tolerance is small compared with the patch size.

LATTICE METHODS

These methods are equivalent to facetting the entire surface and interrogating the facets rather than the original surface. The two variants are curve-order and lattice-order [Payn68; Payn71].

In curve-order lattice methods, a starting point is found by searching facets until one is found that has an intersection. The points where the curve enters and leaves the facet are determined, and a straight line joining them is drawn. Except at the edge, if a curve leaves one facet, it must enter another, and so it may be traced from facet to facet until an edge or the starting facet is found. If each facet traversed is marked, the search for a new starting point can then be resumed until all facets have been examined.

In lattice-order lattice methods, the facets are scanned in some regular sequence. Any that happen to contain pieces of intersection are sectioned.

The second variant is undoubtedly simpler to code and, because the facets are generated in regular sequence, there is no need to have them all explicit at once, thus making it possible to run the method using a relatively small amount of memory. The regular generation may also mean that very fast difference equations can be used to generate the points rather than evaluating every one individually.

However, the pieces of curve are generated in an order unrelated to the curve which they form. This means that, for any purpose requiring a traversal of the curve as a whole (machining along it is a good example), there has to be a sorting process that would probably cost as much as this option saves.

Algorithm (A Curve-order Algorithm)

This algorithm assumes that we have already found a pair of points (u_l, v_l) and (u_r, v_r) on the boundary that are the required parametric lattice size apart and that satisfy

$$f_\ell = \left[\, \vec{P}(u_\ell, v_\ell) - \vec{Q}\,\right] \cdot \vec{A} < 0$$

$$f_r = \left[\, \vec{P}(u_r, v_r) - \vec{Q}\,\right] \cdot \vec{A} \geq 0$$

```
begin      u := (f_r * u_ℓ − f_ℓ * u_r)/(f_r − f_ℓ)
           v := (f_r * v_ℓ − f_ℓ * v_r)/(f_r − f_ℓ)
           append point P(u,v) to the output curve
           until      u_t := u_r + v_ℓ − v_r
                      v_t := v_r + u_ℓ − u_ℓ
           u_t, v_t is outside boundary
           do      P_L := P
                   f_t := [ P(u_t, v_t) − Q ]·A
                   if   f_t < 0
                   then u_ℓ := u_t
                        v_ℓ := v_t
                        f_ℓ := f_t
                   else u_s := u_ℓ + v_ℓ − v_r
                        v_s := v_ℓ + u_r − u_ℓ
                        f_s := [ P(u_s, v_s) − Q ]·A
                        if   f_s < 0
                        then u_ℓ := u_s
                             v_ℓ := v_s
                             f_ℓ := f_s
                             u_r := u_t
                             v_r := v_t
                             f_r := f_t
                        else u_r := u_s
                             v_r := v_s
                             f_r := f_s
                        fi
                   fi
                   u := (f_r * u_ℓ − f_ℓ * u_r)/(f_r − f_ℓ)
                   v := (f_r * v_ℓ − f_ℓ * v_r)/(f_r − f_ℓ)
                   append point P(u,v) to the output curve
           od
end
```

Again, this algorithm may readily be modified to generate intersections with implicit surfaces other than the plane by modifying the assignments to f_t and f_s.

This version assumes that the lattice cell size divides exactly into both parametric dimensions of the surface and, therefore, that there is no need to tidy up the final step to the actual boundary, as there was with the marching algorithm. If it were required, the same method used in the marching algorithm could be applied.

Both variants of this method have the following problems:

(a) There is no guarantee of finding all intersections, since only those which the facetted approximation has will be found.

(b) This is the slowest of the methods because to get an adequate resolution, a dense lattice is required theoretically evaluated all over the surface and not just at the parts near the intersection.

To make the method a practical possibility would require work on ways of adapting the lattice density to the local curvature of the result curve, as well as work on ways of finding all loops without evaluating the whole lattice. The spanning tree idea mentioned above would apply equally here, with the simplification that only the maxima of the facetted approximation need be considered.

Adapting the density is not trivial. The reason for this can be seen in Figure 1; at a boundary where the density changes, the result curve will

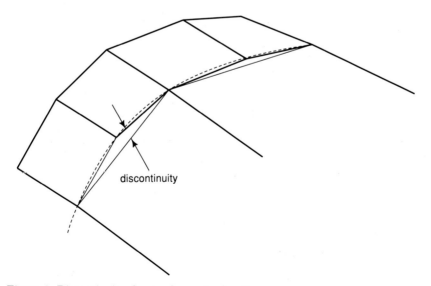

Figure 1. Discontinuity due to change in density.

have a possible discontinuity, since adjacent facets will not, in general, be continuous.

RECURSIVE DIVISION

This is the most recent method. It works on the principle that there is a test that can determine if there is a possibility of the intersection existing across a piece of surface. This test may give false-positives but not false-negatives. If the piece of surface returns a positive from this test, either the piece is simple enough for an approximation that can be interrogated by some simple procedure, or else the piece is divided into parts to which the whole procedure may be applied in turn.

Algorithm

This algorithm assumes that the surface $\mathbf{S}$ has as its representation a set of points whose bounding box also contains all the points of the surface which is represented.

intersection $(\mathbf{S}, (\vec{Q}, \vec{A}))$:

```
begin      if    all points in S have same sign of [P⃗ - Q⃗]·A⃗
                 then return empty intersection
           else if S represents a simple enough surface
                 then return simple intersection (S, (Q⃗,A⃗))
           else divide S into S₁, S₂
                 return union of intersection(S₁,(Q⃗,A⃗))
                              with intersection(S₂,(Q⃗,A⃗))
                 fi
           fi
end
```

Note that this algorithm does *not* generalise immediately to implicit surfaces other than planes, because there is no guarantee that the set of points representing $\mathbf{S}$ spans a range of f including all values found on the surface itself.

The actual implementation of this algorithm depends critically on the data structures for representation of partial curves. This data structure has to be capable of holding pieces of curve that are joined together in the unioning stage of the process.

I strongly recommend following Nasri [Nasr85] and holding with each segment of curve an explicit start point and an explicit end point in u, v coordinates. This greatly facilitates the union procedure. Versions of this algorithm have been published that leave all the unioning until the end. In my view, this creates a sorting difficulty that can be avoided simply by keeping track of the pieces of string at every return from a layer of recursion.

The control of the required pitch length has to be embodied in the criterion for simplicity, and this method will not give quite the same evenness of spacing along the curve as does the marching method.

As typically implemented, this method applies to Bézier patches, possibly derived from a B-spline surface. The test is based on the bounding box of the Bézier control points always containing the surface. In principle, the B-spline control points could be used in a similar way, but the Bézier points give a sharper test (fewer false-positives), which makes the process faster. Some descriptions talk of the use of the convex hull in place of the bounding box (which should also give a sharper test), but the extra complication of evaluation and comparison of convex hulls does not appear to be cost-effective.

Note that, whereas marching and lattice methods apply generally to all parametric surfaces because the surface itself is accessed only through the evaluation at specific parameter values, the subdivision methods do not. Their procedural interface has two parts, the generation of a bounding polyhedron of some kind, and the actual subdivision. Subdivision methods can be applied to other than B-spline and Bézier surfaces, but it takes more work.

For example, suppose that we wish to use this technique to interrogate an offset surface, for simplicity, a simple spherical offset of radius r. The condition that the test for possible intersection should never give false-negatives may be satisfied by expanding each bounding box by r in each direction. If the basic surface lies within the original bounding box, the offset surface must lie within the expanded one. However, as division proceeds, this will give so many false-positives that the algorithm will never terminate. It is necessary to be more subtle, adding to the bounding box the bounding box of only that part of the offset sphere that can be invoked by the surface normals of the piece of surface currently being examined. The OSLO algorithm [Cohe80] is one way of carrying out the division of a B-spline surface into Bézier pieces and then of subdividing them further.

The problem of incompatible density of estimation applies to this method as well as to adaptive lattice methods. It is solvable here because the pieces of curve resulting from interrogation of the two pieces of surface can be rejoined during the return up the tree of recursive calls [Nasr85]. The estimate of the common point resulting from the denser division is always easily identified.

An important issue is that the combination of the test and the division operators is in fact a procedural definition of the surface, just as evaluation of a point from the parameters is a procedural definition of a parametric surface. The universe of shapes so describable has not been properly characterised.

This question of closure is the main problem with this method, since back-of-the-envelope calculations indicate that it should be slower than marching by a small factor only. Its advantages, that all pieces will always be found, and that it is robust, I regard as more important than a factor of two or three in speed [Sabi86].

ADAPTIVE REFINEMENT

A fourth technique, which may best be applied to the leaves of the recursive division tree, first identifies the start and finish points of a segment of intersection curve. The midpoint in parameter space is evaluated and a search made perpendicular to the chord in parameter space until a point satisfying the interrogation condition is found. Each half may be used as a chord in turn until no further densification is required. An obvious variant of this could use the known direction of the curve in parameter space at each end to give Hermite cubic rather than linear interpolation as a first approximation [Geis83].

This method appears to give robustness, although one danger may be that of the solution curve that is almost straight but that has a pimple in the interior. The pimple could easily be missed if allowed to operate at too large a scale.

Once a result in parametric space is determined, it must be evaluated with adequate density in real space for linear interpolation along the result curve to be sufficiently accurate.

HYBRID METHODS

The distinction between these methods is not clearcut. The idea of using the same search methods for starting points for curve-order lattice as for marching has already been mentioned. Another in-between method is a more robust marching method that may also be regarded as an adaptive lattice one.

In this technique, developed from one described by Lodwick and Whittle [Lodw70], there is no evaluation of the derivatives of the point unless they are required explicitly in the interrogation condition. Once two result points $\vec{P}_{n-1}$ and $\vec{P}_{n-2}$ are known, the next $(\vec{A})$ is postulated to be that given by the same step again. It is evaluated and, unless it satisfies the interrogation condition, a small step at right angles in the parameter plane is taken to $\vec{B}$. Hopefully, this will have an interrogation error of the opposite sign, and linear interpolation between the two probe points will give a result point. If not, linear interpolation between the second probe point $(\vec{B})$ and a new probe $(\vec{C})$ a small distance on the same side of the previous result point will give a new result (Figure 2). This method gives good adaptation to variation of curvature along the result.

Another hybrid suggested by Geisow [Geis83] is the use of recursive division down only far enough to ensure that marching will be robust. Yet another is to use marching but have a more robust alternative that can be applied if the marching fails.

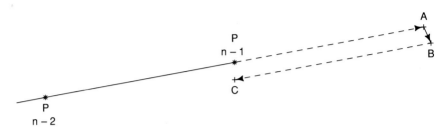

Figure 2. Lodwick and Whittle marching [Lodw70].

SPECIAL CASES WHERE THE CURVES ARE PARAMETRIC

In the context of contouring interpolants of scattered data in two dimensions, methods have been proposed that divide the surface into triangular pieces, each of which has the quadratic form

$$z = ax^2 + by^2 + 2hxy + 2fx + 2gy + c$$

which have conic section contours. The vector-valued analogue of this would have plane cross sections that are all made up of conic section pieces in the parameter plane, and that could therefore be calculated by evaluating some expression for successive values of some curve parameter [Marl76]. I had not encountered use of this in the literature in the free-form surface context until Sederberg started looking at them under the name of Steiner patches [Sede84; Sede85].

Higher order implicit surfaces exist for which all cross sections are rational parametric curves. Unfortunately, cubics with this property are all ruled surfaces. Quartics of this kind have conic section generators. Again, I have not seen these ideas explored in the literature as practical tools for surface representation.

Another idea not elaborated to the point of usefulness is that of parametric curves more complex than the polynomial ones. The intersection of two quadric surfaces does not have a polynomial parametric representation, but it can be parameterised by an expression with one square root [Levi76]. The ambiguity this introduces means that each parameter value corresponds to two points on the curve or to none, and thus separate loops correspond to different parameter intervals in which the expression inside the square root is positive. This method may come into its own when methods of designing arrays of cyclide patches have been devised.

In any case, even when plane sections are rational, the other interrogations would not be expected to be, nor would sections of offset surfaces. Such a property would therefore be an aid only to average speed of operation. One of the other techniques would also be needed for these cases.

Interrogation of Other-than-standard Parametric Surfaces

All the above methods have been described in the context of interrogating some parametric surface, whether it be a complex directrix-generator formulation, a single bicubic patch, or an array of patches in a B-spline surface. Surfaces that do not fit this mould, namely, n-sided patches and the recursive division structures, still have interrogation methods.

Interrogation of n-sided Patches

This requires more complicated implementation of the marching method, since a step is taken in a parameter space more complex than a unit square. A Gregory pentagon [Greg86] has non-isoparametric boundaries, which would probably be quite easy to handle if the main system understood trimmed surfaces.

The Sabin pentagons [Sabi83] require the marching to be done in a parametric space of five variables, but this is not mathematically difficult, as the other three can be evaluated from any adjacent pair. Provided that the smallest pair is used to evaluate the others, this is well conditioned. The logic of the interrogation process is therefore unchanged, and only the implementation is made more complex to handle this extra evaluation and to arrange for the switching of the master parameters as the probe point moves across the surface.

The extra calculation will certainly make progress across the more complex patch slower than across a normal one, but there is no obvious reason to fear any reduction in robustness. Even the extra computing time may not be particularly significant if n-sided patches contribute a small fraction of the surface area.

Lattice methods require that a lattice be defined for the equivalent facetting. This is easy for triangles; for pentagons, the latticing of the five corners as if they were square patches is an obvious solution. The only difficulty is to determine the parameter values of the lattice points, but even this can be overcome by a little algebraic preprocessing.

Because the kind of n-sided patch that embeds in a network of quadrilaterals does not subdivide, there are no recursive division interrogations of these patches except those that are explicitly defined in terms of a recursive subdivision structure.

Interrogation of Recursive Division Surfaces

There are more options here than at first appear. Obviously, the recursive division definition can be used as the basis for a recursive division interrogation. It is also possible to analyse the limit surface in terms of conventional patches, which cluster around the singular points (Figure 3).

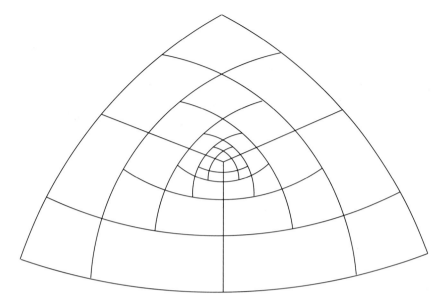

Figure 3. Clustering of patches round a singular point.

At some level of acceptable approximation, it is always possible to use a finite set of such patches and to apply the usual interrogation algorithms within them. The density of a lattice should depend on the level of recursion at which the patch was generated so that the lattice for the entire surface is even overall [Nasr85].

Interrogation of Implicit Surfaces

If a surface equation of the form

$$f(\vec{P}) = 0$$

is to be interrogated, most parametric surface methods have their analogues. In particular, plane sectioning switches the roles of the plane and the surface: the plane becomes the parametric surface and the sculptured surface the implicit one. The intersection of two implicit surfaces requires marching or latticing in three variables instead of four.

Quantitative Estimates of Performance

Because the absolute speed depends on the power of the computer being used to carry out the interrogations, and because intersections vary in difficulty, these comparisons are very coarse estimates. They work by estimating the number of floating point operations needed to give 20 plane sections each of about 25 points (marching equivalent) across a 4×4 array of bicubic patches with curvature continuity.

MARCHING

The computation has two phases, finding the start point and tracing the curve. Finding the start point involves scanning around the boundary, on average halfway, i.e., past nine mesh points, each involving the evaluation of the plane equation (7 flops) as well as the data access. Once the span is found, interpolation along the edge by iterated inverse interpolation may require ten evaluations. Although these could use the curve equation for speed, they are likely to use the full bicubic evaluation (90 flops) for flexibility, together with plane evaluation. The cost of the start point is therefore $(9)(7) + 10(90+7) = 1033$ flops (say, 1000). Each step along the curve takes three evaluations (Prudden's figure), and the evaluation with first derivatives (210 flops) takes about one third of the total time. Thus, each step takes $(9)(210)$ flops $= 1890$ (say, 2000). The full curve is thus estimated to take $1000 + (25)(2000)$, which is 51000 flops. Twenty of these take about 1 Mflop.

If the floating point operations take about half the computing time and the actual time of one flop is 5 microseconds, this would predict a half a second of CPU time per section calculated or 10 seconds of CPU time for the entire nest.

LATTICE

The full facetting of the 4×4 hull surface would probably require at least a 50×50 lattice, giving the evaluation of 2500 points at 90 flops each, or 225000 flops. Tracing one section strictly requires the comparison of each of these with the plane plus the interpolation of, say, 50 points at 12 flops each, giving $(2500)(7) + (50)(12) = 17500 + 600 = 18000$ flops. The total cost is thus $225000 + (20)(18000) = 585000$ flops, or 0.6 times the marching method.

This figure is very sensitive to the density of facetting, for example, 100×100 facetting would quadruple it. It is also sensitive to the number of parallel planes required, as a significant fraction of the time is in preprocessing for the full set of sections.

RECURSIVE DIVISION

This is most easily estimated by working upwards from the final points. Each span requires the evaluation of two end points, together with its contribution to the tree of divisions above it. Assuming binary division, each division adds one to the number of pieces being considered. Thus, the total number of divisions must be the same as the number of pieces plus an allowance for wastage due to the culling out of pieces that are not crossed. Fifty final pieces (they will not be as well distributed as in the marching method) and 100 divisions per section is probably a reasonable estimate.

Each end point will be just a linear interpolation, costing 12 flops, or 24 per span, giving 1200 flops per section. The division process for Bézier bicubics (only the top five divisions are B-spline divisions, which is a complication not worth including) takes 144 flops, and the testing of each half for noninclusion takes 16 plane tests or 118 flops. Thus, each of the 100 divisions takes $144 + (2)(118) = 380$ flops. Testing for simplicity applies only to the retained halves and probably costs another 16 plane tests, giving a total of 498, say, 500 flops per division, or 50000 flops per section.

Twenty sections, therefore, take 20 (50000 + 1200), which is effectively the same 1 Mflop, as in the marching method.

ADAPTIVE REFINEMENT

This requires in its simple form the finding of both ends of each section, followed by a linear search for each issued point. The number of issued points will be somewhat larger than for marching, say, 35. Finding a start point was estimated previously to be 1000 flops, and each linear search will involve some ten point-only evaluations if iterated inverse interpolation is used. The cost per section is therefore $(2)(1000) + (35)(10)(90 + 10) = 2000 + 35000 = 37000$ flops, giving a total cost of 740 Kflops for the 20 sections.

PARAMETRIC SECTIONS

Whenever it is possible to evaluate a curve parametrically the opportunity should be taken. All the above methods take on the order of a million floating point operations in order to display only 500 points, a cost of about 2000 flops per point. A parametric evaluation can afford to be fairly complicated and still beat that figure handsomely.

Other Aspects of Interrogation

METRIC PROPERTIES

Some analyses require properties such as the surface area of a piece of surface or the volume of a region of space bounded by surfaces.

Surface Area

The surface area may be evaluated by integration of elemental areas over the entire region. However, two problems arise. First, the elemental surface area is the modulus of a vector. In fact, $d\vec{P}/du \times d\vec{P}/dv$, the surface normal, gives the oriented area, and integrating this gives a vector whose dot product with any direction gives the projection of area in that direction; this can be done algebraically. The wetted surface area, however, uses the modulus of this, and so there is no simple, closed-form integral.

Second, the region of which the surface area is required may well not be bounded by the natural isoparametric lines that would make closed-form integration easy.

Some numerical integration is therefore necessary, and the obvious candidates are a lattice method and recursive division. The recursive division can be regarded in this case as an adaptive variant of the lattice anyway. The use of a subdivision structure is probably more accurate numerically, as small contributions are added to quantities of about the same size rather than to the (larger) total accumulated area.

The condition for subdividing rather than estimating the surface area of a piece can be based on the fact that, for a piece of positive Gaussian curvature, the area of a triangle is bounded between the area of the chordal triangle and the sum of the areas of the tangent planes (Figure 4).

The analogue of arc length, which is bounded (for unimodal plane curves) from below by the chord, and from above by the length of the two tangent pieces, is a useful one.

Division proceeds if the two bounds are too far apart or if the boundary of the piece is too complicated. Otherwise, an appropriate mean of the two bounds is taken. Twice the chord plus the sum of the lengths of the tangents is a very good approximation to three times the arc length of a reasonably behaved curve.

Enclosed Volume

The obvious way to approach this is to sum the volumes of elemental pyramids over the surface, the only subtlety being the choice of a vertex for

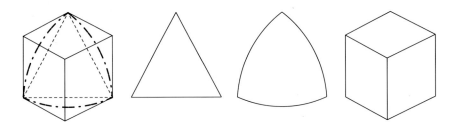

Figure 4. Estimates for surface area.

the pyramids. Numerical accuracy will be lost if the vertex is too far away, so that the required volume appears as the difference of large quantities of opposite sign. The centroid cannot be used, as its determination requires the volume, but the midpoint of the bounding box is likely to be just as good.

Each elemental volume can be expressed as a polynomial in the parameters: no square roots are involved, so algebraic integration is possible, giving the volume as a directly evaluable function of the control points.

A typical problem requiring evaluation of volumes is that of determining the displacement of a candidate hull form for a ship. In this case, it is likely that the displacement will be specified in the requirements for the surface. Provided that the parametric path of the waterline remains unchanged during an interactive perturbation (i.e., x and y perturbations only, or z perturbations restricted to below the waterline) the closed form makes it possible to recompute displacement very fast indeed during dynamic surface modifications. Again, because of the existence of closed-form integration, the recursive division structure need only be invoked as required by the complication of the boundary of the face currently being summed.

The elemental volumes meeting the boundary should take the actual boundary curve geometry into account rather than forward reckoning from its representation in parameter space in order to guarantee that it is handled consistently between the two surfaces that intersect there.

In the case of a plane curve, twice the sum of the areas based on the tangent pieces plus the area based on the chord gives a good approximation of the enclosed area.

Moments of Inertia

These are similar to volume and need a similar structure with slightly different expressions in the core of the evaluation.

PLATE DEVELOPMENT

This interrogation arises when a curved structure is to be clad by flat sheets cut to shape before they are bent. It is necessary to determine the shape to cut them so that when they are bent they have the correct outline [Mann78].

Parametric representation with a single parameter plane provides a convenient structure for the evaluation of plate developments. From the surface definition, S_1, a second definition, S_2, is constructed so that for each point on the first surface there is a point on the second surface with the same parameter values. This second point is the developed position of the first one, and so the development of any curves on the original surface can be constructed by reevaluation on the second.

The two questions are:

(a) how to determine the second surface definition; and

(b) what step length to use when evaluating the curves prior to reevaluation.

The separation of the creation of the second surface from the evaluation of curves across it is both a strength and a weakness. It is a strength because whatever method has the confidence of the customers can be used, even to the point of having a few alternatives. The subsequent reevaluation does not know how its surface was constructed. It is a weakness because in the case of doubly curved plates, the mapping should depend on the outline of the plates that are to be developed. Even the portholes in them will influence how the metal really flows during forming. It is always possible for a distinct developed surface to be derived for each plate, taking the plate shape and the correct physics of deformation into account.

In the later versions of NMG that implemented this facility, the algorithm used was the analogue of marking the parameter lines on the surface with wet ink and then rolling the surface along these lines (without rotation) onto a sheet of blotting paper, noting where the mesh points came and how their control vectors projected into that plane. This rolling started from an operator-selected point somewhere in the middle of the surface and proceeded outward. Apart from the initial rolls outward in the four parametric directions from the start, each point was approached in two directions and a carefully argued reconciliation made between the two estimates.

The approximation in this process can be controlled by having a denser mesh in the derived surface than in the original if it is found to be necessary. The techniques for this are the same as those for controlling approximate offsetting (see Sabin, "Sculptured Surface Definitions," this volume). I do not regard dynamic construction as being useful here, as any purely geometric method will be of doubtful accuracy anyway.

We left the choice of step length in the original evaluation to the operator on the basis that he would look at the developed results and repeat the whole process if the curves showed facetting. It subsequently turned out that this is safe but possibly inefficient, since the developed curves can never have sharper curvature than the originals (the developed shape has only the geodesic curvature, while the original has both geodesic and normal curvature).

Coupling the two processes is possible, so that the reevaluation is done on the fly and the step length controlled by criteria related to the developed curve, but I would not regard it as a high priority.

MESHING FOR FINITE ELEMENTS

The key function in this context is the placing of nodes on the surface. The elements between those nodes will only approximate the surface, but the nodes should lie on it. Any demonstration of meshing that uses element boundaries only along parameter lines should be regarded as unrealistic.

Element boundaries should follow the internal structure. They must be derived from the surface by interrogation in a fully general way.

In NMG we typically calculated the structural curves and then interpolated nodes along them. It would probably have been better to have used these results as first approximations to be finally corrected by reference to the original surface and intersection definition.

MODEL MACHINING BY NUMERICAL CONTROL

Much of the literature on machining of sculptured surfaces assumes that a spherical-ended cutter machines only along isoparametric lines. Some packages are unnecessarily limited in this respect.

The British Aircraft Corporation (BAC) experience was that both the cutting and the computing could be made considerably more efficient by computing good cutting patterns; this significantly improved the productivity of the machine shop responsible for cutting wind tunnel models. Roughing with a fairly sharp-cornered milling cutter removed most of the material from the billet in a single operation, after which any deformation due to stress relief could be measured and new datum faces machined on the billet. For finishing, again, intelligent use of the large projected radius of a toroidal cutter could keep the necessary number of cuts down, and use of patterns other than parallel isoparametric lines avoided inefficient bunching of cuts. Parallel plane sections are fairly good in this respect.

It is interesting that, because the machining process is point contact, complex forms such as advanced marine propellers may be machined efficiently on rather simple numerical control (NC) machine tools with only two simultaneous contouring axes.

Fine detail, such as the withdrawal of the tool at stroke ends by a fraction of a millimetre along the surface normal, avoided dwell marks, which are much more difficult to polish out than a slight 'pip' [Bell74].

What we did not have at the time, which would have been valuable, was the ability to make continuous strokes across a complete configuration of surfaces including fillets between separately defined arrays of patches. The ability to compute such curves in one piece would also be valuable in other contexts, and should therefore be put high on the wish-list.

A further possible complication is that of computing deformed shapes so that the model is cut to such a shape that, under testing loads, it deforms to a correct image of the shape of the original under service loads. Such a facility is in fact straightforward to apply, since the deformations are small enough for simple perturbation of the control points to be accurate enough.

Acknowledgments. Most of the material presented in this paper was derived under contract to the Ministry of Defence, United Kingdom, and thanks are due for their permission to use this material. I would also like to thank Drs. John Duncan and Nicholas Prudden of the Ministry of Defence, Prof. Robin Forrest, and Dr. Alan Ball for their contributions.

Appendix: Variant Tree for Interrogation Methods

Which major method?

Marching

    What start scan?

        Edges only

        Edges plus raster scan for single loop if no edge start

        Max/min extent plus scanning tree

    What major step method?

        Derivative-based

        Repeat of last step plus 10 percent

    What minor step method?

        Newton-Raphson

        Local lattice

Lattice

    What order?

        Curve order

           What start scan?

             As above

           What size grid?

             Coarse with refinement

                What refinement?

                    Linear

                    Cubic Hermite

             Fine

        Raster order

           What size grid?

             As above

Recursive division

    What condition for simplicity?

        Linear interpolation adequate

        Marching provably robust

        Single intersection for refinement

What criteria for division choice?

Alternating

Longest edge

Least simple

What division ratio?

Always equal halves

Patch boundary if one exists, otherwise equal

Adaptive

REFERENCES

[Bell74]
Bell, C., Landi, B., and Sabin, M.A., The programming and use of numerical control to machine sculptured surfaces, in *Proc. of 14th MTDR Conference*, pp. 233–238, New York: Macmillan, 1974.

[Cohe80]
Cohen, E., Lyche, T., and Riesenfeld, R.F., Discrete B-splines and subdivision techniques in computer aided design and computer graphics, *Comput. Graph. Image Process.*, Vol. 14, pp. 87–111, 1980.

[Geis83]
Geisow, A.D., Surface Interrogations, Ph.D. Thesis, University of East Anglia, Norwich, U.K., 1983.

[Greg86]
Gregory, J.A., *N*-sided surface patches, in *The Mathematics of Surfaces*, Gregory, J.A., Ed., pp. 217–232, Oxford, U.K.: Clarendon Press, 1986.

[Levi76]
Levin, J.Z., A parametric algorithm for drawing pictures of solid objects composed of quadric surfaces, *CACM*, Vol. 19, pp. 555–563, 1976.

[Lodw70]
Lodwick, G.D., and Whittle, J., A technique for automatic contouring field survey data, *Austral. Comput. J.*, Vol. 2, pp. 104–109, 1970.

[Mann78]
Manning, J.R., Computerised Pattern Cutting, Shoe and Allied Trades Research Assoc. RR287, Kettering, U.K., July 1978

[Marl76]
Marlow, S., and Powell, M.J.D., A Fortran subroutine for plotting the part of a conic that is inside a given triangle, Report R-8336, Atomic Energy Research Establishment, Harwell, England, 1976.

[Nasr85]
Nasri, A., Polyhedral Subdivision Methods for Free-form Surfaces, Ph.D. Thesis, University of East Anglia, Norwich, U.K., 1985.

[Payn68]
Payne, P.J., A Contouring Program for Coons Surface Patches, CAD Group Document 16, Cambridge University, Cambridge, U.K., 1968.

[Payn71]
Payne, P.J., A Contouring Program for Joined Surface Patches, CAD Group Document 58, Cambridge University, Cambridge, U.K., 1971.

[Prat86]
Pratt, M.J., and Geisow, A.D., Surface/surface intersection problems, in *The Mathematics of Surfaces*, Gregory, J.A., Ed., pp. 117–142, Oxford, U.K.: Clarendon Press, 1986.

[Sabi83]
Sabin, M.A., Non-rectangular surface patches suitable for inclusion in a B-spline surface, in *Proc. of Eurographics 83*, ten Hagen, P.J.W., Ed., pp. 55–70, Amsterdam: Elsevier Science Publishers BV (North Holland), 1983.

[Sabi86]
Sabin, M.A., Recursive division, in *The Mathematics of Surfaces*, Gregory, J.A., Ed., pp. 269–282, Oxford, U.K.: Clarendon Press, 1986.

[Sede84]
Sederberg, T.W., Anderson, D.C., and Goldman, R.N., Implicit representation of parametric curves and surfaces, *Comput. Vision, Graph. Image Process.*, Vol. 28, pp. 22–84, 1984.

[Sede85]
Sederberg, T.W., Piecewise algebraic surface patches, *Comput. Aided Geom. Design*, Vol. 2, pp. 53–59, 1985.

Solid Modelling—Survey and Current Research Issues

M.J. Pratt

Abstract

The material falls into two parts. The first gives a historical introduction to solid modelling and summarises the three most frequently used techniques, cellular subdivision, constructive solid geometry, and boundary representation. The second part of the paper deals with some current research areas in solid modelling, as follows:

The integration of sculptured or free-form surfaces into solid modellers raises a variety of problems. Some of these are mathematical, being concerned with the computation of intersection curves and trimmed surface patches, though significant issues also arise in the user interface context.

Form features have recently been identified as a key concept in the integration of computer aided design and manufacture. Their nature and importance are discussed, techniques for automatic feature recognition are outlined, and the idea of 'design by features' is introduced.

Finally, the paper deals with data exchange between solid modelling systems, an important issue in industrial communications. Progress towards an international standard for 'neutral file' data transfer is described, and the virtues of a standard dynamic or procedural interface is explained.

Historical Introduction

The development of the computer-based CAD/CAM system has led to major changes in the way product data is represented. The traditional means is in terms of manually produced drawings. From the late 1960s computerised draughting systems have been available that produce the same kind of drawings in a different and more efficient manner. Such systems avoid the need for much of the repetitive work inherent in the manual process while permitting the designer to work in terms that remain familiar to him. As was the case with manually produced drawings, drawings produced on CAD/CAM systems are still largely composed of straight lines and circular arcs and are still heavily annotated with dimensions, notes, and other miscellaneous information. The drawing, however, is initially created on a graphics screen rather than on paper, although 'hard copy' may be generated on a plotter. The least familiar aspect of this method of draughting is the need for interaction with the computer, but many traditionally trained draughtsmen have found little difficulty in converting to the new mode of operation.

In the early 1970s further developments occurred that had far-reaching implications. The first such development was the association of depth information with the lines in a 2D drawing generated by a draughting system. This allowed the definition of a class of what are known as $2^1/_2$ D objects, characterised by stepwise dimensional variations in the third dimension; all surfaces of such an object are either vertical or horizontal. At first sight, the enhancement may not seem very significant but, in fact, the computer could now generate a unified representation of the object rather than three complementary partial representations in the form of the orthogonal views traditionally drawn. For the first time we had a *computer model* of the product. Within the computer, a $2^1/_2$ D object was represented as a set of edges in space, and it was rapidly found to be possible to generalise the idea, which enabled the generation of fully 3D models of the same type. These models have become known, for obvious reasons, as *wireframe* models. One immediate advantage of the wireframe representation of an object is that the computer can automatically generate drawings of the object from any point of view and in any projection chosen by the user. If 2D drawings are required, the usual orthogonal projections can be derived from the unified model simply by viewing it in parallel projection in the directions of the three axes. However, because the model consists only of a set of edges, drawings from other points of view can become very congested for complex objects, since all of the edges are drawn; the lack of surface information in the model implies that there is no capability for the automatic generation of the hidden-line or hidden-surface views that make visualisation so much easier.

Most of the CAD systems used today are employed for the generation of 2D drawings or 3D wireframe models. Many of the more powerful CAD systems on the market now also include a capability for defining complex, doubly curved surfaces. The methods used stem from mathematical developments in the late 1950s and early 1960s, mainly in the aircraft industry, but these methods demand considerable computational resources even by today's standards, and it is only comparatively recently that they have become a practical proposition in an interactive design system. Systems of this kind merely model isolated surfaces, however, whereas most engineering objects are bounded by faces lying on a collection of different surfaces.

The next development in this sequence of ways of representing products was the *solid modeller*, which brought together the advantages of the wireframe and surface modellers. The model in the computer now contained information concerning all the faces of the object including the surfaces they lay on and the edge curves that bound them. Furthermore, details of the connectivity between faces, edges, and other elements were stored, as will be described later. The description was sufficiently complete so that a wide range of applications could be performed automatically, at least in principle. From the computer graphics point of view, the computer could now automatically generate hidden-line or hidden-surface pictures of the object represented from any desired point of view. It could also compute the volume, mass, and moments of inertia of the object, which is of great convenience in engineering applications.

The ultimate type of model for engineering purposes is referred to as a *product model*. The earlier types of models may be classed together as *geometric models*, since the information they contain is very largely geometric. The exception is the dimensioning and annotation information on drawings, but it should be recalled that this is intended for human interpretation. In a product model all of this information will be associated with the geometric part of the model in some *machine-understandable* manner, and the model may then be considered to be truly complete for the automation of engineering processes, which may draw all their data from the model and thus operate without human intervention. It should be emphasised that we are still some way from this desirable situation, and much work remains to be done to find appropriate ways of representing nongeometric data in the product model.

The most significant aspect of the progression described is the increasing potential for interpretation of the model by the computer. The manually produced drawing is intended exclusively for human interpretation. Even when a similar drawing is produced using a 2D draughting system, the information in the computer that represents the drawing is not intended for automatic interpretation; it is merely a coding of a human-interpretable drawing. With the wireframe model we have more possibility for automatic use of the data; as already pointed out, the computer can now generate drawings of the object represented from arbitrary viewpoints. However, many applications are still impossible because they require the existence of surface data in the model. Surface modellers usually permit the definition of unconnected surfaces only and not complete object models. They do permit certain applications to be automated, notably, the generation of data for numerically controlled machining, but it is not until we come to the geometrically complete solid model that the potential for automation of a wide range of applications begins to emerge.

Many solid modelling systems are now marketed commercially, and while most of the powerful CAD/CAM systems that have been developed over the last 15 years were originally of the wireframe type, they have now acquired a solid modelling capability. At present, however, the range of applications that have been automated is quite restricted. This is because of early concentration on the purely geometric aspects of modelling; it is only recently that attention has turned to the additional requirements of the informationally complete product model. There are already signs of exciting developments in the automatic generation of manufacturing data in the near future.

Potential applications for product modellers include the following:

(a) automatic finite-element mesh generation obviating the need for the use of an interactive preprocessor;

(b) automatic analysis of the motion of linkages and mechanisms (including robots) for collisions between components or with other objects in their environment;

(c) automatic generation of machining operation and sequence plans for the manufacture of individual parts;

(d) automatic generation of assembly plans.

The above list is by no means exhaustive.

It is clear that, if the integration of CAD and CAM is to be based upon the use of an informationally complete product model, then the system which generates that model must be completely reliable and must provide the information needed by downstream applications in a convenient form. While the modeller will be one of the keystones of the entire process, current systems are not ideal for this purpose, since they possess certain shortcomings both as regards robustness and informational completeness. The second part of this paper discusses some of the research issues that must be tackled to alleviate these problems. Firstly, however, the various types of solid modelling systems in use today are described, since their modes of operation, particularly as regards their underlying data structures, have considerable influence on their suitability for general CAD/CAM purposes.

Techniques of Solid Modelling

TYPES OF SOLID MODELLER

Existing solid modelling systems may be divided into three classes. Firstly, there are systems based on the spatial decomposition of the volume containing the modelled object into an array of cells which may be occupied or empty. These are referred to as *cellular* or *spatial occupancy* systems. Several such systems have been developed, but they are mostly research tools; only one such modeller is commercially available, and it is not primarily intended for engineering purposes. The most highly developed of the cellular techniques is the *octree* method briefly described below.

In the second type of system the modelling process involves the building up of complex objects from relatively simple volumetric building blocks or *primitives*. These primitives retain their explicit representation in the data structure that describes the final model; the various combination operations are also stored, and the overall representation therefore contains a 'history' of the construction of the model. A system of this type is referred to as a *constructive solid geometry* (CSG) modeller.

Thirdly, there are the *boundary representation* (Brep) modellers which, as their name implies, model only the boundary of the modelled object. The boundary changes as the model is built and, by contrast with the CSG approach, details of its constructional 'history' are lost.

In the following sections a review is given of the underlying principles of all three types of modellers.

Cellular Modellers

The basic cellular method is conceptually very simple. A finite volume of space entirely containing the object to be modelled is assumed to be divided into a large number of discrete cuboidal cells. In the simplest case, these are all of the same size so that a regular 3D mesh results. The modelling system then labels each cell as to whether or not it is occupied by material. The appropriate data structure is a 3D matrix in which each element corresponds to one space cell. The value of an element might be 0 for an empty cell and 1 for a full cell.

Clearly this approach has the virtue of simplicity. However, in order to obtain good resolution on the boundary of an object, it is necessary to use a large number of small cells, which leads to problems of computer storage. Figure 1 shows a 2D example illustrating the manner of representation of an object boundary and the problems of resolution. In three dimensions the horizontal and vertical line segments on the boundary of the model will be replaced by horizontal and vertical rectangular facets.

One existing solid modeller based on the cellular approach, the Japanese TIPS-1 system [TIPS78], overcomes the resolution problem by using three classes of cells rather than two. This system uses a coarse regular mesh in which cells are defined as full, empty, or *boundary*; in the last case the cell is partially occupied by material and contains part of the boundary of the

Figure 1. Resolution problem with regular cellular decomposition (cells more than half occupied are considered full).

modelled object. These boundary cells are by far the most important from the applications point of view, and they are treated in various special ways to achieve more effective resolution of the true object boundary. For some purposes the refinement is achieved by making reference to the true underlying surfaces, expressed by implicit equations of the form $f(x, y, z) = 0$. In other cases, for example, in the computation of volume, mass, and moments of inertia, boundary cells are further subdivided into arrays of 125 smaller subcells, each subcell being classed as full or empty. It should be noted that it is only necessary to use this higher resolution for the relatively small proportion of cells that are of the boundary type; there is no virtue in further subdividing the original coarse cells, which are known to be either completely full or completely empty.

It is worth stressing that the boundary of an object is its most important attribute for most applications. Boundary information is needed, for example, for the generation of a shaded surface rendering. Similarly, if one wishes to machine an object from a solid blank of metal, the cutter paths must be determined by reference to the shape of the boundary. It is therefore logical to seek a means for the automatic increase of resolution of the cellular structure in the vicinity of the boundary. The TIPS-1 system achieves this in a fairly crude way, as described above; a more sophisticated approach is now available in the *octree* method [Jack80; Meag82]. Here there are only two classes of cells, full and empty, but the cells are graded in size. An initial coarse regular decomposition is made, and the cells are classified. Some will be full and others empty; those which fall into neither class must contain part of the object boundary, and these are further subdivided into a $2 \times 2 \times 2$ mesh of smaller cells. The classification is now repeated, and subdivision is performed on boundary subcells in a similar manner. This method allows the achievement of any desired order of resolution of the object boundary. The result of the subdivision may be represented as a tree structure having as its root the single original cuboidal cell containing the object. Subdivision of any cell that is neither full nor empty gives rise to eight branches; cells that are found to be full or empty at any level of subdivision are not further subdivided. Figure 2 illustrates the principle for a 2D example—in this case the structure is known as a *quadtree* rather than an octree, since there are four rather than eight subdivisions of the boundary cells. Quadtrees have gained considerable interest in their own right in the field of computer graphics but will not be discussed further here.

Despite the use of large cells in the interior and exterior of an object model, the storage requirements of the octree method are still very large. Phoenix Data Systems have developed specialised hardware for use in this type of modelling and have demonstrated the INSIGHT modeller based on octree principles [John86]. This system is oriented towards medical rather than engineering applications.

It has been shown by Yerry and Shephard [Yerr83; Yerr84] that better boundary resolution can be achieved with smaller storage requirements by

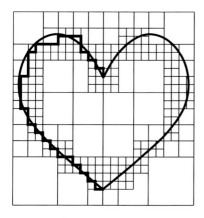

Figure 2. Octree decomposition of the area from Figure 1 (cells more than half occupied are considered full).

the use of *modified quadtrees and octrees*. In this approach the boundary cells at the most refined level of subdivision are replaced by full or empty cells whose shapes have been modified to make them conform more closely to the true boundary of the object. In a modified quadtree representation of a 2D object, the boundary is polygonal and closely follows the contour of the original (see Figure 3), in contrast with the stepwise variation of the boundary illustrated in Figure 2 for the conventional quadtree. The modified octree representation of a solid object is similarly faceted in three dimensions.

More recently, Ayala et al. [Ayal85] and Navazo et al. [Nava86] have proposed the use of an even further refined version of the octree method in which boundary cells contain references to the exact boundary surfaces of the object. It is worth noting that this approach was presaged ten years or more ago in the TIPS-1 system, as described earlier.

Cellular or spatial subdivision methods lend themselves to certain types of engineering applications, and some solid modellers that are not basically of this type nevertheless employ subdivision for specific purposes. The NONAME modeller, developed at Leeds University, is an example. This CSG system uses a cellular method to determine a machining strategy for manufacturing the modelled object [Care83]. A cellular representation is also clearly convenient for the computation of mass properties, since it is only necessary to calculate the properties of an assembly of cuboidal elements that are uniform internally. It is also possible to base the automatic generation of a finite-element mesh on a cell structure; this was, in fact, the main purpose of the work of Yerry and Shephard referred to previously.

Despite these virtues, most solid modellers based on a purely cellular approach are still in the research domain. This appears to be because a satisfactory trade-off has yet to be found between the requirement for accurate boundary resolution needed in engineering applications and the very large storage requirements that this implies. For this reason, the remainder of this paper will concentrate mainly on the CSG and boundary representation approaches to solid modelling.

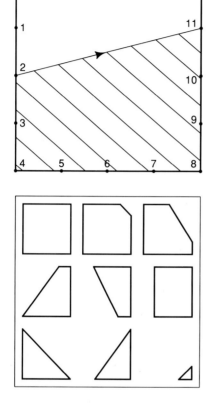

Figure 3. Modified quadtree element: the number pair 2, 11 defines the shaded area. Other possible elements are also shown.

Constructive Solid Geometry (CSG) Modellers

The CSG modellers are those which build a representation of a complex object in terms of representations of simple volumetric primitives. These primitives typically include blocks, cylinders, cones, spheres, and tori. *Boolean* or *set operations* are provided allowing the set union, set difference, or set intersection of volumes (regarded as sets of points in space) to be formed. The data structure for a modeller of this kind is quite compact and is based on what is in graph-theoretic terms known as a *tree*, a particular class of graph structure containing no closed cycles. Figure 4 shows a simple L-shaped bracket together with its CSG tree representation. Each *branch* of the tree ends in a *leaf* corresponding to one of the primitive volumes, and branches meet at *nodes* corresponding to set operators. Conventionally, the root of such a tree (which represents the complete object) is depicted at the top, and the structure is evaluated from the bottom up; thus, the union of block A with block B is formed first, and then the cylinder C is differenced from the result. In practice, the data structure is usually rather more complicated than this, since the same primitive volume is often referenced more than once in the description of a complete object, with translational or rotational transformations applied. Nevertheless, the diagram illustrates the essential nature of the CSG data structure. It should be noted that the geometry of the object modelled is represented entirely in terms of the geometry of the original primitives, and that the data structure incorporates a 'history' of the mode of creation of the part model.

The actual geometry of the primitives is usually represented in terms of what are known as *half-spaces*; these are in effect directed surfaces possessing a concept of an inside and an outside.

The characteristics of CSG modellers derive mainly from the use of the CSG tree as the primary data structure. For many applications, even such a basic one as graphical visualisation, details of the edges and faces of the object are required. The CSG structure is described as *unevaluated*, since these details are not explicitly present in it. When they are required, they must be computed. This process is called *evaluation* and, for a complex object, it can be a very heavy computational task. For example, since the only geometric information present is that concerned with surfaces on which the object faces lie, details of all the edge curves must be calculated (by computing the intersection curves of pairs of surfaces). The edges themselves are bounded segments of these curves, the bounding points being vertices whose positions must be computed as the intersections of three surfaces. All this data must be computed and a secondary evaluated data structure created in order to draw a simple wireframe picture of the object. Once it has been used, this information is discarded again in the simpler CSG systems, although there is now an increasing tendency to

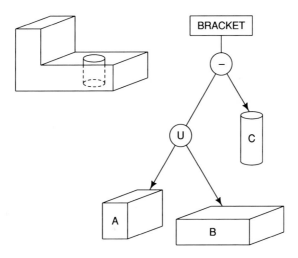

Figure 4. CSG tree structure for an L-shaped bracket defined in terms of two blocks and one cylinder.

retain the evaluated information and to augment it incrementally as the CSG representation is built up.

The CSG approach has distinct advantages in terms of conceptual simplicity and robustness. Furthermore, by virtue of the compact nature and lack of redundancy in the primary data structure, it is possible to represent dimensions of some or all of the primitives by variable parameters rather than fixed numerical values, thereby providing a useful ability for 'family of parts' definition.

On the other hand, the CSG philosophy also has its disadvantages, although time may show that many of them can be overcome. One fundamental problem is that much current thinking on the automation of the interface between design and manufacturing seems to indicate that an evaluated data structure is most appropriate for this type of application. It is important to be able to address individual faces and edges of an object, and the CSG method not only requires an expensive evaluation process to generate the necessary entities, but also sometimes makes it difficult to refer to them in a convenient way. However, it has been found to be possible to automate certain applications (the generation of shaded surface renderings, the generation of finite-element meshes, and the computation of mass properties, for example) by working directly from the CSG tree without evaluating the model. The future may see the development of effective corresponding algorithms in the manufacturing area.

Another disadvantage of the CSG approach as it exists at present is that the constructional operations available to the designer are usually limited to set operations on previously defined volumes, which proves inconvenient for certain types of detailing needed once the gross geometric form of a part has been established. A further problem is the apparent difficulty of implementing 'free-form' surface geometry in a way that is convenient for engineering design.

It has been shown that, provided all Boolean or set operations are regarded as being *regularised* in nature, any object built up from properly defined primitive volumes is itself a valid solid. Regularised operations [Requ80] upon solids defined in terms of closed sets of space points involve a specialised treatment of the boundary points of these sets, which is necessary to ensure that invalid results do not occur. For example, if a small cube is placed on top of a larger one, they share a common set of points, those constituting their area of contact. This point set is in fact the intersection of the two volumes in set-theoretic terms, but it clearly does not constitute a valid solid in its own right. In essence, the performance of a regularised set operation involves three steps, which avoid the occurrence of invalid results:

(a) the boundary points are removed from each set of points to leave an 'open' set;

(b) the set operation is performed on the resulting open sets of points;

(c) boundary points are restored to the result of the operation.

If these steps are followed and the original solid representations were valid, then all subsequent volumes defined will also be valid. In the example given above, it should be noted that the removal of boundary points from both cubes removes the set of points which they have in common so that the regularised intersection operation gives a null result.

Most CSG modellers build a form of boundary representation in situations where evaluated data are required. However, this secondary data structure is often not as complex as that of a pure boundary representation (Brep) system, since it may not be optimised for incremental construction, especially in those systems which compute it from scratch whenever needed. In consequence, there is less to go wrong when this structure is generated. Even when matters do not go smoothly, the system always has the basic CSG representation to fall back on, so all is not lost. By contrast, Brep modellers have no second line of defence and, if an operation fails, may crash completely.

The archetypal CSG solid modeller is PADL-2 developed at the University of Rochester [Brow82]. This system is the basis of two commercial solid modellers, McDonnell Douglas' UNISOLIDS (though this is likely to be based on the Brep system ROMULUS from 1990 onwards) and Autotrol's S7000.

Many algorithms used in PADL-2, particularly for boundary evaluation, use *set membership classification*. This may be illustrated in terms of a space curve passing through a volume; the points on the curve fall into three classes lying, respectively, interior to, exterior to, and on the surface of the volume. The first two classes represent bounded curve segments; if we think of the space curve as being an edge curve of one primitive and the solid as being a second primitive, then these curve segments are candidates for edges resulting from a Boolean operation involving the two primitives. Which are accepted as edges and which rejected depends on the particular Boolean operation. This is the basis of the PADL-2 evaluation process [Tilo80].

Boundary Representation (Brep) Modellers

The boundary representation approach uses an evaluated data structure as the sole description of the object. Details are stored of all the elements that compose the object's boundary (most notably faces, edges, and vertices), together with what is called *topological* information concerning the interconnections between these elements. For a valid solid model the faces of the object should form at least one closed shell dividing its interior from its exterior. There may be more than one shell if interior voids are present. Ideally, it should be the responsibility of the system rather than the user to guarantee that the object boundary is complete.

A typical Brep data structure is a network built from a hierarchy of topological entities, with vertices at the lowest level, then edges, faces, and entire objects. Assemblies may be modelled at a yet higher level as sets of component objects. Entities are linked by means of pointers, for example, from a face to each of its bounding edges, from an edge to its two end vertices, and so on. Vertices, edges, and faces have additional pointers to 'geometrical' entities, namely, points, curves, and surfaces, respectively. The topology alone, as defined by the network structure without the geometry, represents a deformable or 'rubber' object that only becomes rigid when the geometry is specified. Some modellers have additional levels in the hierarchy and specify loops of edges (i.e., face boundary loops) and shells of faces, as in Figure 5.

In a Brep modeller the data structure is built up incrementally as model creation proceeds. This means that a wireframe picture can be drawn quite quickly at any stage; explicit edge details are present in the data structure, and it is only necessary to draw each edge using an appropriate viewing transformation. Most such systems provide Boolean or set operations, but these are computationally expensive since the result has to be evaluated immediately. This necessitates the computation of surface intersections to determine new edge curves, the insertion of new edges and vertices into the data structure, and so on. However, it is comparatively easy to provide a range of other means of object construction in systems of this type, enabling Boolean operations to be avoided to some extent. This is highly desirable, since these operations are not only slow but also less reliable than some of the other procedures.

One of the most powerful methods of object construction is *sweeping*. This requires the definition of a 2D profile curve, which is then swept linearly through space to generate an 'extrusion' or swept rotationally about an axis to create a rotational solid. The method is still more powerful when

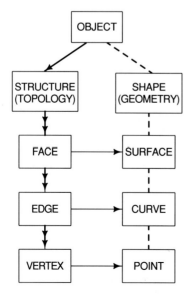

Figure 5. Typical Brep data structure: double arrows denote multiple pointers. Note the topology/geometry separation.

it allows profiles to be defined on plane faces of existing objects and then to be swept inwards to create through holes or depressions or outwards to create protrusions. Some CSG systems provide sweeping operations on profiles for the initial creation of volumes, but none at present implements the extension of the method just described.

Other creation procedures that are available in some Brep modellers include a range of *local operations*. These allow the modification of a localised region of the data structure in an efficient manner. For example, the geometry associated with a single face can be redefined and the result evaluated quickly without the need for a Boolean operation. Similarly, an edge of an object may be bevelled by the replacement of an edge in the data structure with a simple substructure defining a new inserted face with its connected edges and vertices.

The advantages of the Brep approach to solid modelling are as follows:

(a) a wider range of creation techniques may be provided than is the case for CSG systems. Some of these are computationally very efficient;

(b) the data structure provides convenient 'handles' for the attachment of associated nongeometric data, e.g., tolerance data or surface finish or heat treatment requirements for a particular face;

(c) there is efficient access to the geometric information that is needed for many applications purposes, e.g., the automatic generation of manufacturing data;

(d) it is easy in principle to implement the 'sculptured' or free-form geometry required by many engineering parts.

On the other hand there are also disadvantages:

(a) it is less easy than in the CSG case to provide an automatic guarantee of the integrity of a model;

(b) Brep systems are inherently less robust than CSG systems because the generation of the data structure often requires answers to delicate geometric enquiries concerning the coincidence or parallelism of geometric entities, which can give rise to problems of numerical tolerance in the computer;

(c) it is less easy than in the CSG case to provide a facility for the parametric definition of families of parts.

It should be pointed out at this stage that Brep modellers fall into two subclasses distinguished by their use of exact or approximate geometry. Approximating systems generally represent curved object faces by assemblies of planar facets or subfaces. This greatly simplifies the generation of hidden-line drawings, for example, and also means that all surface intersection calculations can be performed entirely in terms of intersections between planes. However, a very fine subdivision of faces into facets will require a great many such computations, which may take even longer than the calculation of the intersection between the underlying exact surfaces. There are obvious disadvantages of faceting when a solid modeller is used for interference analysis between parts in an assembly. Most faceting systems allow the user to choose the tolerance in the approximation, and many also provide some form of exact representation of the approximated surfaces. However, these are not generally used in computer-intensive operations such as Booleans, which are performed on the faceted approximate model. This can, in fact, lead to results that are topologically erroneous when compared with the exact results.

Commercially available Brep systems include PROREN, ROMULUS, and TECHNOVISION (using exact geometry) and CATIA, EUCLID, and GEOMOD (faceting systems). One of the better documented research modellers of the Brep type, BUILD, was originally developed at Cambridge University but is now undergoing further enhancement at Cranfield [Brai79; Ande83].

Brep systems have many advantages, as already pointed out, but they lack the robust primary data structure possessed by the CSG systems. The boundary representation data structure is large, complex, and usually highly redundant in the interests of efficient access for a wide variety of purposes. It has to be optimised for two main classes of operations. Firstly, there are modelling operations, which have the effect of modifying the data structure incrementally as the designer builds the model. Secondly, there are interrogations, which are frequently necessary during the modelling process and are essential for engineering applications interfacing with the modeller. A delicate balance has to be maintained in the design of the data structure, since the implementation of a redundant access path that speeds up a particular interrogation means that there are more pointers to be reset during modelling operations which, in consequence, are likely to be slowed down.

Unlike the CSG systems, Brep modellers do not in general have a simple and robust unevaluated representation to fall back upon when some modelling operation runs into problems. The best that can be done is to store a journal file that records all the modelling functions performed during a design session. If the system crashes, this can then be rerun to reconstruct the model as it was before the failure, and suitable measures can be taken to circumvent the problem that arose. This is often time-consuming and frustrating, and reliability is therefore at a premium. Unfortunately, it has not proved easy to achieve in systems of this type, and the best commercial Brep systems are even now prone to occasional failure despite the many man-years of effort and the wealth of experience that has gone into their development. Fortunately, systems of this type often offer alternative means of achieving the same result, and the perceptive user soon learns the types of situations and operations that may give rise to problems.

Complete validity checking is not easily provided for a Brep model; efficient means have been developed for ensuring topological validity, but geometrical validity still requires expensive computational checks. Consider, for example, a large rectangular plate that has a circular profile defined upon its upper face. This profile is now swept rotationally through 90 degrees about an axis in that face to create a hook-shaped projection. The object is topologically the same if the angle of sweep is anywhere between zero and 180 degrees, since it has the same number of faces, edges, and vertices and they are all connected in the same way. If the angle exceeds 180 degrees, the same situation holds provided we are prepared to accept self-intersecting objects as valid. However, for engineering purposes such objects are not valid, and we must require the system to carry out the geometrical checks that recognise the occurrence of the self-intersection. When this occurs a major topological change takes place; the initial object had genus zero (no through holes) and the new object has genus one, since a through hole has been created (see Figure 6).

The guarantee of topological validity mentioned above can be given provided the model is constructed by means of what are called *Euler operations* [Brai79; Mant82]. These are derived from a generalisation of Euler's law, which in its simplest form $F - E + V = 2$ asserts a relationship between the number of faces, edges, and vertices of a polyhedral object. Its requisite generalisation is the *Euler-Poincaré formula*:

$$F - E + V - H = 2(M - G)$$

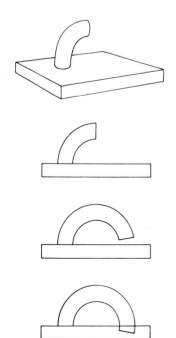

Figure 6. Rotation of profile by 90°, 170°, and 190°, showing self-intersection and the need for geometric checking.

In this equation, the significance of the variables is as follows:

F = number of faces of the object(s),

E = number of edges of the object(s),

V = number of vertices of the object(s),

H = number of hole loops (disjoint interior edge loops of faces of the object(s)),

M = number of objects,

G = total genus (the sum of the numbers of through holes in all the objects).

Note that the relation is valid for assemblies of objects as well as single parts; it is also valid for objects with nonplanar faces.

An Euler operation is any operation that changes the value of two or more of the variables in the Euler-Poincaré formula whilst retaining its validity. For example, we may add 1 to the values of E and V; if the equation was previously valid it will remain valid. This operation corresponds to the creation of a new vertex on an existing edge, which is thereby split into two edges. If we perform this operation on two opposite edges of a face of a cube, we may then create a new edge joining the two new vertices. This splits the face concerned into two faces; the corresponding Euler operation is one which increases both E and F by 1. Infinitely many Euler operations may be defined, but it is usual in modellers that implement them to work in terms of a convenient set of about ten. In such systems, all modelling operations that involve topological changes are broken down into sequences of Euler operations, and the topological integrity of the model is then always assured [Brai79; Mant82].

Unfortunately, in view of the foregoing, the major reliability problems of Brep modellers are concerned with geometry rather than topology. A standard example concerns the intersection of two cylinders (see Figure 7). The intersection curve may be closed and continuous, self-intersecting, or split into two disjoint branches, all three cases arising as the smaller cylinder is displaced through a small distance with respect to the larger one. It is quite possible for numerical tolerance problems in the computation of the intersection curves (see the section on intersections of surfaces under Current Research Issues) to give the wrong result when the true situation is very close to the limiting (self-intersecting) case. In this event, the topology of the model will not agree with its geometry, and dire results are likely to arise if modelling proceeds on the basis of this erroneous situation.

The problems of geometric tolerancing are not significantly less for faceted modellers than for those using exact geometry. For one thing, there are many more faces, edges, and vertices in a faceted model, and the number of coincidences, etc. to be checked is correspondingly higher. Figure 8 depicts a solid modelling benchmark object that presents some interesting

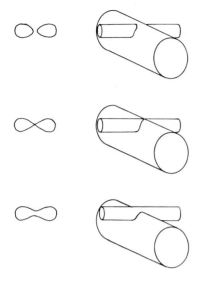

Figure 7. Topological variations in the intersection curve of two cylinders.

problems. The chief of these is the modelling of the blend between the conical body of the object and the toroidal projection. Each boundary of the blend surface will be determined approximately in terms of line segments generated by intersecting facets from the faces on either side. Since the true blend is tangential to the surfaces on either side, the two families of facets will be almost parallel where the intersections occur or even actually parallel to within the angular tolerance of the system. Inevitably, then, computational difficulties will arise due to the ill conditioning of the equations to be solved. Furthermore, the approximate boundary will appear very jagged and irregular when the object is drawn unless some smoothing technique is applied.

Figure 8. The 'Cranfield Object', a benchmark solid modelling part having a cone/torus blend.

Hybrid Modellers

It has been shown that neither of the two major approaches to solid modelling, CSG and Brep, is perfect for all applications. It is hardly surprising, therefore, that hybrid systems are now becoming more common; system developers are trying to get the best of both worlds. The ideal modeller would be one that retains a compact description of the 'history' of the model construction whilst simultaneously providing an evaluated Brep data structure. This implies the incremental generation of the boundary representation as the constructive model is built; early fears that the concurrent building of dual representations might lead to mutual inconsistency appear to have been overstated, since a number of commercial systems now do this quite routinely. One of the chief problems with this philosophy is that the user interface has to be of the CSG type. The efficient Brep local operations cannot be provided, since these can operate only on an evaluated data structure. No effective means has yet been demonstrated of converting back from a Brep to a CSG representation, and hence one of the dual representations would be lost. However, it is quite possible that time will show us how to overcome this problem.

Some Current Research Issues In Solid Modelling

In the last major section of this paper four current research issues in solid modelling are explored. Their choice is entirely subjective on the author's part—they happen to be topics in which he is particularly interested. Two are treated in lesser depth: free-form surfaces because they are the sole subject of a separate presentation in this volume (see Sabin, 'Interrogation Techniques for Parametric Surfaces'), and programming interfaces because this is a relatively new area of work whose significance is only gradually becoming realised. The two remaining topics, form features and CAD data exchange standards, are given a more extended treatment; both are emerging topics of major practical importance.

The choice of subjects also reflects the author's involvement with the research organisation Computer Aided Manufacturing International, Inc. (CAM-I), in particular with its Geometric Modelling Program. Much of CAM-I's work in solid modelling is innovative and highly relevant to the needs of industry; it deserves to be more widely known, and to this end significant CAM-I research results are cited where appropriate.

FREE-FORM SURFACES IN SOLID MODELLING

Even now, after nearly 20 years of solid modeller development, many commercial systems do not possess the capability of defining objects with free-form surfaces. Amongst those which do have this facility, the majority use faceted rather than exact representations. It appears, as mentioned in the previous discussion of CSG modellers, that free-form surfaces are harder to implement in a CSG rather than a Brep environment, although a few recent papers discuss techniques for defining free-form CSG primitives (e.g., Rossignac and Requicha [Ross84] and Saia et al. [Saia87]. The remainder of this section is written with a boundary representation approach in mind, since this allows more flexibility in the provision of appropriate methods for the designer.

Design Methods for Free-form Surfaces

In a recent paper, Várady and Pratt [Vara84] have identified design requirements for four classes of free-form surfaces. These are (a) aesthetic surfaces having few, if any, engineering constraints; (b) generalised duct surfaces having precise constraints along two boundaries; (c) blending surfaces and fillets having precise constraints on all boundaries; and (d) fitted surfaces, which are required to meet constraints not only on their boundaries but also in their interiors. Examples of each class are:

(a) the surface of a work of sculpture;

(b) an exhaust manifold, where the precise constraints occur at the ends of the ducts and the intermediate cross-sections are of lesser importance;

(c) the cone/torus fillet on the Cranfield Object (Figure 8), which must be tangential to the surfaces on either side and have circular arc cross-sections in the plane of symmetry of the object;

(d) a car body shape defined to fit a large number of points digitised from a clay model.

Appropriate methods should be available for the creation of surface geometry in each of these four classes. This matter has been given very little consideration in the literature. There are several well established, but not particularly ideal, user interface techniques for the design of free-form surfaces in isolation, but a much wider range of techniques could be made available in a solid modelling context. One possibility, for example, is to define a nonsculptured object initially and to use this as a 'framework' for the creation of sculptured or free-form regions by the use of local operations. Chiyokura and Kimura [Chiy83] suggest one way of doing this, and another is outlined in Pratt [Prat85b].

The most heavily researched of the four listed surface classes is that of Class (c), blends and fillets. Several papers on this topic have recently appeared, many of them independently proposing variations on a single theme, that of algebraically defined blending surfaces. A good summary of work in this area is given by Woodwark [Wood87].

The motivation behind this work is that the rounding, blending, and filleting of edges in a solid model should be a rapid and automatic operation

requiring very little work by the designer. He should be able to point to
an edge and to ask the system to blend it, possibly specifying blend radii
at the two ends; the system should then do the rest. The only commercial
system possessing blending capabilities of this type is ROMULUS [Rock85].
In some other systems the desired result may be obtained only after a great
deal of tedious work, which is inappropriate, since the operation described
is a conceptually trivial, final detailing operation. Some modellers allow
the blending surface to be created but then require it to be incorporated
in a 'blending solid' that is finally united with the original object using
a Boolean operation. Bearing in mind that a blend surface is tangential
to the two surfaces on either side, and that Boolean operations between
objects with tangential surfaces give rise to numerical tolerance problems,
it is not surprising that such operations are frequently unsuccessful.

Intersections of Surfaces

As increasingly many solid modellers acquire free-form surface capabilities,
the computation of intersection curves between such surfaces becomes more
important. If a face lies on a free-form surface, then its edges will be
intersection curves of this type, and it is therefore necessary to be able
to calculate them accurately, reliably, and quickly. Accuracy is necessary
because the models are intended for engineering purposes; reliability is
necessary in the sense that the intersection algorithms must give complete
rather than partial answers and must not fail in critical situations; and
speed is a *sine qua non* of any interactive graphical system worthy of the
name.

The conventional means of representing free-form geometry is in terms of
parametrically defined curves and surfaces [Faux79]. These provide great
flexibility; indeed, the nonuniform rational B-spline surfaces currently in
vogue can represent all the simple quadric surfaces from the plane and the
cylinder up to the most complex doubly curved surfaces used in designing cars, shoes, or plastic bottles. However, this very generality makes
the calculation of intersections between such surfaces much more complex.
The resulting curves may contain many different disjoint branches, each of
which may exhibit pathological features such as cusps, self-intersections, or
self-tangencies. These two different types of complexity have been referred
to as *global* and *local*, respectively, and both require very careful computational treatment [Prat86; Faro86; Barn87]. No algorithm has yet been
developed that combines the three necessary qualities referred to above.
Many workers have reported methods which combine two of these virtues,
but at present we must tolerate slow intersection calculations, since reliability and accuracy are clearly indispensable in systems for engineering
use. It is possible that parallel processing may come to our aid in speeding
these computations, but nothing has yet been published on this application
to the author's knowledge.

Form Features and Their Applications

Many workers have attempted to state precisely what is meant by a 'form feature'. Although it is easy to give examples, a truly satisfactory general definition remains an elusive goal. The present author's latest attempt is as follows:

> A Form Feature is a related set of elements of a geometric model conforming to characteristic rules allowing its recognition and classification and that, regarded as an independent entity, has some significance during the life cycle of the modelled product.

The 'elements' referred to might be, for example, volumetric primitives in a CSG model or geometric and topological entities in a Brep model. The essence of the definition is that such elements often occur in recognisable patterns when the model is viewed from the point of view of some particular application such as finite-element analysis or process-planning for manufacture. Note that it is possible to define types of features other than *form* features—the latter term implies some content of geometry or shape in the feature definition, which is why the term *geometric* model is used rather than the more general term *product* model. Note, however, that *addition* of feature information to a geometric model is one of the requirements of a product model.

Some examples of form features are provided in the following sections to illuminate the definition given above. In what follows, form features will often be referred to simply as 'features' for the sake of brevity.

Examples of Form Features

Manufacturing Features of Machined Parts

It was in the manufacturing area that the term 'form features' was first used. Machined parts typically exhibit through holes, blind holes, pockets, slots, and grooves, all of which are examples of form features. Their importance for manufacturing planning is that each feature type has associated with it a comparatively small set of possible manufacturing options. The choice between these can be made by consideration of associated technological information (the surface finish required, for example) and of available production resources [Prat84a]. A knowledge of the manufacturing features of a part is therefore a very useful start in the generation of a process plan. This was recently demonstrated by Pavey et al. [Pave86]. A glossary of form features of machined and sheet metal parts was compiled some years ago by CAM-I [CAM-I81a].

It is important to note that each feature type defines a family of specific features; for example, 'flat-bottomed cylindrical blind hole' features may have any combination of radius and depth parameters. It should be noted also that (if we think for the moment in boundary representation terms) such features may be represented at least from the geometric point of view as sets of part faces. For example, a pocket feature comprises a base face and a set of side-wall faces. In this case the faces form a connected set, but features may also be composed of unconnected faces. Consider, for example, a cylindrical shaft with a circumferential groove. The groove separates two cylindrical faces that form a single feature from the manufacturing point of view, since they will normally both be produced by a single manufacturing operation.

Combinations of features are also of great importance. A countersunk hole provides an illustration in which the cylindrical hole and the conical countersink may be regarded as features in their own right, but their combination may be regarded as a 'compound feature'. A pattern of cylindrical holes is an example of another type of compound feature in which the individual holes are all features of the same type but the pattern has some additional special significance.

It is also possible that a feature may be defined in terms of one or more edges or vertices of a part. In a Brep modeller an edge may be labelled in the data structure as 'chamfered' and, in this case, the chamfer feature is associated with the single edge. The modeller may have the capability of evaluating the label, in which case a new angled face will be interpolated in the model to replace the edge. Then the chamfer feature will be associated with the new face. This example shows that there may be more than one way of representing a single feature in a solid modeller. A bevelled corner may be similarly represented, in terms of a labelled vertex.

Design Features

From the designer's point of view features are often concerned with the functionality of a part. A cylindrical hole feature may be a bearing housing, while a compound feature consisting of a set of fins on an engine may be for cooling purposes, to give but two illustrations. The designer's features may sometimes correspond with the manufacturing features, but this will not always be so. A standard example is a wing rib that has a peripheral flange and several stiffening members, as shown in Figure 9. The designer may work with an initial profile prescribed by aerodynamic considerations; he will specify a thickness for the flange, the centrelines and thicknesses of the stiffeners, and the blend radii where they meet the flange. When it comes to manufacturing, however, supposing the part is to be machined from the solid, the process planner will see a set of pocket features rather than a flange and some stiffeners. Matters are yet further complicated by the fact that the thickness of the stiffeners *may* in fact be of importance in a manufacturing context if they are likely to deform under the cutting forces applied.

Analysis Features

Analysis is an integral part of the overall design process, and we will consider a case where the use of finite-element analysis is appropriate. The

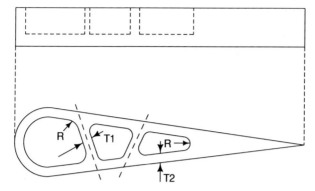

Figure 9. Machined wing rib defined by profile shape, centrelines of stiffeners, thicknesses T1, T2, radius R.

part to be analysed may have certain form features such as mounting lugs whose strength is particularly important, and these will be the salient features for the analysis. But there are also more subtle kinds of features in this context, since the finite-element mesh is usually generated on an idealisation of the original part model rather than on the part model itself. To give a few examples, parts with a high level of symmetry can frequently be analysed in terms of a small section of the original; rotational parts can be analysed in terms of a 2D profile; certain regions of the part may be approximated in terms of beam, plate, or shell elements; and certain design features of the original part (such as small holes in lightly stressed regions) may be neglected altogether. From the analyst's point of view, then, a part may exhibit symmetry features, rotational features, plate or shell features, and so on in addition to the types of features previously described.

Tolerance Features

The designer's dimensioning scheme for a part is usually related to the intended functionality of the part. The attachment of tolerance specifications to dimensions is aimed at ensuring that parts will fulfill their desired role despite the inevitability of process inaccuracies during manufacture. However, the imposition of tolerances lacks real meaning unless the part can be inspected subsequent to manufacture for compliance with those tolerances. There are certain standard types of inspection process, many of which are concerned with checking the dimensions of features such as those previously mentioned, i.e., diameters of holes or shafts, widths and depths of slots, and so forth. However, other types of features also occur, for example, a 'pair of parallel plane faces' feature, which may arise in connection with a tolerance either on distance between two planar faces or on their parallelism.

In modern tolerancing practice tolerances are often specified with respect to datum planes, which may or may not be coincident with planar faces of

386   M.J. Pratt

the part. To handle noncoincident cases it is desirable to associate auxiliary geometry with the part model. This capability is provided by very few solid modelling systems at present.

Assembly Features

These are features having significance in the (possibly automated) assembly of some product from its component parts. Normally, a set of faces on one part will mate with a corresponding set of faces on another; the sets of faces concerned must not only be labelled as features of the individual parts, but these features must also be somehow related in the assembly data structure to indicate their logical relationship. Information concerning tolerances and fits will appropriately be associated with these interfeature relationships. Functionality data could be linked with mating features in many cases, as, for example, with the outer face of a bearing and the cylindrical face of the housing into which it fits. Special methods will probably be needed for the representation of frequently occurring situations such as rivets assembled in rivet holes and similar usages of standard fastener types.

Robotics Features

Under this heading may be grouped those features of importance for robot manipulation. For example, a pair of parallel faces of a part might be labelled as a feature since they may be gripped by the end-effector of a robot involved in the assembly of this part with others.

Form Features in a Solid Modelling Context

As explained earlier in this paper, one of the main virtues of the solid modeller is that it generates product representations which, unlike the traditional engineering drawing, can in principle be interpreted by the computer. The potential therefore exists for the automation of various downstream processes once the initial model has been created. Moreover, we have also seen that several applications such as the generation of finite-element models, the planning of manufacturing methods, and the assessment of manufacturing quality are concerned with form features.

We now consider form features in the context of each of the two major approaches to solid modelling, constructive solid geometry (CSG) and boundary representation (Brep). The first provides a high-level geometric description of parts in terms of their volumetric constituents, while the second provides a low-level description in terms of a structured and connected set of faces, edges, and vertices. A representation of a part in terms of its form features in fact comes midway between the two in terms of the level of information. In the CSG case, a feature is not identical with a single primitive but is generated by the interaction of two or more primitives, as illustrated in Figure 10. While the overall object shape is represented by

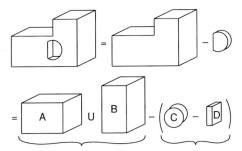

Part body volumes   Feature producing volumes

Figure 10. D-pocket as interaction of 'part body' volume and 'feature-producing' volume.

a global set of Boolean operations on the primitives, the features are represented by more localised, subsidiary Boolean relations on them. In the Brep case a feature is generally represented in terms of a set of faces in the model. The number of features on a given part will usually be considerably smaller than the number of basic topological elements. In this case, then, the feature model is less localised than the individual elements in the basic data structure, whereas in the CSG case it is more localised. It should be emphasized that the foregoing comments apply in the case of a single feature model for use in a specific application. For multiple applications it may be necessary to associate several different feature models with a single underlying solid model.

The point to be drawn from the last two paragraphs is that although feature information is required for the automation of certain applications, the fundamental data structures of existing solid modellers provide information at a level which is either not sufficiently detailed (CSG) or which is too detailed (Brep). There are two possible ways of rectifying this situation: either the existing data structures must be augmented to permit the representation of features, or new data structures must be devised in which feature entities are the basic components. The latter approach has not yet been much studied, although Arbab et al. [Arba82], Patel [Pate86], and Luby et al. [Luby86] describe some initial work in this area.

If we assume that the most appropriate course is to augment existing data structures, then two questions arise. These are (a) how should the feature information be generated in the first place, and (b) how should the data structure be augmented in order to represent it? These topics are the subjects of the two following sections of this paper.

Generation of Feature Information

Three approaches are available for the generation of feature data. Firstly, if the solid model has already been created, then the features existing on it may be recognised *a posteriori*. Secondly, since an individual modelling operation often gives rise to a feature, all such features could be automatically recognised at their time of creation. Thirdly, the designer could actually be allowed to work in terms of features, in which case his intent with regard to features could be captured at the outset and the need for automatic recognition to some extent avoided. The three methods are now examined in more detail, and it will be seen that they all have their advantages and disadvantages; possibly they will all have a place in the product-modelling technology of the future.

A Posteriori Feature Recognition

Feature recognition on a completed geometric model may be either manual or automatic. The manual method simply requires the operator to indicate those entities in the model that he wishes to group together to define a particular feature. It is comparatively easy to implement, and existing systems providing this facility include the Cranfield Testbed Modeller [Hail85; Pave86] and the commercially available systems ROMULUS from Shape Data Ltd. and CIMPLEX from Automated Technology Products.

The implementation of automatic feature recognition is a much more complex undertaking, but historically it was the first approach to be tried. Kyprianou [Kypr80] describes a method that has been implemented with the Brep modeller BUILD (see also [Jare84; Park83]). Features are identified by finding certain patterns of convex and concave edges occurring in the part data structure. To give two simple examples, a square pocket in one face of an object is bounded by a loop of edges that are all convex, while a square boss is bounded by a set of concave edges at its base. These properties are characteristic of depression and protrusion features in general, and a recognition strategy was developed based on these and related observations for the detection of bosses and of blind and through holes.

More recently, other methods have been devised which use a 3D extension of *syntactic pattern recognition*. This requires the specification of a set of rules that must be satisfied by the elements forming a particular type of feature, e.g., opposite pairs of walls of a simple rectangular pocket must be parallel and all adjacent faces (including the floor) must be mutually perpendicular. Henderson [Hend84], for example, translates the information in a ROMULUS model into a set of PROLOG statements and then uses the PROLOG inference facilities to find connected groups of faces conforming to the rules defining various feature types (see also [Choi84; Stal83; Hend84b].

Both of the above methods are implemented with Brep systems, but Woo [Woo82] has published an algorithm for the recognition of features in a CSG context. This has not been implemented in practice because no existing CSG modeller has all the required geometric capabilities, but the approach is interesting in several respects and is certainly worthy of study.

The kinds of 'after the event' feature recognition described here may seem cumbersome and computationally expensive when the possibility exists of generating feature information in the model as it is created. Nevertheless, methods of this type will certainly be needed, since, as pointed out earlier, the designer may think in terms of one set of features as he creates the model, while the finite-element analyst or the process planner may perceive a quite different set. As already mentioned, any part model must ultimately have associated with it several different feature models, one for each required downstream application. The designer can only generate one of these, and many of his features may also correspond to the features required for other applications. When this correspondence is lacking, however, automatic feature recognition must be invoked.

Feature Recognition During Model Creation

As remarked in the section on Brep modellers, some modellers provide the capability of defining profiles on planar faces of the model and sweeping them in, out, or through to create depressions, protrusions, or through holes, respectively. In all these cases each sweep operation creates a feature, which may be classified at its time of creation by analysis of the geometry of the profile and the nature of the sweep. Other related modelling operations permit similar possibilities for building up a feature model as the design proceeds. However, this approach is not a universal answer to feature modelling. Firstly, the features created are purely geometric or 'shape' features that may or may not correspond with the functional features required for application purposes. Secondly, the universally implemented Boolean operations often do not give rise to features of any commonly recognised type, or lead to ambiguous situations. For example, if two coincident cubes are created and one is moved or rotated slightly before the two are unioned, it is difficult to decide what is the basic body of the resulting object and what are the natures of the features arising on it. Alternatively, suppose a cylinder is unioned with a flat disc as shown in Figure 11; have we created a boss on the disc or a flange around the base of the cylinder? Either interpretation may be valid for certain applications.

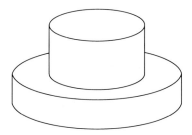

Figure 11. A boss on a disc, or a flange on a cylinder?

Design by Features

There appears to be some virtue in allowing the designer actually to create his model in terms of features. Then, instead of subtracting a block or performing a sweep operation to create a rectangular pocket feature, he could simply pick an option 'RECTANGULAR POCKET' from a feature menu. The system might then call up a generic description of such a pocket and prompt him for details of size, location, and so on before performing the necessary computations and modifying the model appropriately. With this mode of operation the system would know the nature of the feature created, at least as far as the designer's view of it was concerned, and could set up the necessary information in the data structure immediately. The designer's features will in many cases correspond to the features required by subsequent applications. Design by features is therefore likely to lead to greater efficiency in the modeller/application interface. Another advantage is that the designer can specify not only the shape of the feature but also its intended functionality, e.g., a hole could be labelled as a bearing housing. It is not possible using automatic feature recognition to recapture designer intent regarding function; this must be recorded at the outset.

This method of design is not without problems, unfortunately. In particular, extensive geometric checking will have to be provided to ensure that each feature created is of the stated type when the system interprets the designer's input. For example, he may call for a cylindrical blind hole feature but position it with respect to the base object so that its cylindrical face breaks through the boundary, as shown in Figure 12. The feature thus created falls into some class that is not the one originally called for, and the user must be informed of an error. Similar problems arise when the creation of a new feature leads to a modification in some previously existing feature that changes its class. In fact, it appears that the class of any feature may have to be continually monitored throughout the design process using techniques akin to automatic recognition.

The idea of design by features is not new, but many implementations are still very much in the research stage. Some recent work in this area is

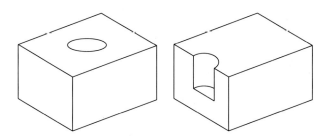

Figure 12. 'Cylindrical blind hole' feature validly and invalidly placed on a block.

described in Grabowski et al. [Grab83; Grab86], Hart et al. [Hart86], Patel [Pate86], and Luby et al. [Luby86]. Commercial systems having some capability in this respect include Applicon's BRAVO!, Automation Technology Products' CIMPLEX, McDonnell Douglas' UNISOLIDS, and Parametric Technology Inc.'s PRO-ENGINEER.

Representation of Features

The obvious way to represent a shape feature in a Brep context is as a collection of topological elements of the model, usually faces. The natural approach in a CSG system is to model features as interactions between volumetric primitives, but this method has been rejected at the University of Rochester, the home of the CSG philosophy, in favour of a boundary-oriented representation [Requ84]. We therefore concentrate on the latter approach.

A feature entity needs to be defined that is capable of storing at least the following information:

(a) pointers to the faces (or other topological entities) involved in the feature;

(b) some indication of the feature type;

(c) some indication of the feature application area.

For certain applications considerably more data are needed. For example, a tolerancing feature may make reference to a set of datum planes, some procedure for setting up the appropriate set of dimensions for the particular feature type (if these are not explicitly available in the model), and the associated tolerance values [CAM-I84]. It is worth noting that design by features may allow much of this information to be generated automatically at the time of feature creation.

It is clearly desirable that the collection of faces making up a feature be structured in some way. For example, in a pocket feature the base and the side faces may be treated in different ways from a manufacturing point of view, e.g., using area clearance and profiling, respectively. A depression feature such as this has a loop of edges that forms its boundary; they are thereby distinguished from the other edges of the feature, and may be thought of as the boundary of a hypothetical face (or set of faces) that closes off the feature and turns it into a self-contained volume. It may be found convenient actually to incorporate such hypothetical 'closure' faces in the feature data structure.

Feature representations of the type described are said to be *explicit* [CAM-I85a]. It will almost certainly be found desirable also to allow *implicit* or unevaluated representations, which simply make reference to the generic description of a feature class together with a set of defining parameters. Such descriptions will undoubtedly be necessary for the implementation of design by features, and they will also provide an economical means of representing a mass of feature detail whose evaluation may not be required for all purposes.

A further type of feature representation takes the form of an attribute attached to one or more topological entities. A common example is a thread attribute associated with the shank of a bolt model; in most cases it would not be desirable to represent the helical geometry of the thread explicitly.

Feature Manipulation

Once feature data structures have been set up in the solid model, many convenient facilities are easily made available for geometric modification. Since a feature can be treated as a self-contained entity, it can, in principle, be deleted, moved, scaled, copied, or instanced [CAM-I85a; Prat88]. Most of these results are readily achieved in CSG systems by editing the underlying textual description of the model and re-evaluating, but, in a Brep system, which does not retain a history of the construction of the model, such operations are either cumbersome or impossible unless features are implemented.

Other Considerations Regarding Features

It was pointed out at the beginning of the current section that a general definition of a form feature is an elusive goal. It must also be emphasised that definitions of individual feature types vary according to environment, being dependent on the particular philosophy and the range of manufacturing resources employed in a given company. For example, a circular blind hole feature may be drilled by Company A, whereas if Company B does not possess a sufficiently large drill it may mill it, treating it as a pocket feature. Such considerations imply that any solid modeller providing feature facilities must allow great flexibility for each user to define in his own terms precisely the set of features he wishes to use.

For manufacturing purposes it appears that feature data alone is not enough for the determination of a complete process plan. If a model of the part is subtracted from a model of the stock material, then what remains is the volume of material to be removed (assuming that the part is machined from the solid). The latter volume must now be decomposed into what are called *delta-volumes*, i.e., volumes removed by individual machining operations [CAM-I82a]. As the final form of the part is approached, the delta-volumes will correspond to (or be determined by) form feature volumes, but initially this will not generally be so. An algorithm for the determination of delta-volumes is given in CAM-I [CAM-I85c]. Work on this generalisation of the feature concept is in its infancy, and many complex problems have to be faced. Not least among these is the fact that certain types of compound features can be decomposed into delta-volumes in more than one way. Consider, for example, the case of a counterbored cylindrical hole. This may be decomposed into two delta-volumes in either of the following ways:

(a) cylindrical hole plus counterbore volume;
(b) large-radius shallow hole plus small-radius deep hole.

In view of the potential importance of form features for automated applications of solid modellers, it is not surprising that they are currently attracting a great deal of attention. It is worth noting that the 1988 ASME Computers in Engineering Conference held in San Francisco in August 1988 contained a major session entirely devoted to this topic.

DATA EXCHANGE BETWEEN SOLID MODELLERS

Standards have been a major issue in computer graphics for several years. However, although solid modellers are usually interactive graphical systems, they are mostly designed for engineering applications. Consequently, any standards developed for solid modellers must take into account not merely the graphical aspects (indeed, GKS and PHIGS are already playing a part here) but also a wide range of different classes of information having significance specifically for engineering applications. One particular problem, that of transferring design data between different CAD systems, has given rise to several national standards, and a draft international standard is currently being developed.

The requirement for CAD data exchange may arise within a company that uses more than one CAD system for different purposes (as many do), or in a contractor/subcontractor situation. Clearly for 2D draughting systems the design data can be exchanged in the form of drawings, but once the sending system has generated a drawing it is time-consuming and error-prone for a human operator to re-enter the same design into the receiving system. For 3D models even three-view drawings cannot usually be made to convey all the required data. In either case it is clearly desirable that details of the computer model can be transmitted automatically to avoid the lengthy manual reconstruction process.

There is a general consensus that a *neutral file* approach to CAD data transfer is appropriate. It is the content and the format of the neutral file which is standardised. Each CAD system must be provided with two translators, a *preprocessor* which translates the native internal format of the sending system into neutral file format, and a *postprocessor* which translates from the neutral file format into the native internal format of the receiving system. This stratagem requires $2N$ translators to be written for all possible transfers between N different systems, as opposed to $N(N-1)$ specialised translators if all possible cases are catered for directly without the use of a neutral file. Since N, the number of commercial CAD systems, is now of the order of 100, the neutral file technique has a clear advantage.

Brief notes are given below on existing CAD data exchange standards and on the status of the international standard. These are followed by remarks on some of the problems specific to data exchange between solid modelling systems.

IGES (Initial Graphics Exchange Specification). This neutral file format was developed rapidly in the United States in 1980, and IGES Version 1 became an ANSI standard in 1982 [ANSI82]. It was followed by Versions 2 and 3, which have not been standardised. Version 4 was published in March 1988 [IGES88]; it is intended to submit this version to ANSI as an updated standard.

The significance of the IGES acronym should be noted. The *I* denotes *I*nitial, reasonably enough, since this was a rapidly developed means of tackling an urgent problem for United States industry. The *G* denotes *G*raphics, and this is especially significant, since in 1980 most CAD systems were essentially draughting systems and the underlying idea was that the information transferred concerned computer representations of *drawings*. Finally, it is noteworthy that the *S* stands for *S*pecification rather than *S*tandard.

The draughting orientation of IGES Version 1 is reflected in the presence of two major classes of entities in the neutral file. These are *geometric entities* (lines, circular arcs, etc.) and *annotation entities* (various types of arrows, witness lines, dimensions, textual notes, etc.). There is also a class of *associativity entities*, allowing very general associations to be set up between entities or groups of entities in the neutral file, but these are little used in practice.

IGES is now in very widespread use, to the extent that it is a *de facto* international standard, but it has a number of serious shortcomings [Prat85a]. Its problems are at least partly due to the rate of development of CAD systems since it was first defined, as these systems often possess new capabilities for which the current version of IGES makes no provision. As already mentioned, Version 1 was concerned mainly with the transfer of 2D and 3D wireframe data; there was also limited provision for transferring curve and surface data based on cubic polynomial splines. Ensuing versions built upon this beginning and also permitted the transfer of applications-oriented data, concerning finite-element models for example. It was not until Version 4 that solid model transfer became possible, and this only for CSG models. Version 5 will be published during 1990 and will cater additionally for Brep solid models.

The recent and projected solid modelling capabilities of IGES are based on a document called the Experimental Solids Proposal (ESP), which was in turn closely related to the pioneering Experimental Boundary File (XBF) specification published and tested by the research organisation Computer Aided Manufacturing International, Inc. [CAM-I81b; CAM-I82b; Prat84b]. This permitted the transfer of boundary representations in terms of geometrical entities and of topological relationships modelled using the IGES associativity mechanism, a vertex being defined in terms of the set of edges meeting there, and so on. The XBF also represented CSG models in terms of primitives and set operations. One major difference between XBF and IGES Version 5 is that the latter defines specialised topological entities (faces, edges, vertices, etc.) and does not use the associativity approach for conveying this class of information.

SET (Système d'Echange et de Transfert). This is a French AFNOR standard [AFNO85] resulting from that country's dissatisfaction with IGES, mainly from the point of view of the very large neutral files that it generates and the consequent long translation times required. SET entities are similar to those of IGES, but a much more compact file structure is used. Translators are available for a range of commercial CAD systems. The initial definition of SET was undertaken by the Aérospatiale company, which continues to preside over its current development. SET is used most notably in the European aerospace industry and is the data transfer means used between the partners of the Airbus A320 project. As with IGES, the initial version could transfer 2D and 3D draughting data; surface capabilities were then added, and a version capable of transferring CSG and Brep solid modelling data has been submitted for standardisation by AFNOR.

VDAFS (Verband der Automobilindustrie Flächenschnittstelle). This German DIN standard is restricted to the transfer of free-form surface data. The standard was formulated because of problems encountered in the German automotive industry in using the facilities provided by IGES for this purpose. Two versions have been published; the second permits transfer of a wider range of entities, but only the first has become a standard [DIN86; VDA86]. Work on further development of VDAFS has now ceased, since the new international STEP standard discussed below will subsume its capabilities.

STEP (Standard for the Exchange of Product Data). This international standard for CAD data transfer is now being developed within the International Standards Organisation, specifically within the ISO subcommittee ISO TC/184/SC4. The main inputs are from the United States, where a new projected standard called PDES (Product Data Exchange Standard) has been worked on since 1984, and from a group of European countries having involvement in ESPRIT Project 322, CAD Interfaces, abbreviated as CAD*I, which also started in 1984. A Draft Proposal for Version 1 of STEP was issued for appraisal by national standards organisations in March 1989 (ISO89).

PDES was initiated in the United States because IGES was recognised to have major limitations, and it was designed from the outset to transfer a very wide spectrum of data covering the entire life cycle of a product. This includes not only 'shape' information and associated textual data, as with IGES, but also information concerning many engineering applications and certain types of administrative data. Applications currently being worked on include architectural engineering and construction, electrical and electronic products, form features, finite element analysis, and mechanical products. The major United States contribution to the STEP standard is in these application areas. There is a consensus within the community of volunteers involved in the development of PDES that, for topics on which agreement has been reached within ISO, PDES and STEP will become identical.

*The ESPRIT CAD*I Project.* This project has 12 participant organisations drawn from six nations of the European Economic Community. It is funded by the European Commission. The CAD*I partners play a key role in the ISO work through membership of their own countries' national standards bodies. Their work is concentrated in two main areas: on a new formally defined neutral file format for the transfer of 'shape' information, designed to avoid the difficulties experienced with IGES, and on standard formats for transferring data between the various stages of the finite-element analysis process. The CAD*I neutral file format has from the outset been designed to transfer wireframe, surface, and solid modelling data. The first-ever transfers of Brep solid models between different systems were demonstrated in 1986 between a Shape Data Ltd. ROMULUS system at Cranfield Institute of Technology in England and a Norsk Data TECHNOVISION system at the Technical University of Denmark.

Much of the CAD*I work has been accepted with little modification as the core of STEP Version 1. Version 3.3 of the CAD*I neutral format has been published [Schl88], and annual reports have been issued by the project since its inception [CADI86; CADI87; CADI88]. As far as solid models are concerned, CSG models are transmitted in terms of primitives and set operations, while Brep models are transmitted in terms of geometric and topological entities.

The development of basic STEP preprocessors for solid modellers has proved fairly easy in those cases in which it has merely been necessary to write out all of the entities composing the transmitted model in the appropriate format for the neutral file. This is possible when all the model entities have corresponding entities in the file specification, and vice versa. However, it is not necessary to look very far for a case where this is not so; ROMULUS possesses a blending capability that uses a highly nonstandard type of algebraically defined surface [Rock85] having no corresponding geometric entity in the STEP specification. The transfer of a blended ROMULUS model would therefore require each blend surface to be approximated by one of the 'standard' surface types, for example, by a nonuniform rational B-spline surface. In a situation such as this, either the modeller must be capable of computing the approximation or this function must be performed by the preprocessor.

Another type of difficulty can arise when the transmitting modeller lacks certain entities that must be present in the neutral file. The STEP neutral format has been designed so that any reasonably conventional Brep data structure will map onto it, and vice versa, but the mechanism for performing the mapping is not always straightforward. For example, the STEP file requires the presence of loop entities, i.e., ordered sets of edges that

form individual face boundaries, whereas the PROREN system marketed
by Isykon GmbH contains no loop entities in its native data structure. The
required information is certainly *implicitly* present in PROREN, but the
preprocessor has to make it explicit in the neutral file, which involves a
large number of interrogations concerning edge and face connectivity.

Postprocessor development for STEP has proved more difficult. One
problem concerns the type of access available in the receiving system to
allow reconstruction of the model from the neutral file information. There
appear to be three possibilities. The first is to write to a new sequential
file having the format used by the receiving system to store its own models on disc. This has the problem that validity checking is difficult; it is
comparatively easy to write the file, but if the modeller then cannot read
it because it has some error or deficiency, the transfer process fails.

The second possibility is to write to a 'program file' containing a sequence
of instructions for rebuilding the model from scratch. This is, in fact, what
is effectively done in the transmission of a neutral file containing CSG data
into a Brep system, which then evaluates it. However, if the transmitting
system is itself a pure Brep system, then the constructional history of the
model has been lost. In this case what is required is the determination
of a CSG (or equivalent procedural) representation corresponding to the
Brep model. Development of an algorithm for this type of representation
conversion is currently an unsolved research problem.

The third approach to model reconstruction is to work through a programming interface of the kind discussed in the next section. Briefly, this
allows access to all the facilities of the modeller for creation, deletion, modification, and interrogation of models and their underlying entities, so that
a Brep model can in principle be reconstructed edge by edge and face by
face in a dynamic manner. This method relies on the 'completeness' of
the programming interface. In the one attempt so far made to use this
approach (at Cranfield Institute of Technology, using ROMULUS) a large
measure of success has been achieved, though models with certain types of
topology/geometry combinations cannot be rebuilt owing to the lack of a
specialised topological operation in the Kernel Interface, as this system's
programming interface is known.

One of the major problems of CAD data transfer is concerned with free-
form parametrically defined surfaces. In fact, this problem led to the development of VDAFS mentioned previously, although even that specialised
standard does not overcome all the difficulties. The problem is now becoming more acute as solid modellers increasingly incorporate free-form
geometric capabilities. The free-form surface types conventionally used in
geometric modelling are either of the pure polynomial or the rational type.
In either case systems differ very considerably in the degree of the polynomials used, which ranges from two to 20 in current commercial systems.
Clearly it is not possible to transfer curve and surface data exactly from a
system using degree 15 into a system restricted to degree three, although

it is possible to go the other way. Further, exact transfer between a rational system and a polynomial system is not possible either, although once again the reverse process may be possible (subject to a proviso on the degrees involved), since polynomials are a subset of the rational functions. Where data transfer is required between mathematically incompatible systems some form of approximation is required by which, for example, a high-degree polynomial or rational surface is subdivided into smaller patches, each of which is represented to within a given tolerance in terms of lower-degree functions. Two approaches to such a method of approximation have been developed within the ESPRIT CAD∗I Project mentioned above [Goul87; Lach88].

There is one further important issue that has emerged during recent experiments in solid model data transfer, and this is concerned with numerical tolerances. Every modeller has certain built-in tolerances of distance and angle that it uses in deciding, for example, whether two points are coincident or whether two lines are collinear. These tolerances vary from one modeller to another and, in some cases, the user is able to adjust them to meet his own requirements. It is therefore possible to transmit a model in which the tolerances are set to large values and to try to receive it in a modeller that uses much smaller values. This implies that points considered to be coincident in the sending system may be interpreted as distinct in the receiving system, in which case the agreement between topology and geometry in the original model may be lost. This problem is a wide-open research topic, since no work has yet been undertaken to overcome the difficulty described.

Programming or Applications Interfaces

As long ago as 1979 the research organisation Computer Aided Manufacturing International, Inc. (CAM-I) perceived the need for a standard means of accessing the full range of capabilities of a solid modeller dynamically via a *programming interface*. Such an interface would allow an applications program (for example, a finite-element mesh generator or an automated process planning system) to make use of all the modeller's facilities for creation, modification, and interrogation of solid models by making calls to a specified set of procedures forming part of the modeller software. If such an interface could be standardised and implemented with a wide selection of commercial modelling systems, then the door would be opened to third-party software vendors to develop applications packages interfacing without modification to all the systems concerned. This will be extremely attractive to companies wishing to develop integrated CAD/CAM configurations on a modular basis, acquiring different modules from different vendors and perhaps writing particularly specialised modules in-house. Specifically, it implies that the choice of applications modules may be made independently of the choice of solid modeller.

CAM-I published its first suggestion for a standard programming interface in 1980 [CAM-I80]; this specification has since become known as the Applications Interface Specification (AIS). The AIS has been revised and extended in the light of further related work. The most recent consolidated version [CAM-I86a] contains all these improvements and has a structure of levels of implementation imposed upon it. Two partial implementations of the interface exist for the CAM-I Testbed Modeller [CAM-I85b] and for the CSG modeller PADL-2 [CAM-I89]. Various demonstrations have been given of applications making use of the interface; one example is concerned with automated process planning of machined parts [CAM-I86b; Pave86].

The AIS in its current form consists of approximately 200 FORTRAN subroutine specifications. Guidelines are also provided for implementation in languages other than FORTRAN; in fact, the Testbed Modeller referred to above is written in PASCAL and can be accessed either through the FORTRAN interface or through the corresponding set of underlying PASCAL procedures. There are several commercial solid modellers possessing programming interfaces with varying degrees of similarity to the CAM-I AIS. The closest is the ROMULUS Kernel Interface; this is hardly surprising, since the 1980 version of the AIS was prepared by Shape Data Ltd., the developers of the ROMULUS modeller. CAM-I is an accredited standards-making body in the United States and intends to submit the AIS for standardisation after a due period of further experimentation, demonstration, and consultation with system vendors.

As presently structured, the AIS has a set of core facilities corresponding to the basic set of operations provided by most commercial systems. Creation operations are available for the conventional set of solid primitives, and subroutines are included for the Boolean operations of union, intersection, and subtraction. Solids may also be created by defining 2D profiles and using linear or rotational sweep operations. Profiles defined upon planar faces of existing solids may be similarly swept. Various types of transformations may be applied to previously defined objects. Most important for applications purposes is the range of interrogation functions provided, which allow determination of connectivity between topological elements and of the geometry associated with any face, edge, or vertex. Some basic utility functions are also provided. The core set of subroutines has been limited to 50 in number.

Additional layers of facilities are provided dealing with (a) assemblies; (b) properties and attributes; (c) additional geometric utilities; (d) further types of implicitly defined geometry; (e) parametric free-form geometry; (f) checks and verification; and (g) Euler operations. The intention is that implementers of modellers and applications programs can specify their level of implementation and their requirements level, respectively, so that it will be easy to ascertain whether a certain modeller is compatible with a particular application program.

REFERENCES

[AFNO85]
AFNOR, Industrial Automation—External Representation of Product Definition Data—Data Exchange and Transfer Standard Specification Version 85-08, AFNOR Standard z68-300, Association française de normalisation, Paris-la-Défense, France, 1985.

[Ande83]
Anderson, C.M., The New BUILD User Guide, CAE Group Document No. CAM-116, Cambridge University Engineering Dept., Cambridge, U.K., 1983 (obtainable from DACAM, Cranfield Institute of Technology, Bedford, U.K.).

[ANSI82]
ANSI, Digital Representation for Communication of Product Definition Data, ANSI Y14.26M-1981 (American National Standard), ASME, New York, NY, 1982.

[Arba82]
Arbab, F., Cantor, D.G., Lichten, L., and Melkanoff, M.A., The MARS CAM-oriented modeling system, in *Proc. Conf. on CAD/CAM Technology in Mechanical Engineering* (Massachusetts Institute of Technology, March 1982), Cambridge, MA: MIT Press, 1982.

[Ayal85]
Ayala, D., Brunet, P., Juan, R., and Navazo, I., Object representation by means of nonminimal division quadtrees and octrees, *ACM Trans. Graph.*, Vol. 4, pp. 41–59, 1985.

[Barn87]
Barnhill, R.E., Farin, G., Jordan, M., and Piper, B.R., Surface/surface intersection, *Comput. Aided Geom. Design*, Vol. 4, pp. 3–16, 1987.

[Brai79]
Braid, I.C., Notes on a Geometric Modeller, CAD Group Document No. CAM-101, Cambridge University Computing Laboratory, Cambridge, U.K., 1979 (obtainable from DACAM, Cranfield Institute of Technology, Bedford, U.K.).

[Brow82]
Brown, C. M., PADL-2: A technical summary, *IEEE Comput. Graph. Appl.* Vol. 2, pp. 69–84, 1982.

[CAD*I86]
CAD*I, ESPRIT Project 322: CAD Interfaces—Status Report 2, Report No. KfK-PFT 121, Kernforschungszentrum Karlsruhe, F.R.G., 1986.

[CAD*I87]
CAD*I, ESPRIT Project 322: CAD Interfaces—Status Report 3, Report No. KfK-PFT 132, Kernforschungszentrum Karlsruhe, F.R.G., 1987.

[CAD*I88]
CAD*I, ESPRIT Project 322: CAD Interfaces—Status Report 4, Report No. KfK-PFT 139, Kernforschungszentrum Karlsruhe, F.R.G., 1988.

[CAM-I80]
CAM-I, An Interface between Geometric Modellers and Applications Programs, 3 Vols., Report No. R-80-GM-04, CAM-I Inc., Arlington, TX, 1980.

[CAM-I81a]
CAM-I, CAM-I's Illustrated Glossary of Workpiece Form Features, Report No. R-80-PPP-02.1, CAM-I Inc., Arlington, TX, 1981.

[CAM-I81b]
CAM-I, CAM-I Geometric Modelling Project Boundary File Design (XBF-2), Report No. R-81-GM-02.1, CAM-I Inc., Arlington, TX, 1981.

[CAM-I82a]
CAM-I, Design of an Advanced Numerical Control Processor, Report No. R-82-ANC-01, CAM-I Inc., Arlington, TX, 1982.

[CAM-I82b]
CAM-I, Implementation and Testing of the CAM-I Geometric Modelling Project Boundary Representation for Solid Objects, Report No. R-82-GM-02, CAM-I Inc., Arlington, TX, 1982.

[CAM-I84]
CAM-I, Dimensioning and Tolerancing Final Report, Report No. R-85-GM-02.2, CAM-I Inc., Arlington, TX, 1984.

[CAM-I85a]
CAM-I, Requirements for the Support of Form Features in a Solid Modelling System, Report No. R-85-ASPP-01, CAM-I Inc., Arlington, TX, 1985.

[CAM-I85b]
CAM-I, Systems Documentation for the Cranfield Testbed Modeller, Vol. 2, Report No. PS-85-GM-01 (2 vols.), CAM-I Inc., Arlington, TX, 1985.

[CAM-I85c]
CAM-I, Volume Decomposition Algorithm, 2 Vols., Report No. R-85-ANC-01, CAM-I Inc., Arlington, TX, 1985.

[CAM-I86a]
CAM-I, The CAM-I Applications Interface Specification: Consolidated and Restructured Version, 2 Vols., Report R-86-GM-01.1, CAM-I Inc., Arlington, TX, 1986.

[CAM-I86b]
CAM-I, Features Extraction and Process Planning, Report No. R-86-PPP-01, CAM-I Inc., Arlington, TX, 1986.

[CAM-I89]
CAM-I, PADL-2/AIS Implementation (2 vols.), Report No. PS-89-ANC/GM/PP-01.1, CAM-I Inc., Arlington, TX, 1989.

[Care83]
Carey, G.C., and de Pennington, A., A study of the interface between CAD and CAM using geometric modelling techniques, in *Proc. 3rd Anglo-Hungarian Seminar on Computer Aided Design* (Cambridge, Sept. 1983), Jared, G.E.M., and Várady, T., Eds., Cambridge, U.K., Cambridge University Engineering Department, 1983.

[Chiy83]
Chiyokura, H., and Kimura, F., Design of solids with free-form surfaces, *Comput. Graph.*, Vol. 17, pp. 289–298, 1983 (SIGGRAPH 83).

[Choi84]
Choi, B.K., Barash, M.M., and Anderson, D.C., Automatic recognition of machined surfaces from a 3D solid model, *Comput. Aided Design*, Vol. 16, pp. 81–86, 1984.

[DIN86]
DIN, *Format zum Austausch geometrischer Information*, DIN Standard 66301, Deutsches Institut für Normung e.v., Berlin, F.R.G., 1986.

[Faro86]
Farouki, R.T., The characterization of parametric surface sections, *Comput. Vision, Graph. Image Proc.*, Vol. 33, pp. 209–236, 1986.

[Faux79]
Faux, I.D., and Pratt, M.J., *Computational Geometry for Design and Manufacture*, Chichester, England: Ellis Horwood, 1979.

[Goul89]
Goult, R.J., Parametric Curve and Surface Approximation, in *The Mathematics of Surfaces III*, Handscomb, D.C., Ed. (Proc. IMA Conf., Oxford, Sept. 1988), Oxford: Oxford University Press, 1989.

[Grab83]
Grabowski, H., and Seiler, W., Preliminary design requirements to communication processing in CAD, *Comput. Graph. Mech. Engrg.*, Vol. 7, pp. 111–123, 1983.

[Grab86]
Grabowski, H., Anderl, R., Pätzold, B., and Rude, S., An Overview for a Concept on Advanced Modelling, WG 5 Report, ESPRIT CAD Interfaces (CAD∗I) Project, Kernforschungszentrum Karlsruhe, F.R.G., 1986.

[Hail85]
Hailstone, S.R., Explicit Form Features in Solid Modelling, Master's Thesis, DACAM, Cranfield Institute of Technology, Bedford, U.K., 1985.

[Hart86]
Hart, N., Bennaton, J., and Acar, S., A CAD engineering language to aid manufacture, in *Computer Aided Production Engineering* (Proc. International Conf., Edinburgh, April 1986) Bury St. Edmunds, England: Mechanical Engineering Publications Ltd., 1986.

[Hend84a]
Henderson, M.R., Extraction of Feature Information from Three Dimensional CAD Data, Ph.D. Dissertation, Purdue University, West Lafayette, IN, May 1984.

[Hend84b]
Henderson, M.R., and Anderson, D.C., Computer recognition and extraction of form features: A CAD/CAM link, *Comput. in Industry*, Vol. 5, pp.315–325, 1984.

[IGES88]

IGES, Initial Graphics Exchange Specification, Version 4.0, National Institute of Standards and Technology, Gaithersburg, MD, 1988.

[ISO89]

Draft Proposal for STEP, DP10303, International Standards Organisation, 1989.

[Jack80]

Jackins, C.L., and Tanimoto, S.L., Oct-trees and their use in representing three-dimensional objects, *Comput. Graph. Image Proc.*, Vol. 14, pp. 249–270, 1980.

[Jare84]

Jared, G.E.M., Shape features in geometric modelling, in *Solid Modelling by Computers* (Proc. General Motors Solid Modeling Symposium, Warren, Michigan, Sept. 1983) New York: Plenum Press, 1984.

[John86]

Johnson, R.H., *Solid Modelling: A State-of-the-Art Report*, 2nd Ed., Amsterdam: North-Holland, 1986.

[Kypr80]

Kyprianou, L.K., Shape Classification in Compruter Aided Design, Ph.D. Dissertation, University of Cambridge, Cambridge, U.K., 1980.

[Lach88]

Lachance, M.A., Chebyshev economisation for parametric surfaces, *Comput. Aided Geom. Design*, Vol. 5, pp. 195–208, 1988.

[Luby86]

Luby, S.C., Dixon, J.R., and Simmons, M.K., Creating and using a features data base, *Comput. Mech. Engrg.*, pp. 25–33, Nov. 1986.

[Mant82]

Mäntylä, M., and Sulonen, R., GWB: A solid modeller with Euler operators, *IEEE Comput. Graph. Appl.*, Vol. 2, pp. 17–31, 1982.

[Meag82]

Meagher, D., Geometric modelling using octree encoding, *Comput. Graph. Image Proc.*, Vol. 19, pp. 129–147, 1982.

[Nava86]

Navazo, I,, Ayala, D., and Brunet, P., A geometric modeller based on the exact octree representation of polyhedra, *Comput. Graph. Forum*, Vol. 5, pp. 91–104, 1986.

[Park83]

Parkinson, A., Feature Recognition and Parts Classification in BUILD, CAD Group Document No. CAM-112, Cambridge University Engineering Dept., Cambridge, U.K., 1983 (obtainable from DACAM, Cranfield Institute of Technology, Bedford, U.K.).

[Pate86]

Patel, R., A Mechanical Engineering Design Interface for Geometric Modelling, Ph.D. Dissertation, Newcastle Polytechnic, Newcastle-upon-Tyne, U.K., 1986.

[Pave86]

Pavey, S.G., Hailstone, S.R., and Pratt, M.J., (1986), An automated interface between CAD and process planning, in *Computer Aided Production Engineering*, (Proc. International Conf., Edinburgh, April 1986), Bury St. Edmunds, England: Mechanical Engineering Publications Ltd., 1986.

[Prat84a]

Pratt, M.J., Solid modelling and the interface between design and manufacture, *IEEE Comput. Graph. Appl.*, Vol. 4, pp. 52–59, 1984.

[Prat84b]

Pratt, M.J., and Wilson, P.R., IGES-based transmission of solid modelling data, in *Proc. MICAD 84 Conf.* (Paris, Feb./Mar. 1984), Paris: Hermes Press, and London: Kogan Page, 1984.

[Prat85a]

Pratt, M.J., IGES: The present state and future trends, *Comput. Aided Engrg J.*, Vol. 2, pp. 130–133, 1985.

[Prat85b]

Pratt, M.J., Automatic blending in solid modelling—An approach based on the use of parametric geometry, in *Proc. 4th Anglo-Hungarian Seminar on Computer Aided Design* (Budapest, Oct. 1985), Renner, G., and Pratt, M.J., Eds., Budapest: Computer and Automation Institute of the Hungarian Academy of Sciences, 1985.

[Prat86]

Pratt, M.J., and Geisow, A.D., Surface/surface intersection problems, in *The Mathematics of Surfaces* (Proc. IMA Conf., Manchester, Sept 1984), Gregory, J.A., Ed., London: Oxford University Press, 1986.

[Prat88]

Pratt, M.J., Synthesis of an optimal approach to form feature modelling, in *Proc. 1988 ASME Computers in Engineering Conf.* (San Francisco, Aug. 1988), New York: American Society of Mechanical Engineers, 1988.

[Requ80]

Requicha, A.A.G., Representations of rigid solids—Theory, methods and systems, *Comput. Surveys*, Vol. 12, pp. 437–464, 1980.

[Requ84]

Requicha, A.A.G., Representation of tolerances in solid modeling: Issues and alternative approaches, in *Solid Modeling by Computers* (Proc. General Motors Solid Modeling Symposium, Warren, Michigan, Sept. 1983), New York: Plenum Press, 1984.

[Rock85]

Rockwood, A.P., Blending surfaces in solid modelling, in *Proc. 4th Anglo-Hungarian Seminar on Computer Aided Design* (Budapest, Oct. 1985), Renner, G., and Pratt, M.J., Eds., Computer and Automation Institute of the Hungarian Academy of Sciences, 1985.

[Ross84]

Rossignac, J.R., and Requicha, A.A.G., Constant radius blending in solid modelling, *Comput. Mech. Engrg.*, pp. 65–73, 1984.

[Saia87]

Saia, A., Bloor, M.S., and de Pennington, A., Sculptured solids in a CSG-based geometric modelling system, in *The Mathematics of Surfaces II* (Proc. 2nd IMA Conf. on the Mathematics of Surfaces, Cardiff, Sept. 1986), Martin, R.R., Ed., London: Oxford University Press, 1987.

[Schl88]

Schlechtendahl, E.G. Ed., *Specification of a CAD*I Neutral File for Solids, Version 3.3*, Berlin: Springer-Verlag, 1988.

[Stal83]

Staley, S.M., Henderson, M.R., and Anderson, D.C., Using syntactic pattern recognition to extract feature information from a solid geometric data base, *Comput. Mech. Engrg.*, pp. 61–66, Sept. 1983.

[Tilo80]

Tilove, R.B., Set membership classification: A unified approach to geometric intersection problems, *IEEE Trans. Comput.*, Vol. C29, pp. 874–883, 1980.

[TIPS78]

TIPS Working Group, TIPS-1 Technical Information Processing System, Institute of Precision Engineering, Hokkaido University, Sapporo, Japan, 1978.

[VDA86]

VDA, VDA-Flächenschnittstelle (VDAFS), Version 2.0, Verband der Automobilindustrie e.v., Frankfurt, F.R.G., 1986.

[Vara84]

Várady, T., and Pratt, M.J., Design techniques for the definition of solid objects with free-form geometry, *Comput. Aided Geom. Design*, Vol. 1, pp. 207–225, 1984.

[Woo82]

Woo, T.C., Feature extraction by volume decomposition, in *Proc. Conf. on CAD/CAM Technology in Mechanical Engineering* (Massachusetts Institute of Technology, March 1982), Cambridge, MA: MIT Press, 1982.

[Wood87]

Woodwark, J.R., Blends in geometric modelling, in *The Mathematics of Surfaces II* (Proc. 2nd IMA Conf. on the Mathematics of Surfaces, Cardiff, Sept. 1986), Martin, R.R., Ed., London: Oxford University Press, 1987.

[Yerr83]

Yerry, M.A., and Shephard, M.S., A modified quadtree approach to finite element mesh generation, *IEEE Comput. Graph. Appl.*, Vol. 3, pp. 39–46, 1983.

[Yerr84]

Yerry, M.A., and Shephard, M.S., Automatic three-dimensional mesh generation by the modified-octree technique, *Internat. J. Numer. Methods Engrg.*, Vol. 20, pp. 1965–1990, 1984.

6 Graphics and Networking

Workstations, Networking, Distributed Graphics, and Parallel Processing

Michael J. Muuss

Abstract

The process of design is iterative in nature; designs are formulated, analyzed, and improved until the goals are met. Modern graphics workstations provide a powerful platform for performing detailed design and limited analysis of solid model designs, with faster computers accessed via network links for full resolution analysis. A broad spectrum of analysis tools exist, and most express their output in graphical form. Their three main styles of graphics display are examined, along with a look at the underlying software mechanisms to support them.

Several enabling technologies are required for analysis tools to run on one computer, with graphical display on another computer, including network-transparent frame buffer capability. The importance of portable external data representations is reviewed, and several specific external data representations are examined in significant detail. By carefully dividing application software into appropriate tools and connecting them with UNIX pipes, a measure of parallel processing can be achieved within one system. In a tool-oriented environment with machine-independent data formats, network-distributed computation can be accomplished.

The next step is to make a single tool execute faster using parallel processing. Many analysis codes are implemented using the ray-tracing paradigm, which is ideal for execution in parallel on tightly coupled shared-memory multiprocessors and loosely coupled ensembles of computers. Both are exploited using different mechanisms. Strategies used for operating on shared-memory multiprocessors such as the Denelcor HEP, Alliant FX/8, and Cray X-MP are presented along with measured performance data.

Strategies used for dividing the work among network-connected, loosely coupled processors (each of which may itself be a parallel processor) are presented, including details of the dispatching algorithm and the design of the distribution protocol. The performance issues of this type of parallel processing are presented, including a set of measured speeds on a variety of hardware.

Introduction

The fundamental purpose of the Ballistic Research Laboratory (BRL) CAD package is to enable designers and engineers to create and analyze highly detailed 3D solid models. These models are considered 'solid models' because the models are a computer description of closed, solid, 3D shapes represented by an analytical framework within which the 3D material is completely and unambiguously defined [Deit83]. Completeness is assured because the representation contains a full description of a piece of solid matter; there is no view-specific information [Muus87c].

The software in the BRL CAD package is grouped into three main categories. First and foremost it includes a complete solid modeling system. Secondly, there is a set of libraries for producing graphical displays on a variety of display hardware. Finally, there is a large collection of software tools, each of which performs a single function quite well and which are easily combined in powerful ways using UNIX pipes [Ritc78].

The purpose of this paper is to describe the graphics tools and graphics support environment necessary to enable visual displays to be the center of the design process, and to discuss how network capabilities and parallel processing are important in such an environment, both to support collaboration and to improve performance. The first section sets the stage by reviewing the design process. A broad spectrum of design analysis tools exist, and most express their output in graphical form. In the second section, the three main styles of graphics display are examined, along with a look at the underlying software mechanisms to support them. In the third section, the extension of these graphics mechanisms to the network environment is examined in significant detail. In the fourth section, the power of parallel processing is exploited for multitool applications, both on multiprocessor hardware and utilizing multiple uniprocessor machines on the network. In the fifth section, shared-memory parallel processing techniques are employed to make *a single application tool* run much faster. Finally, an ensemble of network computers is employed to make a single application tool run much faster.

THE MODERN COMPUTING ENVIRONMENT

The cost of computer power continues to plummet. Therefore, computer systems are becoming more and more prevalent in the modern workplace. They are purchased to improve productivity, lower costs, or improve the quality of the workplace. Due to system proliferation, users are located on different machines separated from each other. It is vitally important that they not become isolated from necessary information, or the proliferation of computer systems will bring a family of new problems.

To exploit the influx of new computer power, *automation systems and facilities, regardless of manufacturer, model, and location, must interoperate.*

This interoperation requires the connection of these systems to data networks. A user should be able to move data between any pair of computers, without physical intervention, using one simple set of commands, regardless of the data's source or destination. Single-vendor networks are impossible in the government arena and difficult elsewhere, forcing computer planners into a systems-integration role. Networking standards are young, or still emerging, so there are many issues still to be resolved. This paper details one powerful set of applications built for a network environment full of computers.

As one of the nation's foremost research and development laboratories, BRL has continued to help advance the state of the art in computer science and computer practice, starting in 1943 with what became the ENIAC project, which resulted in BRL's possessing one of the world's first electronic computers. The proliferation of hardware started immediately thereafter. The diversity of computers installed resulted in BRL scientists having to deal with issues of software portability in the 1950s. In the early 1960s, BRL developed solid modeling and ray-tracing technology which went into production use in 1965. BRL was part of the initial ARPANET in 1967 and, by the advent of the TCP/IP protocols in 1982, had the largest campus area network in the Department of Defense. In 1988, the BRL facility included two supercomputers, a Cray X-MP/48 and a Cray-2, a fiberoptic-based campus area network, dozens of super-minicomputer systems, over a dozen distributed computer facilities, and hundreds of workstations and personal computers (Figure 1). More than 30 high-performance, high-resolution color graphics workstations are located throughout the laboratory. The use of color graphics to combine *advanced modeling* with *scientific visualization* accounts for BRL's continuing ability to increase the pool of human knowledge in times of dwindling funding [McCo87].

The BRL CAD package is BRL's third generation of modeling software and represents over 150,000 lines of C source code written since 1979. Parts of this system have roots in work done over two decades ago [MAGI67], most notably solid modeling and ray tracing. It is highly portable, having run on five distinct generations of hardware running various versions of the UNIX operating system [Muus87a]. As of this writing, this software is known to run on hardware from many different vendors (Table 1) and is in use at over 300 sites worldwide. The nonmilitary portions of this software are available.[†]

The Iterative Nature of Design

Design is an iterative process. Starting with a set of goals, an initial concept is defined. The initial concept is refined until the design is believed to have reached a worthwhile plateau, and then the design is subjected to a variety

---

[†]For details, please contact the author.

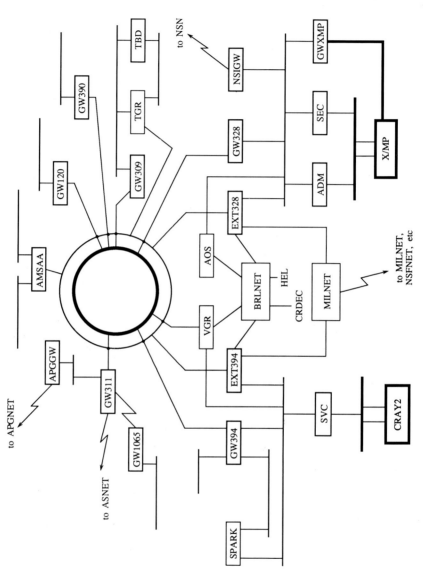

Figure 1. The BRL campus network.

Table 1. Hardware supported by the
BRL CAD package.

Vendor	System
Alliant	FX/4, FX/8, FX/80
Convex	C1, C2
Cray	Cray-1, Cray X-MP, Cray-2
DEC	VAX-11/750, 780, etc.
DEC	VaxStation-II GPX
Denelcor	HEP H-1000
Elxsi	6410, 6420
Gould	PN 6000, PN 9000
ISI	68020
Multiflow	Trace 7/200
Pyramid	90MX
Ridge	330
SGI	3-D (2400, 3030, etc.)
SGI	4-D (4D/60, etc.)
Sun	Sun-2, Sun-3, Sun-4
Tektronix	4132

of analysis techniques in an attempt to determine how well it meets the
original goals. The result of the analysis determines whether the goals have
been met. If the goals have not been met, then the outcome of the analysis
drives another iteration of the refinement process.

In a full-scale solid modeling system, there is no need for initial drawings; the designer expresses the initial structures directly into the modeling
system's editor just as a modern author creates his 'rough draft' directly
into a word processor. At the completion of each version of the design, the
model is subjected to a battery of analyses appropriate to the function of
the object being designed. Strength, volume, weight, level of protection,
and other similar evaluations can be reported along with the production
of a variety of images and/or drawings. These automated analyses help
identify weaknesses or deficiencies in a design *early in the design process.*
By detecting flaws early, the designer has the opportunity to correct his
plans before having invested too much time in a bad design, or the designer
can switch to an entirely different approach that may seem more promising
than the original one. In this way, the solid modeling system allows the
designer to concentrate on the important, creative aspects of the design
process. Freeing the designer of routine analysis permits designs to be finished in less time than previously required, or allows much more rigorously
optimized designs to be delivered in comparable time frames and at the

same cost as unoptimized designs created using older techniques [Deit85].

The creative process that converts goals into designs has been the subject of some study, but the process is not yet well enough understood for there to be much opportunity for automation. However, the analysis of a given design against a fixed set of standards (the design goals) is amenable to a great deal of automation. Given a full description of the geometry of an object and an indication of the material used to construct each part, it is possible to conduct a battery of analyses automatically. These analyses might range from determining the center of mass, to creating an optical image of the object, to performing a detailed structural analysis of the object under various forms of loading. In light of the iterative nature of design and the current lack of deep insight into the creative process, the BRL CAD package is focused on appropriately applying the power of computers to each part of the design loop. Each of these parts are supported by at least one main piece of software.

The designer is provided with powerful, interactive, and vision-oriented tools for specifying the geometry of the objects that they wish to build. The specification and modification of geometry is done using the solid model editor **mged** [Weav80; Muus83].

The application writer is provided a powerful platform upon which to build analysis tools, where the physics of a particular analysis is insulated from the complexities of the shapes under analysis. Analysis tools are built free from the details of the underlying geometry using **librt**, a ray-tracing library for model interrogation.

A broad family of automatic analysis tools are provided to the designer to help assess the merits of each design change. Many analysis tools are built around a generic skeleton of code that provides some common housekeeping functions and thus reduces development costs and helps to provide consistent interfaces.

The output of the analysis tools is provided to the designer in graphical form to permit rapid comprehension of complex assessments. The model analysis tools produce graphical output using **libfb**, a generic frame buffer library with full network display capability, and **libplot3**, a library for the production of 2D and 3D UNIX-Plot files.

The ability to store and manipulate images and signals is provided to permit convenient handling of analysis output and to permit easy comparison of simulation results with actual test data. The handling of all the images and data resulting from the analysis codes is managed via several groups of tools, including a collection of software tools for frame buffer manipulation, a collection of software tools for image processing and analysis, a collection of software tools for handling 2D and 3D UNIX-Plot wireframe plots, and a collection of software tools for signal generation and processing.

A substantial amount of technology and software is required to achieve the environment described in the preceding list. The technology of solid modeling is discussed in much greater detail elsewhere [Muus87c].

OVERVIEW OF ANALYSIS TOOLS

Many phenomena that are ordinarily difficult to model can be handled simply and elegantly with ray tracing. For example, an illumination model based on ray tracing merely needs to fire a ray at each light source to determine the total light energy at each point. By dithering the location of the light sources, this gives a statistically good rendition of shadow penumbra effects. Unlike conventional rendering packages, ray tracing also makes it easy to deal with objects that are partly or entirely reflective and with transparent objects that have varying refractive indices. Furthermore, by applying the proper sorts of dither [Cook84], motion-blur, depth-of-field, translucency, and other effects are easily achieved.

Given that lighting model code exists for making static images, it is straightforward to develop code that can animate the position of the 'eye' (camera) and light sources within the model, and it requires only a modest additional effort to develop the capability of articulating the model geometry itself. Using animation can be very beneficial when trying to gain comprehension of complex geometry, especially when the object being modeled has never actually been physically built. There is nothing that communicates complex structures more clearly than to observe them passing by.

The power of the lighting model code can be further extended by making provision to record the paths of all the rays followed when computing the light intensity for each pixel in an auxiliary file. This capability allows one to follow the path of the light rays passing through lenses reflecting from mirrors while performing image rendering with no additional computation. This makes a fantastic debugging tool. Studying the paths of light rays as they are repeatedly bent by passing from air to glass and back again has traditionally been a painstaking manual procedure for lens designers. By modeling, it becomes possible to predict lens behavior including making a determination of the exact focal length, finding the precise influence of spherical distortions and edge effects, determining the amount of image distortion due to internal reflection and scattering, and finding the level of reflections from the lens mounting hardware. Furthermore, experiments can be conducted to determine the effects of adding or removing baffles, irises, special lens coatings, etc.

In the design of vehicles, moments and products of inertia play a central role. Particularly when designing aircraft, weights, the center of gravity, and parameters related to inertia are vital aspects of creating a stable design with high performance. For ground vehicles and fixed structures these figures are quite significant, providing a good estimate of structural loading and allowing transportation costs to be assessed. Moments of inertia are important in determining under what conditions a vehicle may be overturned by maneuvering or impact, and they can also help predict the vehicle's handling when maneuvering over rough terrain [Deit83].

An important extension to the study of simple static and dynamic loading of structures is to consider dynamic stress caused by the impact of a high-velocity object with the model. This could be as ordinary as a rock striking a car traveling at 80 kilometers per hour, hailstones falling from the sky, or a collision with another vehicle. On the other hand, if the object being designed is intended for use in a military setting, the range of threats that must be considered is greatly enlarged [Weav82].

Synthetic aperture radar (SAR) is a technique by which a variety of image information about a distant object can be obtained by correlating multiple radar samples taken from various positions [Toom82]. While standard radars only report target backscatter and range information, SAR techniques can resolve distinct scattering regions of a target [Deit84].

Tradeoff Analysis

The philosophy adopted at BRL has been to develop a broad set of analyses that are supported from the same geometry database [Deit84]. These analyses cover the spectrum from engineering decision aids, to design validators, to drafting and milling interfaces, to the generation of manufacturing drawings, to image generation for management comprehension and sales advantage. Key analysis capabilities have been developed to assess the strength, weight, protection, and performance levels offered by the structures represented by a solid model. Using this analysis information and additional domain-specific applications tools makes it possible to produce highly detailed designs constructed with a philosophy of *system optimization* right from the start [Deit88]. This allows the rapid development of systems with the desired levels of performance at the best attainable price.

Local Patterns of Use

At any stage of a design, the model can be used to make realistic images and engineering drawings. This capability is so powerful that it ordinarily justifies the expense of constructing the solid model. However, the real payoff from building a geometric model comes when it is time to analyze it. The model can be subjected to numerous engineering analyses, allowing the effects of varying many parameters to be studied in a controlled way.

From the perspective of a designer working in a highly interactive analysis environment, the majority of his time is spent using the graphics screen to interact with the model geometry, contemplating it, viewing it, and changing it. After a significant design change, one or more analyses may be conducted on the new design, with the output images being displayed on the graphics screen as they are computed. Interaction with the model then continues.

Local Viewing of Local Data

MAIN STYLES OF GRAPHICS DISPLAY

There are several distinct types of graphics support that are required to implement the use of the software just described. First, interaction with the model geometry using **mged** is done in a highly interactive mode using wireframe displays. The **mged** program contains a library of *display manager* modules that support a wide variety of hardware types to produce these wireframe displays and to deal with knobs, buttons, mice, joysticks, and other hardware-specific input devices.

Second, many of the applications programs produce full-color shaded images. To free the applications programs from having to deal with the specifics of each type of hardware needed to display these images, a hardware-independent frame buffer library called **libfb** has been built. By using this library, each application can be written to perform abstract operations on an idealized 24-bit deep RGB frame buffer, and the details of managing the particular hardware can be left to the library. This library also allows applications to open an arbitrary number of different frame buffers, where each one may potentially be made by a different manufacturer.

Third, quite a few of the applications programs produce 2D or 3D plots for the designer to view. To provide this capability, the traditional UNIX-Plot capability has been extended to provide 3D plotting, plotting using floating-point coordinates, and plotting in color. This extended UNIX-Plot support is provided to the applications in the form of the library **libplot3**, which will be described in more detail below.

Finally, a number of applications presently under development will produce collections of polygons suitable for display on hardware with intrinsic polygon-drawing capabilities. These faceted objects are stored using the nonmanifold property of the radial-edge data structure.

GRAPHICS STANDARDS VERSUS NEW HARDWARE

There are a great many graphics standards available today, so many as to make a mockery of the word 'standard'. Support for the three main styles of graphic display in the BRL CAD package could perhaps be provided with some effort using one or more standards in existence today. However, most of these capabilities were created *circa* 1980 and were oriented toward providing high performance over a well-defined and moderately limited domain of operations. As a result, the capabilities provided by the BRL CAD package overlap with some of the capabilities that exist in current standard graphics packages. There are a number of compelling reasons for continuing to support the existing BRL styles of operation even in a climate rich with standards. First, there is no known standard that can provide operations with semantics that match the existing operations and capabilities fairly closely. Second, there is no standard that is implemented across as wide a range of hardware as the present BRL library implementations. Third, there is no known implementation of a standard graphics package that can deliver performance roughly comparable to the existing implementations. Finally, implementing support for each new type of display hardware typically requires from four to 40 man-hours of effort, which is significantly less effort than would be required to implement a full standard package on the same hardware, the assumption here being that new hardware does not support the necessary standard packages. New hardware rarely supports the graphics standards of interest.

One of the strongest arguments in favor of standard graphics libraries is based on the notion that if new hardware is always delivered with support for the existing standards, and if all important user code is written to use the existing standards, then moving the existing user code to new hardware should just require recompilation, and everything will work. Unfortunately, in practice several problems have been encountered when attempting to realize this ideal. Graphics hardware is evolving at a fantastic pace. Not only have speeds increased, but completely new features never seen before keep appearing. Standards activities, on the other hand, tend to succeed best in fields of endeavor that have a more moderate growth rate, because establishing standards is a very time-consuming task. Standards are therefore forced to lag behind the 'state of the art' by half a decade or so.

The strategy adopted early in the development of the BRL CAD package was based on the premise that a graphics interface standard with suitable power, flexibility, and performance would probably not emerge during the lifetime of the software. Therefore, it was necessary to be positioned such that new hardware could be supported with great agility. All current BRL applications are satisfied using some combination of the three basic families of graphics operations. In each case, a low-level interface is constructed that provides the absolute minimum set of features possible while retaining the ability to actually accomplish something, following the 'small is beautiful' philosophy [Kern84].

These remarks should not be taken as a global condemnation of standards. Because of the highly focused domain of operations, the lack of committee participation in the design, and the orientation toward performance in favor of generality, the support for graphic displays in the BRL CAD package has been easy to implement, cleanly designed, and highly effective. For uses that fall within the supported domain of operations, these libraries are likely to prove highly satisfying. For other uses, some other solution is required. However, it is important to note that all of the display generation and handling in the BRL CAD package has been built on these abstractions without significant strain.

The **mged** display managers and the **libfb** interface routines both provide capabilities to interactively manipulate display hardware, so high performance is a significant issue. To retain high performance while also achieving good modular software design, an object-oriented interface is used in both cases. While it is possible to use **libplot3** in an interactive setting, the portable machine-independent plot file provides the standard interface. Here, only a single hardware-specific plotfile display program is needed for each type of hardware.

As a result of the graphics interface strategy selected, it is necessary to create three new software modules each time new hardware is to be supported. However, because of the very careful selection of the interfaces, it typically requires less than one man-week of programming effort to support each new type of hardware. Because only several pieces of exciting new hardware appear each year, this strategy has proven to be most effective.

HANDLING FULL-COLOR IMAGES

The Frame-buffer Abstraction

The frame buffer that **libfb** provides is very simple and has only a few assumptions. The display surface is rectangular and is covered with individually addressable pixels. The display surface is *npixels* wide and *nlines* high. Pixels are addressed as (x, y) using first quadrant Cartesian coordinates so that $(0, 0)$ is the lower left corner of the display, with $0 \leq x < npixels$, and $0 \leq y < nlines$.

The rectangular display surface requested must fit entirely on the screen space available for the selected piece of hardware. Therefore, the library does not have to provide any services to clip the display surface to the hardware screen. Multipixel writes start at a given x, y coordinate and proceed to the right (the $+x$ direction) until $x = npixels - 1$. If more pixels remain to be written, the y coordinate is increased by one and the x coordinate is reset to zero so that pixel writing proceeds on the next line *up* on the screen.

Pixels

Each pixel is 24 bits deep, with eight bits assigned to each of Red, Green, and Blue. Pixels are dealt with by **libfb** as atomic units of type `RGBpixel`. The C language declaration for this is:

```
typedef unsigned char RGBpixel[3];
```

where element [0] is Red, [1] is Green, and [2] is Blue. As a result of this, pixels are stored tightly packed in memory, using three bytes per pixel, in a large `unsigned char` array. The sequence of colors in the array is thus Red Green Blue, Red Green Blue....

One seemingly attractive alternative to this format might have been to define the pixel differently as

```
typedef struct {
                unsigned char red;
                unsigned char green;
                unsigned char blue;
} RGBpixel;
```

However, such a choice would invite the compiler to provide structure padding to ensure word alignment of the start of the structure. This could waste a significant amount of memory. The worst case is machines with 64-bit word lengths like the Crays; such a pixel definition would expand each pixel from three to eight bytes!

The Color Map

The eight-bit Red value of a pixel is mapped by a Red color map (color look-up table) with 256 (2^8) entries to determine the actual intensity displayed on the screen. Green and Blue are handled similarly. Each of the 256 color map entries is expected to be 16 bits wide, with the values represented as binary fixed-point notation, with the radix point to the left of bit zero, so that intensities in the color map can be thought of as varying from 0.0 to 1.0 (or an unsigned int varying from 0x0000 to 0xFFFF, in hexadecimal). The color map transformation is generally handled by hardware. When the hardware color map is less than 16 bits wide, the low-order bits are discarded. Where the hardware color map capability is missing, it is simulated by hardware-specific **libfb** routines. Such simulation implies that the hardware-specific routines need to retain a memory copy of the original unmapped pixels to permit the original pixel values to be read back. The color map is important for certain image-processing operations as well as to permit approximate corrections for the nonlinearity of the display device (gamma correction). For details on better methods for achieving the gamma correction, consult Hall [Hall83].

The 'libfb' Interface

The interface to the **libfb** routines is loosely modeled after the interface to the UNIX **stdio** I/O library. In particular, the routine fb_open returns a pointer to an object of the type FBIO. While the contents of the FBIO object are opaque to the application, all other **libfb** routines require that this pointer be provided as the first parameter. All the internal state data for the library routines and the underlying hardware are stored in the FBIO object. With this formalism, it now becomes easy to write applications that utilize an arbitrary number of display devices simultaneously, even if each device is potentially a different type of hardware. The routines that comprise **libfb** are listed in Table 2 [Muus87b].

A set of buffered I/O routines is also provided (Table 3) in which a *band*

Table 2. **libfb** routines.

fb_open(device,width,height)	open the device
fb_close(fbp)	close the device
fb_read(fbp,x,y,buf,count)	read count pixels at x, y
fb_write(fbp,x,y,buf,count)	write count pixels at x, y
fb_clear(fbp,color)	clear to an optional color
fb_rmap(fbp,color map)	read a color map
fb_wmap(fbp,color map)	write a color map
fb_window(fbp,x,y)	place x, y at center
fb_zoom(fbp,xzoom,yzoom)	pixel replicate zoom
fb_getwidth(fbp)	actual device width in pixels
fb_getheight(fbp)	actual device height
fb_cursor(fbp,mode,x,y)	cursor in image coords
fb_scursor(fbp,mode,x,y)	cursor in screen coords
fb_log(format,arg,...)	user replaceable error logger

of scanlines is kept in memory, with the library transparently providing band exchanges via bulk frame buffer reads and writes. While using these routines can speed up programs that make 'well-behaved' single pixel reads and writes, it does not make the drawing of vertical lines significantly faster, since such a line could run through quite a few bands, causing many band exchanges. In practice, very few programs use buffered I/O but, because it can be provided by the library independent of the specifics of the underlying display hardware, it seemed appropriate to implement it as a general capability.

Specifying a Particular Frame Buffer

The display to be used is selected by the string parameter *device* in the call to fb_open(). If that parameter is a null string, the UNIX runtime environment variable FB_FILE is used. If FB_FILE is undefined, the default display for that system type is selected (a library compile-time option).

Table 3. **libfb** buffered I/O.

fb_ioinit(fbp)	set up a memory buffer
fb_seek(fbp,x,y)	move to an x, y location
fb_tell(fbp,xp,yp)	gives the current location
fb_rpixel(fbp,pixelp)	read a pixel and bump location
fb_wpixel(fbp,pixelp)	write and bump current location
fb_flush(fbp)	bring display up to date

The format of the *device* string is

$$[\texttt{host :}]/\texttt{dev}/device\_name[\#]$$

to designate a hardware device (where the square brackets '[]' denote an optional parameter), or simply

<code>disk_filename</code>

to specify the name of an ordinary file to act as a virtual frame buffer (with the image conveniently being stored in **pix**(5) format into that file). The string prefix '/**dev**/' is used to identify that this request is for a hardware display device as opposed to naming an ordinary file. In such cases, the *device_name* part generally will *not* correspond to actual system hardware entries in the directory /**dev**. If the /**dev** prefix is not given, then a pathname to an ordinary disk file is assumed.

If a hostname is given, a network connection is opened to the frame buffer library daemon (**rfbd**) on that machine. The remaining part of the string is passed to the remote daemon to complete the open (this generalizes the open to allow multiple 'hops' in order to reach a desired host). More about this later.

The *debug* interface prints a message each time a library routine is called as an aid to debugging. The disk file interface is used to directly manipulate images in a **pix**(5) format file as if that image were in a frame buffer. Support for specific display hardware is optional and is determined by compile-time configuration options. The current list of supported devices is given in Table 4.

Because the model of the display is that of a traditional frame buffer, providing support for much simpler display devices like Sun workstations requires a lot of software simulation because of the many features that are not implemented in the hardware. The first device supported (in 1981) was an Ikonas (now Adage RDS-3000), which operates as either a 512×512 or 1024×1024 display with 24-bit pixels. The Ikonas hardware does not allow the current display resolution to be sensed from software, so that any program opening the display must 'know' whether the frame buffer should be opened in low- or high-resolution mode. As a result, every program that deals with a frame buffer, even those which have little to do with display size (such as those which read or write color maps), includes a $-\mathbf{h}$ 'high-resolution' flag (for 1024×1024 operation) and a default resolution of 512×512 to make it convenient to open the display with the proper resolution.

Wireframe Display Support in MGED

The **mged** editor is used to specify and modify the geometry in the solid model database. The editor presents a representation of the geometry using wireframe displays.

Table 4. **libfb**-supported interfaces.

Standard	
file	Manipulate disk image
debug	Print library calls

Optional	
remote	Network access to remote display
adage	Adage RDS-3000 ('Ikonas')
sgi	SGI Iris display (3D)
sgi	SGI Iris display (4D)
sun	SunView interface (bw and color)
X	MIT X Windows interface, for X11
ptty	AT&T 5620 w/special Moss layer
rat	Raster Technology One/80
ug	Ultra Graphics

Support for a variety of display hardware is achieved through the use of an object-oriented programming interface between the main **mged** program and the *display manager* routines. When objects are first called up for view, vector representations of the wireframes are created in an internal form and made available to the currently attached display manager.

Display managers for two main families of display systems are built with a single common formalized interface. First, display systems with displaylist capability are supported. When objects are first called up for view, the internal vector lists are converted to device-specific formats and placed into displaylist memory. All subsequent operations are performed by transmitting displaylist updates and replacing viewing matrices. Second, display systems with no displaylist memory are supported. For these displays, each time the main **mged** program signals that the screen needs to be updated, the current viewing matrices are combined with the internal vector list and the vectors are clipped and output to the display. At present, all versions of **mged** have support for these types of display devices by default:

plot	any UNIX-Plot filter
tek	Tektronix 4014 and family
tek4109	Tektronix 4109

These optional display devices are also supported, when specifically configured:

sgi	Silicon Graphics Iris 4D
sgi	Silicon Graphics Iris 3D
sun	Sun Microsystems
X	MIT X-Windows X11R3
X10	MIT X-Windows X10R4
vg	Vector General 3300

mg	Megatek 7250
rat	Raster Tech One/180, 380
rat80	Raster Tech One/80
ps	Evans & Sutherland Picture System 300
mer	Megatek Merlin 9200
sab	Saber Technology

libplot3: PLOTTING SUPPORT

UNIX systems have traditionally supported device-independent plotting on a variety of displays, using the **libplot**(3) library routines to produce **plot**(5) format plot files. These plot files can be displayed on a variety of displays using the **plot**(1) program (renamed **tplot**(1) in SystemV). Standard device support on SystemV includes the DASI 300, DASI 450, and Versatec D1200A. Standard device support on Berkeley UNIX includes the Tektronix 4013, 4014, DASI 450, DASI 300, AED 512, BBN Bitgraph, Imagen laserprinter, HP 2648, Versatec D1200A, and the Benson Varian plotter. Crude plots can also be printed on any terminal with cursor-addressing capability. The BRL SystemV extensions [Gwyn85] provide support for the Selanar HiREZ-100, HP 2648, HP 7750A plotter, HP 2686A LaserJet, Megatek 7255, Tektronix 4014, Tektronix 4105, Trilog ColorPlot II, Teletype 5620, and Digital Engineering's Retrographics VT100.

The standard plotting interface permits plotting in two dimensions using 16-bit signed integer coordinates. The intervals to be used in x and y must be specified in advance. There is support for text strings, circles, arcs, points, and lines, with an option for selecting line types. Plot files created using **libplot** are binary and portable to other machines. Unfortunately, due to the origins of this software on the PDP-11 and the VAX, the integers are written in VAX ('Little-Endian') byte order.

BRL's **libplot3**(3) library provides a great many additional features over the standard UNIX **libplot**(3) library. Colors may be specified as 24-bit RGB quantities. Additional routines exist to plot using three coordinates. The 2D and 3D integer-valued routines have been supplemented with routines that take floating-point values. These floating-point values are written into the plot file in a transportable, machine-independent binary format using **htond**(3). The 3D floating-point routines have two interface styles, one where each coordinate is a formal parameter to the subroutine, and one where location in space is passed as a pointer to a vector. The second form is especially convenient when using the vector mathematics routines.

The **libplot3**(3) library provides a powerful and portable mechanism for creating 2D and 3D plot files that are upwards (but not downwards) compatible with the original UNIX **libplot**(3) library. In addition to the low-level routines mentioned so far, additional library routines exist for drawing coordinate axes, scaling data, etc., so that this capability can be used for traditional data plotting [Muus78] as well as for representing 3D wireframes.

Viewing of Remote Data

THE MOTIVATION FOR COMPLICATING GRAPHICS BY ADDING NETWORKING

Collaboration is a very important aspect of creative endeavors, both scientific and artistic. Collaboration implies having more than one person involved, which implies that there is probably more than one workstation or computer involved, which implies that some form of machine communication is required.

In 'the old days', graphics displays were either terminals attached to a mainframe with an ordinary serial line, such as the Tektronix 4014, or high-speed peripherals connected directly to an I/O channel, such as the Evans & Sutherland PS-1. Networking involved little more than connecting all the terminals to *the* computer. In either case, sharing of data between users was automatic, because all users used the same computer.

Such simplicity no longer exists. In the modern computing environment, computers are everywhere. To retain the benefits of synergistic interaction, the barriers between machines must be removed.[†]

The Modern Computing Environment

The state of most computer facilities in the late 1980s can be best summarized by the word 'diversity' [Quar86]. A single computer is no longer able to serve the needs of an entire facility; in many cases a single computer may be allocated to serve the needs of a small group of people or even an individual. Fortunately, the cost per unit of processing power has fallen steadily and rapidly for the last 15 years. As a result of the increase in demand and decrease in cost, computer systems have proliferated wildly, appearing in all aspects of business, education, and government.

Proliferation of computer systems within organizations has served to highlight the importance of networking. Some organizations have opted to depend on a single vendor for all their hardware needs; such organizations have typically been able to enjoy a reasonable degree of interoperability between their systems, but often at a sharp expense of having to forgo more powerful or less expensive offerings from other vendors. Educational and government institutions, always forced to be very short-term cost-conscious, have often been forced to diversify. Having a collection of

---

[†]For authorized users. A sensible security posture must still prevail, but that is a topic for some other paper.

dissimilar machines has complicated the task of achieving communication between them.

Accomplishing communication between different vendor-specific communication systems has always been possible, although often expensive. The development of the vendor-independent TCP/IP protocol family [Fein85], the use of TCP/IP on the ARPANET, and the development of fast, inexpensive local area network (LAN) technologies like Ethernet [Xero80] has resulted in a common communication standard that is in widespread use. The TCP/IP protocol family took the promise of Open Systems Interconnection (OSI) from an ideal to a production capability in 1982, and TCP/IP has been in widespread use ever since. Through the use of the TCP/IP protocols, computers from any manufacturer can communicate reliably, effectively, and efficiently with all other computers on the network.

With processing power getting less expensive, computers becoming physically smaller, and the invention of Ethernet making local area networking inexpensive enough to be practical in any facility, the emergence of the workstation was inevitable. Personal computers (PCs) and workstations share the common trait of having a processor, main memory, and video display dedicated to working on the problems of a single user. A workstation is distinguished from a personal computer mainly by the ability to multiprogram, i.e., the workstation has the ability to interleave the running of more than one program without interference. The ability to multiprogram is necessary to make a computer system into a good network citizen. The network environment is populated by many 'daemon' programs that provide services to, and demand services of, other machines on the network; these programs use a small amount of processor time on an ongoing basis to conduct those services.

Workstations are a commonplace item in all current computer installations. Recent advances in VLSI have made it clear that the workstation is the heir apparent to the throne once held by the ordinary terminal. For example, the Sun-3/50 is a 1–1.5 million instruction per second (MIPS) Motorola 68020-based machine with a Motorola 68881 floating-point unit, 4 Mbytes of main memory, a 10 million bit per second (Mbps) Ethernet interface, and an 1152×896 pixel display—yet, as of this writing, the selling price in the United States is only four thousand dollars, a fraction of the cost of a graphics terminal only a decade earlier. Furthermore, high-performance workstations offer compute performance that rivals that of many common minicomputers, often at a small fraction of the price. What is happening in the computer industry is that, while the super-minicomputers grow upwards to compete with the supercomputers, the workstations grow upwards to compete with the conventional minicomputer.

Computer Categories

A properly balanced computer network has a mix of different resources. For a laboratory working on science and engineering problems, the resources typically fall into three categories: supercomputers, super-minicomputers, and workstations (Table 5). It can sometimes be difficult to distinguish between different types of computers, so a small diversion to define terms is necessary.

Supercomputers. A supercomputer represents the fastest processing and I/O capabilities available. The instruction set is optimized for scientific processing. The supercomputer processor is best utilized primarily for computationally intensive processing loads because of the long time needed to quench the processor pipelines and save the state of the processor. Due to the complexity of the processor, some machine-specific software development is often necessary to obtain maximum performance.

Mini-supercomputers. A mini-supercomputer is a processor that executes the exact same instruction set and binary software as a supercomputer but at a much slower speed and at a much lower cost. These systems are typically purchased to offload software development from supercomputers, or in circumstances where a full supercomputer is not required or would be prohibitively expensive. Having the exact same hardware complexity as a full supercomputer, similar machine-specific software development is necessary for maximum performance.

Mainframe computers. A mainframe computer typically has an instruction set balanced for general-purpose programming and business applications and usually runs a business-oriented operating system.

Super-minicomputers. A super-minicomputer is a very large minicomputer architecture device utilizing lower performance I/O devices and a collection of minicomputer processing elements to make a system that has a substantial aggregate processing power but retains the low-overhead, interactive orientation of the minicomputer architecture. They are suitable for highly interactive tasks (especially graphics display) as well as medium

Table 5. Processor categorization.

Category	MFLOPS	I/O
Supercomputer	>500	High-performance I/O
Mini-supercomputer	>50	channels with dedicated
Mainframe	3–50	I/O processors; 3–15
		Mbytes/sec per channel
Super-minicomputer	7–100	Medium-performance I/O
Minicomputer	0.5–7	controlled by same CPU(s)
		that run user code; 1–3
		Mbytes/sec per channel;
		hardware error recovery
Workstation	0.1–3	Low cost; low-speed I/O
Microcomputer	0.0–0.5	controlled by CPU; < 1
		Mbytes/sec per channel;
		software error correction

scale numeric processing. I/O devices are typically controlled by the same processors that run users' programs, with hardware to perform I/O error correction.

Minicomputers. A minicomputer is intended for interactive computing, to be shared between a small- to medium-sized community of users. The hardware is optimized for interactive processing and is generally low cost, with modest I/O bandwidths. I/O devices are typically controlled by the same processor that runs users' programs, with hardware to perform I/O error correction.

Workstations. A workstation is intended for a single user at a time, with high-resolution monochrome or medium-resolution color displays, and high interactivity for a single application. Only small amounts of processing can be performed local to the workstation.

Microcomputers. A microcomputer is cheap. Typically they lack multiprogramming and TCP/IP network support, making the effective utilization of multiple microcomputers difficult. However, they are often extremely cost-effective sources of computing power for clerical and administrative applications.

Network Concepts, Standard Protocols

The International Standards Organization (ISO) has adopted a reference model for Open Systems Interconnection (OSI) that divides network service into seven layers of abstraction to permit the different aspects of a complete network implementation to be more easily considered [Tane81].

7	Application	(User)
6	Presentation	Data transformation
5	Session	Create connections
4	Transport	Segmentation and reliability
3	Network	Routing
2	Link	Build bit streams
1	Physical	Electrical transitions

Except for the discussion about network bandwidth, which is primarily determined by the characteristics of the hardware that is providing a particular physical layer, this paper assumes that a reliable, full duplex, eight-bit binary path is available between pairs of computers, on demand, and that the session layer and lower layers handle all necessary details. Here, the focus is on the activities in the presentation and application layers, i.e., to take the raw network capability and use it to provide meaningful graphics across network links.

There are quite a few network protocol families in existence that can be viewed using the ISO model (with varying degrees of success). Most are vendor-specific, and two are standards devised by nonvendors (Table 6).

Table 6. Standard network protocols.

Organization	Protocol
Xerox	NS
Digital	DECNET
IBM	SNA
U.S. Govt.	TCP/IP
ISO	TP4

The Need for Bandwidth

People who are tasked with planning for network bandwidth requirements generally are not prepared for the volume of data that graphical applications generate and consume. At BRL, there are two functional requirements for network bandwidth that define the minimum acceptable performance of a network. They are based on user impatience factors [IBM82]. Any user should be able to achieve file transfer rates of one Mbyte per minute, or 140 Kbits per second. A CAD user should be able to retrieve a 512×512 24-bit deep image in 30 seconds, or 210 Kbits per second. These values are bare minimums. More reasonable performance would be to transfer data at the rate of one Mbyte per ten seconds, or 838 Kbits per second, with the image transfer happening in three seconds, or two Mbits per second. While the minimum values are no problem (see Table 7), the more desirable speeds begin to approach the limits of conventional technology (considering that the network supports hundreds of users).

Fortunately, for graphics there is an upper bound on the amount of network bandwidth that is likely to be required per user. In this case, the limiting factor is the bandwidth of the human eye-brain system, which has been estimated at approximately 10 Gbits per second (10,000 Mbits per second). For most purposes, the eye can be deceived with images of

Table 7. Various Local Area Network speeds (Mbits per second).

0.056	Point-to-Point
1.544	Point-to-Point
10	Ethernet
10	ProNet-10 Ring
16	DEC PCL-11
50	Hyperchannel
80	ProNet-80 Ring
100	FDDI
1200	UltraNet

significantly lower resolution. The best example of this is the 4.2 MHz bandwidth of an NTSC television signal [Conr80], which provides low but very usable image quality. For computer graphics applications, more spatial resolution than that provided by NTSC is often desirable, while 30 frames per second animation rates are only needed for the most demanding work. Table 8 [Rica87] provides data rates for several types of animation.

There are not many computers that can compute animation sequences in real time, although there are quite a few that have I/O systems capable of reading, postprocessing, and displaying precomputed data at these data rates. The first line in the table describes a data rate comparable to the maximum throughput of the new generation of LAN technology, the proposed FDDI (fiberoptic data distribution interconnect), 100 Mbits per second. To date, only the Ultra device is capable of operating in this range of data rates, with a peak speed of 1200 Mbits per second, but a variety of other devices of comparable bandwidth are presently in development [McCo87].

THE BRL REMOTE FRAME BUFFER CAPABILITY

The machine at BRL that had the nicest display hardware on it had one of the slowest processors (a VAX 11/780). To allow computation and display to occur on separate machines, the **libfb** frame buffer library was given support for an extra type of display hardware: the remote frame buffer. The goal of this capability was to be able to direct graphics operations to any display screen attached to the network merely by specifying in the *device* string the name of the host computer and the name of the display device. (Refer back to the section on **libfb** for a discussion of the three methods for providing the *device* string, and the syntax.) The details of establishing the network connection to the appropriate computer, as well as the hardware-specific display support, should all be entirely transparent to the user, except perhaps for some performance variations.

Detection that the given *device* string indicates the use of a network display is handled by the **libfb** routines that implement the fb_open() function. Rather than vectoring to a module to support a local display, the fb_open() function forces all operations to vector through the if_remote.c module. When the if_remote.c module is called to open the frame buffer,

Table 8. Data rates for various resolutions

Resolution	Frames per second	Data rate (Mbits per second)
$512 \times 512 \times 24$	15	95
$512 \times 512 \times 24$	30	190
$1024 \times 1024 \times 24$	15	375
$1024 \times 1024 \times 24$	30	755
$1024 \times 1024 \times 24$	60	1510
$2048 \times 2048 \times 24$	24	2415

it assumes the role of a 'network client' and causes a network connection to be established to the 'network server' on the indicated remote machine. The client then passes the hardware device specification to the server. The server process calls fb_open() on its copy of **libfb** and returns the status code (success or failure) to the client, which returns the status code to the calling application.

The routines in the if_remote module convert all the parameters in the library calls into machine-independent messages. These messages are sent from the client to the server using the 'package' (PKG) protocol [Muus87b]. When the server receives a message, it determines which operation is being requested, converts the machine-independent values in the message back into the native format of the server machine, and then invokes the intended library routine.

The definition of the protocol exchanged by the client and server machines is a level-seven (application) protocol that depends on level-six services (presentation) for the external data representation conversions. The machine-independent messages generated by this protocol are transmitted via **libpkg**, which provides level-six (presentation) and level-five (session) services. **libpkg** provides capabilities for the transmission of both synchronous messages and asynchronous messages. Synchronous messages are used by the if_remote protocol when return codes from the server are significant. In this case, the client library routine does not return until a reply message has been received from the server. For significantly improved performance, the fb_write() routine uses asynchronous messages so that the client library routine returns a 'success' indication immediately while the network and server continue to work on displaying the data. This allows the production of data and the display of the data to proceed at the maximum possible rate. With this design, the library depends on reliable delivery services from the level-four (transport) services of the particular communication protocol.

One of the delightful features of this design is that the remote frame buffer capability can be stacked to an arbitrary depth. That is to say, one could specify the *device* as

$$host1 : host2 : /dev/device\_name[\#]$$

In this case, the original client would contact *host1* as a server. *host1*, in processing the remainder of the *device* string, would vector to if_remote.c, thus acting as a client, and would contact *host2*, which would perform as the actual server. This sort of an arrangement is a good test of the symmetry of the protocol and ensures that no implementation details have been overlooked. Stacking servers in this manner is rarely useful, but the capability comes in handy just often enough so as to be worth keeping around. One use is to bridge across a change in underlying protocols. For example, assume three hosts, A, B, and C, where A and B communicate via the TCP/IP protocols, and B and C communicate via the DECNET protocols. There is no way for an image to be transmitted directly from A to C. However, in this case, machine B can act as an application-level 'relay' and bridge the gap. Another use for stacking servers is to bypass network software or traffic-routing problems by forcing the data to flow through a suitable intermediary.

By careful implementation, the use of remote frame buffers across reasonably high-performance network connections has a level of performance that is only slightly slower than local display performance. The network frame buffer concept is a very powerful one; once accustomed to it, users refuse to deal with more restrictive environments. This capability has been used to conduct data analysis at NASA facilities, with live graphics transmitted from BRL computers, miles away.

Will new standards like the MIT X Window System make the BRL frame buffer library unnecessary? In the short term, no. X Version 11 does not support 24-bit color images, nor does it provide a powerful enough interface for controlling many important frame buffer operations such as color maps, pan, and zoom. However, to provide compatibility with X-based systems, an if_X module implementing the frame buffer library functions is being developed so that all systems that run X will have **libfb** support.

THE REMOTE MGED DISPLAY MANAGER

In a manner similar to that just described for **libfb**, there is a special display manager for **mged** called `dm-net.c` that communicates with an **mged** server process on a remote machine and facilitates network execution of **mged**. This software is still considered experimental, but it has been demonstrated to work correctly. However, the proper level of interactive response depends on having a network path between the client and the server with low latency and low packet loss, so that display motions remain smooth.

The underlying mechanism is very similar to that just described for **libfb**, with specially formatted messages carried via **libpkg** between the client and server processes. It will not be described further here.

THE PKG PROTOCOL

The 'package' (PKG) protocol is a critical 'enabling technology' upon which a great many BRL network applications are built. The **libpkg** services bridge levels six (presentation) and five (session) in the OSI model and are layered on top of a virtual circuit provided by the level-five and -four (transport) capabilities of the native operating system. One of the main purposes of **libpkg** is to insulate the applications programmer from the details of establishing and managing a network connection.

libpkg frees the programmer from concerns about storage and buffer management and other details relating to the network communications internals by allowing exchange of messages of any size (up to $2^{32} - 1$ bytes), with automatic allocation of sufficient dynamic memory for the receive buffer handled by the library. Thus, messages exchanged by users of **libpkg** may be of arbitrary size. There is no requirement for different messages of the same type to have the same size. It is perfectly reasonable to transmit messages with no data, for example, to signal that a particular event has happened. The **libpkg** interface supports a dynamic mix of synchronous and asynchronous message transmission paradigms, allowing the implementation of traditional blocking remote procedure call operations, as well as permitting nonblocking operations (such as used by the fb_write() operation described above) and 'surprise' asynchronous operations (such as used by the fb_log() operation).

Each message is transmitted across the virtual circuit with an eight-byte header to permit the receiving **libpkg** routines to properly receive and dispatch the message (Figure 2). All three header fields are transmitted in Big-Endian byte order; the format of the data field is determined by the calling application and is opaque to the **libpkg** routines. The *magic number* field is set to the value 0x41FE in hexadecimal and is used by the receiver routines to defend against various system failures such as an application program writing data to the wrong file descriptor (the network connection, in this case). The *type* field is provided by the caller of pkg_send() (see Table 9) and is used on the receiving end to appropriately dispatch the message: either a blocking read is satisfied by the arrival of the appropriate message type, or an asynchronous event is vectored through the pkg_switch table and the message is dispatched to an application-specific handler.

Typically, PKG is layered on top of a TCP connection, although PKG has also been run over DECNET and X.25. Multiple PKG connections per process are supported, which is used by **remrt**. When using TCP, the TCP option SO_KEEPALIVE is enabled so that all communications failures and remote system failures are noticed by the TCP layer after an appropriate time interval, avoiding the need for application-level timeouts. **libpkg** handles the incremental aggregation of received data into full messages, freeing the calling application from having to handle the details of

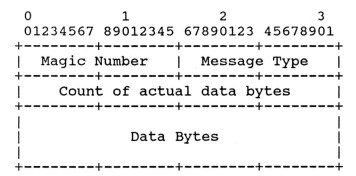

Figure 2. Format of the PKG protocol message header.

Table 9. **libpkg** routines.

pkg_open	Open net connection to host
pkg_permserver	Be permanent server, and listen
pkg_transerver	Be transient server, and listen
pkg_getclient	Server: accept new connection
pkg_close	Close net connection
pkg_send	Send message
pkg_waitfor	Get specific msg, do others
pkg_bwaitfor	Get specific msg, user buffer
pkg_get	Read bytes, assembling msg
pkg_block	Wait for full msg to be read

short reads. The Berkeley UNIX **select**(3) system call provides the ability to easily handle asynchronous communications traffic on multiple connections. This protocol had originally been developed to make the remote **mged** display possible, but later uses were found in command and control experiments [Cham86], distributed processing programs [Muus87d], and other network applications. The degree of functionality provided by **libpkg** is not significantly greater than that provided by the virtual circuit support of the basic operating system and amounts to only about 1300 lines of source code, yet it provides a convenient and worthwhile abstraction of the underlying network mechanism that makes the implementation of distributed applications very much simpler.

EXTERNAL DATA REPRESENTATION

When transmitting information on a network, careful attention must be given to the format and order of the data transmitted. In a heterogeneous network the internal processor architectures of the communication end points are likely to be different, yet effective and accurate transmission of data is still desired.

Moving binary data between disparate computer architectures is not a new idea and has been done for at least three decades. So far, the communication has typically involved specific pairs of computers, typically a mainframe or supercomputer sending results to some kind of 'front-end'. In such cases, one machine would be given the task of always converting the data to and from the format used by the other machine. When constructing distributed applications that run on a wide variety of hardware that can all communicate with each other, it is no longer possible to predict in advance how the machines may be coupled together.

Two strategies exist for coping with such heterogeneity. Either (a) all machines can agree to adopt a single standard for communication, or (b) all machines must have the software to enable them to convert internal data to the internal formats of all other machine types. The first strategy is weakest when two computers of similar type wish to communicate, where their internal format is not the standard format. Transmission of a block of data would therefore require converting it to the standard format, sending it, and converting it back to the internal format, when using the internal format would have been acceptable *in this case*. The second strategy always performs well when similar machines converse, because no format conversion is required. However, this strategy creates a significant software coding and testing burden on the implementors when the number of different formats, N, becomes significant, i.e., when N is greater than 3, because of the need to write N^2 conversion routines. Also, the task of adding support for a new type of machine becomes formidable: N new conversion routines must be written, and every existing machine needs to be updated to support the new format.

The overall strategy favored by the DARPA Network Research community has been to establish a single standard representation for each type of communication and then to have all machines communicate using that single standard. The BRL CAD package has continued in this tradition. The external data representation described here fits into level-six (presentation) of the OSI reference model and serves generally the same purpose as the ISO X.409 Abstract Syntax Notation (ASN.1). Note that both the data representation described here and the Sun XDR standard [Sun87] use implicit typing, i.e., no indication of the data format becomes part of the external data representation, while the ASN.1 standard includes many details of the data format and data structuring in the external representation of the data.

Ordering and Numbering Bits in a Byte

In the discussion that follows, it is assumed that the underlying hardware handles the disassembly and reassembly of serial bit streams into eight-bit bytes in a transparent manner. In this document, the left-most bit in a diagram is the high-order or most significant bit (MSB), and this bit is labeled bit zero. For example, the diagram in Figure 3 represents the value 170 decimal, 0xCC hex, 0252 octal.

Transmitting Sequences of Bytes

The organization and order of transmission of data described in this document is specified at the byte level. The order of transmission of a group of bytes is the normal order in which they are read in English. In Figure 4

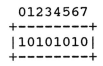

Figure 3. Numbering bits in a byte.

the bytes are transmitted in ascending numerical order (i.e., 1, 2, 3, ...). This convention is often referred to as the 'Big-Endian' order [Cohe80] because the big (most significant) end of the binary number is transmitted first. Big-Endian notation is the standard order in the TCP/IP protocols of the DARPA InterNet [Post81], now formalized as MIL-STD-1777 [DCA83]. The Big-Endian order is also the internal format commonly used by IBM, Gould, Sun, SGI, Alliant, Apple, and many other computers. For these reasons, the Big-Endian order is used for the BRL CAD package external data representation.

Transmitting Integers

All integers are transmitted in Big-Endian or 'network order' regardless of the internal representation of the particular machines. To send a signed 16-bit quantity, the number is represented in twos-compliment form, and the byte sequence is as shown in Figure 5, where S is the sign bit, MSB is the most significant bit, and LSB is the least significant bit. Byte 1 is transmitted first, and byte 2 is transmitted second.

To send a 32-bit signed integer, the number is represented in twos-compliment form, and the byte sequence is as shown in Figure 6. Unsigned integers are encoded similarly, occupying either 16- or 32-bit positions.

Transmitting Strings

Character strings are represented using the ASCII character set. They are placed into the external message without regard for alignment and are terminated by a zero byte (all bits off). There is no limit to the length of a character string (Figure 7).

Floating-point Representations

The most portable representation of a floating-point number would be to encode it as a printable ASCII string. However, using a printable ASCII representation would require 16 decimal digits to contain the mantissa, two digits for the signs of the exponent and mantissa, three decimal digits for the exponent, and at least two additional characters for the mantissa decimal (radix) point and the exponent marker. Such an encoding would look like '−1.234567890123456e−103' and would require at least 23 characters (bytes).

Exchanging floating-point numbers in binary form is a very compact representation using a small and constant amount of bandwidth: eight bytes. Therefore, using an eight-byte binary format requires about one third the network bandwidth as the printable ASCII representation. In addition to the significant bandwidth savings, using a binary format is also likely to require significantly less computer time for format conversion to machine-specific formats because of the strong similarities in internal binary formats and the simplicity of using bit operations to implement the conversions.

```
0                   1                   2                   3
01234567 89012345 67890123 45678901
+--------+--------+--------+--------+
|    1   |    2   |    3   |    4   |
+--------+--------+--------+--------+
|    5   |    6   |    7   |    8   |
+--------+--------+--------+--------+
|    9   |   10   |   11   |   12   |
+--------+--------+--------+--------+
```

Figure 4. Numbering a sequence of bytes.

```
0                   1
01234567 89012345
+--------+--------+
|    1   |    2   |
+--------+--------+

+--------+--------+
|S|MSB        LSB|
+--------+--------+
```

Figure 5. Network representation of 16-bit signed integer.

```
0                   1                   2                   3
01234567 89012345 67890123 45678901
+--------+--------+--------+--------+
|    1   |    2   |    3   |    4   |
+--------+--------+--------+--------+

+--------+--------+--------+--------+
|S|MSB                           LSB|
+--------+--------+--------+--------+
```

Figure 6. Network representation of 32-bit signed integer.

```
+--------+--//---+--------+--------+--------+
| Byte 1 |  ...  |Byte N-1| Byte N |00000000|
+--------+--//---+--------+--------+--------+
```

Figure 7. Network representation of a character string.

Binary Floating-point Representations

Virtually all modern computers utilize twos-compliment binary format as
the internal representation for integers. Thus, the only issue with transmitting integers was to define a byte order; the underlying representation
was already common to all the computers. In the case of floating-point
numbers, the situation is more complex. Not only does the byte ordering
need to be defined, but the network representation of the floating-point
number itself needs to be defined.

Just as integers come in various sizes, floating-point numbers also come
in different sizes, the most common of which are called 'single precision'
(typically 32 bits) and 'double precision' (typically 64 bits). This discussion
focuses entirely on the double-precision format.

Between the various vendors, there have been quite a few different internal representations for floating-point numbers. Typically, each format has
several advantages over the others. The main alternatives are as follows.

IEEE Standard 754

The IEEE Standard 754 double-precision floating point (see Figure 8) is
most popularly used in new microprocessor designs and is found in a wide
variety of new computer systems, especially new workstations. As stated
by Kahan [Kaha86] "This standard is on its way to becoming more widely
adopted than any other design for computer arithmetic. VLSI chips that
conform to some version of that standard have been produced by a host of
manufacturers, among them Intel i8087, i80287, Motorola 68881, National
Semiconductor 32081, Weitek WTL-1032 and WTL-1165, Western Electric
(AT&T) WE32106, Zilog Z8070" and MIPS FPS2000. The radix is 11 bits
wide, in base 2, excess-1023 format. The fraction has 52 significant bits,
a 'hidden' leading one to the left of the high-order bit, and a radix point
to the *right* of the hidden bit, giving roughly 16 decimal digits of significance. Overflow threshold is 2.0^{1024}, or 1.8e+308. Underflow threshold
is 0.5^{1022}, or 2.2e−308. There are explicit representations for *infinity* and
not-a-number (NaN), both signaling NaN and quiet NaN. When the exponent is 2047 (all bits set), a special condition exists. If all fraction bits are
zero, the value is infinity times the sign. If the fraction is non-zero, and
the MSB (bit 12) of the fraction is zero, then this represents a signaling
NaN; otherwise, this represents a quiet NaN.

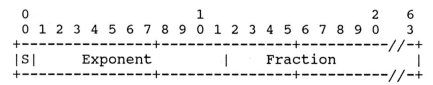

Figure 8. IEEE Standard 754 floating point format.

IBM System/360

IBM System/360 double-precision (eight-byte, or 'long') floating point [IBM70] (see Figure 9) is also used by other vendors such as Gould. The radix is 7 bits wide, in base 16, excess-64 format. The fraction has 56 significant bits, having a radix point to the left of the high-order bit, with no hidden bits, giving roughly 17 decimal digits of significance. Overflow threshold is 16.0^{63}, or $7.2e+75$. Underflow threshold is 16.0^{-65}, or $5.4e-79$. There is no representation of *infinity*. There is no representation of not-a-number (NaN).

DEC VAX-11 'D' Format

Digital Equipment Corporation's VAX-11 double-precision 'D' format (see Figure 10) was also used on the earlier PDP-11 machines. The radix is 8 bits wide, in base 2, excess-128 format. The fraction has 56 significant bits, with a 'hidden' leading bit, giving roughly 17 decimal digits of significance. Overflow threshold is 2.0^{127}, or $1.7e+38$. Underflow threshold is 0.5^{128}, or $2.9e-39$. This range of representable numbers is comparatively narrow. There is no representation of *infinity*. There are reserved values to represent signaling NaN [DEC76]. Note that the actual fraction is made by combining (left to right) Fract_A, Fract_B, Fract_C, and Fract_D. Also note that this ordering is neither pure 'Big-Endian' nor 'Little-Endian' but a peculiar mixture of the two, being Big-Endian within each 16-bit unit but Little-Endian when combining the 16-bit sections.

Cray Research Inc.

In Cray Research Incorporated's full-precision floating point (Figure 11), the radix is 15 bits wide, in base 2, excess-16384 format. The fraction has 48 significant bits, having a radix point to the left of the high-order bit, with no hidden bits, giving at least 14 decimal digits of significance. Overflow threshold is 2.0^{8191}, or $1.0e+2466$. Underflow threshold is 0.5^{8192}, or $1.0e-2466$. There is no representation of *infinity*. There are reserved values to represent NaN. Whether the NaN is signaling or quiet depends on the setting of the hardware Floating-point Mode flag [Cray82].

DEC VAX-11 'G' Format

Digital Equipment Corporation's VAX-11 double-precision 'G' format (see Figure 12) is considered optional and is not supported on all VAX machines, with hardware support available only on some models. Thus, it is used much less frequently than the DEC 'D' format, even though it is very close to the IEEE format. The radix is 11 bits wide, in base 2, excess-1024 format. The fraction has 52 significant bits, having a 'hidden' leading one to the left of the high-order bit, and a radix point to the *left* of the hidden bit, giving roughly 15 decimal digits of significance. Overflow threshold is 2.0^{1023}, or $8.9e+307$. Underflow threshold is 0.5^{1024}, or $5.5e-309$. There

440   Michael J. Muuss

is no representation of *infinity*. There are reserved values to represent signaling NaN [DEC82].

Convex

The native double-precision format of the Convex machines (see Figure 13) (some of which also have IEEE capability) is a Big-Endian version of Digital Equipment Corporation's VAX-11 double-precision 'G' format described above, and has the same properties [Conv88].

Summary. The salient features of these different formats are summarized in Table 10.

A Standard for Network Floating-point Numbers

From all of the possibilities just mentioned, the ANSI/IEEE Standard 754 for Binary Floating-Point Arithmetic [IEEE85] was chosen. This choice was made on the basis of the IEEE format's overall technical merits including extended dynamic range, its status as an accepted and respected standard, and its widespread implementation in common graphics workstations. This choice was made even though this format has a few less bits in the fraction than other formats, most notably that of the VAX, and thus delivers slightly less accuracy. The differences in accuracy were considered to be small enough not to matter; depending on more than 15 decimal digits of accuracy is an impediment to portability in any case and cannot be improved upon in the external data representation.

Therefore, when communicating binary floating-point data across a network connection, all floating-point values must be converted from the host-specific representation to the 64-bit IEEE representation before transmission and, upon reception, all floating-point values must be converted from the 64-bit IEEE representation to the host-specific representation. When the IEEE representation is transmitted, it is to be transmitted in Big-Endian byte order. That is, bits 0–7 are transmitted in the first byte, bits 8–15 are transmitted in the second byte, and so forth.

Table 10. Various formats for internal representation of floating-point numbers.

Format	Radix Bits	Fraction Bits	Decimal Digits	Overflow Threshold	Underflow Threshold
IEEE	11	52+1	16	1.8e+308	2.2e−308
IBM 360	7	56,53	17	7.2e+75	5.4e−79
VAX 'D'	8	56+1	17	1.7e+38	2.9e−39
Cray	15	48	14	1.0e+2466	1.0e−2466
VAX 'G'	11	52+1	15	8.9e+307	5.5e−309
Convex	11	52+1	15	8.9e+307	5.5e−309

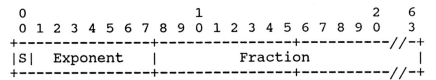

Figure 9. IBM System/360 floating point format.

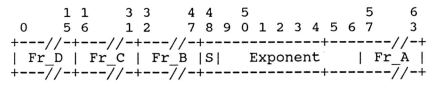

Figure 10. DEC VAX-11 'D' floating point format.

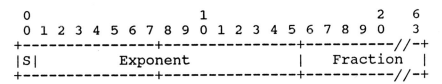

Figure 11. Cray research floating point format.

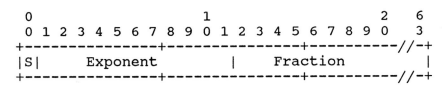

Figure 12. DEC VAX-11 'G' floating point format.

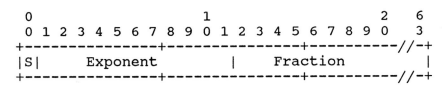

Figure 13. Convex native floating point format.

Floating-point Converter Interface

A pair of library routines have been written (in the C programming language [Ritc78b; Kern78]) to convert between a local host computer's C **double** data type (typically 64-bit double precision) and the *network floating-point format*, which is the 64-bit IEEE double precision representation in 'network' (i.e., Big-Endian) order. The subroutines are defined in C as

```
htond( netptr, hostptr, count );
unsigned char  * netptr;
unsigned char  * hostptr;
int count;

ntohd( hostptr, netptr, count );
unsigned char  * hostptr;
unsigned char  * netptr;
int count;
```

The names are acronyms for Host TO Network Double (`htond`) and Network TO Host Double (`ntohd`), in the style of the existing Berkeley network data representation subroutines, such as `htons` (host to network short), `htonl` (host to network long), etc. However, unlike their Berkeley counterparts, these routines have two significant differences. First, neither the input nor output buffers need to be word aligned to permit the greatest flexibility in converting the data, even though this may impose a speed penalty on some architectures. This property can be especially useful when creating tightly packed network messages containing mixed data types, freeing the programmer from the necessity to add 'pad' bytes to ensure alignment. The concept of alignment is hard to make both portable and storage-efficient and is thus properly avoided as a subroutine constraint. Second, these subroutines operate on a sequential block of numbers rather than on just a single value. This allows entire arrays to be conveniently converted with a single subroutine call, thus improving the clarity of the code, saving on subroutine linkage execution costs, and allowing the hope for effective vectorization of the subroutines on those machines with vector hardware capability.

Significance

The significance of having established a standard for exchanging floating-point numbers should not be underestimated. Most existing network applications restrict themselves to the transmission of integers, either for reasons of efficiency or to simplify the conversion problem. For the purposes of scientific computing, converting data to integers is rarely acceptable because of the requirement for having a large dynamic range available while also maintaining many digits of significance.

Having the capability to conveniently and efficiently transmit floating-point numbers over the the network has given rise to a whole variety of important new capabilities. One example, which has already had significant impact, was the result of including the 3D floating-point plotting capabilities of **libplot3**, which provides a machine-independent 'metafile' capability for plots of full resolution, allowing arbitrary amounts of zooming to examine extraordinarily fine details in the data.

The `htond` and `ntohd` routines have been implemented and tested on a wide variety of machine families including the Cray X-MP, Cray-2, Alliant, Sun-3, Silicon Graphics 3D and 4D, DEC VAX, and Gould PowerNode. When combined with the Berkeley routines `htons`, `ntohs`, `htonl`, and `ntohl`, or with the **libpkg** versions (`pkg_gshort`, `pkg_pshort`, `pkg_glong`, and `pkg_plong`), it becomes possible to easily read and write messages in a portable, machine-independent format. This capability is the cornerstone of the successful growth of the BRL CAD package software into networked environments.

Comparison with Sun XDR

This paper has described a standard for the encoding of data without making any attempt to provide a mechanism for describing the data, either in the program source code or in the transmitted external representation. The format described specifically assumes that the external representation does not have any alignment restrictions, so that strings and binary data may be mixed freely.

The Sun Microsystems XDR standard [Sun87] is very similar to the encoding proposed here, with a few significant differences. It is worthwhile noting that the BRL encoding was selected in 1984 and developed independently of the work at Sun. It is therefore interesting that, with the exception of alignment issues and the representation of strings, the same external format was selected. This is almost certainly due to the exhortations of Cohen [Cohe80]. Therefore, with some careful coding, it is possible for XDR software and BRL CAD package software to interoperate.

XDR assumes that all quantities are aligned on four-byte boundaries for the greatest efficiency of processing on 32-bit word-addressable computers. XDR also prefixes all variable-length fields with a 32-bit length indicator and then pads the variable field. These choices consume some additional network bandwidth but, in most cases, the difference in bandwidth requirements is small (for cases seen to date, XDR generates between 0 percent and 20 percent more bytes in the external representation).

Sun XDR goes a step further than just defining a standard representation for data exchange; XDR also provides a syntax for describing the external data structure. This description is preprocessed to produce compilable code that automatically converts data between the internal and external formats, using the description of the data to be exchanged. This is a very nice feature indeed and certainly makes the exchange of complex data structures much more convenient than an explicit conversion strategy. The XDR preprocessing step presumes a much closer coupling to the compiler environment than the BRL CAD approach, which may result in some additional (one-time) portability efforts to support each new type of system. In summary, it seems that either interface can be readily used, with the BRL CAD interface being easier to use for simpler data structures, with a few less restrictions, while the Sun XDR is far better at handling complex data structures.

Pipeline-oriented Distributed Computation

Carefully dividing application software into appropriate tools provides significant rewards for software developers and maintainers in terms of decreased program complexity, decreased incidence of bugs, and increased maintainability [Kern76]. For the user, having the ability to combine a set of software tools in arbitrary ways provides the potential for performing functions never imagined by the original software designers.

Traditional operating systems require that each command in a multicommand sequence be run sequentially, with the output from each command stored in a temporary file for input into later steps. In the UNIX system, this style of operation can be improved upon if the data passing between pairs of commands is originally stored in a single temporary file. In this case, pairs of commands can be connected together using UNIX pipes. In so doing, not only is the requirement for managing the temporary files (and their attendant storage) eliminated, but a degree of parallelism is introduced as well. As an example, this three command sequence:

```
step1 < input  > tmp1
step2 < tmp1   > tmp2
step3 < tmp2   > output
rm tmp1 tmp2
```

can be reduced to this pipeline:

```
step1 < input | step2 | step3 > output
```

Standard UNIX shell notation is used here, with < meaning 'read from' (redirect standard input), > meaning 'write to' (redirect standard output), and | meaning 'pipe standard output from command on the left into standard input of command on the right'.

Systems with multiple processors have existed since the 1960s. Experimental UNIX systems with multiple processors existed in the late 1970s [Muus79]. The Dual-VAX work at Purdue University [Gobl81] popularized the use of multiple processors with the UNIX system and paved the way for widespread commercial support. Multiprocessor UNIX systems are now common, with most major vendors supporting at least one model with multiple processors. Vendors like Alliant and Sequent have based their entire product lines on parallel processing. Utilizing the UNIX pipeline constructs permits convenient and transparent exploitation of local multiprocessor resources with no reprogramming.

TOOL-ORIENTED IMAGE PROCESSING

A large number of simple tools for manipulating images and frame buffers are provided in the CAD package. They are written in the traditional UNIX software tools fashion: each performs a single basic function and is intended to be connected together with other tools to achieve an overall goal. A fair amount of effort went into making a standard interface to the tools. All tools provide a usage message if executed with no arguments. A common collection of flags is defined for all of the tools. If a tool expects to see binary data and discovers that the binary data is routed to a user's terminal, the tool aborts rather than splattering a binary stream on an unsuspecting terminal.

The use of software tools for computer graphics is not new. Recent systems advocating this tools-based approach include those of Duff [Duff85] and Peterson [Pete86]. The BRL CAD package is extremely flexible as a result of this approach. Generally, a new tool is added whenever the existing ones are found to be inadequate. Success is claimed if users can easily achieve day-to-day tasks without having to write any new programs.

FILE FORMATS

Effective construction of software tools depends on having agreed upon standards for the format of the data that is passed between the various tools. It is important to note that UNIX itself does not impose any form on data files; there are no end-of-record markers or other operating system generated information. Therefore, the interpretation of bytes within a file is implicit and left entirely up to the programs used to read the file. The tools that are provided with the UNIX system are primarily intended for dealing with data stored in ASCII text files. These tools are quite powerful in their problem domain, but representing graphics constructs in a printable ASCII form typically yields an unacceptable performance penalty. Therefore, it is necessary to define a variety of file formats that are more appropriate to the graphical tasks at hand. For efficiency reasons, binary formats are generally to be preferred, both in terms of being a compact representation and also requiring the least processing time to handle by virtue of needing little or no conversion before use. Significantly more stringent requirements are placed on the specification of file formats if files containing binary data are to be portable between different types of machines without need for explicit data conversion.

Storing Images: **pix**(5) and **bw**(5) files

By far the most common image formats are either eight-bit per pixel black and white **bw**(5) or 24-bit per pixel color **pix**(5) formats. These files have the simplest possible format in order to enable rapid development of new tools. As a result of pixel arrays being stored tightly packed in memory in the well-defined order of RGB, the `RGBpixel` definition is a useful format for storing pixels in files. `RGBpixels` are tightly packed arrays with three `unsigned char` elements. Values in each byte are viewed as intensities from 0 (off) through 255 (full on). Therefore, **pix**(5) format picture files are defined as being a sequence of `RGBpixels`. The ordering of the pixels in the file is first quadrant Cartesian and corresponds to the pixel-writing order of **libfb**. The first pixel has coordinates $(0, 0)$ and is the lower left corner of the image. The second pixel has coordinates $(1, 0)$, and subsequent pixels are stored left to right. The first pixel after the end of the first scanline has coordinates $(0, 1)$. Subsequent scanlines are stored bottom to top. This can be more simply thought of as a byte stream composed of repeated RGB triples, e.g., RGBRGBRGB.... Because **pix** files are defined as a byte stream, they are inherently portable to all machines with eight-bit bytes.

A close relative of the **pix**(5) format file is the **bw**(5) format file. This is used for storing eight-bit-deep monochrome ('black and white') images. **bw** files are stored in the same first quadrant layout as **pix** files, with the exception that each pixel is only one byte wide instead of being three bytes wide.

The **pix**(5) and **bw**(5) file formats have no header. The use of a simple headerless image format is the only fundamental design choice that has continued to be debated. The primary advantage of the headerless format is the ease of connecting tools together with pipes and the ease of creating new tools without having to use I/O routines specific to the reading and writing of images. Each program is simply handed data, and the interpretation of the data is implicit in the definition of the tool used and the active options. This also allows the whole wealth of UNIX tools to be applied to images as well, as there is no special-purpose header that has to be skipped. More importantly, tools don't have to know how to do the 'right thing' with the header information in the presence of seemingly contradictory information from either the definition of the tool or from the command line options. For example, processing a **pix** image with a **bw** tool like **bwmod** is often done. If files had headers, tools would almost certainly balk at being feed input with the wrong pixel depth, which in this example would be very frustrating. However, having tools infer how to do the 'right thing' could also be extremely complicated if the header contains very much information, such as with the NASA FITS image format.

Having 'raw' headerless data does have its price. It is difficult to tell whether a given image is color or not, what its dimensions are, etc. Consistent file-naming conventions (using '.bw' or '.pix' as filename suffixes) address the first issue; doing most work in 'standard sizes' of 512×512 or 1024×1024 pixels helps alleviate the second issue. In general, only the scanline length needs to be known, as the number of scanlines can then be found by dividing the file size by the scanline length. The algorithms of many tools simply run until all of the data is gone, and some don't even care about scanline lengths at all, so the inconvenience of having headerless files tends to be minor. Using a good shell with history and commandline screen editing features, or writing sets of simple goal-specific shell scripts tends to minimize the aggravation of having to repetitively specify unusual image sizes on every command.

libplot3 Files

The original UNIX **plot**(5) format file was machine independent, although with the unfortunate choice of Little-Endian (VAX) byte ordering for the 16-bit integers. The extensions to the file format to provide all of the additional features (3D, floating-point coordinates, color) described above were all done in such a way as to preserve the machine-independent property of UNIX-plot files. In this way, not only is it possible to view plot files on displays attached to local computers, but it is also very convenient to produce images on remote displays.

Image Compression: The Utah RLE Format

Another format for storing images is the University of Utah's Run Length Encoded **rle** images, which typically have a file suffix of '.rle'. This is the standard image format of the Utah Raster Toolkit [Pete86]. Because this format typically requires less disk storage than the equivalent **pix** or **bw** file and the compression operation takes some processor time, this format is typically used for long-term image storage and image exchange with other institutions that use the Utah Raster Toolkit. Institutions that have neither the Utah nor BRL image-processing tools often have an easier time importing images in **pix** format because it is so simple.

Model Databases

Model databases are normally stored in a machine-specific binary form with a typical filename extension of '.g', with portable ASCII versions of those databases having a filename extension of '.asc'. It is beyond the scope of this paper to describe the format in detail other than to note that **mged** and **librt** know how to read the model databases, and that programs that wish to create geometry using procedural methods may do so with the services of the **libwdb** library for writing databases.

Frame Buffer Tools

Typically, image manipulation and processing is performed either on data streams or on disk files. This is done in order to separate the operations for handling a display device from the generic operations of image handling. A common beginning to a processing pipeline is a **fb-pix** command to get an image from a frame buffer, just as a common end of a processing pipeline is a **pix-fb** command to display the final result. Several useful operations can be performed with direct interaction with a frame buffer, so some device-independent tools are provided, including tools to allow changing colormaps, panning and zooming through an image, moving a pointer, adding labeling, etc. (Table 11). Where tools require the user to move a cursor or the image and cursor support is not available, both **emacs**-style and **vi**-style keyboard motion commands are accepted by all programs.

Image Manipulation

A substantial collection of tools for image manipulation are provided as part of the package. These can generate statistics, histograms, extract parts of an image, rotate, scale, and filter them, etc. Space does not permit a discussion of all of the types of manipulation supported, but some of the more interesting tools are listed in Table 12.

Format Conversion

The N^2 problem of format conversion between all the different 'external' file formats is simplified by providing tools to convert all external file formats into the simple **pix** and **bw** formats. A selection of these conversion tools is listed in Table 13. In all of the tables, the tool for the reverse conversion is omitted, e.g., in addition to the **rle-pix** tool, there is also a **pix-rle** for converting color images into **rle** format. Also, only the color (**pix**) version of a tool has been listed even though most have black and white (**bw**) equivalents.

Most of the tools listed have a wide variety of options consistent with their basic function. For example, the tool to convert a color image to a black and white image (**pix-bw**) allows selection of color-blending values: equal weighting, NTSC weighting, or 'typical CRT' weighting. It also allows arbitrary weights to be given for selecting or mixing of the color planes in any way desired.

User Interface

Using software tools effectively comes with experience. The BRL CAD package has tried to ease the difficulty of learning a new set of tools by using a common set of flags and common tool-naming conventions throughout

Table 11. Selected frame buffer tools.

fb-pix	frame buffer to color image
fb-bw	frame buffer to black and white
fb-cmap	read a frame buffer color map
fbcmap	can load several 'standard' color maps
fbclear	clear to an optional RGB color
fbgamma	load or apply gamma-correcting color maps
fbzoom	general zoom and pan routine
fbpoint	select pixel coordinates
fblabel	put a label on an image
fbcolor	a color-selecting tool
fbscanplot	scanline RGB intensity plotter
fbanim	a 'postage-stamp' animator
fbcmrot	a color map rotator
fbed	a frame buffer image editor

the package. The 'user interface' is ultimately the Unix shell and its conventions for establishing pipes, passing arguments to programs, etc. A shell with history recall and screen-oriented command editing, such as the **tcsh**, is a major convenience when constructing complicated command pipelines.

Constructing very complex interconnections between processing tools from the command line is sometimes difficult. One limitation is the single-input, single-output notion of a Unix pipe. Image manipulation often calls for three or more channels of data, as with **pix-bw3**. The most common solution to this problem is the use of intermediate files. Other approaches

Table 12. Selected image tools.

pixstat	statistics—min, max, mean, etc.
pixhist	histogram
pixhist3d	RGB color space cube histogram
pixfilter	apply selected 3×3 filters
pixrect	extract a rectangle
pixrot	rotate, reverse, or invert
pixscale	scale up or down
pixdiff	compare two images
pixmerge	merge two/three images
pixtile	mosaic images together
gencolor	source a byte pattern
bwmod	apply expressions to each byte

Table 13. Selected format conversion tools.

g2asc	model database to portable ASCII form
bw-pix	black and white to color image
bw3-pix	three black and whites to color RGB
rle-pix	Utah's RLE format to color image
ap-pix	Applicon Ink-Jet to color image
sun-pix	Sun bit map to color or black and white
mac-pix	MacIntosh MacPaint bit maps to color

include extensions to the **tee** program, or a special tool such as **chan** [Moor85] which demultiplexes a stream, feeds each channel to a different program, and remultiplexes the results.

PIPELINE PROCESSING

Systems which facilitate the coupling of dataflow-oriented tools allow complex custom applications to be put together without writing any code. Consider this simple image-processing example:

```
pixinterp2x  − s512  < image.pix | \
pixfilter  − s1024  − lo | \
pixmerge  − n63/0/127  − −  − background.pix | \
pixrot  − r  − i 1024 1024 | \
pix−fb  − h
```

which roughly says: take the 512×512 color picture file in *image.pix* and perform bilinear interpolation to increase the image size to 1024×1024. Low-pass filter the large image with a 3×3 filter kernel, composite the filtered image with an existing color picture in *background.pix* with background replacement done on all pixels with RGB value 63/0/127, and then rotate the image 180 degrees and display it on the current frame buffer.

Note how no intermediate images are stored in disk files throughout the whole procedure. In this example, this may not be significant because the image at most stages required only 3 Mbytes of storage; but this becomes more important when manipulating 400 Mbyte image data, which is processed in exactly the same way.

It is also worth noting that for larger images, this type of image processing can take a significant amount of time. While operations like this could be performed in a batch mode, there is a significant advantage to being able to observe the progress of the computation. As the results arrive on the display, the opportunity exists to abort the whole process if something is going wrong. In addition to the savings of significant amounts of computer time, there is also the potential to save 'people time' by increasing the number of cases that can be attempted. Thus, the speed of the project (assuming that the computer-processing requirements are part of the critical path of the project) is increased.

This type of interactive processing works most effectively in an environment where each graphics user has his own multiwindow workstation (not necessarily a graphics workstation) so that the user can switch to another window and continue working while monitoring the progress of the graphics output. For example, a group of ten people, each with a dedicated, inexpensive monochrome workstation, might share the services of two or three color workstations using the network capabilities described below.

GENERAL NETWORK COMPUTING

Using UNIX interactively on a Cray is pretty heady stuff. Simply being able to open a 'Cray X-MP' window or a 'Cray-2' window on a workstation and having the same environment (shells, screen editors, compilers, source code tools, TCP networking, etc.) as on all the rest of the the network machines (Suns, SGIs, VAXen, Goulds, Alliants, etc.) is worth a lot. However, being able to rsh an image-processing command over to a Cray without having to make special arrangements to put the files over on the Cray first or having to submit a batch job harnesses the power of supercomputing without having to pay a stiff premium in inconvenience. For people acquainted with the Berkeley UNIX networking capabilities, the capabilities described in this section may seem trivial and almost not worthy of mention. People not acquainted with the ease and power of the Berkeley rsh remote shell command may be surprised at the hidden synergistic power that appears when this capability is combined with a good collection of tools.

While logged in on the console of an SGI workstation, in order to dynamically produce some plot data and then locally view the resulting **plot** file, this pipeline is needed:

```
cruncher | pl-sgi
```

In this case, 'cruncher' is assumed to produce a **plot** file on its standard output (*stdout*). The pl-sgi program reads a **plot** file on standard input (*stdin*) and produces a color wireframe display in a new window. However, if the computational speed of the workstation were inadequate, a slight variation could be used:

```
rsh Cray.arpa cruncher | pl-sgi
```

Simply by directing remote execution (via the rsh command) and naming the remote machine to perform the computation (in this case 'Cray.arpa'), the power of another machine is brought to bear on the task. The rsh command [Leff83] provides a number of significant features: (a) it connects to the specified machine and validates access permission; (b) it passes the specified command to a shell on the specified machine for parsing and execution; (c) it copies its standard input to the remote command; (d) the standard output of the remote command is copied to **rsh**'s standard output; (e) the standard error output of the remote command is returned separately and is copied to **rsh**'s standard error output; (f) local interrupt, quit, and terminate signals are propagated to the remote command; (g) **rsh** exits when the remote command does, returning the remote exit status. Therefore, performing an operation on a remote machine with **rsh** produces an effect that is indistinguishable from performing the same operation locally.

Another variation of this example might be useful if, instead of being logged in on the graphics workstation, you were logged in directly on the Cray and, after having finished some code development, you wished to see an image. In this case, the command would be:

```
cruncher | rsh Vax.arpa pl − fb
```

This would send the **plot** file to the machine 'Vax.arpa' and cause it to be displayed on a frame buffer. To generate a videotape to display the effect of varying a parameter in a simulation running on the Cray, with the display and videotape capability on the VAX, consider the following modest shell script (typed at the keyboard or run from a file):

```
for parm in 'loop 1 100 2'
do
      cruncher $parm | rsh Vax.arpa 'pl − fb; vas4 record 1'
done
```

This simple script runs the **loop** tool to generate all the integers between 1 and 100 inclusive, with an increment of 2, and assigns them to the shell variable **parm**. For each value of **parm**, the **cruncher** program is run with **parm** as a formal argument. The **plot** format output is sent to the VAX, displayed on the frame buffer, and then the **vas4** directs the Lyon-Lamb video animation controller to record the image onto one frame of videotape.

Now, consider this variation on the earlier image-processing example:

```
pixinterp2x − s512  <  image.pix | \
rsh Cray.arpa 'pixfilter − s1024 − lo' | \
rsh Alliant.arpa 'pixmerge − n 63/0/127 − − − background.pix' | \
rsh Vax.arpa 'pixrot − r − i 1024 1024 | pix−fb − h'
```

which roughly says: grab an image on my local machine, perform bilinear interpolation locally, send it first to the Cray for low-pass filtering, send it secondly to the Alliant for compositing with a background image, and then send it to a trusty VAX to (a) rotate the image 180 degrees and (b) display it on the frame buffer.

Having learned about `rsh`, the possibilities of such combinations of different tools running on different machines are staggering. With the proper infrastructure of computers, operating systems, display hardware, network software, and image-processing tools all connected together in compatible ways, the tremendous potential of distributed computing can be easily harnessed without users having to write any programs!

Shared-memory Parallel Processing

In the preceding section, we have seen how different processors can be harnessed to achieve a single goal. The discussion so far has focused on using multiple processors (a) within a single, multi-CPU system through the use of UNIX pipes, and (b) by distributing different tools in a pipeline to different machines on the network. This section extends the investigation into parallel processing one level further in order to harness the power of multiple processor machines to make a single application run faster. For the purposes of this discussion, the application to be parallelized is a ray-tracing program, but the techniques developed here are quite general.

THE NEED FOR SPEED

Images created using ray tracing have a reputation for consuming large quantities of computer time. For complex models, 10 to 20 hours of processor time to render a single frame on a DEC VAX-11/780–class machine is not uncommon. Using the ray-tracing paradigm for engineering analysis [Muus87c] often requires many times more processing than rendering a view of the model. Examples of such engineering analyses include the predictive calculation of radar cross-sections, heat flow, and bistatic laser reflectivity. For models of real-world geometry, running these analyses approaches the limits of practical execution times even with modern supercomputers. Three main strategies are being employed to attempt to decrease the amount of elapsed time it takes to ray trace a particular scene.

Advances in Algorithms for Ray Tracing

Newer techniques in partitioning space [Kapl85] and in taking advantage of ray-to-ray coherence [Arvo87] promise to continue to yield algorithms that do fewer and fewer ray/object intersections that do not contribute to the final results. Significant work remains to be done in this area, and an order of magnitude performance gain remains to be realized. However, there is a limit to the gains that can be made in this area.

Acquiring Faster Processors

A trivial method for decreasing the elapsed time to run a program is to purchase a faster computer. However, even the fastest general-purpose computers such as the Cray X-MP and Cray-2 do not execute fast enough to permit practical analysis of all real-world models in appropriate detail. Furthermore, the speed of light provides an upper bound on the fastest computer that can be built out of modern integrated circuits; this is already a significant factor in the Cray X-MP and Cray-2 processors, which operate with 8.5 ns and 4.3 ns clock periods, respectively.

Using Multiple Processors

By engaging the resources of multiple processors to work on a single problem, the speed-of-light limit is circumvented. However, the price is that explicit attention must be paid to the distribution of data to the various processors, synchronization of the computations, and collection of results.

Parallel processing is still a relatively young art, and presently only limited support is available for the automatic parallelization of existing code, with newer vendors like Alliant leading the crowd. For now, there are few general techniques for taking programs intended for serial operation on a single processor and automatically adapting them for operation on multiple processors [Ohr86]. The **Worm** program developed at Xerox PARC [Shoc82] is one of the earliest known network image-rendering applications. More recently at Xerox PARC, Frank Crow has attempted to distribute the rendering of a single image across multiple processors [Crow86] but discovered that communication overhead and synchronization problems limited parallelism to about 30 percent of the available processing power. A good summary of work to date has been collected by Peterson [Pete87].

Ray-tracing analysis of a model has the very nice property that the computations for each ray/model intersection are entirely independent of other ray/model intersection calculations. Therefore, it is easy to see how the calculations for each ray can be performed by separate, independent processors. The underlying assumption is that each processor has read-only access to the entire model database. While it is possible to partition the ray-tracing algorithm in such a way as to require only a portion of the model database being resident in each processor, this significantly increases the complexity of the implementation as well as the amount of synchronization and control traffic needed. Such a partitioning has therefore not yet been seriously attempted.

It is the purpose of the research reported in the rest of this paper to explore the performance limits of parallel operation of ray-tracing algorithms where available processor memory is not a limitation. While it is not expected that this research will result in a general-purpose technique for distributing arbitrary programs across multiple processors, the issues of the control and distribution of work and providing reliable results in a potentially unreliable system are quite general. The techniques used here are likely to be applicable to a large set of other applications.

RAY-TRACING BACKGROUND

The origins of modern ray tracing come from work at MAGI under contract to BRL initiated in the early 1960s. The initial results were reported by MAGI [MAGI67] in 1967. Extensions to the early developments were undertaken by a Department of Defense Joint Technical Coordinating Group effort, resulting in publications in 1970 [JTCG70] and 1971 [JTCG71]. A detailed presentation of the fundamental analysis and implementation of the ray-tracing algorithm can be found in these two documents. Also see [Appe68].

More recently, interest in ray tracing has developed in the academic community, with Kay's thesis in 1979 [Kay79] being a notable early work. One of the central papers in the ray-tracing literature is the work of Whitted [Whit80]. Model sampling techniques can be improved to provide substantially more realistic images by using the 'distributed ray tracing' strategy [Cook84]. For an excellent, concise discussion of ray tracing, consult Rogers [Roge85, pp. 363–381].

There are several implementation strategies for interrogating the model by computing ray/geometry intersections. The traditional approach has been batch-oriented, with the user defining a set of 'viewing angles', turning loose a big batch job to compute all the ray intersections, and then postprocessing all the ray data into some meaningful form. However, the major drawback of this approach is that the application has no dynamic control over ray paths, making another batch run necessary for each level of reflection, etc.

In order to be successful, applications need (a) dynamic control of ray paths to naturally implement reflection, refraction, and fragmentation into multiple subsidiary rays and (b) the ability to fire rays in arbitrary directions from arbitrary points. Nearly all nonbatch ray-tracing implementations have a specific, closely coupled application (typically, a model of illumination), which allows efficient and effective control of the ray paths. However, the most flexible approach is to implement the ray-tracing capability as a general-purpose library in order to make the function available to any application as needed. This is the approach taken in the BRL CAD package [Muus87b]. The ray-tracing library is called **librt**, while the ray-tracing application of interest here (an optical spectrum lighting model) is called **rt**.

THE STRUCTURE OF **librt**

In order to give all applications dynamic control over the ray paths and to allow the rays to be fired in arbitrary directions from arbitrary points, BRL has implemented its third-generation ray-tracing capability as a set of library routines. **librt** exists to allow application programs to intersect rays with model geometry. There are four parts to the interface: three preparation routines and the actual ray-tracing routine. The first routine that must be called is rt_dirbuild(), which opens the database file and builds the in-core database table of contents. The second routine to be called is rt_gettree(), which adds a database sub-tree to the active model space. rt_gettree() can be called multiple times to load different parts of the database into the active model space. The third routine is rt_prep(), which computes the space-partitioning data structures and does other initialization chores. Calling this routine is optional, as it is called by rt_shootray() if needed. rt_prep() is provided as a separate routine to allow independent timing of the preparation and ray-tracing phases of applications.

To compute the intersection of a ray with the geometry in the active model space, the application must call rt_shootray() once for each ray. Ray path selection for perspective, reflection, refraction, etc. is entirely determined by the application program. The only parameter for rt_shootray() is a **librt** 'application' structure, which contains five major elements: the vector a_ray.r_pt, which is the starting point of the ray to be fired; the vector a_ray.r_dir, which is the unit-length direction vector of the ray; the pointer *a_hit(), which is the address of an application-provided routine called when the ray intersects the model geometry; the pointer *a_miss(), which is the address of an application-provided routine called when the ray does not hit any geometry; and the flag a_onehit, which is set nonzero to stop ray tracing as soon as the ray has intersected at least one piece of geometry (useful for lighting models). Also included are various locations for each application to store state variables (recursion level, colors, etc.). Note that the integer returned from the application-provided a_hit()/a_miss() routine is the formal return of the function rt_shootray(). The rt_shootray() function is prepared for full recursion so that the a_hit()/a_miss() routines can themselves fire additional rays by calling rt_shootray() recursively before deciding their own return value.

In addition, the function rt_shootray() is serially and concurrently reentrant, using only registers, local variables allocated on the stack, and dynamic memory allocated with rt_malloc(). The rt_malloc() function serializes calls to **malloc**(3). By having the ray-tracing library fully prepared to run in parallel with other instances of itself in the same address space, applications can take full advantage of parallel hardware capabilities where such capabilities exist.

A Sample Ray-tracing Program

A simple application program that fires one ray at a model and prints the result is included below to demonstrate the simplicity of the interface to **librt**.

```
#include < brlcad/raytrace.h >
struct application ap;
main(){
    rt_dirbuild("model.g");
    rt_gettree("car");
    rt_prep();
    ap.a_point  =  [ 100,  0,  0 ];
    ap.a_dir  =  [ −1,  0,  0 ];
    ap.a_hit  =  &hit_geom;
    ap.a_miss  =  &miss_geom;
    ap.a_onehit  =  1;
    rt_shootray( &ap );
}
hit_geom(app,  part)
struct application  * app;
struct partition  * part;
{
    printf("Hit%s",  part− > pt_forw− > pt_regionp− > reg_name);
}
miss_geom(){
    printf("Missed");
}
```

NORMAL OPERATION: SERIAL EXECUTION

When running the **rt** program on a serial processor, the code of interest is the top of the subroutine hierarchy. The function **main()** first calls **get_args()** to parse any command line options, then **rt_dirbuild()** to acquaint **librt** with the model database and **view_init()** to initialize the application (in this case, a lighting model, which may call **mlib_init()** to initialize the material-property library). Finally, **rt_gettree()** is called repeatedly to load the model treetops. For each frame produced, the viewing parameters are processed, and **do_frame()** is called.

Within **do_frame()**, initialization is handled on a per-frame basis by calling **rt_prep()**, **mlib_setup()**, **grid_setup()**, and **view_2init()**. Then, **do_run()** is called with the linear pixel indices of the start and end locations in the image; typically, these values are zero and (width×length)−1 except for the ensemble computer case. In the nonparallel cases, the **do_run()** routine initializes the global variables **cur_pixel** and **last_pixel**, and calls worker(). At the end of the frame, view_end() is called to handle any final output and to print some statistics.

The worker() routine obtains the index of the next pixel that needs to be computed by incrementing cur_pixel, and calls rt_shootray() to interrogate the model geometry. view_pixel is called to output the results for that pixel. worker() loops, computing one pixel at a time, until cur_pixel > last_pixel, after which it returns.

When rt_shootray() hits some geometry, it calls the a_hit() routine listed in the application structure to determine the final color of the pixel. In this case, colorview() is called. colorview() uses view_shade() to do the actual computation. Depending on the properties of the material hit and the stack of shaders that are being used, various material-specific renderers may be called, followed by a call to rr_render() if reflection or refraction is needed. Any of these routines may spawn multiple rays, and/or recurse on colorview().

PARALLEL OPERATION ON SHARED-MEMORY MACHINES

By capitalizing on the serial and concurrent reentrancy of the **librt** routines, it is very easy to take advantage of shared-memory machines where it is possible to initiate multiple 'streams of execution' or 'threads' within the address space of a single process. In order to be able to ensure that global variables are only manipulated by one instruction stream at a time, all such shared modifications are enclosed in critical sections. For each type of processor, it is necessary to implement the routines RES_ACQUIRE() and RES_RELEASE() to provide system-wide semaphore operations. When a processor acquires a resource and any other processors need that same resource, they wait until it is released, at which time exactly one of the waiting processors then acquires the resource.

In order to minimize contention between processors over the critical sections of code, all critical sections are kept as short as possible, typically, to only a few lines of code. Furthermore, there are different semaphores for each type of resource accessed in critical sections. res_syscall is used to interlock all UNIX system calls and some library routines, such as **write**(2), **malloc**(3), **printf**(3), etc. res_worker is used by the function worker() to serialize access to the variable cur_pixel, which contains the index of the next pixel to be computed. res_results is used by the function view_pixel to serialize access to the result buffer. This is necessary because few processors have hardware multiprocessor interlocking on byte operations within the same word. res_model is used by the **libspl** spline library routines to serialize operations which cause further model refinement during the ray-tracing process, so that data structures remain consistent.

Application of the usual client-server model of computing suggests that one stream of execution be dedicated to dispatching the next task, while the rest of the streams of execution are used for ray-tracing computations. However, in this case, the dispatching operation is trivial and a 'self-dispatching' algorithm is used, with a critical section used to protect the shared variable cur_pixel. The real purpose of the function do_run() is to perform whatever machine-specific operation is required to initiate *npsw* streams of execution within the address space of the **rt** program, and then to have each stream call the function worker(), each with appropriate local stack space.

Each worker() function loops until no more pixels remain, taking the next available pixel index. For each pass through the loop, RES_ACQUIRE (res_worker) is used to acquire the semaphore, after which the index of the next pixel to be computed, cur_pixel, is acquired and incremented before the semaphore is released, i.e.,

```
worker() {
    while(1) {
        RES_ACQUIRE( & rt_g.res_worker );
        my_index  =  cur_pixel + +;
        RES_RELEASE( &rt_g.res_worker );
        if( my_index  >  last_pixel )
            break;
        a.a_x  =  my_index%width;
        a.a_y  =  my_index/width;
        ... compute ray parameters ...
        rt_shootray(&a);
    }
}
```

On the Denelcor HEP H-1000 each word of memory has a full/empty tag bit in addition to 64 data bits. RES_ACQUIRE is implemented using the Daread() primitive, which uses the hardware capability to wait until the semaphore word is full, then read it, and mark it as empty. RES_RELEASE is implemented using the Daset() primitive, which marks the word as full. do_run() starts additional streams of execution using the Dcreate (worker) primitive, which creates another stream that immediately calls the worker() function.

On the Alliant FX/8, RES_ACQUIRE is implemented using the hardware instruction test-and-set (TAS), which tests a location for zero. As an atomic operation, if the location is zero it sets it nonzero and sets the condition codes appropriately. RES_ACQUIRE embeds this test-and-set instruction in a polling loop to wait for acquisition of the resource. RES_RELEASE just zeros the semaphore word. Parallel execution is achieved by using the hardware capability to spread a loop across multiple processors, so a simple loop from zero to seven which calls **worker()** is executed in hardware concurrent mode. Each concurrent instance of **worker()** is given a separate stack area in the 'cactus stack'.

On the Cray X-MP and Cray-2, the Cray multitasking library is used. **RES_ACQUIRE** maps into **LOCKON**, and **RES_RELEASE** maps into **LOCKOFF**, while **do_run()** just calls **TSKSTART(worker)** to obtain extra workers.

PERFORMANCE MEASUREMENTS

An important part of the BRL CAD package is a set of five benchmark model databases and associated viewing parameters, which permit the relative performance of different computers and configurations to be made using a significant production program as the basis of comparison. For the purposes of this paper, only the 'Moss' database is used for comparison. Since this benchmark generates pixels the fastest, it places the greatest demands on any parallel processing scheme. The benchmark image is computed at 512×512 resolution.

The relative performance figures for running **rt** in the parallel mode with Release 1.20 of the BRL CAD package are presented below (Table 14). The Alliant FX/8 machine is brl-vector.arpa configured with eight Computational Elements (CEs), six 68012 Interactive Processors (IPs), and 32 Mbytes of main memory running Concentrix 2.0, a port of 4.2 BSD UNIX. The Cray X-MP/48 machine is brl-patton.arpa, serial number 213, with four processors, eight Mwords of main memory, and a clock period of 8.5 ns running UNICOS 2.0, a port of System V UNIX. Unfortunately, no comprehensive results are available for the Denelcor HEP, the only other parallel computer known to have run this code.

The multiple-processor performance of **rt** increases nearly linearly for shared-memory machines with small collections of processors. The slight speedup of the Alliant when the fifth processor is added comes from the fact that the first four processors share one cache memory, while the second four share a second cache memory. To date, **rt** holds the record for the best achieved speedup for parallel processing on both the Cray X-MP/48 and the Alliant. Measurements on the HEP before it was dismantled indicated that near-linear improvements continued through 128 streams of execution. This performance is due to the fact that the critical sections are very small, typically just a few lines of code, and that they account for an insignificant portion of the computation time. When **rt** is run in parallel and the number of processors is increased, the limit to overall performance is determined by the total bandwidth of the shared memory and by memory conflicts over popular regions of code and data.

Table 14. Parallel **rt** speedup versus number of processors.

No. of Processors	Alliant FX/8	Efficiency	Cray X-MP/48	Efficiency
1	1.00	100%	1.00	100%
2	1.84	92.0%	1.99	99.5%
3	2.79	93.0%	2.96	98.7%
4	3.68	92.0%	3.86	96.5%
5	4.80	96.0%		
6	5.70	95.0%		
7	6.50	92.9%		
8	7.46	93.3%		

Distributed Computation on Loosely-coupled Ensembles of Processors

The basic assumption of this design is that network bandwidth is modest, so that the number of bytes and packets of overhead should not exceed the number of bytes and packets of results. The natural implementation would be to provide a remote procedure call (RPC) interface to rt_shootray(), so that when additional subsidiary rays are needed, more processors could potentially be utilized. However, measurements of this approach on VAX, Gould, and Alliant computers indicates that the system-call and communications overhead is comparable to the processing time for one ray/model intersection calculation. This much overhead rules out the RPC-per-ray interface for practical implementations. On some tightly coupled ensemble computers, there might be little penalty for such an approach but, in general, some larger unit of work must be exchanged.

It was not the intention of the author to develop another protocol for remote file access, so the issue of distributing the model database to the **rtsrv** server machines is handled outside of the context of the **remrt** and **rtsrv** software. In decreasing order of preference, the methods for model database distribution that are currently used are Sun NFS, Berkeley **rdist**, Berkeley **rcp**, and ordinary DARPA **ftp**. Note that the binary databases need to be converted to a portable format before they are transmitted across the network, because **rtsrv** runs on a wide variety of processor types. Except for the model databases and the executable code of the **rtsrv** server process itself, no file storage is used on any of the server machines.

DISTRIBUTION OF WORK

The approach used in **remrt** involves a single dispatcher process, which communicates with an arbitrary number of server processes. Work is assigned in groups of scanlines. As each server finishes a scanline, the results are sent back to the dispatcher, where they are stored. Completed scanlines are removed from the list of scanlines to be done and from the list of scanlines currently assigned to that server. Different servers may be working on entirely different frames. Before a server is assigned scanlines from a new frame, it is sent a new set of options and viewpoint information.

The underlying communications layer used is the package (PKG) protocol, provided by the **libpkg** library, so that all communications are known to be reliable, and communication disruptions are noticed. Whenever the dispatcher is notified by the **libpkg** routines that contact with a server has been lost, all unfinished scanlines assigned to that server are requeued at the head of the 'work to do' queue, so that they will be assigned to the very next available server, allowing tardy scanlines to be finished quickly.

Distribution Protocol

When a server process **rtsrv** is started, the host name of the machine running the dispatcher process is given as a command line argument. The server process is started from a command in the dispatcher **remrt**, which uses **system**(3) to run the **rsh** program, or directly via some other mechanism. This avoids the need to register the **rtsrv** program as a system network daemon and transfers issues of access control, permissions, and accounting onto other, more appropriate tools. Initially, the **rtsrv** server initiates a PKG connection to the dispatcher process and then enters a loop reading commands from the dispatcher. Some commands generate no response at all, some generate one response message, and some generate multiple response messages. However, note that the server does not expect to receive any additional messages from the dispatcher until after it has finished processing a request, so that requests do not have to be buffered in the server. While this simplifies the code, it has some performance implications, which are discussed later.

In the first stage, the message received must be of type MSG_START, with string parameters specifying the pathname of the model database and the names of the desired treetops. If all goes well, the server responds with a MSG_START message; otherwise, diagnostics are returned as string parameters to a MSG_PRINT message and the server exits.

In the second stage, the message received must be of type MSG_OPTIONS or MSG_MATRIX. MSG_OPTIONS specifies the image size and shape, hypersampling, stereo viewing, perspective versus orthographic view, and control of randomization effects (the 'benchmark' flag), using the familiar UNIX command line option format. MSG_MATRIX contains the 16 ASCII floating-point numbers for the 4×4 homogeneous transformation matrix which represents the desired view.

In the third stage, the server waits for messages of type MSG_LINES, which specify the starting and ending scanline to be processed. As each scanline is completed, it is immediately sent back to the dispatcher process to minimize the amount of computation that could be lost in case of server or

communications failure. Each scanline is returned in a message of type
MSG_PIXELS. The first two bytes of that message contain the scanline number in network-order 16-bit binary. Following that are the 3 bytes of RGB
data that represent the scanline. When all the scanlines specified in the
MSG_LINES command are processed, the server again waits for another message, either another MSG_LINES command or a MSG_OPTIONS/MSG_MATRIX
command to specify a new view.

At any time, a MSG_RESTART message can be received by the server, which
indicates that it should close all of its files and immediately re-**exec**(2)
itself, either to prepare for processing an entirely new model or as an error
recovery aid. A MSG_LOGLVL message can be received at any time to enable
and disable the issuing of MSG_PRINT output. A MSG_END message suggests
that the server should commit suicide, courteously.

DISPATCHING ALGORITHM

The dispatching (scheduling) algorithm revolves around two main lists, the
first being a list of currently connected servers and the second being a list
of frames still to be done. For each unfinished frame, a list of scanlines
remaining to be done is maintained. For each server, a list of the currently
assigned scanlines is kept. Whenever a server returns a scanline, it is
removed from the list of scanlines assigned to that server and stored in the
output image and also in the optional attached frame buffer. (It can be
quite entertaining to watch the scanlines racing up the screen, especially
when using processors of significantly different speeds.) If the arrival of
this scanline completes a frame, then the frame is written to disk on the
dispatcher machine, timing data is computed, and that frame is removed
from the list of work to be done.

When a server finishes the last scanline of its assignment and more work
remains to be done, the list of unfinished frames is searched and the next
available increment of work is assigned. Work is assigned in blocks of
consecutive scanlines up to a per-server maximum assignment size. The
block of scanlines is recorded as the server's new assignment and is removed
from the list of work to be done.

RELIABILITY ISSUES

If the **libpkg** communications layer looses contact with a server machine,
or if **remrt** is commanded to drop a server, then the scanlines remaining in
the assignment are requeued at the head of the list of scanlines remaining
for that frame. They are placed at the head of the list so that the first
available server will finish the tardy work, even if it had gone ahead to
work on a subsequent frame.

Presently, adding and dropping server machines is a manual (or script-
driven) operation. It would be desirable to develop a separate machine-
independent network mechanism that **remrt** could use to inquire about

the current loading and availability of server machines, but this has not been done. This would permit periodic status requests to be made, and automatic reacquisition of eligible server machines could be attempted. Peterson's Distrib System [Pete87] incorporates this as a built-in part of the distributed computing framework, but it seems that using an independent transaction-based facility such as Pistritto's Host Monitoring Protocol (HMP) facility [Nata84] is a more general solution.

If the dispatcher fails, all frames that have not been completed are lost; on restart, execution resumes at the beginning of the first uncompleted frame. By carefully choosing a machine that has excellent reliability to run the dispatcher on, the issue of dispatcher failure can be largely avoided. However, typically no more than two frames are lost, minimizing the impact. For frames that take extremely long times to compute, it would be reasonable to extend the dispatcher to snapshot the work queues and partially assembled frames in a disk file to permit operation to resume from the last 'checkpoint'.

DISTRIBUTED **remrt** PERFORMANCE

Ten identical Sun-3/50 systems were used to test the performance of **remrt**. All had 68881 floating-point units and 4 Mbytes of memory, and all were in normal time-sharing mode, unused except for running the tests and the slight overhead imposed by /etc/update, **rwhod**, etc. To provide a baseline performance figure for comparison, the benchmark image was computed in the normal way using **rt** to avoid any overhead that might be introduced by **remrt**. The elapsed time to execute the ray-tracing portion of the benchmark was 2639 seconds; the preparation phase was not included but amounted to only a few seconds.

The 'speedup' figure of 0.993 for 1 CPU (Table 15) shows the loss of performance of 0.7 percent introduced by the overhead of the **remrt** to **rtsrv** communications versus the nondistributed **rt** performance figure. The primary result of note is that the speedup of the **remrt** network-distributed application is very close to the theoretical maximum speedup, with a total efficiency of 97.8 percent for the ten Sun case! The very slight loss of performance noticed (2.23 percent) is due mostly to 'new assignment latency' discussed further below. Even so, it is worth noting that the speedup achieved by adding processors with **remrt** was even better than the performance achieved by adding processors in parallel mode with **rt**. This effect is due mostly to the lack of memory and semaphore contention between the **remrt** machines.

Unfortunately, time did not permit configuring and testing multiple Alliants running **rtsrv** in full parallel mode, although such operation is supported by **rtsrv**.

When **remrt** is actually being used for producing images, many different types of processors can be used together. The aggregate performance of all

Table 15. **remrt** Speedup versus number of processors.

No. of	Ratios		Elapsed Seconds			
CPUs	Theory	Sun-3/50	Theory	Sun-3/50	Total Speedup	Efficiency
1	1.0000	1.0072	2639.0	2658	0.993	99.3%
2	0.5000	0.5119	1319.5	1351	1.953	97.7%
3	0.3333	0.3357	879.6	886	2.979	99.3%
4	0.2500	0.2524	659.7	666	3.949	98.7%
5	0.2000	0.2027	527.8	535	4.916	98.3%
6	0.1666	0.1686	429.8	445	5.910	98.5%
7	0.1429	0.1470	377.0	388	6.778	96.8%
8	0.1250	0.1266	329.9	334	7.874	98.4%
9	0.1111	0.1133	293.2	299	8.796	97.7%
10	0.1000	0.1019	263.9	269	9.777	97.8%

the available machines on a campus network is truly awesome, especially when a Cray or two is included! Even in this case, the network bandwidth required does not exceed the capacity of an Ethernet (yet). The bandwidth requirements are sufficiently small so that it is practical to run many **rtsrv** processes distributed over the ARPANET/MILNET. On one such occasion in early 1986, 13 Gould PN9080 machines were used all over the East Coast to finish some images for a publication deadline.

PERFORMANCE ISSUES

The policy of making work assignments in terms of multiple adjacent scanlines reduces the processing requirements of the dispatcher and also improves the efficiency of the servers. As a server finishes a scanline, it gives the scanline to the local operating system to send to the dispatcher machine, while the server continues with the computation, allowing the transmission to be overlapped with more computation. When gateways and wide-area networks are involved (with their accompanying increase in latency and packet loss), this is an important consideration. In the current implementation, assignments are always blocks of three scanlines because there is no general way for the **rtsrv** process to know what kind of machine it is running on and how fast it is likely to go. Clearly, it would be worthwhile to assign larger blocks of scanlines to the faster processors so as to minimize idle time and control traffic overhead. Seemingly the best way to determine this would be to measure the rate of scanline completion and dynamically adjust the allocation size. This is not currently implemented.

By increasing the scanline block assignment size for the faster processors, the amount of time the server spends waiting for a new assignment (termed 'new assignment latency') is diminished but not eliminated. Because the current design assumes that the server does not receive another request until the previous request has been fully processed, no easy solution exists. Extending the server implementation to buffer at least one additional request would permit this limitation to be overcome, and the dispatcher would then have the option of sending a second assignment before the first one had been completed to always keep the server 'pipeline' full. For the case of very large numbers of servers, this pipelining will be important to keep delays in the dispatcher from affecting performance. In the case of very fast servers, pipelining will be important in achieving maximum server utilization by overcoming network and dispatcher delays.

To obtain an advantage from the pipeline effect of the multiple scanline work assignments, it is important that the network implementations in both the servers and the dispatcher have adequate buffering to hold an entire scanline (typically 3K bytes). For the dispatcher, it is a good idea to increase the default TCP receive space (and thus the receive window size) from 4K bytes to 16K bytes. For the server machines, it is a good idea to increase the default TCP transmit space from 4K bytes to 16K bytes. This can be accomplished by modifying the file /sys/netinet/tcp_usrreq.c to read:

$$\texttt{int tcp\_sendspace} = 1024 * 16;$$

$$\texttt{int tcp\_recvspace} = 1024 * 16;$$

or to make suitable modifications to the binary image of the kernel using *adb*(1):

```
adb  − w  − k  /vmunix
tcp_sendspace?W  0x4000
tcp_recvspace?W  0x4000
```

The dispatcher process must maintain an active network connection to each of the server machines. In all systems there is some limit to the number of open files that a single process may use (symbol NOFILE); in 4.3 BSD UNIX, the limit is 64 open files. For the current implementation, this places an upper bound on the number of servers that can be used. As many campus networks have more than 64 machines available at night, it would be nice if this limit could be eased. One approach is to increase the limit on the dispatcher machine. Another approach is to implement a special 'relay server' to act as a fan-in/fan-out mechanism, although the additional latency could get to be an issue. A third approach is to partition the problem at a higher level. For example, having the east campus do the beginning of a movie and the west campus do the end would reduce the open file problem. Additionally, if gateways are involved, partitioning the problem may be kinder to the campus network.

Conclusions

Parallel computing is good. This paper has shown how it is possible to implement good graphics interfaces within the confines of a single uniprocessor machine. With the adoption of a 'software tools' approach when providing data handling capabilities, it was shown how to transparently take advantage of multiprocessor machines and to thus realize a speed advantage. Furthermore, the careful selection of file formats permitted realizing a further speed advantage in the accomplishment of a single task by utilizing multiple systems located across a network.

Carrying the theme of increased speed further, multiprocessor systems were examined as a vehicle for making single image-generation tools operate faster. An important result was to note that when operation in a shared-memory parallel environment was an initial design goal, the implementation of concurrently reentrant code did not significantly increase the complexity of the software. Having code with such properties allows direct utilization of nearly any shared-memory multiprocessor with a minimum of system-specific support, namely, the RES_ACQUIRE and RES_RELEASE semaphore operations and some mechanism for starting multiple streams of execution within the same address space.

Finally, collections of processors connected only by conventional speed network links are considered as the final environment for making a single tool operate faster using multiprocessing. It was shown that network-distributed computing need not be inefficient or difficult. The protocol and dispatching mechanism described in the preceding sections has been shown to be very effective at taking the computationally intensive task of generating ray-traced images and distributing it across multiple processors connected only by a communications network. There are a significant number of other application programs that could directly utilize the techniques and control software implemented in **remrt** to achieve network-distributed operation. However, the development and operation of this type of program is still a research effort; the technology is not properly packaged for widespread, everyday use. Furthermore, it is clear that the techniques used in **remrt** are not sufficiently general to be applied to all scientific problems. In particular, problems where each 'cell' has dependencies on some or all of the neighboring cells will require different techniques.

Massive proliferation of computers is a trend that is likely to continue through the 1990s and beyond. Developing software to utilize significant numbers of network-connected processors is the coming challenge. This paper has presented a strategy that meets this challenge and provides a simple, powerful, and efficient method for distributing a significant family of scientific analysis codes across multiple computers.

Acknowledgments. The author would like to thank Dr. Paul Deitz for providing unflagging support and encouragement, Phil Dykstra, Paul Stay, Gary Moss, Chuck Kennedy, and Bob Reschly for the long hours as we designed and built this software, and Prof. Dave Rogers for once again persuading me to write it all down.

The following strings that have been included in this paper are known to enjoy protection as trademarks; the trademark ownership is acknowledged in the table below.

Trademark	Trademark Owner
Cray	Cray Research, Inc.
Ethernet	Xerox Corporation
FX/8	Alliant Computer Systems Corporation
IBM 370	International Business Machines Corporation
MacIntosh	Apple Computer, Inc.
MacPaint	Apple Computer, Inc.
NFS	Sun Microsystems, Inc.
PowerNode	Gould, Inc.
ProNet	Proteon, Inc.
Sun Workstation	Sun Microsystems, Inc.
SunView	Sun Microsystems, Inc.
UNIX	AT&T Bell Laboratories
UNICOS	Cray Research, Inc.
VAX	Digital Equipment Corporation
VaxStation	Digital Equipment Corporation
X Window System	Massachusetts Institute of Technology

REFERENCES

[Appe68]
Appel, A., Some techniques for shading machine renderings of solids, *AFIPS 1968 Spring Joint Computer Conf.*, Vol. 32, pp. 37–45, 1968.

[Arvo87]
Arvo, J., and Kirk, D., Fast ray tracing by ray classification, *Comput. Graph.* (SIGGRAPH 87), Vol. 21, pp. 55–64, 1987.

[Cham86]
Chamberlain, S., Muuss, M.J., and Pistritto, J., *The BRL Fire Support Application for ADDCOMPE*, BRL Special Publication BRL-SP-53, April 1986.

[Cohe80]
Cohen, D., *On Holy Wars and a Plea for Peace, IEN-137*, DDN Network Information Center, Menlo Park, CA, April 1980.

[Conr80]
Conrac, *Raster Graphics Handbook*, New York: Van Nostrand Reinhold, 1980.

[Conv88]
Convex, *Convex Vector C Compiler User's Guide*, Convex Computer Corporation, Doc 720-630-200, Richardson, TX, January 1988.

[Cook84]
Cook, R.L., Porter, T., and Carpenter, L., Distributed ray tracing, *Comput. Graph.* (SIGGRAPH 84), Vol. 18, pp. 137–145, 1984.

[Cray82]
Cray, *Cray-1 Computer Systems Mainframe Reference Manual*, Cray Research Inc., HR-0029, Mendota Heights, MN, November 1982.

[Crow86]
Crow, F.C., *Experiences in Distributed Execution: A Report on Work in*

Progress, SIGGRAPH '86 Tutorial, Advanced Image Synthesis, Dallas, TX, August 1986.

[DCA83]
DCA, *MIL-STD-1777: Internet Protocol*, Defense Communications Agency, U.S. Government Printing Office, 12 August 1983.

[DEC76]
DEC, *Digital PDP-11/70 Processor Handbook*, Digital Equipment Corporation, Maynard, MA, 1976.

[DEC82]
DEC, *VAX Technical Summary*, Digital Equipment Corporation, Maynard, MA, 1982.

[Deit83]
Deitz, P.H., *Solid Geometric Modeling—The Key to Improved Materiel Acquisition from Concept to Deployment*, Defense Computer Graphics 83, Washington DC, 10–14 October 1983.

[Deit84]
Deitz, P.H., *Predictive Signature Modeling via Solid Geometry at the BRL*, Sixth KRC Symposium on Ground Vehicle Signatures, Houghton, MI, 21–22 August 1984.

[Deit85]
Deitz, P.H., *The Future of Army Item-Level Modeling*, Army Operations Research Symposium XXIV, Ft. Lee, VA, 8–10 October 1985.

[Deit88]
Deitz, P.H., Mermagen, W., Jr., and Stay, P., An integrated environment for Army, Navy, and Air Force target description support, *Proceedings of the Tenth Annual Symposium on Survivability/ Vulnerability*, April 1988.

[Duff85]
Duff, T., Compositing 3-D rendered images, *Comput. Graph.* (SIGGRAPH 85), Vol. 19, pp. 41–44, 1985.

[Fein85]
Feinler, E.J., Jacobsen, O.J., Stahl, M.K., and Ward, C.A., *DDN Protocol Handbook, NIC 50004*, DDN Network Information Center, Menlo Park, CA, December 1985.

[Gobl81]
Goble, G.H., and Marsh, M.H., *A Dual Processor VAX 11/780*, Purdue University Technical Report TR-EE 81-31, September 1981.

[Gwyn85]
Gwyn, D.A., ED., VLD(VMB) UNIX Supplementary Manual for System V, BRL Internal Publication, October 1985.

[Hall83]
Hall, R.A., *A Methodology for Realistic Image Synthesis*, MS Dissertation, Cornell University, Ithaca, NY, 1983.

[IBM70]
IBM, *IBM System/370 Principles of Operation*, International Business Machines Corporation, GA22-7000-4, Poughkeepsie, NY, 1970.

[IBM82]

IBM, *The Economic Value of Rapid Response Time*, International Business Machines Corporation, Poughkeepsie, NY, 1982.

[IEEE85]

IEEE, *ANSI/IEEE Standard 754 for Binary Floating-Point Arithmetic*, Institute of Electrical and Electronic Engineers, Piscataway, NJ, August 1985.

[JTCG70]

JTCG, *MAGIC Computer Simulation, Vol. 1, User Manual*, Joint Technical Coordinating Group for Munitions Effectiveness, 61JTCG/ME-71-7-1, July 1970.

[JTCG71]

JTCG, *MAGIC Computer Simulation, Vol. 2, Analyst Manual*, Joint Technical Coordinating Group for Munitions Effectiveness, 61JTCG/ME-71-7-2-1, May 1971.

[Kaha86]

Kahan, W., Liu, Z-S.A., McDonald, S., Ng, K-C., and Tang, P., *Introduction to Mathematical Library Functions*, The 4.3 Berkeley Software Distribution, Berkeley, CA, May 1986.

[Kapl85]

Kaplan, M.R., *Space-Tracing, a Constant Time Ray-Tracer*, SIGGRAPH 85 Tutorial, State of the Art in Image Synthesis, San Francisco, CA, July 1985.

[Kay79]

Kay, D.S., *Transparency, Refraction, and Ray Tracing for Computer Synthesized Images*, Master's Thesis, Cornell University, Ithaca, NY, January 1979.

[Kern76]

Kernighan, B.W., and Plauger, P.J., *Software Tools*, Reading, MA: Addison-Wesley, 1976.

[Kern78]

Kernighan, B.W., and Ritchie, D.M., *The C Programming Language*, AT&T Bell Laboratories, Murray Hill, NJ, 1978.

[Kern84]

Kernighan, B.W., and Pike, R., *The UNIX Programming Environment*, p. viii, Englewood Cliffs, NJ: Prentice Hall, 1984.

[Leff83]

Leffler, S.J., *Bug Fixes and Changes in 4.2BSD*, The 4.2 Berkeley Software Distribution, Berkeley, CA, July 1983.

[MAGI67]

MAGI, *A Geometric Description Technique Suitable for Computer Analysis of Both Nuclear and Conventional Vulnerability of Armored Military Vehicles*, MAGI Report 6701, AD847576, August 1967.

[McCo87]

McCormick, B.H., DeFanti, T.A., and Brown, M.D., Visualization in scientific computing, *Comput. Graph.*, Vol. 21, pp. C-7-8, 1987.

[Moor85]
Moore, R.F., *CARL Startup Kit*, Computer Audio Research Laboratory, University of California at San Diego, San Diego, CA, 1985.

[Muus78]
Muuss, M.J., *The Terminal Independent Graphics Package: System Design and Operation*, Army Research Office Report, September 1978.

[Muus79]
Muuss, M.J., *The Implementation of a Multi-Processor UNIX System: Preliminary Design*, Army Research Office Report No. 1127, October 1979.

[Muus83]
Muuss, M.J., Applin, K.A., Suckling, R.J., Moss, G.S., Weaver, E.P., and Stanley, C., *GED: An Interactive Solid Modeling System for Vulnerability Analysis*, BRL Technical Report ARBRL-TR-02480, NTIS AD No. A-126-657, March 1983.

[Muus87a]
Muuss, M.J., Why buy UNIX? *New Zealand Computer Scene and Office Automation*, No. 7, pp. 74–78, 1987.

[Muus87b]
Muuss, M.J., Dykstra, P., Applin, K., Moss, G., Davisson, E., Stay, P. and Kennedy, C., *Ballistic Research Laboratory CAD Package, Release 1.21*, BRL Internal Publication, Aberdeen, MD, June 1987.

[Muus87c]
Muuss, M.J., Understanding the preparation and analysis of solid models, in *Techniques for Computer Graphics*, Rogers, D.F., and Earnshaw, R.A., Eds., New York: Springer-Verlag, 1987.

[Muus87d]
Muuss, M.J., RT and REMRT—Shared memory parallel and network distributed ray-tracing programs, in *USENIX: Proceedings of the Fourth Computer Graphics Workshop*, October 1987.

[Nata84]
Natalie, R., Muuss, M.J., Kingston, D., Kennedy, C., and Gwyn, D., *The First BRL VAX UNIX Manual*, BRL Internal Publication, Aberdeen, MD, Fall 1984.

[Ohr86]
Ohr, S., Minisupercomputers mix vector speed, scalar flexibility, *Electronic Des.*, Vol. 34, pp. 107–114, 1986.

[Pete86]
Peterson, J.W., Bogart, R.G., and Thomas, S.W., The Utah raster toolkit, in *USENIX: Proceedings of the Third Computer Graphics Workshop*, 1986.

[Pete87]
Peterson, J.W., *Distributed Computation for Computer Animation*, Technical Report UUCS 87-014, University of Utah, Salt Lake City, UT, June 1987.

[Post81]
Postel, J., Internet Protocol Specification, RFC-791, in *DDN Protocol Handbook, Vol 2, NIC 50004*, DDN Network Information Center, Menlo Park, CA, September 1981.

[Quar86]
Quarterman, J.S., and Hoskins, J.C., Notable computer networks, *CACM*, Vol. 29, pp. 932–971, 1986.

[Rica87]
Ricart, G., Research university bandwidth estimates, in *A Report to the Congress on Computer Networks to Support Research in the United States: A Study of Critical Problems and Future Options, Volume III, A Compendium of Supporting Technical Data*, Federal Coordinating Council on Science, Engineering, and Technology, June 1987.

[Ritc78a]
Ritchie, D.M., and Thompson, K., The UNIX time-sharing system, *Bell Sys. Tech. J.*, Vol. 57, pp. 1905–1929, 1978.

[Ritc78b]
Ritchie, D.M., Johnson, S.C., Lesk, M.E., and Kernighan, B.W., The C programming language, *Bell Sys. Tech. J.*, Vol. 57, pp. 1991–2019, 1978.

[Roge85]
Rogers, D.F., *Procedural Elements for Computer Graphics*, New York: McGraw-Hill, 1985.

[Shoc82]
Shoch, J.F., and Hupp, J.A., The Worm programs—Early experience with a distributed computation, *CACM*, Vol. 25, p. 172, 1982.

[Sun87]
Sun, *XDR: External Data Representation Standard, RFC-1014*, DDN Network Information Center, Menlo Park, CA, June 1987.

[Tane81]
Tanenbaum, A.S., *Computer Networks*, Englewood Cliffs, NJ: Prentice-Hall, 1981.

[Toom82]
Toomay, J.C., *Radar Principles for the Non-Specialist*, London: Lifetime Learning Publications, 1982.

[Weav80]
Weaver, E.P., and Muuss, M.J., *Interactive Construction of COM-GEOM Targets*, BRL Spring Technical Conference, 1980.

[Weav82]
Weaver, E.P., and Deitz, P.H., Solid Modeling in Survivability/Vulnerability, *Proceedings of the Second Joint Technical Coordinating Group for Aircraft Survivability, Workshop on Survivability and Computer-Aided Design*, Vol. 1, U.S. Air Force Museum, Wright-Patterson AFB, Ohio, 1982.

[Whit80]
Whitted, J.T., An improved illumination model for shaded display, *CACM*, Vol. 23, pp. 343–349, 1980.

[Xero80]
Xerox, *The Ethernet, a Local Area Network: Data Link Layer and Physical Layer Specification*, X3T51/80-50, Xerox, Stamford, CT, October 1980.

7 Graphics Standards

Standardization in Computer Graphics

Günther E. Pfaff

Abstract

Standardization in computer graphics is already very important and will become still more significant in the future. Standardized interfaces allow the user to employ a great variety of different computers, graphics devices, and operating systems without changing the graphics application programs for each new system. Graphics data can be transferred between different systems, new devices can be plugged into existing configurations, and results are predictable when moving to a new environment. This report will outline the essential aspects of existing standards as well as standards-to-be.

Introduction

Since the Graphical Kernel System (GKS) has successfully become a standard, a flood of further standardization activities has followed. These activities are mainly concentrated on GKS-adjacent fields, but part of them also show intersections with GKS.

The five main systems will be introduced in this paper and will be compared using a meta-concept developed for today's graphics standards.

The standards and standard proposals described are:

the Graphical Kernel System (GKS);

the extension of GKS by 3D functions (GKS-3D);

the Programmer's Hierarchical Interactive Graphics System (PHIGS);

the Computer Graphics Metafile (CGM);

the Computer Graphics Interface CGI.

The structure of an overall system as shown in Figure 1 will first be discussed.

When an application program accesses graphics functions to generate a picture on a graphics device or to allow a graphics interaction with an operator at a device, any or all of the following components may be engaged:

the application program itself;

a graphics system—ISO standards for graphics systems are GKS, GKS-3D, and PHIGS;

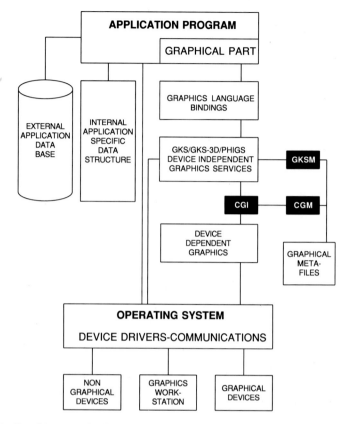

Figure 1. Graphics standards: overall structure.

the language binding for a graphics system—for all ISO graphics standards, representations of the functions are specified in the major programming languages such as FORTRAN, C, PASCAL, and ADA;

the graphics workstation, which translates functions of the particular graphic system at its workstation interface into the functions of the graphics device. The extent of this processing depends both on the functionality of the standard as well as on the functionality available in the device being driven. If a device conforms to the full CGI definition, the workstation software in a GKS system will be greatly reduced;

the graphics device, which can consist of hardware, firmware, and/or software. It is capable of presenting a physical representation of a picture and handling the physical interaction by an operator. Some devices have only output capabilities, e.g., plotters, some have only input capabilities, e.g., digitizers, and some have both, e.g., terminals;

metafiles—instead of presenting a picture on a device, a description of the picture can be routed to an archiving facility. Graphic metafiles are used to store pictures for later display or further processing.

This paper can certainly give but an introductory overview of graphics standards. For further information, the reader should consult the references, particularly [Ende87; Temp85].

Meta-concepts for Graphics Standards

Today's standards, including proposed standards, are all based on the same concepts, which were formed in the course of the discussion of GKS.

All systems are based on the concepts of workstations, output elements called primitives and primitive attributes, pictures, picture structuring and manipulations, coordinate systems and transformations , and input and interaction. A short introduction to these concepts is given below to make comparison of the different systems possible. These standards all have the same objectives:

the independence of programming of physical graphics devices, which allows portability of programs to be maintained and protects the investment in programs everywhere a graphics standard is used;

the efficient use of existing computer and device functions;

provision of suitable functions to solve application problems;

interchange of information between different systems, applications, and users. Pictures, programs, and programming knowledge can thus be repeatedly used which, in turn, protects investments and saves money.

Workstations

In general, workstations are abstractions of graphics devices. They are used to combine the different characteristics of physical devices with abstract and higher order characteristics. The applications are then programmed with 'logical devices' or workstations instead of using pen plotters or raster plotters, bitmap screens or color raster screens, or digitizers or keyboards.

The workstation concept is thus the real basis for portability of programs.

Graphics Output

Pictures are always set up using either vectors and/or raster graphics. The standards define graphic primitives to represent graphic objects on the different output media. Attributes are used to describe the appearance of the graphics elements.

Input and Interaction

Logical input devices are defined for programming of interactive graphics applications. Strictly speaking, logical input devices are input data types. The application program thus defines only the required data type but not the method by which the user inputs data into the program. The realization of the logical input devices using the large number of available physical input devices is determined by the implementations of the standards.

Attributes

Every graphics standard distinguishes between primitive attributes and picture structure attributes. Primitive attributes are either statically allocated to output elements, or they may be dynamically modified during picture representation. The attributes of picture structures can always be dynamically modified.

Picture Structuring and Picture Manipulation

Interactive applications typically have to manipulate pictures and picture parts. The relevant standards, therefore, include possibilities for picture structuring. The degree of picture structuring is application-dependent. Highly interactive applications with fast picture modifications require very complex capabilities for structuring the objects to be manipulated, while applications with emphasis on picture output need little or no structuring. The range of functionality with picture structuring, therefore, comprises single-stage mechanisms (overall picture–output elements) and two-level structuring (overall picture–segments–output elements) as well as hierarchical structures.

Coordinate Systems and Transformations

Every system distinguishes between device coordinates, virtual picture coordinates, world coordinates, and modelling coordinates. Depending on its scope, a standard will include only the first two of the above coordinate systems (metafiles and graphics drivers) or the first three of the above coordinate systems if the coordinates additionally serve to define and manipulate pictures. All of the coordinate systems listed above will be included if the standard also covers the modelling of graphics objects.

GKS

In July 1985, GKS became an international standard [ISO85]. This standard has been adopted as a national standard by many countries. Several language bindings have been defined for GKS and have been published as additional standards, e.g., for FORTRAN, PASCAL, ADA, and C. The GKS standard defines a standard interface between an application program and the graphic system. GKS offers the basic capabilities of generating 2D graphic representations. It supports interactive graphic data processing with functions for interactive control and for data input by the operator, for picture structuring and manipulation, and for the storing and retrieving of pictures.

The Applications of GKS

The applications of GKS comprise the generation of technical and commercial data representations as 2D and 3D drawings (Figures 2–4). GKS also supports applications of cartography, process control, and the various CAx-areas. Obviously, the large variety of applications place different requirements on GKS implementations as well as its use by computer and graphics devices.

Output Primitives

GKS offers six output primitives to draw lines, to mark a set of points, to output text, to display areas with a homogeneous structure, and to display a structure defined on a raster level. The sixth primitive is a generalized drawing primitive that allows nonstandardized display capabilities. The basic elements are as follows (see Figure 5):

POLYLINE—GKS generates a polyline with given corner points;

POLYMARKER—GKS generates at each point of a given set of points a centered symbol;

TEXT—GKS generates a character string at a given position;

Figure 2. GKS cartographic application.

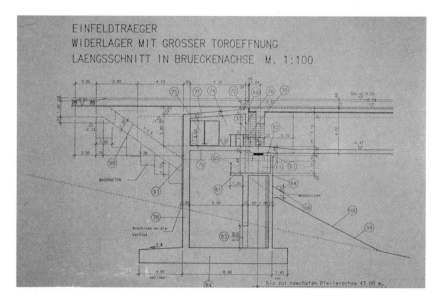

Figure 3. GKS CAD application.

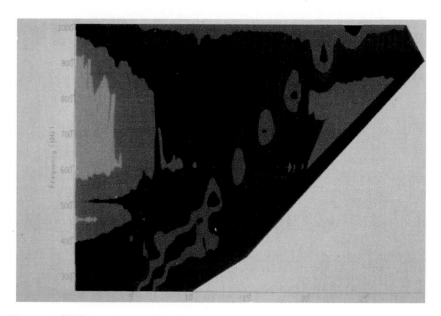

Figure 4. GKS mapping application.

FILL AREA—GKS generates an area defined by a given set of points. The area may be filled with a uniform color, a pattern, or a hatch or by only drawing the boundary;

CELL ARRAY—GKS generates a raster picture out of a given cell array;

GENERALIZED DRAWING PRIMITIVE—This element allows the address of output capabilities of devices not covered by the other output primitives, such as the drawing of interpolation curves and circular arcs. GKS does not interpret the parameters but only passes them to single workstations which generate the corresponding picture elements from the parameters. GKS sends additional data that enables the workstation to correctly transform and clip the element.

ATTRIBUTES FOR PRIMITIVES

GKS defines two kinds of attributes: global attributes that are valid on all connected workstations and workstation-specific attributes that are valid only on a specific workstation. Global attributes are immediately linked to the primitives and can thus no longer be modified after the primitive has been displayed. Workstation-specific attributes are chosen via so-called bundle indices from a bundle table. This indirect attribute setting allows attributes to be redefined and thus causes dynamic modification of attributes. An example is the dynamic modification of color via the color look-up table of color raster devices; the picture thus already drawn changes dynamically.

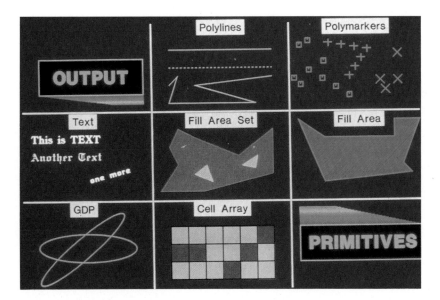

Figure 5. Output Primitives.

Global attributes are:

POLYLINE:	polyline index
	— linetype
	— line width scale factor
	— polyline color index
	pick identifier
POLYMARKER:	polymarker index
	— marker type
	— marker size scale factor
	— polymarker color index
	pick identifier
TEXT:	text index
	— text font and precision
	— character expansion factor
	— character spacing
	— text color index
	character height
	character up vector
	text path
	text alignment
	pick identifier
FILL AREA:	fill area index
	— interior style
	— style index
	— fill area color index
	pattern size
	pattern reference point
	pick identifier
CELL ARRAY:	pick identifier
GENERALIZED DRAWING PRIMITIVE:	several sets of (a) to (d) or none with the except that the pick identifier is always an attribute

GKS defines the following workstation-specific attribute tables:

polyline bundle table;

polymarker bundle table;

text bundle table;

fill area bundle table;

pattern table;

color table.

Their content is always addressed via an index, e.g., polyline index, fill area index, color index. The 13 workstation attributes included in the bundle tables may also be used as global direct attributes. A simultaneous use of these attributes as global and as workstation-specific attributes is, of course, not possible. The user may indicate via the *aspect source flag* for each of the 13 attributes whether the attribute is to be an individually set global attribute or a workstation-specific attribute taken from a bundle of a bundle table.

COORDINATE SYSTEMS AND TRANSFORMATIONS

GKS defines the following coordinate systems:

world coordinates;
normalized device coordinates;
device coordinates (see Figure 6).

In a first step, the world coordinates passed with each output primitive are mapped onto an abstract display space which is described by normalized device coordinates (NDC). This display space is used for segment storage and metafile storage.

The normalized device coordinate system is conceptually designed without boundaries, although only the unit square [0,1 × 0,1] or parts of it can be mapped onto the specified display space of a workstation. Segments outside the unit square can, however, be returned into the interior via segment manipulation and thus can be made visible.

In a second step, normalized device coordinates are mapped onto device coordinates (DC). The device coordinates describe the display space and/or

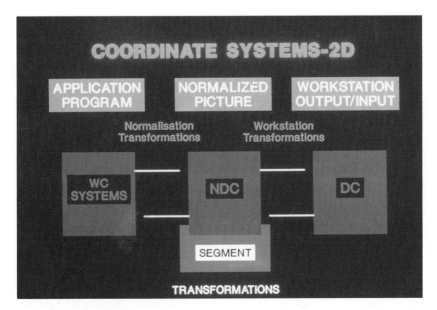

Figure 6. Transformations.

the input space on a specified workstation. Because specified areas are always limited, the device coordinate space is also limited. The unit for device coordinates is meters. They are mainly used to draw accurately scaled pictures. Devices such as projectors, which cannot be allocated an exact size in display space, can use other units.

The mapping of world coordinates onto normalized device coordinates is executed via the normalization transformation; the mapping of normalized device coordinates onto device coordinates is done via the workstation transformation. All output elements execute this mapping. Coordinate input executes the mapping backwards so that the coordinates entered on the device level are returned in world coordinates and can then be used directly to define new output primitives.

Both transformations are defined using rectangles parallel to the coordinate axes. The normalization transformation is specified by a 'window' in world coordinates and a 'viewport' in normalized device coordinates, and the workstation transformation by a 'workstation window' in normalized device coordinates and a 'workstation viewport' in device coordinates.

Apart from the two transformations described above, transformations exist that are applied to segments and that map normalized device coordinates onto normalized device coordinates. These transformations are described later.

GRAPHICS WORKSTATIONS

GKS is based on the concept of abstract graphics workstations (Figure 7). The application program controls the physical devices via the logical interface formed by the workstation. Certain special graphics workstations offer the capabilities of storing and exchanging graphics information (segment storage and metafiles) .

Each workstation available in a GKS implementation (except for specific graphics workstations) has its own workstation description table which describes its capabilities and characteristics. The application program can inquire as to what capabilities are available and can thus adapt its behavior. Each graphics workstation belongs to one of the following six categories:

output workstation—has one display surface but no possibilities of input (e.g., a plotter);

input workstation—has at least one input device but does not offer any output capabilities (e.g., a digitizer);

input/output workstation—combines the capabilities of an output workstation with the capabilities of an input workstation. It therefore has at least one input device and a display surface that is generally used to display primitives as well as dialogue information. Examples of those workstations are most terminals that have input devices such as a keyboard, mouse, light pen, tablet, crosshair, etc.;

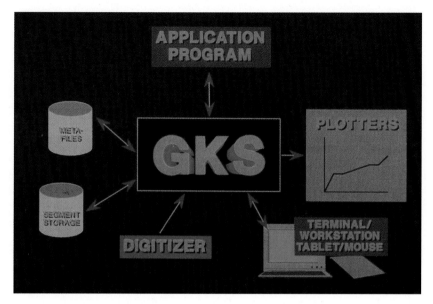

Figure 7. Workstation Concept.

workstation-independent segment storage—serves to temporarily store GKS segments, which can then be copied to all other GKS output workstations or which can be reused for segment definition;

GKS metafile output—the metafile serves for long-term storage of graphics information in a standard format and can be transmitted between suitable GKS systems;

GKS metafile input—the GKS workstation is separately defined to read in and interpret a GKS metafile.

GRAPHICS INPUT

An application program receives graphics input data via logical input devices. These are controlled by the operator and deliver logical input data.

A logical input device is defined by the workstation identifier, an input class, and a device number. The implementor determines the implementation of the logical input devices to one or more physical devices.

GKS defines six input classes, which correspond to the six possible input data types possible:

Locator—The locator device delivers a position in world coordinates and the normalization transformation number of the viewport in which the position entered is located. When this position is situated in several viewports at the same time, the viewport with the highest priority is chosen. Suitable physical input devices are a crosshair, mouse, tablet, digitizer, and light pen but also keyboards to input the coordinates.

Stroke—The stroke device delivers a sequence of positions in world co-ordinates and the normalization transformation number of the viewport with the highest priority in which the positions are located. All physical input devices capable to input positions can be used for the implementations of stroke devices (as with the locator).

Valuator—The valuator device delivers a real value. The operator can adjust this number at a graphics device (e.g., at a potentiometer), enter the number (e.g., via the keyboard), or adjust it using a simulation technique and another graphics device (e.g., a ruler with a pointing device).

Choice—The choice device delivers a positive integer value chosen out of a number of alternatives. Input devices often used are function keyboards, screen menus, tablets, or digitizers.

Pick—The pick device delivers a segment name and a pick identifier as well as a status indicating whether or not a segment has been picked. Output elements that are not stored in segments cannot be picked. Segments are usually picked by positioning a crosshair on an output element within the segment using a tablet or a mouse.

String—The string device delivers a character string which is usually entered via an alphanumeric keyboard.

Each logical input device can be operated in three different modes, the so-called operating modes; the application program can always select one of these modes. The three operating modes are REQUEST, SAMPLE, and EVENT. Depending on the operating mode, input values are differently entered and passed to the application program:

REQUEST—A call to the REQUEST function reads a logical input value from the logical input device specified. GKS waits until the operator has entered the input or has caused an interrupt by pressing, for instance, a special break key.

SAMPLE—On calling a SAMPLE function, the current logical input value of the logical input device specified is reported without waiting for an operator action.

EVENT—GKS maintains an input queue containing chronologically ordered event reports. An event report contains the identification of the logical input device and the logical input value. The event report is asynchronously generated by operating the active input devices.

The functions described above may only be called if the input device addressed is in the relevant operating mode. Figure 8 shows an interactive GKS application using CHOICE and LOCATOR input functions.

SEGMENTS

Segments are used to create structures within pictures. Segments can be addressed and manipulated via segment operations. In GKS, output elements can both be grouped in segments and generated outside segments.

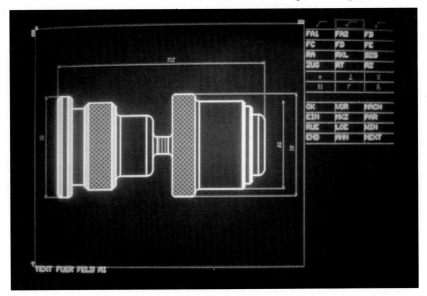

Figure 8. Interactive GKS Application (GKSCAD).

Each segment is characterized by a segment name, which is defined by the application. The segment operations possible are copying (COPY SEGMENT TO WORKSTATION, ASSOCIATE SEGMENT WITH WORKSTATION), transformations (SET SEGMENT TRANSFORMATION), renaming (RENAME SEGMENT), delete (DELETE SEGMENT, DELETE SEGMENT FROM WORKSTATION), detectability (SET DETECTABILITY), priority modification (SET SEGMENT PRIORITY), highlighting (SET HIGHLIGHTING), insertion (INSERT SEGMENT), and visibility modification (SET VISIBILITY).

A GKS segment is stored on all workstations active at the time of segment generation. In case a graphics device does not offer segment storage (such as a plotter or storage tube) this will be handled within GKS. All GKS workstations thus have the same functional behavior. After a segment has been closed, primitives within it can neither be modified nor can new segments be added. A function to enlarge a segment after it has been closed is also not provided. Geometric transformations, modifications of a segment's characteristics as well as changes of the workstation-specific attributes used within the segment are, on the other hand, possible.

Every output primitive within a segment has a pick identifier associated with it. This forms a second level of naming. They are used to identify parts within segments. Such parts are distinguished only during input; they cannot be individually manipulated. This stage of naming is intended to support applications for which a large number of picture parts must be distinguished during input but which need not be manipulated.

Segments can be modified via segment attributes. Those are visibility, highlighting, segment priority, detectability, and segment transformation.

Workstation-dependent and Workstation-independent Segment Storage

A workstation-dependent segment storage is conceptually available for every output workstation and input/output workstation from GKS level 1a and up. It guarantees that segment attributes can be altered or segments can be deleted.

Only one workstation-independent segment storage (WISS) is defined to store and transmit output primitives and attributes within a segment from one graphics workstation to another or to insert them into an open segment. The segments stored in the WISS can be re-used via the functions COPY SEGMENT TO WORKSTATION, ASSOCIATE SEGMENT WITH WORKSTATION, and INSERT SEGMENT. The implementor must decide whether to realize the workstation-independent segment storage within GKS or to use the capabilities of a specific device and the relevant device driver.

The GKS Metafile

GKS provides functions to read and write a metafile, the so-called GKS metafile (GKSM). A metafile is a means to transmit and store pictures in an application- and device-independent way. A metafile has the following tasks:

to store graphic information in machine-readable form—the metafile is the basis for spooling and for graphics editor systems which allow the plotting of pictures on peripherals or the modification or processing of pictures later in a session;

to transport graphic information from one place to another via a storage medium (for instance, via a magnetic tape) as well as via networks;

to exchange pictures between different graphic configurations;

to save graphic information and reboot applications that were interrupted by a system breakdown. The metafile then serves as a log file for the pictures generated or modified by the user.

The GKS functions to read and write a GKS metafile are part of the GKS standard. The format of the metafile is described in an appendix of the GKS document. This appendix, however, is not part of the GKS standard. There is, on the other hand, an independent metafile standard defined by ISO. It describes both the contents and the format of pictures and can be used by GKS systems. (See the later section on the Computer Graphics Metafile.)

During output, graphics metafile data sets are generated by calling GKS output and attribute functions. User data sets with contents specified by the application may be stored on the metafile by calling the function WRITE ITEM TO GKSM.

The Graphical Kernel System-3D

In 1983, the ISO-WG2 started to work on an extension of the graphics standard GKS. This extension was to have, among others, the following characteristics:

all GKS application programs must run on GKS-3D implementations without any modifications;

the GKS concepts such as workstations, segments, logical input functions, and logical output functions are to be extended by 3D concepts such as camera model and logical 3D functions for input and output.

In 1987 a description of GKS-3D was published by ISO [ISO87a] which became an international standard in 1988.

APPLICATION OF GKS-3D

Many applications involving graphic representations and interactions with the user are based on 3D user models. Classic examples are:

models of buildings in the construction industry;

models of building parts in mechanical engineering;

representation models of physical objects (e.g., molecular structures);

statistical data or functions to be displayed in 3D representations.

GKS-3D can support these applications in several aspects:

Display—GKS-3D supports perspective or parallel display of 3D output elements such as lines and areas (Figure 9). It allows the definition of any view as well as the display of several simultaneous views on one device. As an optional function, the removal of hidden lines and hidden surfaces is available.

Picture manipulation—GKS-3D allows the definition of 3D segments that can be transformed in space (e.g., rotated). In addition, the user may freely choose his viewing position. It is thus possible to move objects once generated by the application program (e.g., a vehicle) or to look at objects (e.g., a building) from different sides without regenerating the picture (Figure 10).

Input—Three-dimensional positions or point sequences can be input via the combination of 2D input devices such as a tablet plus keyboard or 3D input devices such as a joystick with rotation around the Z-axis. They can also be input via real 3D input devices such as scanning devices. These input values may be used for controlling picture modifications as well as for the input of coordinates for application programs.

GKS-3D naturally offers the same advantages as GKS(-2D), for instance, device-independence or the possibility of picture storage and picture exchange on the metafile level. The definition of the GKS-3D standard is discussed in more detail below.

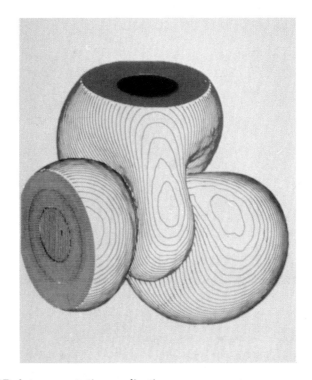

Figure 9. 3D data presentation application.

GRAPHIC OUTPUT

Just as does GKS, GKS-3D contains device-independent output elements to display points, lines, areas, and text. The application program uses these functions to generate a logical 3D picture. Points and lines are nonplanar primitives located in 3D space; areas and texts, however, are planar output elements located on 2D planes in 3D space.

GKS-3D also supports the GKS(-2D) display functions to preserve compatibility with GKS. These functions are mapped onto a predefined plane in 3D space. It is thus possible to integrate existing 2D applications into new GKS-3D applications with a minimum of effort.

An additional primitive has been defined in GKS-3D: **FILL AREA SET**. This function allows display of areas with holes. A separate set of attributes has been defined for these primitives. For the interior, the attributes correspond to the **FILL AREA** attributes. For the boundaries, the new attributes (**EDGE** representation) correspond to the **POLYLINE** attributes.

GRAPHIC INPUT

This group of functions defines a device-independent interface between the operator and the application program. GKS-3D maps the set of different

Figure 10. 3D design object viewing application.

physical input devices onto eight logical input device classes. First, there are coordinate-independent input devices for text input (e.g., a keyboard), choice (e.g., menu input), value input (e.g., a joystick), and the input of segment names. They are identical to the corresponding logical input devices of GKS.

On the other hand, GKS(-2D) and GKS-3D offer the possibility of point input as well as the input of point sequences. The logical 3D input devices correspond to only a few physical 3D input devices. As a result, most of the time they have to be simulated on a GKS-3D workstation using available 2D physical input devices.

GRAPHICS WORKSTATIONS

The workstation concept of GKS-3D is identical to that of GKS(-2D). Workstations in GKS-3D, however, always have 3D capabilities, i.e., they accept and store output elements in 3D normalized coordinates and they perform the projections from 3D to 2D coordinates, and vice versa for input. They also support graphics devices with integrated 3D capabilities (oscillating mirrors, holographic devices, etc.).

COORDINATE SYSTEMS AND TRANSFORMATIONS

GKS-3D defines five different coordinate systems. The application program passes all the output elements in the world coordinate system (WC3) to

GKS-3D. This is the coordinate system in which the object to be displayed is defined (the units may, for instance, be meters when displaying a house or light years when displaying a star system). An application may also identify several world coordinate systems. All world coordinate systems are mapped into the normalized coordinate system (NDC3). The objects of the different 'worlds' are combined there into a 3D picture. Groups of defined output elements may still be moved or rotated in 3D space (in general, transformed) via the segment transformation.

The coordinate systems that follow can best be compared with photography. The transmission from NDC3 to the viewing reference coordinates (VRC) does not alter the object but determines the position and the viewing direction, as does a photographer. In similar manner, viewing reference coordinates allow the user to freely move around his object and to look at it from different angles and distances.

The next transformation describes the projection of the 3D picture from the viewer's position. Projection parameters are the projection window (depending on the focal length of the lens) and the selection of perspective or parallel projection. The projected picture is created in the normalized projection coordinate system (NPC) (Figure 11). This coordinate system is three-dimensional, but the third dimension is used only as depth information for hidden line/hidden surface (HL/HS) processing which starts here. Projection can be avoided for real 3D devices (e.g., holography) so that the NPC system forms a real 3D coordinate system for this device class.

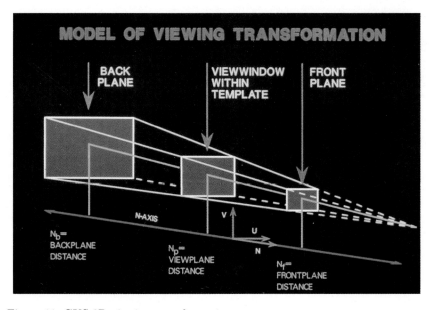

Figure 11. GKS-3D viewing transformations.

The device transformation, the last transformation, maps the generated picture onto the device surface, the device coordinates. This transformation no longer allows any distortion. It merely serves as an optimum mapping of the device-independent NPC onto the different physical output systems.

To sum up:

the mapping of world coordinates onto normalized device coordinates allows the generation of 3D pictures of different objects;

the segment transformation serves to move subpictures as representations of objects (e.g., to rotate the wheels of a car);

in the viewing reference coordinate system the observer positions himself in front of the object;

the normalized projection coordinate system contains the projected picture;

the device transformation maps the picture onto the graphics output device.

Hidden line/hidden surface algorithms calculate all visible parts for a picture on a graphics workstation and display them on the output surface. Hidden elements are suppressed. GKS-3D does not define the details of hidden line/hidden surface algorithms nor does it require the existence of such algorithms in a GKS-3D implementation.

Picture Structuring and Picture Manipulation

The segment concept of GKS-3D is, apart from some minor extensions, identical to that of GKS.

Segments are groups of output elements defined by each individual application. If such a subpicture is to be highlighted interactively on the display or to be rotated with the segment transformation, only an attribute of this segment must correspondingly be redefined.

Segments in GKS-3D are always 3D definitions. This applies even if segments are only generated from 2D output elements (which exist in GKS-3D for reasons of compatibility). The segment transformation in GKS-3D consists of a 4×4 matrix. Two utility functions are available to set this matrix.

Picture Archiving

A GKS Metafile (GKSM-3D) is defined in GKS-3D that fulfills the same functionality of picture archiving as does the GKSM in GKS.

GKSM-3D contains 3D output elements as well as the corresponding attributes. Furthermore, GKSM-3D contains all segment functions, attribute functions, and control functions corresponding to GKSM.

The GKSM(-2D) cannot fulfill the required functionality of picture archiving in a GKS-3D system, since it cannot store the 3D picture. GKSM(-2D) can, however, be connected as a special workstation to store device-independent 2D pictures, e.g., to produce device-specific plotfiles from the GKSM files.

Programmer's Hierarchical Interactive Graphics System

Simultaneous to GKS-3D, PHIGS has been defined by the American National Standards Institute (ANSI) and brought forward to the ISO WG2 [ISO87b]. The concepts of PHIGS were strongly influenced by today's graphics hardware technologies. In certain areas, PHIGS was consciously made incompatible with the GKS standard for the sake of performance and functionality as will be shown below. PHIGS became a draft international standard in 1987 and was adopted as an international standard in late 1988.

The PHIGS standard comprises the following concepts:

system and workstation control;
output elements;
bundle attributes;
individual attributes;
attribute filters;
transformations;
structure definitions;
structure modifications;
structure display;
structure storage;
request input, sample input, event input;
inquiry functions;
error handling.

It is obvious that PHIGS basically has the same concepts that were defined in GKS. Differences arise with

the possibilities of picture structuring;
the concept of centralized structure storage;
the possibilities of picture editing;
the precision and control of picture structure attributes;
the modelling transformation.

The basic difference, i.e., the concept of the centralized structure storage, will be discussed first.

In the GKS philosophy, model data are stored outside of GKS in the application. GKS serves to display and possibly store the representations of the current model data. The smallest unit that can then be modified is a segment—the single-stage combination of output elements and attributes.

This picture is available and, conceptually, is stored on all workstations. This results in *decentralized* picture storage. Global storage may additionally be available (the workstation-independent segment storage) from which pictures and picture parts can be copied to the workstations.

In the PHIGS philosophy, model data are kept inside the graphic system. Data is stored in the centralized structure storage (or at least the graphics part of the model) and kept at a central place within the system. The different workstations connected *do not*, conceptually, stoi ? the pictures. For each workstation a processor (traverser) running through the centralized structure storage interprets the pictures and generates output. Picture parts (substructures) may be interpreted and displayed separately for reasons of efficiency. PHIGS thus offers the concept of a *central* picture storage that holds arbitrarily structured pictures stored hierarchically.

While, in GKS, picture definition and picture output are combined (except for the output buffer command), PHIGS distinguishes between picture definition, picture editing, and picture representation. Figure 12 shows the model.

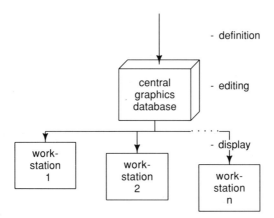

Figure 12. PHIGS organizational model.

Application of PHIGS

The emphasis in the application of PHIGS is, as its name indicates, put on interactive applications with high requirements on execution time and possibilities of picture manipulation (Figures 13 and 14). Examples are:

robotics (simulation and control);

the modelling of molecular structures;

graphics systems for command and control;

simulation systems for the control of aircraft, ships, and automotive vehicles;

process control systems;

finite element systems;

3D CAD systems in mechanics, architecture, etc.

PHIGS applications obviously overlap with those of GKS and GKS-3D. The complexity of PHIGS certainly makes it less appropriate for 2D graphics applications as well as for 3D applications in which the objects to be processed do not have a hierarchical data structure. It should, furthermore,

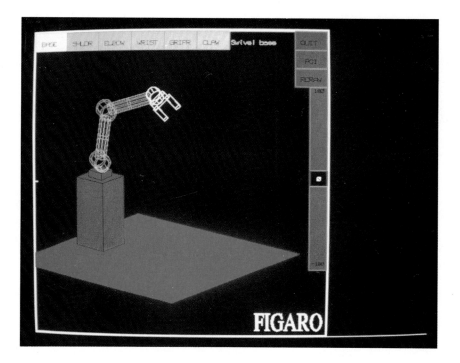

Figure 13. PHIGS robotic application.

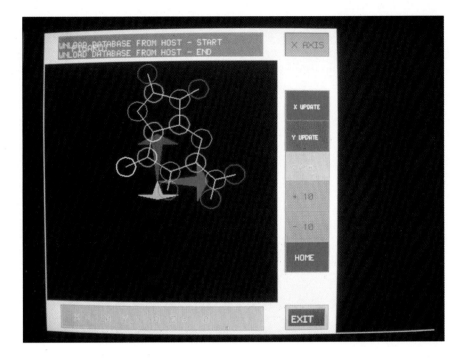

Figure 14. PHIGS molecular modelling application.

be pointed out that efficiency of execution depends on the use of graphics devices with PHIGS hardware or PHIGS firmware. PHIGS can, in addition, be realized efficiently on simple graphics devices (without their own graphics storage). Those graphics devices with their own segment storage and hardware transformations that are put forward today and have been optimized for GKS cannot run efficiently with PHIGS.

GRAPHIC OUTPUT

The graphic output facilities of PHIGS are identical to those of GKS-3D. It thus offers the following primitives:

POLYLINE—PHIGS generates a polyline connecting the given points in 3D space.

POLYMARKER—PHIGS generates a sequence of symbols at the set of points in 3D space.

TEXT—PHIGS generates a character string at a given position that is located in a defined plane in 3D space.

FILL AREA—PHIGS generates an area that is defined by a given set of points. The area may be filled with a uniform color, a pattern, or a hatch or, with low-performance devices, indicated by drawing only the boundaries. The area is located on a defined plane in 3D space.

FILL AREA SET—PHIGS generates an area defined by a given set of points. Areas with holes can thus be defined. The fill area set has its own attribute set which allows the indication of the display of the area's interior (uniform color, pattern, hatch, or empty) and the adjustment of the display of the boundaries (linetype, line width, color). The fill area set is located on an implicitly defined plane in 3D space (as is the case with fill area).

CELL ARRAY—PHIGS generates a raster picture from a given pixel array. Devices which do not support raster capabilities need only to draw the boundaries. The cell array is located on an implicitly defined plane in 3D space.

GENERALIZED DRAWING PRIMITIVE—This basic element allows addressing the output capabilities of devices not covered by other output elements, such as the drawing of interpolation curves and interpolation surfaces, circles, and circular arcs but also volumes such as cylinders, balls, etc.

GRAPHIC INPUT

PHIGS is also identical to GKS-3D as to graphic input facilities. PHIGS defines six different input classes that correspond to the six possible input data types. They are determined as follows:

Locator—The locator delivers a position in world coordinates and gives the viewing transformation number of the viewport in which the position entered is located. When the position is situated in several viewports at the same time, the viewport with the highest priority is chosen. Suitable physical input devices are a crosshair, mouse, tablet, digitizer, and light pen but also a keyboard to input the coordinates.

Stroke—Stroke delivers a sequence of positions in world coordinates and gives the viewing transformation number of the viewport with the highest priority in which all positions entered are located. All physical input devices are suitable to input positions (as with the locator).

Valuator—A valuator delivers a real number. The operator can adjust this number at a graphics device (e.g., a potentiometer), enter the number (e.g., via the keyboard), or adjust it using a simulation and a graphics device (e.g., a scale with a pointer).

Choice—Choice delivers a positive integer chosen out of a number of alternatives. Input devices often used are function keyboards and menus on screens, tablets, or digitizers.

Pick—Pick delivers a pick path, the name of the substructure in a hierarchical structure, and the length of the pick path as well as a status indication. Objects are usually picked by positioning a crosshair on an output element within the object by using a tablet or mouse.

String—String delivers a character string, which is usually entered via the alphanumeric keyboard.

Each logical input device can be operated in three different modes, the so-called operating modes; the application program can always select one of these modes. The three operating modes are REQUEST, SAMPLE, and EVENT. Input values are entered differently and are passed to the application program depending on the operating mode.

REQUEST—A call to the REQUEST function tries to read a logical input value from the logical input device specified. PHIGS waits until the operator has entered the input or has caused an interrupt by pressing, for instance, a special key.

SAMPLE—On calling the SAMPLE function, the current logical input value of the logical input device specified is reported without waiting for an operator action.

EVENT—PHIGS maintains an input queue containing chronologically ordered event reports. An event report contains the identification of the logical input device as well as the logical input value. The event report is asynchronously generated by operating an input device.

The functions described may only be called if the input device addressed is in the relevant operating mode.

Graphics Workstations

The workstation concept of PHIGS is similar to that of GKS-3D. PHIGS, however, knows only three workstation categories: INPUT, OUTPUT and INPUT/OUTPUT. As in GKS-3D, they are defined by description tables, state lists, as well as functionality. In contrast with GKS, PHIGS workstations do not have workstation-dependent picture storage: the graphics information is always taken and displayed from the centralized structure storage. An implementation would realize local picture storage only for reasons of efficiency.

Another contrast with GKS is that PHIGS does not recognize any metafile workstations (this functionality is replaced by a data archive function). Also, PHIGS does not have workstation-independent segment storage (this is replaced by the centralized structure storage.

Coordinate Systems and Transformations

The underlying principle used when defining the GKS standard was the separation of modelling and viewing. Unlike GKS, PHIGS includes modelling in the system. This results in defining the following coordinate systems:

modelling coordinates;

world coordinates;

viewing coordinates;

normalized projection coordinates;

device coordinates.

PHIGS application programs define a picture by combining separate parts. Each part may be defined in its own coordinate system (a modelling coordinate system). The resulting picture is mapped via the modelling transformation into one single coordinate system, the so-called PHIGS world coordinate system, which corresponds to normalized device coordinates in GKS.

Picture Structuring and Picture Manipulation

Picture Structuring

The PHIGS application program defines graphic objects that are stored in the centralized structure storage. The PHIGS picture definition is based on hierarchical structures. The entire picture belongs to one root, and every subpicture is a node (child) which, in turn, can again be a root (parent) for another subpicture definition.

Each root is called a structure. Each structure is a sequence of elements that is opened by OPEN STRUCTURE and closed by CLOSE STRUCTURE. The connection to a node is defined by the element EXECUTE STRUCTURE.

Elements used to define a picture in PHIGS are the output elements and attributes of GKS and GKS-3D as well as the following additional functions:

Structure definition—A structure is opened via OPEN STRUCTURE and closed via CLOSE STRUCTURE. Only one structure can be open at any time.

Output elements—POLYLINE, POLYMARKER, TEXT, FILL AREA, FILL AREA SET, CELL ARRAY, GENERALIZED DRAWING PRIMITIVE (GDP).

Functions to set output element attributes.

Labels—Labels can be defined that are referenced during the editing process.

Name sets—PHIGS recognizes name sets where the names can be set as attributes for the separate picture elements. Functions are available to add names to name sets or to delete them from these sets within the centralized storage structure.

Transformation matrices—Graphic information is stored in PHIGS in modelling coordinates (world coordinates), in contrast to GKS. This allows transformation matrices to be stored in the centralized storage structure; these elements are called 'modelling matrices'.

Structure references—The actual picture hierarchy is realized via structure references. Other structures may be pointed at within structures. At processing time, the structure reference is interpreted as a subroutine. When a structure reference is not available it is interpreted as an empty structure at runtime.

Application data sets—A command to enter application data into the centralized storage structure is available.

Structure copies—As with the GKS command INSERT SEGMENT, a structure can also be copied into another in PHIGS.

Examples of graphics object stored in the PHIGS-CSS are given in Figure 15.

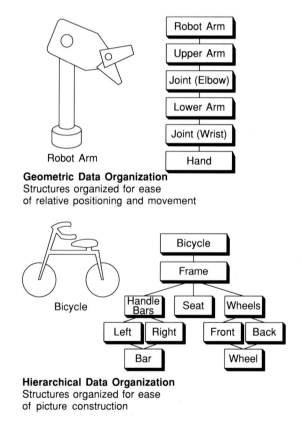

Figure 15. Examples of graphics object storing in PHIGS-CSS.

Picture Manipulation

PHIGS allows direct access to the modification of the entries in the centralized storage structure. Editing functions are available to position a pointer
in the centralized storage structure and to delete and insert elements or a
range of elements at the current pointer position.

Picture Display

The display of a picture on a workstation is initialized via the function
POST ROOT. A processor (traverser) then processes the structure below the
root indicated.

Every structure element is interpreted according to the predefined standard attributes valid when PHIGS is initialized. The elements are sequentially interpreted. When a substructure has to be interpreted, the following
operations are executed by calling the command EXECUTE STRUCTURE:

the interpretation of the current structure is interrupted;

the current state (attributes, local and global transformations, name sets,
etc.) is stored;

the substructure indicated is processed;

the attributes stored are reloaded on returning from the substructure;

the current structure is further interpreted.

Certain attributes of a parent structure are passed on calling a substructure:

attributes;

name sets;

the current concatenated transformation matrix; this is the global transformation matrix in the substructure;

viewing index.

PICTURE ARCHIVING

PHIGS allows the archiving of structures from the centralized structure
storage in an external file as well as the rereading of structures. The archive
file, however, is not a separate workstation as in GKS.

While in GKS, the contents of a metafile is read in by the application program record by record and may be checked and modified and is then passed
to GKS for interpretation. PHIGS offers functions to move entire picture
structures between PHIGS and external files. Functions for decomposition
are available to solve possible naming problems.

At present, PHIGS does not have any format definition for archive storage so `that a manufacturer-independent exchange of archive files is not
yet possible.

Computer Graphics Metafile

THE CGM STANDARD

CGM is an ISO standard [ISO87c] that defines a metafile format for the storage and transfer of picture description information. The file format consists of a set of elements (items) that support the representation of a wide range of pictures independent of graphics devices. The elements are split into groups which delimit major structures (metafiles and pictures), specify the representations used within the metafile, control the display of the picture, perform basic drawing actions, control the attributes of the basic drawing actions, and provide access to nonstandard device capabilities. The CGM standard currently does not allow the structuring of pictures (e.g., segments) nor 3D elements. This will be covered in two addenda, which are currently in preparation.

Three different data encoding forms, binary encoding, character encoding, and clear text encoding, are defined within the standard. Each of the three encodings is capable of representing the full functionality of CGM. Translation between the encodings is possible without loss of picture information, although subsequent translation back into the original encoding may not result in precisely the same data stream due to different quantizations of precisions in the different encodings.

The character encoding used is intended to provide an encoding of minimum size. It conforms to the rules of ISO 646 [ISO646] and ISO 2022 [ISO2022] and is particularly suitable for transfer through networks which cannot support binary transfers.

The binary encoding used provides an encoding that, on many systems, requires the least effort to generate and interpret. It is, therefore, intended to minimize the processing overhead while slightly increasing the size of the metafile.

The clear text encoding used provides an encoding in a human-readable form. Metafiles using this encoding can be created, viewed, and edited with standard text editors. It is, therefore, also suitable for transfer through networks which only support the transfer of text files.

The CGM standard defines the form (syntax) and functional behavior (semantics) of a set of elements that may occur in the CGM. The following eight classes of elements exist:

Delimiter elements—These separate different metafiles in one file (BEGIN PICTURE, END PICTURE). The delimiter elements are present to allow random access to individual metafiles and pictures;

Metafile descriptor elements—These elements are used to identify a metafile and to describe the functional capabilities required to interpret a particular CGM. The CGM interpreter is thus informed of the capabilities required to successfully interpret a Computer Graphics Metafile;

Picture descriptor elements—They are used to declare the parameter modes of other elements, to configure the portion of coordinate space of interest, and to set the background color;

Control elements—These elements are to specify address space, clipping boundaries, and format descriptions of the CGM elements. Control elements may occur repeatedly within a picture;

Graphics picture elements;

Attribute elements;

Escape elements which describe device-dependent or system-dependent data;

External elements, which do not communicate information not directly related to the generation of a graphic image. These elements comprise the MESSAGE elements, the APPLICATION DATA elements, the ESCAPE elements, and the GDP elements.

Application of CGM

CGM can be used both without another graphics system or in connection with standards such as GKS, GKS-3D, PHIGS, or CGI. The following usages are typical.

Generation of CGM files by application programs for communicating graphic data representations. These files can then be transferred to other systems, e.g., for use in documentation and publishing systems, catalogues, databases, and data retrieval systems or for previewing and printing applications.

Picture capture file in GKS, PHIGS, or CGI applications. A picture is created by an application program (batch) or interactively by a user (e.g., with a graphics editor or CAD system) and stored in the graphic system. GKS or PHIGS can then copy pictures or picture parts onto a CGM workstation for later use.

CGM file creating and editing. In a program environment consisting of GKS or PHIGS and a graphics editor, a user interactively creates general-purpose drawings or loads existing metafiles and continues modification and editing of the pictures. The final results may be output on any graphics device (plotter, laser printer, display, etc.) in total or in part using different formats. Common examples of such systems are desktop publishing packages in which the graphics editor is integrated in alphanumeric data-processing systems.

Output Elements

The number of output elements considerably exceeds the functional range of GKS. A brief overview will, therefore, be given. CGM output elements are:

POLYLINE—a sequence of points are connected by a polyline;

DISJOINT POLYLINE—each two succeeding points of a sequence of points are connected by a line;

POLYMARKER—a centered symbol is displayed at a set of points;

TEXT—a text string as in GKS;

RESTRICTED TEXT—a text string that is mapped into a given parallelogram;

APPEND TEXT—this text function allows the addition of a string to the last text, restricted text, or to append a text element. Font, precision, text size, color, etc., can be changed between any text and the append text function;

POLYGON—same as GKS fill area;

CELL ARRAY—a raster matrix in the form of a parallelogram. Different specification formats for the color or color index values (runlength, packed format) are available depending on the encoding.

GENERALIZED DRAWING PRIMITIVE—used to extend the different forms of output elements;

RECTANGLE, CIRCLE and four different kinds of circular arcs; ELLIPSE and two different kinds of elliptic arcs—some of these are displayed as vector primitives, i.e., using the polyline attributes; others are displayed as raster primitives, i.e., using the fill area attributes. These functions are special elements of the generalized drawing primitive.

OUTPUT ELEMENT ATTRIBUTES

The abilities of the CGM standard to display graphics elements with different attributes also considerably exceed that of the GKS. The display attributes that CGM and GKS have in common are:

bundled and individual attributes are available;

the GKS line attributes, marker attributes, text attributes, and polygon attributes are available.

Additional capabilities of CGM are:

line width and marker size cannot only be scaled via a scaling factor, but their width and size, respectively, can also be set absolutely;

colors can be indicated via index and color tables as well as directly via their RGB value;

so-called auxiliary colors as well as a transparency flag are introduced; this offers the possibility of displaying the gaps of polylines with interrupted linetypes either in background color or auxiliary colors;

a character base vector is included in addition to the character up vector for displaying text; it is thus possible to map a character from a rectangle into a parallelogram. Besides the font indicating the character font, a character set as well as an alternative character set are offered;

fill attributes and edge attributes are available to display polygon and polygon sets as in GKS-3D and PHIGS. These make it possible to separately control the area's interior and the area's boundaries.

Computer Graphics Interface (CGI)

THE CGI STANDARD

CGI is the draft proposed standard DP 9636 [ISO88] currently under development at ISO, which describes the interface between the device-independent and device-dependent parts of a graphic system. The device-independent part can, for instance, be GKS or other device-independent graphics applications. The device-dependent part is the driver for a certain device. An implementation of CGI is, therefore, a device driver with a standardized interface as defined by CGI.

CGI describes a set of functions for control and data exchange from and to the device through this interface. These functions can be made available in a subroutine library. The subroutine calling conventions are defined in a language binding. They can, on the other hand, be implemented on a terminal driven from a host computer through a communication link and the CGI functions are accessed using a data stream binding.

The CGI standard defines the form (syntax) and functional behavior (semantics) of a set of functions that may occur in CGI:

Control functions, which specify the modes of operation of certain other functions and the address space to be used, select the protocols for the exchange of data, provide for session initialization and termination, and control the device's operation;

Graphic primitive functions, which describe the visual components of a picture on the device;

Attribute functions, which describe the appearance of graphic primitive functions;

Escape functions, which describe device-dependent functions or implementation-dependent functions used to construct a picture;

External functions, which communicate information which is not directly related to the generation of a graphic image;

Segmentation functions, which can be used to store and manipulate groups of primitives and their attributes;

Input functions, which provide the ability to obtain graphic input from the virtual device in different ways and control the form and timing of this acquisition;

Raster functions, which can be used to generate and manipulate images on raster devices.

Application of CGI

CGI allows implementations either with a software-to-software interface (procedural binding, data-stream binding in a network) or with a software-to-hardware interface (data-stream binding to CGI devices). This allows for the use of CGI implementations as stand-alone packages in an application (they then serve as application programming interfaces) as well as their integration as standard device drivers into a standard graphics environment.

CGI packages are useful for:

graphic system designers or programmers who define a GKS environment consisting of the GKS kernel and various drivers for the different graphics peripherals; both development systems and target application systems can thus be configured;

graphic system designers, programmers, and end users loading new CGI drivers into their GKS system when connecting a new graphics device;

graphic system programmers who want to use the CGI library directly for programming their application in a single device environment, e.g., on a PC or workstation;

manufacturers of graphics boards, devices, or systems who want to offer a standard graphics device interface for their equipment by loading tailored CGI drivers onto their system.

Implementation of CGI in a Distributed Environment

In many cases graphic applications will run in a host–subsystem configuration, where the main program runs on the host and the subsystem, e.g., a terminal is used for graphic output and graphic input. In this configuration performance can be increased substantially by implementing high-level functions on the subsystem.

CGI can be implemented locally on a subsystem to provide this high level functionality. A communication interface between host and terminal is then required.

Communication between Host and CGI-Subsystem

The communication interface realizes a data stream binding. Each CGI function is encoded into a stream of bytes which are sent either to the subsystem via RS232 or other communication links, or stored in a shared memory and directly accessed by the subsystem. The data stream binding conforms to CGM for functions which are identical in CGI and CGM.

CGI Host Interface

The application running on the host computer has access to CGI functions through a CGI language binding which is identical to the one running on the terminal. This is important for applications which are ported to different systems, it allows an application to run in a host–terminal environment as well as locally on a graphics workstation without any modification. The communication link and the data stream binding are completely transparent to the application.

Encoding and Decoding

Instead of directly calling the CGI modules, the host language binding calls an encoding module which generates the data stream to be sent to the terminal. The encoding module is called once for each CGI function. It encodes each function by sending a function code number and then the parameters for this function according to the CGM character coding format. The resulting byte stream is sent to the terminal via RS232 or another communication link.

On the terminal side, a similar decoder is available to receive the data stream and retrieve the original functions with their parameters. An interpreter program is running in a continuous loop always performing the three steps GET, DECODE, and INTERPRET. The next function code number is received from the host in the GET step. The parameters for this function are received and decoded in the DECODE step, and the appropriate function in the CGI system is called with these parameters in the INTERPRET step.

The GET and DECODE steps are both executed in the decoding module, which has a single entry interface for all possible CGI functions. A function code number and a pointer to a parameter block is passed in this interface; the size and format of this parameter block depend on the function code number. A single entry interface is much more convenient for decoding purposes because the actual parameter list is available only after the function has been completely received and decoded.

INPUT and INQUIRY functions are used to return data to the host. This requires an encoding module on the terminal side and a decoding module on the host side. Because the host as well as the terminal require an encoding module and a decoding module, the software on both sides is actually very similar. The single entry interface is identical on host and terminal and only some tables are changed to provide the different functionality.

CGI and CGM are defined to have identical functionality with regard to output and attribute functions. Additional CGI features provided are mainly input and raster functions. The segmentation concept is almost identical to that of GKS except for the presence of an extra function to reopen a segment and to add graphics elements to it. There are more differences with input and raster functions, as explained below.

INPUT FUNCTIONS

While GKS defines three methods of obtaining input data, CGI input functions control and perform four methods of input from a virtual device.

REQUEST—return an input on a signal from the operator of the device;

SAMPLE—immediately return the current value from a continuously operated device;

EVENT—save input events from multiple input devices in an event queue;

ECHO REQUEST—similar to **REQUEST**, with additional features to permit echoing on a remote device.

CGI also defines two more input classes than do the other standards, i.e., *General* and *Area*. A list of the eight input classes is given in Table 1.

CGI allows the increased modelling of input devices. There are a number of functions to control input device states independently of each other, e.g., echo state, prompt state, acknowledgment state, measure state, etc. Input devices can also be dynamically configured. There exists a function to associate a set of triggers to a logical input device at runtime.

RASTER FUNCTIONS

The CGI standard defines a set of elements for creating, modifying, retrieving, and displaying image portions defined as pixel data below the CGI. A bitmap (or raster) is a rectangular array of elements (points) called 'pixels', each holding an independent color or intensity.

One bitmap may be selected for modification by subsequent output functions. When applying output operations to a bitmap, the resulting value of a pixel is determined by combining the value of the drawing color with the current value of the pixel in the bitmap. The rule which defines how pixel values are combined is called the *drawing mode*. A variety of drawing modes is provided to be used by the client. In addition, 'transparency' may be used to modify some pixels while leaving others untouched.

Table 1. Overview of the CGI Input Classes.

Input Class	Data Returned	Example
Choice	An integer from a discrete range of alternatives	Button, menu box
Locator	A single VDC point	Digitizer, mouse
String	A character string	Alphanumeric keyboard
Stroke	A sequence of VDC points	Digitizer
Valuator	A number from a continuous range of alternatives	Potentiometer
Pick	A pick status and the segment structure, containing the pick identifier and a segment identifier	Light pen, mouse
General	A data report	Voice input
Area	A pixel array	Scanner

Exactly one bitmap is displayed on the view surface at one time. A device may offer more than one depictable bitmap (e.g., to support 'double buffering') any of which may be selected as the display bitmap. The depictable bitmap's physical characteristics are device-dependent in both the numbers of pixels along each axis and the number of bits per pixel.

Other bitmaps may be created at the request of the CGI client. A client-defined bitmap is not depictable, but portions may be transferred onto or combined with a depictable bitmap.

Bitblock transfer functions support the movement and combination of rectangular regions of bitmaps parallel to the axes. A bitmap region may be replicated as a tile so as to fill a larger destination area; bitmaps may also be used as an interior style when rendering fill area output primitives.

Trends in Graphics Standards

PROBLEMS APPLYING TODAY'S GRAPHICS STANDARDS

Since GKS officially became an ISO standard and has been accepted internationally by industry, research, and science, more application programs based on GKS than on any de facto graphics standard exist world-wide today. GKS has become particularly well established with large companies, which have standardized their graphics basis for mainframes and workstations. Every major computer manufacturer now offers a GKS implementation for their system.

However, the success of GKS has produced new problems.

Implementation

The market offers many graphics devices such as plotters, graphics printers, digitizers, graphics cards, graphics terminals with more or less local graphics intelligence, microfilm equipment, typesetting machines, etc. GKS is supposed to run on all these devices. However, the GKS drivers of the various suppliers are not compatible. The device manufacturers cannot offer drivers, because an interface is not defined. Some of them, therefore, offer their own GKS implementations, thus adding to the confusion about how to connect these implementations with devices from other manufacturers.

Overhead

A graphics standard such as GKS requires a certain overhead as to storage capacity and execution time; less than 50 functions out of the total of 210 are usually used. Part of every portable GKS implementation is written device independently and, therefore, is not as optimized as the device-specific graphic libraries of the manufacturers. This can only be balanced by intensive optimization by the suppliers of GKS, a process only a few suppliers will be able to survive. However, the problem of overhead is reduced by the fall in hardware prices (costs of memory and processing capacity); this parallel development has considerably encouraged the acceptance of graphics standards.

Current

A standard defines the 'state of the art' at the time it is developed. Once published, it is meant to remain stable for a certain time. The average lifetime of a graphics hardware product today is less than 12 months. This requires continuous extension and interpretation of the standard. The relevant implementations have to keep up with hardware development; the average release cycle of GKS implementations is therefore approximately six months.

In the meantime, standards in other areas, e.g., communication standards, user interface techniques, workstation technologies, increased intelligence of graphics processors, etc., have evolved. Certain problems now have to be solved for GKS, such as

embedding GKS into window management systems such as the X Window system;

realizing new user interfaces with GKS such as 'pop-up menus';

using the growing intelligence of graphics processors;

flexibly distributing GKS systems on different processors (host–PC environment, several processors on one bus, transputers).

New Applications

The rapidly increasing use of graphics software requires a growing functionality. Graphics applications that generate realistic pictures using the computer are spreading, especially in the United States. The fields of applications are, for instance:

CAD systems to display results in aircraft construction, ship building, automobile construction, etc., as exactly as possible;

simulation of operations such as the simulation of movements, steering mechanisms for aircraft, ships, and cars, or computer games;

animation of scenes, such as in the film and advertising industries.

These applications, for instance, require 3D displays, efficient raster graphics, and algorithms for shading and lighting. The GKS standard no longer suffices.

User Interfaces

The modern development of man–machine interfaces has begun to have practical applications in graphics. When designing interactive systems, importance is increasingly being attached to screen and dialogue layout.

Window standards, originally designed to facilitate operation on workstations and PCs, are being developed simultaneously with computer graphics standards. They allow several independent processes to operate at the same time with each process having its own window. When designing graphics applications with sophisticated user interfaces, the screen often must be divided into several windows; some of them remain unchanged while others change during program execution. The question is how to use window systems for graphics applications, i.e., how to integrate windows and graphics standards.

MANUFACTURERS AND GRAPHICS STANDARDS

How do manufacturers of computer systems deal with graphics standards today? At first sight, several tendencies can be made out, all of which would prefer to be detached from the others by manufacturers—'we cannot use the others' developments for our applications'.

Graphics Boards

Above all, there are the manufacturers of graphics boards. Their market is developing positively despite an enormous fall in prices. These boards solely serve OEM-purposes and mainly are integrated into systems with a standard bus (IBM-PC, VME-Bus, Multibus, Q-Bus, etc.). The application software or existing graphics packages on the host usually have to operate directly on the graphic functions of the cards. To serve the different applications, the manufacturers offer all standards and de facto standards relevant for their market, e.g., CGI/VDI, GEM/VDI, EGA, CGA, Hercules, and DGIS. These suppliers are obviously GKS-oriented. PHIGS is much too complex, windowing is supported by hardware (X would then run very inefficiently), and standards do not yet exist for picture processing.

Workstations

The workstation manufacturers feel restricted in achieving technological progress by standards such as CGI and GKS; PHIGS+++ may still offer certain marketing advantages over the competition. X Windows is accepted as a basic systems, though the compatibility will be limited to their own operating system by offering supersets of X Windows.

Mainframes

For manufacturers of mainframes the graphic component is of less importance. Today's computer architectures are tailored to high-performance numeric calculations and data administration. To visualize such data, a graphics standard such as GKS is often used to display pictures applying various data representation algorithms. For higher performance requirements such as process control applications, workstations are connected to mainframes to visualize the data using local processing power. Communication standards then play an increasing role. Supercomputers are, on the other hand, used for movie generation applying fast picture-processing algorithms. A likely standard for this has yet to evolve.

TRENDS IN THE COMPUTER GRAPHICS MARKET

Four striking developments of the recent past are described below, each of which is linked to one trend in the computer graphics market, to show the development of graphic systems and thus graphics standards-to-be.

the availability of programmable graphics processors;

the introduction by several major manufacturers at the same time of new workstations on a RISC architecture with 10 MIPS and more processing capacity;

the de facto standardization of the X Window system;

the developments in the generation of realistic pictures, which are almost industrially applicable.

The resulting trends in the computer graphics market have followed.

Programmable Processors

First of all, special processors in silicon have developed into programmable processors on a chip-set basis in graphics hardware. Programming can be done in standard languages such as 'C'. A graphics board can pack enough memory to locally load and perform a program such as the CGI standard. Thus, the transformation of a 'plain' graphics board into a CGI terminal remains a question of a few man-weeks of development for the manufacturer or OEM. Consequently, the increase in performance is very high since the host no longer needs to process graphic commands. Further development shows that graphics boards will have CPUs such as Motorola 68030, Intel 80386, and NSC-CPUs or special chips to support complex operations such as 3D transformations, pixel operations, area shadings, ray tracing, Z buffering, etc. It will take but a few years for graphics boards with computer capacities of several 100 MIPS to be available (systems with 40 MIPS already exist), which will carry out complex picture displays in real time. The 'local intelligence' required will be developed in a high-level programming language, cross-compiled and loaded onto the board or kept there in the EPROM.

RISC Workstations

Demonstrations of the new RISC workstations showed that it is now possible to execute programs controlling moving objects (e.g., flight operations) in real time on a 'standard workstation'. The application program was written in FORTRAN on a device-independent and computer-independent

FORTRAN implementation of the graphics standard PHIGS (it could just as well have been written in GKS-3D without performance differences). This clearly shows the following. First, the advantages of programming with a graphics standard package can also be used to develop applications that required machine programming on special hardware (e.g., with gambling machines) some years ago. Second, the doubts about the performance of standard packages often mentioned become completely irrelevant if clean programming techniques are used.

X Windows

Most important workstation and terminal manufacturers have agreed on a standard for window management systems (X Windows). The basic version of X is public domain software and can be installed on a Unix environment within a few man-weeks. This rather inefficient version is quickly spreading. Workstation manufacturers are optimizing their respective versions for their own hardware. With graphics software, however, this window management system is most inefficient (X then produces direct bitmap data even with intelligent graphics processors). At present, several companies in the United States and Europe enhance the X definition by adding 2D and 3D graphics functions. This will probably lead to a period of incompatibility, which will result in a new standard.

Realistic Image Generation

For the most part, research has left behind the fields of vector and raster graphics and is now concentrating on systems to generate realistic representations of models held on the computer. Ray tracing and shading and lighting algorithms have been developed sufficiently so that pictures generated on the computer can hardly be distinguished from photographs. These capacities for animation of objects (such as the modelling of facial expressions), simulation of events (such as flight simulators), or CAD/CIM applications (to display objects under design in real time) can now be offered by workstation manufacturers; they have only been supplied by supercomputer manufacturers until now. Now that these functions are established, they can be included in a graphics standard. The United States workstation manufacturers have already started to define PHIGS++, which contains the functions mentioned above. In ISO, the GKS review has been started which will lead to a new standard 'GKS 9x'. This will probably include GKS extensions of new important functions of the current state of the art.

FUTURE DEVELOPMENT

The trend toward standardization continues to grow even in the technology market of the United States. Considering current developments, the following scenario for graphics standards in the next few years becomes likely.

The concept of CGI for 2D applications and a derivative of PHIGS++ will be accepted for future graphics boards. They will perform all transformations, clipping at arbitrary planes and hidden line/hidden surface functions locally. First, the elements will be taken from GKS-3D/PHIGS; then, more complex surface elements will be added with shading, lighting, transparency, etc. of PHIGS++ (and possibly GKS 9x), and, finally, display elements of a higher order.

The graphic system will be integrated with a window standard (X Window with 2D/3D extensions). The subsystem will receive the data via the X protocol; the display speed will amount to more than 100,000 picture elements per second. Thus, picture refresh from device-dependent picture elements will be possible, i.e., transformations, clipping, hidden surface, and displaying of elements will take place with every picture refresh; the system is supplied with the necessary data 'from above'.

Graphics standards such as GKS, GKS-3D, and PHIGS will merge into two systems (2D and 3D) and become application-oriented tools. They will interface to the device standards mentioned above.

The functionality of the three graphics standards will be combined into one reference standard having several subsets. An applicant for such a system is GKS 9x, which will be developed along with the GKS review within the next few years. Application systems will use the graphics standard tools according to their requirements, i.e., they will select the appropriate subset.

REFERENCES

[ISO646]
  ISO, Information Processing, 7-bit coded character set for information exchange, IS646.

[ISO2022]
  ISO, Information Processing, ISO 7-bit and 8-bit coded character sets—Code extension techniques, IS2022.

[ISO85]
  ISO, Graphical Kernel System (GKS), IS 7942, 1985.

[ISO87a]
  ISO, Graphical Kernel System 3D (GKS-3D), DIS 8805, 1987.

[ISO87b
  ISO, Programmer's Hierarchical Interactive Graphics System (PHIGS), DIS 9592, 1987.

[ISO87c]
  ISO, Computer Graphics Metafile (CGM), IS 8632, 1987.

[ISO88]
  ISO, Computer Graphics Interface (CGI), DP 9636, April 1988.

[Ende87]
  Enderle, G., Kansy, K., and Pfaff, G., *Computer Graphics Programming*,

GKS—The Graphics Standard, 2nd Ed., Berlin, Heidelberg, New York: Springer-Verlag, 1987.

[Temp85]
TEMPLATE, Understanding PHIGS, GTS-GRAL, Darmstadt, West Germany, 1985.

Biographies

Biographies

Computer Graphics Techniques –
Theory and Practice

David F. Rogers

David F. Rogers is Professor of Aerospace Engineering at the U.S. Naval Academy. In 1959, he earned a Bachelor of Aeronautical Engineering degree from Rensselaer Polytechnic Institute and subsequently was awarded the M.S.AE and Ph.D. degrees from the same Institute.

Dr. Rogers is the author of three textbooks on computer graphics, including *Mathematical Elements for Computer Graphics* and *Procedural Elements for Computer Graphics*. He is a member of SIGGRAPH, ACM, the Society of Naval Architects and Marine Engineers, and an Associate Fellow of the American Institute of Aeronautics and Astronautics. Dr. Rogers is the founder and former Director of the Computer Aided Design/Interactive Graphics Group at the U.S. Naval Academy. He is editor for the Springer-Verlag Series *Monographs in Visual Communication* and is the editor of *Computers & Education*. He also is a member of the editorial boards of *The Visual Computer* and of the *Computer Aided Design Journal*.

Professor Rogers was Co-Chair of the BCS/ACM International Summer Institute on *State of the Art in Computer Graphics* held in Scotland in 1986. He was also co-chairman of ICCAS '82, The International Conference on Computer Applications in the Automation of Shipyard Operation and Ship Design. He is a member of the International Program Committee for ICCAS. He was also co-chairman of the International Program Committee for Computer Graphics Tokyo '85.

Professor Rogers was Fujitsu Research Fellow at the Royal Melbourne Institute of Technology in Melbourne, Australia in 1987 and a Visiting Professor at the University of New South Wales, Sydney, Australia in 1982. He was an Honorary Research Fellow at University College London in England during 1977-78 where he studied Naval Architecture.

Professor Rogers was one of the original faculty who established the Aerospace Engineering Department at the U.S. Naval Academy in 1964. He has both an experimental and a theoretical research background. He has research interests in the areas of highly interactive graphics, computer aided design and manufacturing, numerical control, computer aided education, hypersonic viscous flow, boundary layer theory, and computational fluid mechanics.

Rae A. Earnshaw

Dr. Rae Earnshaw is Head of Computer Graphics at the University of Leeds, with interests in graphics algorithms, integrated graphics and text, display technology, CADCAM, and human-computer interface issues. He has been a Visiting Professor at IIT, Chicago, USA; Northwestern Polytechnical University, Xian, China; and George Washington University, Washington, DC, USA. He was a Director of the NATO ASI on *Fundamental Algorithms for Computer Graphics* held in England in 1985, and a Co-Chair of the BCS/ACM International Summer Institute on *State of the Art in Computer Graphics* held in Scotland in 1986. He was also a Director of the NATO ASI on *Theoretical Foundations of Computer Graphics and CAD* held in Italy in 1987.

He is a member of SIGGRAPH, ACM, IEEE, IEEE Computer Society, an Associate Fellow of the Institute of Mathematics and its Applications, and a Fellow of the British Computer Society.

Jack E. Bresenham

Jack Bresenham is Professor of Computer Science at Winthrop College in Rock Hill, South Carolina, USA. His work in computer graphics dates from 1962. His research interest is incremental algorithms for raster graphics. Prior to joining the faculty at Winthrop, Dr. Bresenham spent twenty-seven years working at various IBM development laboratories and headquarters. From 1981 through 1984 he worked on the IBM 3270 PC/GX graphic workstation project in Hursley, England. Since 1985 he has been a member of the X3H3.3 CGI graphics standards committee. He is a member of ACM, IEEE, Sigma Xi, and Phi Kappa Phi.

Frank C. Crow

Frank Crow is with the Imaging Area in the Computer Science Laboratory at Xerox Palo Alto Research Center (Xerox PARC) in Palo Alto, California. Previously he taught at Ohio State University and the University of Texas. He has spent considerable effort on developing algorithms for realistic image synthesis, and on systems and architectures for realizing them. He has a longstanding interest in parallel algorithms and architectures for computer display.

Roy Hall

Roy Hall graduated from Rensselaer Polytechnic Institure in 1976 with a B. Architecture and a B.S. Civil Engineering. He was introduced to computer graphics as a design tool for finite element analysis of large deflection tensile and inflated structures. He graduated from Cornell in 1983 with an M.S. from the Program of Computer Graphics where he concentrated on realistic image synthesis. Roy Hall has written image generation systems for Robert Abel & Associates, Vertigo Computer Imagery, and Wavefront Technologies where he was Director of Software Development. He has published in IEEE Computer Graphics and Applications and in The Visual Computer, and is a member of ACM and IEEE. He has lectured at numerous conferences on the subjects of rendering, realism, illumination models, and color science as applied to computer graphics. He has recently published a book, *Illumination and Color in Computer Generated Imagery*, Springer-Verlag 1989. He is currently on the Faculty at Cornell University in Ithaca, New York.

Gary W. Meyer

Gary Meyer is an assistant professor of computer and information science at the University of Oregon. He is particularly interested in the visual perceptual issues that are involved in both the interpretation of computer generated displays and the production of realistic images. His research has involved color monitor calibration, the reproduction of perceptually uniform color spaces, the efficient synthesis of color for realistic images, and the perceptual comparison of real scenes with computer generated pictures. Professor Meyer has received the Bachelor of Science from the University of Michigan and the Master of Science from Stanford University. He was employed by Bell Telephone Laboratories prior to receiving his Ph.D. while studying at the Cornell University Program of Computer Graphics. He is a member of ACM, IEEE, SID, SMPTE, and OSA.

Michael J. Muuss

Michael Muuss has 15 years of experience in working with advanced computer systems. Since 1981, he has been leading the Ballistic Research Laboratory's (BRL) Advanced Computer Systems Team in research projects concerning Networking, Graphics, CAD/CAE, Operating Systems, Parallel Architectures, and Command and Control. He is the principal architect of BRL's second-generation constructive solid geometry based CAD system, which is now in use at over 150 sites, and the primary author of the model editor 'MGED' and the advanced ray-tracing package 'RT'. He is the architect for both processing and communications within BRLNET, BRL's extensive campus network of computers ranging from workstations through super-minicomputers up to a Cray X-M/P48 and Cray-2.

Gunther E. Pfaff

Gunther Pfaff, Diplom Informatiker, born October 12, 1951, completed his studies in computer science at the Technical University of Darmstadt in 1979 with a diploma degree. After that he worked for five years as a research assistant in the area of interactive graphics systems with Prof. Encarnacao, University of Darmstadt, where in 1984 he received a Ph.D. in this subject. Dr. Pfaff is an active member of the DIN and ISO committees on graphics standards as well as a member of Eurographics and ACM-SIGGRAPH. He has co-authored and edited several books and published many papers in the area of computer graphics and given lectures and tutorials at international level at SIGGRAPH, Eurographics, IFIP, BCS, GI, CAMP, CAPE and others. Since 1985 Dr. Pfaff has been a partner and Managing Director of GTS-GRAL GmbH and is in charge of research and development and international product marketing.

Michael J. Pratt

Mike Pratt is Professor of Computer Aided Engineering (CAE) at Cranfield Institute of Technology, U.K. His specialisation in CAE grew out of an interest in applications of geometry in the early 1970's. He has written many research papers and is part author of several books including (with I. D. Faux) *Computational Geometry for Design and Manufacture.* Current research interests include curve and surface modelling, engineering applications of solid modelling (with particular emphasis on the use of form features) and CAD data exchange. He recently spent six months as a Visiting Fellow at the General Electric Corporate R & D Center, Schenectady, N.Y. working on representations of form features. He is a member of the Royal Aeronautical Society, the Institute of Mathematics and its Applications, the British Computer Society, and the Eurographics Association.

Malcolm A. Sabin

Malcolm Sabin has been active in the applications of computer graphics since the mid-1960's, when he wrote a sculptured surface software system still in use today. Since then he has been concerned with part programming systems and control software for numerically controlled machine tools, and with mesh generation for finite element analysis. He has been Chairman of the BCS CAD Specialist Group, and a member of IFIP WG 5.2. He is now on the Editorial Boards of CAD, CAGD, and Computer Journal. He consults for SERC and CAE, and retains his technical interests in the numerical representation of shape, being particularly interested in methods for the interrogation of parametric and recursive-division surfaces. He is Technical Director of Fegs Ltd.

Maureen A. Stone

Maureen Stone is a member of the research staff of the Xerox Palo Alto Research Center, Palo Alto, California, USA. Her research interests are color, especially color reproduction, interactive graphics, and spline curves. She has been an employee of the Xerox Corporation since graduating in

1978 with an MS/CS from the California Institute of Technology. Prior to attending Caltech, she was a student and research assistant in the Electrical Engineering Department of the University of Illinois, Urbana, Illinois. The projects she is involved in at Xerox focus on interactive document creation, digital printing, and electronic publishing. She is a member of ACM, and was the SIGGRAPH'87 Technical Program Chair.

Brian Wyvill

Brian Wyvill received his Ph.D. from the University of Bradford in 1975 and continued his interest in computer animation as a Research Fellow at the Royal College of Art. He is now an Associate Professor at the University of Calgary where he leads the Graphicsland animation research team, and has been extensively involved in the design of the JADE graphics system and the Ray Tracing Machine. His research interests include hierarchical graphics systems, algorithms for synthesizing visual images, animation and man-machine interface design. Current interests include 'soft' objects, motion control, and recursive data structures for computer animation. He is a member of ACM, CGS, SIGGRAPH, and is on the Editorial Board of the Visual Computer.

Index

Index